# 4th Workshop on Multilingual Representation Learning (MRL 2024)



Miami, Florida, USA
16 November 2024

ISBN: 979-8-3313-0848-3

**Printed from e-media with permission by:**

Curran Associates, Inc.
57 Morehouse Lane
Red Hook, NY 12571

**Some format issues inherent in the e-media version may also appear in this print version.**



Printed with permission by Curran Associates, Inc. (2025)



Association for Computational Linguistics
209 N. Eighth Street
Stroudsburg, Pennsylvania 18360

Phone: 1-570-476-8006
Fax: 1-570-476-0860

acl@aclweb.org

**Additional copies of this publication are available from:**

Curran Associates, Inc.
57 Morehouse Lane
Red Hook, NY 12571 USA
Phone: 845-758-0400
Fax: 845-758-2633
Email: curran@proceedings.com
Web: www.proceedings.com

MRL 2024

# The 4th Workshop on Multilingual Representation Learning

## Proceedings of the Workshop

November 16, 2024

Order copies of this and other ACL proceedings from:

Association for Computational Linguistics (ACL)
317 Sidney Baker St. S
Suite 400 - 134
Kerrville, TX 78028
USA
Tel: +1-855-225-1962
acl@aclweb.org

# Organizing Committee

**Organizers**

David Ifeoluwa Adelani, McGill University, Canada
Duygu Ataman, New York University, USA
Mammad Hajili, Microsoft, USA
Raghav Mantri, New York University, USA
David Stap, University of Amsterdam, Netherlands
Jonne Sälevä, Brandeis University, USA
Francesco Tinner, University of Amsterdam, Netherlands
Abraham Owodunni, Ohio State University, USA

# Program Committee

**Reviewers**

David Ifeoluwa Adelani, Manuel Bobie Amankwatia, Catherine Arnett

Travis M. Bartley, Vishal Bhalla

Jiajing Chen, Xupeng Chen, Olutosoye Taiwo Christian, Zoltan Csaki

Konstantin Dobler, Koel Dutta Chowdhury

Yassine El Kheir, Abdellah El Mekki

Senkang Hu

Yusif Ibrahimov, Mironshoh Inomjonov, Jafar Isbarov

Ainaz Jamshidi, Jiby Mariya Jose

Yixiao Kang, Zhengjian Kang, Christopher Klamm, Hongzhi Kuai

Senyu Li, Yueqian Lin, Weisi Liu

Pranita Yogesh Mahajan, Nimshi Venkat Meripo

Muhammad Amin Nadim, Usman Nawaz

Esther Odunayo Oduntan, Peter Oseghale Ohue, Yewande Ojo

Chester Palen-Michel

Shaibal Saha, Shubham Shukla, Janet Yunchen Sung, Jonne Sälevä

Shaomu Tan, Wenjia Tan, Yihang Tao, Shailja Thakur

Vajratiya Vajrobol, Deepali Verma

Sahil Walia, Azmine Toushik Wasi, Di Wu

Sadia Zaib, Zhehao Zhang, Xufeng Zhao, Huichi Zhou, Ziqi Zhou

## Keynote Talk
# Invited talk 1

**Karen Livescu**
TTI at Chicago
**2024-11-16 9:10 –**

**Bio:** Karen Livescu is a Professor at the Toyota Technological Institute at Chicago (TTIC). Her research focuses on speech and language processing and related areas of machine learning. She obtained her PhD in Computer Science MIT 2005, working in the Spoken Language Systems group of the Computer Science and Artificial Intelligence Laboratory.

# Keynote Talk
# Invited talk 2

**Hila Gonen**
University of Washington
**2024-11-16 9:50 –**

**Bio:** Hila Gonen is a postdoctoral Researcher at the Paul G. Allen School of Computer Science & Engineering at the University of Washington working on Natural Language Processing. Her research focuses on two goals: (1) making cutting-edge language technology available and fair across speakers of different languages and users of different socio-demographic groups; (2) developing algorithms and methods for controlling the model's behavior. Prior to joining UW, she completed a Ph.D in Computer Science at the NLP lab at Bar Ilan University.

## Keynote Talk

# Invited talk 3

**Sebastian Ruder**
Cohere for AI
**2024-11-16 16:00 –**

**Bio:** Sebastian Ruder is a research scientist at Cohere based in Berlin, Germany working on making large language models (LLMs) multilingual. He completed his PhD in Natural Language Processing and Deep Learning at the Insight Research Centre for Data Analytics.

# Table of Contents

# Program

**Saturday, November 16, 2024**

| | |
|---|---|
| 09:00 - 09:10 | *Opening Remarks* |
| 09:10 - 09:50 | *Invited Talk by Karen Livescu* |
| 09:50 - 10:30 | *Invited Talk by Hila Gonen* |
| 10:30 - 11:00 | *Coffee Break* |
| 11:00 - 12:30 | *Poster Session* |
| 12:30 - 14:00 | *Lunch Break* |
| 14:00 - 14:15 | *Findings Paper* |
| 14:15 - 14:30 | *Winning Team Presentation* |
| 14:30 - 15:00 | *Best Paper* |
| 15:00 - 15:30 | *Honorable Mentions* |
| 15:30 - 16:00 | *Coffee Break* |
| 16:00 - 16:50 | *Invited Talk by Sebastian Ruder* |
| 16:50 - 17:00 | *Closing Remarks* |

# SambaLingo: Teaching Large Language Models New Languages

**Zoltan Csaki, Bo Li, Jonathan Li, Qiantong Xu, Pian Pawakapan Leon Zhang**
**Yun Du, Hengyu Zhao, Changran Hu, Urmish Thakker**
SambaNova Systems
zoltan.csaki@sambanovasystems.com

## Abstract

Despite the widespread availability of LLMs, there remains a substantial gap in their capabilities and availability across diverse languages. One approach to address these issues has been to take an existing pre-trained LLM and continue to train it on new languages. While prior works have experimented with language adaptation, many questions around best practices and methodology have not been covered. In this paper, we present a comprehensive investigation into the best practices for adapting LLMs to new languages. Our study explores the key components in this process, including vocabulary extension and initialization of new tokens, direct preference optimization and the data scarcity problem for human alignment in low-resource languages. We scale these experiments across 9 languages and 2 parameter scales (7B and 70B). We compare our models against Llama 2, Aya-101, XGLM, BLOOM and existing language experts, outperforming all prior published baselines. Additionally, all evaluation code[1] and checkpoints[2] are made public to facilitate future research.

## 1 Introduction

New state of the art large language models are being released at a breakneck speed, yet their training data, tokenizer, and evaluations remain primarily centered around a few popular languages such as English, Chinese, French and Arabic. In principle, the way to create large language models for specific languages is to pre-train models from scratch (Sengupta et al., 2023; Zhang et al., 2020). However, it is difficult to obtain a large amount of compute resources and a vast quantity of data in diverse languages. Researchers have tackled this problem by training monolithic multi-lingual models that cover a wide range of languages (Workshop et al., 2023; Lin et al., 2022; Shliazhko et al., 2023; Xue et al., 2021). These models can still struggle to achieve uniformly good results across all languages due to various factors such as the curse of multilinguality (Chang et al., 2023; Conneau et al., 2020) and the scarcity of pre-training data in many languages (Chung et al., 2023).

Recently, adapting English centric models to new languages has gained prominence (Blevins et al., 2024; Yong et al., 2023; Ebrahimi and Kann, 2021; Pires et al., 2023; Pipatanakul et al., 2023; Lin et al., 2024). The resulting models can outperform large multilingual models and even language specific models pre-trained from scratch. Adaptation requires various design choices around the tokenizer, data, alignment and evaluation strategies. This paper aims to provide a comprehensive study to help inform these decisions, outlining a clear protocol to adapt a pre-trained model to a new language. We show that our methodology works by training models across 9 languages and 2 parameter scales (7B and 70B) and comparing them against publicly available models. Figure 1 and 2 show that our methodology can lead to better models than existing state of the art models in these languages.

The key studies and contributions include:

- Best practices for adapting existing LLMs to new languages scaled across 9 typologically and linguistically diverse languages including Arabic, Bulgarian, Hungarian, Japanese, Russian, Serbian, Slovenian, Thai, and Turkish
  - Expanding the vocabulary for the target language improves the tokenizer fertility (12), but does not have a siginficant impact on downstream accuracy (5.1.1)
  - Various embedding initialization methods have minimal impact on accuracy,

[1] Fork of lm-evaluation-harness Gao et al., 2023 with new multilingual benchmarks: lm-evaluation-harness

[2] All SambaLingo Checkpoints: SambaLingo Checkpoints



*Proceedings of the Fourth Workshop on Multilingual Representation Learning (MRL 2024)*, pages 1–21
November 16, 2024 ©2024 Association for Computational Linguistics

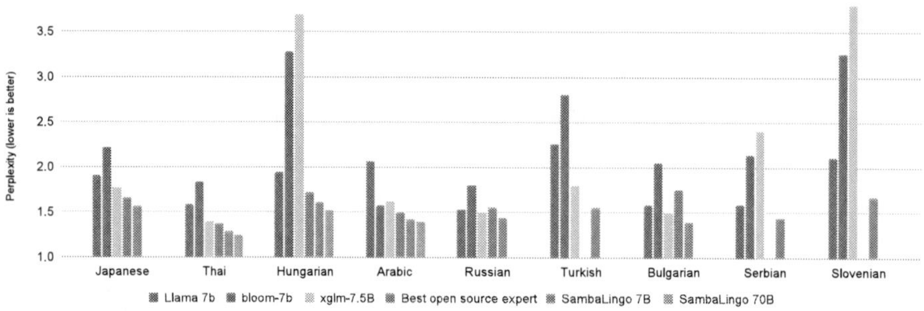


Figure 1: Evaluation perplexity on hold out dataset, we also evaluate perplexity over wikipedia and Mc4 in appendix F. Open source expert baselines: Japanese - Swallow-7b-hf (TokyoTech, 2023), Thai: typhoon-7b (Pipatanakul et al., 2023), Arabic: jais-13b (Sengupta et al., 2023), Hungarian: PULI-GPTrio (Yang et al., 2023), Russian: saiga-7b (Gusev, 2023), Bulgarian: mGPT-bulgarian(Shliazhko et al., 2023). We could not find Serbian, Slovenian and Turkish languages models with low enough perplexity that would fit the graph so we chose to omit them here to ensure readability.

but sub word averaging accelerates training loss convergence (5.1.2)

  - The quality of the base checkpoint on English benchmarks can improve downstream language adaptation results (5.3)

- A recipe for human preference alignment in any language using open source data
  - Aligning the adapted model requires minimal data from the target language, reducing the need of gathering expensive alignment data (5.2.1)
  - The choice of translated versus human written alignment data does not have a large impact on win rates (5.2.2)

- Open sourcing code and checkpoints to promote future research
  - State of the art models adapted from Llama 2 in 9 languages and 2 parameter scales (7B, 70B)[2]
  - Integration of FLORES-200, SIB-200, EXAMS and multilingual perplexity benchmarks with lm-eval-harness[1] (Gao et al., 2023)

## 2 Related Work

While prior work has explored adapting pre-trained LLMs to new languages, they do not extensively study the methodology to do so. None of these works explore the design choices around aligning models in new languages, for example the mixture of data in the base models language and the new language or the impact of translated data on qualitative evaluation. Pires et al. (2023) and Cui et al. (2023b) adapt Llama models to Portuguese and Chinese respectively, but they do not explore the impact of vocabulary extension and/or initialization. Blevins et al. (2024) explores training language experts to break the curse of multilinguality starting from a pre-trained model, but they do not explore the impact of vocabulary extension, initialization and quality of the base model. Extension of vocabulary was discussed in Zhao et al. (2024b); Tikhomirov and Chernyshev (2023), however they do not explore token embedding initialization strategies or impact of quality of base model. Lin et al. (2024) studies simultaneous language adaptation to 500 languages. Nevertheless, they also do not answer questions around alignment or token initialization strategy. Ye et al. (2023) studies language adaptation of a wide variety of English-centric and multilingual models, however they only focus on finetuning XNLI tasks.

There has been a significant body of work around open-source multi-lingual models (Workshop et al., 2023; Lin et al., 2022; Shliazhko et al., 2023). Our work differs from the aforementioned studies as we solely focus on adapting pre-trained LLMs to new languages and not on pre-training from scratch. Notably, these multilingual open-source models tend to be pretrained on significantly fewer tokens than the base models we adapt from. As the models in this work tend to outperform these multilingual models, this presents a promising path forward for obtaining the state of the art in new languages.

## 3 Adaptation Methodology

We present our methodology to adapt large languages models to a new language, with state of the art results in 9 target languages: Arabic, Thai, Turkish, Japanese, Hungarian, Russian, Bulgarian, Serbian and Slovenian. We select these languages because they provide a mix of high resource and lower resources languages with diverse character sets and linguistic patterns. We additionally limit the scope of the languages studied in this paper to languages with easily available text datasets from CulturaX (Nguyen et al., 2023). See Section 4 for evaluation results on the final checkpoints produced by this methodology, and Section 5 for ablations justifying our methods.

We use the term *initial language* to describe the original language that the base model was trained on (in this case, English) and the term *target language* as the new language this model is being adapted to.

### 3.1 Selecting a Base Model

Our methodology starts with an existing base checkpoint instead of pre-training from scratch. Previous work has shown that starting from an existing checkpoint leads to faster training convergence, better downstream evaluation accuracy and lower compute/data requirements (Pires et al., 2023; Lin et al., 2024; Csaki et al., 2023). Section 5.3 demonstrates that it is important to select a starting checkpoint with the best results for the initial language, as that will improve the downstream results for the target language. Based on these observations, we chose Llama2 7B as our base model to adapt to target languages, the best open source model available at the time of the experiments.

We additionally scale this methodology to Llama 2 70B. Given compute restrictions, we only do this for 3 languages - Arabic, Thai and Hungarian. See Section 4.2 for in-depth comparisons of our 7B and 70B models.

### 3.2 Extending Model Vocabulary

Llama 2 (et al, 2023) was trained predominantly on English text, and has poor tokenizer efficiency for other languages (see Section 5.1). To address this inefficiency, we chose to extend the vocabulary of the Llama 2 tokenizer by adding non overlapping tokens from the target language and initializing them using sub-word embeddings from the original tokenizer. See Section 5.1 for experiments that justify our approach.

### 3.3 Continual Pre-training

We train each language independently on data that consists of a 1:3 mixture of English and target language web data biased towards the target language. Pretraining data for all languages, including English, is sourced from CulturaX (Nguyen et al., 2023). These decisions are grounded in results from previous works: Zhao et al. (2024b); Csaki et al. (2023) show that mixing in data from the base model domain helps downstream accuracy and training stability, Gupta et al. (2023) find that including a higher proportion of data from the target distribution helps improve the convergence in the target distribution, Almazrouei et al. (2023) showed the importance of cleaned web data. Additionally, hyperparameters used for training can be found in Appendix A.

### 3.4 Aligning To Human Preferences In Other Languages

To train a chat-aligned version of the model, we follow the two-stage approach from Tunstall et al. (2023) - supervised finetuning (SFT) followed by direct preference optimization (DPO). More details about hyperparameters for each of these phases used can be found in Appendix A.

- For SFT, we use `ultrachat-200k` (Tunstall et al., 2023), in a 1:1 ratio with a Google translated version of `ultrachat-200k`.
- For human preference alignment, we use the `ultrafeedback` (Cui et al., 2023a) and `cai-conversation-harmless` dataset (Huang et al., 2024). We mix these datasets with a 10:1 ratio of English to machine translated data. Section 5.2.1 shows that this ratio of data performs almost as well as other ratios and section 5.2.2 shows that machine-translated data can perform as well as human written data.

## 4 Evaluation

### 4.1 Quantitative Evaluation

We use a wide variety of benchmarks to quantitatively evaluate the performance of our models and compare them to prior work. See Table 1 for the full list of quantitative benchmarks. In summary, we evaluate language modeling with perplexity on a holdout set of CulturaX (Nguyen et al.,

| Datasets | Task Category | Num Few-Shot | Number Of Languages | Metric |
|---|---|---|---|---|
| mc4 , Wikipedia | Perplexity | - | 323 | Perplexity |
| FLORES-200 | Translation | 8 | 200 | CHRF |
| SIB-200 | Text Classification | 3 | 200 | Accuracy |
| BELEBELE | Question Answering | 3 | 122 | Accuracy |
| Exams | Knowledge | 3 | 11 | Accuracy |
| XNLI<br>XStoryCloze<br>XCOPA<br>XWinograd<br>PAWS-X | Natural Language Understanding | 0 | 25+ | Accuracy |

Table 1: Multi-lingual evaluation suite

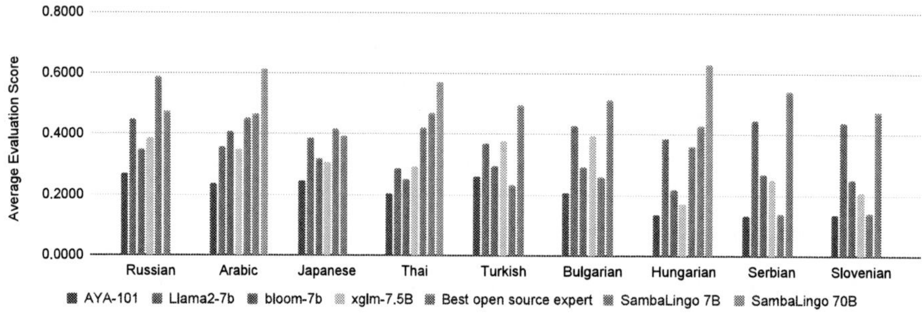


Figure 2: Quantitative evaluation results. The "best open source experts" are the same as ones specified in Figure 1. See Appendix F for the full breakdown.

2023), translation with CHRF (Popović, 2015) on FLORES-200 (Goyal et al., 2021; Zhu et al., 2023), text classification accuracy on SIB-200 (Adelani et al., 2024; Lin et al., 2024), open-book question answering on BELEBELE (Bandarkar et al., 2023), closed-book question answering on EXAMS (Hardalov et al., 2020), and a variety of natural language understanding benchmarks (XNLI (Conneau et al., 2018), XStoryCloze (Lin et al., 2022), XCOPA (Ponti et al., 2020), XWinograd (Emelin and Sennrich, 2021), and PAWS-X (Yang et al., 2019)).

All quantitative evaluations are performed on our adapted models after continuous pretraining, but before the alignment stage. We evaluate each checkpoint only on the language that it was trained on. Note that not all of our target languages are covered across all benchmarks. However, each language we examine has evaluations in at least 4 of these benchmarks. We ensured that perplexity measurements were done on a held out set in the target language, and verify that evaluating perplexity on different domains of text such as Wikipedia and MC4 (Raffel et al., 2019) have very similar results in appendix F.

#### 4.1.1 Quantitative Results

We compare our continuously pretrained models against the best open source models available in each target language and state of the art multilingual models. Figure 1 shows that our SambaLingo models have a lower perplexity across all existing baselines on a holdout set from our training data. Perplexity on other domains also follows the same trend as shown in appendix F. Figure 2 shows the average evaluation score across the evaluation benchmarks introduced in Section 4.1, where we see our models outperform all other models in 7/9 languages.

### 4.2 Scaling to 70B

Scaling to 70B consistently leads to better results as seen in table 2. The 70B models in the table have trained on fewer tokens than the 7B models.

Additionally, we evaluate compute-matched checkpoints of our 7B and 70B Llama 2 models

| Language | Checkpoint | ppl (↓) | FLORES EN→X (↑) | FLORES X→EN (↑) | Belebele (↑) | SIB-200 (↑) | XNLI (↑) | XStoryCloze (↑) |
|---|---|---|---|---|---|---|---|---|
| Arabic | 70B | **1.44** | **54.25** | **65.60** | **0.78** | **0.69** | 0.33 | **0.68** |
| | 7B | **1.44** | 53.67 | 61.66 | 0.29 | 0.26 | **0.34** | 0.65 |
| Hungarian | 70B | **1.57** | **58.81** | **64.03** | **0.82** | **0.64** | - | - |
| | 7B | 1.63 | 52.70 | 58.31 | 0.33 | 0.25 | - | - |

Table 2: This table compares compute matched 7B and 70B checkpoints. We look at intermediate checkpoint results and compare 7B models trained for 40B tokens with 70B models trained for 4B tokens.

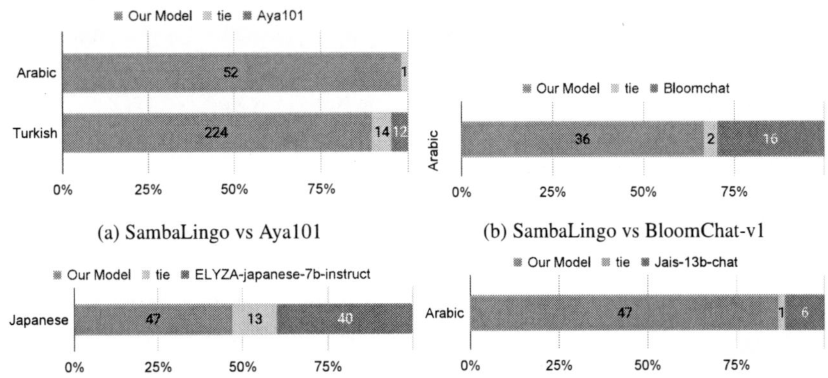


(a) SambaLingo vs Aya101

(b) SambaLingo vs BloomChat-v1

(c) SambaLingo vs ELEYZA-7b-instruct

(d) SambaLingo vs Jais-13b-chat

Figure 3: GPT4 evaluation result

in table 2. The compute-matched 70B checkpoints are trained for 10x fewer steps (4B tokens vs 40B tokens) and perform as well as or better than 7B variants trained over 40B tokens in every benchmark across Arabic and Hungarian.

## 4.3 Evaluating Human Aligned Checkpoints

### 4.3.1 GPT-4 as a Judge

To test our human aligned models' ability to generate high quality responses to real user prompts, we use GPT-4 (OpenAI and et al, 2024) as a judge. This method was first introduced by Zheng et al. (2023) to evaluate English models, and then used by Üstün et al. (2024) as a method to evaluate multilingual models. The resulting model generations are shuffled and fit to the prompting style suggested by (Zheng et al., 2023) before being fed to GPT-4. See Appendix D for the manually collected prompts and section 4.3.2 for the evaluation results.

GPT-4 as a judge has been widely accepted by the community as a way to evaluate chat models (Zheng et al., 2023; Verga et al., 2024), and we extend this to multilingual models. To ensure that GPT-4 is understanding the multilingual text we have native speakers read through a few examples of GPT-4 explaining its decision making process. The native speakers unanimously agree that GPT-4 clearly understands the content in other languages. In appendix D.2 we include example model generations along with GPT-4's corresponding preferences and explanations. Further work is needed to do a large scale study to see how GPT-4 preferences align with human preferences in other languages.

### 4.3.2 Qualitative Results

Measuring win-rate using GPT-4 as a judge only works in scenarios where a human aligned or instruction tuned model is available in a language. Given this constraint, we were only able to find relevant comparisons for Arabic, Japanese and Turkish, and do not have qualitative evaluations for our models in the other 6 languages. We do not compare to llama2-chat because we found that Llama2-chat and other open source English foundation chat models reply in English when prompted in the target language, instead of replying back in the target language. The results of our evaluation are shown in Figure 3. Our SambaLingo models consistently outperform other models in the same language. For details about the native speaker-curated prompts, see Appendix D. We additionally run evaluations with Claude Opus (Anthropic, 2024) as a judge to ensure that there is no bias by GPT-4 and find very similar results in appendix D.1

| Added Tokens | Hungarian | Russian | Turkish | Bulgarian | Arabic | Japanese | Thai |
|---|---|---|---|---|---|---|---|
| 0 | 2.70 | 2.28 | 3.28 | 2.36 | 4.23 | 2.07 | 4.84 |
| 1000 | 2.52 | 2.25 | 2.56 | 2.19 | 2.11 | 1.75 | 2.10 |
| 4000 | 2.14 | 2.05 | 2.20 | 1.92 | 1.67 | 1.23 | 1.50 |
| 25000 | 1.78 | 1.78 | 1.77 | 1.66 | 1.26 | 0.93 | 1.10 |

Table 3: Number of added tokens vs fertility (average number of tokens per "word")

| Language | Tokenizer | ppl (↓) | FLORES EN→X (↑) | FLORES X→EN (↑) | Belebele (↑) | SIB-200 (↑) | XNLI (↑) | XStoryCloze (↑) |
|---|---|---|---|---|---|---|---|---|
| Arabic | Original | 1.50 | 48.27 | 57.35 | 0.27 | 0.27 | **0.34** | 0.63 |
| | Expanded | **1.46** | **52.66** | **61.05** | **0.32** | **0.35** | **0.34** | **0.64** |
| Hungarian | Original | **1.61** | **52.70** | **58.31** | **0.33** | 0.26 | - | - |
| | Expanded | 1.63 | 51.82 | 57.12 | 0.30 | **0.34** | - | - |
| Serbian | Original | **1.403** | 56.15 | 64.89 | 0.32 | **0.59** | - | - |
| | Expanded | 1.435 | **58.30** | **66.35** | **0.37** | 0.52 | - | - |

Table 4: Accuracy after training with expanded vocabulary vs original tokenizer

# 5 Ablations

In this section, we present ablations of our design decisions in Section 3. Section 5.1 presents experiments motivating the modifications we make to the base model's tokenizer and how we initialize its new embeddings. Section 5.2 ablates the amount of target language data and use of machine translated data in the DPO phase of our methodology. Finally, section 5.3 looks at the impact of the quality of the base model.

## 5.1 Vocabulary Expansion

The Llama2 tokenizer is centered towards English. While this tokenizer can encode characters in any language, it will be very inefficient for non-English text. In fact, the BPE tokenizer may tokenize non-Latin characters as multiple independent bytes. One way to mitigate this problem is to extend the vocabulary of the base model by adding new tokens that represent the target language to it, and start adaptation training with this expanded vocabulary. This method also helps improve the inference efficiency in the target language. We explore different sizes for the expanded vocabulary and their impacts on fertility (Ács, 2019) in Table 3 and Figure 12. We chose to expand the vocabulary by 25,000 tokens for all languages as it yields the lowest fertility for all languages and highest throughput on the hardware platform.

### 5.1.1 Vocabulary Expansion vs Original Tokenizer

To measure the impact of vocabulary expansion on accuracy, we train two models—one using an expanded vocabulary and the other using the original vocabulary—across two three languages: Hungarian, Arabic and Serbian. We find that expanding the vocabulary does not have significant impact on the downstream accuracy. Nonetheless, given the benefit that the expanded vocabulary has for inference and sequence length utilization in the target language, we chose to expand the vocabulary of the base model.

### 5.1.2 Initializing new token embeddings

We experiment with 4 different token initialization strategies for the new tokens added to the vocabulary across 3 languages - Hungarian Arabic and Thai. For each experiment, we train the model for 10 billion tokens and compare the loss values. Let $V$ be the set of tokens in the original vocabulary, and $E(t)$ the embedding vector of a token $t \in V$. The four token initialization methods we consider are as follows:

- `gaussian`: $\mathcal{N}(0, 0.02)$
- `xavier_uniform`
- `avg_all` (Hewitt, 2021): For each new token $t'$, initialize $E(t') = \text{mean}(\{E(t)\forall t \in V\})$
- `avg_subwords` (Liu et al., 2024; Koto et al., 2021): For each new token $t'$, let $L_{t'} = [t_1, ..., t_k]$ be the list of $k$ tokens that $t'$ would have been tokenized as under the original tokenizer. Initialize the new embedding with $E(t') = \text{mean}([E(t_1), ..., E(t_k)])$.

Figure 4 shows that after continuous pretraining for 10B tokens, all methods converge to similar loss values, with `avg_subwords` showing faster convergence. Table 5 shows the impact on downstream

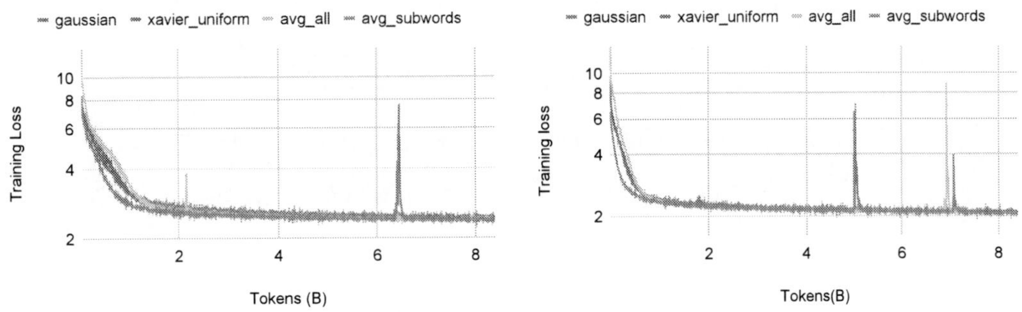


(a) Arabic

(b) Hungarian

Figure 4: Training loss for different token initialization methods

| Language | Initialization Method | ppl (↓) | FLORES EN→X (↑) | FLORES X→EN (↑) | Belebele (↑) | SIB-200 (↑) | XNLI (↑) | XStoryCloze (↑) |
|---|---|---|---|---|---|---|---|---|
| Arabic | gaussian | 1.50 | 48.48 | 57.31 | 0.34 | 0.25 | 0.34 | 0.61 |
| | xavier_uniform | 1.49 | 50.46 | 58.90 | 0.36 | 0.26 | 0.33 | 0.62 |
| | avg_all | **1.48** | 50.54 | 58.29 | 0.34 | 0.25 | **0.35** | 0.63 |
| | avg_subwords | **1.48** | **50.87** | **59.62** | **0.38** | **0.27** | 0.34 | **0.64** |
| Hungarian | gaussian | **1.65** | **51.42** | **56.92** | 0.32 | **0.50** | - | - |
| | xavier_uniform | **1.65** | 49.52 | 55.81 | **0.34** | 0.42 | - | - |
| | avg_all | 1.76 | 51.39 | 56.86 | **0.34** | 0.45 | - | - |
| | avg_subwords | **1.65** | 50.79 | 56.77 | 0.33 | 0.30 | - | - |
| Thai | gaussian | 1.31 | 51.50 | 52.95 | 0.33 | 0.53 | 0.44 | - |
| | xavier_uniform | 1.31 | 52.88 | 55.34 | 0.32 | 0.30 | 0.38 | - |
| | avg_all | 1.31 | 52.89 | 55.36 | 0.35 | **0.60** | **0.46** | - |
| | avg_subwords | **1.30** | **53.34** | **55.36** | **0.37** | 0.35 | **0.46** | - |

Table 5: Multilingual evaluations across token embedding initialization methods

benchmarks. For Thai and Arabic, avg_subwords achieves marginally better scores while for Hungarian the results are mixed. These results show that the choice of initialization has minimal impact on the accuracy of end model when trained for 10 billion tokens. However avg_subwords gives faster training loss convergence, so we chose to initialize the new embeddings using avg_subwords.

## 5.2 Direct Preference Optimization

### 5.2.1 DPO Data Mixture

There is a lack of supervised finetuning and human alignment data across different languages. Collecting such data can be difficult and expensive. Given that the models obtained from our methodology are bilingual, we explore the question of how much of the human alignment data can be English and how much of it has to be from the target language. We run DPO on data mixtures of the English/Target language data ratio across 100:1, 10:1, 10:3 and 1:1, and observe the resulting win-rate in pairwise comparisons with the model trained on a 1:1 data ratio. For each experiment we keep the amount of English data the same and downscale the target language. We run these experiments on two languages: Hungarian and Arabic, with results in Table 6. We show that a 10:1 data ratio can perform almost as well as 1:1 data ratio for Hungarian. For Arabic, even a 10:3 data ratio still falls behind the performance of 1:1. One hypothesis is that Hungarian is more linguistically similar to English than Hungarian so there is more language transfer during fine tuning, but further research is needed to understand how the language impacts optimal alignment data mixture ratio.

### 5.2.2 Impact of Translated Human Preference Data

Results in Table 6 are based on translated data from the target language. Üstün et al. (2024) emphasized the importance of human written prompt completion pairs and claim that translated data does not perform as well. However, their work does not start with a high quality pretrained base model, nor do they use DPO. In order to understand whether machine translated data is a viable option for human alignment, we explore the impact of alignment using both approaches. We use Google translated ultrafeedback-200k data for one run and human-written data from Open Assistant Conversations (OASST1) (Köpf et al., 2023) for the other. We run this study on Russian, as it is has the most hu-

| Target Language: English Ratio | 100:1 | 10:1 | 10:3 | 1:1 |
|---|---|---|---|---|
| Arabic | 30.39% | 35.00% | 34.62% | 50.00% |
| Hungarian | 39.29% | 45.18% | 45.78% | 50.00% |

Table 6: DPO data mixture result (win-rate compared with 1:1 data mixture)

| Base Model | ppl(↓) | FLORES EN→X(↑) | FLORES X→en(↑) | Belebele(↑) | SIB-200(↑) |
|---|---|---|---|---|---|
| GPT-13B | 1.80 | 37.94 | 48.99 | 0.28 | **0.25** |
| Llama-2-7b | **1.61** | **53.72** | **58.65** | **0.34** | **0.25** |

Table 7: Performance of GPT-13B and Llama 2 7B on Hungarian benchmarks after adaptation

man written data from OASST1 (Köpf et al., 2023). The model trained using translated data attains a 50.47% win rate compared to the model trained with OASST1. This comparison does not control for the diversity and quality of the question answer pairs in the dataset because chat datasets with parallel human translated data in multiple languages. so this comparison is not meant to illustrate that translated data is as good or better than native data, but rather to show that human written data is not a silver bullet required to obtain good quality aligned models in other languages.

### 5.3 Importance Of Base Model Quality

To explore the relationship between the quality of the base model employed for language adaptation and its subsequent impact on accuracy in the target language, we ablate using two different base models - Llama 2 7B and GPT-13B (Srinivasan et al., 2023). The GPT-13B model is trained on much fewer tokens compared to llama2. We measure the GPT-13B model on some commonly accepted English benchmarks instead of our multilingual evaluation suite because these benchmarks are used more frequently to compare English checkpoints. GPT-13B lags behind Llama 2 7B in every English evaluation tasks we measured in Table 9.

We adapt both of these models to Hungarian. Table 7 illustrates that using a higher quality base model (Llama 2 7B) leads to better downstream performance in the target language. These results show that many of the benefits of training come from the base model quality not just the continuous training we do. This additionally indicates that as newer higher quality models become available, there is value in applying our proposed adaptation methodology on new base models.

## 6 Limitations

Our work has several limitations, including the need for extensive data from the target language, which is often unavailable for many languages. We study 9 diverse languages, but further research is required to address multilingual data scarcity and generalize our recipe. Due to compute and time constraints, our ablation studies focus on around 3 languages each, assuming similar results for other languages, although linguistic diversity and data availability may affect this. Additionally, we evaluate our chat-based model using GPT-4 as a judge, and while this has been shown to strongly correlate with human preferences in English, we are uncertain how well this works in other languages. We acknowledge that publicly releasing LLMs is risky because they can inadvertently generate harmful or biased content, compromise privacy, and be exploited for malicious purposes such as spreading misinformation. Moreover, while our models are adapted to other languages and cultures, the English base model, data biases, and use of translation may prevent them from fully capturing the nuances of cultures and languages from around the world.

## 7 Conclusion

We present a methodology to adapt pretrained LLMs to new languages. The methodology encompasses both continuous pretraining and alignment to human preferences in the target language. We present experimental results to justify our design choices and scale our methodology to 9 typologically diverse languages and 2 parameter scales. We make our evaluation scripts and final checkpoints publically available to facilitate future research, and we hope this work outlines a clearer path towards attaining state of the art language models in every language.

## References

David Adelani, Hannah Liu, Xiaoyu Shen, Nikita Vassilyev, Jesujoba Alabi, Yanke Mao, Haonan Gao, and En-Shiun Lee. 2024. SIB-200: A simple, inclusive, and big evaluation dataset for topic classification in 200+ languages and dialects. In *Proceedings of the 18th Conference of the European Chapter of the Association for Computational Linguistics (Volume 1: Long Papers)*, pages 226–245, St. Julian's, Malta. Association for Computational Linguistics.

Ebtesam Almazrouei, Hamza Alobeidli, Abdulaziz Alshamsi, Alessandro Cappelli, Ruxandra Cojocaru, Mérouane Debbah, Étienne Goffinet, Daniel Hesslow, Julien Launay, Quentin Malartic, et al. 2023. The falcon series of open language models. *arXiv preprint arXiv:2311.16867*.

AI Anthropic. 2024. The claude 3 model family: Opus, sonnet, haiku. *Claude-3 Model Card*.

Lucas Bandarkar, Davis Liang, Benjamin Muller, Mikel Artetxe, Satya Narayan Shukla, Donald Husa, Naman Goyal, Abhinandan Krishnan, Luke Zettlemoyer, and Madian Khabsa. 2023. The belebele benchmark: a parallel reading comprehension dataset in 122 language variants. *arXiv preprint arXiv:2308.16884*.

Terra Blevins, Tomasz Limisiewicz, Suchin Gururangan, Margaret Li, Hila Gonen, Noah A. Smith, and Luke Zettlemoyer. 2024. Breaking the curse of multilinguality with cross-lingual expert language models. *Preprint*, arXiv:2401.10440.

Tyler A. Chang, Catherine Arnett, Zhuowen Tu, and Benjamin K. Bergen. 2023. When is multilinguality a curse? language modeling for 250 high- and low-resource languages. *Preprint*, arXiv:2311.09205.

Hyung Won Chung, Noah Constant, Xavier Garcia, Adam Roberts, Yi Tay, Sharan Narang, and Orhan Firat. 2023. Unimax: Fairer and more effective language sampling for large-scale multilingual pretraining. *Preprint*, arXiv:2304.09151.

Alexis Conneau, Kartikay Khandelwal, Naman Goyal, Vishrav Chaudhary, Guillaume Wenzek, Francisco Guzmán, Edouard Grave, Myle Ott, Luke Zettlemoyer, and Veselin Stoyanov. 2020. Unsupervised cross-lingual representation learning at scale. *Preprint*, arXiv:1911.02116.

Alexis Conneau, Ruty Rinott, Guillaume Lample, Adina Williams, Samuel Bowman, Holger Schwenk, and Veselin Stoyanov. 2018. XNLI: Evaluating cross-lingual sentence representations. In *Proceedings of the 2018 Conference on Empirical Methods in Natural Language Processing*, pages 2475–2485, Brussels, Belgium. Association for Computational Linguistics.

Zoltan Csaki, Pian Pawakapan, Urmish Thakker, and Qiantong Xu. 2023. Efficiently adapting pretrained language models to new languages. *Preprint*, arXiv:2311.05741.

Ganqu Cui, Lifan Yuan, Ning Ding, Guanming Yao, Wei Zhu, Yuan Ni, Guotong Xie, Zhiyuan Liu, and Maosong Sun. 2023a. Ultrafeedback: Boosting language models with high-quality feedback. *Preprint*, arXiv:2310.01377.

Yiming Cui, Ziqing Yang, and Xin Yao. 2023b. Efficient and effective text encoding for chinese llama and alpaca. *Preprint*, arXiv:2304.08177.

Abteen Ebrahimi and Katharina Kann. 2021. How to adapt your pretrained multilingual model to 1600 languages. *Preprint*, arXiv:2106.02124.

Denis Emelin and Rico Sennrich. 2021. Wino-X: Multilingual Winograd schemas for commonsense reasoning and coreference resolution. In *Proceedings of the 2021 Conference on Empirical Methods in Natural Language Processing*, pages 8517–8532, Online and Punta Cana, Dominican Republic. Association for Computational Linguistics.

Hugo Touvron et al. 2023. Llama 2: Open foundation and fine-tuned chat models. *Preprint*, arXiv:2307.09288.

Leo Gao, Jonathan Tow, Baber Abbasi, Stella Biderman, Sid Black, Anthony DiPofi, Charles Foster, Laurence Golding, Jeffrey Hsu, Alain Le Noac'h, Haonan Li, Kyle McDonell, Niklas Muennighoff, Chris Ociepa, Jason Phang, Laria Reynolds, Hailey Schoelkopf, Aviya Skowron, Lintang Sutawika, Eric Tang, Anish Thite, Ben Wang, Kevin Wang, and Andy Zou. 2023. A framework for few-shot language model evaluation.

Naman Goyal, Cynthia Gao, Vishrav Chaudhary, Peng-Jen Chen, Guillaume Wenzek, Da Ju, Sanjana Krishnan, Marc'Aurelio Ranzato, Francisco Guzmán, and Angela Fan. 2021. The flores-101 evaluation benchmark for low-resource and multilingual machine translation.

Kshitij Gupta, Benjamin Thérien, Adam Ibrahim, Mats L. Richter, Quentin Anthony, Eugene Belilovsky, Irina Rish, and Timothée Lesort. 2023. Continual pre-training of large language models: How to (re)warm your model? *Preprint*, arXiv:2308.04014.

Ilya Gusev. 2023. Saiga 7b.

Momchil Hardalov, Todor Mihaylov, Dimitrina Zlatkova, Yoan Dinkov, Ivan Koychev, and Preslav Nakov. 2020. EXAMS: A multi-subject high school examinations dataset for cross-lingual and multilingual question answering. In *Proceedings of the 2020 Conference on Empirical Methods in Natural Language Processing (EMNLP)*, pages 5427–5444, Online. Association for Computational Linguistics.

John Hewitt. 2021. Initializing new word embeddings for pretrained language models.

Edward J Hu, Yelong shen, Phillip Wallis, Zeyuan Allen-Zhu, Yuanzhi Li, Shean Wang, Lu Wang, and Weizhu Chen. 2022. LoRA: Low-rank adaptation of large language models. In *International Conference on Learning Representations*.

Shengyi Huang, Lewis Tunstall, Edward Beeching, Leandro von Werra, Omar Sanseviero, Kashif Rasul, and Thomas Wolf. 2024. Constitutional ai recipe. *Hugging Face Blog*.

Srinivasan Iyer, Xi Victoria Lin, Ramakanth Pasunuru, Todor Mihaylov, Daniel Simig, Ping Yu, Kurt Shuster, Tianlu Wang, Qing Liu, Punit Singh Koura, Xian Li, Brian O'Horo, Gabriel Pereyra, Jeff Wang, Christopher Dewan, Asli Celikyilmaz, Luke Zettlemoyer, and Ves Stoyanov. 2022. OPT-IML: scaling language model instruction meta learning through the lens of generalization. *CoRR*, abs/2212.12017.

Fajri Koto, Jey Han Lau, and Timothy Baldwin. 2021. Indobertweet: A pretrained language model for indonesian twitter with effective domain-specific vocabulary initialization. *Preprint*, arXiv:2109.04607.

Andreas Köpf, Yannic Kilcher, Dimitri von Rütte, Sotiris Anagnostidis, Zhi-Rui Tam, Keith Stevens, Abdullah Barhoum, Nguyen Minh Duc, Oliver Stanley, Richárd Nagyfi, Shahul ES, Sameer Suri, David Glushkov, Arnav Dantuluri, Andrew Maguire, Christoph Schuhmann, Huu Nguyen, and Alexander Mattick. 2023. Openassistant conversations – democratizing large language model alignment. *Preprint*, arXiv:2304.07327.

Peiqin Lin, Shaoxiong Ji, Jörg Tiedemann, André F. T. Martins, and Hinrich Schütze. 2024. Mala-500: Massive language adaptation of large language models. *Preprint*, arXiv:2401.13303.

Xi Victoria Lin, Todor Mihaylov, Mikel Artetxe, Tianlu Wang, Shuohui Chen, Daniel Simig, Myle Ott, Naman Goyal, Shruti Bhosale, Jingfei Du, Ramakanth Pasunuru, Sam Shleifer, Punit Singh Koura, Vishrav Chaudhary, Brian O'Horo, Jeff Wang, Luke Zettlemoyer, Zornitsa Kozareva, Mona Diab, Veselin Stoyanov, and Xian Li. 2022. Few-shot learning with multilingual language models. *Preprint*, arXiv:2112.10668.

Mingjie Liu, Teodor-Dumitru Ene, Robert Kirby, Chris Cheng, Nathaniel Pinckney, Rongjian Liang, Jonah Alben, Himyanshu Anand, Sanmitra Banerjee, Ismet Bayraktaroglu, Bonita Bhaskaran, Bryan Catanzaro, Arjun Chaudhuri, Sharon Clay, Bill Dally, Laura Dang, Parikshit Deshpande, Siddhanth Dhodhi, Sameer Halepete, Eric Hill, Jiashang Hu, Sumit Jain, Ankit Jindal, Brucek Khailany, George Kokai, Kishor Kunal, Xiaowei Li, Charley Lind, Hao Liu, Stuart Oberman, Sujeet Omar, Sreedhar Pratty, Jonathan Raiman, Ambar Sarkar, Zhengjiang Shao, Hanfei Sun, Pratik P Suthar, Varun Tej, Walker Turner, Kaizhe Xu, and Haoxing Ren. 2024. Chipnemo: Domain-adapted llms for chip design. *Preprint*, arXiv:2311.00176.

Niklas Muennighoff, Alexander M. Rush, Boaz Barak, Teven Le Scao, Aleksandra Piktus, Nouamane Tazi, Sampo Pyysalo, Thomas Wolf, and Colin Raffel. 2023. Scaling data-constrained language models. *Preprint*, arXiv:2305.16264.

Thuat Nguyen, Chien Van Nguyen, Viet Dac Lai, Hieu Man, Nghia Trung Ngo, Franck Dernoncourt, Ryan A. Rossi, and Thien Huu Nguyen. 2023. Culturax: A cleaned, enormous, and multilingual dataset for large language models in 167 languages. *Preprint*, arXiv:2309.09400.

OpenAI and Josh Achiam et al. 2024. Gpt-4 technical report. *Preprint*, arXiv:2303.08774.

Kunat Pipatanakul, Phatrasek Jirabovonvisut, Potsawee Manakul, Sittipong Sripaisarnmongkol, Ruangsak Patomwong, Pathomporn Chokchainant, and Kasima Tharnpipitchai. 2023. Typhoon: Thai large language models. *Preprint*, arXiv:2312.13951.

Ramon Pires, Hugo Abonizio, Thales Sales Almeida, and Rodrigo Nogueira. 2023. *Sabiá: Portuguese Large Language Models*, page 226–240. Springer Nature Switzerland.

Edoardo Maria Ponti, Goran Glavaš, Olga Majewska, Qianchu Liu, Ivan Vulić, and Anna Korhonen. 2020. XCOPA: A multilingual dataset for causal commonsense reasoning. In *Proceedings of the 2020 Conference on Empirical Methods in Natural Language Processing (EMNLP)*, pages 2362–2376, Online. Association for Computational Linguistics.

Maja Popović. 2015. chrF: character n-gram F-score for automatic MT evaluation. In *Proceedings of the Tenth Workshop on Statistical Machine Translation*, pages 392–395, Lisbon, Portugal. Association for Computational Linguistics.

Colin Raffel, Noam Shazeer, Adam Roberts, Katherine Lee, Sharan Narang, Michael Matena, Yanqi Zhou, Wei Li, and Peter J. Liu. 2019. Exploring the limits of transfer learning with a unified text-to-text transformer. *arXiv e-prints*.

Together Computer SambaNova Systems. 2023. BLOOMChat: a New Open Multilingual Chat LLM.

Akira Sasaki, Masato Hirakawa, Shintaro Horie, and Tomoaki Nakamura. 2023. Elyza-japanese-llama-2-7b.

Neha Sengupta, Sunil Kumar Sahu, Bokang Jia, Satheesh Katipomu, Haonan Li, Fajri Koto, William Marshall, Gurpreet Gosal, Cynthia Liu, Zhiming Chen, Osama Mohammed Afzal, Samta Kamboj, Onkar Pandit, Rahul Pal, Lalit Pradhan, Zain Muhammad Mujahid, Massa Baali, Xudong Han, Sondos Mahmoud Bsharat, Alham Fikri Aji, Zhiqiang Shen, Zhengzhong Liu, Natalia Vassilieva, Joel Hestness, Andy Hock, Andrew Feldman, Jonathan Lee, Andrew Jackson, Hector Xuguang Ren, Preslav Nakov, Timothy Baldwin, and Eric Xing. 2023. Jais and jais-chat: Arabic-centric foundation and instruction-tuned open generative large language models. *Preprint*, arXiv:2308.16149.

Oleh Shliazhko, Alena Fenogenova, Maria Tikhonova, Vladislav Mikhailov, Anastasia Kozlova, and Tatiana Shavrina. 2023. mgpt: Few-shot learners go multilingual. *Preprint*, arXiv:2204.07580.

Venkat Srinivasan, Darshan Gandhi, Urmish Thakker, and Raghu Prabhakar. 2023. Training large language models efficiently with sparsity and dataflow. *Preprint*, arXiv:2304.05511.

Xianghui Sun, Yunjie Ji, Baochang Ma, and Xiangang Li. 2023. A comparative study between full-parameter and lora-based fine-tuning on chinese instruction data for instruction following large language model. *arXiv preprint arXiv:2304.08109*.

SambaNova Systems. 2023a. x-self-instruct-seed-32.

SambaNova Systems. 2023b. xoa22.

Mikhail Tikhomirov and Daniil Chernyshev. 2023. Impact of tokenization on llama russian adaptation. *Preprint*, arXiv:2312.02598.

TokyoTech. 2023. Swallow 7b.

Lewis Tunstall, Edward Beeching, Nathan Lambert, Nazneen Rajani, Kashif Rasul, Younes Belkada, Shengyi Huang, Leandro von Werra, Clémentine Fourrier, Nathan Habib, Nathan Sarrazin, Omar Sanseviero, Alexander M. Rush, and Thomas Wolf. 2023. Zephyr: Direct distillation of lm alignment. *Preprint*, arXiv:2310.16944.

Pat Verga, Sebastian Hofstatter, Sophia Althammer, Yixuan Su, Aleksandra Piktus, Arkady Arkhangorodsky, Minjie Xu, Naomi White, and Patrick Lewis. 2024. Replacing judges with juries: Evaluating llm generations with a panel of diverse models. *Preprint*, arXiv:2404.18796.

BigScience Workshop, :, and Teven Le Scao et al. 2023. Bloom: A 176b-parameter open-access multilingual language model. *Preprint*, arXiv:2211.05100.

Linting Xue, Noah Constant, Adam Roberts, Mihir Kale, Rami Al-Rfou, Aditya Siddhant, Aditya Barua, and Colin Raffel. 2021. mt5: A massively multilingual pre-trained text-to-text transformer. *Preprint*, arXiv:2010.11934.

Yinfei Yang, Yuan Zhang, Chris Tar, and Jason Baldridge. 2019. PAWS-X: A cross-lingual adversarial dataset for paraphrase identification. In *Proceedings of the 2019 Conference on Empirical Methods in Natural Language Processing and the 9th International Joint Conference on Natural Language Processing (EMNLP-IJCNLP)*, pages 3687–3692, Hong Kong, China. Association for Computational Linguistics.

Zijian Győző Yang, László János Laki, Tamás Váradi, and Gábor Prószéky. 2023. Mono- and multilingual gpt-3 models for hungarian. In *Text, Speech, and Dialogue*, Lecture Notes in Computer Science, pages 94–104, Plzeň, Czech Republic. Springer Nature Switzerland.

Jiacheng Ye, Xijia Tao, and Lingpeng Kong. 2023. Language versatilists vs. specialists: An empirical revisiting on multilingual transfer ability. *Preprint*, arXiv:2306.06688.

Zheng-Xin Yong, Hailey Schoelkopf, Niklas Muennighoff, Alham Fikri Aji, David Ifeoluwa Adelani, Khalid Almubarak, M Saiful Bari, Lintang Sutawika, Jungo Kasai, Ahmed Baruwa, Genta Indra Winata, Stella Biderman, Edward Raff, Dragomir Radev, and Vassilina Nikoulina. 2023. Bloom+1: Adding language support to bloom for zero-shot prompting. *Preprint*, arXiv:2212.09535.

Zhengyan Zhang, Xu Han, Hao Zhou, Pei Ke, Yuxian Gu, Deming Ye, Yujia Qin, Yusheng Su, Haozhe Ji, Jian Guan, Fanchao Qi, Xiaozhi Wang, Yanan Zheng, Guoyang Zeng, Huanqi Cao, Shengqi Chen, Daixuan Li, Zhenbo Sun, Zhiyuan Liu, Minlie Huang, Wentao Han, Jie Tang, Juanzi Li, Xiaoyan Zhu, and Maosong Sun. 2020. Cpm: A large-scale generative chinese pre-trained language model. *Preprint*, arXiv:2012.00413.

Jiawei Zhao, Zhenyu Zhang, Beidi Chen, Zhangyang Wang, Anima Anandkumar, and Yuandong Tian. 2024a. Galore: Memory-efficient llm training by gradient low-rank projection. *arXiv preprint arXiv:2403.03507*.

Jun Zhao, Zhihao Zhang, Luhui Gao, Qi Zhang, Tao Gui, and Xuanjing Huang. 2024b. Llama beyond english: An empirical study on language capability transfer. *Preprint*, arXiv:2401.01055.

Lianmin Zheng, Wei-Lin Chiang, Ying Sheng, Siyuan Zhuang, Zhanghao Wu, Yonghao Zhuang, Zi Lin, Zhuohan Li, Dacheng Li, Eric P. Xing, Hao Zhang, Joseph E. Gonzalez, and Ion Stoica. 2023. Judging llm-as-a-judge with mt-bench and chatbot arena. *Preprint*, arXiv:2306.05685.

Wenhao Zhu, Hongyi Liu, Qingxiu Dong, Jingjing Xu, Shujian Huang, Lingpeng Kong, Jiajun Chen, and Lei Li. 2023. Multilingual machine translation with large language models: Empirical results and analysis. *Preprint*, arXiv:2304.04675.

Judit Ács. 2019. Exploring bert's vocabulary.

Ahmet Üstün, Viraat Aryabumi, Zheng-Xin Yong, Wei-Yin Ko, Daniel D'souza, Gbemileke Onilude, Neel Bhandari, Shivalika Singh, Hui-Lee Ooi, Amr Kayid, Freddie Vargus, Phil Blunsom, Shayne Longpre, Niklas Muennighoff, Marzieh Fadaee, Julia Kreutzer, and Sara Hooker. 2024. Aya model: An instruction finetuned open-access multilingual language model. *Preprint*, arXiv:2402.07827.

## A Hyperparameters

- **Continuous Pre-training**: We pack the pretraining mixture into sequences of length 4096 and pretrain with *document attention* as described in Section 3.2 of Iyer et al. (2022) to ensure we only attend to tokens in the context of the corresponding text document. We train with a global batch size of 1024, sequence length of 4096, maximum learning rate of 1e-4 with cosine decay, warm-up ratio of 0.01 and a weight decay of 0.1. Each expert is trained for a maximum of 4 epochs, following (Muennighoff et al., 2023). Notably, we train all model parameters, foregoing use of PEFT methods such as LoRA (Hu et al., 2022), which are known to be inferior to full parameter training (Zhao et al., 2024a)(Sun et al., 2023).

- **Supervised Finetuning**: We use a global batch size of 512 and a maximum sequence length of 2048 tokens. We used a linear decay learning rate of 2e-5 with 10% warm up

- **Direct Preference Optimization**: We train with a global batch size 32 for 3 epochs, a linear decay learning rate of 5e-7, 10% warmup and $\beta = 0.1$ as the regularization factor for DPO

## B Language Experts vs Monolith Multilingual Model

"The Curse Of Multilinguality" (Chang et al., 2023; Conneau et al., 2020) is the idea that LLMs have a fixed capacity with which to learn various languages. This theory claims that as one expands the number of languages a model is trained on, the various languages compete for the capacity of the model, therefore degrading the models performance across all languages. Blevins et al. (2024) attempt to address this phenomenon by adapting multiple small-scale language experts from XGLM-1.7B (Lin et al., 2022), one for each language, and show that each expert outperforms training a single monolithic model trained simultaneously on one language. We build on these results by scaling this study to 7B parameters and use more comprehensive evaluation metrics than just perplexity. We compare our 9 Llama 2 7B language experts against a monolith Llama 2 7B model continuously pretrained on all 9 languages. We ensure that each language is represented equally in the monolith's training data and the vocabulary is expanded to represent all 9 languages evenly.

For comparison's sake, we select intermediate model checkpoints such that each individual language expert has used the same amount of compute as the monolith multilingual model. This means that the experts required 9x more compute to train then the monolith. Table 8 averages the evaluation results across all 9 languages and finds that the monolith model and language experts have very similar performance. This implies that if one wants to adapt to many languages at once, it may be more compute-efficient to continuously train a multi-linugal model rather then independent experts. Further work is warranted to determine how this result scales with an increasing number of target languages.

| **Benchmark (Num Shots)** | **Llama2-7b Avg** | **Multilingual Monolith Avg** | **Language Expert Avg** |
|---|---|---|---|
| $\downarrow$ Holdout PPL | 1.75 | 1.55 | **1.50** |
| $\uparrow$ FLORES (8) | 40.42% | 50.69% | **51.71%** |
| $\uparrow$ Belebele (3) | **36.24%** | 33.36% | 32.09% |
| $\uparrow$ SIB-200(3) | 26.67% | **38.04%** | 33.43% |
| $\uparrow$ XNLI (0) | 39.00% | **43.44%** | 43.04% |
| $\uparrow$ XStoryCloze (0) | 56.35% | 65.75% | **68.03%** |
| $\uparrow$ XWinograd (0) | 69.48% | **72.39%** | 71.97% |
| $\uparrow$ PAWS-X (0) | 51.00% | **54.40%** | 53.50% |
| $\uparrow$ MGSM (3) | **5.40%** | 4.00% | 4.20% |

Table 8: Monolith multilingual continuous training vs language experts, averaged over all 9 languages.

## C Base Model English Evaluation

| | HellaSwag(↑) | OpenBookQA(↑) | ARC-E(↑) | ARC-C(↑) | PiQA(↑) | Winogrande(↑) |
|---|---|---|---|---|---|---|
| GPT-13B | 0.60 | 0.36 | 0.53 | 0.30 | 0.76 | 0.60 |
| Llama-2-7B | **0.76** | **0.57** | **0.73** | **0.48** | **0.80** | **0.70** |

Table 9: Performance of GPT-13B and Llama-2-7B on English NLU benchmarks

## D Qualitative Results

For Arabic, we compare our 7B arabic expert with aya-101 (Üstün et al., 2024), Jais-13b-chat (Sengupta et al., 2023), and Bloomchat-v1 (SambaNova Systems, 2023) and use prompts from x-self-instruct-seed-32 (Systems, 2023a) and xOA22 (Systems, 2023b). Our Arabic chat model reaches 87.96% win rate compared to Jais-13B-chat, 99.06% win rate compared to Aya101, and 68.52% compared to Bloomchat-v1. For Japanese, we compare our Japanese chat model with ELYZA-japanese-Llama-2-7b-instruct (Sasaki et al., 2023) on 100 randomly sampled prompts aya dataset (Üstün et al., 2024), reaching a win rate of 53.5% For Turkish, we compare our Turkish chat model against aya-101 (Üstün et al., 2024) using prompts from the test set of aya dataset (Üstün et al., 2024), leading to win-rate of 92.4%.

### D.1 Evaluating Chat Models With Claude

We run evaluations using the same prompt as GPT-4 as a judge, but use Claude Opus (Anthropic, 2024) as a judge. Figure 5 shows the evaluations to be in line with our previous results with GPT-4 as a judge 3. This shows that there is no strong bias in using GPT-4 as a judge.

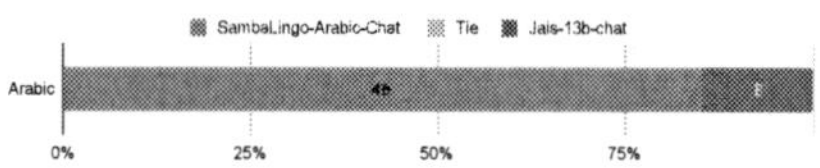


(a) SambaLingo vs Jais-13b-chat

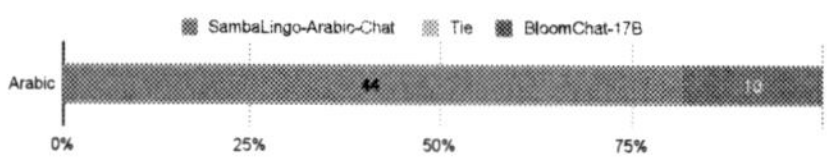


(b) SambaLingo vs BloomChat-v1

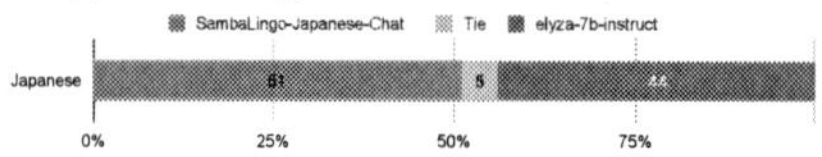


(c) SambaLingo vs ELEYZA-7b-instruct

Figure 5: Claude Opus evalution results

### D.2 GPT-4 As A Judge

Below are some examples of how GPT-4 judged two candidate responses in Japanese, Arabic and Turkish. See figures 6, 7, 8, 9, 10, 11

| Prompt | Model 1 Completion | Model 2 Completion | GPT4 Judge |
|---|---|---|---|
| １８６９年に開通した世界最長の運河の名前は何でしょう? | １８６９年に開通した世界最長の運河の名前は、「グランド・キャニオン・アンド・サンタフェ・アンド・トレイル・パス運河」です。<br><br>この運河はアメリカ合衆国のアリゾナ州とニューメキシコ州を結ぶ全長約435kmの運河です。<br><br>ちなみに、現在世界最長の運河は、アフリカ大陸とアジア大陸を結ぶ「スエズ運河」です。 | 世界最長の運河は、1869 年に開通したスエズ運河です。 | Assistant A's response is incorrect. The canal opened in 1869 is the Suez Canal, not the "Grand Canyon and Santa Fe and Trail Pass Canal" as stated by Assistant A. Furthermore, the Suez Canal is not only the longest canal opened in 1869, but it is also currently the longest canal in the world. Assistant B correctly identifies the Suez Canal as the longest canal opened in 1869. Therefore, Assistant B's response is more accurate and relevant to the user's question. |

Figure 6: Japanese Example 1

| Prompt | Model 1 Completion | Model 2 Completion | GPT4 Judge |
|---|---|---|---|
| 俳句は全部で１７文字からなりますが、短歌は全部で何文字からなるでしょう? | 短歌は通常、俳句よりも長く、全編で少なくとも 31 文字あります。 | 短歌は、全部で５文字からなる「五七五」が基本です。 | Assistant A's response is correct. A Tanka (短歌) in Japanese poetry is composed of 31 syllables (or "on" in Japanese), not 5 as Assistant B incorrectly states. Assistant B seems to be confusing Tanka with Haiku, which is composed of 17 syllables and is often structured as 5-7-5. Therefore, Assistant A provides a more accurate and relevant answer to the user's question. |

Figure 7: Japanese Example 2

| Prompt | Model 1 Completion | Model 2 Completion | GPT4 Judge |
| --- | --- | --- | --- |
| من 1 إلى 10 ما هو تأثير Novalgin على تخفيف الألام إعتماداً على الإحصائيات المتاحة | لا توجد إحصائيات دقيقة لتقييم مدى تم شركة Google Inc.، المعروفة ببساطة باسم \"Google\"، هي شركة أمريكية متعددة الجنسيات متخصصة في مجال الإعلان المرتبط بخدمات الإنترنت والبحث.<br><br>تأسست الشركة في 4 سبتمبر 1998 من قبل Larry Page و Sergey Brin ، وهما طالبا الدكتوراه في جامعة ستانفورد . يقع مقرها الرئيسي في Menlo Park ، كاليفورنيا ، الولايات المتحدة الأمريكية .<br><br>دأت Google كشركة خاصة ، وتم طرح أسهمها للاكتتاب العام في 19 أغسطس 2004. اعتبارًا من 3 يناير 2023 ، تعد Alphabet Inc. الشركة الأم لشركة Google.<br><br>في غضون بضع سنوات من تأسيسه ، أصبح Google أحد أكثر الأسماء شهرة وشعبية بين مستخدمي الإنترنت حول العالم. بحلول عام 2021 ، احتفظ Google بأكثر من 95٪ من حصة السوق العالمية لمحركات البحث ، مما جعله المهيمن بلا منازع في هذا المجال. | نشاء Google في عام 1998 على يد سيرجي برين ولاري بيج عندما كانا طالبين في جامعة ستانفورد. لقد بدأوا كمشروع بحثي في جامعة ستانفورد، وسرعان ما أدركوا إمكانات محرك البحث الذي قاموا بإنشائه. في عام 1998، قاموا بتسجيل Google كشركة، وفي عام 1999، تم إطلاق Google كمحرك بحث عام.<br><br>كان أحد العوامل الرئيسية التي ساهمت في هيمنة Google على محركات البحث هو تركيزها على تزويد المستخدمين بنتائج بحث عالية الجودة وذات صلة. لقد استثمروا بكثافة في تطوير خوارزميات البحث الخاصة بهم، والتي تم تصميمها لتحديد مواقع الويب الأكثر صلة واستجابة لاستعلامات المستخدم. بالإضافة إلى ذلك، قدمت Google ميزات مثل التصفية الجغرافية، واقتراحات البحث التلقائية، ونتائج البحث الفوري، والتي جعلت من السهل على المستخدمين العثور على المعلومات التي يحتاجون إليها بسرعة.<br><br>هناك عامل آخر ساهم في نجاح Google وهو تركيزها على تجربة المستخدم. لقد أدركوا أن المستخدمين يريدون نتائج بحث سريعة ودقيقة وسهلة الاستخدام، وقد استثمروا في إنشاء واجهة سهلة الاستخدام وبديهية. لقد قاموا أيضًا بدمج العديد من الميزات التي جعلت من السهل على المستخدمين التنقل في نتائج البحث الخاصة بهم، مثل شريط البحث، ونتائج البحث المنسدلة، ونتائج البحث المنسدلة.<br><br>بشكل عام، كان الجمع بين خوارزميات البحث عالية الجودة، وتجربة المستخدم الرائعة، والتركيز على الابتكار هو الذي ساعد Google على أن تصبح محرك البحث الأكثر شعبية في العالم. | Both assistants provided relevant and accurate information about the effectiveness of Novalgin in pain relief. However, Assistant A provided a more comprehensive response by mentioning a specific study published in a pain research journal in 2016, and also discussed the factors that might affect the effectiveness of Novalgin. Assistant B also mentioned some studies, but the information provided was less detailed and less specific compared to Assistant A. Therefore, Assistant A's response is more helpful and detailed.<br><br>Final Verdict: [[A]] |

Figure 8: Arabic Example 1

| Prompt | Model 1 Completion | Model 2 Completion | GPT4 Judge |
|---|---|---|---|
| من 1 إلى 10 ما هو تأثير Novalgin على تخفيف الألام إعتماداً على الإحصائيات المتاحة | لا توجد إحصائيات دقيقة لتقييم مدى فعالية النوفالجين في تسكين الألم. ومع ذلك، فإن بعض الدراسات تشير إلى أن النوفالجين قد يكون فعالًا مثل مضادات الالتهاب غير الستيرويدية (NSAIDs) الأخرى في علاج آلام الأسنان والتهاب المفاصل.<br><br>وقد وجدت دراسة صغيرة عام 2013 أن النوفالجين كان أكثر فعالية من دواء وهمي في تقليل ألم عصب الضرس بعد خلعه. ووجدت دراسة أخرى عام 2014 أن النوفالجين كان له نفس الفعالية مثل الإيبوبروفين في علاج التهاب مفصل الفك الصدغي.<br><br>ومع ذلك، هناك حاجة لمزيد من الأبحاث لتحديد مدى فعالية النوفالجين في تسكين الألم بشكل دقيق. | لا يمكنني الوصول إلى أحدث الإحصائيات، ولكن وفقًا لدراسة نشرت في مجلة أبحاث الألم في عام 2016، فإن نوفالاجين فعال في تخفيف الألم المعتدل إلى الشديد لدى المرضى الذين يعانون من آلام ما بعد الجراحة. وجدت الدراسة أن نوفالاجين كان أكثر فعالية من العلاج الوهمي في تقليل شدة الألم ومدته. ومع ذلك، قد تختلف فعالية نوفالاجين في تخفيف الألم اعتمادًا على عوامل مثل شدة الألم، ومدة الألم، والحالة الصحية العامة للمريض. من الأفضل دائمًا استشارة أخصائي الرعاية الصحية لتحديد أفضل خيارات إدارة الألم بناءً على احتياجات الفرد الخاصة. | Both assistants provided relevant and accurate information about the effectiveness of Novalgin in pain relief. However, Assistant A provided a more comprehensive response by mentioning a specific study published in a pain research journal in 2016, and also discussed the factors that might affect the effectiveness of Novalgin. Assistant B also mentioned some studies, but the information provided was less detailed and less specific compared to Assistant A. Therefore, Assistant A's response is more helpful and detailed.<br><br>Final Verdict: [[A]] |

Figure 9: Arabic Example 2

| Prompt | Model 1 Completion | Model 2 Completion | GPT4 Judge |
|---|---|---|---|
| Cilt bakımında buhar kaç dakika verilir? | ika arasında yapılır. | Cilt bakımı rutinine buhar uygulaması genellikle 5-10 dakika kadar kısa bir süre için yapılır. Buhar, gözeneklerin açılmasına ve cildin nemlendirilmesine yardımcı olur, bu da onu cilt bakımı rutininin önemli bir parçası haline getirir. Ancak cilt tipine ve kişisel tercihe bağlı olarak buhar süresi ayarlanabilir. Buhar uygulaması sırasında ciltte herhangi bir rahatsızlık veya tahriş hissedilirse, buhar uygulaması durdurulmalı ve bir dermatoloğa veya cilt bakımı uzmanına danışılmalıdır. | Assistant A's response is incomplete and does not provide any useful information to the user's question. On the other hand, Assistant B provides a detailed and informative response, explaining that steam is typically applied for 5-10 minutes during a skincare routine, the benefits of steam, and advice on what to do if discomfort or irritation is experienced. Therefore, Assistant B's response is more helpful, relevant, and accurate. My final verdict is: [[B]] |

Figure 10: Turkish Example 1

| Prompt | Model 1 Completion | Model 2 Completion | GPT4 Judge |
|---|---|---|---|
| Sütçü İmam Üniversitesi ne zaman kuruldu? | li ilçesinde, Sivas Valisi Süleyman Demirel'in talimatıyla, Sivas'ın tanınmış tarihi ve kültürel değerlerine sahip, Sivas'ın ilk ve tek devlet üniversitesi olarak kurulmuştur. | Kahramanmaraş Sütçü İmam University (KSÜ) was founded in 1986 and is located in the city of Kahramanmaraş in southeastern Turkey. | Assistant A provides a direct and accurate answer to the user's question, stating that Sütçü İmam University was established in 1986 and is located in Kahramanmaraş in southeastern Turkey. On the other hand, Assistant B's response is irrelevant and confusing, as it talks about a university in Sivas and mentions Süleyman Demirel, who was not related to the establishment of Sütçü İmam University. Therefore, Assistant A's response is more helpful, relevant, and accurate.<br><br>Final Verdict: [[A]] |

Figure 11: Turkish Example 2

# E Expanded Vocabulary Tokenizer Fertility

## E.1 Expanded Vocabulary Tokenizer Fertility

In figure 12 We measure the fertility of the tokenizer as we expand the vocabulary, and see that we can improve the fertility from about 4.8 to 1.1 on Thai. This is about a 4.35x improvement, implies that inference speeds can improve up to 4.35x compared to the Llama2 tokenizer.

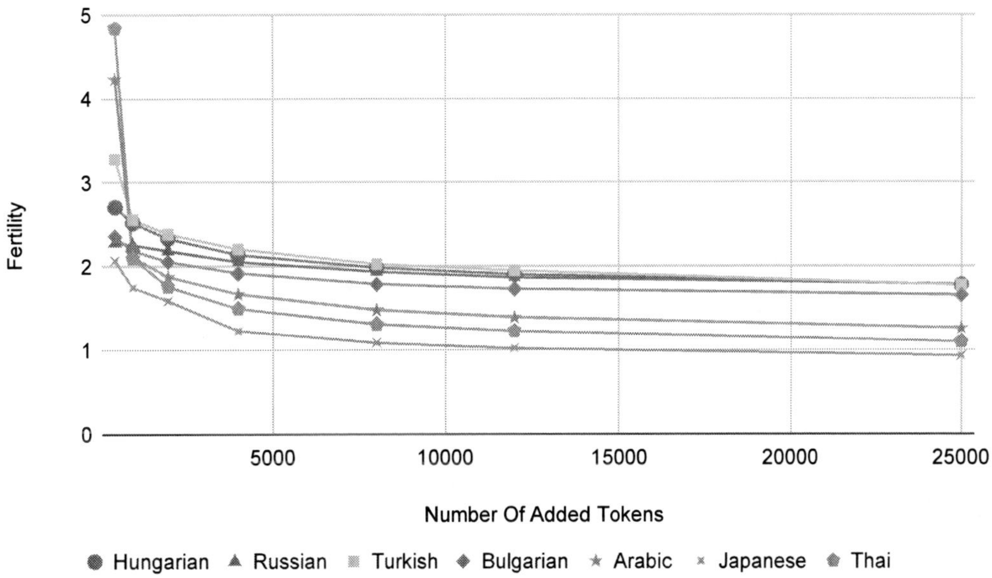


Figure 12: Tokenizer Fertility: the average number of tokens per "word" (Ács, 2019)

## F Main Results Details

See tables 13 and 14 for all evaluation results

| Langauge | Checkpoint | Holdout PPL | MC4 PPL | Wikipedia PPL | FLORES EN->X 8 shot CHRF | FLORES X->en 8 shot CHRF | FLORES EN->X 8 shot BLEU | FLORES X->en 8 shot BLEU | Belebele 3 shot | SIB-200 3 shot | Exams 3 shot | XNLI 0 shot | XStory Cloze 0 shot | XWinograd 0 shot | PAWS-X 0 shot | XCOPA 0 shot | MGSM 3 shot | Average |
|---|---|---|---|---|---|---|---|---|---|---|---|---|---|---|---|---|---|---|
| Russian | Our-Russian-7b | 1.44 | 1.35 | 1.30 | 54.90 | 61.13 | 27.67 | 35.07 | 0.35 | 0.43 | | 0.36 | 0.72 | 0.69 | | | 0.09 | 0.47 |
| Russian | Our Monolith | 1.48 | 1.37 | 1.35 | 53.45 | 59.72 | 25.57 | 31.93 | 0.34 | 0.44 | | 0.50 | 0.69 | 0.67 | | | 0.05 | 0.48 |
| Russian | Saiga-7b | 1.56 | 1.73 | 2.89 | 52.95 | 61.70 | 24.28 | 34.09 | 0.75 | 0.63 | | 0.50 | 0.69 | 0.67 | | | 0.33 | 0.59 |
| Russian | Llama2-7b | 1.53 | 1.49 | 1.36 | 49.59 | 59.55 | 21.83 | 33.70 | 0.42 | 0.26 | | 0.41 | 0.63 | 0.69 | | | 0.08 | 0.45 |
| Russian | bloom-7b1 | 1.51 | 1.40 | 1.38 | 28.22 | 44.75 | 5.60 | 18.07 | 0.27 | 0.25 | | 0.43 | 0.53 | 0.57 | | | 0.02 | 0.35 |
| Russian | xglm-7.5B | 1.80 | 1.79 | 1.81 | 32.62 | 50.64 | 4.33 | 17.48 | 0.25 | 0.26 | | 0.46 | 0.63 | 0.63 | | | 0.02 | 0.39 |
| Russian | AYA-101 | | | | 0.45 | 1.04 | 0.00 | 0.00 | 0.23 | 0.28 | | 0.40 | 0.60 | 0.63 | | | 0.00 | 0.27 |
| Arabic | Our-Arabic-70B | 1.39 | | | 57.67 | 66.99 | 26.05 | 41.21 | 0.74 | 0.73 | | 0.35 | 0.69 | | | | | 0.63 |
| Arabic | Our-Arabic-Base | 1.42 | 1.40 | 1.38 | 54.11 | 63.09 | 22.71 | 38.86 | 0.34 | 0.29 | | 0.34 | 0.66 | | | | | 0.47 |
| Arabic | Our Monolith | 1.52 | 1.49 | 1.49 | 49.39 | 58.39 | 69.82 | 54.70 | 0.31 | 0.36 | | 0.33 | 0.62 | | | | | 0.45 |
| Arabic | Jais-13b | 1.50 | 1.44 | 1.39 | 49.39 | 58.39 | 18.92 | 33.35 | 0.31 | 0.36 | | 0.33 | 0.62 | | | | | 0.45 |
| Arabic | Llama2-7b | 1.81 | 1.93 | 1.89 | 28.06 | 44.96 | 3.40 | 21.12 | 0.31 | 0.26 | | 0.35 | 0.50 | | | | | 0.36 |
| Arabic | bloomz-7 | 1.57 | 1.57 | 1.52 | 44.11 | 54.88 | 14.60 | 29.37 | 0.28 | 0.25 | | 0.34 | 0.59 | | | | | 0.41 |
| Arabic | xglm-7.5 | 1.60 | 1.60 | 1.59 | 18.87 | 49.39 | 1.17 | 22.80 | 0.25 | 0.26 | | 0.34 | 0.56 | | | | | 0.35 |
| Arabic | AYA-101 | | | | 0.37 | 0.88 | 0.00 | 0.00 | 0.23 | 0.28 | | 0.33 | 0.56 | | | | | 0.24 |
| Japanese | Our-Japanese-7B | 1.56 | 1.54 | 1.59 | 36.64 | 52.10 | 2.10 | 23.43 | 0.28 | 0.26 | | | | 0.77 | 0.54 | | 0.02 | 0.39 |
| Japanese | Our Monolith | 1.66 | 1.56 | 1.65 | 34.97 | 49.88 | 0.77 | 20.88 | 0.33 | 0.40 | | | | 0.78 | 0.54 | | 0.03 | 0.42 |
| Japanese | ELYZA-japanese-Llama | 1.75 | 1.76 | 1.72 | 16.88 | 43.94 | 0.01 | 15.24 | 0.34 | 0.43 | | | | 0.77 | 0.49 | | 0.02 | 0.38 |
| Japanese | Swallow | 1.65 | 1.77 | 1.75 | 39.58 | 50.87 | 1.12 | 22.16 | 0.39 | 0.27 | | | | 0.81 | 0.44 | | 0.10 | 0.42 |
| Japanese | Llama2-7b | 1.90 | 2.03 | 1.67 | 30.44 | 48.92 | 1.30 | 20.93 | 0.39 | 0.29 | | | | 0.70 | 0.51 | | 0.02 | 0.39 |
| Japanese | bloom-7b1 | 2.26 | 2.44 | 2.20 | 14.25 | 39.44 | 0.23 | 12.17 | 0.26 | 0.25 | | | | 0.59 | 0.55 | | 0.04 | 0.32 |
| Japanese | xglm-7.5B | 1.80 | 1.72 | 1.80 | 19.68 | 30.04 | 0.01 | 4.58 | 0.27 | 0.25 | | | | 0.65 | 0.48 | | 0.00 | 0.31 |
| Japanese | AYA-101 | | | | 0.32 | 0.94 | 0.00 | 0.00 | 0.23 | 0.29 | | | | 0.63 | 0.56 | | 0.00 | 0.25 |
| Thai | Our-Thai-70B | 1.24 | | | 55.41 | 62.45 | 11.92 | 36.13 | 0.74 | 0.77 | | 0.44 | | | | 0.64 | 0.24 | 0.57 |
| Thai | Our-Thai-7B | 1.29 | 1.23 | 1.22 | 54.21 | 56.07 | 11.64 | 29.94 | 0.38 | 0.65 | | 0.45 | | | | 0.61 | 0.08 | 0.47 |
| Thai | Our Monolith | 1.35 | 1.28 | 1.26 | 51.79 | 54.17 | 11.35 | 27.02 | 0.31 | 0.40 | | 0.48 | | | | 0.60 | 0.06 | 0.42 |
| Thai | typhoon-7b | 1.37 | 1.41 | 1.40 | 50.16 | 26.28 | 5.95 | 6.10 | 0.60 | 0.30 | | 0.42 | | | | 0.61 | 0.27 | 0.42 |
| Thai | Llama2-7b | 1.59 | 1.55 | 1.55 | 19.85 | 29.78 | 2.24 | 8.80 | 0.31 | 0.25 | | 0.36 | | | | 0.56 | 0.04 | 0.29 |
| Thai | bloom-7b1 | 1.83 | 1.78 | 1.83 | 13.56 | 18.92 | 0.13 | 1.33 | 0.27 | 0.25 | | 0.34 | | | | 0.55 | 0.02 | 0.25 |
| Thai | xglm-7.5B | 1.40 | 1.30 | 1.27 | 30.24 | 24.10 | 0.50 | 5.13 | 0.24 | 0.25 | | 0.42 | | | | 0.59 | 0.01 | 0.29 |
| Thai | AYA-101 | | | | 0.68 | 0.81 | 0.00 | 0.00 | 0.23 | 0.26 | | 0.35 | | | | 0.58 | 0.00 | 0.21 |
| Turkish | Our-Turkish-7B | 1.56 | 1.59 | 1.55 | 54.22 | 58.27 | 20.47 | 31.95 | 0.37 | 0.33 | | 0.45 | | | | 0.70 | | 0.50 |
| Turkish | Our Monolith | 1.63 | 1.69 | 1.66 | 51.61 | 55.98 | 77.91 | 60.55 | 0.30 | 0.41 | | 0.49 | | | | 0.66 | | 0.49 |
| Turkish | TURNA | | | | 0.00 | 0.02 | 0.00 | 0.00 | 0.23 | 0.25 | | 0.37 | | | | 0.56 | | 0.24 |
| Turkish | Llama2-7b | 2.27 | 2.44 | 2.16 | 27.61 | 43.03 | 161.70 | 76.56 | 0.32 | 0.26 | | 0.37 | | | | 0.55 | | 0.37 |
| Turkish | bloom-7b1 | 2.95 | 3.24 | 3.00 | 12.75 | 24.78 | 351.11 | 121.72 | 0.29 | 0.25 | | 0.35 | | | | 0.51 | | 0.30 |
| Turkish | xglm-7.5B | 1.83 | 1.91 | 1.80 | 28.63 | 42.99 | 485.24 | 113.21 | 0.25 | 0.25 | | 0.47 | | | | 0.58 | | 0.38 |
| Turkish | AYA-101 | | | | 1.02 | 1.13 | 98.59 | 98.58 | 0.23 | 0.31 | | 0.40 | | | | 0.60 | | 0.26 |

Figure 13: Main results, evaluation benchmarks described in 4.1.This data is averaged to create 2.

| Langauge | Checkpoint | Holdout PPL | MC4 PPL | Wikipedia PPL | FLORES EN->X 8 shot CHRF | FLORES X->en 8 shot CHRF | FLORES EN->X 8 shot BLEU | FLORES X->en 8 shot BLEU | Belebele 3 shot | SIB-200 3 shot | Exams 3 shot | XNLI 0 shot | XStory Cloze 0 shot | XWinograd 0 shot | PAWS-X 0 shot | XCOPA 0 shot | MGSM 3 shot | Average |
|---|---|---|---|---|---|---|---|---|---|---|---|---|---|---|---|---|---|---|
| Bulgarian | Our-Bulgarian-Base | 1.42 | 1.35 | 1.29 | 62.94 | 65.06 | 36.25 | 39.31 | 0.36 | 0.43 | 0.52 | 0.49 | | | | | | 0.51 |
| Bulgarian | Our Monolith | 1.46 | 1.44 | 1.34 | 61.92 | 64.50 | 34.45 | 38.28 | 0.35 | 0.45 | 0.49 | 0.47 | | | | | | 0.50 |
| Bulgarian | mGPT-1.3B-bulgarian | 1.75 | 1.65 | 1.53 | 18.53 | 24.78 | 2.89 | 4.19 | 0.23 | 0.25 | 0.30 | 0.34 | | | | | | 0.26 |
| Bulgarian | Llama2-7b | 1.59 | 1.61 | 1.39 | 51.55 | 62.43 | 23.12 | 36.55 | 0.37 | 0.27 | 0.38 | 0.41 | | | | | | 0.43 |
| Bulgarian | bloom-7b1 | 2.06 | 2.14 | 2.10 | 23.08 | 35.55 | 2.20 | 10.91 | 0.28 | 0.25 | 0.26 | 0.39 | | | | | | 0.29 |
| Bulgarian | xglm-7.5B | 1.50 | 1.48 | 1.36 | 45.05 | 58.48 | 10.38 | 28.13 | 0.23 | 0.25 | 0.41 | 0.45 | | | | | | 0.40 |
| Bulgarian | AYA-101 | | | | 0.60 | 0.86 | 0.00 | 0.00 | 0.23 | 0.30 | 0.33 | 0.37 | | | | | | 0.21 |
| Hungarian | Our-Hungarian-70B | 1.52 | | | 57.18 | 63.40 | 25.89 | 37.07 | 0.76 | 0.56 | | | | | | | | 0.63 |
| Hungarian | Our-Hungarian-7B | 1.61 | 1.63 | 1.56 | 53.72 | 58.65 | 22.84 | 31.64 | 0.34 | 0.25 | | | | | | | | 0.43 |
| Hungarian | Our Monolith | 1.66 | 1.78 | 1.67 | 52.81 | 57.06 | 21.00 | 29.52 | 0.30 | 0.35 | | | | | | | | 0.44 |
| Hungarian | PULI-GPTrio | 1.72 | 1.74 | 1.67 | 46.33 | 48.23 | 15.81 | 21.05 | 0.24 | 0.25 | | | | | | | | 0.36 |
| Hungarian | Llama2-7b | 1.95 | 2.24 | 1.78 | 42.47 | 53.89 | 13.47 | 27.26 | 0.33 | 0.25 | | | | | | | | 0.39 |
| Hungarian | bloom-7b1 | 3.02 | 3.75 | 3.68 | 12.55 | 23.73 | 0.62 | 4.15 | 0.27 | 0.25 | | | | | | | | 0.22 |
| Hungarian | xglm-7.5B | 3.36 | 4.36 | 4.17 | 6.40 | 11.87 | 0.15 | 0.36 | 0.23 | 0.27 | | | | | | | | 0.17 |
| Hungarian | AYA-101 | | | | 0.51 | 0.87 | 0.00 | 0.00 | 0.23 | 0.30 | | | | | | | | 0.14 |
| Serbian | Our-Serbian-7B | 1.44 | 1.35 | 1.26 | 56.16 | 64.89 | 29.03 | 40.51 | 0.32 | 0.59 | 0.59 | | | | | | | 0.54 |
| Serbian | Our Monolith | 1.45 | 1.46 | 1.35 | 58.53 | 65.43 | 31.05 | 40.19 | 0.35 | 0.41 | 0.37 | | | | | | | 0.47 |
| Serbian | sr-gpt2 | | | | 0.15 | 7.49 | 0.00 | 0.03 | 0.23 | 0.25 | | | | | | | | 0.14 |
| Serbian | Llama2-7b | 1.60 | 1.67 | 1.42 | 49.19 | 63.98 | 20.65 | 39.52 | 0.39 | 0.25 | | | | | | | | 0.44 |
| Serbian | bloom-7b1 | 2.13 | 2.33 | 2.21 | 22.08 | 32.80 | 1.68 | 9.64 | 0.28 | 0.25 | | | | | | | | 0.27 |
| Serbian | xglm-7.5B | 2.39 | 2.60 | 2.42 | 19.38 | 31.24 | 0.47 | 6.84 | 0.24 | 0.27 | | | | | | | | 0.25 |
| Serbian | AYA-101 | | | | 0.64 | 1.03 | 0.00 | 0.00 | 0.23 | 0.29 | | | | | | | | 0.13 |
| Slovenian | Our-Slovenian-7B | 1.68 | 1.69 | 1.70 | 54.37 | 58.60 | 26.39 | 32.54 | 0.35 | 0.43 | | | | | | | | 0.48 |
| Slovenian | Our Monolith | 1.72 | 1.62 | 1.80 | 55.79 | 60.12 | 27.59 | 33.43 | 0.30 | 0.51 | | | | | | | | 0.49 |
| Slovenian | sl-gpt2 | | | | 9.84 | 8.62 | 0.06 | 0.01 | 0.24 | 0.15 | | | | | | | | 0.14 |
| Slovenian | Llama2-7b | 2.11 | 2.08 | 1.86 | 44.45 | 57.57 | 15.77 | 31.73 | 0.38 | 0.36 | | | | | | | | 0.44 |
| Slovenian | bloom-7b1 | 3.40 | 3.44 | 3.66 | 17.26 | 30.21 | 1.25 | 7.02 | 0.28 | 0.25 | | | | | | | | 0.25 |
| Slovenian | xglm-7.5B | 4.42 | 4.66 | 4.58 | 10.94 | 23.84 | 0.32 | 2.70 | 0.24 | 0.25 | | | | | | | | 0.21 |
| Slovenian | AYA-101 | | | | 0.93 | 1.22 | 0.00 | 0.00 | 0.23 | 0.30 | | | | | | | | 0.14 |

Figure 14: Main results, evaluation benchmarks described in 4.1.This data is averaged to create 2.

# What an Elegant Bridge: Multilingual LLMs are Biased Similarly in Different Languages

**Viktor Mihaylov** **Aleksandar Shtedritski**

Oxford Artificial Intelligence Society, University of Oxford

## Abstract

This paper investigates biases of Large Language Models (LLMs) through the lens of grammatical gender. Drawing inspiration from seminal works in psycholinguistics, particularly the study of gender's influence on language perception, we leverage multilingual LLMs to revisit and expand upon the foundational experiments of Boroditsky (2003). Employing LLMs as a novel method for examining psycholinguistic biases related to grammatical gender, we prompt a model to describe nouns with adjectives in various languages, focusing specifically on languages with grammatical gender. In particular, we look at adjective co-occurrences across gender and languages, and train a binary classifier to predict grammatical gender given adjectives an LLM uses to describe a noun. Surprisingly, we find that a simple classifier can not only predict noun gender above chance but also exhibit cross-language transferability. We find a strong social influence of language on the way multilingual LLMs reason.

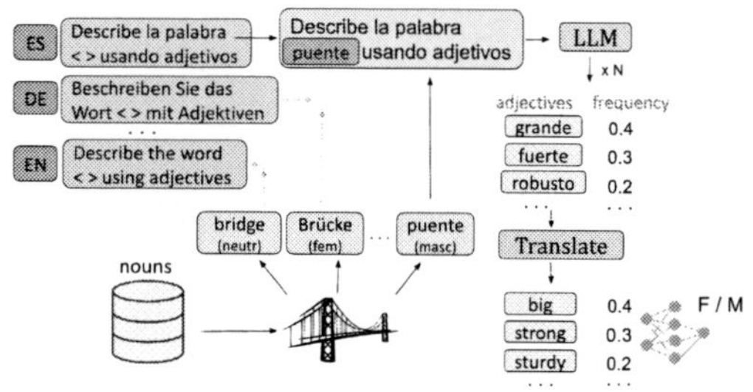


Figure 1: **Probing the bias of multilingual LLMs.** We prompt a LLM to describe gendered nouns using adjectives. This allows us to study psycholinguistic biases of LLMs. For example, if the generated adjectives are predictive of the nouns's gender, we can, by training a binary classifier, predict grammatical gender by only looking at the adjectives a LLM uses to describe a word.

## 1 Introduction

The way we perceive the world is not only affected by our culture (Oyserman and Lee, 2008; Masuda et al., 2008), but also the language we speak (Boroditsky et al., 2003; Boroditsky, 2001). The relationship between cognition and language has been of interest for a long time (Langacker, 1993), especially through the lens of gender (Boroditsky et al., 2003; Gygax et al., 2008). Recent advances in Large Language Models (LLMs), that match human performance on multiple tasks, provide an exciting opportunity to study the relationship between the psycholinguistic biases of humans and those of machines. While it is unclear whether the latter relationship exists, it would be a more scalable, affordable, and even ethical (Banyard and Flanagan, 2013) alternative to human studies.

In this work, we revisit the study of (Boroditsky et al., 2003) in the era of LLMs. To see how grammatical gender affects cognition, Boroditsky et al. (2003) ask speakers of languages with grammatical gender (where nouns have assigned genders) to describe various objects, finding that the language a person speaks affects the attribution of masculine or feminine characteristics to objects. For example, a Spanish speaker (where "bridge" is masculine) might describe a bridge with words like "strong" or "sturdy", while a German speaker (where "bridge" is feminine) might use terms like "elegant" or "beautiful". However, several subsequent studies fail to replicate such results (Haertlé; Mickan et al., 2014; Samuel et al., 2019), which is but a symptom of the replication crisis in psychology (Wiggins and Christopherson, 2019; Shrout and Rodgers, 2018; Maxwell et al., 2015). Similarly, studies in the field of NLP that examine the way gendered nouns are used in text corpora (Williams et al., 2021; Kann, 2019), find conflicting evidence on whether there is a relationship between grammatical gender and cognition.

The existence of gender bias has been well stud-



*Proceedings of the Fourth Workshop on Multilingual Representation Learning (MRL 2024)*, pages 22–29
November 16, 2024 ©2024 Association for Computational Linguistics

ied for word embeddings (Bolukbasi et al., 2016; Basta et al., 2019; Caliskan et al., 2017), as well as a range of NLP systems, such as ones for machine translation (Stanovsky et al., 2019; Vanmassenhove et al., 2018), image and video captioning (Tatman, 2017; Hall et al., 2023), or sentiment analysis (Kiritchenko and Mohammad, 2018). More recently, the social biases of LLMs have been studied (Kirk et al., 2021). While the multilingual capabilities of LLMs have been extensively evaluated, showing they perform well on machine translation (Hendy et al., 2023; Jiao et al., 2023; Wang et al., 2023) as well as various multilingual benchmarks (Ahuja et al., 2023; Bang et al., 2023), the evaluation of biases in the multilingual setting is less mature. Contrary to recent work showing that multilingual LLMs have different biases for different languages Mukherjee et al. (2023), we find that when it comes to gendered nouns, LLMs are biased in a similar way, as the biases are predictive of each other.

In this paper, we loosely follow the protocol of Boroditsky et al. (2003) and prompt LLMs to describe nouns using adjectives in different languages. Specifically, we focus on open-sourced LLMs (Llama-2 (Touvron et al., 2023) and Mistral (Jiang et al., 2023)). We select 10 languages that have grammatical gender (e.g, German and Spanish), and use the LLMs to describe gendered nouns using adjectives. This allows us to see how adjectives co-occur across languages. Our most important findings are that (i) a simple classifier can predict the gender of a noun using the adjectives used to describe it, and (ii) such a classifier reliably transfers across languages, suggesting LLMs are biased similarly in different languages.

## 2 Method

In this work, we are interested in the adjectives a multilingual LLM uses to describe gendered nouns when asked in different languages. Here, we describe how we generate such adjectives, and how we examine whether they are predictive of the grammatical gender of the nouns.

### 2.1 Describing nouns in different languages

We show our pipeline for describing gendered nouns with adjectives in Figure 1. More formally, for a language $l$ we have a database of K gendered nouns $\mathcal{N}^l = \{n_1^l, n_2^l, ..., n_K^l\}$, with corresponding grammatical genders $g(n_i^l) = \{\mathrm{f}, \mathrm{m}\}$ for feminine and masculine, respectively. We prompt the LLM to describe a noun $n_k^l$ using adjectives, which we parse into a list of $M$ adjectives $\mathcal{A}(n_k^l) = \{a_1^l, a_2^l, ..., a_M^l\}$. For every noun $n$, we repeat the prompting $N$ times and compute the frequencies $f$ with which the adjectives appear:

$$f(a_i) = \frac{\sum_{j=1}^{N} \mathbb{1}(a_i \in \mathcal{A}(n_j))}{N}. \quad (1)$$

Finally, we keep the adjectives with top-$p$ frequencies. In practice, we use $N = 50$ and $p = 50$.

### 2.2 Predicting gender from descriptions

To examine to what extent the adjectives an LLM uses to describe a noun are predictive of its grammatical gender, we train a binary classifier $\Phi$ to predict grammatical gender:

$$\hat{g}(n_i^l) = \Phi\left(\sum_{i=1}^{p} f\left(a_i^l\right) e_g\left(a_i^l\right)\right),$$

where the input to the classifier are GloVe (Pennington et al., 2014) word embeddings $e_g$ of the adjectives weighted by the adjectives frequencies $f$. In practice, we use a modified version of $f$, where $f' = -30/\log(f)$ to give us a better scaling. The classifier $\Phi$ is a 2-layer MLP and we train it with binary cross-entropy loss.

As shown in Figure 1, we first translate the generated adjectives to English. We do this for two reasons. Firstly, adjectives in some languages are also gendered and that would help the classifier learn this shortcut (e.g. *pretty* in Spanish is *bonito* and *bonita* for masculine and feminine, respectively). Adjectives in English are not gendered, so the classifier $\Phi$ has no way of inferring the gender of the noun from the grammatical form. Secondly, this allows for easy transfer of the classifier across languages – e.g. we can train $\Phi$ on words generated in Hindi, and evaluate on Italian.

## 3 Experiments

### 3.1 Implementation details

**Languages** We conduct experiments on the languages Bulgarian, Czech, French, German, Greek, Hindi, Italian, Latvian, Portuguese, and Spanish.

**Nouns** We automatically collect commonly used nouns from every language, and their corresponding grammatical gender. For details on the way we collect those nouns, and the number of nouns per language, please refer to the Appendix. We exclude neuter nouns as such nouns do not exist

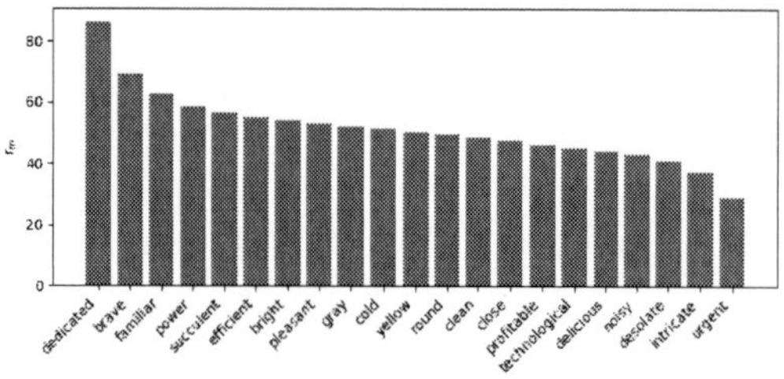


Figure 2: **Bias when describing gendered nouns.** Here we prompt an LLM in Spanish and for a random sample of adjectives, show the percentage of *masculine* nouns they were used for.

in every language. We subsample the feminine or masculine nouns in each gender to ensure a uniform distribution for each language.

**LLMs** In our experiments we use the open-sourced Mistral-7B (Jiang et al., 2023) model, unless stated otherwise. We also repeat our experiments with Llama2-7B (Touvron et al., 2023).

**Prompts** We prompt the LLM to describe the given noun in the corresponding language using comma-separated adjectives. In practice, we use few-shot prompts, which we show in the Appendix.

**Translation** Where we translate nouns, adjectives, or prompts, we use Google Translate [1].

### 3.2 Bias in generated adjectives

First, we look at adjectives that commonly occur for masculine or feminine nouns.

For every adjective $a_i$, we look at the ratio $r_m$:

$$r_m(a_i) = \frac{\sum_{n \in \mathcal{N}, g(n)=\mathrm{m}} \mathbb{1}(a_i \in \mathcal{A}(n)))}{\sum_{n \in \mathcal{N}} \mathbb{1}(a_i \in \mathcal{A}(n)))}, \quad (2)$$

which shows the proportion of masculine words it was used to describe. We randomly sample adjectives and show their $r_m$ in Figure 2. We see that adjectives like intricate and desolate are associated with feminine nouns, whereas adjectives like dedicated and brave are associated with masculine nouns. We show more examples for different languages in the Appendix.

### 3.3 Do languages show similar biases?

Next, we explore whether adjectives describing masculine and feminine nouns tend to co-occur in different languages. To this end, we compute a gendered-adjective similarity score $S_{pq}$ for every language pair of languages $l_p$ and $l_q$. We

[1]Google Translate, `https://translate.google.com/`

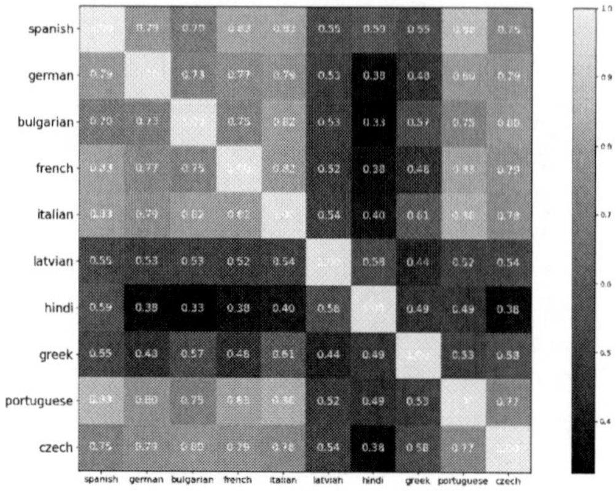


Figure 3: **Gendered adjective similarity sccores.**

do that as follows. We take the set of $N$ adjectives $a_1, a_2, ..., a_N$ that are used to describe at least 15 nouns in both $l_p$ and $l_q$. Then for both languages, we construct a gendered-adjective score vector $\sigma \in \mathbb{R}^N$, where $\sigma[i] = r_m(a_i)$. Now, $\sigma_p$ and $\sigma_q$ contain the gender ratio for all $N$ adjectives. Finally, we define the gendered-adjective similarity score $S_{pq}$ as the cosine similarity between $\sigma_p$ and $\sigma_q$.

In Figure 3 we show the score $S$ for all language pairs. We see that in Romance languages (Spanish, Italian, French Portuguese), Slavic languages (Bulgarian, Czech), and Germanic languages (German), the LLM shows a high gendered-adjective similarity score, meaning that the adjectives in these languages tend to have similar value of $r_m$. On the other hand, Greek, Hindi and Latvian have a low score between themselves and others.

### 3.4 Predicting the gendered nouns

Can we predict the gender of a noun in some language given the adjectives used to describe it? Following Section 2.2, we train binary classifiers to predict the grammatical gender of a noun from the adjectives used to describe it (translated to English). We train a separate classifier for each language. As seen in Table 1, for all languages the classifier reliably does better than random – meaning that the adjectives are predictive of gender.

### 3.5 Transfer between languages

If we train a grammatical gender classifier, like in Section 3.4, can we predict the gender of a noun in an **unseen** language? To answer this, where we train grammatical gender classifiers on adjectives from 9 languages (translated to English), and eval-

| Language | F1 | Accuracy | | |
|---|---|---|---|---|
| | | Overall | Masc. | Fem. |
| Bulgarian | 0.64 | 68.4% | 72.4% | 63.3% |
| Czech | 0.52 | 59.0% | 58.3% | 60.2% |
| French | 0.63 | 56.5% | 55.8% | 56.8% |
| German | 0.60 | 60.0% | 52.7% | 69.4% |
| Greek | 0.68 | 69.0% | 62.7% | 77.6% |
| Hindi | 0.53 | 54.3% | 57.5% | 51.2% |
| Italian | 0.46 | 68.2% | 73.0% | 54.3% |
| Latvian | 0.64 | 62.6% | 60.0% | 65.0% |
| Portuguese | 0.55 | 62.0% | 62.7% | 60.1 % |
| Spanish | 0.62 | 63.3% | 59.6% | 68.0% |

Table 1: **Predicting grammatical gender.** We train a classifier to predict the gender of nouns given the adjectives the LLM uses to describe them.

| Language | F1 | Accuracy | | |
|---|---|---|---|---|
| | | Overall | Masc. | Fem. |
| Bulgarian | 0.56 | 62.5% | 64.4% | 59.8% |
| Czech | 0.45 | 60.6% | 70.6% | 43.5% |
| French | 0.62 | 54.8% | 50.3% | 57.3% |
| German | 0.54 | 58.6% | 73.1% | 46.0% |
| Greek | 0.64 | 60.6% | 47.8% | 75.3% |
| Hindi | 0.53 | 48.8% | 37.9% | 60.2% |
| Italian | 0.40 | 60.1% | 61.6% | 55.6% |
| Latvian | 0.41 | 51.7% | 81.2% | 29.7% |
| Portuguese | 0.55 | 62.8% | 63.0% | 62.4% |
| Spanish | 0.59 | 58.8% | 56.7% | 60.1% |

Table 2: **Unseen Language Results.** We train on all other languages and predict the genders of nouns in the given language. We train a separate leave-one-out classifier for each language.

uate on the final language. As we see in Table 2, such classifiers can reliably predict gender across languages. Interestingly, they even work better than random for Greek, Hindi and Latvian, despite the results reported in Section 3.3. We suggest that although the LLM uses different adjectives to describe masculine and feminine nouns in different languages (hence low $S_{pq}$), they are semantically similar (hence high accuracy when evaluating the classifier on an unseen language).

## 4 Discussion

### 4.1 Reproducibility

Studying the phenomena relating cognition to grammatical gender in psychology has led to inconclusive results(Boroditsky, 2001; Haertlé; Mickan et al., 2014; Samuel et al., 2019). These could be explained by different experimental settings with speakers of different languages, which are difficult to control in a human study. Similarly, prior works that examine text corpora using NLP techniques show conflicting results (Williams et al., 2021; Kann, 2019). The results of these works heavily depend on the text corpora analyzed, and the methods used to identify adjective-noun pairs, which might be subpar for languages other than English. Our method presents more consistent results by ensuring consistent evaluation across languages.

| LLM | Eval | F1 | Accuracy | | |
|---|---|---|---|---|---|
| | | | Overall | Masc. | Fem. |
| Mistral-7B | Same | 0.59 | 62.3% | 61.5% | 62.6% |
| Llama2-7B | Same | 0.59 | 64.6% | 67.9% | 59.9% |
| Mistral-7B | Unseen | 0.53 | 57.9% | 60.7% | 55.1% |
| Llama2-7B | Unseen | 0.54 | 59.1% | 62.6% | 54.9% |

Table 3: **Evaluating Llama-2.** We compare grammatical gender classifiers Llama-2 to Mistral when tested on the *same* language (as in Section 3.4), or an *unseen* language (as in Section 3.5). We show mean results over all 10 languages. We see that we observe a similar predictive performance on adjectives used by Llama-2 as those by Mistral.

### 4.2 Importance of our results

Our results are only valid for noun-adjective associations in LLMs. However, these associations have been learnt through co-occurences of these words in text corpora, which have been produced by speakers of the respective languages. Future work should study how well such biases in LLMs are predictive of biases of humans.

The results we present suggest a consistent bias that associates nouns with adjectives, depending on their grammatical gender. This could be important when LLMs are used to describe humans using objects, or vice versa (anthropomorphism, personification, metaphors, ...), where traits of these objects are transferred to the human. Furthermore, using LLMs to perform machine translation of such phrases could lead to a loss of meaning or unexpected biases.

## 5 Conclusion

In this work, we revisit the psycholinguistic experiments of Boroditsky et al. (2003), confirming the hypothesis of their work applies to LLMs, where different words are used to described masculine and feminine nouns. Our most surprising finding is that we can reliably zero-shot transfer a classifier that predicts grammatical gender across languages. This shows that while LLMs might think differently on different languages, they are biased similarly when it comes to grammatical gender. We hope this work inspires others to explore psycholonguistic experiments applied to LLMs, and to drive a discussion of whether such results can be useful to inform or motivate human experiments.

## 6 Limitations

We only conducted experiments and observed these effects for the opens-sourced Mistral-7B and Llama2-7B models. It is not clear if similar effects can be observed in larger LLMs, or commercial LLMs such as GPT-4. While we ensured to cover a wide range of languages, the ones we used are by no means exhaustive and only cover indo-european languages. Finally, we only explore the biases of general-purpose, multilingual LLMs. Looking into specialised LLMs, fine-tuned for the specific language, might be more representative of what models would be used in practice.

## 7 Acknowledgements

This work has been completed with the support of the Oxford AI student society, the EPSRC Centre for Doctoral Training in Autonomous Intelligent Machines Systems [EP/S024050/1] (A.S.) and compute resources from the AWS Responsible AI Grant.

## References

Kabir Ahuja, Rishav Hada, Millicent Ochieng, Prachi Jain, Harshita Diddee, Samuel Maina, Tanuja Ganu, Sameer Segal, Maxamed Axmed, Kalika Bali, et al. 2023. Mega: Multilingual evaluation of generative ai. *arXiv preprint arXiv:2303.12528*.

Yejin Bang, Samuel Cahyawijaya, Nayeon Lee, Wenliang Dai, Dan Su, Bryan Wilie, Holy Lovenia, Ziwei Ji, Tiezheng Yu, Willy Chung, et al. 2023. A multitask, multilingual, multimodal evaluation of chatgpt on reasoning, hallucination, and interactivity. *arXiv preprint arXiv:2302.04023*.

Philip Banyard and Cara Flanagan. 2013. *Ethical issues in psychology*. Routledge.

Christine Basta, Marta R Costa-Jussà, and Noe Casas. 2019. Evaluating the underlying gender bias in contextualized word embeddings. *arXiv preprint arXiv:1904.08783*.

Tolga Bolukbasi, Kai-Wei Chang, James Y Zou, Venkatesh Saligrama, and Adam T Kalai. 2016. Man is to computer programmer as woman is to homemaker? debiasing word embeddings. *Advances in neural information processing systems*, 29.

Lera Boroditsky. 2001. Does language shape thought?: Mandarin and english speakers' conceptions of time. *Cognitive psychology*, 43(1):1–22.

Lera Boroditsky, Lauren A Schmidt, and Webb Phillips. 2003. Sex, syntax, and semantics. *Language in mind: Advances in the study of language and thought*, 22:61–79.

Aylin Caliskan, Joanna J Bryson, and Arvind Narayanan. 2017. Semantics derived automatically from language corpora contain human-like biases. *Science*, 356(6334):183–186.

Pascal Gygax, Ute Gabriel, Oriane Sarrasin, Jane Oakhill, and Alan Garnham. 2008. Generically intended, but specifically interpreted: When beauticians, musicians, and mechanics are all men. *Language and cognitive processes*, 23(3):464–485.

Izabella Haertlé. Does grammatical gender influence perception? a study of polish and french speakers. *Psychology of Language and Communication*, 21(1):386–407.

Siobhan Mackenzie Hall, Fernanda Gonçalves Abrantes, Hanwen Zhu, Grace Sodunke, Aleksandar Shtedritski, and Hannah Rose Kirk. 2023. Visogender: A dataset for benchmarking gender bias in image-text pronoun resolution.

Amr Hendy, Mohamed Abdelrehim, Amr Sharaf, Vikas Raunak, Mohamed Gabr, Hitokazu Matsushita, Young Jin Kim, Mohamed Afify, and Hany Hassan Awadalla. 2023. How good are gpt models at machine translation? a comprehensive evaluation. *arXiv preprint arXiv:2302.09210*.

Albert Q Jiang, Alexandre Sablayrolles, Arthur Mensch, Chris Bamford, Devendra Singh Chaplot, Diego de las Casas, Florian Bressand, Gianna Lengyel, Guillaume Lample, Lucile Saulnier, et al. 2023. Mistral 7b. *arXiv preprint arXiv:2310.06825*.

Wenxiang Jiao, Wenxuan Wang, Jen-tse Huang, Xing Wang, and Zhaopeng Tu. 2023. Is chatgpt a good translator? a preliminary study. *arXiv preprint arXiv:2301.08745*.

Katharina Kann. 2019. Grammatical gender, neowhorfianism, and word embeddings: A data-driven approach to linguistic relativity. *arXiv preprint arXiv:1910.09729*.

Svetlana Kiritchenko and Saif M Mohammad. 2018. Examining gender and race bias in two hundred sentiment analysis systems. *arXiv preprint arXiv:1805.04508*.

Hannah Rose Kirk, Yennie Jun, Filippo Volpin, Haider Iqbal, Elias Benussi, Frederic Dreyer, Aleksandar Shtedritski, and Yuki Asano. 2021. Bias out-of-the-box: An empirical analysis of intersectional occupational biases in popular generative language models. *Advances in neural information processing systems*, 34:2611–2624.

Ronald W Langacker. 1993. Universals of construal. In *Annual Meeting of the Berkeley Linguistics Society*, volume 19, pages 447–463.

Takahiko Masuda, Mikako Akase, MH Radford, and Huaitang Wang. 2008. Effect of contextual factors on patterns of eye-movement: Comparing sensitivity to background information between japanese and westerners. *Shinrigaku Kenkyu: The Japanese Journal of Psychology*, 79(1):35–43.

Scott E Maxwell, Michael Y Lau, and George S Howard. 2015. Is psychology suffering from a replication crisis? what does "failure to replicate" really mean? *American Psychologist*, 70(6):487.

Anne Mickan, Maren Schiefke, and Anatol Stefanowitsch. 2014. Key is a llave is a schlüssel: A failure to replicate an experiment from boroditsky et al. 2003. *Yearbook of the German Cognitive Linguistics Association*, 2(1):39–50.

Anjishnu Mukherjee, Chahat Raj, Ziwei Zhu, and Antonios Anastasopoulos. 2023. Global voices, local biases: Socio-cultural prejudices across languages. *arXiv preprint arXiv:2310.17586*.

Daphna Oyserman and Spike WS Lee. 2008. Does culture influence what and how we think? effects of priming individualism and collectivism. *Psychological bulletin*, 134(2):311.

Jeffrey Pennington, Richard Socher, and Christopher Manning. 2014. GloVe: Global vectors for word representation. In *Proceedings of the 2014 Conference on Empirical Methods in Natural Language Processing (EMNLP)*, pages 1532–1543, Doha, Qatar. Association for Computational Linguistics.

Steven Samuel, Geoff Cole, and Madeline J Eacott. 2019. Grammatical gender and linguistic relativity: A systematic review. *Psychonomic bulletin & review*, 26:1767–1786.

Patrick E Shrout and Joseph L Rodgers. 2018. Psychology, science, and knowledge construction: Broadening perspectives from the replication crisis. *Annual review of psychology*, 69:487–510.

Gabriel Stanovsky, Noah A. Smith, and Luke Zettlemoyer. 2019. Evaluating gender bias in machine translation. In *Proceedings of the 57th Annual Meeting of the Association for Computational Linguistics*, pages 1679–1684, Florence, Italy. Association for Computational Linguistics.

Rachael Tatman. 2017. Gender and dialect bias in YouTube's automatic captions. In *Proceedings of the First ACL Workshop on Ethics in Natural Language Processing*, pages 53–59, Valencia, Spain. Association for Computational Linguistics.

Hugo Touvron, Louis Martin, Kevin Stone, Peter Albert, Amjad Almahairi, Yasmine Babaei, Nikolay Bashlykov, Soumya Batra, Prajjwal Bhargava, Shruti Bhosale, et al. 2023. Llama 2: Open foundation and fine-tuned chat models. *arXiv preprint arXiv:2307.09288*.

Eva Vanmassenhove, Christian Hardmeier, and Andy Way. 2018. Getting gender right in neural machine translation. In *Proceedings of the 2018 Conference on Empirical Methods in Natural Language Processing*, pages 3003–3008, Brussels, Belgium. Association for Computational Linguistics.

Longyue Wang, Chenyang Lyu, Tianbo Ji, Zhirui Zhang, Dian Yu, Shuming Shi, and Zhaopeng Tu. 2023. Document-level machine translation with large language models. *arXiv preprint arXiv:2304.02210*.

Bradford J Wiggins and Cody D Christopherson. 2019. The replication crisis in psychology: An overview for theoretical and philosophical psychology. *Journal of Theoretical and Philosophical Psychology*, 39(4):202.

Adina Williams, Ryan Cotterell, Lawrence Wolf-Sonkin, Damián Blasi, and Hanna Wallach. 2021. On the relationships between the grammatical genders of inanimate nouns and their co-occurring adjectives and verbs. *Transactions of the Association for Computational Linguistics*, 9:139–159.

# Appendix

## A Collecting nouns

We collect words in German [2] and Spanish [3] from a blog post that lists commonly used words in these languages, and shows their grammatical gender. For Bulgarian [4], Greek [5], Czech [6], French [7], Hindi [8], Italian [9], Latvian [10] and Portuguese [11], we take a list of words and their grammatical gender from Wikipedia. Following that, we only select words whose English translation is in the list of commonly used words in either German or Spanish.

| Language | Total | Masc. | Fem. |
|---|---|---|---|
| Bulgarian | 1414 | 839 | 575 |
| Czech | 2383 | 1501 | 882 |
| French | 2763 | 996 | 1767 |
| German | 2031 | 952 | 1089 |
| Greek | 1257 | 670 | 587 |
| Hindi | 830 | 425 | 405 |
| Italian | 2919 | 2219 | 700 |
| Latvian | 1223 | 522 | 701 |
| Portuguese | 1766 | 1119 | 647 |
| Spanish | 1758 | 896 | 862 |

Table 4: **Dataset Statistics.** We present the number of masculine and feminine words we consider for all 10 languages. The languages are sorted alphabetically.

We show the number of collected nouns per language in Table 4. We use 90% of the nouns in each language for training, and 10% for testing.

## B Excluding animate nouns

Following prior works that look into grammatical gender by looking at word co-occurrence in text corpora (Williams et al., 2021), we exclude animate nouns from our datasets in all languages (e.g. "uncle", "cashier", "engineer", etc.). We repeat the experiments from Section 3.4 in Table 6, and see that the inclusion of animate nouns does not affect overall results.

| LLM | F1 | Accuracy Overall | Accuracy Male | Accuracy Female |
|---|---|---|---|---|
| Mistral-7B | 0.57 | 55.0% | 50.0% | 60.0% |
| Llama2-7B | 0.70 | 65.0% | 50.0% | 80.0% |

Table 5: **Evaluating the agreement with native English.** We evaluate the agreement of our classifier trained on 10 gendered languages to the perceived grammatical gender of native English speakers, which we treat as ground truth.

| Language | F1 | Accuracy Overall | Accuracy Masc. | Accuracy Fem. |
|---|---|---|---|---|
| Bulgarian | 0.70 | 71.1% | 73.8% | 68.3% |
| German | 0.69 | 63.8% | 63.1% | 64.2% |
| Spanish | 0.56 | 55.3% | 56.2% | 54.4% |
| Italian | 0.51 | 65.2% | 64.5% | 67.1% |
| Czech | 0.55 | 57.2% | 54.3% | 61.2% |
| Greek | 0.68 | 69.5% | 79.6% | 60.1% |
| Portuguese | 0.60 | 61.1% | 56.7% | 67.2% |
| Hindi | 0.59 | 58.1% | 67.7% | 51.2% |
| Latvian | 0.70 | 63.2% | 60.0% | 64.8% |
| French | 0.60 | 57.0% | 58.8% | 55.8% |

Table 6: **Gendered Nouns Predictions.** This table is for the filtered dictionaries, i.e. without jobs/mother/father etc.

## C Gendered adjectives

We show more examples of adjectives that are predominantly used for masculine (or feminine) nouns in Figure 4, similarly to Section 3.2.

## D Promps

The prompt we use in English is as follows:

```
***Question***: Describe the word “bottle” using comma-separated adjectives. ***Answer***: glass, sleek, thin, brittle, elegant, transparent, clear, tall, fragile, shiny
***Question***: Describe the word “stone” using comma-separated adjectives. ***Answer***: round, old, strong, cold, solid, ancient, sturdy, dense, natural, durable
***Question***: Describe the word <> using comma-separated adjectives. ***Answer***:
```

For the other languages we translate the prompt, e.g. in Spanish we use:

```
***Pregunta***: Describe la palabra “botella” usando adjetivos separados por comas. ***Respuesta***: vidrio, liso, delgado, quebradizo, elegante, transparente, claro, alto, frágil, brillante
```

[2]https://frequencylists.blogspot.com/2016/01/the-2980-most-frequently-used-german.html

[3]https://frequencylists.blogspot.com/2015/12/the-2000-most-frequently-used-spanish.html

[4]https://en.wiktionary.org/wiki/Category:Bulgarian_nouns_by_gender

[5]https://en.wiktionary.org/wiki/Category:Greek_nouns_by_gender

[6]https://en.wiktionary.org/wiki/Category:Czech_nouns_by_gender

[7]https://en.wiktionary.org/wiki/Category:French_nouns_by_gender

[8]https://en.wiktionary.org/wiki/Category:Hindi_nouns_by_gender

[9]https://en.wiktionary.org/wiki/Category:Italian_nouns_by_gender

[10]https://en.wiktionary.org/wiki/Category:Latvian_nouns_by_gender

[11]https://en.wiktionary.org/wiki/Category:Portuguese_nouns_by_gender

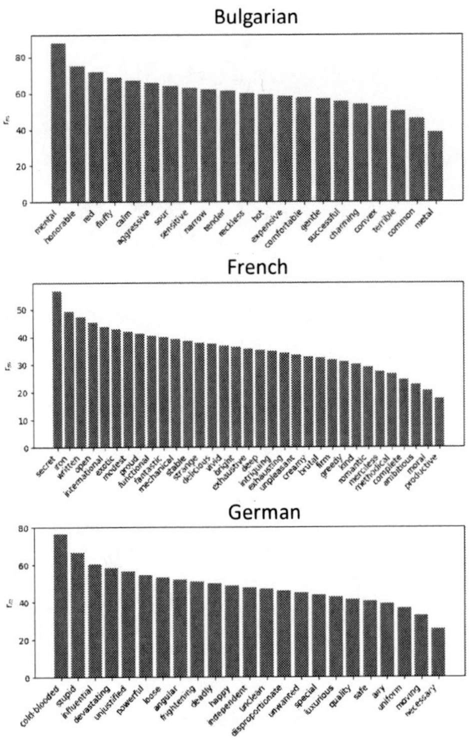


Figure 4: **Bias when describing gendered nouns**. Here we prompt an LLM in Bulgarian, French, and German and for a random sample of adjectives, show the percentage of masculine nouns they were used for.

```
***Pregunta***: Describe la palabra "piedra" usando adjetivos separados por comas. ***Respuesta***: redondo, viejo, fuerte, frío, sólido, antiguo, robusto, denso, natural, duradero
***Pregunta***: Describe la palabra <> usando adjetivos separados por comas. ***Respuesta***:
```

# Adapting Open-Source Generative Large Language Models for Low-Resource Languages: A Case Study for Turkish

**Cagri Toraman**
Computer Engineering Department
Middle East Technical University, Ankara, Turkey
ctoraman@ceng.metu.edu.tr

## Abstract

Despite advancements in English-dominant generative large language models, further development is needed for low-resource languages to enhance global accessibility. The primary methods for representing these languages are monolingual and multilingual pretraining. Monolingual pretraining is expensive due to hardware requirements, and multilingual models often have uneven performance across languages. This study explores an alternative solution by adapting large language models, primarily trained on English, to low-resource languages. We assess various strategies, including continual training, instruction fine-tuning, task-specific fine-tuning, and vocabulary extension. The results show that continual training improves language comprehension, as reflected in perplexity scores, and task-specific tuning generally enhances performance of downstream tasks. However, extending the vocabulary shows no substantial benefits. Additionally, while larger models improve task performance with few-shot tuning, multilingual models perform worse than their monolingual counterparts when adapted.

## 1 Introduction

The performance of proprietary generative large language models (LLMs) is better than open-source ones in most cases as this article is written (Xu et al., 2022; Sun et al., 2024), though there are efforts to develop open-source generative LLMs in terms of high performance and human ethics alignment (Touvron et al., 2023a; Jiang et al., 2023; Almazrouei et al., 2023).

The progress is more significant in the English language compared to other languages as the aforementioned open-source models are mostly trained by English corpora (Wang et al., 2023; Zhang et al., 2023a). To make natural language processing technology more inclusive and accessible globally, research and development should be dedicated to the techniques that improve the performance of large language models in low-resource languages.

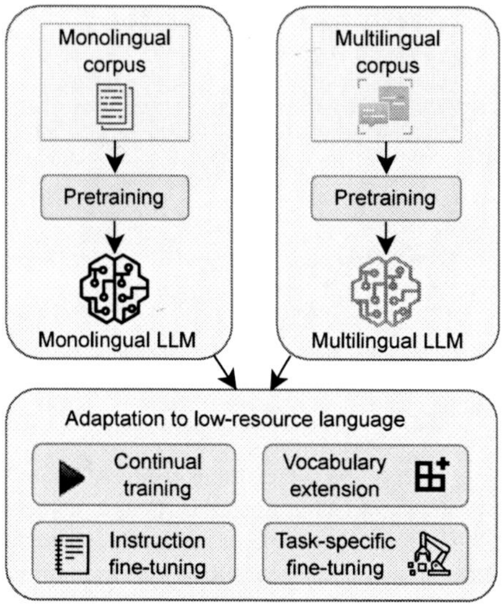


Figure 1: Adapting generative large language models for low-resource languages.

Monolingual (Yang et al., 2023b; Nagoudi et al., 2023; Pires et al., 2023; Uludoğan et al., 2024; Corrêa et al., 2024; Kesgin et al., 2024) and multilingual pretraining (Shliazhko et al., 2023; Scao et al., 2022; Lin et al., 2024b; Blevins et al., 2024) of generative LLMs are two main solutions for representing low-resource languages. However, monolingual pretraining is too costly due to hardware requirements for generative LLMs (Zhao et al., 2023a). On the other hand, multilingual LLMs have uneven performance across different languages mostly due to imbalanced training corpus (Zhang et al., 2023a; Qin et al., 2024). Our proposed solution is to adapt open-source generative LLMs for low-resource languages, illustrated in Figure 1.

In this regard, this study examines how to adapt open-source LLMs for low-resource languages in



*Proceedings of the Fourth Workshop on Multilingual Representation Learning (MRL 2024)*, pages 30–44
November 16, 2024 ©2024 Association for Computational Linguistics

a systematic way. We focus on the benefits of using different methodologies, both individually and together, including continual training, supervised fine-tuning, and vocabulary extension, to adapt generative LLMs for low-resource languages.

For the sake of efficiency, we use Llama (Touvron et al., 2023a) in the experiments. We select the Turkish language as a low-resource language. We therefore refer to the model family used in this study as `LlamaTurk`. The model size and language selection are affordable when the number of experiments is considered in this study[1]. Also, Llama is trained mostly with English data, which can provide better investigation for adapting non-English languages. The Turkish language can be categorized under low-resource languages when training corpus of open-source generative LLMs are considered (Touvron et al., 2023a), yet the recipes given in this study can also be used for other low-resource languages since the methods are independent of language itself.

We further examine adaptation in terms of two more aspects: Model size and multilinguality. Model size is important for scalability and performance (Zhao et al., 2023a; Yang et al., 2023a). We provide an analysis of the adaptation of Llama-7b and 13b in this respect. Moreover, multilingual LLMs, such as BLOOM (Scao et al., 2022), Yi (AI et al., 2024), Aya (Üstün et al., 2024), and MaLA (Lin et al., 2024a), can provide an opportunity to adapt low-resource languages easier than English-dominant ones due to multilingual corpus and vocabulary. Since BLOOM and Yi do not involve Turkish in training and Aya is larger than MaLA in terms of model parameters, we use MaLA for an analysis of multilingual LLMs.

The main contributions of this study can be summarized as follows. We (i) analyze the adaptation of generative LLMs for low-resource language systematically to understand advantages and disadvantages in terms of continual training, instruction fine-tuning, task-specific fine-tuning, and vocabulary extension, (ii) investigate model size and multilingual models for adaptation, and (iii) publish all resources including source codes, datasets, and generative models reported in the experiments[2].

[1]Two NVIDIA RTX 2080Tis and four A4000s are employed in the experiments.

[2]https://github.com/metunlp/llamaturk

## 2 Related Work

Generative LLMs are either proprietary or open-source. Although proprietary LLMs have currently outstanding performance (Sun et al., 2024), there are also efforts to develop competitive open-source models (Touvron et al., 2023a; Jiang et al., 2023).

The majority language of open-source generative LLMs is English. Their pretraining text corpus mostly includes text in the English language. For adapting LLMs pretrained with English data for low-resource languages, the following methods are examined. (i) The training phase is continued using non-English raw data to learn the language properties of the new language (Ebrahimi and Kann, 2021; Larcher et al., 2023; Csaki et al., 2023; Cui et al., 2024; Zhao et al., 2024; Acikgoz et al., 2024). (ii) The knowledge of large language model is transferred by supervised fine-tuning on a non-English instruction or downstream-task dataset (Santilli and Rodolà, 2023; Holmström and Doostmohammadi, 2023; Kohli et al., 2023; Csaki et al., 2023; Zhao et al., 2024; Garcia et al., 2024; Kuulmets et al., 2024). (iii) The vocabulary of large language model is extended to include non-English tokens (Cui et al., 2023; Zhao et al., 2024).

These methods are employed in different studies and languages, resulting in a lack of understanding advantages and disadvantages of each in a controlled experimental framework. Different from these studies, we provide a comprehensive experimental setup on the benefits of different methodologies for adapting generative LLMs for low-resource languages. Moreover, we focus on model size and multilingual models for adaptation.

## 3 Adaptation Methods

In this section, we explain the methods to adapt open-source generative LLMs for low-resource languages in detail.

### 3.1 Continual Training

Continual training is the process of extending the pretraining phase of LLMs by incorporating new data corpus (Gupta et al., 2023). The main objective is to minimize the loss on this new data while having relatively lower loss scores on previous data since continual training is open to catastrophic forgetting (French, 1999; Li and Lee, 2024). Continual training can therefore capture implicit language structures and text semantics.

Previous studies (Qin et al., 2022) show that continual training improves the performance of domain adaptation for BERT-like encoder-based LLMs (Devlin et al., 2019). It is also used for adapting decoder-based generative LLMs to low-resource (Cui et al., 2023; Zhao et al., 2024), code-mixed (Owen et al., 2024), non-Latin (Husain et al., 2024), and multilingual (Lin et al., 2024a) settings.

In this study, similar to previous studies, we employ Low-Rank Adaptation (LoRA) (Hu et al., 2021) for efficient training due to limited resources. We use a raw Wikipedia corpus[3] from November 2023 with a size of 534,988 Turkish articles.

We set the input sequence length as 512 tokens and the batch size as 128 instances. We use 32 gradient accumulation steps and 100 linear warmup steps. We train with a learning rate of 3e-4 for a single epoch. LoRA's R is set to 8, alpha to 16, and dropout to 0.05. Since continual training is costly and the study has a limited budget, we employ continual training for only Llama-7b[4] with 8-bit quantization. A single run of continual training takes approximately 206 hours with these settings using four NVIDIA RTX A4000s.

### 3.2 Instruction Fine-tuning

Instruction tuning is a supervised fine-tuning method that improves the ability of LLMs to follow instructions (Wei et al., 2021; Ouyang et al., 2022; Zhang et al., 2024). During training, the model is presented with many pairs of instructions and corresponding responses. The main objective is to teach the model to generate accurate responses based on the given instructions, rather than continuing from the previous text.

Different from previous instruction-tuning efforts, Stanford's Alpaca (Taori et al., 2023) is a leading model that shows major improvements by instruction fine-tuning an open-source generative LLM, namely (Touvron et al., 2023a). While Alpaca and similar models such as Vicuna (Chiang et al., 2023) have an instruction set constructed by prompting proprietary LLMs, other models such as Dolly (Conover et al., 2023) employ human labor for constructing a more reliable instruction set. The majority of these efforts are for the English language, yet there are instruction-tuned models to adapt English-supported LLMs for low-resource settings (Cui et al., 2023; Zhao et al., 2024; Azime et al., 2024).

In this study, we construct an instruction set by translating Alpaca's 52k instructions from English to Turkish by using Google Translate[5]. The quality of the translated set is inadequate for training since we observe many issues such as translation errors (e.g. missing letters and untranslated words), keyword translations (e.g. reserved keywords specific to programming languages should not be translated), and semantic mismatching (e.g. original instruction asks for a phrase with five words, but correct translation has less than five words). We therefore manually validate and correct the quality of the instruction set. We publish our instruction set[6]. We also provide a prompting example for instruction fine-tuning in Appendix A.1.

We employ instruction tuning for all LLMs examined in this study, namely Llama-7b[7], Llama-13b[8], and MaLA-10b[9]. We use 8-bit quantization with LoRA (resulting in training 12.4% of LLM parameters) and the same hyperparameters as in continual training, except that we use a smaller input sequence length (256 tokens) and train for two epochs. A single run of instruction tuning takes approximately 17.5 hours for Llama-7b with these settings using two NVIDIA RTX 2080Tis.

### 3.3 Task-Specific Fine-tuning

Task-specific tuning is a type of instruction tuning, where a fine-tuning set involves task-related instructions and ground-truth answers (Budzianowski and Vulić, 2019; Wang et al., 2024), rather than adapting a general-purpose instruction set. Task-specific tuning of generative LLMs is proven to be successful in different domains including text editing (Raheja et al., 2023), sentiment analysis (Inserte et al., 2024), and machine translation (Zheng et al., 2024). However, task-specific tuning have the potential of deteriorating the language capabilities of LLMs (Zhang et al., 2023b; Zhao et al., 2023b).

We follow instruction fine-tuning with a task-specific dataset for the downstream task of sentiment analysis. We choose sentiment analysis since it is a widely applicable task that represents a fundamental natural language processing capability (Liu, 2012). For this purpose, we create an instruction set for sentiment analysis. To create a balanced set, we downsample 2,500 instances for both neg-

[3]https://huggingface.co/datasets/wikipedia
[4]https://huggingface.co/huggyllama/llama-7b
[5]https://translate.google.com
[6]https://github.com/metunlp/llamaturk
[7]https://huggingface.co/huggyllama/llama-7b
[8]https://huggingface.co/huggyllama/llama-13b
[9]https://huggingface.co/MaLA-LM/mala-500-10b-v1

| | Data | Size | Tokens |
|---|---|---|---|
| Continual training | Wiki | 535.0k | 273.9m |
| Instruction tuning | Alpaca | 52.0k | 13.3m |
| Task-specific tuning | Sentiment | 5.0k | 1.3m |
| Vocabulary extension | BPE | 28.6k | 28.6k |

Table 1: **Data statistics for adaptation methods**. The columns represent the type of data used (Data), the total number of instances (Size), and the total number of tokens (Tokens), respectively.

ative and positive sentiment classes, a total of 5k instances from the TRSAv1 dataset (Aydoğan and Kocaman, 2023). We then use a prompt manually crafted for the task of sentiment analysis[10]. We provide the prompt in Appendix A.2.

We employ task-specific tuning for all LLMs examined in this study. We use all models in 8-bit quantization. We also use LoRA (resulting in training 12.4% of LLM parameters) and the same hyperparameters as in instruction tuning. A single run of task-specific tuning takes approximately 2.5 hours for Llama-7b with these settings using two NVIDIA RTX 2080Tis.

### 3.4 Vocabulary Extension

Vocabulary embeddings are a major component of how LLMs understand and process natural language text by capturing semantic meanings and relationships among subwords called tokens (Toraman et al., 2023). Vocabulary tokens are determined by tokenization algorithms such as WordPiece (Schuster and Nakajima, 2012) and Bype Pair Encoding (BPE) (Sennrich et al., 2016).

Llama has a vocabulary size of 32k tokens based on BPE tokenization (Touvron et al., 2023a). The majority of tokens in its vocabulary are English. The remaining small portion involves European languages with Latin and Cyrillic symbols.

In this study, we extend Llama's vocabulary by merging with low-resource language tokens. Specifically, we use the Turkish tokenizer with 28,600 tokens trained by BPE algorithm (Toraman et al., 2023) (We publish the tokenizer[6]).

Merging the original Llama tokenizer with low-resource vocabulary yields 59,773 tokens, meaning that 827 tokens are overlapping. This results in adding almost 228m new parameters to be trained into the model due to the extended vocabulary embeddings. We employ vocabulary extension with above-mentioned methods when Llama-7b is used with LoRA due to limited resources.

[10]We run prompts from existing resources (Bach et al., 2022) but decided to use a manually crafted one by observing better performance in preliminary experiments.

### 3.5 Combinations

A summary of data statistics used for the adaptation methods is given in Table 1. In addition to a single examination of these methods, we also report the results of using them in combination to leverage better performance. We particularly employ the following combinations using Llama-7b with LoRA. Hyperparameters are set the same as explained in the previous subsections.

*Continual Training with Instruction Fine-tuning:* We first obtain a model by continual training using raw Wiki data as explained in Section 3.1. We then apply instruction fine-tuning as explained in Section 3.2. The motivation is to boost the potential of instruction tuning when the backbone model is trained with low-resource raw text beforehand.

*Continual Training with Task-Specific Fine-tuning:* With a similar motivation to the previous approach, we first obtain a model by continual training using raw Wiki data. We then apply task-specific fine-tuning as explained in Section 3.3.

*Continual Training with Instruction and Task-Specific Fine-tuning:* The motivation is to boost the performance of task-specific tuning when the model is trained by both raw text and instruction-set in low-resource language beforehand. We first obtain a model by continual training using raw Wiki data. We then apply instruction tuning and task-specific fine-tuning respectively.

*Instruction and Task-Specific Fine-tuning:* This approach avoids continual training but examines using both instruction and then task-specific tuning respectively. The motivation is to boost the performance of task-specific tuning when the model is trained by only instruction-set in low-resource language beforehand.

*Vocabulary Extension with Instruction Fine-tuning:* We extend the vocabulary with low-resource language tokens as explained in Section 3.4. We then apply instruction tuning to understand the impact of vocabulary extension on instruction tuning.

*Vocabulary Extension with Task-Specific Fine-tuning:* With a similar motivation to the previous approach, we extend the vocabulary with low-resource language tokens and then apply task-specific tuning to understand the impact of vocabulary extension on task-specific tuning.

*Vocabulary Extension with Continual Training:*

| | xquad question | xquad context | dbricks instruction | dbricks response |
|---|---|---|---|---|
| Size | 1.2k | 1.2k | 15.0k | 15.0k |
| Chars | 74.7k | 965.4k | 1.1m | 5.4m |
| Tokens | 37.4k | 458.3k | 549.8k | 2.4m |

Table 2: **Dataset statistics for perplexity**. The xquad dataset has question and context subsets. The databricks (dbricks) dataset has instruction and response subsets.

We extend the vocabulary with low-resource language tokens and then apply continual training to understand its impact on continual training.

## 4 Experiments

In this section, we evaluate the performance of different methods to adapt generative large language models for low-resource language. We particularly conduct both intrinsic and extrinsic evaluations in order to understand the performance of both language comprehension and downstream tasks. We also run benchmark LLM evaluation by using appropriate datasets. This section further involves the results of using varying model sizes and applying multilingual models for the adaptation.

### 4.1 Intrinsic Evaluation

Intrinsic evaluation of generative LLMs involves a perplexity score that represents how well a language model can predict the next word in a sequence of text (Jurafsky and Martin, 2009):

$$\text{perplexity} = 2^{-\frac{1}{N}\sum_{i=1}^{N}\log_2 P(w_i|w_1,\ldots,w_{i-1})} \quad (1)$$

where $N$ is the total number of words and $P(w_i|w_1, w_2, \ldots, w_{i-1})$ is the probability assigned by the model to the $i$-th word given the preceding text context.

A lower perplexity score indicates that language model is better able to predict the next word, and thus has a better understanding of the language.

We calculate the perplexity scores on different data collections than the ones used in Section 3. Specifically, we use the Turkish question and context subsets of `xquad` (Artetxe et al., 2019), and the instruction and response subsets of `databricks-dolly-15k` (Conover et al., 2023) using a Turkish translated version[11]. The detailed statistics of the data used for calculating perplexity scores are given in Table 2. The reason for reporting the perplexity scores for different subsets is that the characteristics of each subset can be helpful to understand the applied method's impact on the adaptation. For instance, `xquad-question` has instances of questions while `xquad-context` has longer paragraphs of task descriptions. Similarly, `databricks-instruction` has instruction-type questions, while `databricks-response` has answers or responses to those questions.

In Table 3, we provide the perplexity scores. The main observations can be summarized as follows.

**Continual training reduces perplexity scores.** In all cases, perplexity scores are improved by continual training (`LlamaTurk-7b-c`). The lowest perplexity scores are also obtained by continual training in the majority of cases (three of four data collections). A possible reason is that the model could gradually accumulate language knowledge as it is exposed to more raw text. This incremental learning process can allow the model to become more robust and adaptable.

**Instruction tuning improves perplexity but not task-specific tuning.** Perplexity scores are improved by instruction tuning (`LlamaTurk-7b-i`). The only exception is `xquad-context`, yer instruction tuning has still a very close perplexity score to the original `Llama-7b`. Our instruction-tuning set is based on Alpaca, which has general-purpose instructions and responses. On the other hand, task-specific tuning (`LlamaTurk-7b-t`) deteriorates perplexity scores in all cases. We argue that, by training on task-specific instructions, generative LLMs might become overly specialized and optimized for those specific instructions, rather than maintaining a more general understanding of language.

**Combinations fail in most cases but depends on data types.** The combinations that include task-specific tuning have poor perplexity scores. On the other hand, continual training and instruction tuning improve perplexity. We therefore expect to have a better performance by using them together (`LlamaTurk-7b-c-i`) but perplexity scores get worse than the case when they are applied alone. However, when perplexity is measured on an instruction set (`databricks-instruction`), continual training together with instruction tuning has the lowest perplexity score. This observation can support that generative LLMs adapt to different data types, and one should consider target data type before selecting adaptation method.

[11]https://huggingface.co/datasets/atasoglu/databricks-dolly-15k-tr

| Model | Continual Training | Instruction Tuning | Task Tuning | Vocabulary Extension | Data: xquad question | xquad context | dbricks instruction | dbricks response |
|---|---|---|---|---|---|---|---|---|
| Llama-7b | | | | | 6.6916 | 1.5487 | 9.5845 | 9.0259 |
| LlamaTurk-7b-c | ✓ | | | | **5.5088** | **1.5064** | 8.4364 | **7.0924** |
| LlamaTurk-7b-i | | ✓ | | | 6.3260 | 1.5674 | 8.3131 | 7.9351 |
| LlamaTurk-7b-t | | | ✓ | | 9.2267 | 1.7850 | 13.7173 | 13.2289 |
| LlamaTurk-7b-c-i | ✓ | ✓ | | | 7.0676 | 1.5978 | **8.2488** | 9.4570 |
| LlamaTurk-7b-i-t | | ✓ | ✓ | | 9.0380 | 1.8194 | 13.0113 | 11.8501 |
| LlamaTurk-7b-c-t | ✓ | | ✓ | | 7.7305 | 1.7181 | 12.5591 | 10.7188 |
| LlamaTurk-7b-c-i-t | ✓ | ✓ | ✓ | | 8.0855 | 1.6666 | 11.5441 | 10.6943 |
| LlamaTurk-7b-v-i | | ✓ | | ✓ | 18.6241 | 3.8897 | 22.1750 | 24.3312 |
| LlamaTurk-7b-v-t | | | ✓ | ✓ | 28.7707 | 5.8666 | 37.6394 | 43.7040 |
| LlamaTurk-7b-v-c | ✓ | | | ✓ | 17.3135 | 3.6807 | 23.9212 | 23.2612 |

Table 3: **Perplexity scores**. The models have different adaptation methods: Continual Training (c), Instruction Tuning (i), Task-specific Tuning (t), and Vocabulary Extension (v). The xquad dataset has question and context subsets. The databricks (dbricks) dataset has instruction and response subsets. The best (lowest) perplexity scores for each dataset are given in bold.

**Vocabulary extension has poor perplexity.** In all models where vocabulary extension is applied (Llama-7b-v), perplexity scores get higher than the original (Llama-7b). We argue that without sufficient training data and fine-tuning, the model can struggle to effectively incorporate the new vocabulary into its internal representations and learning processes. Similarly, (Zhao et al., 2024) observes negative impact of vocabulary extension, and also suggests that vocabulary extension might not be a suitable choice for small-scale continual training such as in our continual training with 0.2 billion tokens of the training data. Another reason could be the number of additional tokens in vocabulary (28k tokens), merged with the original tokenizer (32k tokens). More experimentation is needed to understand if a different number of new tokens in vocabulary works better in adaptation (Csaki et al., 2023).

## 4.2 Extrinsic Evaluation

Generative LLMs employ human evaluations as an evaluation method to align with human judgments (Ouyang et al., 2022). However, human-based evaluation is labor-intensive, making it costly and less feasible for low-resource languages. On the other hand, LLM evaluation benchmarks offer reliable evaluation for downstream NLP tasks such as GLUE (Wang et al., 2018) and SuperGLUE (Wang et al., 2019). Similarly, there are evaluation frameworks and tools such as LM Evaluation Harness (Gao et al., 2023) and MLflow[12]. However, they mostly support English benchmark datasets. Although multilingual datasets are published by

| Model | 0-shot | 1-shot | 2-shot | 3-shot |
|---|---|---|---|---|
| Llama-7b | 0.00 | 0.50 | 0.53 | 0.50 |
| LlamaTurk-7b-c | 0.00 | 0.47 | 0.54 | 0.51 |
| LlamaTurk-7b-i | 0.06 | 0.48 | 0.48 | 0.56 |
| LlamaTurk-7b-t | 0.90• | 0.84∘ | 0.61 | 0.78 |
| LlamaTurk-7b-c-i | 0.10 | 0.52 | 0.50 | 0.54 |
| LlamaTurk-7b-i-t | 0.83∘ | 0.90• | 0.93• | 0.89• |
| LlamaTurk-7b-c-t | 0.82 | 0.60 | 0.62 | 0.86∘ |
| LlamaTurk-7b-c-i-t | 0.62 | 0.52 | 0.56 | 0.51 |
| LlamaTurk-7b-v-i | 0.35 | 0.44 | 0.49 | 0.53 |
| LlamaTurk-7b-v-t | 0.44 | 0.50 | 0.53 | 0.53 |

Table 4: **Accuracy scores on sentiment analysis**. The darker cell color gets, the better task performance. The symbol "•" indicates statistically significant difference at a 95% interval in pairwise comparisons between the highest performing method and others (except with "∘").

some benchmarks, either they do not include the language used in this study, or the data size is small for task-specific tuning. We therefore craft an evaluation on sentiment analysis in this subsection[13].

For this purpose, we extract 100 instances (50 instances for both positive and negative classes) from the Turkish sentiment analysis dataset used in task-specific tuning (Aydoğan and Kocaman, 2023). We avoid selecting from 5k instances used in task-specific tuning explained in Section 3.3. Since inference is time costly, we use a small subset of this dataset for the evaluation. However, we take the average of five different runs by using random seeds. We thereby validate statistically significant differences in the average performances with the two-tailed paired t-test at a 95% interval.

We also craft inference prompts for different scenarios including zero-shot to few-shot prompts. We check the generated text if it equals to positive or

[12]https://github.com/mlflow/mlflow

[13]We also provide a benchmark evaluation for available datasets from LLM benchmarks in Section 4.3.

| Model | XCOPA | | | | Belebele | | | |
|---|---|---|---|---|---|---|---|---|
| | 0-shot | 1-shot | 2-shot | 3-shot | 0-shot | 1-shot | 2-shot | 3-shot |
| Llama-7b | 0.53 | 0.51 | 0.48 | 0.52 | 0.23 | 0.23 | 0.23 | 0.24 |
| LlamaTurk-7b-i | **0.58** | 0.51 | 0.50 | 0.55 | 0.24 | 0.27 | 0.25 | **0.28** |
| LlamaTurk-7b-c-i | 0.52 | 0.52 | 0.53 | 0.50 | 0.24 | 0.25 | 0.23 | 0.27 |
| LlamaTurk-7b-v-i | 0.55 | 0.53 | 0.54 | 0.54 | 0.24 | 0.27 | 0.23 | **0.28** |

Table 5: **Accuracy scores on benchmark datasets**. The highest scores for each dataset are given in bold.

negative, and calculate the accuracy score accordingly. We measure accuracy since the inference dataset is fully balanced. We provide the inference prompts in Appendix A.3.

During inference, we load the models with 8-bit quantization due to limited hardware. Generation configuration involves the following hyperparameters. The temperature is set to 0.2. Beam search is applied with four beams, and top-p is set to 0.75. A single run of inference takes approximately from six hours (zero-shot) to eight hours (3-shot) for Llama-7b with these settings using two NVIDIA RTX 2080Tis. In Table 4, we provide the accuracy scores for all methods.

**Task-specific tuning improves the performance of downstream task.** We find that task-specific tuning cannot help improve perplexity scores previously. However, our extrinsic evaluation shows that task-specific tuning improves the performance of sentiment analysis. Specifically, we observe that task-specific tuned model (`LllamaTurk-7b-t`) is good at zero-shot inference, suggesting that task-specific instructions provide sufficient knowledge for zero-shot evaluation.

**Instruction tuning boosts the performance of downstream task when used together with task-specific tuning.** When instruction tuning is employed alone, it has no significant impact on the performance of downstream task. However, the highest accuracy is obtained when instruction and task-specific tuning are together employed. Moreover, `LllamaTurk-7b-i-t` has a better few-shot performance compared to other methods including task-specific tuning.

**Continual training can help task-tuning.** When continual training is employed alone (`LllamaTurk-7b-c`), we observe no significant improvement in the performance of downstream task. However, the performance is promising when it is used together with task-specific tuning (`LllamaTurk-7b-c-t`). This suggests further examination of continual training with task-specific tuning in different downstream tasks and datasets.

**Vocabulary extension has poor downstream performance.** Similar to the perplexity experiments, we observe that vocabulary extension has no improvement on the performance of downstream task.

### 4.3 Benchmark Evaluation

In this subsection, we report the performance results on benchmark datasets. Since LLM evaluation benchmarks mostly include English datasets, we examine multilingual datasets in available LLM benchmarks. For this purpose, we use the Turkish subsets of XCOPA (Ponti et al., 2020) and Belebele (Bandarkar et al., 2023) datasets provided by LM Evaluation Harness (Gao et al., 2023). XCOPA is a benchmark to evaluate the ability of machine learning models to transfer commonsense reasoning. Belebele is a multiple-choice machine reading comprehension dataset, and each question has four multiple-choice. We modify the default prompts given in LM Evaluation Harness to align with our instruction prompting. We provide the inference prompts in Appendix A.4 and A.5.

Since the dataset sizes are small, we are not able to apply task-specific tuning in these benchmark datasets. Specifically, we observe almost no change in performance scores when XCOPA's 600 and Belebele's 900 instances are fine-tuned for the Turkish language, while the performance is improved in Section 4.2 with 5k instances. We thereby report the results for instruction tuning and related methods. Table 5 reports the accuracy scores on the XCOPA and Belebele datasets.

The results show that instruction tuning (`LlamaTurk-7b-i`) improves the performance of downstream task in both datasets. However, continual training and vocabulary extension have no significant benefits. The results thereby align with the results reported in Section 4.2.

### 4.4 Model Size

We provide an analysis of the impact of model size on adapting generative LLMs. For this purpose, we employ Llama models with 7b and 13b parameters. Figure 2 shows a histogram depicting the compari-

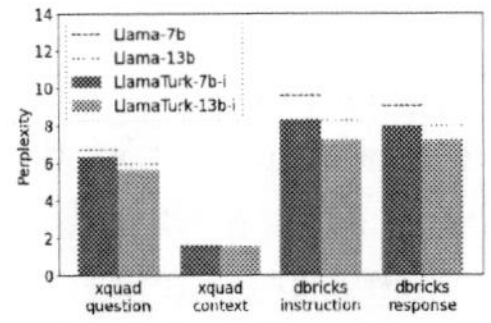


(a) Perplexity of instruction tuning (lower is better)

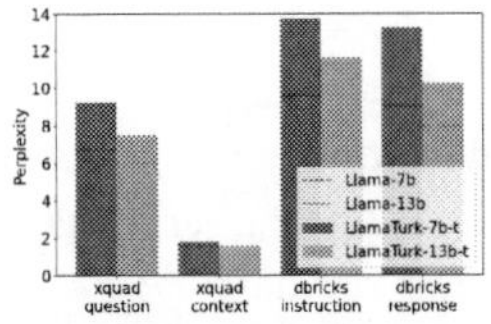


(b) Perplexity of task-specific tuning (lower is better)

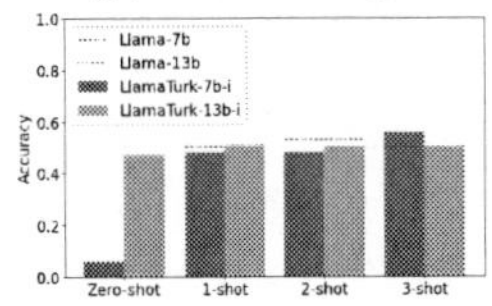


(c) Accuracy of instruction tuning (higher is better)

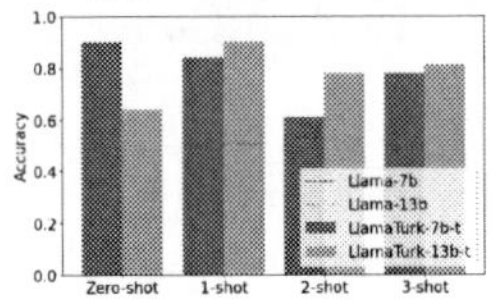


(d) Accuracy of task-specific tuning (higher is better)

Figure 2: **Model size comparison for adaptation.**

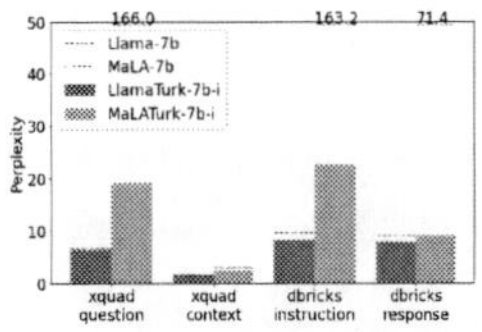


(a) Perplexity of instruction tuning (lower is better).

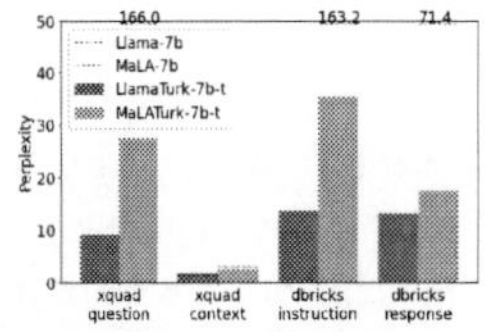


(b) Perplexity of task-specific tuning (lower is better).

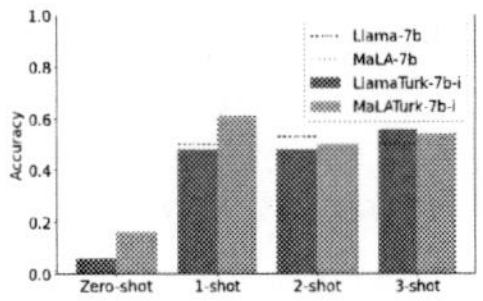


(c) Accuracy of instruction tuning (higher is better).

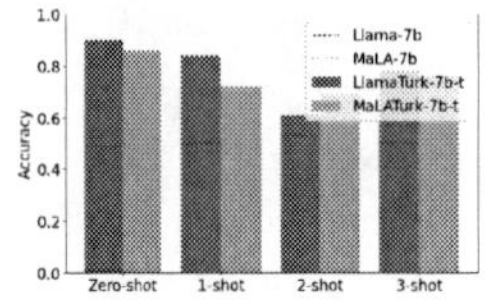


(d) Accuracy of task-specific tuning (higher is better).

Figure 3: **Multilingual comparison for adaptation.**

son between the fine-tuned models for instruction tuning (`LlamaTurk-7b-i` and `LlamaTurk-13b-i`) and task-specific tuning (`LlamaTurk-7b-t` and `LlamaTurk-13b-t`).

**Perplexity is improved by adapting a larger model.** In both cases of applying instruction or task-specific tuning, we find that `LlamaTurk-13b` improves perplexity scores in all cases. However, task-specific tuning (`LlamaTurk-13b-t`) is still outperformed by the original Llama model `Llama-13b` in most cases.

**Task performance is improved by adapting a larger model when few-shot tuning is applied.** We find that `LlamaTurk-13b` improves the performance of downstream task when it is applied with task-specific tuning and few-shot evaluation. On the other hand, the adaptation of a larger model with instruction tuning has no significant impact on the performance of downstream task.

### 4.5 Multilingual Models

We also provide an analysis for the impact of multilingual generative LLMs on adapting generative LLMs. For this purpose, we fine-tune a multilingual model, MaLA-500 (Lin et al., 2024b). MaLA is developed to cover 534 languages by using vocabulary extension and continual training on Llama2 (Touvron et al., 2023b). Analyzing a multilingual LLM with an enriched vocabulary can provide more insights into LLM adaptation for low-resource languages.

Figure 3 shows a histogram depicting the comparison between the fine-tuned models for instruction tuning (`LlamaTurk-7b-i` and `MaLATurk-7b-i`) and task-specific tuning (`LlamaTurk-7b-t` and `MaLATurk-7b-t`).

**Adapting multilingual LLM has no significant improvements.** Perplexity and accuracy scores of the original `MaLA-7b` model are improved by adapting `MaLATurk-7b` in both instruction and task-specific tuning. However, the perplexity of adapting a monolingual model `LlamaTurk-7b` is still better than adapting a multilingual model in all cases. Similarly, monolingual adaptation has better accuracy scores of task-specific tuning in most cases. The only benefit of adapting multilingual LLM is observed when instruction tuning is applied. Note that the results are obtained under the assumption that the number of pretraining data instances and their quality differ between Llama and MaLA. Further investigations are needed to fully understand the comparison between monolingual and multilingual setups for adaptation.

## 5 Conclusion

This study examines different methods for adapting English-dominant generative large language models to low-resource languages.

The results show that continual training with raw text can improve perplexity. Vocabulary extension has no significant impact on adaptation performance under a small scale of continual training set. Another factor can be 8-bit quantization with LoRA that trains a subset of model weights for new vocabulary token embeddings (Dobler and de Melo, 2023).

We also find that the adaptation with general-purpose instruction tuning has promising results in both perplexity and accuracy scores, while downstream task performance can be boosted by task-specific tuning. Furthermore, adapting a larger model with 13b parameters improves task performance with few-shot tuning. However, we observe no significant improvements by adapting a multilingual model.

In future work, we plan to adapt other open-source language models such as Llama2 (Touvron et al., 2023b) and Gemini (Team et al., 2024) to generalize our results to different models. Other adaptation methods can also be studied such as modification of model architecture since different model layers and tokenization algorithms might change the outcomes.

## 6 Limitations

This study employs a particular family of generative large language models (Llama and MaLA) for adapting open-source generative monolingual and multilingual LLMs to a low-resource language using the 8-bit quantization with LoRA. Other generative models and non-quantization might have different results in the experiments. Similarly, we use Turkish language for the target of adaptation. Other languages might have different experimental results depending on the tuning and inference datasets with prompt examples. We therefore acknowledge the effect of the instruction set and prompting templates in the results.

Continual training is done by using Wikipedia in this study. However, other data types can be used such as comprehensive multilingual datasets (Nguyen et al., 2024) and filtering methods can also be applied for training corpus. Also, sequence length is limited up to 512 tokens in this study for the sake of efficiency but Llama supports up to 2048 tokens. This might result in losing some information specifically in continual training where longer Wikipedia articles are used compared to the prompts in instruction and task-specific sets.

The evaluation sets used for calculating perplexity scores involve questions, instructions, and responses. Evaluation results might differ with other raw data such as Common Crawl. Benchmark evaluation is limited to extracting Turkish subsets from multilingual datasets in this study due to the unavailability of benchmark datasets for the target language[14].

Moreover, we would like to emphasize the limited hardware resources the experiments were conducted, which restricts using a variety of models including larger sizes (higher than 13b) and different model types (rather than Llama), and larger evaluation sets.

## 7 Ethical Concerns

This study employs a low-resource language, Turkish, and our findings can guide to other researchers studying low-resource languages. We also provide performance evaluations that can be considered for deploying generative LLMs in similar tasks.

To provide transparency, we explain all details regarding text collections used in pretraining and fine-tuning our generative language models. Moreover, we report the details of the models and configurations with hyperparameters.

Since the training corpus of generative LLMs involves a huge amount of raw text from different resources including the world wide web, it is inevitable to observe a risk of cultural and ethical bias towards different individuals and communities in the generated text of the published models in this study (Kasneci et al., 2023; Cetinkaya et al., 2024). Moreover, training texts are contaminated with more problematic biases and polluted with a large amount of synthetic text generated by LLMs (Denning and Rousse, 2024). Possible bias can be removed by filtering the corpus, however, we leave the study of such filtering to future work since it would require a dedicated effort but the scope of this study is to compare the adaptation methods of generative LLMs for low-resource languages.

Lastly, we estimate the carbon footprint of our study based on the energy usage of GPUs. We consider execution time in hours and electrical energy consumption in kWh, and assume that power consumption during training is equal to the maximum power drain of GPUs by operating at maximum power utilization (0.25 MW for 2080Ti, and 0.14 MW for A4000). We assume that 1 MWh is equivalent to 0.439 ton CO2eq[15]. Our estimation ignores the carbon footprint of CPU utilization and the manufacturing costs of the hardware.

Social carbon cost is approximately 50.64, 3.84, and 0.55 kg CO2eq for a single run of continual training, instruction tuning, and task-specific tuning, respectively.

[14] After this study was submitted, a new Turkish benchmark was published (Yüksel et al., 2024).

[15] https://enerji.gov.tr/evced-cevre-ve-iklim-elektrik-uretim-tuketim-emisyon-faktorleri

**Acknowledgements** The work was partially done at Aselsan, Ankara, Turkey.

## References

Emre Can Acikgoz, Mete Erdogan, and Deniz Yuret. 2024. Bridging the bosphorus: Advancing turkish large language models through strategies for low-resource language adaptation and benchmarking.

01. AI, :, Alex Young, Bei Chen, Chao Li, Chengen Huang, Ge Zhang, Guanwei Zhang, Heng Li, Jiangcheng Zhu, Jianqun Chen, Jing Chang, Kaidong Yu, Peng Liu, Qiang Liu, Shawn Yue, Senbin Yang, Shiming Yang, Tao Yu, Wen Xie, Wenhao Huang, Xiaohui Hu, Xiaoyi Ren, Xinyao Niu, Pengcheng Nie, Yuchi Xu, Yudong Liu, Yue Wang, Yuxuan Cai, Zhenyu Gu, Zhiyuan Liu, and Zonghong Dai. 2024. Yi: Open foundation models by 01.ai.

Ebtesam Almazrouei, Hamza Alobeidli, Abdulaziz Alshamsi, Alessandro Cappelli, Ruxandra Cojocaru, Mérouane Debbah, Étienne Goffinet, Daniel Hesslow, Julien Launay, Quentin Malartic, Daniele Mazzotta, Badreddine Noune, Baptiste Pannier, and Guilherme Penedo. 2023. The falcon series of open language models.

Mikel Artetxe, Sebastian Ruder, and Dani Yogatama. 2019. On the cross-lingual transferability of monolingual representations. *CoRR*, abs/1910.11856.

Murat Aydoğan and Veysel Kocaman. 2023. Trsav1: a new benchmark dataset for classifying user reviews on Turkish e-commerce websites. *Journal of Information Science*, 49(6):1711–1725.

Israel Abebe Azime, Mitiku Yohannes Fuge, Atnafu Lambebo Tonja, Tadesse Destaw Belay, Aman Kassahun Wassie, Eyasu Shiferaw Jada, Yonas Chanie, Walelign Tewabe Sewunetie, and Seid Muhie Yimam. 2024. Enhancing amharic-llama: Integrating task specific and generative datasets. *arXiv preprint arXiv:2402.08015*.

Stephen H. Bach, Victor Sanh, Zheng-Xin Yong, Albert Webson, Colin Raffel, Nihal V. Nayak, Abheesht Sharma, Taewoon Kim, M Saiful Bari, Thibault Fevry, Zaid Alyafeai, Manan Dey, Andrea Santilli, Zhiqing Sun, Srulik Ben-David, Canwen Xu, Gunjan Chhablani, Han Wang, Jason Alan Fries, Maged S. Al-shaibani, Shanya Sharma, Urmish Thakker, Khalid Almubarak, Xiangru Tang, Dragomir Radev, Mike Tian-Jian Jiang, and Alexander M. Rush. 2022. Promptsource: An integrated development environment and repository for natural language prompts.

Lucas Bandarkar, Davis Liang, Benjamin Muller, Mikel Artetxe, Satya Narayan Shukla, Donald Husa, Naman Goyal, Abhinandan Krishnan, Luke Zettlemoyer, and Madian Khabsa. 2023. The belebele benchmark: a parallel reading comprehension dataset in 122 language variants.

Terra Blevins, Tomasz Limisiewicz, Suchin Gururangan, Margaret Li, Hila Gonen, Noah A Smith, and Luke Zettlemoyer. 2024. Breaking the curse of multilinguality with cross-lingual expert language models. *arXiv preprint arXiv:2401.10440*.

Paweł Budzianowski and Ivan Vulić. 2019. Hello, it's gpt-2–how can i help you? towards the use of pretrained language models for task-oriented dialogue systems. *arXiv preprint arXiv:1907.05774*.

Yusuf Mucahit Cetinkaya, Emre Kulah, Ismail Hakki Toroslu, and Hasan Davulcu. 2024. Targeted marketing on social media: utilizing text analysis to create personalized landing pages. *Soc. Netw. Anal. Min.*, 14(77).

Wei-Lin Chiang, Zhuohan Li, Zi Lin, Ying Sheng, Zhanghao Wu, Hao Zhang, Lianmin Zheng, Siyuan Zhuang, Yonghao Zhuang, Joseph E. Gonzalez, Ion Stoica, and Eric P. Xing. 2023. Vicuna: An open-source chatbot impressing gpt-4 with 90%* chatgpt quality.

Mike Conover, Matt Hayes, Ankit Mathur, Jianwei Xie, Jun Wan, Sam Shah, Ali Ghodsi, Patrick Wendell, Matei Zaharia, and Reynold Xin. 2023. Free dolly: Introducing the world's first truly open instruction-tuned llm.

Nicholas Kluge Corrêa, Sophia Falk, Shiza Fatimah, Aniket Sen, and Nythamar de Oliveira. 2024. Teenytinyllama: open-source tiny language models trained in brazilian portuguese.

Zoltan Csaki, Pian Pawakapan, Urmish Thakker, and Qiantong Xu. 2023. Efficiently adapting pretrained language models to new languages.

Yiming Cui, Ziqing Yang, and Xin Yao. 2023. Efficient and effective text encoding for chinese llama and alpaca. *arXiv preprint arXiv:2304.08177*.

Yiming Cui, Ziqing Yang, and Xin Yao. 2024. Efficient and effective text encoding for chinese llama and alpaca.

Peter Denning and B Scot Rousse. 2024. Can machines be in language? *Communications of the ACM*, 67(3):32–35.

Jacob Devlin, Ming-Wei Chang, Kenton Lee, and Kristina Toutanova. 2019. Bert: Pre-training of deep bidirectional transformers for language understanding. In *Proceedings of the 2019 Conference of the North American Chapter of the Association for Computational Linguistics: Human Language Technologies, Volume 1 (Long and Short Papers)*, pages 4171–4186.

Konstantin Dobler and Gerard de Melo. 2023. Focus: Effective embedding initialization for monolingual specialization of multilingual models. In *Proceedings of the 2023 Conference on Empirical Methods in Natural Language Processing*, page 13440–13454. Association for Computational Linguistics.

Abteen Ebrahimi and Katharina Kann. 2021. How to adapt your pretrained multilingual model to 1600 languages. In *Proceedings of the 59th Annual Meeting of the Association for Computational Linguistics and the 11th International Joint Conference on Natural Language Processing, ACL/IJCNLP 2021, (Volume 1: Long Papers), Virtual Event, August 1-6, 2021*, pages 4555–4567. Association for Computational Linguistics.

Robert M French. 1999. Catastrophic forgetting in connectionist networks. *Trends in cognitive sciences*, 3(4):128–135.

Leo Gao, Jonathan Tow, Baber Abbasi, Stella Biderman, Sid Black, Anthony DiPofi, Charles Foster, Laurence Golding, Jeffrey Hsu, Alain Le Noac'h, Haonan Li, Kyle McDonell, Niklas Muennighoff, Chris Ociepa, Jason Phang, Laria Reynolds, Hailey Schoelkopf, Aviya Skowron, Lintang Sutawika, Eric Tang, Anish Thite, Ben Wang, Kevin Wang, and Andy Zou. 2023. A framework for few-shot language model evaluation.

Gabriel Lino Garcia, Pedro Henrique Paiola, Luis Henrique Morelli, Giovani Candido, Arnaldo Cândido Júnior, Danilo Samuel Jodas, Luis Afonso, Ivan Rizzo Guilherme, Bruno Elias Penteado, and João Paulo Papa. 2024. Introducing bode: A finetuned large language model for portuguese prompt-based task. *arXiv preprint arXiv:2401.02909*.

Kshitij Gupta, Benjamin Thérien, Adam Ibrahim, Mats L Richter, Quentin Anthony, Eugene Belilovsky, Irina Rish, and Timothée Lesort. 2023. Continual pre-training of large language models: How to (re) warm your model? *arXiv preprint arXiv:2308.04014*.

Oskar Holmström and Ehsan Doostmohammadi. 2023. Making instruction finetuning accessible to non-English languages: A case study on Swedish models. In *Proceedings of the 24th Nordic Conference on Computational Linguistics (NoDaLiDa)*, pages 634–642, Tórshavn, Faroe Islands. University of Tartu Library.

Edward J Hu, Yelong Shen, Phillip Wallis, Zeyuan Allen-Zhu, Yuanzhi Li, Shean Wang, Lu Wang, and Weizhu Chen. 2021. Lora: Low-rank adaptation of large language models. *arXiv preprint arXiv:2106.09685*.

Jaavid Aktar Husain, Raj Dabre, Aswanth Kumar, Jay Gala, Thanmay Jayakumar, Ratish Puduppully, and Anoop Kunchukuttan. 2024. Romansetu: Efficiently unlocking multilingual capabilities of large language models models via romanization.

Pau Rodriguez Inserte, Mariam Nakhlé, Raheel Qader, Gaetan Caillaut, and Jingshu Liu. 2024. Large language model adaptation for financial sentiment analysis.

Albert Q. Jiang, Alexandre Sablayrolles, Arthur Mensch, Chris Bamford, Devendra Singh Chaplot, Diego de las Casas, Florian Bressand, Gianna Lengyel, Guillaume Lample, Lucile Saulnier, Lélio Renard Lavaud, Marie-Anne Lachaux, Pierre Stock, Teven Le Scao, Thibaut Lavril, Thomas Wang, Timothée Lacroix, and William El Sayed. 2023. Mistral 7b.

Daniel Jurafsky and James H. Martin. 2009. *Speech and Language Processing (2nd Edition)*. Prentice-Hall, Inc., USA.

Enkelejda Kasneci, Kathrin Seßler, Stefan Küchemann, Maria Bannert, Daryna Dementieva, Frank Fischer, Urs Gasser, Georg Groh, Stephan Günnemann, Eyke Hüllermeier, et al. 2023. Chatgpt for good? on opportunities and challenges of large language models for education. *Learning and individual differences*, 103:102274.

H. Toprak Kesgin, M. Kaan Yuce, Eren Dogan, M. Egemen Uzun, Atahan Uz, H. Emre Seyrek, Ahmed Zeer, and M. Fatih Amasyali. 2024. Introducing cosmosgpt: Monolingual training for turkish language models.

Guneet Singh Kohli, Shantipriya Parida, Sambit Sekhar, Samirit Saha, Nipun B Nair, Parul Agarwal, Sonal Khosla, Kusumlata Patiyal, and Debasish Dhal. 2023. Building a llama2-finetuned llm for odia language utilizing domain knowledge instruction set.

Hele-Andra Kuulmets, Taido Purason, Agnes Luhtaru, and Mark Fishel. 2024. Teaching llama a new language through cross-lingual knowledge transfer.

Celio Larcher, Marcos Piau, Paulo Finardi, Pedro Gengo, Piero Esposito, and Vinicius Caridá. 2023. Cabrita: closing the gap for foreign languages.

Chen-An Li and Hung-Yi Lee. 2024. Examining forgetting in continual pre-training of aligned large language models. *arXiv preprint arXiv:2401.03129*.

Peiqin Lin, Shaoxiong Ji, Jörg Tiedemann, André FT Martins, and Hinrich Schütze. 2024a. Mala-500: Massive language adaptation of large language models. *arXiv preprint arXiv:2401.13303*.

Peiqin Lin, Shaoxiong Ji, Jörg Tiedemann, André F. T. Martins, and Hinrich Schütze. 2024b. Mala-500: Massive language adaptation of large language models.

Bing Liu. 2012. *Sentiment Analysis and Opinion Mining*. Morgan & Claypool Publishers.

El Moatez Billah Nagoudi, Muhammad Abdul-Mageed, AbdelRahim Elmadany, Alcides Alcoba Inciarte, and Md Tawkat Islam Khondaker. 2023. Jasmine: Arabic gpt models for few-shot learning.

Thuat Nguyen, Chien Van Nguyen, Viet Dac Lai, Hieu Man, Nghia Trung Ngo, Franck Dernoncourt, Ryan A. Rossi, and Thien Huu Nguyen. 2024. CulturaX: A cleaned, enormous, and multilingual dataset for large language models in 167 languages. In *Proceedings of the 2024 Joint International Conference on Computational Linguistics, Language Resources and Evaluation (LREC-COLING 2024)*, pages 4226–4237, Torino, Italia. ELRA and ICCL.

Long Ouyang, Jeffrey Wu, Xu Jiang, Diogo Almeida, Carroll Wainwright, Pamela Mishkin, Chong Zhang, Sandhini Agarwal, Katarina Slama, Alex Ray, et al. 2022. Training language models to follow instructions with human feedback. *Advances in neural information processing systems*, 35:27730–27744.

Louis Owen, Vishesh Tripathi, Abhay Kumar, and Biddwan Ahmed. 2024. Komodo: A linguistic expedition into indonesia's regional languages.

Ramon Pires, Hugo Abonizio, Thales Sales Almeida, and Rodrigo Nogueira. 2023. Sabiá: Portuguese large language models. In *Intelligent Systems*, pages 226–240, Cham. Springer Nature Switzerland.

Edoardo M. Ponti, Goran Glavaš, Olga Majewska, Qianchu Liu, Ivan Vulić, and Anna Korhonen. 2020. XCOPA: A multilingual dataset for causal commonsense reasoning. In *Proceedings of the 2020 Conference on Empirical Methods in Natural Language Processing (EMNLP)*.

Libo Qin, Qiguang Chen, Yuhang Zhou, Zhi Chen, Yinghui Li, Lizi Liao, Min Li, Wanxiang Che, and Philip S. Yu. 2024. Multilingual large language model: A survey of resources, taxonomy and frontiers.

Yujia Qin, Jiajie Zhang, Yankai Lin, Zhiyuan Liu, Peng Li, Maosong Sun, and Jie Zhou. 2022. Elle: Efficient lifelong pre-training for emerging data. In *Findings of the Association for Computational Linguistics: ACL 2022*, pages 2789–2810.

Vipul Raheja, Dhruv Kumar, Ryan Koo, and Dongyeop Kang. 2023. Coedit: Text editing by task-specific instruction tuning.

Andrea Santilli and Emanuele Rodolà. 2023. Camoscio: An italian instruction-tuned llama. *arXiv preprint arXiv:2307.16456*.

Teven Le Scao, Angela Fan, Christopher Akiki, Ellie Pavlick, Suzana Ilić, Daniel Hesslow, Roman Castagné, Alexandra Sasha Luccioni, François Yvon, and Matthias Gallé et al. 2022. BLOOM: A 176b-parameter open-access multilingual language model.

Mike Schuster and Kaisuke Nakajima. 2012. Japanese and korean voice search. In *2012 IEEE International Conference on Acoustics, Speech and Signal Processing (ICASSP)*, pages 5149–5152.

Rico Sennrich, Barry Haddow, and Alexandra Birch. 2016. Neural machine translation of rare words with subword units. In *Proceedings of the 54th Annual Meeting of the Association for Computational Linguistics (Volume 1: Long Papers)*, pages 1715–1725, Berlin, Germany. Association for Computational Linguistics.

Oleh Shliazhko, Alena Fenogenova, Maria Tikhonova, Vladislav Mikhailov, Anastasia Kozlova, and Tatiana Shavrina. 2023. mgpt: Few-shot learners go multilingual.

Lichao Sun, Yue Huang, Haoran Wang, Siyuan Wu, Qihui Zhang, Chujie Gao, Yixin Huang, Wenhan Lyu, Yixuan Zhang, Xiner Li, et al. 2024. Trustllm: Trustworthiness in large language models. *arXiv preprint arXiv:2401.05561*.

Rohan Taori, Ishaan Gulrajani, Tianyi Zhang, Yann Dubois, Xuechen Li, Carlos Guestrin, Percy Liang, and Tatsunori B. Hashimoto. 2023. Stanford alpaca: An instruction-following llama model. `https://github.com/tatsu-lab/stanford_alpaca`.

Gemini Team, Rohan Anil, Sebastian Borgeaud, Jean-Baptiste Alayrac, Jiahui Yu, Radu Soricut, Johan Schalkwyk, Andrew M. Dai, Anja Hauth, Katie Millican, et al. 2024. Gemini: A family of highly capable multimodal models.

Cagri Toraman, Eyup Halit Yilmaz, Furkan Şahinuç, and Oguzhan Ozcelik. 2023. Impact of tokenization on language models: An analysis for Turkish. *ACM Transactions on Asian and Low-Resource Language Information Processing*, 22(4):1–21.

Hugo Touvron, Thibaut Lavril, Gautier Izacard, Xavier Martinet, Marie-Anne Lachaux, Timothée Lacroix, Baptiste Rozière, Naman Goyal, Eric Hambro, Faisal Azhar, Aurelien Rodriguez, Armand Joulin, Edouard Grave, and Guillaume Lample. 2023a. Llama: Open and efficient foundation language models.

Hugo Touvron, Louis Martin, Kevin Stone, Peter Albert, Amjad Almahairi, Yasmine Babaei, Nikolay Bashlykov, Soumya Batra, Prajjwal Bhargava, Shruti Bhosale, et al. 2023b. Llama 2: Open foundation and fine-tuned chat models. *arXiv preprint arXiv:2307.09288*.

Gökçe Uludoğan, Zeynep Yirmibeşoğlu Balal, Furkan Akkurt, Melikşah Türker, Onur Güngör, and Susan Üsküdarlı. 2024. Turna: A Turkish encoder-decoder language model for enhanced understanding and generation.

Alex Wang, Yada Pruksachatkun, Nikita Nangia, Amanpreet Singh, Julian Michael, Felix Hill, Omer Levy, and Samuel R. Bowman. 2019. *SuperGLUE: a stickier benchmark for general-purpose language understanding systems*. Curran Associates Inc., Red Hook, NY, USA.

Alex Wang, Amanpreet Singh, Julian Michael, Felix Hill, Omer Levy, and Samuel Bowman. 2018. GLUE: A multi-task benchmark and analysis platform for natural language understanding. In *Proceedings of the 2018 EMNLP Workshop BlackboxNLP: Analyzing and Interpreting Neural Networks for NLP*, pages 353–355, Brussels, Belgium. Association for Computational Linguistics.

Wenxuan Wang, Zhaopeng Tu, Chang Chen, Youliang Yuan, Jen tse Huang, Wenxiang Jiao, and Michael R. Lyu. 2023. All languages matter: On the multilingual safety of large language models.

Yizhong Wang, Hamish Ivison, Pradeep Dasigi, Jack Hessel, Tushar Khot, Khyathi Chandu, David Wadden, Kelsey MacMillan, Noah A Smith, Iz Beltagy, et al. 2024. How far can camels go? exploring the state of instruction tuning on open resources. *Advances in Neural Information Processing Systems*, 36.

Jason Wei, Maarten Bosma, Vincent Y Zhao, Kelvin Guu, Adams Wei Yu, Brian Lester, Nan Du, Andrew M Dai, and Quoc V Le. 2021. Finetuned language models are zero-shot learners. *arXiv preprint arXiv:2109.01652*.

Frank F. Xu, Uri Alon, Graham Neubig, and Vincent Josua Hellendoorn. 2022. A systematic evaluation of large language models of code. In *Proceedings of the 6th ACM SIGPLAN International Symposium on Machine Programming*, MAPS 2022, page 1–10, New York, NY, USA. Association for Computing Machinery.

Jingfeng Yang, Hongye Jin, Ruixiang Tang, Xiaotian Han, Qizhang Feng, Haoming Jiang, Shaochen Zhong, Bing Yin, and Xia Hu. 2023a. Harnessing the power of llms in practice: A survey on chatgpt and beyond. *ACM Transactions on Knowledge Discovery from Data*.

Zijian Győző Yang, László János Laki, Tamás Váradi, and Gábor Prószéky. 2023b. Mono-and multilingual gpt-3 models for hungarian. In *International Conference on Text, Speech, and Dialogue*, pages 94–104. Springer.

Arda Yüksel, Abdullatif Köksal, Lütfi Kerem Şenel, Anna Korhonen, and Hinrich Schütze. 2024. Turkishmmlu: Measuring massive multitask language understanding in turkish.

Shengyu Zhang, Linfeng Dong, Xiaoya Li, Sen Zhang, Xiaofei Sun, Shuhe Wang, Jiwei Li, Runyi Hu, Tianwei Zhang, Fei Wu, and Guoyin Wang. 2024. Instruction tuning for large language models: A survey.

Xiang Zhang, Senyu Li, Bradley Hauer, Ning Shi, and Grzegorz Kondrak. 2023a. Don't trust ChatGPT when your question is not in English: A study of multilingual abilities and types of LLMs. In *Proceedings of the 2023 Conference on Empirical Methods in Natural Language Processing*, pages 7915–7927, Singapore. Association for Computational Linguistics.

Zheng Zhang, Chen Zheng, Da Tang, Ke Sun, Yukun Ma, Yingtong Bu, Xun Zhou, and Liang Zhao. 2023b. Balancing specialized and general skills in llms: The impact of modern tuning and data strategy.

Jun Zhao, Zhihao Zhang, Luhui Gao, Qi Zhang, Tao Gui, and Xuanjing Huang. 2024. Llama beyond english: An empirical study on language capability transfer.

Wayne Xin Zhao, Kun Zhou, Junyi Li, Tianyi Tang, Xiaolei Wang, Yupeng Hou, Yingqian Min, Beichen Zhang, Junjie Zhang, Zican Dong, Yifan Du, Chen Yang, Yushuo Chen, Zhipeng Chen, Jinhao Jiang, Ruiyang Ren, Yifan Li, Xinyu Tang, Zikang Liu, Peiyu Liu, Jian-Yun Nie, and Ji-Rong Wen. 2023a. A survey of large language models.

Xujiang Zhao, Jiaying Lu, Chengyuan Deng, Can Zheng, Junxiang Wang, Tanmoy Chowdhury, Li Yun, Hejie Cui, Zhang Xuchao, Tianjiao Zhao, et al. 2023b. Domain specialization as the key to make large language models disruptive: A comprehensive survey. *arXiv preprint arXiv:2305.18703*.

Jiawei Zheng, Hanghai Hong, Xiaoli Wang, Jingsong Su, Yonggui Liang, and Shikai Wu. 2024. Fine-tuning large language models for domain-specific machine translation.

Ahmet Üstün, Viraat Aryabumi, Zheng-Xin Yong, Wei-Yin Ko, Daniel D'souza, Gbemileke Onilude, Neel Bhandari, Shivalika Singh, Hui-Lee Ooi, Amr Kayid, Freddie Vargus, Phil Blunsom, Shayne Longpre, Niklas Muennighoff, Marzieh Fadaee, Julia Kreutzer, and Sara Hooker. 2024. Aya model: An instruction finetuned open-access multilingual language model.

# A Appendix

## A.1 Instruction Fine-tuning Prompt

The prompt used in instruction tuning is given as follows (translated prompt is given in parenthesis).

```
Aşağıda, daha geniş bir bağlam sağlayan
girdiyle birlikte bir görevi açıklayan
talimat bulunmaktadır. Talimatı yeterince
sağlayan bir çıktı yaz.
(Below is an instruction explaining a task
with input that provides more context.
Write an output that satisfies
the instruction)

### Talimat (Instruction):
[INSTRUCTION]

### Girdi (Input):
[INPUT]

### Çıktı (Output):
[OUTPUT]
```

## A.2 Task-Specific Fine-tuning Prompt

The prompt used in task-specific (sentiment analysis) fine-tuning is given as follows (translated prompt is given in parenthesis).

```
Aşağıda bir görevi açıklayan talimat
bulunmaktadır. Talimatı yeterince
```

```
sağlayan bir çıktı yaz.
(Below are instructions describing a task.
Write an output that satisfying
the instruction)

### Talimat:
Lütfen verilen yorumun olumlu ya da
olumsuz olduğunu çıktı olarak belirtin.
(Please indicate whether the given comment
is positive or negative.)

### Yorum (Comment):
[INPUT]

### Çıktı (Output):
[OUTPUT]
```

### A.3 Task-Specific Inference Prompt

For sentiment analysis, the prompt used in zero-shot inference is the same as the prompt used for task-specific fine-tuning given in A.2. Few-shot prompting (one-shot for example) is given as follows (translated prompt is given in parenthesis).

```
Aşağıda bir görevi açıklayan talimat
bulunmaktadır. Talimatı yeterince
sağlayan bir çıktı yaz.
(Below are instructions describing a task.
Write an output that satisfies
the instruction)
### Talimat (Instruction):
Lütfen verilen yorumun olumlu ya da
olumsuz olduğunu çıktı olarak belirtin.
(Please indicate whether the given
comment is positive or negative.)

### Yorum (Comment):
çok güzel, sağlıklı, temiz, ferah
(very beautiful, healthy, clean,
spacious)

### Çıktı (Output):
olumlu
(positive)

### Talimat (Instruction):
Lütfen verilen yorumun olumlu ya da
olumsuz olduğunu çıktı olarak belirtin.
(Please indicate whether the given
comment is positive or negative.)

### Yorum (Comment):
[INPUT]

### Çıktı (Output):
[OUTPUT]
```

### A.4 XCOPA Inference Prompt

Few-shot prompting (one-shot for example) is given as follows (translated prompt is given in parenthesis).

```
Aşağıda bir görevi açıklayan talimat
bulunmaktadır. Talimatı yeterince
sağlayan bir çıktı yaz.
(Below are instructions describing a task.
Write an output that satisfies
the instruction)

### Talimat (Instruction):
Verilen cümlenin sebebi nedir?
(What is the reason for the given
sentence?)
Kadın kötü bir ruh halindeydi bu yüzden
(The woman was in a bad mood so)

### Girdi (Input):
arkadaşıyla biraz konuştu.
(she talked to her friend for a while.)
arkadaşına onu yalnız bırakmasını söyledi.
(she told her friend to leave her alone.)

### Çıktı (Output):
Kadın kötü bir ruh halindeydi bu yüzden
arkadaşına onu yalnız bırakmasını söyledi.
(The woman was in a bad mood so she told
her friend to leave her alone.)

Aşağıda bir görevi açıklayan talimat
bulunmaktadır. Talimatı yeterince
sağlayan bir çıktı yaz.
(Below are instructions describing a task.
Write an output that satisfies
the instruction)

### Talimat (Instruction):
Verilen cümlenin sebebi nedir?
(What is the reason for the given
sentence?)
[INPUT]

### Girdi (Input):
[OPTION1]
[OPTION2]
```

```
### Çıktı (Output):
Ürün balonlu naylonla paketlenmişti
bu yüzden [OUTPUT]
(The product was packaged with
bubble wrap so [OUTPUT])
```

### A.5 Belebele Inference Prompt

Few-shot prompting (one-shot for example) is given as follows (translated prompt is given in parenthesis).

```
Aşağıda bir görevi açıklayan talimat
bulunmaktadır. Talimatı yeterince
sağlayan bir çıktı yaz.
(Below are instructions describing a task.
Write an output that satisfies
the instruction)

### Talimat (Instruction):
Tüm notalara doğru şekilde basmaya devam
ederken elinizin mümkün olduğu kadar
rahat olduğundan emin olun - aynı zamanda
parmaklarınızla fazladan hareketler
yapmamaya çalışın. Bu şekilde kendinizi
olabildiğince az yormuş olacaksınız.
Unutmayın ki piyanoda olduğu gibi daha
fazla ses için tuşlara çok güçlü
vurmanıza gerek yoktur. Akordeon
üzerinde, ekstra hacim elde etmek için
körüğü daha fazla basınç veya hızda
kullanırsınız. Akordeonu çalarken
aşağıdakilerden hangisi sesin
yükselmesini sağlar?
(Make sure your hand is as relaxed as
possible while still hitting all the
notes correctly - at the same time,
try not to make extra movements with
your fingers. This way, you will tire
yourself as little as possible.
Remember that you don't need to hit
the keys too hard to get more sound,
like on the piano. On the accordion,
you use the bellows with more pressure
or speed to get extra volume.
Which of the following makes the sound
rise when playing the accordion?)

### Girdi (Input):
A: Daha fazla hız (more speed)
B: Daha fazla güç (more power)
C: Daha az basınç (less pressure)
D: Daha az parmak hareketi
(less finger movement)

### Çıktı (Output):
A

Aşağıda bir görevi açıklayan talimat
bulunmaktadır. Talimatı yeterince
sağlayan bir çıktı yaz.
(Below are instructions describing a task.
Write an output that satisfies
the instruction)

### Talimat (Instruction):
Tüm notalara doğru şekilde basmaya
devam ederken elinizin mümkün olduğu
kadar rahat olduğundan emin olun -
aynı zamanda parmaklarınızla fazladan
hareketler yapmamaya çalışın. ...
Akordeonu çalarken aşağıdakilerden
hangisi sesin yükselmesini sağlar?
(Make sure your hand is as relaxed as
possible while still hitting all the
notes correctly - at the same time,
try not to make extra movements with
your fingers. ... Which of the
following makes the sound rise
when playing the accordion?)

### Girdi (Input):
[OPTION1]
[OPTION2]
[OPTION3]
[OPTION4]

### Çıktı (Output):
[OUTPUT]
```

# An Efficient Approach for Studying Cross-Lingual Transfer in Multilingual Language Models

**Fahim Faisal, Antonios Anastasopoulos**
Department of Computer Science, George Mason University
{ffaisal,antonis}@gmu.edu

## Abstract

The capacity and effectiveness of pre-trained multilingual models (MLMs) for zero-shot cross-lingual transfer is well established. However, phenomena of positive or negative transfer, and the effect of language choice still need to be fully understood, especially in the complex setting of massively multilingual LMs. We propose an *efficient* method to study transfer language influence in zero-shot performance on another target language. Unlike previous work, our approach *disentangles downstream tasks from language*, using dedicated adapter units. Our findings suggest that some languages do not largely affect others, while some languages, especially ones unseen during pre-training, can be extremely beneficial or detrimental for different target languages. We find that no transfer language is beneficial for all target languages. We do, curiously, observe languages previously unseen by MLMs consistently benefit from transfer from *almost any* language. We additionally use our modular approach to quantify negative interference efficiently and categorize languages accordingly. Furthermore, we provide a list of promising transfer-target language configurations that consistently lead to target language performance improvements. [1]

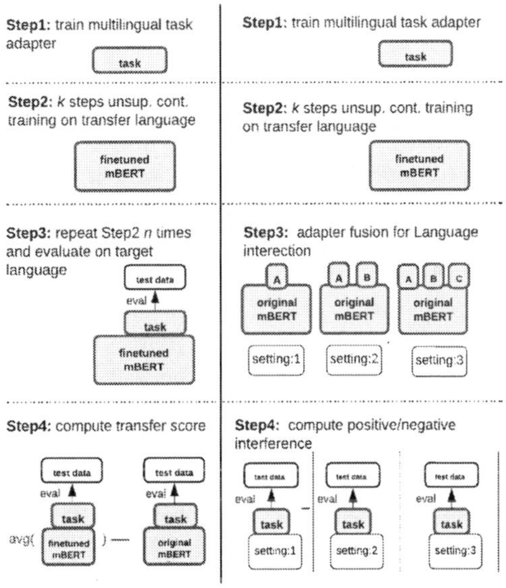


Figure 1: Our approach uses efficient few-step continued tuning (left) and adapter modules (right) to disentangle the effect of *task* and *language* to quantify the effect of a *transfer* language for a given task and model. The left panel depicts the framework for our cross-lingual transfer, while the right panel represents the scenario of multiple language interactions followed by quantifying negative interference.

## 1 Introduction

Pretrained Multilingual Models (MLMs) perform surprisingly well in terms of zero-shot cross-lingual transfer even though no explicit cross-lingual signal was present during pretraining. Subword fertility (Deshpande et al., 2022), token sharing (Dufter and Schütze, 2020), script (Muller et al., 2021), as well as balanced language representation (Rust et al., 2021) contribute to this effectiveness. But, by and large, the most important component seems to be the combination of languages the model is trained and evaluated on. It is important, hence, to understand why and when cross-lingual transfer is successful at the language level.

Previous attempts at studying cross-lingual transfer fall into two categories. First, the most popular approaches are those which, given a task and a MLM, task-tune the MLM on annotated data from a *transfer* language and then evaluate on a *target* language (e.g. Lin et al., 2019). The problem with such approaches is that (a) they do not disentangle the effect of task and language, since they train directly on the task using *annotated* data in the transfer language, and (b) it is expensive to task-tune the whole model for all possible transfer languages.

Second, other approaches tackle the inefficiency

[1]Code and data are publicly available: https://github.com/ffaisal93/neg_inf



*Proceedings of the Fourth Workshop on Multilingual Representation Learning (MRL 2024)*, pages 45–92
November 16, 2024 ©2024 Association for Computational Linguistics

problem by relying on bilingual approximations: Malkin et al. (2022) for instance train bi-lingual BERT (Devlin et al., 2019) models, task-tune them on the transfer language and then evaluate on the *target* one, and contrast this performance to a monolingual target-language BERT. While this approach ignores the fact that language interactions can be different in multilingual and bilingual models (Wang et al., 2020; Papadimitriou et al., 2022), it does correlate decently with transfer performance on multilingual models. However, it still does not disentangle task from language and is quite expensive, as studying $n$ languages requires training $n^2 + n$ BERT models.

In this work, we propose an *efficient* approach to study cross-lingual transfer, outlined in Figure 1, that also disentangles the effect of task-tuning and the effect of language, while operating within the framework of the same MLM. Our approach relies on learning a separate *task* adapter module to perform the downstream task, which needs to only be trained once (hence it is efficient). We then perform unsupervised finetuning on unannotated transfer language data for a minimal number of steps. Comparing the performance of the model on the target language with and without the previous step results in a direct assessment of the effect of the transfer language without changing the conditions under which the downstream task was learned. In addition, we extend this framework to quantify the negative interference resulted from the interaction of multiple languages (Figure 1(right)). With the aid of adapter-fusion tuning (Pfeiffer et al., 2021), we compare different combinations of language adapters and compute the interference occurring due to increased interactions.

We perform extensive analysis using this efficient approach on five downstream tasks using dozens of transfer and target languages (*184 in total*) and devise a metric (which we dub *transfer score*) to quantify which languages have/receive positive or adverse effects on/from others. Last, we focus our analysis on cross-lingual transfer for languages unseen during the pre-training of the MLM.

## 2 Methodology

Adapters (Pfeiffer et al., 2022) are light-weight parameter-efficient modules that can be injected between the layers of pretrained models. In their typical usecase, the rest of the model is frozen and only the adapter modules are trained, to adapt a model to a new language, domain, or task. Importantly, for our goals, these adapters are also composable: one can stack an independently trained language adapter and task adapter to achieve decent performance for that language on that task. First we use an adapter-based setting to perform our analysis on cross-lingual transfer. Furthermore, we extend our study to negative interference and language interaction through another adapter-fusion-based setting.

**Cross-Lingual Transfer** The composable property of adapters allows us to disentangle learning a task from the language representations (the process is also outlined in Figure 1). In step 1, we first train a task-specific adapter `[T]` (e.g. named entity recognition), on data from as many languages as possible. This module will be responsible for performing the downstream task independently of input language. We then (step 2) finetune the `[base]` model (e.g. `mBERT`) on a transfer language $\alpha$ with only a few steps (1, 10, or 100) using masked language modeling, obtaining $[\texttt{base}^{\alpha}]$. Now the language representations of this finetuned model will be (slightly) biased towards the transfer language.

Last, in step 3 we reinsert the task adapter in both the finetuned and the original pretrained model, and use both models to test and evaluate on target language data $\beta$. The difference in performance between these two models $\text{score}(\beta\,; [\texttt{base+t}]^{\alpha}) - \text{score}(\beta\,; [\texttt{base+t}])$ will reveal whether transfer language $\alpha$ benefits (if positive) or hurts (if negative) target language $\beta$.

An obvious caveat of our approach so far is that a single update (or 10 or 100) with a randomly sampled batch in any language does not allow for any robust conclusions. To avoid this issue, we repeat the above process $n$=10 times for each transfer language with different data and aggregate these scores.

Our final transfer score $\text{ts}(\alpha \rightarrow \beta\,; \texttt{base}, \texttt{t})$ for a given model `base` and task `t` turns the difference of the finetuned and original model into a percentage of the original baseline performance, for fairer comparisons at different levels of performance:

$$\text{ts}(\alpha \rightarrow \beta\,; \texttt{base}, \texttt{t}) = \frac{\frac{\sum_1^{10} \text{score}(\beta\,; [\texttt{base+t}]^{\alpha})}{n} - \text{score}(\beta\,; [\texttt{base+t}])}{\text{score}(\beta\,; [\texttt{base+t}])}$$

**Negative Interference** The typical definition of negative interference describes it as the phenomenon when batches in different languages produce opposite gradients during training. We instead focus on downstream performance, in line with most studies focusing on cross-lingual transfer, assuming that a negative effect on performance implies negative interference. Another reason is that, in $n$ dimensional spaces, there extremely high probability of two random vectors being orthogonal; hence any two gradient vectors could certainly be orthogonal without necessarily impacting downstream performance.

To quantify negative interference, we follow a modular-based approach depicted in Figure 1(right). Like before, we separate the task and language, followed by performing interaction among multiple languages. However, we use language adapters at this time instead of continuously finetuning the base model. This strategy allows us to efficiently train multiple language sub-parts only once (Step2) followed by mixing those modules through adapter fusion (Pfeiffer et al., 2021). In our experiments, we train a set of language adapters and make either monolingual settings or a combination of bilingual/trilingual interactions (Step3). Then we stack previously trained task adapter while only changing the underlying language combination. Finally, we extract the interference score from the difference between already computed multilingual and monolingual counterparts (Step4).

Having these interference scores at hand, we can tell whether a language actually gets benefits or not while influencing the associated languages in a positive/negative manner. For example, consider language A interacting with language B. We can easily quantify the interference of language A by calculating the loss/gain of this bilingual interaction [AB]: a score increase for $A$ compared to its monolingual counterpart (i.e. $+\mathtt{A} = +_{\mathtt{[AB]}-\mathtt{[A]}}$) means positive interference for A in this particular setting. We can further extend this to a trilingual setting as well (i.e. $+\mathtt{A} = +_{\mathtt{[ABC]}-\mathtt{[A]}}$). Using these scores, we can get different combinations of interference scenarios by counting the co-occurred positive/negative interference. We use $|+\mathtt{A},+\mathtt{B}|$ to denote the number of cases where A benefits both itself and B, presenting all possible rules in Table 1. Utilizing these rules, we can identify how much language A actually gains or loses during its bilingual/trilingual interactions while providing substantial interference to other languages.

Moreover, we can use these interference combination counts to project languages in an interference representation space. For example, consider a 2-D space of bilingual interaction where the X-axis represents the negative/positive interference a language receives from one such interaction and the Y-axis is for the interference it provides to other languages. We can project a language using the dot product of counts (eg. $|+\mathtt{A},-\mathtt{B}|$) with its corresponding quadrant identifier $[1,-1]$. As a result, the projection coordinates $(x_A, y_A)$ for language $A$ in a bilingual interaction could be obtained as follows:

$$
\begin{aligned}
\mathtt{C} =& |-\mathtt{A},-\mathtt{B}| + |-\mathtt{A},+\mathtt{B}| + |+\mathtt{A},-\mathtt{B}| \\
&+ |+\mathtt{A},+\mathtt{B}| \\
(\mathtt{x_A},\mathtt{y_A}) =& \frac{1}{\mathtt{C}} \times (|-\mathtt{A},-\mathtt{B}| \cdot [-1,-1] \\
&+ |-\mathtt{A},+\mathtt{B}| \cdot [-1,1] + |+\mathtt{A},-\mathtt{B}| \cdot [1,-1] \\
&+ |+\mathtt{A},+\mathtt{B}| \cdot [1,1])
\end{aligned}
$$

Using the above-mentioned projections, we visualize a language in a way that represents how much interference it provides as well as receives (see example with each step of the calculation in Appendix §F). We can further extend this strategy to the trilingual setting, but now we have to deal with eight axes instead of four. In Figure 4 of the result section, we present the language interaction visualizations for bilingual and trilingual scenarios.

| Notations (+: win, −: loss) |
|---|
| 1. $|+\mathtt{A}|$ = *count*( A gains in interaction [AB] or [ABC]) |
| 2. $|-\mathtt{A}|$ = *count*(A losses in interaction [AB] or [ABC]) |
| 3. $|+\mathtt{A},+\mathtt{B}|$ = *count*(Both language gets benefit). In other words, A gains. At the same time, B receives benefits while interacting with A. |

| Bilingual Interactions | Trilingual Interactions | |
|---|---|---|
| $|-\mathtt{A},-\mathtt{B}|$ | $|-\mathtt{A},-\mathtt{B},-\mathtt{C}|$ | $|-\mathtt{A},-\mathtt{B},+\mathtt{C}|$ |
| $|-\mathtt{A},+\mathtt{B}|$ | $|-\mathtt{A},+\mathtt{B},-\mathtt{C}|$ | $|-\mathtt{A},+\mathtt{B},+\mathtt{C}|$ |
| $|+\mathtt{A},-\mathtt{B}|$ | $|+\mathtt{A},-\mathtt{B},-\mathtt{C}|$ | $|+\mathtt{A},-\mathtt{B},+\mathtt{C}|$ |
| $|+\mathtt{A},+\mathtt{B}|$ | $|+\mathtt{A},+\mathtt{B},-\mathtt{C}|$ | $|+\mathtt{A},+\mathtt{B},+\mathtt{C}|$ |

Table 1: Interference calculation for language A. $|+\mathtt{A}|$ means the number of cases where A itself gets benefits. If the setting is bilingual, then $|+\mathtt{A}| = \text{count}(+_{[\mathtt{AB}]-[A]})$ (i.e. if the evaluation score on task language A: $[\mathtt{AB}] - [\mathtt{A}] > 0$ for the combination [AB], we get a +A.)

## 3 Experimental Setup

We conduct our experiments in two different settings targeted to perform two different analyses: first understanding the language effect on cross-lingual transfer and then, extending this to quantify language-language interaction.

Primarily, we use multilingual BERT as our base model and report XLM-R results for comparative model evaluation. We use a total of 38 transfer languages (11 unseen during pretraining) to finetune the MLM using masked language modeling with the process described above. Using these transfer languages, we do monolingual finetuning on mBERT for either 1, 10, 100, or 1000 steps and each experiment is repeated for 10 times. At the sametime, we trained multilingual task adapters followed by task evaluation on the following tasks:

- **Token-level:** Dependency Parsing (DEP), Part-of-Speech (POS) tagging and Named Entity Recognition (NER). Parsing and POS tagging are evaluated on a set of 114 languages from Universal Dependencies v2.11 (de Marneffe et al., 2021). For NER, we use 125 languages from the Wikiann (Pan et al., 2017) dataset.
- **Sentence-level:** Natural Language Inference (NLI) evaluated on XNLI (Conneau et al., 2018) and AmericasNLI (ANLI) (Ebrahimi et al., 2022) datasets.
- **Extractive Question Answering:** Evaluated on TyDiQA (Clark et al., 2020) gold task.

Additionally, we train 38 language adapters to perform the experiment on language-to-language interaction and negative interference. Here, we stack the previously trained task adapter on top of either one or a combination of double or triple language adapters (Figure 1(b)) and then perform the evaluation on the transfer languages having task data available. All training and evaluation datasets, implementation and hyper-parameter details are provided in Appendices C-E (Table 24-29).

| Lang. | Base | Continious Steps k=10 | k=1000 | Lang. Interaction [1A] | [2A] | [3A] |
|---|---|---|---|---|---|---|
| | | | **Parsing** | | | |
| pcm | **81.1** | 79.1 | 77.9 | 79.3 | 79.5 | 79.5 |
| wol | **69.5** | 68.1 | 67.3 | 68.9 | 69.1 | 69.1 |
| kmr | 31.9 | 31.7 | **45.3** | 32.6 | 32.1 | 32.0 |
| bam | 29.9 | 30.9 | **38.1** | 30.8 | 30.8 | 30.8 |
| gub | 21.7 | 20.9 | **34.5** | 23.8 | 23.73 | 23.5 |
| | | | **POS Tagging** | | | |
| pcm | **92.9** | 92.2 | 91.2 | 92.3 | 92.5 | 92.6 |
| wol | **85.6** | 84.2 | 82.1 | 84.1 | 84.7 | 84.8 |
| kmr | 40.2 | 40.5 | **55.8** | 41.1 | 40.8 | 40.7 |
| bam | 30.3 | 30.8 | **49.5** | 30.7 | 30.5 | 30.5 |
| gub | 28.5 | 28.7 | **36.7** | 28.8 | 28.8 | 28.9 |
| | | | **NER** | | | |
| ibo | **61.1** | 57.2 | 55.4 | 57.5 | 57.8 | 57.7 |
| pms | 88.2 | **88.9** | 87.6 | 88.2 | 87.5 | 87.6 |
| kin | **72.4** | 71.8 | 68.5 | 70.5 | 71.1 | 71.9 |

Table 2: Task results for transfer languages unseen by mBERT. **base:** zero-shot with task adapter [T]. **Continuous Steps:** do $k$ steps of finetuning on that language plus [T]. **Lang. Interaction:** introducing language adapters; [1A]: just 1 adapter (in language) and evaluate on it; [2A]: 2 language adapters, the target lang. and one test (the result is averaged for all transfer langs.); [3A]: 3 lang. adapters (results are average again). The highest obtained score for each language is bolded.

## 4 Results and Discussion

First, in 4.1, we present a comparative scenario in between continuous training and language interaction in terms of performance improvement over the baseline model. Then in 4.2, we discuss the findings of continuous training in the context of cross-lingual transfer. After that, in 4.3, we present the representation of language interactions as well as interference following the strategy discussed in Section 2.

### 4.1 Continuous Training vs Language Interaction

Here we present 8 sets of scores for each token-level task. The baseline is where we stack the task adapter on the base pretrained mBERT (i.e. zero-shot task on pretrained mBERT+ [T]). Then for all the evaluation languages, we perform 4 sets of cross-lingual transfers (i.e. 1, 10, 100, and 1000 steps of continuous training). For the language-language interaction experiment, we only perform the evaluation on transfer languages where either 1, 2 or 3 language adapters are fused together before stacking the task adapter (i.e. [1A], [2A], [3A]).

**Only Unseen Transfers** In Table 2, we present our token-level evaluation report for transfer languages unseen during the pretraining phase. For the [2A] and [3A] language interaction results, we compute and report the average score where the evaluation language is also present in the [2A] or [3A] adapter fusion. For tasks where word-to-word relation plays a critical role (parsing and pos tagging), we observe similar patterns of improvement over baseline in both Cont. steps and lang. interaction settings. Whereas, for a task like NER, we do not observe any improvement over baseline both in sustained cont. (k=1000) and interaction settings. Even though we are evaluating the same language after continuous masked language modeling (mlm) or adapter fusion with another high-resource language, there is no clear winning formula that can

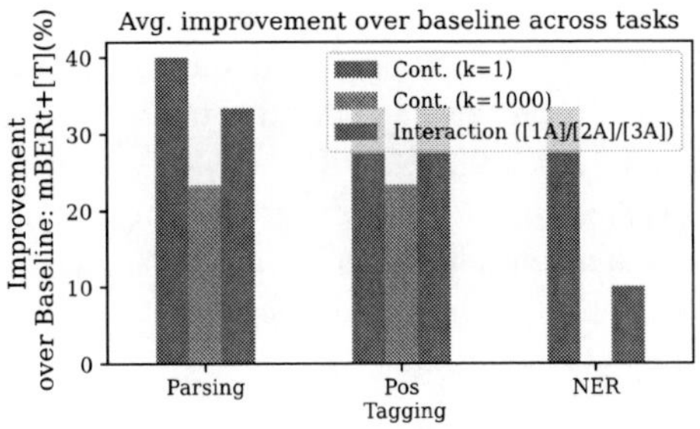


Figure 2: Average score improvement over baseline across tasks for the transfer languages (evaluated on itself). We observe a spike of over 33% positive score at continuous training step 1. Among these, only 23.3% cases result in sustained improvement after 1000 steps (0% in NER). On the contrary, standard language adapter interaction stays at 25% average improvement.

always serve the unseen low-resource languages.

**Unseen+Seen Transfers** On the other hand, when we consider the case of both unseen and seen languages together in token-level tasks, we see a spike of 33% average improvement over baseline with just 1 step of mlm training. However, this improvement percentage gets down to a sustained 23.3% (except task NER) when we evaluate again after having 1000 steps of training. Whereas, in language interaction settings where we fuse standard well-trained language adapters, we generally observe improvement for those languages which also get benefited from continuous training. The improvement percentage averaged over all 38 transfer languages is presented in Figure 2. In addition, we present all the scores for all 38 transfer languages and token-level tasks in App. Tables 7, 9, and 11.

## 4.2 Takeaways from Continuous Training

**No Universal Donor** First, we search for transfer languages that can be used for positive transfer for a large set of languages. However, we find no language out of 38 that can positively influence almost all languages using mBERT as base model. For this experiment, we rank the transfer languages based on their averaged transfer score (i.e. `aggregated-transfer`). In Table 3, we list the top 5 ranked transfer languages with their transfer score (base model: mBERT) and the percentage of target languages that do benefit from them (more details in Appendix H). We observe, most languages benefit within the range of 30-45% of target languages across tasks except NLI. However, we did not receive any positive transfer for

| | Lang. | ts | +(%) | Lang. | ts | +(%) | Lang. | ts | +(%) |
|---|---|---|---|---|---|---|---|---|---|
| | **Parsing** | | | **POS Tagging** | | | **NER** | | |
| 1 | mya | 0.33 | 40.4 | **kin** | 0.41 | 35.1 | zho | 0.16 | 49.6 |
| 2 | ell | 0.15 | 31.6 | **kmr** | 0.36 | 36.9 | tel | 0.08 | 32.8 |
| 3 | **kmr** | 0.14 | 35.9 | **mos** | 0.27 | 34.2 | hun | 0.08 | 40.8 |
| 4 | yor | 0.14 | 33.3 | hye | 0.27 | 36.9 | heb | 0.04 | 34.4 |
| 5 | **pcm** | 0.13 | 31.6 | cym | 0.22 | 37.7 | est | 0.03 | 36.8 |
| | **XNLI** | | | **ANLI** | | | **TyDiQA** | | |
| 1 | **hau** | -34.4 | 0.0 | **bam** | -15.0 | 0.0 | zho | 0.7 | 77.8 |
| 2 | **bam** | -34.9 | 0.0 | **hau** | -17.8 | 0.0 | jpn | 0.1 | 44.4 |
| 3 | **gub** | -36.4 | 0.0 | **gub** | -18.4 | 0.0 | gle | -0.1 | 44.4 |
| 4 | **ewe** | -36.7 | 0.0 | deu | -19.8 | 0.0 | **wol** | -0.1 | 44.4 |
| 5 | hin | -37.1 | 0.0 | fin | -19.9 | 0.0 | cym | -0.1 | 33.3 |

Table 3: Top 5 transfer languages per task ranked using the aggregated transfer score (`ts` columns; see App. H for computation). Unseen ones are **bolded**. *+(%)* is the percentage of languages receiving positive transfer. No transfer language helps all target languages. (Complete rank with transfer scores: Table 15-18).

| | Parsing | Pos Tagging | NER | XNLI | ANLI | TyDiQA |
|---|---|---|---|---|---|---|
| mBERT | 30.6 | 31.0 | 31.8 | 0 | 0 | 30.1 |
| xlmr | 20.5 | 33.2 | 41.1 | 44.4 | 41.6 | 17.0 |

Table 4: Average percentage of languages receiving positive transfer (avg. *+(%)*) across models. Unlike mBERT, xlmr provides positive transferring in NLI.

both of the two different NLI task datasets (XNLI and ANLI). The maximum positive transfer percentage is from zho in both NER and TyDiQA. Interestingly, low-resourced unseen languages perform well in general as transfer languages: 31.7% (token-level) and 28.3% (sentence-level) of top 20 transfer languages are unseen languages.

**Base Model and Task Matters** To further investigate the discrepancy observed in NLI task, we replace the base model mBERT with XLM-R (Table 4). Unlike mBERT, XLM-R in NLI provides superior performance (XNLI: +44.4% and ANLI: +41.6%). This signifies how the choice of the base model in a setting with a disentangled language-task effect could drastically change the cross-lingual transfer performance of certain tasks.

Moreover, we observe the above-discussed rankings of transfer languages vary across tasks. To investigate the underlying similarity, we select a large subset of languages (the common 62 target languages across three token-level tasks) and rank the transfer languages as before. We then compute the Spearman rank correlation and statistical significance (`p<0.05`) of their transfer scores tasks (see Appendix Table 21). Only parsing and NER are positively correlated ($\rho$=0.4) whereas POS tag-

| Rank | Lang. # (max, min) | ts | Var. | Type |
|---|---|---|---|---|
| 1 | **ibo** (10, 10) | 0.05 | 23.5 | (+ *and* -) |
| 3 | **bam** (11, 15) | 0.02 | 21.5 | (+ *and* -) |
| 6 | **mos** (13, 2) | 0.09 | 16.1 | (+) |
| 8 | **pcm** (1, 11) | 0.13 | 13.4 | (-) |
| 26 | eng (0, 0) | -0.22 | 6.4 | neutral |
| 36 | ara (0, 0) | -0.12 | 5.1 | neutral |

Table 5: Example of transfer languages ranked with their `aggregated-transfer (ts)` score variance (task: parsing). Unseen languages (**bold** font) exhibit high variance. # (max) represents the language count receiving maximum positive transfer. (see Appendix L)

ging is negatively correlated with the other two tasks. This is somewhat surprising, because we use the same underlying dataset for the parsing and POS tagging tasks. We find only a few transfer languages could effectively provide positive transfer simultaneously across tasks. The 5 common languages in the top 20 across tasks are: `yor`, **`mos`**, **`kin`**, **`hau`**, and `tel`. In sort, languages unseen by `mBERT` (in **boldface**), exhibit similar ranking across tasks (see Table 15-18), whereas others vary. For example, `zho` is the lowest-ranked one in parsing while being top-ranked in NER! Appendix Figure 6 shows the number of common languages across tasks.

**Unseen Languages Transfer with High Variance** We observe that transfer languages with high variance mainly fall into one of three categories:

1. (+ *and* -): boost performance for some languages while hurt significantly some others;
2. (+): mostly (small) positive transfer, significantly hurts only a few languages;
3. (-): mostly (small) negative transfer, significantly helps only a few languages.

See examples in Table 5 and Appendix L for details. Though unseen languages perform well as transfer languages, they usually exhibit the traits of high-variance transfer. Around 90% of unseen transfer languages are within top-20 languages sorted by variance (see Appendix Figure 7).

**Target Language Differences** Unlike transfer languages, we find target languages that are almost universal recipients of positive cross-lingual transfer, many of which are unseen by `mBERT`. On the other hand, some languages do not receive any benefit from the diverse set of transfer languages. In Figure 3(a), we plot the target languages based on the percentage of languages from which they receive positive or negative transfer (see additional maps in Appendix Figure 5). We find around one-third of target languages across three token-level tasks never receive any positive transfer (parsing: 35.1%, POS: 28.1%, NER: 32.8%). Nevertheless, there are target languages (mostly unseen by `mBERT`) that benefit from all transfer languages (eg. `nap`, `mpu` in parsing). See Appendix I and Table 19 for additional results.

**Seen vs Unseen Languages** Transferring from either seen or unseen languages to unseen languages (i.e. `transfer(seen/unseen→ unseen)`) generally helps. For this experiment, we use the large set of token-level task evaluation and 11 transfer languages unseen during `mBERT` pertaining from diverse families including Indo-European, Afro-Asiatic, Mande, Niger-Congo and Tupian. We observe, that transferring to a large and diverse set of seen languages from unseen languages (i.e. `transfer(unseen→ seen)`) does not provide any substantial utility. Among the three tasks, we get the average transfer as positive for unseen transfer languages just once (dependency parsing, `transfer(unseen→ unseen)`). See Figure 8 for the difference of utility provided when the transfer-/target languages are seen vs unseen.

**Sustained Cross-Lingual Transfer** Our approach limits step 2 (continued training on the transfer language) to a minimal number of steps. For this section, we extend this to 1000 steps. In the vast majority of transfer-target language combinations, this leads to (small) negative transfer under our setting. We suspect this is due to the underlying model undergoing the first steps of catastrophic forgetting (McCloskey and Cohen, 1989).

There are some languages, though, mostly unseen ones (eg. `nap`, `gun`, `tpn`, `aqz`) that benefit more from this extended setting. See Appendix J Table 20, where we report the target language receiving the highest benefit from each transfer language for each setting (1,10,100,1000 steps). All the max-utility recipients aside from `bar` and `nds` are unseen languages. Figure 3(b) presents the training step progression of `aggregated-transfer` scores for `Mossi`, one of the most donating transfer languages, and Appendix N (Figures 9-18) shows the transfer progression graphs for all transfer languages. At the task level, POS tagging always ends up having comparatively higher target language performance variance with more training steps, while NER almost always ends up with negative results with longer training.

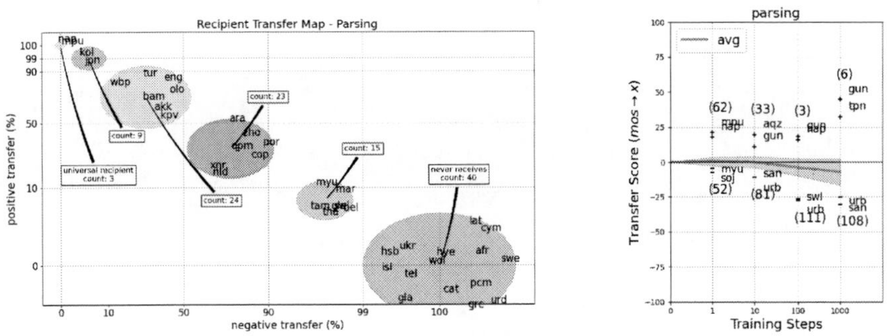


(a) Target languages mapped based on percentage of receiving positive/negative transfers.

(b) `Aggregated-transfer` score line with standard deviations through different training steps for Mossi (mos) as transfer language.

Figure 3: (a) Some languages exhibit universal recipient nature (yellow) while some never receive positive transfer (red). (b) Shown are the top and bottom two languages receiving maximum/minimum scores (eg. gun, `tpn` at 1000 steps) at each step, with total positive/negative transfers (in parenthesis) also shown. See Appendix N for other transfer language score lines.

### 4.3 Takeaway from Language Interactions

We plot all the transfer languages in a 2d axis for both two-language interactions and three-language interactions as shown in Figure 4.

**Bilingual Interactions** First of all, we observe most of the languages mainly fall into either one of the two categories: (1) A(+), B(+): getting benefits from interactions and helping others at the same time, (2) A(-), B(+): Helping other languages but do not get benefits from those languages. Secondly, there are resemblances in how certain languages from specific categories interfere across all 3 tasks. For example, consider the case of `zho`, `swe`, `spa` and `fra`. These languages fall to the lower right part of all three graphs. However, there are languages like `ara` that do not uniformly get benefits across three tasks while maintaining it's positive interfering status. Although, there are debates whether English (eng) is an appropriate "hub" language or not (Anastasopoulos and Neubig, 2020), `eng` maintains its status in the upper right quarter making it a good transfer language in all Latin script majority settings.

**Trilingual Interactions** Now we increase the number of languages for a specific transfer language to influence. When we compare the bilingual settings with the trilingual ones (Figure 4 (2)), the left-right categorization remains the same. However, many languages receive an uplifting position meaning the strength of performing positive interference increases for those languages (eg. `are` in dependency parsing, `zho` in NER). Moreover, we observe an overall decrease in the lower-right corner for both dependency parsing and NER. However, there are languages like `wol` in POS tagging that goes from upper-left to lower-left. Nonetheless, very few different colored points (i.e. negative coordinate for 3rd language) signify the fact that a multilingual setting is beneficial towards a larger group of recipients.

## 5 Recommendations

Based on our above findings, we make a number of recommendations in choosing the appropriate transfer language and training scheme for a low-resource setting.

1. There is no universal donor but having multiple transfer languages in the training scheme helps in terms of language interference.
2. For universal recipient languages (eg. Typologically diverse unseen ones), including almost any language in the transfer scheme help.
3. Low resource unseen languages generally transfer with high variance. A good idea is to include them with other seen languages in the transfer scheme to stabilize the transfer output across a large number of target languages.
4. Only some of the unseen low-resource ones show sustained transfer toward other low-resource languages through continuous thousand-step training. Usually, the deviation happens during an early stage of training. So just continuing pretraining for longer is not optimal for a scenario with mixed-category languages.
5. The patterns of receiving positive transfer are similar when we use either one language small-

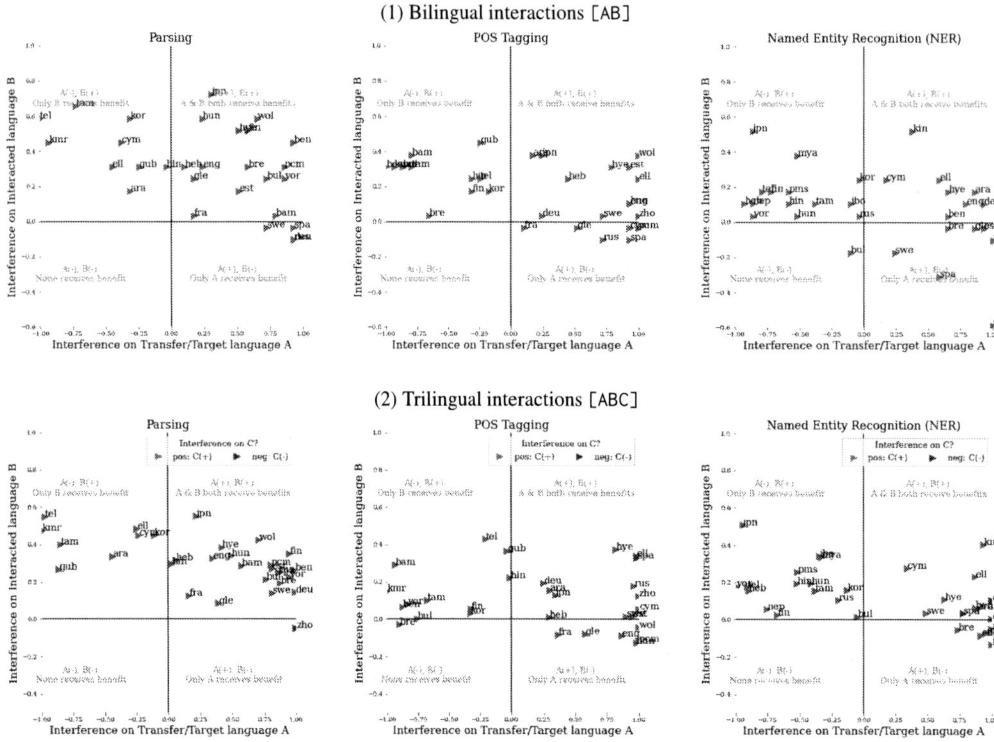


Figure 4: Language interaction representation for bilingual and trilingual settings. To identify the language coordinates, we use two and three adapters (i.e. [2A], [3A]) jointly fused. In [3A] plots, we show the position only for one interacted language B along with transfer/target language A. For the 3rd language C, we use color variation (red/blue) to depict whether C receives positive transfer or not.

step continuous training or 2/3 standard adapter fusion. So using a large set of trained language adapters fused together according to the need is a simpler way to deal with a large set of mixed-category target languages.

## 6 Conclusion and Future Work

We devise an efficient approach to study cross-lingual transfer in multilingual models for various tasks that disentangles task and language effects. We believe this disentanglement coupled with few-step fine-tuning has the potential to uncover currently uncharted model behaviors (eg. NLI evaluation). Our findings suggest languages unseen by MLMs clearly exhibit different behavioral pattern compared to other languages in general: they are universal as target, exhibit high variance as transfer language, and their behavior follows similar patterns across tasks. In addition, we do not find a universal donor (a language that benefits all others). Last, we find that some languages consistently benefit from settings that resemble "catastrophic forgetting" for other languages, an observation we believe merits a dedicated follow-up study.

We hope that our approach will allow for further study of cross-lingual transfer for more languages and MLMs, and we plan to extend this in future work, as our findings suggest interesting differences in the behavior of languages used in pre-training and unused ones. Eventually, we hope that our study will also lead to guidelines for selecting appropriate transfer languages, as well as more informed methods for the adaptation of MLMs to new under-served languages. While our proposed approach being highly efficient to expand the paradigm of cross-lingual transfer evaluation, the findings shed light onto the easy adaptation of MLMs for new languages in a low-resource setting.

## Limitations

In this work, we primarily experiment with encoder models like mBERT and XLM-R, token-level syntactic tasks and two sentence-level tasks. In future, we would expand this work to recent large language models and tasks involving natural language understanding. Moreover, our work only focus on low-resource setting with small-scale training data and parameter-efficient adapters. In future, instead of monolingual finetuning we will use this parameter efficient approach for multilingual finetuning thus unfolding effective multilingual pretraining configurations. As the base-language model choice, we only use mBERT. The evaluation of cross-lingual transfer needed to be expand to decoder based language models.

## Acknowledgements

This work has been generously supported by the National Science Foundation under grants IIS-2125466 and IIS-2327143. We are thankful to the anonymous reviewers and area chairs for their constructive feedback. This project was supported by resources provided by the Office of Research Computing at George Mason University (`https://orc.gmu.edu`) and funded in part by grants from the National Science Foundation (Awards Number 1625039 and 2018631).

## References

Julien Abadji, Pedro Ortiz Suarez, Laurent Romary, and Benoît Sagot. 2022. Towards a Cleaner Document-Oriented Multilingual Crawled Corpus. *arXiv e-prints*, page arXiv:2201.06642.

David Adelani, Jesujoba Alabi, Angela Fan, Julia Kreutzer, Xiaoyu Shen, Machel Reid, Dana Ruiter, Dietrich Klakow, Peter Nabende, Ernie Chang, Tajuddeen Gwadabe, Freshia Sackey, Bonaventure F. P. Dossou, Chris Emezue, Colin Leong, Michael Beukman, Shamsuddeen Muhammad, Guyo Jarso, Oreen Yousuf, Andre Niyongabo Rubungo, Gilles Hacheme, Eric Peter Wairagala, Muhammad Umair Nasir, Benjamin Ajibade, Tunde Ajayi, Yvonne Gitau, Jade Abbott, Mohamed Ahmed, Millicent Ochieng, Anuoluwapo Aremu, Perez Ogayo, Jonathan Mukiibi, Fatoumata Ouoba Kabore, Godson Kalipe, Derguene Mbaye, Allahsera Auguste Tapo, Victoire Memdjokam Koagne, Edwin Munkoh-Buabeng, Valencia Wagner, Idris Abdulmumin, Ayodele Awokoya, Happy Buzaaba, Blessing Sibanda, Andiswa Bukula, and Sam Manthalu. 2022. A few thousand translations go a long way! leveraging pre-trained models for African news translation. In *Proceedings of the 2022 Conference of the North American Chapter of the Association for Computational Linguistics: Human Language Technologies*, pages 3053–3070, Seattle, United States. Association for Computational Linguistics.

Antonios Anastasopoulos and Graham Neubig. 2020. Should all cross-lingual embeddings speak English? In *Proceedings of the 58th Annual Meeting of the Association for Computational Linguistics*, pages 8658–8679, Online. Association for Computational Linguistics.

Jonathan H. Clark, Eunsol Choi, Michael Collins, Dan Garrette, Tom Kwiatkowski, Vitaly Nikolaev, and Jennimaria Palomaki. 2020. TyDi QA: A benchmark for information-seeking question answering in typologically diverse languages. *Transactions of the Association for Computational Linguistics*, 8:454–470.

Alexis Conneau, Ruty Rinott, Guillaume Lample, Adina Williams, Samuel Bowman, Holger Schwenk, and Veselin Stoyanov. 2018. XNLI: Evaluating cross-lingual sentence representations. In *Proceedings of the 2018 Conference on Empirical Methods in Natural Language Processing*, pages 2475–2485, Brussels, Belgium. Association for Computational Linguistics.

Marie-Catherine de Marneffe, Christopher D. Manning, Joakim Nivre, and Daniel Zeman. 2021. Universal Dependencies. *Computational Linguistics*, 47(2):255–308.

Ameet Deshpande, Partha Talukdar, and Karthik Narasimhan. 2022. When is BERT multilingual? isolating crucial ingredients for cross-lingual transfer. In *Proceedings of the 2022 Conference of the North American Chapter of the Association for Computational Linguistics: Human Language Technologies*, pages 3610–3623, Seattle, United States. Association for Computational Linguistics.

Jacob Devlin, Ming-Wei Chang, Kenton Lee, and Kristina Toutanova. 2019. BERT: Pre-training of deep bidirectional transformers for language understanding. In *Proceedings of the 2019 Conference of the North American Chapter of the Association for Computational Linguistics: Human Language Technologies, Volume 1 (Long and Short Papers)*, pages 4171–4186, Minneapolis, Minnesota. Association for Computational Linguistics.

Philipp Dufter and Hinrich Schütze. 2020. Identifying elements essential for BERT's multilinguality. In *Proceedings of the 2020 Conference on Empirical Methods in Natural Language Processing (EMNLP)*, pages 4423–4437, Online. Association for Computational Linguistics.

Abteen Ebrahimi, Manuel Mager, Arturo Oncevay, Vishrav Chaudhary, Luis Chiruzzo, Angela Fan, John Ortega, Ricardo Ramos, Annette Rios, Ivan Vladimir Meza Ruiz, Gustavo Giménez-Lugo, Elisabeth Mager, Graham Neubig, Alexis Palmer, Rolando Coto-Solano, Thang Vu, and Katharina Kann. 2022. AmericasNLI: Evaluating zero-shot natural language understanding of pretrained multilingual models in truly low-resource languages. In *Proceedings of the 60th Annual Meeting of the Association for Computational Linguistics (Volume 1: Long Papers)*, pages 6279–6299, Dublin, Ireland. Association for Computational Linguistics.

Fahim Faisal and Antonios Anastasopoulos. 2022. Phylogeny-inspired adaptation of multilingual models to new languages. In *Proceedings of the 2nd Conference of the Asia-Pacific Chapter of the Association for Computational Linguistics and the 12th International Joint Conference on Natural Language Processing (Volume 1: Long Papers)*, pages 434–452, Online only. Association for Computational Linguistics.

Yoshinari Fujinuma, Jordan Boyd-Graber, and Katharina Kann. 2022. Match the script, adapt if multilingual: Analyzing the effect of multilingual pretraining on cross-lingual transferability. In *Proceedings of the 60th Annual Meeting of the Association for Computational Linguistics (Volume 1: Long Papers)*, pages 1500–1512, Dublin, Ireland. Association for Computational Linguistics.

Yu-Hsiang Lin, Chian-Yu Chen, Jean Lee, Zirui Li, Yuyan Zhang, Mengzhou Xia, Shruti Rijhwani, Junxian He, Zhisong Zhang, Xuezhe Ma, Antonios Anastasopoulos, Patrick Littell, and Graham Neubig. 2019. Choosing transfer languages for cross-lingual learning. In *Proceedings of the 57th Annual Meeting of the Association for Computational Linguistics*, pages 3125–3135, Florence, Italy. Association for Computational Linguistics.

Dan Malkin, Tomasz Limisiewicz, and Gabriel Stanovsky. 2022. A balanced data approach for evaluating cross-lingual transfer: Mapping the linguistic blood bank. In *Proceedings of the 2022 Conference of the North American Chapter of the Association for Computational Linguistics: Human Language Technologies*, pages 4903–4915, Seattle, United States. Association for Computational Linguistics.

Michael McCloskey and Neal J Cohen. 1989. Catastrophic interference in connectionist networks: The sequential learning problem. In *Psychology of learning and motivation*, volume 24, pages 109–165. Elsevier.

Benjamin Muller, Antonios Anastasopoulos, Benoît Sagot, and Djamé Seddah. 2021. When being unseen from mBERT is just the beginning: Handling new languages with multilingual language models. In *Proceedings of the 2021 Conference of the North American Chapter of the Association for Computational Linguistics: Human Language Technologies*, pages 448–462, Online. Association for Computational Linguistics.

Xiaoman Pan, Boliang Zhang, Jonathan May, Joel Nothman, Kevin Knight, and Heng Ji. 2017. Cross-lingual name tagging and linking for 282 languages. In *Proceedings of the 55th Annual Meeting of the Association for Computational Linguistics (Volume 1: Long Papers)*, pages 1946–1958, Vancouver, Canada. Association for Computational Linguistics.

Isabel Papadimitriou, Kezia Lopez, and Dan Jurafsky. 2022. Multilingual bert has an accent: Evaluating english influences on fluency in multilingual models. arXiv:2210.05619.

Jonas Pfeiffer, Naman Goyal, Xi Lin, Xian Li, James Cross, Sebastian Riedel, and Mikel Artetxe. 2022. Lifting the curse of multilinguality by pre-training modular transformers. In *Proceedings of the 2022 Conference of the North American Chapter of the Association for Computational Linguistics: Human Language Technologies*, pages 3479–3495, Seattle, United States. Association for Computational Linguistics.

Jonas Pfeiffer, Aishwarya Kamath, Andreas Rücklé, Kyunghyun Cho, and Iryna Gurevych. 2021. AdapterFusion: Non-destructive task composition for transfer learning. In *Proceedings of the 16th Conference of the European Chapter of the Association for Computational Linguistics: Main Volume*, pages 487–503, Online. Association for Computational Linguistics.

Jonas Pfeiffer, Andreas Rücklé, Clifton Poth, Aishwarya Kamath, Ivan Vulić, Sebastian Ruder, Kyunghyun Cho, and Iryna Gurevych. 2020. AdapterHub: A framework for adapting transformers. In *Proceedings of the 2020 Conference on Empirical Methods in Natural Language Processing: System Demonstrations*, pages 46–54, Online. Association for Computational Linguistics.

Phillip Rust, Jonas Pfeiffer, Ivan Vulić, Sebastian Ruder, and Iryna Gurevych. 2021. How good is your tokenizer? on the monolingual performance of multilingual language models. In *Proceedings of the 59th Annual Meeting of the Association for Computational Linguistics and the 11th International Joint Conference on Natural Language Processing (Volume 1: Long Papers)*, pages 3118–3135, Online. Association for Computational Linguistics.

Zirui Wang, Zachary C. Lipton, and Yulia Tsvetkov. 2020. On negative interference in multilingual models: Findings and a meta-learning treatment. In *Proceedings of the 2020 Conference on Empirical Methods in Natural Language Processing (EMNLP)*, pages 4438–4450, Online. Association for Computational Linguistics.

Thomas Wolf, Lysandre Debut, Victor Sanh, Julien Chaumond, Clement Delangue, Anthony Moi, Pierric Cistac, Tim Rault, Remi Louf, Morgan Funtowicz, Joe Davison, Sam Shleifer, Patrick von Platen, Clara Ma, Yacine Jernite, Julien Plu, Canwen Xu, Teven Le Scao, Sylvain Gugger, Mariama Drame, Quentin Lhoest, and Alexander Rush. 2020. Transformers: State-of-the-art natural language processing. In *Proceedings of the 2020 Conference on Empirical Methods in Natural Language Processing: System Demonstrations*, pages 38–45, Online. Association for Computational Linguistics.

## A Related Works

**Cross-Lingual Transfer** Studying cross-lingual transfer to prepare a better pretraining configuration is a well-explored topic. Malkin et al. (2022) propose a balanced-data approach to identify effective set of languages for model training through constructing bilingual language graph. They formulate the problem in terms of linguistic blood bank where language can either play the role of donor or receiver. This study comprises over a large set of languages while training a large number of bilingual models. However, how a large multilingual model (eg. mBERT) having a shared representation space larger than bilingual models perform in similar setting is not evaluated yet. Fujinuma et al. (2022) points out it is always better to have a diverse set of languages during pretraining for zero-shot adaptation. At the same-time, language relatedness in pretraining configuration always helps.

**Adaptation to Unseen Languages** The idea of performing effective zero-shot transfer is highly beneficial for model adaptation to new languages. According to Muller et al. (2021), transfer learning helps some new languages while some hard languages does not get the benefit mainly because of the difference in writing systems. Transliterating those languages to a more familiar form is a useful approach in this case.

**Parameter Efficiency** Recently parameter-efficient language modeling approaches are becoming more and more popular and capable. Adapter units (Pfeiffer et al., 2022) are such modular units containing small trainable set of parameters. Using adapters resolve the problem of model-capacity and training bottleneck. In addition, most of the parameters remain unchanged thus preventing the problem of negative interference. The most important benefit of adapter untis are it's modular design. It is also possible to train the adapters using language-phylogeny information (Faisal and Anastasopoulos, 2022) thus extending the base model capacity to unseen new language in an informed manner.

## B Terminologies

**Transfer Language:** The languages we use to perform monolingual finetuning of the base language model (mBERT) using masked language modeling.

**Target Language:** The languages we use to evaluate both the pretrained as well as finetuned mBERT on downstream tasks.

**Negative Transfer:** The scenario where language model performance drops because of finetuning it on a transfer language.

**Cross-lingual Transfer:** The established method of finetuning a language model on one transfer language and deploy it on another target language.

**Unseen Languages** Any language that were not part of the original pretraining step.

## C Dataset Details

### C.1 Transfer Languages

We perform mono-lingual finetuning as well as language adapter training on 38 transfer languages. Each language dataset contains 10k lines of text. We use texts from several corpus including OSCAR (Abadji et al., 2022) and African News Translation dataset (Adelani et al., 2022). 11 out of these 38 languages are unseen by mBERT during pretraining steps. The list is provided in Table 24.

### C.2 Adapter Training Dataset

**Dependency Parsing** We train a task adapter for performing dependency parsing task. For this step, we use Universal Dependency training dataset v2.11 (de Marneffe et al., 2021). To keep the data distribution balanced, we use not more than a thousand examples per language. Combining all these data together, we train a multilingual dependency tagging task adapter. The complete list of data-source languages for training this adapter is presented in Table 25.

**Parts-of-Speech Tagging** Here we also use the Universal Dependency training dataset v2.11 (de Marneffe et al., 2021). The languages are also the same ones used for dependency parsing previously.

**Named Entity Recognition** We use Wikiann (Pan et al., 2017) dataset for training a NER task adapter. The complete language lists are provided in Table 26.

**Natural Language Inference** We use XNLI (Conneau et al., 2018) dataset for training a NLI task adapter. The complete language lists are provided in Table 27.

**Extractive Question Answering** We use TyDiQA (Clark et al., 2020) dataset for training an Extractive Question Answering task adapter. The complete language lists are provided in Table 28.

### C.3 Evaluation Dataset

We use 125 languages for evaluating NER task from Wikiann. For udp and pos-tagging tasks we use 114 languages from Universal Dependency dataset. There are 62 languages which are common between these two sets of 125 and 114 languages. For NLI evaluation, we use 15 languages from XNLI (Conneau et al., 2018) dataset and 10 low-resource South American indigenous languages from Americas NLI (ANLI) (Ebrahimi et al., 2022) dataset. For the question answering task, we take 9 languages from TydiQA (Clark et al., 2020) to evaluate. The complete list of 184 evaluation languages are provided in Table 29.

## D Implementation Details

For all of our experiments, we use as well as modify the scripts from huggingface (Wolf et al., 2020) and adapterhub (Pfeiffer et al., 2020). For base language model, we use the model `bert-base-multilingua-uncased` from huggingface model repository.

## E Hyper-parameters

**Masked Language Modeling finetuning**
- Train batch size: 8
- Evaluation batch size: 8
- Training Steps: 1, 10, 100 and 1000
- Learning Rate: 5e-5
- Maximum Sequence Length: 512

**Language Adapter Training: Language Interaction**
- Train batch size: 8
- Evaluation batch size: 8
- Training Epochs: 3
- Learning Rate: 5e-4
- Maximum Sequence Length: 256
- Adapter Parameter Reduction Factor: 16

**Task Adapter Training: Dependency Parsing**
- Train batch size: 36
- Evaluation batch size: 8
- Training Epochs: 5
- Learning Rate: 5e-4
- Maximum Sequence Length: 256
- Adapter Parameter Reduction Factor: 16

| Combination | Count |
|---|---|
| $\|-A, -B\|$ | 1 |
| $\|-A, +B\|$ | 1 |
| $\|+A, -B\|$ | 3 |
| $\|+A, +B\|$ | 2 |

Table 6: Bilingual interaction counts

**Task Adapter Training: POS Tagging**
- Train batch size: 36
- Evaluation batch size: 8
- Training Epochs: 5
- Learning Rate: 5e-4
- Maximum Sequence Length 256
- Adapter Parameter Reduction Factor: 16

**Task Adapter Training: NER**
- Train batch size: 36
- Evaluation batch size: 8
- Training Epochs: 5
- Learning Rate: 5e-4
- Maximum Sequence Length: 256
- Adapter Parameter Reduction Factor: 16

**Task Adapter Training: NLI**
- Train batch size: 32
- Evaluation batch size: 8
- Training Epochs: 5
- Learning Rate: 5e-5
- Maximum Sequence Length: 128
- Adapter Parameter Reduction Factor: 16

**Task Adapter Training: Extractive QA**
- Train batch size: 32
- Evaluation batch size: 8
- Training Epochs: 5
- Learning Rate: 3e-5
- Maximum Sequence Length: 384
- Document Stride: 128
- Adapter Parameter Reduction Factor: 16

## F Language Interference Projection (an example)

For example, consider the case of Arabic [A] that interacts with Bengali [B] in a bilingual setting [AB]. The count from pair combinations of positive and negative interference counts are as follows:

So for language A we get,

$$\begin{aligned}\mathtt{C} =& 1+1+3+2\\ =& 7\\ (\mathtt{x_A},\mathtt{y_A}) =& \frac{1}{7}\times(1\cdot[-1,-1]+1\cdot[-1,1]\\ &+3\cdot[1,-1]+2\cdot[1,1])\\ =&(0.43,-0.14)\end{aligned}$$

Here, $|+A,+B|=2$ means, in total two cases, Arabic gets positive interference score while the other associated language (Bengali) also gets positive interference. Similarly, $|-A,-B|=1$ means, for one language, both Arabic and Bengali get negative interference scores. Now $(X_A,Y_A)=(0.43,-0.14)$. So Arabic will be in the lower-right quartile of the graph (+x, -y) means, Arabic generally gets positive interference but it does not equally beneficial to other languages (gets penalized for cases $|-A,-B|,|+A,-B|$). Here we consider only Bengali as a language to interact with. In practice, we use a set of other transfer languages to compute the total count of each combination for one specific language.

## G Comparison

## H Transfer Language Ranking

We rank the transfer languages by aggregating all the transfer scores. For example, consider getting transfer scores $\{ts_1,..ts_i,..ts_n\}$ for a set of $n$ target languages $L_{tg}$ where $i\in L_{tg}$ and the transfer language is $tf$. Then the aggregated transfer score for $tf$ would be:

$$\mathtt{aggregated}-\mathtt{transfer(tf)}=\frac{\sum_{i=1}^{n}ts_i}{n}$$

The ranking of all transfer languages across three tasks are presented in Table **??**. In addition, we report the percentage of positive transfers for each transfer language. Both in parsing and POS tagging, we observe significant presence of unseen languages in high ranked positions (percentage of unseen languages in top 10: parsing: 40%, POS tagging: 40%, NER: 20%). At the sametime, they provide positive scores similar to the cases of seen languages. On the contrary, in NER, we observe most of the unseen African languages are at the lower ranked positions.

## I Recipient Transfer Maps

In a similar manner of calculating the `aggregated-transfer`, we calculate `aggregated-target`. For example, if a target language $tg$ receives scores $\{ts_1,..ts_i,..ts_m\}$ from a set of $m$ transfer languages $L_{tf}$ where $i\in L_{tf}$. Then the aggregated target score for $tf$ would be:

$$\mathtt{aggregated}-\mathtt{target(tg)}=\frac{\sum_{i=1}^{n}ts_i}{n}$$

This way we identify how much a target language get benefited from all the transfer languages. In Figure 5, we present the Recipient Transfer Maps across tasks. We plot the percentage of positive/negative `aggregated-target` scores and corresponding target languages. Now looking at these maps, we observe the presence of universal target languages (2-5 %) which always receive positive transfer from all of the 38 source languages in two out of three tasks (exception: POS tagging). Wheres, around 28% languages in parsing and tagging, 32.8% in NER never receive any positive transfer. We observe out of 40 languages which receive positive transfer in more than 90% times, 25 languages are unseen low resourced languages. The complete list of target languages which never receive and which almost always receive positive transfer is presented in Table 19.

## J Maximum Score Recipients are low-resourced

In Table 20, we report all the recipients those receive maximum transfer scores at different steps of mlm fine-tuning. From the results, it is evident that, a multilingual model almost always benefits certain unseen, low-resource as well as endangered languages largely. We observe out of 19 max-recipients, 17 are `mBERT`-unseen languages. Moreover, the two other seen-languages: Bavarian German and Low German are also low-resourced languages.

## K Task Matters

In Figure 6, we present the commonality graph of transfer language ranking across all three tasks. Spearman rank correlation with p value is presented in Table 21.

## L Transfer Languages with High Variance

In Figure 7, we present the violin plots for all the transfer languages sorted by their

| | Dependency Parsing | | | | | | | | | | |
|---|---|---|---|---|---|---|---|---|---|---|---|
| | mBERT | Continious Steps | | | | Lang. Interaction | | | Improvement | | |
| lang | base | 1 | 10 | 100 | 1000 | [1A] | [2A] | [3A] | $Imp_{c:1}$ | $Imp_{c:1000}$ | $Imp_i$ |
| ell | 92.82 | 92.73 | 92.39 | 92.09 | 91.46 | 91.97 | 91.91 | 91.98 | no | no | no |
| tel | 90.15 | 89.33 | 89.43 | 87.92 | 85.01 | 89.74 | 89.44 | 89.46 | no | no | no |
| spa | 90.02 | 89.87 | 89.42 | 89.00 | 88.16 | 89.09 | 89.20 | 89.24 | no | no | no |
| hin | 89.04 | 88.77 | 88.35 | 87.76 | 87.09 | 88.28 | 88.22 | 88.29 | no | no | no |
| hun | 87.20 | 87.14 | 86.49 | 85.65 | 85.06 | 86.25 | 86.29 | 86.36 | no | no | no |
| heb | 85.59 | 85.36 | 85.06 | 84.56 | 83.82 | 85.01 | 84.96 | 84.97 | no | no | no |
| swe | 85.45 | 85.32 | 85.03 | 84.88 | 84.30 | 84.76 | 84.81 | 84.88 | no | no | no |
| tam | 84.48 | 84.37 | 82.84 | 83.04 | 81.68 | 83.70 | 83.46 | 83.40 | no | no | no |
| cym | 83.26 | 83.15 | 82.58 | 82.45 | 81.95 | 83.11 | 83.06 | 83.10 | no | no | no |
| hye | 82.27 | 81.88 | 81.49 | 81.08 | 80.22 | 80.95 | 81.02 | 81.02 | no | no | no |
| **pcm** | 81.04 | 80.32 | 79.11 | 78.47 | 77.91 | 79.32 | 79.50 | 79.52 | no | no | no |
| est | 80.78 | 80.68 | 80.03 | 79.80 | 79.03 | 79.88 | 79.96 | 80.04 | no | no | no |
| gle | 79.65 | 79.21 | 79.03 | 78.66 | 78.99 | 79.09 | 79.09 | 79.14 | no | no | no |
| zho | 70.42 | 70.41 | 70.10 | 69.66 | 70.17 | 64.74 | 70.06 | 70.46 | no | no | yes |
| **wol** | 69.46 | 68.66 | 68.09 | 64.63 | 67.32 | 68.96 | 69.05 | 69.10 | no | no | no |
| ara | 31.25 | 31.15 | 31.29 | 30.99 | 29.97 | 30.45 | 30.38 | 30.37 | no | no | no |
| fra | 27.84 | 27.56 | 26.46 | 24.70 | 24.19 | 24.92 | 24.96 | 24.95 | no | no | no |
| jpn | 22.54 | 22.50 | 22.52 | 22.73 | 22.49 | 22.43 | 22.43 | 22.42 | no | no | no |
| deu | 89.37 | 89.40 | 88.67 | 88.39 | 87.43 | 89.10 | 89.28 | 89.35 | yes | no | no |
| bul | 89.32 | 89.32 | 89.01 | 89.01 | 89.09 | 89.12 | 89.18 | 89.21 | yes | no | no |
| rus | 88.09 | 88.14 | 87.96 | 87.53 | 87.03 | 87.82 | 87.88 | 87.94 | yes | no | no |
| eng | 79.62 | 79.76 | 79.56 | 79.39 | 78.86 | 80.18 | 80.18 | 80.24 | yes | no | yes |
| ben | 75.31 | 76.69 | 73.53 | 73.00 | 69.31 | 74.69 | 75.71 | 75.87 | yes | no | yes |
| bre | 70.79 | 71.90 | 69.82 | 71.04 | 72.12 | 73.58 | 73.76 | 73.86 | yes | yes | yes |
| kor | 64.02 | 64.33 | 64.31 | 63.76 | 65.02 | 64.33 | 64.35 | 64.43 | yes | yes | yes |
| fin | 63.54 | 64.58 | 63.45 | 63.26 | 63.84 | 64.22 | 64.37 | 64.45 | yes | yes | yes |
| yor | 40.92 | 42.80 | 40.40 | 42.17 | 47.59 | 42.55 | 42.84 | 42.93 | yes | yes | yes |
| **kmr** | 31.94 | 32.44 | 31.73 | 32.75 | 45.30 | 32.54 | 32.10 | 32.03 | yes | yes | yes |
| **bam** | 29.99 | 30.43 | 30.87 | 29.95 | 38.13 | 30.74 | 30.81 | 30.78 | yes | yes | yes |
| **gub** | 21.64 | 21.97 | 20.96 | 22.92 | 34.52 | 23.83 | 23.73 | 23.52 | yes | yes | yes |

Table 7: Dependency Parsing results. Improvement: $Imp_{c:1}$ cont. step 1-base. $Imp_{c:1000}$: cont. steps 1000-base. $Imp_i$: improvement in language interactions ([1A]/[2A]/[3A]) versus baseline. Languages unseen by mBERT are in **bold** font.

| Dependency Parsing (Model Comparison) | | | | | | | | | | |
|---|---|---|---|---|---|---|---|---|---|---|
| | mBERT | | | | | XLM-R | | | | |
| lang | base | 1 | 10 | 100 | 1000 | base_x | 1_x | 10_x | 100_x | 1000_x |
| ell | 92.82 | 92.73 | 92.39 | 92.09 | 91.46 | 93.33 | 93.27 | 93.01 | 92.59 | 92.86 |
| tel | 90.15 | 89.33 | 89.43 | 87.92 | 85.01 | 88.49 | 87.88 | 86.34 | 85.99 | 86.41 |
| spa | 90.02 | 89.87 | 89.42 | 89.00 | 88.16 | 89.66 | 89.70 | 89.38 | 88.92 | 89.26 |
| deu | 89.37 | 89.40 | 88.67 | 88.39 | 87.43 | 89.71 | 89.63 | 89.09 | 88.74 | 89.30 |
| bul | 89.32 | 89.32 | 89.01 | 89.01 | 89.09 | 90.19 | 90.31 | 90.22 | 89.73 | 90.19 |
| hin | 89.04 | 88.77 | 88.35 | 87.76 | 87.09 | 89.46 | 89.50 | 89.13 | 88.06 | 88.41 |
| rus | 88.09 | 88.14 | 87.96 | 87.53 | 87.03 | 88.72 | 88.76 | 88.62 | 88.16 | 88.45 |
| hun | 87.20 | 87.14 | 86.49 | 85.65 | 85.06 | 89.16 | 89.13 | 88.78 | 88.40 | 88.73 |
| heb | 85.59 | 85.36 | 85.06 | 84.56 | 83.82 | 86.22 | 86.14 | 85.87 | 85.54 | 85.69 |
| swe | 85.45 | 85.32 | 85.03 | 84.88 | 84.30 | 85.88 | 85.84 | 85.55 | 85.18 | 85.47 |
| tam | 84.48 | 84.37 | 82.84 | 83.04 | 81.68 | 84.59 | 84.66 | 84.32 | 84.35 | 85.35 |
| cym | 83.26 | 83.15 | 82.58 | 82.45 | 81.95 | 83.53 | 83.32 | 82.75 | 82.38 | 83.11 |
| hye | 82.27 | 81.88 | 81.49 | 81.08 | 80.22 | 84.61 | 84.54 | 84.18 | 83.79 | 84.28 |
| pcm | 81.04 | 80.32 | 79.11 | 78.47 | 77.91 | 79.58 | 79.38 | 78.48 | 77.87 | 79.37 |
| est | 80.78 | 80.68 | 80.03 | 79.80 | 79.03 | 83.96 | 83.96 | 83.52 | 83.20 | 83.55 |
| gle | 79.65 | 79.21 | 79.03 | 78.66 | 78.99 | 81.38 | 81.42 | 80.62 | 80.05 | 80.79 |
| eng | 79.62 | 79.76 | 79.56 | 79.39 | 78.86 | 78.99 | 78.77 | 78.42 | 77.86 | 78.27 |
| ben | 75.31 | 76.69 | 73.53 | 73.00 | 69.31 | 69.06 | 69.09 | 68.88 | 66.28 | 69.94 |
| bre | 70.79 | 71.90 | 69.82 | 71.04 | 72.12 | 63.88 | 63.51 | 62.70 | 61.99 | 65.45 |
| zho | 70.42 | 70.41 | 70.10 | 69.66 | 70.17 | 70.47 | 70.59 | 70.39 | 70.11 | 70.31 |
| wol | 69.46 | 68.66 | 68.09 | 64.63 | 67.32 | 67.95 | 67.78 | 66.51 | 64.33 | 64.88 |
| kor | 64.02 | 64.33 | 64.31 | 63.76 | 65.02 | 63.83 | 63.58 | 63.19 | 63.59 | 64.54 |
| fin | 63.54 | 64.58 | 63.45 | 63.26 | 63.84 | 69.12 | 68.73 | 68.07 | 68.63 | 69.62 |
| yor | 40.92 | 42.80 | 40.40 | 42.17 | 47.59 | 23.22 | 22.70 | 22.70 | 24.24 | 38.40 |
| kmr | 31.94 | 32.44 | 31.73 | 32.75 | 45.30 | 64.53 | 64.08 | 62.50 | 64.94 | 66.41 |
| ara | 31.25 | 31.15 | 31.29 | 30.99 | 29.97 | 9.42 | 9.54 | 10.04 | 9.84 | 8.82 |
| bam | 29.99 | 30.43 | 30.87 | 29.95 | 38.13 | 29.68 | 29.70 | 29.28 | 29.16 | 34.20 |
| fra | 27.84 | 27.56 | 26.46 | 24.70 | 24.19 | 19.59 | 19.99 | 18.49 | 16.18 | 19.34 |
| jpn | 22.54 | 22.50 | 22.52 | 22.73 | 22.49 | 7.87 | 7.65 | 7.84 | 7.30 | 6.91 |
| gub | 21.64 | 21.97 | 20.96 | 22.92 | 34.52 | 22.22 | 21.82 | 22.09 | 23.43 | 36.49 |
| Avg. | 69.26 | 69.34 | 68.67 | 68.37 | 69.24 | 68.28 | 68.17 | 67.70 | 67.36 | 69.16 |

Table 8: Dependency Parsing results comparison using mBERT and XLM-R (for languages present in both transfer and target set.)

| | | POS Tagging | | | | | | | | | |
|---|---|---|---|---|---|---|---|---|---|---|---|
| | mBERT | Continious Steps | | | | Lang. Interaction | | | Improvement | | |
| lang | base | 1 | 10 | 100 | 1000 | [1A] | [2A] | [3A] | $Imp_{c:1}$ | $Imp_{c:1000}$ | $Imp_i$ |
| spa | 97.84 | 97.80 | 97.66 | 97.60 | 97.41 | 97.67 | 97.71 | 97.72 | no | no | no |
| ell | 97.25 | 97.16 | 97.17 | 96.99 | 96.87 | 97.02 | 97.09 | 97.10 | no | no | no |
| heb | 95.22 | 95.07 | 94.91 | 94.72 | 94.52 | 94.86 | 94.89 | 94.89 | no | no | no |
| swe | 95.17 | 95.04 | 95.00 | 94.92 | 94.90 | 94.97 | 95.01 | 95.02 | no | no | no |
| hun | 94.28 | 94.17 | 94.03 | 93.94 | 93.82 | 93.91 | 94.01 | 94.03 | no | no | no |
| rus | 94.10 | 94.08 | 94.03 | 93.84 | 93.59 | 93.89 | 93.92 | 93.94 | no | no | no |
| **pcm** | 92.98 | 92.77 | 92.17 | 91.84 | 91.23 | 92.25 | 92.46 | 92.55 | no | no | no |
| hin | 92.23 | 92.00 | 91.76 | 91.61 | 91.39 | 91.98 | 92.00 | 92.01 | no | no | no |
| est | 91.12 | 90.90 | 90.65 | 90.48 | 90.65 | 90.68 | 90.77 | 90.80 | no | no | no |
| hye | 91.08 | 90.78 | 90.50 | 90.13 | 89.58 | 90.74 | 90.86 | 90.89 | no | no | no |
| cym | 89.69 | 89.36 | 89.03 | 88.83 | 88.60 | 88.96 | 89.15 | 89.22 | no | no | no |
| tel | 88.60 | 88.42 | 88.46 | 87.83 | 87.81 | 87.94 | 87.95 | 87.93 | no | no | no |
| gle | 88.29 | 88.08 | 87.62 | 87.13 | 87.49 | 87.72 | 87.81 | 87.83 | no | no | no |
| **wol** | 85.58 | 84.85 | 84.16 | 82.06 | 82.08 | 84.11 | 84.64 | 84.82 | no | no | no |
| eng | 84.65 | 84.64 | 84.63 | 84.62 | 84.58 | 84.62 | 84.74 | 84.77 | no | no | yes |
| tam | 83.10 | 82.74 | 82.19 | 82.39 | 82.38 | 82.87 | 82.72 | 82.70 | no | no | no |
| ben | 80.34 | 79.35 | 78.56 | 79.29 | 79.56 | 81.10 | 80.43 | 80.39 | no | no | yes |
| **bam** | 30.30 | 30.27 | 30.74 | 33.92 | 49.49 | 30.65 | 30.51 | 30.45 | no | yes | yes |
| **gub** | 28.49 | 28.11 | 28.66 | 30.02 | 36.64 | 28.82 | 28.77 | 28.85 | no | yes | yes |
| jpn | 7.85 | 7.73 | 7.80 | 7.91 | 7.84 | 7.58 | 7.67 | 7.68 | no | no | no |
| bul | 96.12 | 96.13 | 96.07 | 96.08 | 96.12 | 96.05 | 96.01 | 96.01 | yes | no | no |
| deu | 90.55 | 90.56 | 90.47 | 90.13 | 90.22 | 90.68 | 90.69 | 90.70 | yes | no | yes |
| zho | 80.45 | 80.50 | 80.54 | 80.55 | 79.72 | 79.34 | 79.71 | 79.91 | yes | no | no |
| fin | 77.98 | 78.30 | 77.83 | 77.78 | 78.36 | 77.82 | 77.83 | 77.83 | yes | yes | no |
| bre | 66.91 | 67.28 | 67.67 | 68.15 | 70.26 | 68.02 | 67.79 | 67.72 | yes | yes | yes |
| kor | 56.28 | 56.42 | 56.49 | 56.61 | 57.72 | 56.59 | 56.58 | 56.57 | yes | yes | yes |
| yor | 45.91 | 48.22 | 46.73 | 51.24 | 57.28 | 45.71 | 45.45 | 45.45 | yes | yes | no |
| **kmr** | 40.16 | 40.35 | 40.49 | 42.76 | 55.82 | 41.04 | 40.79 | 40.64 | yes | yes | yes |
| fra | 16.35 | 16.47 | 16.66 | 16.63 | 16.24 | 16.77 | 16.79 | 16.79 | yes | no | yes |
| ara | 8.61 | 8.70 | 8.76 | 8.53 | 5.17 | 8.74 | 8.86 | 8.88 | yes | no | yes |

Table 9: POS Tagging results. Improvement: $Imp_{c:1}$ cont. step 1-base. $Imp_{c:1000}$: cont. steps 1000-base. $Imp_i$: improvement in language interactions ([1A]/[2A]/[3A]) versus baseline. Languages unseen by mBERT are in **bold** font.

| POS Tagging (Model Comparison) | | | | | | | | | | |
|---|---|---|---|---|---|---|---|---|---|---|
| | mBERT | | | | | XLM-R | | | | |
| lang | base | 1 | 10 | 100 | 1000 | base_x | 1_x | 10_x | 100_x | 1000_x |
| spa | 97.84 | 97.80 | 97.66 | 97.60 | 97.41 | 97.80 | 97.78 | 97.74 | 97.65 | 97.61 |
| ell | 97.25 | 97.16 | 97.17 | 96.99 | 96.87 | 97.51 | 97.50 | 97.47 | 97.43 | 97.45 |
| bul | 96.12 | 96.13 | 96.07 | 96.08 | 96.12 | 96.79 | 96.75 | 96.68 | 96.58 | 96.58 |
| heb | 95.22 | 95.07 | 94.91 | 94.72 | 94.52 | 96.41 | 96.30 | 96.16 | 96.16 | 96.24 |
| swe | 95.17 | 95.04 | 95.00 | 94.92 | 94.90 | 96.22 | 96.20 | 96.29 | 96.26 | 96.17 |
| hun | 94.28 | 94.17 | 94.03 | 93.94 | 93.82 | 95.53 | 95.57 | 95.51 | 95.24 | 95.17 |
| rus | 94.10 | 94.08 | 94.03 | 93.84 | 93.59 | 94.45 | 94.40 | 94.30 | 94.32 | 94.32 |
| pcm | 92.98 | 92.77 | 92.17 | 91.84 | 91.23 | 93.44 | 93.20 | 91.91 | 92.24 | 92.39 |
| hin | 92.23 | 92.00 | 91.76 | 91.61 | 91.39 | 93.47 | 93.42 | 93.31 | 92.96 | 93.12 |
| est | 91.12 | 90.90 | 90.65 | 90.48 | 90.65 | 93.46 | 93.42 | 93.30 | 93.16 | 93.35 |
| hye | 91.08 | 90.78 | 90.50 | 90.13 | 89.58 | 93.76 | 93.80 | 93.70 | 93.43 | 93.52 |
| deu | 90.55 | 90.56 | 90.47 | 90.13 | 90.22 | 90.04 | 90.03 | 90.01 | 90.00 | 90.00 |
| cym | 89.69 | 89.36 | 89.03 | 88.83 | 88.60 | 91.92 | 91.83 | 91.60 | 91.55 | 91.50 |
| tel | 88.60 | 88.42 | 88.46 | 87.83 | 87.81 | 91.58 | 91.78 | 91.17 | 90.91 | 91.38 |
| gle | 88.29 | 88.08 | 87.62 | 87.13 | 87.49 | 91.51 | 91.49 | 91.13 | 90.79 | 91.22 |
| wol | 85.58 | 84.85 | 84.16 | 82.06 | 82.08 | 84.14 | 83.84 | 83.21 | 81.84 | 81.99 |
| eng | 84.65 | 84.64 | 84.63 | 84.62 | 84.58 | 86.30 | 85.83 | 84.72 | 85.59 | 86.40 |
| tam | 83.10 | 82.74 | 82.19 | 82.39 | 82.38 | 85.55 | 85.71 | 85.79 | 85.76 | 85.73 |
| zho | 80.45 | 80.50 | 80.54 | 80.55 | 79.72 | 85.44 | 85.32 | 85.29 | 85.56 | 85.36 |
| ben | 80.34 | 79.35 | 78.56 | 79.29 | 79.56 | 83.65 | 83.36 | 83.37 | 83.35 | 84.36 |
| fin | 77.98 | 78.30 | 77.83 | 77.78 | 78.36 | 83.76 | 83.57 | 83.35 | 83.59 | 83.38 |
| bre | 66.91 | 67.28 | 67.67 | 68.15 | 70.26 | 61.11 | 60.97 | 61.72 | 61.73 | 64.70 |
| kor | 56.28 | 56.42 | 56.49 | 56.61 | 57.72 | 57.17 | 57.06 | 57.06 | 57.10 | 57.17 |
| yor | 45.91 | 48.22 | 46.73 | 51.24 | 57.28 | 26.88 | 26.41 | 26.37 | 27.63 | 45.90 |
| kmr | 40.16 | 40.35 | 40.49 | 42.76 | 55.82 | 74.85 | 74.96 | 75.78 | 76.26 | 76.95 |
| bam | 30.30 | 30.27 | 30.74 | 33.92 | 49.49 | 29.46 | 29.22 | 29.49 | 29.61 | 36.49 |
| gub | 28.49 | 28.11 | 28.66 | 30.02 | 36.64 | 29.97 | 30.17 | 31.05 | 31.48 | 41.21 |
| fra | 16.35 | 16.47 | 16.66 | 16.63 | 16.24 | 14.16 | 14.14 | 14.28 | 13.84 | 13.59 |
| ara | 8.61 | 8.70 | 8.76 | 8.53 | 5.17 | 8.15 | 8.27 | 8.36 | 8.38 | 7.03 |
| jpn | 7.85 | 7.73 | 7.80 | 7.91 | 7.84 | 7.61 | 7.60 | 7.44 | 7.46 | 7.34 |
| Avg. | 72.92 | 72.87 | 72.71 | 72.95 | 74.24 | 74.40 | 74.33 | 74.25 | 74.26 | 75.59 |

Table 10: POS Tagging results comparison using mBERT and XLM-R (for languages present in both transfer and target set.)

| NER | | | | | | | | | | | |
|---|---|---|---|---|---|---|---|---|---|---|---|
| | mBERT | Continious Steps | | | | Lang. Interaction | | | Improvement | | |
| lang | base | 1 | 10 | 100 | 1000 | [1A] | [2A] | [3A] | $Imp_{c:1}$ | $Imp_{c:1000}$ | $Imp_i$ |
| spa | 90.66 | 90.56 | 90.18 | 89.41 | 87.74 | 90.20 | 90.26 | 90.26 | no | no | no |
| bul | 89.40 | 89.28 | 89.07 | 88.62 | 87.54 | 89.09 | 89.09 | 89.10 | no | no | no |
| fra | 88.14 | 87.95 | 87.56 | 86.53 | 85.19 | 87.63 | 87.77 | 87.80 | no | no | no |
| fin | 87.63 | 87.60 | 87.44 | 87.15 | 86.43 | 87.54 | 87.46 | 87.46 | no | no | no |
| est | 87.40 | 87.27 | 86.93 | 86.28 | 85.36 | 86.92 | 87.04 | 87.10 | no | no | no |
| ell | 85.81 | 85.71 | 84.95 | 84.36 | 83.02 | 85.44 | 85.50 | 85.54 | no | no | no |
| gle | 83.97 | 82.50 | 81.96 | 80.24 | 80.10 | 81.84 | 82.40 | 82.58 | no | no | no |
| ara | 83.69 | 83.50 | 82.73 | 80.85 | 79.29 | 83.04 | 83.18 | 83.23 | no | no | no |
| bre | 83.20 | 83.10 | 82.00 | 80.45 | 79.60 | 82.50 | 82.71 | 82.74 | no | no | no |
| hin | 82.53 | 82.31 | 81.87 | 80.21 | 76.62 | 82.56 | 82.40 | 82.41 | no | no | yes |
| kor | 81.67 | 81.66 | 81.27 | 79.75 | 78.22 | 81.43 | 81.41 | 81.42 | no | no | no |
| eng | 79.43 | 79.33 | 79.03 | 78.52 | 74.96 | 79.07 | 79.18 | 79.20 | no | no | no |
| nep | 78.33 | 77.32 | 77.97 | 75.63 | 69.80 | 78.15 | 77.71 | 77.62 | no | no | no |
| tam | 78.10 | 77.42 | 77.11 | 74.53 | 72.03 | 77.20 | 77.00 | 77.04 | no | no | no |
| heb | 76.53 | 76.41 | 75.92 | 75.09 | 73.56 | 76.19 | 76.04 | 76.07 | no | no | no |
| tel | 76.04 | 75.37 | 75.12 | 70.86 | 68.86 | 75.54 | 75.06 | 75.03 | no | no | no |
| mya | 73.15 | 72.92 | 70.71 | 69.51 | 63.59 | 71.88 | 71.54 | 71.70 | no | no | no |
| zho | 72.07 | 71.94 | 71.62 | 69.65 | 64.61 | 62.44 | 69.03 | 70.95 | no | no | no |
| **ibo** | 61.06 | 57.30 | 57.21 | 53.72 | 55.40 | 57.52 | 57.76 | 57.70 | no | no | no |
| jpn | 59.85 | 59.59 | 58.38 | 56.79 | 53.38 | 58.93 | 58.65 | 58.68 | no | no | no |
| swe | 91.41 | 91.47 | 91.25 | 90.86 | 90.06 | 91.27 | 91.29 | 91.32 | yes | no | no |
| hye | 90.10 | 90.59 | 90.23 | 87.55 | 83.25 | 90.32 | 90.46 | 90.50 | yes | no | yes |
| hun | 88.42 | 88.49 | 88.30 | 87.49 | 86.78 | 88.40 | 88.35 | 88.37 | yes | no | no |
| **pms** | 88.22 | 89.09 | 88.90 | 88.25 | 87.59 | 88.15 | 87.47 | 87.61 | yes | no | no |
| cym | 85.75 | 85.91 | 85.23 | 83.19 | 81.81 | 85.25 | 85.34 | 85.39 | yes | no | no |
| deu | 85.53 | 85.62 | 85.38 | 84.67 | 83.32 | 85.07 | 85.25 | 85.32 | yes | no | no |
| rus | 84.76 | 84.78 | 84.38 | 83.56 | 80.82 | 84.51 | 84.49 | 84.51 | yes | no | no |
| ben | 84.75 | 84.85 | 83.32 | 80.53 | 72.14 | 83.12 | 83.62 | 83.73 | yes | no | no |
| **kin** | 72.38 | 72.74 | 71.76 | 68.79 | 68.50 | 70.48 | 71.11 | 71.85 | yes | no | no |
| yor | 67.53 | 70.33 | 72.11 | 69.40 | 51.34 | 79.11 | 77.58 | 76.04 | yes | no | yes |

Table 11: NER results. Improvement: $Imp_{c:1}$ cont. step 1-base. $Imp_{c:1000}$: cont. steps 1000-base. $Imp_i$: improvement in language interactions ([1A]/[2A]/[3A]) versus baseline. Languages unseen by mBERT are in **bold** font.

| NER (Model Comparison) | | | | | | | | | | |
|---|---|---|---|---|---|---|---|---|---|---|
| | mBERT | | | | | XLM-R | | | | |
| lang | base | 1 | 10 | 100 | 1000 | base_x | 1_x | 10_x | 100_x | 1000_x |
| swe | 91.41 | 91.47 | 91.25 | 90.86 | 90.06 | 89.83 | 89.91 | 89.96 | 89.71 | 89.61 |
| spa | 90.66 | 90.56 | 90.18 | 89.41 | 87.74 | 87.37 | 87.44 | 87.44 | 87.21 | 87.13 |
| hye | 90.10 | 90.59 | 90.23 | 87.55 | 83.25 | 89.85 | 89.77 | 89.56 | 89.98 | 89.88 |
| bul | 89.40 | 89.28 | 89.07 | 88.62 | 87.54 | 87.63 | 87.70 | 87.66 | 87.49 | 87.50 |
| hun | 88.42 | 88.49 | 88.30 | 87.49 | 86.78 | 86.59 | 86.58 | 86.26 | 86.29 | 86.07 |
| pms | 88.22 | 89.09 | 88.90 | 88.25 | 87.59 | 87.12 | 87.42 | 87.17 | 88.22 | 90.54 |
| fra | 88.14 | 87.95 | 87.56 | 86.53 | 85.19 | 84.54 | 84.53 | 84.28 | 84.18 | 84.20 |
| fin | 87.63 | 87.60 | 87.44 | 87.15 | 86.43 | 85.95 | 85.80 | 85.65 | 85.87 | 85.67 |
| est | 87.40 | 87.27 | 86.93 | 86.28 | 85.36 | 85.13 | 85.18 | 85.07 | 84.78 | 84.87 |
| ell | 85.81 | 85.71 | 84.95 | 84.36 | 83.02 | 84.16 | 84.25 | 84.09 | 84.07 | 83.96 |
| cym | 85.75 | 85.91 | 85.23 | 83.19 | 81.81 | 82.74 | 82.21 | 82.37 | 82.06 | 82.25 |
| deu | 85.53 | 85.62 | 85.38 | 84.67 | 83.32 | 83.08 | 83.17 | 83.33 | 82.81 | 82.78 |
| rus | 84.76 | 84.78 | 84.38 | 83.56 | 80.82 | 82.84 | 82.72 | 82.38 | 82.17 | 82.28 |
| ben | 84.75 | 84.85 | 83.32 | 80.53 | 72.14 | 81.42 | 81.82 | 81.52 | 80.14 | 80.20 |
| gle | 83.97 | 82.50 | 81.96 | 80.24 | 80.10 | 81.69 | 81.01 | 80.79 | 80.17 | 80.73 |
| ara | 83.69 | 83.50 | 82.73 | 80.85 | 79.29 | 80.97 | 80.91 | 80.56 | 80.23 | 80.24 |
| bre | 83.20 | 83.10 | 82.00 | 80.45 | 79.60 | 77.32 | 76.92 | 76.97 | 75.94 | 76.81 |
| hin | 82.53 | 82.31 | 81.87 | 80.21 | 76.62 | 80.92 | 80.76 | 81.66 | 81.33 | 80.86 |
| kor | 81.67 | 81.66 | 81.27 | 79.75 | 78.22 | 75.20 | 75.25 | 75.07 | 74.77 | 74.73 |
| eng | 79.43 | 79.33 | 79.03 | 78.52 | 74.96 | 76.56 | 76.56 | 76.82 | 76.21 | 75.35 |
| nep | 78.33 | 77.32 | 77.97 | 75.63 | 69.80 | 76.54 | 75.98 | 77.00 | 74.79 | 74.74 |
| tam | 78.10 | 77.42 | 77.11 | 74.53 | 72.03 | 76.35 | 76.24 | 76.25 | 75.92 | 75.79 |
| heb | 76.53 | 76.41 | 75.92 | 75.09 | 73.56 | 73.41 | 73.20 | 73.10 | 72.91 | 72.80 |
| tel | 76.04 | 75.37 | 75.12 | 70.86 | 68.86 | 76.07 | 76.27 | 75.78 | 74.77 | 74.09 |
| mya | 73.15 | 72.92 | 70.71 | 69.51 | 63.59 | 73.03 | 73.12 | 74.27 | 74.43 | 72.31 |
| kin | 72.38 | 72.74 | 71.76 | 68.79 | 68.50 | 71.23 | 72.72 | 72.00 | 67.94 | 63.44 |
| zho | 72.07 | 71.94 | 71.62 | 69.65 | 64.61 | 64.44 | 64.66 | 64.16 | 63.25 | 62.07 |
| yor | 67.53 | 70.33 | 72.11 | 69.40 | 51.34 | 72.10 | 72.07 | 74.73 | 68.77 | 76.73 |
| ibo | 61.06 | 57.30 | 57.21 | 53.72 | 55.40 | 63.68 | 63.15 | 60.89 | 57.25 | 61.05 |
| jpn | 59.85 | 59.59 | 58.38 | 56.79 | 53.38 | 54.92 | 54.80 | 54.31 | 53.07 | 52.81 |
| Avg. | 81.25 | 81.10 | 80.66 | 79.08 | 76.36 | 79.09 | 79.07 | 79.04 | 78.22 | 78.38 |

Table 12: NER results comparison using mBERT and XLM-R (for languages present in both transfer and target set.)

| XNLI | | | | | |
|---|---|---|---|---|---|
| | | Continious Steps | | | |
| lang | base | 1 | 10 | 100 | 1000 |
| mBERT | | | | | |
| eng | 81.02 | 45.42 | 45.01 | 42.86 | 43.18 |
| spa | 77.33 | 46.59 | 47.52 | 44.87 | 40.96 |
| deu | 76.27 | 46.79 | 47.71 | 46.63 | 39.57 |
| zho | 75.43 | 46.45 | 44.74 | 43.23 | 40.07 |
| bul | 75.13 | 46.57 | 46.70 | 44.85 | 36.58 |
| ell | 73.89 | 44.51 | 44.38 | 44.21 | 36.28 |
| rus | 73.59 | 45.78 | 46.28 | 44.24 | 38.53 |
| ara | 71.36 | 42.82 | 41.44 | 41.37 | 39.34 |
| hin | 67.68 | 41.74 | 42.61 | 40.19 | 35.02 |
| XLM-R | | | | | |
| eng | 84.03 | 83.91 | 83.87 | 83.38 | 83.54 |
| spa | 80.60 | 80.67 | 80.92 | 80.26 | 80.38 |
| bul | 80.24 | 80.24 | 80.16 | 79.72 | 80.45 |
| deu | 79.38 | 79.33 | 79.32 | 78.79 | 79.20 |
| rus | 78.10 | 78.20 | 78.43 | 78.05 | 78.05 |
| ell | 77.82 | 77.77 | 77.61 | 77.22 | 77.59 |
| zho | 77.41 | 77.44 | 77.33 | 77.49 | 77.37 |
| ara | 75.63 | 75.47 | 75.15 | 74.55 | 74.91 |
| hin | 74.81 | 74.67 | 74.35 | 74.02 | 74.55 |

Table 13: XNLI results for (continuous training) languages present in both transfer and target set.

| TyDiQA | | | | | |
|---|---|---|---|---|---|
| | | Continious Steps | | | |
| lang | base | 1 | 10 | 100 | 1000 |
| mBERT | | | | | |
| tel | 58.45 | 58.19 | 57.53 | 56.55 | 56.50 |
| eng | 56.14 | 55.89 | 55.91 | 53.05 | 53.89 |
| ara | 54.83 | 54.73 | 54.40 | 49.28 | 50.99 |
| rus | 50.37 | 49.93 | 49.15 | 36.16 | 43.74 |
| fin | 50.13 | 50.09 | 50.45 | 44.16 | 46.85 |
| kor | 47.83 | 46.59 | 46.74 | 44.09 | 44.38 |
| ben | 45.13 | 46.11 | 48.05 | 45.13 | 44.78 |
| XLM-R | | | | | |
| tel | 56.20 | 56.46 | 55.65 | 55.72 | 56.35 |
| eng | 52.50 | 52.82 | 53.18 | 52.89 | 52.70 |
| ara | 51.57 | 51.69 | 49.16 | 48.02 | 51.13 |
| rus | 47.41 | 47.32 | 45.04 | 44.19 | 46.26 |
| fin | 45.65 | 46.24 | 45.88 | 45.10 | 45.19 |
| ben | 44.25 | 42.39 | 43.27 | 40.97 | 43.45 |
| kor | 42.03 | 42.32 | 42.90 | 43.01 | 43.22 |

Table 14: TyDiQA results (continuous training)for languages present in both transfer and target set.

| Transfer Languages Ranking using mBERT (Token Classification) | | | | | | | | | |
|---|---|---|---|---|---|---|---|---|---|
| Rank | **Parsing** | | | **POS Tagging** | | | **NER** | | |
| | Lang | ts | +(%) | lang | ts | +(%) | lang | ts | +(%) |
| 1 | mya | 0.33 | 40.35 | **kin** | 0.41 | 35.09 | zho | 0.16 | 49.6 |
| 2 | ell | 0.15 | 31.58 | **kmr** | 0.36 | 36.84 | tel | 0.08 | 32.8 |
| 3 | **kmr** | 0.14 | 35.96 | **mos** | 0.27 | 34.21 | hun | 0.08 | 40.8 |
| 4 | yor | 0.14 | 33.33 | hye | 0.27 | 36.84 | heb | 0.04 | 34.4 |
| 5 | **pcm** | 0.13 | 31.58 | cym | 0.22 | 37.72 | est | 0.03 | 36.8 |
| 6 | nep | 0.12 | 35.96 | jpn | 0.18 | 37.72 | cym | 0.03 | 40.0 |
| 7 | rus | 0.11 | 32.46 | mya | 0.17 | 39.47 | eng | 0.02 | 38.4 |
| 8 | **mos** | 0.09 | 42.11 | nep | 0.12 | 31.58 | **mos** | 0.00 | 32.0 |
| 9 | **pms** | 0.09 | 30.70 | **pms** | 0.08 | 37.72 | tam | 0.00 | 35.2 |
| 10 | heb | 0.08 | 30.70 | zho | -0.04 | 34.21 | **hau** | -0.07 | 35.2 |
| 11 | tel | 0.05 | 26.32 | kor | -0.07 | 31.58 | gle | -0.07 | 32.8 |
| 12 | **ibo** | 0.05 | 31.58 | ben | -0.08 | 32.46 | jpn | -0.08 | 33.6 |
| 13 | **hau** | 0.04 | 37.72 | bul | -0.08 | 24.56 | kor | -0.09 | 35.2 |
| 14 | gle | 0.03 | 28.07 | **bam** | -0.12 | 30.70 | swe | -0.11 | 29.6 |
| 15 | **wol** | 0.03 | 35.96 | ell | -0.13 | 33.33 | nep | -0.13 | 31.2 |
| 16 | **bam** | 0.02 | 32.46 | hin | -0.13 | 32.46 | mya | -0.17 | 35.2 |
| 17 | est | 0.00 | 28.95 | tam | -0.14 | 32.46 | hye | -0.17 | 32.0 |
| 18 | hye | -0.03 | 31.58 | **ibo** | -0.14 | 32.46 | bul | -0.18 | 27.2 |
| 19 | cym | -0.03 | 28.95 | **wol** | -0.14 | 27.19 | deu | -0.20 | 32.8 |
| 20 | ben | -0.06 | 31.58 | **pcm** | -0.16 | 29.82 | bre | -0.23 | 35.2 |
| 21 | **kin** | -0.06 | 29.82 | yor | -0.16 | 36.84 | spa | -0.28 | 28.0 |
| 22 | **ewe** | -0.08 | 38.60 | heb | -0.26 | 30.70 | fin | -0.29 | 27.2 |
| 23 | hin | -0.10 | 32.46 | rus | -0.28 | 28.07 | ell | -0.29 | 34.4 |
| 24 | ara | -0.12 | 31.58 | hun | -0.29 | 25.44 | **pms** | -0.29 | 32.0 |
| 25 | deu | -0.13 | 31.58 | ara | -0.30 | 31.58 | ara | -0.32 | 30.4 |
| 26 | **gub** | -0.14 | 34.21 | tel | -0.31 | 28.95 | yor | -0.32 | 27.2 |
| 27 | spa | -0.18 | 30.70 | **hau** | -0.34 | 29.82 | rus | -0.34 | 26.4 |
| 28 | jpn | -0.19 | 27.19 | gle | -0.34 | 28.07 | **wol** | -0.41 | 32.8 |
| 29 | bul | -0.21 | 25.44 | **gub** | -0.34 | 23.68 | ben | -0.54 | 27.2 |
| 30 | swe | -0.21 | 28.95 | fin | -0.35 | 25.44 | **ibo** | -0.54 | 29.6 |
| 31 | eng | -0.22 | 27.19 | eng | -0.35 | 26.32 | **kin** | -0.56 | 31.2 |
| 32 | bre | -0.23 | 28.95 | est | -0.35 | 29.82 | fra | -0.59 | 29.6 |
| 33 | hun | -0.23 | 21.93 | bre | -0.39 | 31.58 | **kmr** | -0.61 | 25.6 |
| 34 | tam | -0.24 | 21.05 | fra | -0.41 | 28.95 | **pcm** | -0.69 | 25.6 |
| 35 | fin | -0.26 | 26.32 | deu | -0.44 | 26.32 | **bam** | -0.69 | 30.4 |
| 36 | fra | -0.37 | 24.56 | spa | -0.53 | 25.44 | hin | -0.72 | 21.6 |
| 37 | kor | -0.38 | 26.32 | swe | -0.66 | 27.19 | **ewe** | -0.76 | 24.8 |
| 38 | zho | -0.48 | 17.54 | **ewe** | -0.79 | 23.68 | **gub** | -0.98 | 24.8 |

Table 15: Transfer Languages ranked by aggregated transfer scores (ts) overall target languages across token classification tasks using mBERT. Languages unseen by mBERT are in **bold** font.

| Transfer Languages Ranking using XLM-R (Token Classification) | | | | | | | | | |
|---|---|---|---|---|---|---|---|---|---|
| Rank | **Parsing** | | | **POS Tagging** | | | **NER** | | |
| | Lang | ts | +(%) | lang | ts | +(%) | lang | ts | +(%) |
| 1 | nep | 0.02 | 23.68 | hin | 0.18 | 39.47 | rus | 1.15 | 40.0 |
| 2 | zho | -0.00 | 34.21 | ben | 0.10 | 36.84 | ell | 1.04 | 41.6 |
| 3 | mya | -0.01 | 21.93 | mya | 0.04 | 34.21 | tel | 0.76 | 41.6 |
| 4 | ben | -0.08 | 26.32 | nep | 0.01 | 34.21 | heb | 0.70 | 46.4 |
| 5 | hin | -0.09 | 29.82 | bul | 0.01 | 40.35 | ben | 0.64 | 36.0 |
| 6 | tam | -0.09 | 27.19 | eng | -0.00 | 35.96 | tam | 0.48 | 44.0 |
| 7 | bre | -0.11 | 23.68 | bre | -0.01 | 42.11 | hin | 0.47 | 44.0 |
| 8 | tel | -0.13 | 20.18 | ara | -0.05 | 37.72 | **pms** | 0.44 | 40.8 |
| 9 | deu | -0.13 | 24.56 | gle | -0.12 | 36.84 | bul | 0.43 | 48.0 |
| 10 | kor | -0.21 | 21.93 | cym | -0.13 | 42.98 | hye | 0.36 | 40.0 |
| 11 | est | -0.25 | 24.56 | rus | -0.13 | 31.58 | ara | 0.33 | 43.2 |
| 12 | swe | -0.25 | 22.81 | hye | -0.16 | 36.84 | swe | 0.32 | 48.8 |
| 13 | **pms** | -0.25 | 31.58 | tam | -0.17 | 39.47 | **kmr** | 0.31 | 46.4 |
| 14 | hye | -0.29 | 21.05 | heb | -0.17 | 41.23 | fra | 0.27 | 44.0 |
| 15 | jpn | -0.34 | 21.93 | zho | -0.24 | 25.44 | eng | 0.25 | 51.2 |
| 16 | fin | -0.35 | 18.42 | **hau** | -0.24 | 38.60 | cym | 0.22 | 48.8 |
| 17 | cym | -0.36 | 18.42 | fra | -0.25 | 36.84 | mya | 0.22 | 45.6 |
| 18 | heb | -0.37 | 22.81 | tel | -0.26 | 40.35 | gle | 0.21 | 46.4 |
| 19 | eng | -0.39 | 23.68 | ell | -0.30 | 39.47 | jpn | 0.20 | 40.0 |
| 20 | bul | -0.42 | 19.30 | deu | -0.31 | 41.23 | fin | 0.18 | 40.0 |
| 21 | rus | -0.47 | 17.54 | kor | -0.31 | 42.11 | hun | 0.17 | 40.8 |
| 22 | **hau** | -0.50 | 16.67 | swe | -0.32 | 41.23 | est | 0.16 | 47.2 |
| 23 | yor | -0.50 | 14.91 | spa | -0.32 | 30.70 | spa | 0.16 | 44.8 |
| 24 | ell | -0.52 | 18.42 | est | -0.34 | 38.60 | deu | 0.15 | 42.4 |
| 25 | **kin** | -0.54 | 19.30 | **pms** | -0.43 | 29.82 | nep | 0.13 | 44.0 |
| 26 | gle | -0.55 | 16.67 | fin | -0.50 | 29.82 | bre | 0.13 | 40.0 |
| 27 | fra | -0.56 | 20.18 | hun | -0.54 | 28.07 | **hau** | 0.12 | 42.4 |
| 28 | ara | -0.57 | 19.30 | **kin** | -0.56 | 28.95 | kor | -0.02 | 44.0 |
| 29 | spa | -0.66 | 17.54 | **kmr** | -0.57 | 28.07 | **pcm** | -0.04 | 38.4 |
| 30 | hun | -0.66 | 14.91 | **pcm** | -0.70 | 16.67 | **wol** | -0.11 | 36.8 |
| 31 | **bam** | -0.74 | 15.79 | jpn | -0.72 | 32.46 | **ibo** | -0.12 | 36.0 |
| 32 | **kmr** | -0.85 | 19.30 | **mos** | -0.84 | 28.07 | **gub** | -0.17 | 36.0 |
| 33 | **mos** | -0.90 | 18.42 | **ewe** | -0.88 | 21.93 | **mos** | -0.19 | 32.0 |
| 34 | **gub** | -0.95 | 15.79 | **bam** | -0.89 | 20.18 | zho | -0.20 | 30.4 |
| 35 | **ibo** | -1.22 | 14.91 | yor | -0.90 | 26.32 | yor | -0.20 | 37.6 |
| 36 | **wol** | -1.40 | 14.91 | **wol** | -0.97 | 22.81 | **ewe** | -0.32 | 30.4 |
| 37 | **pcm** | -1.55 | 10.53 | **ibo** | -1.00 | 23.68 | **kin** | -0.34 | 29.6 |
| 38 | **ewe** | -1.83 | 14.04 | **gub** | -1.05 | 20.18 | **bam** | -0.41 | 32.0 |

Table 16: Transfer Languages ranked by aggregated transfer scores (ts) overall target languages across token classification tasks using XLM-R. Languages unseen by mBERT are in **bold** font.

| Transfer Languages Ranking using mBERT (Sentence Classification & QA) | | | | | | | | | |
|---|---|---|---|---|---|---|---|---|---|
| Rank | **XNLI** | | | **ANLI** | | | **TyDiQA** | | |
| | Lang | ts | +(%) | lang | ts | +(%) | lang | ts | +(%) |
| 1 | **hau** | -34.42 | 0.0 | **bam** | -14.97 | 0.0 | zho | 0.67 | 77.78 |
| 2 | **bam** | -34.85 | 0.0 | **hau** | -17.82 | 0.0 | jpn | 0.08 | 44.44 |
| 3 | **gub** | -36.40 | 0.0 | **gub** | -18.35 | 0.0 | gle | -0.08 | 44.44 |
| 4 | **ewe** | -36.73 | 0.0 | deu | -19.79 | 0.0 | **wol** | -0.12 | 44.44 |
| 5 | hin | -37.08 | 0.0 | fin | -19.93 | 0.0 | cym | -0.14 | 33.33 |
| 6 | deu | -37.33 | 0.0 | hun | -20.01 | 0.0 | mya | -0.15 | 22.22 |
| 7 | kor | -37.86 | 0.0 | kor | -20.15 | 0.0 | **mos** | -0.15 | 44.44 |
| 8 | spa | -38.17 | 0.0 | zho | -20.20 | 0.0 | hun | -0.19 | 22.22 |
| 9 | **kmr** | -38.25 | 0.0 | hin | -20.27 | 0.0 | fin | -0.19 | 44.44 |
| 10 | fin | -38.32 | 0.0 | **pms** | -20.28 | 0.0 | **kin** | -0.22 | 33.33 |
| 11 | rus | -38.34 | 0.0 | yor | -20.37 | 0.0 | est | -0.25 | 33.33 |
| 12 | **pms** | -38.35 | 0.0 | **kin** | -20.63 | 0.0 | hye | -0.25 | 33.33 |
| 13 | hun | -38.57 | 0.0 | spa | -20.66 | 0.0 | tel | -0.26 | 33.33 |
| 14 | heb | -38.72 | 0.0 | mya | -20.68 | 0.0 | eng | -0.28 | 33.33 |
| 15 | swe | -38.86 | 0.0 | heb | -20.68 | 0.0 | ell | -0.29 | 22.22 |
| 16 | est | -38.86 | 0.0 | **ewe** | -20.74 | 0.0 | **ewe** | -0.30 | 33.33 |
| 17 | gle | -38.87 | 0.0 | rus | -20.74 | 0.0 | yor | -0.30 | 33.33 |
| 18 | bul | -38.90 | 0.0 | est | -20.91 | 0.0 | heb | -0.33 | 22.22 |
| 19 | fra | -38.91 | 0.0 | swe | -20.93 | 0.0 | **pms** | -0.34 | 22.22 |
| 20 | yor | -38.94 | 0.0 | gle | -20.99 | 0.0 | tam | -0.38 | 22.22 |
| 21 | ell | -39.24 | 0.0 | bul | -21.07 | 0.0 | ben | -0.39 | 22.22 |
| 22 | **kin** | -39.37 | 0.0 | ell | -21.10 | 0.0 | bul | -0.41 | 33.33 |
| 23 | zho | -39.44 | 0.0 | ara | -21.11 | 0.0 | deu | -0.41 | 22.22 |
| 24 | ara | -39.50 | 0.0 | **kmr** | -21.11 | 0.0 | **gub** | -0.42 | 22.22 |
| 25 | mya | -39.56 | 0.0 | nep | -21.17 | 0.0 | nep | -0.42 | 33.33 |
| 26 | eng | -39.74 | 0.0 | fra | -21.22 | 0.0 | swe | -0.43 | 33.33 |
| 27 | hye | -40.04 | 0.0 | eng | -21.28 | 0.0 | kor | -0.45 | 22.22 |
| 28 | bre | -40.07 | 0.0 | cym | -21.39 | 0.0 | hin | -0.47 | 22.22 |
| 29 | cym | -40.13 | 0.0 | jpn | -21.43 | 0.0 | bre | -0.48 | 11.11 |
| 30 | nep | -40.25 | 0.0 | tam | -21.45 | 0.0 | ara | -0.51 | 33.33 |
| 31 | tel | -40.31 | 0.0 | tel | -21.51 | 0.0 | **ibo** | -0.57 | 33.33 |
| 32 | ben | -40.31 | 0.0 | hye | -21.62 | 0.0 | **bam** | -0.61 | 22.22 |
| 33 | jpn | -40.53 | 0.0 | bre | -21.65 | 0.0 | **kmr** | -0.62 | 33.33 |
| 34 | **mos** | -41.04 | 0.0 | **mos** | -21.65 | 0.0 | spa | -0.66 | 22.22 |
| 35 | tam | -41.04 | 0.0 | **wol** | -22.23 | 0.0 | rus | -0.67 | 22.22 |
| 36 | **wol** | -42.67 | 0.0 | **pcm** | -22.24 | 0.0 | **hau** | -0.89 | 22.22 |
| 37 | **pcm** | -43.37 | 0.0 | **ibo** | -22.36 | 0.0 | fra | -1.04 | 11.11 |
| 38 | **ibo** | -44.78 | 0.0 | ben | -23.37 | 0.0 | **pcm** | -1.10 | 22.22 |

Table 17: Transfer Languages ranked by aggregated transfer scores (ts) overall target languages across Sentence Classification & QA tasks using mBERT. Languages unseen by mBERT are in **bold** font.

| Transfer Languages Ranking using mBERT (Sentence Classification & QA) | | | | | | | | | |
|---|---|---|---|---|---|---|---|---|---|
| Rank | **XNLI** | | | **ANLI** | | | **TyDiQA** | | |
| | Lang | ts | +(%) | lang | ts | +(%) | lang | ts | +(%) |
| 1 | **ewe** | 0.44 | 93.33 | hin | 2.25 | 100.0 | **pcm** | -0.42 | 55.56 |
| 2 | bre | 0.36 | 93.33 | ell | 1.34 | 80.0 | ell | -0.44 | 22.22 |
| 3 | **bam** | 0.30 | 93.33 | nep | 1.33 | 100.0 | fin | -0.46 | 44.44 |
| 4 | **pcm** | 0.30 | 93.33 | ara | 1.31 | 80.0 | zho | -0.47 | 44.44 |
| 5 | **ibo** | 0.28 | 80.00 | swe | 1.31 | 100.0 | heb | -0.47 | 11.11 |
| 6 | rus | 0.22 | 73.33 | tam | 1.03 | 70.0 | **ewe** | -0.51 | 55.56 |
| 7 | **wol** | 0.20 | 80.00 | bul | 0.93 | 70.0 | tam | -0.52 | 11.11 |
| 8 | **hau** | 0.13 | 73.33 | fra | 0.73 | 70.0 | eng | -0.53 | 33.33 |
| 9 | heb | 0.08 | 66.67 | hun | 0.39 | 60.0 | hin | -0.55 | 22.22 |
| 10 | **kmr** | 0.08 | 66.67 | cym | 0.36 | 60.0 | fra | -0.56 | 33.33 |
| 11 | **pms** | 0.06 | 60.00 | deu | 0.25 | 60.0 | tel | -0.56 | 11.11 |
| 12 | jpn | 0.05 | 60.00 | eng | 0.17 | 70.0 | deu | -0.64 | 11.11 |
| 13 | zho | 0.05 | 60.00 | tel | 0.13 | 60.0 | swe | -0.67 | 11.11 |
| 14 | bul | 0.03 | 53.33 | fin | 0.10 | 40.0 | nep | -0.67 | 11.11 |
| 15 | fra | -0.00 | 53.33 | spa | -0.08 | 60.0 | hun | -0.69 | 11.11 |
| 16 | spa | -0.01 | 46.67 | kor | -0.10 | 50.0 | est | -0.70 | 22.22 |
| 17 | mya | -0.04 | 53.33 | rus | -0.10 | 50.0 | **kmr** | -0.71 | 44.44 |
| 18 | **kin** | -0.04 | 40.00 | heb | -0.10 | 50.0 | rus | -0.72 | 0.00 |
| 19 | hye | -0.05 | 53.33 | est | -0.14 | 60.0 | gle | -0.73 | 22.22 |
| 20 | deu | -0.09 | 33.33 | mya | -0.14 | 40.0 | **hau** | -0.77 | 22.22 |
| 21 | eng | -0.11 | 33.33 | ben | -0.19 | 50.0 | ben | -0.77 | 11.11 |
| 22 | gle | -0.11 | 26.67 | gle | -0.27 | 30.0 | kor | -0.78 | 0.00 |
| 23 | est | -0.11 | 33.33 | **hau** | -0.48 | 60.0 | spa | -0.79 | 0.00 |
| 24 | **mos** | -0.11 | 40.00 | zho | -1.00 | 0.0 | bul | -0.81 | 0.00 |
| 25 | swe | -0.12 | 33.33 | **kmr** | -1.07 | 30.0 | hye | -0.91 | 0.00 |
| 26 | tel | -0.13 | 40.00 | hye | -1.14 | 20.0 | cym | -0.92 | 22.22 |
| 27 | cym | -0.14 | 33.33 | jpn | -1.32 | 10.0 | **gub** | -1.02 | 11.11 |
| 28 | ara | -0.18 | 26.67 | **pcm** | -1.53 | 10.0 | **wol** | -1.02 | 11.11 |
| 29 | ben | -0.20 | 20.00 | bre | -2.10 | 0.0 | **ibo** | -1.03 | 33.33 |
| 30 | **gub** | -0.23 | 13.33 | **gub** | -2.19 | 20.0 | ara | -1.08 | 0.00 |
| 31 | nep | -0.23 | 20.00 | **pms** | -2.60 | 0.0 | **bam** | -1.12 | 11.11 |
| 32 | kor | -0.36 | 6.67 | yor | -2.88 | 0.0 | **mos** | -1.15 | 11.11 |
| 33 | hin | -0.39 | 6.67 | **kin** | -4.28 | 0.0 | jpn | -1.15 | 0.00 |
| 34 | ell | -0.45 | 0.00 | **mos** | -4.54 | 10.0 | bre | -1.19 | 11.11 |
| 35 | yor | -0.45 | 13.33 | **bam** | -4.87 | 0.0 | **pms** | -1.22 | 0.00 |
| 36 | fin | -0.46 | 6.67 | **wol** | -5.01 | 0.0 | **kin** | -1.30 | 11.11 |
| 37 | tam | -0.47 | 6.67 | **ewe** | -5.02 | 10.0 | mya | -1.49 | 0.00 |
| 38 | hun | -0.70 | 0.00 | **ibo** | -5.95 | 0.0 | yor | -1.57 | 11.11 |

Table 18: Transfer Languages ranked by aggregated transfer scores (ts) overall target languages across Sentence Classification & QA tasks using XLM-R. Languages unseen by mBERT are in **bold** font.

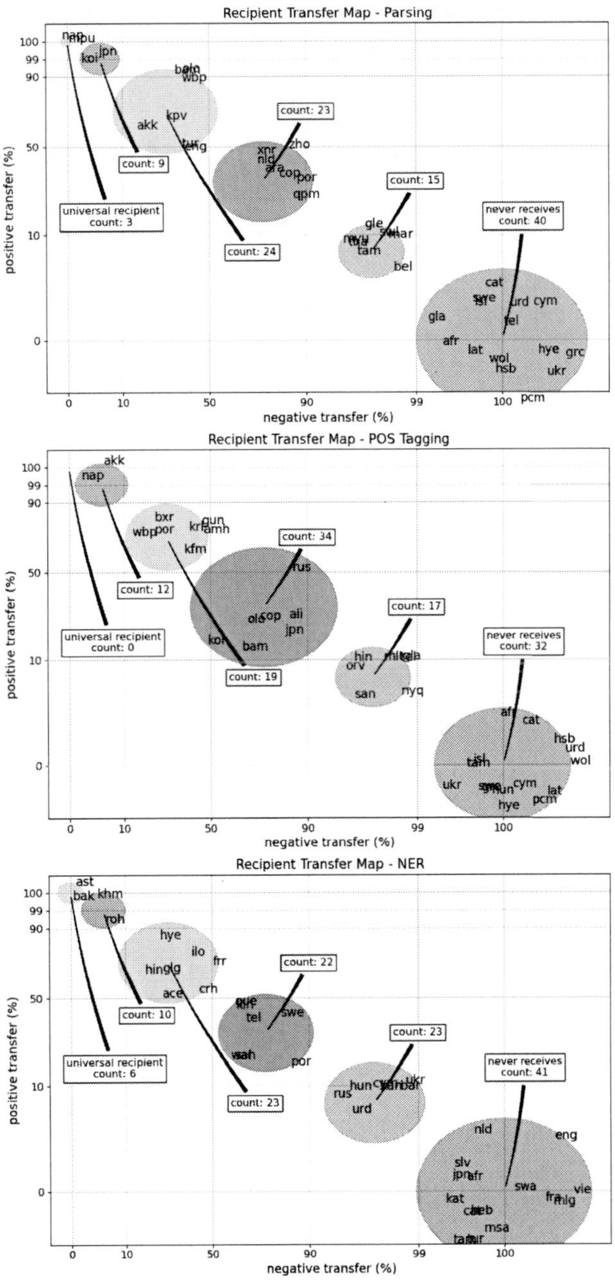


Figure 5: Recipient Transfer Map: we observe universal positive recipients as well as languages those never receive positive transfer across tasks. Circle size represents the percentage of languages fall to a transfer range.

| Tasks | Never Receives | Positive Transfer (%) (90-99] | Universal Recipient |
|---|---|---|---|
| Dependency Parsing | ell, isl, **grc**, **mlt**, fra, **qtd**, hrv, lav, **urb**, **fas**, ukr, spa, cym, tel, **pcm**, afr, swe, est, **nor**, **hsb**, **orv**, cat, slv, **chu**, **sme**, eus, slk, hye, **gla**, urd, hin, **fro**, lit, lat, **san**, **wol**, **lij**, **got**, srp, **lzh** | **tpn**, **koi**, **glv**, kor, **krl**, **mdf**, jpn, **amh**, sqi | **mpu**, **gun**, **nap** |
| POS Tagging | ell, nld, isl, **grc**, lav, **fas**, ukr, spa, cym, hun, **pcm**, afr, swe, est, **nor**, **hsb**, tam, cat, **chu**, **sme**, eus, hye, urd, ben, ita, ron, lit, lat, **wol**, **got**, srp, **lzh** | fra, eng, **qhe**, dan, **myu**, **glv**, kor, tur, kaz, **akk**, **myv**, **nap** | |
| NER | nld, ell, tgl, fra, ces, bul, zho, msa, sun, lav, gle, **fas**, kat, spa, heb, hbs, afr, est, **yid**, eng, tam, bre, vie, jpn, cat, **tha**, slv, ceb, tur, mlg, slk, swa, ben, uzb, ita, ron, tat, pol, **zea**, **lin**, **ibo** | **ksh**, **pms**, aze, **mzn**, **oci**, tgk, **roh**, **khm**, **aym**, **csb** | bak, ast, **uig**, kaz, nds, **amh** |

Table 19: We find 25 languages out of 40 which receives positive transfer from almost any transfer languages (i.e. column 90-99% and 100%) are unseen by mbert. (language codes in **bold** font are the unseen ones)

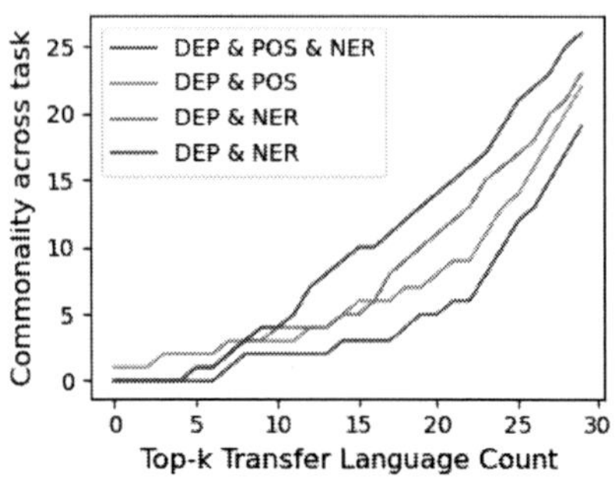


Figure 6: Extent of commonality of top-transfer languages across task. Unseen languages perform generally well while the other language rankings mostly vary across tasks.

`aggregated-transfer` score variance. We observe, the unseen languages (bold font) are the ones having large amount of variances across all three tasks. We find the languages with high variance can provide superior transfer for some languages but at the same time hurt significantly some other languages. For example, if we consider the case of depndency parsing, we find ibo (rank-1) and bam (rank-3) are two languages with high variance. They provide maximum amount of positive transfer some universal low-resourced target languages like akk, koi, apu, tpn from diverse families including afro-asiatic, uralic, tupian. At the same time, ibo also hurts a large number of languages (10) including fra, nyq, sme, san etc providing minimum amount of negative transfer. On the other hand, there can be languages with high variance providing either mostly positive `aggregated-transfer` scores like mos or mostly negative score like pcm. Interestingly, if we look at the `aggregated-transfer` score and variance of pcm in Table 22, we find the transfer is positive overall. Nevertheless it provides minimum negative scores to 11 languages thus making it a transfer language with high variance. On the other

| Transfer Language | Parsing | | | | POS Tagging | | | | NER | | | |
|---|---|---|---|---|---|---|---|---|---|---|---|---|
| | 1 | 10 | 100 | 1000 | 1 | 10 | 100 | 1000 | 1 | 10 | 100 | 1000 |
| gub | mpu | mpu | gun | **gub** | aqz | nap | nap | **nap** | amh | amh | **amh** | bar |
| est | nap | tpn | gun | **gun** | nap | nap | nap | **nap** | amh | amh | **amh** | som |
| bre | nap | nap | gun | **gun** | nap | nap | nap | **nap** | amh | amh | **amh** | amh |
| eng | nap | mpu | gun | **gun** | nap | nap | nap | **nap** | amh | sin | **amh** | nds |
| ben | nap | nap | nap | **gun** | cop | nap | nap | **nap** | amh | sin | amh | **amh** |
| kmr | nap | mpu | gun | **kmr** | urb | nap | nap | **nap** | amh | amh | **amh** | amh |
| spa | nap | mpu | gun | **gun** | nap | nap | **nap** | nap | amh | amh | **amh** | roh |
| bul | nap | nap | nap | **gun** | nap | nap | nap | **amh** | amh | amh | **amh** | som |
| pms | nap | **nap** | nap | mpu | nap | nap | nap | **nap** | amh | amh | **amh** | amh |
| gle | nap | nap | mpu | **gun** | aqz | nap | nap | **nap** | amh | amh | **amh** | som |
| nep | nap | tpn | gun | **gun** | aqz | urb | nap | **nap** | amh | sin | **amh** | roh |
| cym | nap | nap | gun | **gun** | nap | nap | nap | **amh** | amh | **sin** | amh | som |
| fin | nap | nap | tpn | **gun** | nap | nap | nap | **nap** | amh | sin | **amh** | som |
| hye | nap | nap | nap | **gun** | nap | nap | nap | **nap** | uig | sin | **amh** | som |
| mya | nap | nap | wbp | **gun** | aqz | urb | nap | **nap** | amh | amh | **amh** | amh |
| hin | nap | tpn | gun | **gun** | aqz | aqz | nap | **nap** | amh | amh | **amh** | som |
| tel | nap | nap | gun | **gun** | aqz | nap | nap | **amh** | amh | sin | **amh** | roh |
| tam | nap | nap | gun | **gun** | nap | nap | nap | **nap** | amh | sin | **amh** | som |
| kor | tpn | mpu | mpu | **tpn** | nap | nap | nap | **nap** | amh | amh | **amh** | roh |
| ell | nap | tpn | nap | **gun** | nap | nap | nap | **nap** | amh | amh | **amh** | som |
| hun | nap | mpu | gun | **gun** | nap | nap | nap | **nap** | amh | amh | **amh** | som |
| heb | nap | nap | nap | **gun** | nap | nap | nap | **nap** | amh | amh | **amh** | som |
| zho | tpn | nap | nap | **mpu** | nap | nap | nap | **nap** | amh | amh | **amh** | amh |
| ara | nap | nap | gun | **gun** | nap | nap | nap | **nap** | uig | amh | **amh** | amh |
| swe | nap | nap | gun | **gun** | nap | nap | nap | **nap** | amh | sin | **amh** | som |
| jpn | nap | mpu | mpu | **tpn** | nap | nap | nap | **nap** | amh | amh | amh | **amh** |
| fra | nap | mpu | gun | **gun** | nap | nap | nap | **nap** | amh | amh | **amh** | som |
| deu | tpn | mpu | gun | **gun** | nap | nap | nap | **nap** | amh | amh | **amh** | som |
| rus | nap | nap | gun | **gun** | nap | nap | **nap** | nap | amh | sin | **amh** | roh |
| bam | mpu | wbp | **wbp** | gun | nap | **nap** | amh | bam | amh | uig | amh | **amh** |
| ewe | nap | gun | tpn | **gun** | nap | **nap** | amh | nap | amh | sin | **amh** | nds |
| hau | mpu | nap | gun | **gun** | aqz | **nap** | nap | amh | amh | sin | amh | **amh** |
| ibo | tpn | mpu | gun | **gun** | aqz | **nap** | nap | mpu | sin | amh | amh | **amh** |
| kin | mpu | **nap** | nap | tpn | nap | nap | nap | **nap** | amh | amh | **amh** | amh |
| mos | mpu | aqz | gun | **gun** | nap | **nap** | amh | nap | sin | sin | **amh** | amh |
| pcm | nap | nap | wbp | **gun** | kfm | nap | nap | **nap** | amh | amh | **amh** | amh |
| wol | nap | aqz | gun | **gun** | nap | nap | nap | **amh** | amh | sin | **amh** | nds |
| yor | nap | nap | wbp | **gun** | nap | nap | nap | **nap** | amh | amh | **amh** | som |

Table 20: Only bar and nds are seen by mbert. All other languages receiving maximum benefits continuously are unseen by mbert (kfm, urb, gun, aqz, cop, roh, bam, tpn, som, kmr, uig, mpu, amh, sin, wbp, gub, nap). The maximum score across different steps of training are **bolded**.

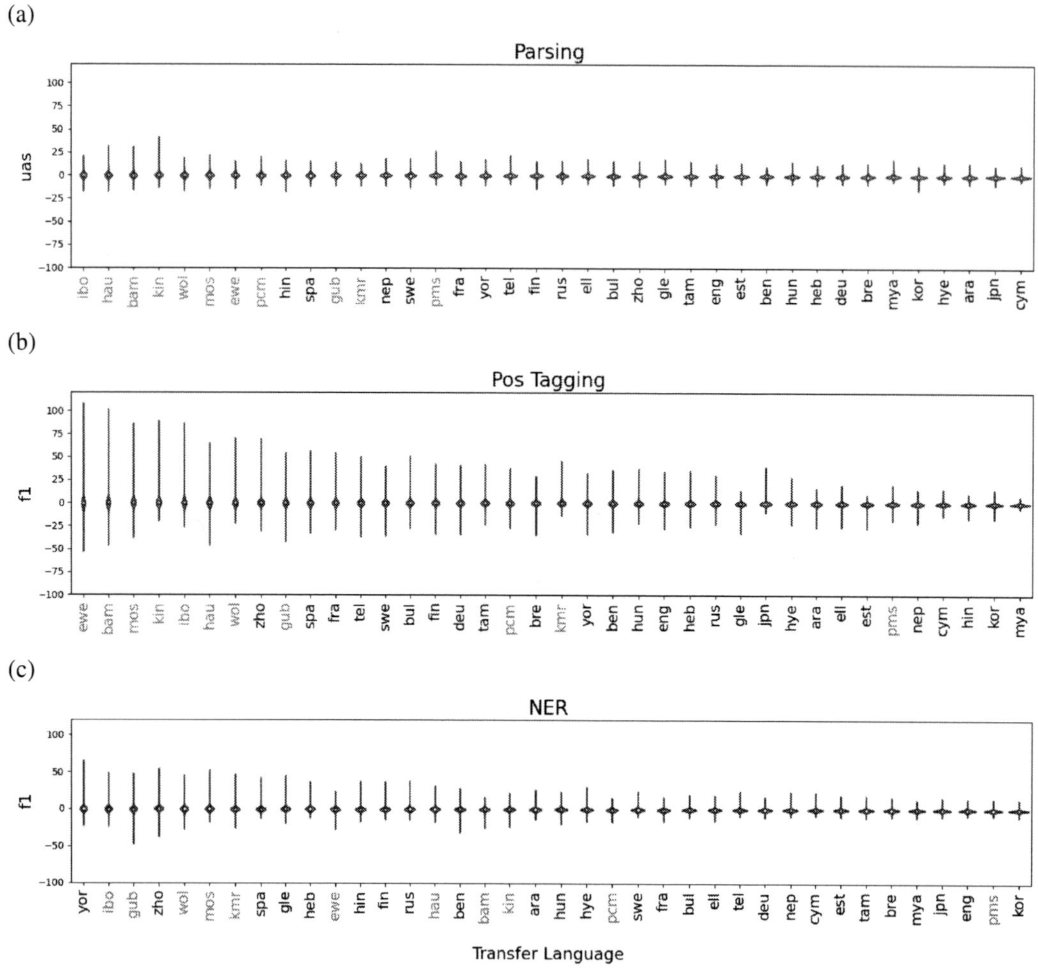


Figure 7: Violin plots of transfer languages sorted by transfer score variance. mBERT unseen languages are in red color font.

| | DEP | POS | NER |
|---|---|---|---|
| DEP | - | **(-0.34, 0.04)** | **(0.40, 0.01)** |
| POS Tagging | **(-0.34, 0.04)** | - | (-0.15, 0.37) |
| NER | **(0.40, 0.01)** | (-0.15, 0.37) | -) |

Table 21: (Spearman Rank correlation, p value) for correlation of transfer language ranking across token-classification tasks. Statistically significant relations are in **bold** font.

hand, low variance languages are the ones those do not significantly affect any transfer languages like arabic (rank 37). Though the overall transfer score is negative (-0.12) for arabic, it fails to provide maximum or minimum transfer score to any target language making it neutral. So, overall it is evident that, transfer languages with high variance are the ones with either (i) mostly positive while significantly hurting a few, (ii) mostly negative while significantly boosting performance for a few, or (iii) Performing both (i) and (ii) concurrently being highly influential as well as detrimental at the same time. Languages unseen by mBERT during pretraining exhibit all three kinds of characteristics with high intensity (see Table 23 for examples). In Table 22, we report the transfer score with variance as well as the count of maximum/minimum transfer score recipients for all transfer languages across tasks.

## M Seen vs Unseen Languages

In Figure 8, we report the aggregated and averaged transfer scores we get for mBERT seen vs unseen languages.

| Rank | Parsing | | | POS Tagging | | | NER | | |
|---|---|---|---|---|---|---|---|---|---|
| | Lang | Transfer (Var.) | (Max, Min) # | Lang | Transfer (Var.) | (Max, Min) # | Lang | Transfer (Var.) | (Max, Min) # |
| 1 | **ibo** | 0.05 (23.5) | (10, 10) | **ewe** | -0.79 (120.4) | (5, 31) | yor | -0.32 (44.4) | (2, 6) |
| 2 | **hau** | 0.04 (22.7) | (2, 2) | **bam** | -0.12 (101.2) | (5, 0) | **ibo** | -0.54 (42.0) | (3, 18) |
| 3 | **bam** | 0.02 (21.5) | (11, 15) | **mos** | 0.27 (69.8) | (4, 3) | **gub** | -0.98 (41.2) | (3, 14) |
| 4 | **kin** | -0.06 (21.4) | (3, 1) | **kin** | 0.41 (69.1) | (3, 0) | zho | 0.16 (32.7) | (46, 3) |
| 5 | **wol** | 0.03 (17.6) | (5, 6) | **ibo** | -0.14 (68.0) | (5, 10) | **wol** | -0.41 (32.4) | (5, 6) |
| 6 | **mos** | 0.09 (16.1) | (13, 2) | **hau** | -0.34 (52.5) | (1, 3) | **mos** | 0.0 (29.5) | (2, 1) |
| 7 | **ewe** | -0.08 (14.5) | (4, 5) | **wol** | -0.14 (51.9) | (8, 10) | **kmr** | -0.61 (25.6) | (3, 8) |
| 8 | **pcm** | 0.13 (13.4) | (1, 11) | zho | -0.04 (45.6) | (26, 7) | spa | -0.28 (24.5) | (1, 1) |
| 9 | hin | -0.1 (13.1) | (4, 3) | **gub** | -0.34 (41.3) | (3, 4) | gle | -0.07 (21.1) | (1, 1) |
| 10 | spa | -0.18 (11.5) | (2, 3) | spa | -0.53 (39.6) | (0, 2) | heb | 0.04 (21.1) | (3, 0) |
| 11 | **gub** | -0.14 (10.7) | (5, 3) | fra | -0.41 (37.2) | (2, 6) | **ewe** | -0.76 (19.0) | (0, 5) |
| 12 | **kmr** | 0.14 (10.2) | (0, 1) | tel | -0.31 (36.6) | (0, 1) | hin | -0.72 (18.6) | (1, 12) |
| 13 | nep | 0.12 (10.1) | (8, 1) | swe | -0.66 (32.2) | (1, 3) | fin | -0.29 (18.3) | (0, 1) |
| 14 | swe | -0.21 (10.0) | (0, 2) | bul | -0.08 (28.9) | (0, 0) | rus | -0.34 (17.4) | (0, 1) |
| 15 | **pms** | 0.09 (9.7) | (3, 1) | fin | -0.35 (28.9) | (0, 1) | **hau** | -0.07 (17.1) | (7, 0) |
| 16 | fra | -0.37 (9.1) | (1, 8) | deu | -0.44 (26.0) | (0, 0) | ben | -0.54 (17.0) | (4, 3) |
| 17 | yor | 0.14 (8.9) | (3, 3) | tam | -0.14 (22.9) | (0, 0) | **bam** | -0.69 (16.1) | (4, 1) |
| 18 | tel | 0.05 (8.7) | (1, 2) | **pcm** | -0.16 (22.1) | (3, 14) | **kin** | -0.56 (13.2) | (1, 3) |
| 19 | fin | -0.26 (8.6) | (1, 1) | bre | -0.39 (21.4) | (1, 0) | ara | -0.32 (13.1) | (0, 1) |
| 20 | rus | 0.11 (8.5) | (0, 1) | **kmr** | 0.36 (21.2) | (11, 6) | hun | 0.08 (12.2) | (2, 0) |
| 21 | ell | 0.15 (8.3) | (1, 0) | yor | -0.16 (21.0) | (1, 1) | hye | -0.17 (12.1) | (0, 1) |
| 22 | bul | -0.21 (6.9) | (1, 1) | ben | -0.08 (20.6) | (3, 2) | **pcm** | -0.69 (11.8) | (6, 25) |
| 23 | zho | -0.48 (6.9) | (5, 10) | hun | -0.29 (20.4) | (3, 1) | swe | -0.11 (10.1) | (0, 0) |
| 24 | gle | 0.03 (6.8) | (1, 1) | eng | -0.35 (18.8) | (2, 1) | fra | -0.59 (9.5) | (0, 5) |
| 25 | tam | -0.24 (6.7) | (1, 3) | heb | -0.26 (17.3) | (0, 1) | bul | -0.18 (9.0) | (0, 1) |
| 26 | eng | -0.22 (6.4) | (0, 0) | rus | -0.28 (15.3) | (0, 0) | ell | -0.29 (8.8) | (1, 1) |
| 27 | est | 0.0 (6.1) | (1, 1) | gle | -0.34 (13.7) | (0, 2) | tel | 0.08 (8.6) | (1, 0) |
| 28 | ben | -0.06 (6.0) | (3, 1) | jpn | 0.18 (13.6) | (11, 0) | deu | -0.2 (8.4) | (0, 0) |
| 29 | hun | -0.23 (5.9) | (0, 2) | hye | 0.27 (12.8) | (2, 0) | nep | -0.13 (8.1) | (1, 1) |
| 30 | heb | 0.08 (5.8) | (0, 1) | ara | -0.3 (11.7) | (0, 0) | cym | 0.03 (7.8) | (2, 1) |
| 31 | deu | -0.13 (5.7) | (1, 4) | ell | -0.13 (11.1) | (1, 0) | est | 0.03 (7.8) | (0, 0) |
| 32 | bre | -0.23 (5.7) | (1, 1) | est | -0.35 (9.1) | (1, 1) | tam | 0.0 (7.1) | (3, 0) |
| 33 | mya | 0.33 (5.6) | (9, 0) | **pms** | 0.08 (8.8) | (2, 0) | bre | -0.23 (5.6) | (1, 0) |
| 34 | kor | -0.38 (5.6) | (0, 1) | nep | 0.12 (8.4) | (6, 0) | mya | -0.17 (5.3) | (5, 2) |
| 35 | hye | -0.03 (5.4) | (0, 2) | cym | 0.22 (6.7) | (0, 0) | jpn | -0.08 (5.3) | (4, 1) |
| 36 | ara | -0.12 (5.1) | (0, 0) | hin | -0.13 (6.4) | (0, 3) | eng | 0.02 (5.1) | (5, 1) |
| 37 | jpn | -0.19 (3.9) | (14, 2) | kor | -0.07 (5.8) | (1, 0) | **pms** | -0.29 (5.0) | (1, 0) |
| 38 | cym | -0.03 (2.9) | (1, 3) | mya | 0.17 (2.7) | (3, 1) | kor | -0.09 (4.4) | (7, 1) |

Table 22: Transfer languages are sorted by transfer score variance (mBERT unseen languages are in **bold** font). # Max Transfer and # Min Transfer denote the count of target languages which receive maximum and minimum transfer from this particular transfer language.

## N Transfer Progression Graphs

From Figure 9 to 18, we present the transfer progression graphs for all 38 transfer languages. We observe POS tagging always have comparatively larger deviation which increase with the progression of training steps. In addition, for different time steps in each graph, we provide percentage of positive/negative transfers and the top performing target languages. This way, we observe top target languages that can get continuous improvement for each transfer language even after thousands of steps.

| Type | Transfer Language | Variance | max(+)→ | min(-)→ |
|---|---|---|---|---|
| (+ *and* -) | ibo | high | aii, ajp, apu, arr, ces, gle, gub, koi, krl, yor | grc, hsb, hye, kfm, otk, san, sme, sqi, srp, urb |
| (+ *and* -) | bam | high | bho, bam, bre, bxr, kfm, kmr, kpv, mpu, rus, soj, wbp | ajp, ara, chu, gla, got, krl, lzh, nld, orv, qpm, qtd, swl, tha, tgl, zho |
| (+) | mos | high | aqz, bel, bul, eng, ind, ita, kaz, lit, myv, pol, tam, tgl, ukr | arr, wbp |
| (-) | pcm | high | tha | aii, bho, ell, eng, eus, hrv, isl, lat, lit, nor, qhe |
| neutral | eng | low | - | - |
| neutral | ara | low | - | - |

Table 23: Characteristics of example transfer languages with different intensity of variance derived from dependency parsing task results. max(+)→ represents set of target language which receive maximum score for the specific transfer language wheres, min(-)→ represents the complete oposite.

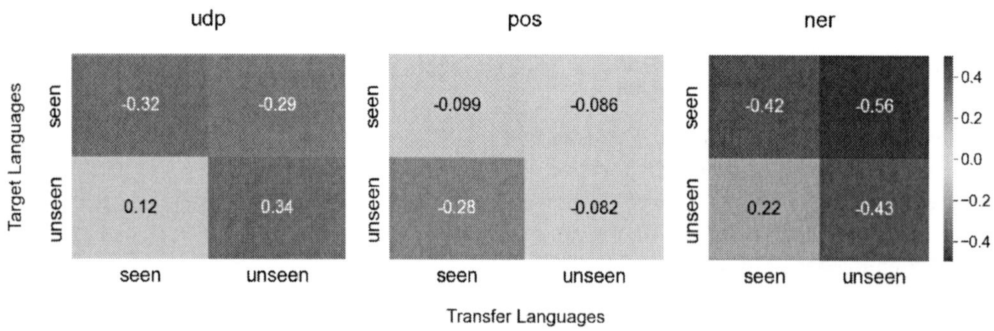


Figure 8: Transfer-Target Heatmap for mbert seen and unseen languages

| Language | iso-639 | Family | Genus | Script | mBERT-seen? |
|---|---|---|---|---|---|
| Hebrew | heb | Afro-Asiatic | Semitic | Hebr | |
| Arabic | ara | Afro-Asiatic | Semitic | Arab | |
| Hausa | hau | Afro-Asiatic | West Chadic | Latn | ✗ |
| Telugu | tel | Dravidian | Dravidian | Telu | |
| Tamil | tam | Dravidian | Dravidian | Taml | |
| Armenian | hye | Indo-European | Armenian | Armn | |
| Breton | bre | Indo-European | Celtic | Latn | |
| Irish | gle | Indo-European | Celtic | Latn | |
| Welsh | cym | Indo-European | Celtic | Latn | |
| English | eng | Indo-European | Germanic | Latn | |
| Swedish | swe | Indo-European | Germanic | Latn | |
| German | deu | Indo-European | Germanic | Latn | |
| Modern Greek (1453-) | ell | Indo-European | Greek | Grek | |
| Bengali | ben | Indo-European | Indic | Beng | |
| Nepali (macrolanguage) | nep | Indo-European | Indic | Deva | |
| Hindi | hin | Indo-European | Indic | Deva | |
| Northern Kurdish | kmr | Indo-European | Iranian | Arab | ✗ |
| French | fra | Indo-European | Romance | Latn | |
| Spanish | spa | Indo-European | Romance | Latn | |
| Piemontese | pms | Indo-European | Romance | Latn | ✗ |
| Bulgarian | bul | Indo-European | Slavic | Cyrl | |
| Russian | rus | Indo-European | Slavic | Cyrl | |
| Japanese | jpn | Japanese | Japanese | Jpan | |
| Korean | kor | Korean | Korean | Kore | |
| Bambara | bam | Mande | Western Mande | Latn | ✗ |
| Kinyarwanda | kin | Niger-Congo | Bantu | Latn | ✗ |
| Yoruba | yor | Niger-Congo | Defoid | Latn | |
| Ewe | ewe | Niger-Congo | Gbe | Latn | ✗ |
| Igbo | ibo | Niger-Congo | Igboid | Latn | ✗ |
| Mossi | mos | Niger-Congo | Oti-Volta | Latn | ✗ |
| Wolof | wol | Niger-Congo | Wolof | Latn | ✗ |
| Burmese | mya | Sino-Tibetan | Burmese-Lolo | Mon–Burmese | |
| Chinese | zho | Sino-Tibetan | Chinese | Chinese | |
| Guajajára | gub | Tupian | Maweti-Guarani | Latn | ✗ |
| Estonian | est | Uralic | Finnic | Latn | |
| Finnish | fin | Uralic | Finnic | Latn | |
| Hungarian | hun | Uralic | Ugric | Latn | |
| Nigerian Pidgin | pcm | other | Creoles and Pidgins | Latn | ✗ |

Table 24: Transfer Languages we use in our study for mBERT fine-tuning

**UDP and POS Tagging Task Adapter Training Dataset**

| Language | iso-639 | UD Identifier | # Examples | Family | Genus | Script |
|---|---|---|---|---|---|---|
| Coptic | cop | cop_scriptorium | 403 | Afro-Asiatic | Egyptian-Coptic | Coptic |
| Arabic | ara | ar_nyuad | 1963 | Afro-Asiatic | Semitic | Arab |
| Hebrew | heb | he_htb | 491 | Afro-Asiatic | Semitic | Hebr |
| Maltese | mlt | mt_mudt | 518 | Afro-Asiatic | Semitic | Latn |
| Kazakh | kaz | kk_ktb | 1047 | Altaic | Turkic | Cyrl |
| Turkish | tur | tr_gb | 2880 | Altaic | Turkic | Latn |
| Uighur | uig | ug_udt | 900 | Altaic | Turkic | Uighur |
| Vietnamese | vie | vi_vtb | 800 | Austro-Asiatic | Vietic | Latn |
| Indonesian | ind | id_pud | 1000 | Austronesian | Malayo-Sumbawan | Latn |
| Basque | eus | eu_bdt | 1799 | Basque | Basque | Latn |
| Turkish German | qtd | qtd_sagt | 805 | Code switching | Code switching | Latn |
| Tamil | tam | ta_mwtt | 534 | Dravidian | Dravidian | Taml |
| Telugu | tel | te_mtg | 146 | Dravidian | Dravidian | Telu |
| Armenian | hye | hy_armtdp | 278 | Indo-European | Armenian | Armn |
| Latvian | lav | lv_lvtb | 1823 | Indo-European | Baltic | Latn |
| Lithuanian | lit | lt_alksnis | 684 | Indo-European | Baltic | Latn |
| Welsh | cym | cy_ccg | 953 | Indo-European | Celtic | Latn |
| Scottish Gaelic | gla | gd_arcosg | 538 | Indo-European | Celtic | Latn |
| Irish | gle | ga_idt | 454 | Indo-European | Celtic | Latn |
| Gothic | got | got_proiel | 1029 | Indo-European | Germanic | Gothic |
| Afrikaans | afr | af_afribooms | 425 | Indo-European | Germanic | Latn |
| Danish | dan | da_ddt | 565 | Indo-European | Germanic | Latn |
| German | deu | de_hdt | 18459 | Indo-European | Germanic | Latn |
| English | eng | en_ewt | 2077 | Indo-European | Germanic | Latn |
| Faroese | fao | fo_oft | 1208 | Indo-European | Germanic | Latn |
| Icelandic | isl | is_icepahc | 5157 | Indo-European | Germanic | Latn |
| Dutch | nld | nl_lassysmall | 875 | Indo-European | Germanic | Latn |
| Norwegian | nor | no_bokmaal | 1939 | Indo-European | Germanic | Latn |
| Swedish | swe | sv_talbanken | 1219 | Indo-European | Germanic | Latn |
| Modern Greek (1453-) | ell | el_gdt | 456 | Indo-European | Greek | Grek |
| Ancient Greek (to 1453) | grc | grc_perseus | 1306 | Indo-European | Greek | Grek |
| Urdu | urd | ur_udtb | 535 | Indo-European | Indic | Arab |
| Sanskrit | san | sa_vedic | 1473 | Indo-European | Indic | Brahmi |
| Hindi | hin | hi_hdtb | 1684 | Indo-European | Indic | Deva |
| Marathi | mar | mr_ufal | 47 | Indo-European | Indic | Deva |
| Persian | fas | fa_perdt | 1455 | Indo-European | Iranian | Arab |
| Northern Kurdish | kmr | kmr_mg | 734 | Indo-European | Iranian | Arab |
| Latin | lat | la_ittb | 2101 | Indo-European | Italic | Latn |
| Catalan | cat | ca_ancora | 1846 | Indo-European | Romance | Latn |
| French | fra | fr_ftb | 2541 | Indo-European | Romance | Latn |
| Old French (842-ca. 1400) | fro | fro_srcmf | 1927 | Indo-European | Romance | Latn |
| Galician | glg | gl_ctg | 861 | Indo-European | Romance | Latn |
| Italian | ita | it_vit | 1067 | Indo-European | Romance | Latn |
| Portuguese | por | pt_gsd | 1204 | Indo-European | Romance | Latn |
| Romanian | ron | ro_nonstandard | 1052 | Indo-European | Romance | Latn |
| Spanish | spa | es_ancora | 1721 | Indo-European | Romance | Latn |
| Belarusian | bel | be_hse | 889 | Indo-European | Slavic | Cyrl |
| Bulgarian | bul | bg_btb | 1116 | Indo-European | Slavic | Cyrl |
| Old Russian | orv | orv_torot | 1756 | Indo-European | Slavic | Cyrl |
| Russian | rus | ru_syntagrus | 6491 | Indo-European | Slavic | Cyrl |
| Serbian | srp | sr_set | 520 | Indo-European | Slavic | Cyrl |
| Ukrainian | ukr | uk_iu | 892 | Indo-European | Slavic | Cyrl |
| Church Slavic | chu | cu_proiel | 1141 | Indo-European | Slavic | Glag+Latn |
| Czech | ces | cs_pdt | 10148 | Indo-European | Slavic | Latn |
| Croatian | hrv | hr_set | 1136 | Indo-European | Slavic | Latn |
| Upper Sorbian | hsb | hsb_ufal | 623 | Indo-European | Slavic | Latn |
| Polish | pol | pl_pdb | 2215 | Indo-European | Slavic | Latn |
| Pomak | qpm | qpm_philotis | 635 | Indo-European | Slavic | Latn |
| Slovak | slk | sk_snk | 1061 | Indo-European | Slavic | Latn |
| Slovenian | slv | sl_sst | 1110 | Indo-European | Slavic | Latn |
| Japanese | jpn | ja_bccwj | 7871 | Japanese | Japanese | Jpan |
| Korean | kor | ko_kaist | 2287 | Korean | Korean | Kore |
| Russia Buriat | bxr | bxr_bdt | 908 | Mongolic | Altic | Cyrl |
| Wolof | wol | wo_wtb | 470 | Niger-Congo | Wolof | Latn |
| Cusco Quechua | qhe | qhe_hiencs | 225 | Quechuan | Quechuan | Latn |
| Literary Chinese | lzh | lzh_kyoto | 4469 | Sino-Tibetan | Chinese | Chinese |
| Chinese | zho | zh_hk | 1004 | Sino-Tibetan | Chinese | Chinese |
| Estonian | est | et_edt | 3214 | Uralic | Finnic | Latn |
| Finnish | fin | fi_ood | 2122 | Uralic | Finnic | Latn |
| Livvi | olo | olo_kkpp | 106 | Uralic | Finnic | Latn |
| Northern Sami | sme | sme_giella | 865 | Uralic | Saami | Latn |
| Hungarian | hun | hu_szeged | 449 | Uralic | Ugric | Latn |
| Nigerian Pidgin | pcm | pcm_nsc | 972 | other | Creoles and Pidgins | Latn |
| Swedish Sign Language | swl | swl_sslc | 34 | other | Sign Languages | |

Table 25: Task Adapter training dataset details (taken from Universal Dependency v2.11 (de Marneffe et al., 2021)) for dependency parsing and pos tagging.

| NER Task Adapter Training Dataset | | | | |
|---|---|---|---|---|
| Language | iso-639 | Family | Genus | Script |
| Somali | som | Afro-Asiatic | Lowland East Cushitic | Latn |
| Arabic | ara | Afro-Asiatic | Semitic | Arab |
| Amharic | amh | Afro-Asiatic | Semitic | Ethi |
| Hebrew | heb | Afro-Asiatic | Semitic | Hebr |
| Maltese | mlt | Afro-Asiatic | Semitic | Latn |
| Mongolian | mon | Altaic | Mongolic | Mongolian |
| Bashkir | bak | Altaic | Turkic | Cyrl |
| Chuvash | chv | Altaic | Turkic | Cyrl |
| Kazakh | kaz | Altaic | Turkic | Cyrl |
| Yakut | sah | Altaic | Turkic | Cyrl |
| Crimean Tatar | crh | Altaic | Turkic | Cyrl+Latn+Arab |
| Kirghiz | kir | Altaic | Turkic | Kyrgyz+Cyrl |
| Azerbaijani | aze | Altaic | Turkic | Latn |
| Tatar | tat | Altaic | Turkic | Latn |
| Turkmen | tuk | Altaic | Turkic | Latn |
| Turkish | tur | Altaic | Turkic | Latn |
| Uzbek | uzb | Altaic | Turkic | Latn |
| Uighur | uig | Altaic | Turkic | Uighur |
| Khmer | khm | Austro-Asiatic | Khmer | Khmer |
| Vietnamese | vie | Austro-Asiatic | Vietic | Latn |
| Malagasy | mlg | Austronesian | Barito | Latn |
| Cebuano | ceb | Austronesian | Greater Central Philippine | Latn |
| Tagalog | tgl | Austronesian | Greater Central Philippine | Latn |
| Waray (Philippines) | war | Austronesian | Greater Central Philippine | Latn |
| Javanese | jav | Austronesian | Javanese | Latn+Javanese |
| Achinese | ace | Austronesian | Malayo-Sumbawan | Latn |
| Malay (macrolanguage) | msa | Austronesian | Malayo-Sumbawan | Latn |
| Sundanese | sun | Austronesian | Malayo-Sumbawan | Latn |
| Iloko | ilo | Austronesian | Northern Luzon | Latn |
| Maori | mri | Austronesian | Oceanic | Latn |
| Aymara | aym | Aymaran | Aymaran | Latn |
| Basque | eus | Basque | Basque | Latn |
| Kannada | kan | Dravidian | Dravidian | Kannada |
| Malayalam | mal | Dravidian | Dravidian | Malayalam |
| Tamil | tam | Dravidian | Dravidian | Taml |
| Telugu | tel | Dravidian | Dravidian | Telu |
| Albanian | sqi | Indo-European | Albanian | Latn |
| Armenian | hye | Indo-European | Armenian | Armn |
| Latvian | lav | Indo-European | Baltic | Latn |
| Lithuanian | lit | Indo-European | Baltic | Latn |
| Breton | bre | Indo-European | Celtic | Latn |
| Welsh | cym | Indo-European | Celtic | Latn |
| Scottish Gaelic | gla | Indo-European | Celtic | Latn |
| Irish | gle | Indo-European | Celtic | Latn |
| Western Frisian | fry | Indo-European | Germanic | West Frisian |
| Afrikaans | afr | Indo-European | Germanic | Latn |
| Bavarian | bar | Indo-European | Germanic | Latn |
| Danish | dan | Indo-European | Germanic | Latn |
| German | deu | Indo-European | Germanic | Latn |
| English | eng | Indo-European | Germanic | Latn |
| Faroese | fao | Indo-European | Germanic | Latn |
| Northern Frisian | frr | Indo-European | Germanic | Latn |
| Icelandic | isl | Indo-European | Germanic | Latn |
| Kölsch | ksh | Indo-European | Germanic | Latn |
| Luxembourgish | ltz | Indo-European | Germanic | Latn |
| Low German | nds | Indo-European | Germanic | Latn |
| Dutch | nld | Indo-European | Germanic | Latn |
| Norwegian | nor | Indo-European | Germanic | Latn |
| Swedish | swe | Indo-European | Germanic | Latn |
| Yiddish | yid | Indo-European | Germanic | Latn |
| Zeeuws | zea | Indo-European | Germanic | Latn |
| Modern Greek (1453-) | ell | Indo-European | Greek | Grek |
| Sindhi | snd | Indo-European | Indic | Arab |
| Urdu | urd | Indo-European | Indic | Arab |
| Assamese | asm | Indo-European | Indic | Assamese |
| Bengali | ben | Indo-European | Indic | Beng |
| Hindi | hin | Indo-European | Indic | Deva |
| Marathi | mar | Indo-European | Indic | Deva |
| Nepali (macrolanguage) | nep | Indo-European | Indic | Deva |
| Gujarati | guj | Indo-European | Indic | Gujarati |
| Oriya (macrolanguage) | ori | Indo-European | Indic | Odia |
| Panjabi | pan | Indo-European | Indic | Shahmukh |
| Sinhala | sin | Indo-European | Indic | Sinhala |
| Dhivehi | div | Indo-European | Indic | Thaana |
| Persian | fas | Indo-European | Iranian | Arab |
| Ossetian | oss | Indo-European | Iranian | Cyrl |
| Tajik | tgk | Indo-European | Iranian | Cyrl+Latn |
| Kurdish | kur | Indo-European | Iranian | Latn+Sorani |
| Mazanderani | mzn | Indo-European | Iranian | Persian |
| Pushto | pus | Indo-European | Iranian | Pushto |
| Asturian | ast | Indo-European | Romance | Latn |
| Catalan | cat | Indo-European | Romance | Latn |
| French | fra | Indo-European | Romance | Latn |
| Galician | glg | Indo-European | Romance | Latn |
| Italian | ita | Indo-European | Romance | Latn |
| Ligurian | lij | Indo-European | Romance | Latn |
| Neapolitan | nap | Indo-European | Romance | Latn |
| Occitan (post 1500) | oci | Indo-European | Romance | Latn |
| Piemontese | pms | Indo-European | Romance | Latn |
| Portuguese | por | Indo-European | Romance | Latn |
| Romansh | roh | Indo-European | Romance | Latn |
| Romanian | ron | Indo-European | Romance | Latn |
| Spanish | spa | Indo-European | Romance | Latn |
| Belarusian | bel | Indo-European | Slavic | Cyrl |
| Bulgarian | bul | Indo-European | Slavic | Cyrl |

| | | | | |
|---|---|---|---|---|
| Macedonian | mkd | Indo-European | Slavic | Cyrl |
| Russian | rus | Indo-European | Slavic | Cyrl |
| Ukrainian | ukr | Indo-European | Slavic | Cyrl |
| Czech | ces | Indo-European | Slavic | Latn |
| Kashubian | csb | Indo-European | Slavic | Latn |
| Serbo-Croatian | hbs | Indo-European | Slavic | Latn |
| Upper Sorbian | hsb | Indo-European | Slavic | Latn |
| Polish | pol | Indo-European | Slavic | Latn |
| Slovak | slk | Indo-European | Slavic | Latn |
| Slovenian | slv | Indo-European | Slavic | Latn |
| Japanese | jpn | Japanese | Japanese | Jpan |
| Georgian | kat | Kartvelian | Kartvelian | Georgian |
| Mingrelian | xmf | Kartvelian | Kartvelian | Latn |
| Korean | kor | Korean | Korean | Kore |
| Chechen | che | Nakh-Daghestanian | Nakh | Cyrl |
| Kinyarwanda | kin | Niger-Congo | Bantu | Latn |
| Lingala | lin | Niger-Congo | Bantu | Latn |
| Swahili (macrolanguage) | swa | Niger-Congo | Bantu | Latn |
| Yoruba | yor | Niger-Congo | Defoid | Latn |
| Igbo | ibo | Niger-Congo | Igboid | Latn |
| Quechua | que | Quechuan | Quechuan | Latn |
| Tibetan | bod | Sino-Tibetan | Bodic | Tibetan |
| Burmese | mya | Sino-Tibetan | Burmese-Lolo | Mon–Burmese |
| Chinese | zho | Sino-Tibetan | Chinese | Chinese |
| Thai | tha | Tai-Kadai | Kam-Tai | Thai |
| Guarani | grn | Tupian | Maweti-Guarani | Latn |
| Estonian | est | Uralic | Finnic | Latn |
| Finnish | fin | Uralic | Finnic | Latn |
| Veps | vep | Uralic | Finnic | Latn |
| Hungarian | hun | Uralic | Ugric | Latn |

Table 26: Task Adapter training dataset details (taken from Wikiann (Pan et al., 2017)) for Named Entity Recognition.

| **NLI Task Adapter Training Dataset** | | | | |
|---|---|---|---|---|
| Language | iso-639 | Family | Genus | Script |
| Arabic | ara | Afro-Asiatic | Semitic | Arab |
| Turkish | tur | Altaic | Turkic | Latn |
| Vietnamese | vie | Austro-Asiatic | Vietic | Latn |
| German | deu | Indo-European | Germanic | Latn |
| English | eng | Indo-European | Germanic | Latn |
| Modern Greek (1453-) | ell | Indo-European | Greek | Grek |
| Urdu | urd | Indo-European | Indic | Arab |
| Hindi | hin | Indo-European | Indic | Deva |
| French | fre | Indo-European | Romance | Latn |
| Spanish | spa | Indo-European | Romance | Latn |
| Bulgarian | bul | Indo-European | Slavic | Cyrl |
| Russian | rus | Indo-European | Slavic | Cyrl |
| Swahili (macrolanguage) | swa | Niger-Congo | Bantu | Latn |
| Chinese | zho | Sino-Tibetan | Chinese | Chinese |
| Thai | tha | Tai-Kadai | Kam-Tai | Thai |

Table 27: Task Adapter training dataset details (taken from XNLI (Conneau et al., 2018)) for Natural Language Inference.

| **Extractive Question Answering Task Adapter Training Dataset** | | | | |
|---|---|---|---|---|
| Language | iso-639 | Family | Genus | Script |
| Arabic | ara | Afro-Asiatic | Semitic | Arab |
| Indonesian | idn | Astronesian | Malay | Latn |
| Telugu | tel | Dravidian | Dravidian | Telu |
| English | eng | Indo-European | Germanic | Latn |
| Bengali | ben | Indo-European | Indic | Beng |
| Russian | rus | Indo-European | Slavic | Cyrl |
| Korean | kor | Korean | Korean | Kore |
| Swahili (macrolanguage) | swa | Niger-Congo | Bantu | Latn |
| Finnish | fin | Uralic | Finnic | Latn |

Table 28: Task Adapter training dataset details (taken from TyDiQA (Clark et al., 2020)) for Extractive Question Answering.

| | Evaluation Languages | | | | | | |
|---|---|---|---|---|---|---|---|
| | Language | iso-639 | NER | UDP and POS | XNLI | ANLI | TyDiQA |
| 1 | Achinese | ace | | X | X | X | X |
| 2 | Afrikaans | afr | | | X | X | X |
| 3 | Assyrian Neo-Aramaic | aii | X | | X | X | X |
| 4 | South Levantine Arabic | ajp | X | | X | X | X |
| 5 | Akkadian | akk | X | | X | X | X |
| 6 | Amharic | amh | | | X | X | X |
| 7 | Apurinã | apu | X | | X | X | X |
| 8 | Akuntsu | aqz | X | | X | X | X |
| 9 | Arabic | ara | | | X | X | |
| 10 | Karo (Brazil) | arr | X | | | X | X |
| 11 | Assamese | asm | | X | X | X | X |
| 12 | Asturian | ast | | X | X | X | X |
| 13 | Aymara | aym | | X | X | | X |
| 14 | Azerbaijani | aze | | X | X | X | X |
| 15 | Bashkir | bak | | X | X | X | X |
| 16 | Bambara | bam | X | | X | X | X |
| 17 | Bavarian | bar | | X | X | X | X |
| 18 | Belarusian | bel | | | X | X | X |
| 19 | Bengali | ben | | | X | X | |
| 20 | Bhojpuri | bho | X | | X | X | X |
| 21 | Tibetan | bod | | X | X | X | X |
| 22 | Breton | bre | | | X | X | X |
| 23 | Bulgarian | bul | | | X | X | X |
| 24 | Russia Buriat | bxr | X | | | X | X |
| 25 | Catalan | cat | | | X | X | X |
| 26 | Cebuano | ceb | | X | X | X | X |
| 27 | Czech | ces | | | X | X | X |
| 28 | Chechen | che | | X | X | X | X |
| 29 | Church Slavic | chu | X | | X | X | X |
| 30 | Chuvash | chv | | X | X | X | X |
| 31 | Chukot | ckt | X | | X | X | X |
| 32 | Coptic | cop | X | | X | X | X |
| 33 | Crimean Tatar | crh | | X | X | X | X |
| 34 | Kashubian | csb | | X | X | X | X |
| 35 | Welsh | cym | | | X | X | X |
| 36 | Danish | dan | | | X | X | X |
| 37 | German | deu | | | | X | X |
| 38 | Dhivehi | div | | X | X | X | X |
| 39 | Modern Greek (1453-) | ell | | | | X | X |
| 40 | English | eng | | | | X | |
| 41 | Estonian | est | | | X | X | X |
| 42 | Basque | eus | | | X | X | X |
| 43 | Faroese | fao | | | X | X | X |
| 44 | Persian | fas | | | X | X | X |
| 45 | Finnish | fin | | | X | X | |
| 46 | French | fra | | | | X | X |
| 47 | Old French (842-ca. 1400) | fro | X | | X | X | X |
| 48 | Northern Frisian | frr | | X | X | X | X |
| 49 | Western Frisian | fry | | X | X | X | X |
| 50 | Scottish Gaelic | gla | | | X | X | X |
| 51 | Irish | gle | | | X | X | X |
| 52 | Galician | glg | | | X | X | X |
| 53 | Manx | glv | X | | X | X | X |
| 54 | Gothic | got | X | | X | X | X |
| 55 | Ancient Greek (to 1453) | grc | X | | X | X | X |
| 56 | Guarani | grn | | X | X | | X |
| 57 | Swiss German | gsw | X | | X | X | X |
| 58 | Guajajára | gub | X | | X | X | X |
| 59 | Gujarati | guj | | X | X | X | X |
| 60 | Mbyá Guaraní | gun | X | | X | X | X |
| 61 | Serbo-Croatian | hbs | | X | X | X | X |
| 62 | Hebrew | heb | | | X | X | X |
| 63 | Hindi | hin | | | | X | X |
| 64 | Croatian | hrv | X | | X | X | X |

| | | | | | | | |
|---|---|---|---|---|---|---|---|
| 65 | Upper Sorbian | hsb | | | X | X | X |
| 66 | Hungarian | hun | | | X | X | X |
| 67 | Armenian | hye | | | X | X | X |
| 68 | Igbo | ibo | | X | X | X | X |
| 69 | Iloko | ilo | | X | X | X | X |
| 70 | Indonesian | ind | X | | X | X | |
| 71 | Icelandic | isl | | | X | X | X |
| 72 | Italian | ita | | | X | X | X |
| 73 | Javanese | jav | | X | X | X | X |
| 74 | Japanese | jpn | | | X | X | X |
| 75 | Kannada | kan | | X | X | X | X |
| 76 | Georgian | kat | | X | X | X | X |
| 77 | Kazakh | kaz | | | X | X | X |
| 78 | Khunsari | kfm | X | | X | X | X |
| 79 | Khmer | khm | | X | X | X | X |
| 80 | Kinyarwanda | kin | | X | X | X | X |
| 81 | Kirghiz | kir | | X | X | X | X |
| 82 | Northern Kurdish | kmr | X | | X | X | X |
| 83 | Komi-Permyak | koi | X | | X | X | X |
| 84 | Korean | kor | | | X | X | |
| 85 | Komi-Zyrian | kpv | X | | X | X | X |
| 86 | Karelian | krl | X | | X | X | X |
| 87 | Kölsch | ksh | | X | X | X | X |
| 88 | Kurdish | kur | | X | X | X | X |
| 89 | Latin | lat | X | | X | X | X |
| 90 | Latvian | lav | | | X | X | X |
| 91 | Ligurian | lij | | | X | X | X |
| 92 | Lingala | lin | | X | X | X | X |
| 93 | Lithuanian | lit | | | X | X | X |
| 94 | Luxembourgish | ltz | | X | X | X | X |
| 95 | Literary Chinese | lzh | X | | X | X | X |
| 96 | Malayalam | mal | | X | X | X | X |
| 97 | Marathi | mar | | | X | X | X |
| 98 | Moksha | mdf | X | | X | X | X |
| 99 | Macedonian | mkd | | X | X | X | X |
| 100 | Malagasy | mlg | | X | X | X | X |
| 101 | Maltese | mlt | | | X | X | X |
| 102 | Mongolian | mon | | X | X | X | X |
| 103 | Makuráp | mpu | X | | X | X | X |
| 104 | Maori | mri | | X | X | X | X |
| 105 | Malay (macrolanguage) | msa | | X | X | X | X |
| 106 | Burmese | mya | | X | X | X | X |
| 107 | Mundurukú | myu | X | | X | X | X |
| 108 | Erzya | myv | X | | X | X | X |
| 109 | Mazanderani | mzn | | X | X | X | X |
| 110 | Neapolitan | nap | | | X | X | X |
| 111 | Low German | nds | | | X | X | X |
| 112 | Nepali (macrolanguage) | nep | | X | X | X | X |
| 113 | Dutch | nld | | | X | X | X |
| 114 | Norwegian | nor | | | X | X | X |
| 115 | Nayini | nyq | X | | X | X | X |
| 116 | Occitan (post 1500) | oci | | X | X | X | X |
| 117 | Livvi | olo | X | | X | X | X |
| 118 | Oriya (macrolanguage) | ori | | X | X | X | X |
| 119 | Old Russian | orv | X | | X | X | X |
| 120 | Ossetian | oss | | X | X | X | X |
| 121 | Old Turkish | otk | X | | X | X | X |
| 122 | Panjabi | pan | | X | X | X | X |
| 123 | Nigerian Pidgin | pcm | X | | X | X | X |
| 124 | Piemontese | pms | | X | X | X | X |
| 125 | Polish | pol | | | X | X | X |
| 126 | Portuguese | por | | | X | X | X |
| 127 | Pushto | pus | | X | X | X | X |
| 128 | Cusco Quechua | qhe | X | | X | X | X |
| 129 | Pomak | qpm | X | | X | X | X |
| 130 | Turkish German | qtd | X | | X | X | X |
| 131 | Quechua | que | | X | X | | X |
| 132 | Romansh | roh | | X | X | X | X |

| | | | | | | | | |
|---|---|---|---|---|---|---|---|---|
| 133 | Romanian | ron | | | | X | X | X |
| 134 | Russian | rus | | | | | X | |
| 135 | Yakut | sah | | X | | X | X | X |
| 136 | Sanskrit | san | X | | | X | X | X |
| 137 | Sinhala | sin | | X | | X | X | X |
| 138 | Slovak | slk | | | | X | X | X |
| 139 | Slovenian | slv | | | | X | X | X |
| 140 | Northern Sami | sme | X | | | X | X | X |
| 141 | Skolt Sami | sms | X | | | X | X | X |
| 142 | Sindhi | snd | | X | | X | X | X |
| 143 | Soi | soj | X | | | X | X | X |
| 144 | Somali | som | | X | | X | X | X |
| 145 | Spanish | spa | | | | | X | X |
| 146 | Albanian | sqi | | | | X | X | X |
| 147 | Serbian | srp | X | | | X | X | X |
| 148 | Sundanese | sun | | X | | X | X | X |
| 149 | Swahili (macrolanguage) | swa | | X | | | X | |
| 150 | Swedish | swe | | | | X | X | X |
| 151 | Swedish Sign Language | swl | X | | | X | X | X |
| 152 | Tamil | tam | | | | X | X | X |
| 153 | Tatar | tat | | X | | X | X | X |
| 154 | Telugu | tel | | | | X | X | |
| 155 | Tajik | tgk | | X | | X | X | X |
| 156 | Tagalog | tgl | | | | X | X | X |
| 157 | Thai | tha | | | | | X | X |
| 158 | Tupinambá | tpn | X | | | X | X | X |
| 159 | Turkmen | tuk | | X | | X | X | X |
| 160 | Turkish | tur | | | | | X | X |
| 161 | Uighur | uig | | | | X | X | X |
| 162 | Ukrainian | ukr | | | | X | X | X |
| 163 | Urubú-Kaapor | urb | X | | | X | X | X |
| 164 | Urdu | urd | | | | | X | X |
| 165 | Uzbek | uzb | | X | | X | X | X |
| 166 | Veps | vep | | X | | X | X | X |
| 167 | Vietnamese | vie | | | | | X | X |
| 168 | Waray (Philippines) | war | | X | | X | X | X |
| 169 | Warlpiri | wbp | X | | | X | X | X |
| 170 | Wolof | wol | X | | | X | X | X |
| 171 | Mingrelian | xmf | | X | | X | X | X |
| 172 | Kangri | xnr | X | | | X | X | X |
| 173 | Yiddish | yid | | X | | X | X | X |
| 174 | Yoruba | yor | | | | X | X | X |
| 175 | Cantonese | yue | X | | | X | X | X |
| 176 | Zeeuws | zea | | X | | X | X | X |
| 177 | Chinese | zho | | | | | X | X |
| 178 | Bribri | bzc | X | X | | X | | X |
| 179 | Asháninka | cni | X | X | | X | | X |
| 180 | Huichol | hch | X | X | | X | | X |
| 181 | Nahuatl | nah | X | X | | X | | X |
| 182 | Otomí | oto | X | X | | X | | X |
| 183 | Shipibo-Konibo | shp | X | X | | X | | X |
| 184 | Rarámuri | tar | X | X | | X | | X |

Table 29: Evaluation languages for all six tasks.

## O FAQ

1. What are the main contributions of this study and the difference of our approach with other methods?

    - First, note that our paper introduces a method for studying cross-lingual transfer, not necessarily a method for improving cross-lingual transfer. We deviate from this "standard" way of using adapters for two reasons:

        (a) Training a task adapter on many languages, as a preliminary step, allows this component to learning the `task`, regardless of language. This is necessary for disentangling the effect of task and language in our analysis.

        (b) We then finetune the whole model (and not introduce a new adapter) exactly because we now want to study the effect of the language. While introducing a new language adapter might have a similar effect, there's additional hurdles to do so: the language adapter would need more data to be trained, as it would be randomly initialized; our approach instead can work even with a single batch/update, so it is applicable even for very, very low-resource scenarios.

    - Secondly, we propose a strategy to visually represent the language-language interaction utilizing the adapter-based fusion method. In general, training fully bilingual or trilingual for a different combination of languages are very expensive. This is why, we opt to have trained language adapter modules and then fuse together according to the need in an efficient manner.

2. What is the reason for selecting the 38 transfer languages, including the 11 unseen languages? Why why include the 11 unseen languages from pre-training?

    - **Language selection**: No other particular reasons except selecting a broader range of transfer languages covering language families and typological diversity. These 38 languages in total cover 10 language families, 26 genus and 14 script variations.

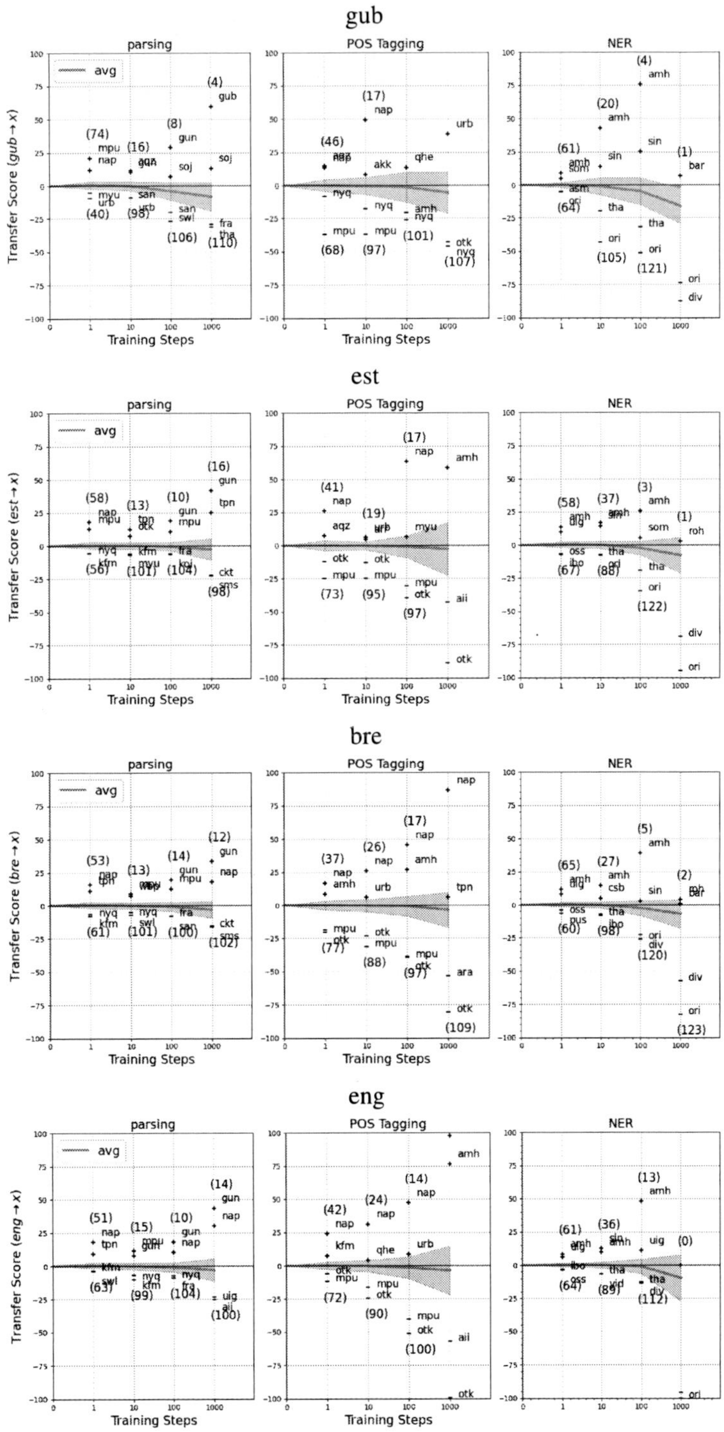


Figure 9: Aggregated Transfer Progression through training steps

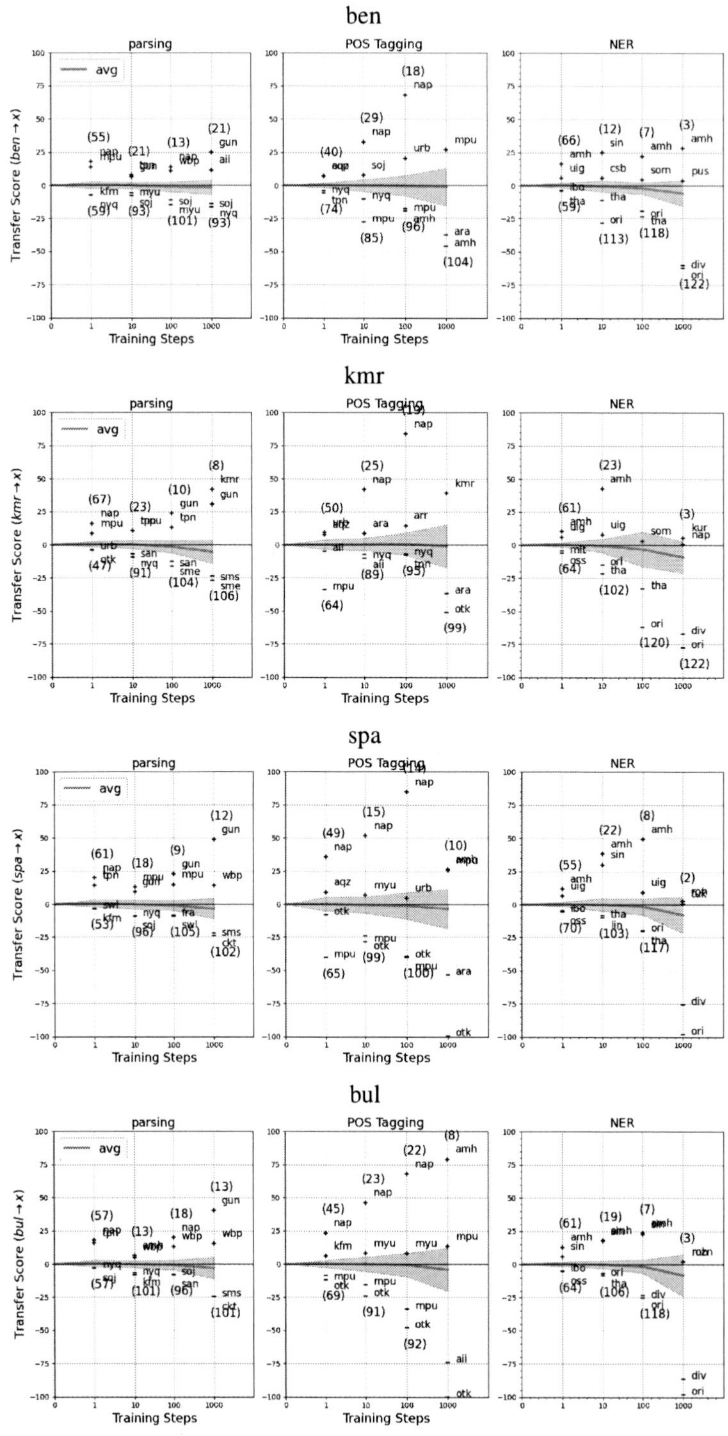


Figure 10: Aggregated Transfer Progression through training steps

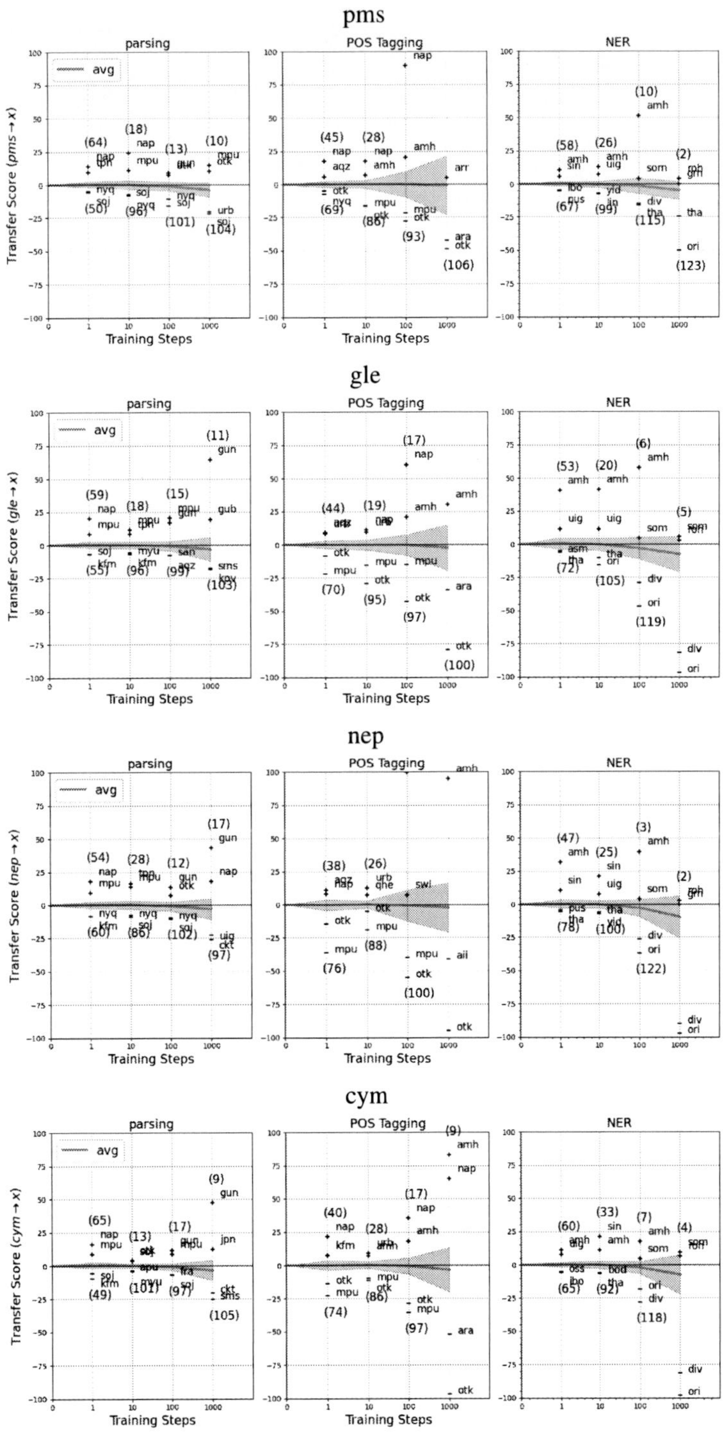


Figure 11: Aggregated Transfer Progression through training steps

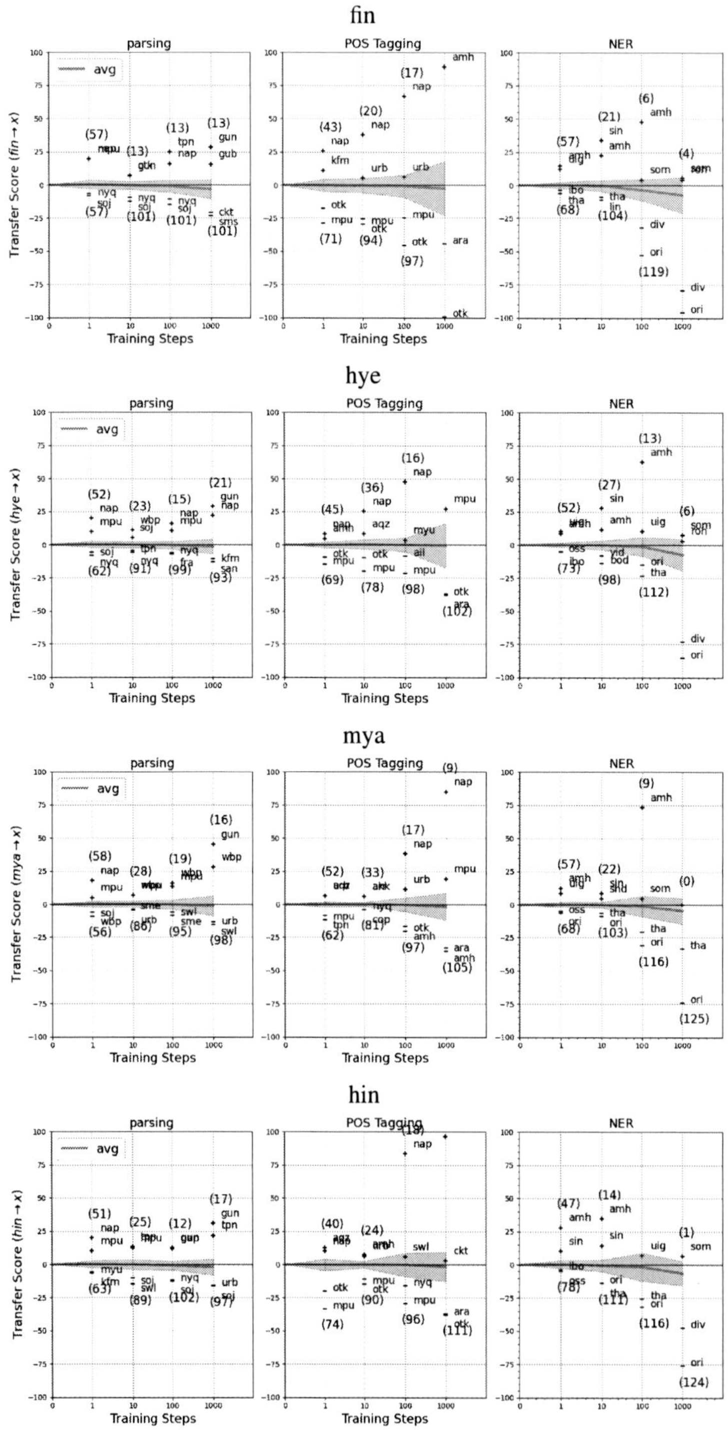


Figure 12: Aggregated Transfer Progression through training steps

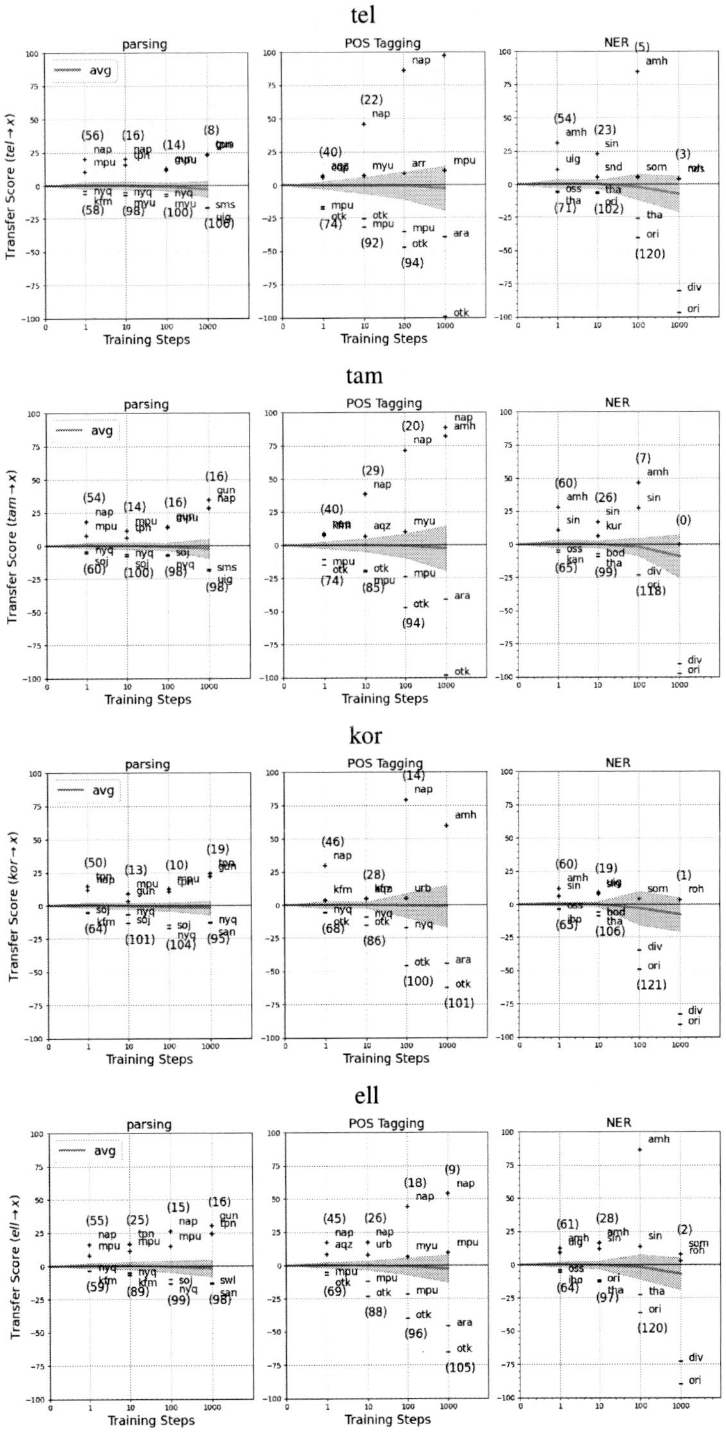


Figure 13: Aggregated Transfer Progression through training steps

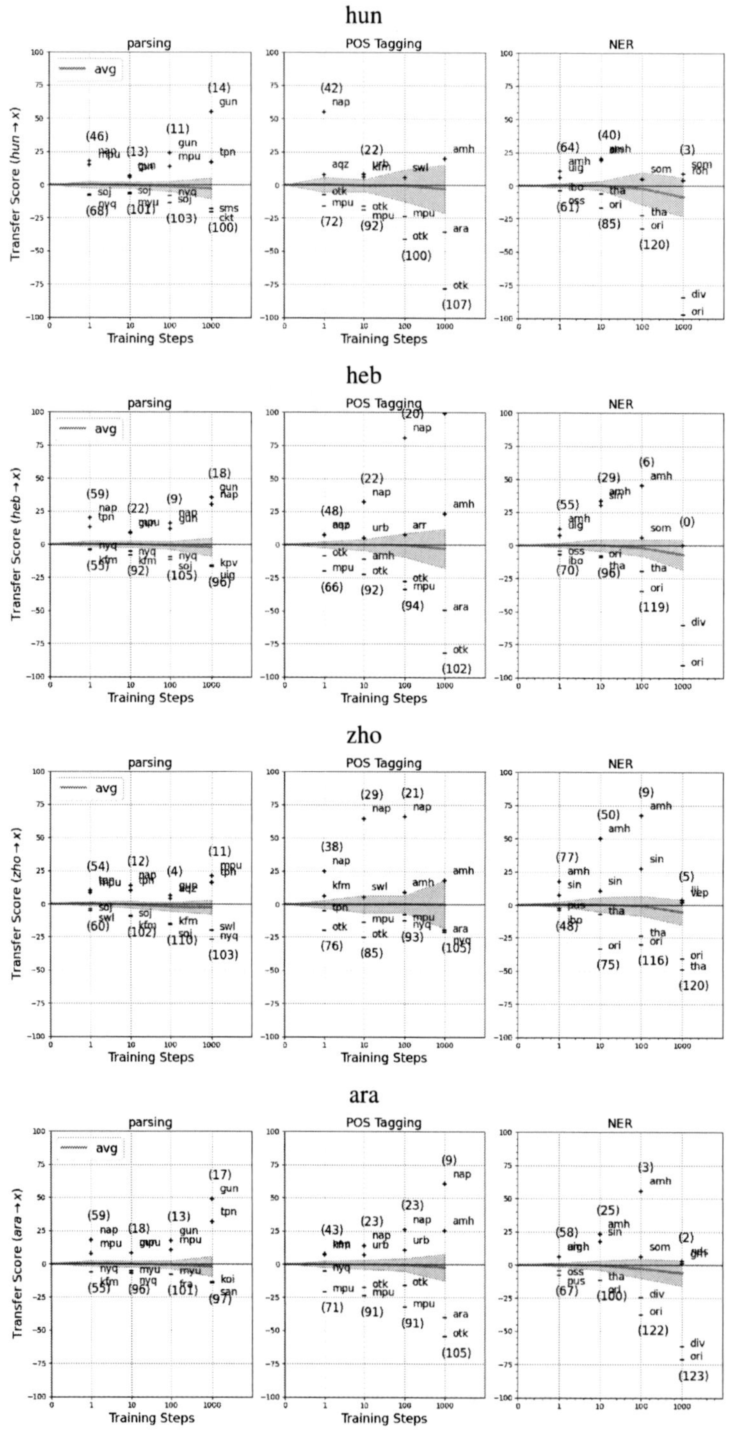


Figure 14: Aggregated Transfer Progression through training steps

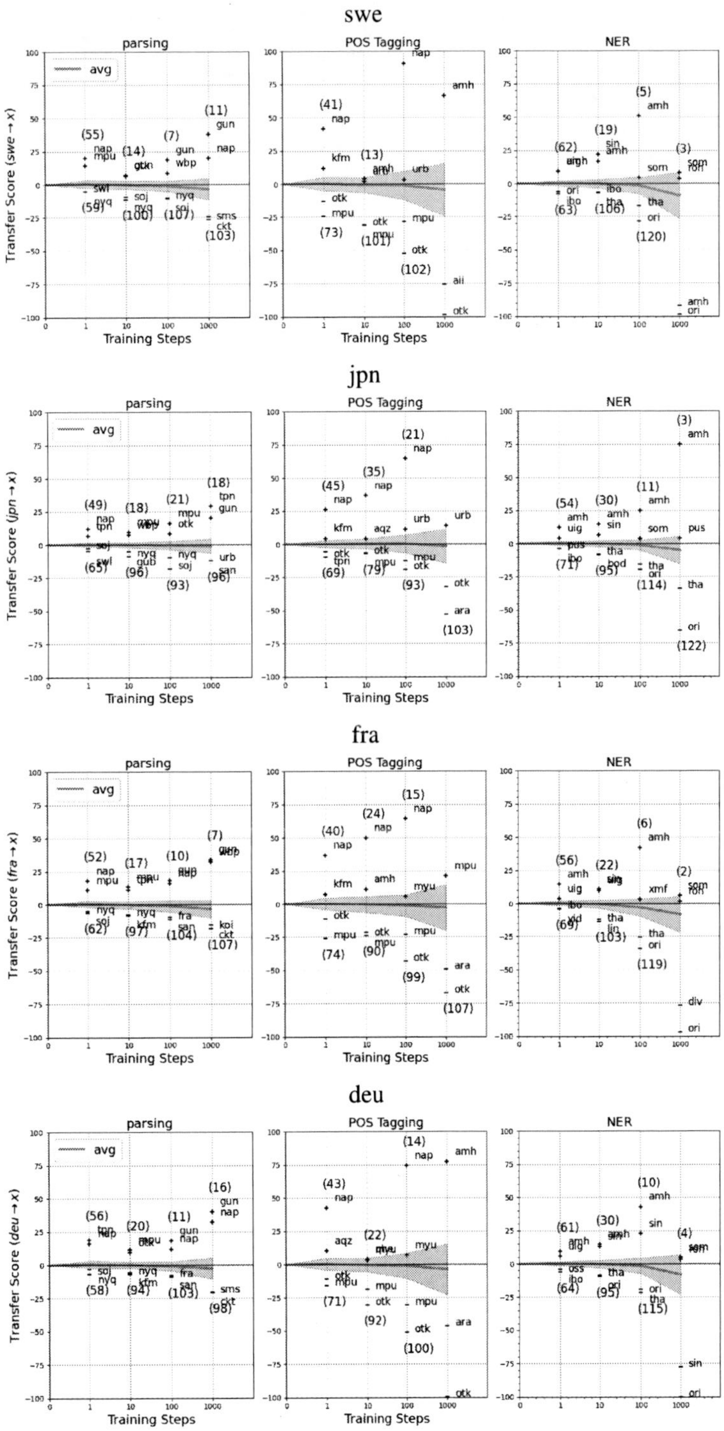


Figure 15: Aggregated Transfer Progression through training steps

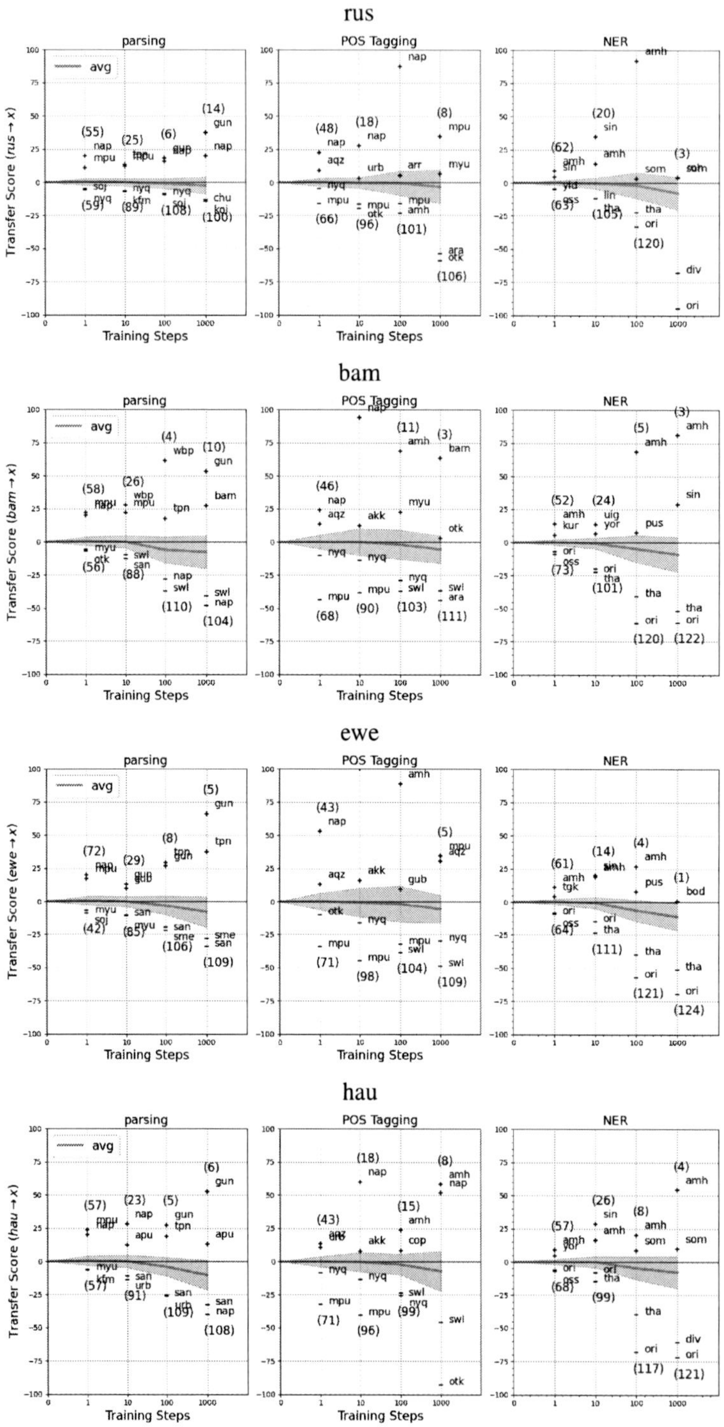


Figure 16: Aggregated Transfer Progression through training steps

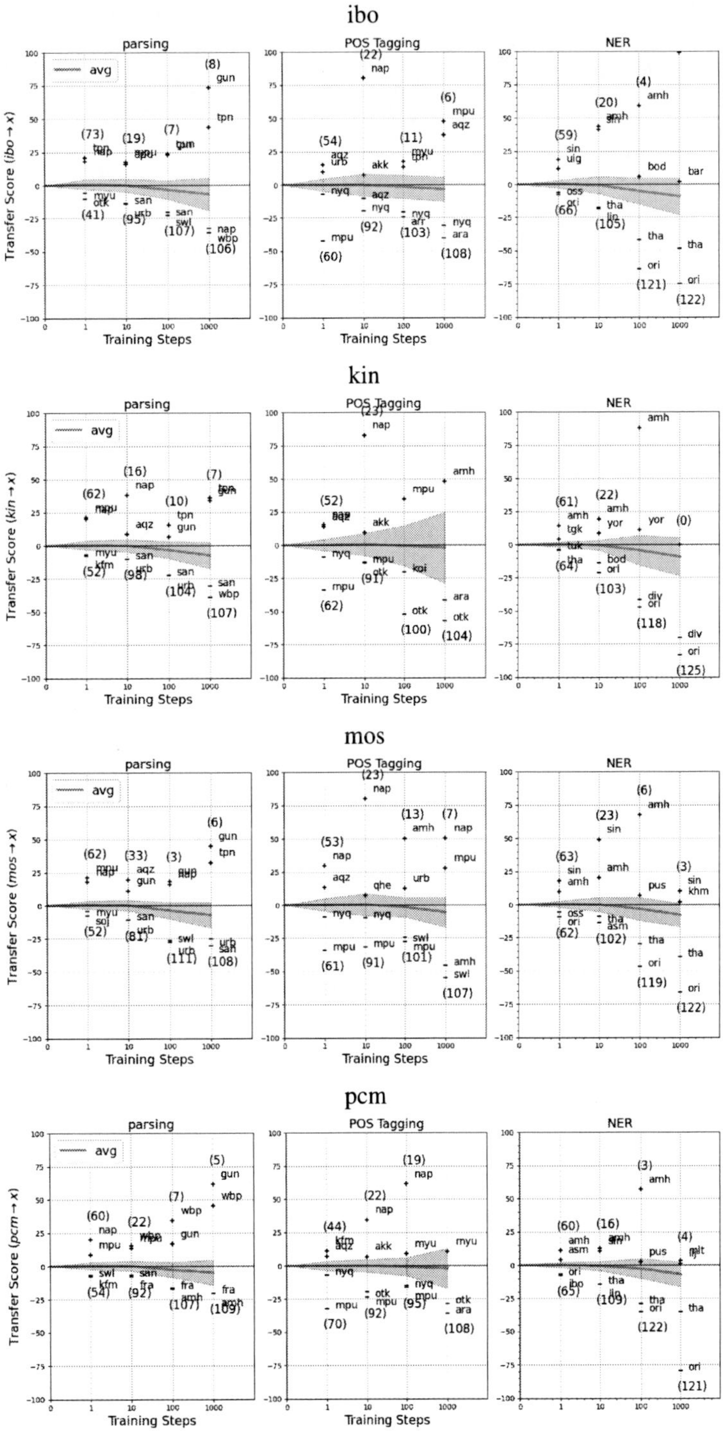


Figure 17: Aggregated Transfer Progression through training steps

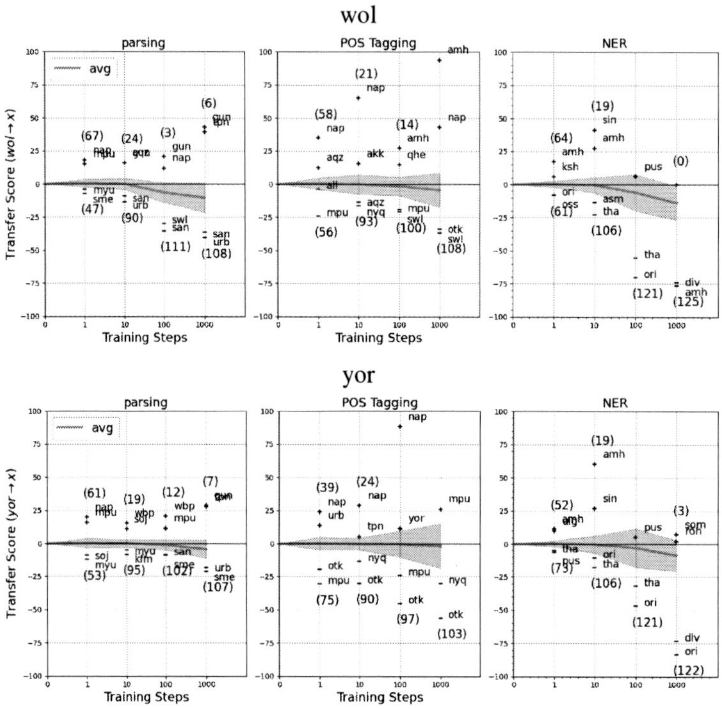

Figure 18: Aggregated Transfer Progression through training steps

# Are You Sure? Rank Them Again: Repeated Ranking For Better Preference Datasets

**Peter Devine**
Lightblue Inc. (Tokyo, Japan)
peter@lightblue-tech.com

## Abstract

Training Large Language Models (LLMs) with Reinforcement Learning from AI Feedback (RLAIF) aligns model outputs more closely with human preferences. This involves an evaluator model ranking multiple candidate responses to user prompts. However, the rankings from popular evaluator models such as GPT-4 can be inconsistent.

We propose the Repeat Ranking method, in which we evaluate the same responses multiple times and train only on those responses which are consistently ranked. Using 2,714 training prompts in 62 languages, we generated responses from 7 top multilingual LLMs and had GPT-4 rank them five times each. Evaluating on MT-Bench chat benchmarks in six languages, our method outperformed the standard practice of training on all available prompts.

Our work highlights the quality versus quantity trade-off in RLAIF dataset generation and offers a stackable strategy for enhancing dataset and thus model quality.

## 1 Introduction

Reinforcement learning has been shown to improve large language model (LLM) performance significantly (Yao et al., 2023; Havrilla et al., 2024), with this form of learning instructing an LLM both how *to* and how *not to* generate text.

This has come in the forms of Reinforcement Learning from Human Feedback (RLHF) (Ouyang et al., 2022) and Reinforcement Learning from Artificial Intelligence Feedback (RLAIF) (Bai et al., 2022b; Lee et al., 2023), where a human or AI is used, respectively, to determine the relative quality of multiple responses to a given prompt. Based on these quality rankings, high quality and low quality responses are defined as "positive" and "negative" and this preference dataset is then used to train an LLM either with the help of a reward model or by directly training using a method such as Proximal Policy Optimisation (PPO) (Schulman et al., 2017), Direct Policy Optimisation (DPO) (Rafailov et al., 2024), or Odds Ratio Preference Optimisation (ORPO) (Hong et al., 2024). This style of training has lead to many of the improvements in recent years in LLM training, with both GPT-3.5 (Ouyang et al., 2022), trained with RLHF, and Starling (Zhu et al., 2023), trained with RLAIF, demonstrating gains upon previous state-of-the-art performance across many evaluation benchmarks.

Most publicly available preference data is monolingual, but we hypothesize that training a model on multilingual preference data will improve the resultant model's multilingual capabilities. This prompted us to create a multilingual preference dataset.

We follow previous methods for creating HLAIF preference datasets such as Nectar (Zhu et al., 2023) by first sampling human generated prompts from public datasets before generating various responses to each prompt using seven state-of-the-art LLMs. We then use a state-of-the-art LLM, GPT-4, to evaluate the relative ranking of each response.

However, we found that when the evaluation process was repeated on the same responses, different rankings were sometimes output by GPT-4. This suggested that the definition of positive and negative labels in these instances had a lower confidence than instances where GPT-4 would consistently output the same ranking given a set of responses.

Therefore, we hypothesized that training only on rankings that GPT-4 consistently outputs over multiple evaluations would lead to greater downstream evaluation performance compared to training on all rankings, both consistent and inconsistent. This lead us to propose the Repeat Ranking method, whereby responses are evaluated multiple times and the consistency of the rankings is used as a filter for inclusion or exclusion from the training set. A representation of our Repeated Ranking method can be found in Fig. 1.

We conducted experiments in which 2,714 mul-



*Proceedings of the Fourth Workshop on Multilingual Representation Learning (MRL 2024)*, pages 93–105
November 16, 2024 ©2024 Association for Computational Linguistics

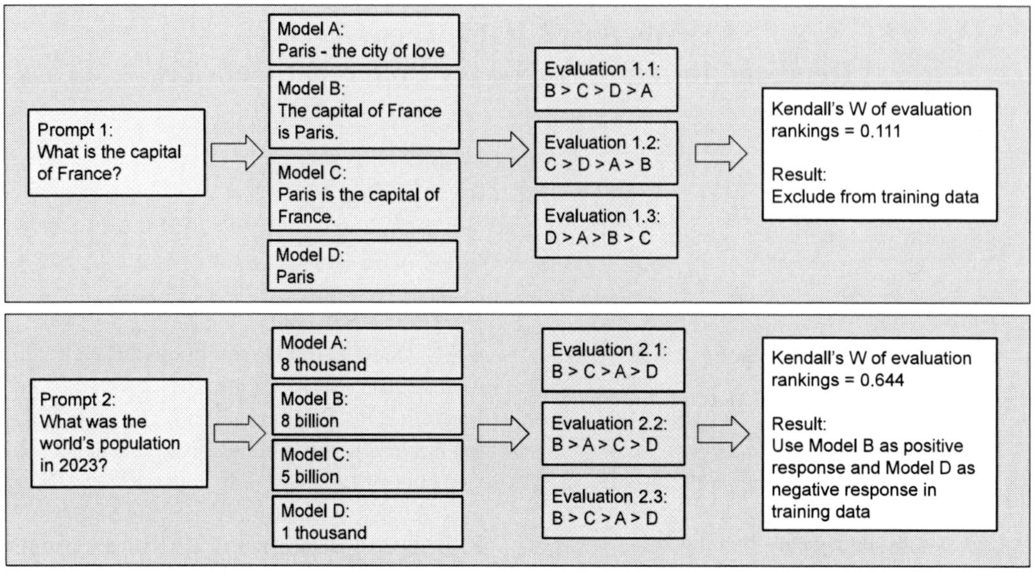


Figure 1: A visual description of how we select our data for training. We use our Repeat Ranking method to repeat the evaluations of the models multiple times and then only train on the best and worst responses which have a high Kendall's W, a measure of ranking agreement, associated with their ranking.

tilingual prompts were selected and 7 LLMs were used to generate responses for each prompt. We then evaluated each set of 7 responses 5 times using GPT-4. Finally, we propose a novel method for filtering evaluated preferences by measuring the consistency of the set of rankings for each evaluation using Kendall's W (Kendall and Smith, 1939). We conducted experiments training an LLM using all rankings, as well as the 75%, 50%, and 25% most consistent rankings. We then evaluated each trained model using the MT-Bench benchmark across 6 languages.

Our results show that training on the more consistently ranked responses gives greater downstream evaluation performance compared to training on all data for a majority of languages tested.

Our findings inform the creation of future preference datasets and offer a method of improving the quality of existing preference datasets. This may open up exciting new avenues for training LLMs and highlights the importance of high quality positive and negative data when training using RLAIF.

We make our training data[1], training code[2], and trained models[3] available online.

## 2 Related Work

LLM chat performance has been improved by training on RLHF datasets in multiple works within the literature.

The RLHF dataset used to train InstructGPT was created by having users and paid annotators evaluate multiple responses to a given prompt and indicating their preferred prompt (Ouyang et al., 2022). This work stated that "most comparisons are only labeled by 1 contractor for cost reasons" and that "having examples labeled multiple times could help identify areas where our contractors disagree, and thus where a single model is unlikely to align to all of them", indicating the seeming importance of having consistently similarly ranked preference data when training with RLHF.

In contrast, the OpenAssistant Conversations (OASST1) dataset (Köpf et al., 2024), contains conversation prompts and responses that are written by volunteers, with the responses evaluated by multiple volunteers. While this is a large dataset of more than 10,000 individual messages, over 70% of these conversations are in either English or Spanish, reducing OASST1's applicability to training a

[1]https://huggingface.co/datasets/lightblue/mitsu

[2]https://github.com/lightblue-tech/suzume/tree/main/mitsu

[3]https://huggingface.co/lightblue/suzume-llama-3-8B-multilingual-orpo-borda-half

multilingual model.

Generating data using human labellers is also costly, which is why several datasets have been constructed for RLAIF.

Previous work includes the use of "Constitutional AI" (Bai et al., 2022b) whereby an LLM is prompted to respond to a prompt before being tasked with revising that response to be less harmful and in line with principles set by researchers. The LLM then generates a less harmful response and the original and revised responses are then used to train another LLM using reinforcement learning.

Further work showed that training using RLAIF can lead to similar human evaluation scores compared to RLHF (Lee et al., 2023). This work also showed that RLAIF by training directly on response evaluation scores elicited from LLMs achieves greater down-stream task performance compared to the Constitutional AI approach of having an LLM revise existing responses.

Nectar (Zhu et al., 2023) is a preference dataset which first samples prompts from a variety of open source datasets, before generating responses based on these prompts using seven state-of-the-art LLMs (GPT-4, GPT-3.5-turbo, GPT-3.5-turbo-instruct, Command R+, Command R, LLama-2-7B-chat, and Mistral-7B-Instruct). These responses are then ranked once by GPT-4 and these rankings are used to train the Starling Alpha and Beta models using reinforcement learning. These prompts and responses are also all in English, meaning that this dataset is not suitable for training a multilingual model.

Due to the paucity of high quality multilingual models existing within the literature, we create one, which we call Mitsu.

Previous work has also shown that filtering reinforcement learning data can lead to higher downstream task accuracy (Morimura et al., 2024). However, this approach relies on an external reward model to choose which data to filter, limiting the application of this approach to domains and languages that no existing reward model has been trained on.

## 3 Method

The overall objective of this piece of work was to create an LLM that was more proficient at multilingual chat than previous LLMs. In the course of creating such an LLM, we generated also insights into the process of creating high quality preference datasets. This section details how we used our Repeated Ranking method to make our training dataset named Mitsu, how we trained our model, and finally how we evaluated our LLM.

### 3.1 Preference Dataset Creation with Repeated Rankings

We create our Mitsu dataset by first following the process of how Nectar (Zhu et al., 2023) was developed by sampling human generated prompts derived from open source datasets such as the LMSYS-Chat-1M dataset (Zheng et al., 2023). Specifically, we select the multilingual stratified sample of prompts from the Tagengo dataset (Devine, 2024), which consists of 76,338 diverse human generated prompts in 74 languages. In order to reduce the costs of generating the dataset, we further stratify by languages, randomly sampling a maximum of 100 prompts per language. For languages with less than 100 prompts in the original dataset, we used all prompts for that language. This resulted in 2,996 prompts in total being selected.

Following the method used in the creation of the Nectar dataset, we used our sampled prompts to generate responses from seven state-of-the-art models. These were GPT-4 (gpt-4-0125-preview) (Achiam et al., 2023), GPT-3.5 Turbo (gpt-35-turbo-0301) (Ouyang et al., 2022), Command R (Gomez, 2024)[4], Command R+ (Gomez, 2024)[5], Qwen 1.5 32B Chat (Bai et al., 2023)[6], Qwen 1.5 72B Chat (Bai et al., 2023)[7], Starling 7B Beta (Zhu et al., 2023)[8].

These models were all chosen for their ability to output at least some multilingual text, which is why we did not consider using high performing but monolingual models such as Llama 3 (AI@Meta, 2024).

Our text generation settings were as follows. We set the generation temperature to 0 for all models, as some models such as Qwen have been shown to require smaller generation temperatures due to their larger vocabulary size and in order to make the generation deterministic to some extend. Future work could explore using more sophisticated tem-

[4]https://huggingface.co/CohereForAI/c4ai-command-r-v01

[5]https://huggingface.co/CohereForAI/c4ai-command-r-plus

[6]https://huggingface.co/Qwen/Qwen1.5-32B-Chat

[7]https://huggingface.co/Qwen/Qwen1.5-72B-Chat

[8]https://huggingface.co/Nexusflow/Starling-LM-7B-beta

perature set-ups per model, language, or prompt. We set our maximum number of tokens to generate as 2,048, and we discard any responses that have not been completed within this token limit. This was done to reduce both generation and evaluation time and costs, but future work could explore using longer generated sequences for a preference dataset. We used the popular vLLM library (Kwon et al., 2023) to generate responses with our local models, which were all models except GPT-4 and GPT-3.5-turbo. For GPT-4 and GPT-3.5-turbo, we generated responses using the Azure OpenAI endpoint. This resulted in 2,762 prompts having 7 full responses (one from each model), which we then ranked.

Our response evaluation again was conducted similarly to Nectar, where we used a similar system message describing the criteria for evaluating prompts as the original Nectar system message. We added one additional evaluation criteria to the original system message, which was "Is the response written naturally and fluently in the language that the prompter would expect?". This was added to make sure that highly rated responses were not correct but English responses to non-English prompts, which can occur in some LLMs.

Aside from our response evaluation criteria, we included a statement in the system message that instructed GPT-4 to output both a short explanation of the merits and drawbacks of each response, before outputting a ranking of the responses. This ranking consisted of responses labelled by alphabet character, using greater than ('>') and equals ('=') signs to determine which responses were evaluated as better and which were of equal quality. To avoid a systematic bias in our evaluations, responses were input to GPT-4 in a randomised order, with the responses being labelled A-G in order. We also take inspiration from work in generating the Nectar dataset in which randomised pairwise comparisons were used by instructing GPT-4 to write the explanation of the ranking in a dictated randomised order. The system message that we used in this work can be found in Figure 3 in the Appendix.

This ranking was generated by using a generation temperature of 0 and a maximum number of generated tokens as 1,024 with the gpt-4-0125-preview version of GPT-4. This resulted in a ranking for each set of 7 responses for each prompt.

Initial experiments investigating the reliability of this ranking showed that the ranking was liable to change significantly for some prompts. We rationalise this as follows. Imaging that a user asked three models "What is the capital of France?", and the responses were "Paris", "Lyon", and "Delhi". In this case, most human evaluators would be able rank the "Paris" answer as being the best answer and "Delhi" as being the worst answer. However, if the responses were instead more indistinguishable in terms of response quality, for example "Paris", "The capital city of France is Paris", and "Paris is the capital of France.", then even human evaluators may struggle to agree on which constituted the best and worst answers given the prompt. We hypothesize that for the same reason, AI evaluators give inconsistent rankings when faced with responses that are more indistinguishable from one another. Reinforcement learning techniques such as ORPO (Hong et al., 2024), which performs monolithic preference optimization without a reference model, rely on sufficiently different positive and negative training labels that an LLM can learn the contrast between the two. Therefore, training on too-similar positive and negative labels may result in a degeneracy of the model overall. Hence, when we observed the lack of consistency in GPT-4's rankings for some responses, we hypothesized that training on only the more consistently ranked outputs would lead to a better evaluation performance than training on all rankings. Therefore, we repeat the ranking process five times, only changing the random order of the responses and the instructed random order of the ranking explanation each time. We discarded any cases in which a generation failed or where the ranking could not be parsed from the generated evaluation, leaving 2,714 individual prompts. We found that only 8.4% of all top responses were ranked top all 5 times, and only 20.2% of bottom responses were ranked bottom all 5 times, which again motivates our work in generating multiple evaluations for each set of responses per prompt.

With these responses, we calculated the Kendall's W (Kendall and Smith, 1939) for each set of rankings. According to Field, "Kendall's Coefficient of Concordance, W, is a measure of the agreement between several judges who have rank ordered a set of entities" (Field, 2005), and we use it to determine how well the repeated evaluation rankings agree. We justify using Kendall's W as a measure of inter-ranker agreement due to its previous use as a measure of ranking agreement within

| Model name | Average Borda Count |
|---|---|
| GPT-3.5 Turbo | 15.91 |
| Starling 7B Beta | 16.57 |
| Qwen 1.5 32B | 18.17 |
| Command R | 20.47 |
| Qwen 1.5 72B | 20.51 |
| Command R + | 21.54 |
| GPT-4 | 26.78 |

Table 1: Average Borda count per model across 5 evaluations.

the mathematical literature. However, since we ultimately just use the top and bottom responses from our rankings, we consider that comparing only the rankings of those two responses directly could possibly be simpler and could potentially lead to better results. We leave this for future work to explore this avenue.

We use this W score to generate three training subsets of Mitsu, where we only trained on responses with the top 25% (674 prompts), 50% (1,350 prompts), 75% (2,018 prompts) of W scores. We also trained a model using the entire Mitsu dataset (2,714 prompts).

In order to train using ORPO, we selected positive and negative responses to prompts. These effectively train a model to generate outputs similar to the positive responses and dissimilar to the negative responses. We selected these responses by calculating the Borda Count (Borda, 1781; Reilly, 2002) of each response over the 5 evaluations, and then selecting the models with the highest and lowest Borda counts for positive and negative, respectively. We randomly sample in cases where there is a tie in the Borda score between the multiple best or worst scores.

Table 1 shows the average Borda score for each model evaluated and Fig. 2 shows the amount of times each model's response was used as the positive and negative response.

We make the top 25%, top 50%, top 75%, and full training datasets available online[9].

### 3.2 Training

We train using our prepared datasets on Suzume 8B Multilingual (Devine, 2024), a multilingual finetune of Llama 3 (AI@Meta, 2024), using ORPO. We chose to train using ORPO due to its demonstrated greater performance compared to the most popular other current RLAIF method, DPO (Hong et al., 2024). We trained using the ORPO settings made available on the Axolotl LLM training package[10] which uses the TRL (von Werra et al., 2020) implementation of the ORPO algorithm. We chose to train on the Suzume 8B Multilingual model as it has the highest MT-Bench scores for a majority of evaluation languages compared to other commercially usable open source models under 10 billion parameters. We train for one epoch for each dataset with an ORPO alpha value set to 0.1, our maximum token sequence length was set to 8,192, and our learning rate was set to 8e-6. The full training configuration for each model can be found on their model cards[11].

For convenience, we refer to the models trained on the top 25%, 50%, 75%, and 100% of W score subsets as Suzume-ORPO-25, Suzume-ORPO-50, Suzume-ORPO-75, and Suzume-ORPO-100, respectively.

### 3.3 Evaluation

We evaluate our models using the multilingual version of the MT-Bench score over 6 languages (Chinese, English, French, German, Japanese, and Russian). This evaluation tests a model's ability to perform tasks such as writing, roleplay, extraction, reasoning, math, coding, STEM knowledge, and humanities knowledge in a given language, using GPT-4-Turbo as the evaluator of the model's responses. Each category contains 10 prompts, with each response being ranked out of 10, to give a final average score over all prompts. We report the 2-turn scores on this benchmark. Note that we do not report Russian performance on math, coding, and reasoning questions as reference answers were not available for these questions. We evaluate all four of our ORPO trained models (Suzume-ORPO-25, Suzume-ORPO-50, Suzume-ORPO-75, and Suzume-ORPO-100), as well as our base model (Suzume-Base) on the MT-Bench benchmark over all 6 languages. As a further baseline, we also evaluate the GPT-3.5-Turbo model (Ouyang et al., 2022) on each language.

As an additional evaluation, we evaluate over

[9]Available at in https://huggingface.co/collections/lightblue/mitsu-datasets-67076f8293b57ae8b2c17293

[10]https://github.com/OpenAccess-AI-Collective/axolotl

[11]Available at https://huggingface.co/collections/lightblue/orpo-experiments-6707702969a9340fa312405f

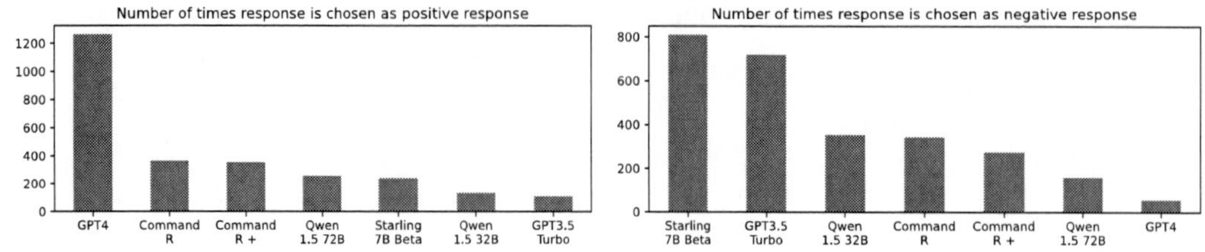


(a) Positive responses

(b) Negative responses

Figure 2: Plots of how often each model's response was chosen as the positive/negative response for training using the Borda count. We observe that a plurality but not a majority of our positive training data comes from GPT-4, while the vast majority of our negative training data comes from responses by Starling and GPT-3.5-Turbo.

the Belebele benchmark, which is a log-probability based benchmark which calculates the probabilities for generating the correct answer tokens given a prompt compared to the probabilities of generating three possible incorrect answers (Bandarkar et al., 2023). We report the accuracy, which is the percentage of test examples where the probability of generating the correct answer from the prompt was higher than the probability of outputting any of the wrong answers. We apply this benchmark over the 6 languages we use in our MT-Bench evaluation, as well as 6 other languages that we selected at random: Arabic, Azerbaijani, Bangla, Croatian, Norwegian, and Thai. Note that this does not test an LLM's chat abilities, but rather tests an LLM's ability to output factual information.

## 4 Results

Table 2 presents the MT-Bench scores across 6 languages for our 4 ORPO subsets compared to the base model and GPT-3.5-Turbo.

All ORPO models surpassed the base model in nearly every language, underscoring the value of ORPO training for enhancing chat capabilities. Furthermore, Suzume-ORPO-50 outperformed Suzume-ORPO-100 in 5 out of 6 languages, despite being trained on half the data. Suzume-ORPO-25 and Suzume-ORPO-75 achieved the highest scores in one language each, but Suzume-ORPO-50 provided the best overall balance.

While the base model did not exceed GPT-3.5-Turbo in any language, Suzume-ORPO-50 outperformed GPT-3.5-Turbo in 4 out of 6 languages, demonstrating that ORPO training enables LLMs match or surpass GPT-3.5-Turbo on chat benchmarks. However, GPT-3.5-Turbo still led in English and Japanese.

We also conducted other small scale tests to further probe the effects of ORPO training. One notable test (Suzume-ORPO-GPT on Table 4) was training using all prompt responses from the models with the best and worst Borda scores, GPT-4 and GPT-3.5 respectively, but we found that this lead to a lower average MT-Bench scores compared to the Suzume-ORPO-100 model. This indicates the importance of model diversity and selecting appropriate responses when generating RLAIF datasets.

Another test (Llama-ORPO-50 on Table 4) we conducted was directly ORPO training a Llama 3 8B Instruct model on the same dataset as Suzume-ORPO-50, but we found that this model had lower MT-Bench scores across all languages. This demonstrates the continued necessity for finetuning before conducting ORPO training.

The final small scale test (Suzume-ORPO-random-50 on Table 4) we conducted was training a model on a randomly selected half of the entire Mitsu dataset. This allowed us to isolate the effects of example selection by using Kendall's W, as this model was trained on the same amount of data as Suzume-ORPO-50. We find that Suzume-ORPO-random-50 model has lower MT-Bench scores across all languages compared to Suzume-ORPO-50, indicating the importance of selecting training prompts based on Kendall's W score.

The Belebele scores for each of our trained models can be found in Table 3. We observe that the base model exhibits greater or equal performance on average on this benchmark compared to Suzume-ORPO-100. This contrasts with our MT-Bench scores which showed that ORPO training unambiguously improved chat performance compared to the base model. However, despite the observed drop in Belebele score when performing full ORPO training, we also observe that Suzume-ORPO-75 and Suzume-ORPO-25 are able to largely achieve

| Language | GPT-3.5-Turbo | Suzume-Base | Suzume-ORPO-100 | Suzume-ORPO-75 | Suzume-ORPO-50 | Suzume-ORPO-25 |
|---|---|---|---|---|---|---|
| Chinese | 7.55 | 7.11 | 7.65 | **7.77** | 7.74 | 7.44 |
| English | **8.26** | 7.73 | 7.98 | 7.94 | 7.98 | 8.22 |
| French | 7.74 | 7.66 | **7.84** | 7.46 | 7.78 | 7.81 |
| German | 7.68 | 7.26 | 7.28 | 7.64 | 7.70 | **7.71** |
| Japanese | **7.84** | 6.56 | 7.20 | 7.12 | 7.34 | 7.04 |
| Russian | 7.94 | 8.19 | 8.30 | 8.74 | **8.94** | 8.81 |
| Mean | 7.83 | 7.42 | 7.71 | 7.78 | **7.91** | 7.84 |

Table 2: The MT-Bench chat benchmark scores for each model evaluated across each language. Bolded values are greatest in their row. We improve upon base model evaluation performance across all languages for nearly all ORPO models. Interestingly, we find that training on the 50% most consistently evaluated prompts leads to greater than or equal evaluation scores than training on all prompts for 5 of 6 languages evaluated.

comparable or better performance with the base model on many languages in this benchmark. This indicates that our ORPO training data selection criteria may be beneficial to mitigating some of the issues we demonstrate of lower performance on log-probability based for ORPO trained models.

We also observe that Suzume Base performs better on two languages (Chinese and Thai) than any ORPO trained model. This may simply be due to the fact that OPRO training, and particularly naive ORPO training (i.e. Suzume ORPO-100), seems to result in reduced performance in Belebele and so even when selecting training examples using Kendall's W, the drop in performance is too large to compensate for.

## 5 Discussion

Our results demonstrate the importance of ORPO training in improving the chat abilities of finetuned models. This, in turn, highlights the importance of creating high quality preference datasets to train LLMs using the ORPO method. Our results showing that model trained on less, but more consistently evaluated, preferences can achieve greater chat benchmark performance than training on all the data. This has the double benefits of increasing performance while reducing training cost by as much as four times for training on our 25% training subset. However, the extra inference computation required to rank responses multiple times is an increased cost with this method of dataset creation.

This could benefit both current and future datasets, with datasets such as Nectar (Zhu et al., 2023) potentially being improved by re-evaluating the dataset's responses and filtering out less consistently evaluated rows.

We theorize that the correct balance between consistency and data volume (i.e. where the cut-off for Kendall's W would be) may vary between tasks, but we have shown that for our multilingual chat setting the benefit on evaluation performance of having a threshold above which we keep our data.

Our results are also purely dataset-based, meaning that they might be able to be stacked with other recent LLM training methods such as SimPO (Meng et al., 2024) and ExPO (Zheng et al., 2024a).

## 6 Future Work

Our results suggest that the technique of repeated evaluations on preference data and only keeping the consistently evaluated prompts and responses for training could be applied to other RLAIF and RLHF datasets. Future work could include investigating whether training only using prompts and responses with high agreement in the evaluations from human annotators could lead to higher accuracy than training on all prompts and responses.

Another potential avenue for future work is using more than one evaluator model for ranking responses. In this work, we only used GPT-4, but there are other state-of-the-art LLMs such as Claude 3 (Anthropic, 2024) and Gemini 1.5 Pro (Reid et al., 2024). We theorize that combining the evaluations of multiple high performance LLMs could serve to create more robust evaluations of responses and mitigate the demonstrated bias that any one LLM exhibits (Feng et al., 2023; Cao et al., 2023). The Mitsu dataset that we use to train our model is single-turn, meaning that each example

| | Suzume Base | Suzume ORPO-100 | Suzume ORPO-75 | Suzume ORPO-50 | Suzume ORPO-25 |
|---|---|---|---|---|---|
| Arabic | 64.3 | 52.6 | **65.3** | 54.7 | 64.6 |
| Azerbaijani | 50.3 | 37.6 | **52.3** | 45.3 | 52.1 |
| Bangla | 46.0 | 37.0 | **49.7** | 43.2 | 46.3 |
| Chinese | **78.0** | 64.4 | 76.1 | 70.0 | 75.7 |
| Croatian | 59.4 | 47.4 | 60.7 | 53.0 | **61.1** |
| English | 84.2 | 75.2 | 83.2 | 83.0 | **84.7** |
| French | 77.3 | 64.4 | 75.7 | 72.2 | **77.6** |
| German | 68.0 | 53.8 | 67.9 | 65.9 | **68.8** |
| Japanese | 66.7 | 57.1 | 63.7 | 58.2 | **68.0** |
| Norwegian | 67.0 | 52.4 | 67.2 | 62.2 | **67.7** |
| Russian | 71.6 | 51.9 | 71.4 | 57.3 | **72.9** |
| Thai | **63.3** | 47.9 | 61.3 | 57.1 | 63.0 |
| **Mean** | 66.4 | 53.5 | 66.2 | 60.2 | **66.9** |

Table 3: Belebele scores for each trained model across the 12 languages that we evaluate on. We observe that full ORPO training leads to much lower Belebele scores compared to the base fine-tuned model. However, we also observe that our method of selecting fewer ORPO training examples is able to marginally improve on the performance of the base model for most languages.

consists of a single prompt-response pair for both positive and negative responses. Future work could expand on this to add multi-turn conversations, as was done by Nectar (Zhu et al., 2023).

The Mitsu dataset also consists of prompts sampled from the Tagengo dataset (Devine, 2024), which are derived from users prompts to LLMs hosted on a demo site. We theorize that these prompts are a mixture of easy and difficult for an LLM to answer. Training on tasks that LLMs are already highly proficient at might be a waste of training resources, so future work could filter prompts based on their perceived difficulty for LLMs. We believe that this may improve LLMs abilities on these difficult tasks.

In our experiments, we chose to rank responses 5 times due to that being the financial limit of our experiment. However, future work could empirically find an optimal number of times to repeat evaluations to obtain a reliable Kendall's W score.

A slight limitation of the Repeated Ranking approach is the increased inference cost in evaluating responses multiple times as an analogue for determining the confidence of the ranking model in the ranking. Future work could explore mitigating this effect by evaluating the combined log probability of a single ranking output and training using only the responses from rankings with the highest probability.

Tools and agents have also been shown to augment the abilities of LLMs (Parisi et al., 2022; Gao et al., 2023; Schick et al., 2024). Future work could explore using tools or agents to enhance the evaluation abilities of the evaluator LLM when evaluating prompt responses. For example, a search tool could determine the veracity of factual claims, or a calculator tool would be able to confirm the mathematical results of an LLM. We theorize that this would lead to more accurate evaluation and would ultimately lead to more accurate LLMs.

## 7 Conclusion

In this study, we explored the impact of repeated rankings from an AI evaluator (GPT-4) on training reinforcement learning from AI feedback (RLAIF) models for multilingual chat capabilities. We found that responses evaluated consistently by GPT-4 led to higher downstream performance across multiple languages, compared to training on all data regardless of evaluation consistency. Our findings indicate that selective training based on evaluation consistency can enhance chat performance and offer a method to improve existing preference datasets. This highlights the balance between quality and quantity when constructing datasets for RLAIF. Our work opens avenues for further optimizing RLAIF datasets and refining training methodologies to develop more proficient multilingual LLMs.

## Limitations

One limitation of this work was the size of the data that we trained upon. Our Mitsu dataset, in total, consisted of less than 3k examples, whereas many popular preference datasets such as Nectar (Zhu et al., 2023) and the HH-RLHF (Bai et al., 2022a) dataset consist of hundreds of thousands of examples. Therefore, we are yet to show whether our proposed response selection technique extends to datasets of that size.

Secondly, the differences in our results are relatively small. While we show relatively consistent improvement in chat performance in models trained over our selected subsets (Suzume-ORPO-25, Suzume-ORPO-50, Suzume-ORPO-75) over the model trained on the whole dataset (Suzume-ORPO-100), these differences are small in magnitude (largely <10% difference). It is nevertheless notable that even demonstrating that chat performance does not decrease with fewer training examples is a useful result that can inform more efficient ORPO training in the future. Therefore, it remains for future work to determine if the improvements in chat ability increase with a larger training set.

Finally, a limitation of this research is that we rely on GPT-4 for our evaluation using the MT-Bench benchmark. This could bias the model as GPT-4 has been shown to exhibit self-enhancement bias (Zheng et al., 2024b), where it evaluates its own responses higher compared to human evaluation, indicating that we may be overfitting to GPT-4's preferences rather than general human ones. However, GPT-4 is the current state-of-the-art for LLMs and has been shown to have very high correlation with human preferences (Zheng et al., 2024b). Moreover, our evaluations using Belebele dataset do not use an LLM for evaluation and again indicate that the accuracy of some of our ORPO trained models over many languages increases compared to the base model.

## Ethics Statement

We have considered the ethical implications of releasing both our training data and trained models. There is the potential for LLMs and training data to be misused, but since we demonstrate that our final LLM is comparable to a publicly available LLM (GPT-3.5-Turbo) that has since been superceded by more recent LLMs (GPT-4, Llama 405B (Dubey et al., 2024) etc.), we assume that the risk impact of our sharing these models and data is minimal.

## References


Josh Achiam, Steven Adler, Sandhini Agarwal, Lama Ahmad, Ilge Akkaya, Florencia Leoni Aleman, Diogo Almeida, Janko Altenschmidt, Sam Altman, Shyamal Anadkat, et al. 2023. Gpt-4 technical report. *arXiv preprint arXiv:2303.08774*.

AI@Meta. 2024. Llama 3 model card.

AI Anthropic. 2024. The claude 3 model family: Opus, sonnet, haiku. *Claude-3 Model Card*.

Jinze Bai, Shuai Bai, Yunfei Chu, Zeyu Cui, Kai Dang, Xiaodong Deng, Yang Fan, Wenbin Ge, Yu Han, Fei Huang, Binyuan Hui, Luo Ji, Mei Li, Junyang Lin, Runji Lin, Dayiheng Liu, Gao Liu, Chengqiang Lu, Keming Lu, Jianxin Ma, Rui Men, Xingzhang Ren, Xuancheng Ren, Chuanqi Tan, Sinan Tan, Jianhong Tu, Peng Wang, Shijie Wang, Wei Wang, Shengguang Wu, Benfeng Xu, Jin Xu, An Yang, Hao Yang, Jian Yang, Shusheng Yang, Yang Yao, Bowen Yu, Hongyi Yuan, Zheng Yuan, Jianwei Zhang, Xingxuan Zhang, Yichang Zhang, Zhenru Zhang, Chang Zhou, Jingren Zhou, Xiaohuan Zhou, and Tianhang Zhu. 2023. Qwen technical report. *arXiv preprint arXiv:2309.16609*.

Yuntao Bai, Andy Jones, Kamal Ndousse, Amanda Askell, Anna Chen, Nova DasSarma, Dawn Drain, Stanislav Fort, Deep Ganguli, Tom Henighan, et al. 2022a. Training a helpful and harmless assistant with reinforcement learning from human feedback. *arXiv preprint arXiv:2204.05862*.

Yuntao Bai, Saurav Kadavath, Sandipan Kundu, Amanda Askell, Jackson Kernion, Andy Jones, Anna Chen, Anna Goldie, Azalia Mirhoseini, Cameron McKinnon, et al. 2022b. Constitutional ai: Harmlessness from ai feedback. *arXiv preprint arXiv:2212.08073*.

Lucas Bandarkar, Davis Liang, Benjamin Muller, Mikel Artetxe, Satya Narayan Shukla, Donald Husa, Naman Goyal, Abhinandan Krishnan, Luke Zettlemoyer, and Madian Khabsa. 2023. The belebele benchmark: a parallel reading comprehension dataset in 122 language variants. *arXiv preprint arXiv:2308.16884*.

J. Borda. 1781. Mémoire sur les élections au scrutin. *Histoire de L'Académie Royale des Sciences, Paris*.

Yong Cao, Li Zhou, Seolhwa Lee, Laura Cabello, Min Chen, and Daniel Hershcovich. 2023. Assessing cross-cultural alignment between chatgpt and human societies: An empirical study. *arXiv preprint arXiv:2303.17466*.

Peter Devine. 2024. Tagengo: A multilingual chat dataset. *arXiv preprint arXiv:2405.12612*.

Abhimanyu Dubey, Abhinav Jauhri, Abhinav Pandey, Abhishek Kadian, Ahmad Al-Dahle, Aiesha Letman, Akhil Mathur, Alan Schelten, Amy Yang, Angela Fan, et al. 2024. The llama 3 herd of models. *arXiv preprint arXiv:2407.21783*.

Shangbin Feng, Chan Young Park, Yuhan Liu, and Yulia Tsvetkov. 2023. From pretraining data to language models to downstream tasks: Tracking the trails of political biases leading to unfair nlp models. *arXiv preprint arXiv:2305.08283*.

Andy P Field. 2005. Kendall's coefficient of concordance. *Encyclopedia of statistics in behavioral science*, 2:1010–11.

Luyu Gao, Aman Madaan, Shuyan Zhou, Uri Alon, Pengfei Liu, Yiming Yang, Jamie Callan, and Graham Neubig. 2023. Pal: Program-aided language models. In *International Conference on Machine Learning*, pages 10764–10799. PMLR.

Aidan Gomez. 2024. Command R: Retrieval-Augmented Generation at Production Scale.

Alex Havrilla, Yuqing Du, Sharath Chandra Raparthy, Christoforos Nalmpantis, Jane Dwivedi-Yu, Maksym Zhuravinskyi, Eric Hambro, Sainbayar Sukhbaatar, and Roberta Raileanu. 2024. Teaching large language models to reason with reinforcement learning. *arXiv preprint arXiv:2403.04642*.

Jiwoo Hong, Noah Lee, and James Thorne. 2024. Reference-free monolithic preference optimization with odds ratio. *arXiv preprint arXiv:2403.07691*.

Maurice G Kendall and B Babington Smith. 1939. The problem of m rankings. *The annals of mathematical statistics*, 10(3):275–287.

Andreas Köpf, Yannic Kilcher, Dimitri von Rütte, Sotiris Anagnostidis, Zhi Rui Tam, Keith Stevens, Abdullah Barhoum, Duc Nguyen, Oliver Stanley, Richárd Nagyfi, et al. 2024. Openassistant conversations-democratizing large language model alignment. *Advances in Neural Information Processing Systems*, 36.

Woosuk Kwon, Zhuohan Li, Siyuan Zhuang, Ying Sheng, Lianmin Zheng, Cody Hao Yu, Joseph E. Gonzalez, Hao Zhang, and Ion Stoica. 2023. Efficient memory management for large language model serving with pagedattention. In *Proceedings of the ACM SIGOPS 29th Symposium on Operating Systems Principles*.

Harrison Lee, Samrat Phatale, Hassan Mansoor, Kellie Lu, Thomas Mesnard, Colton Bishop, Victor Carbune, and Abhinav Rastogi. 2023. Rlaif: Scaling reinforcement learning from human feedback with ai feedback. *arXiv preprint arXiv:2309.00267*.

Yu Meng, Mengzhou Xia, and Danqi Chen. 2024. Simpo: Simple preference optimization with a reference-free reward. *arXiv preprint arXiv:2405.14734*.

Tetsuro Morimura, Mitsuki Sakamoto, Yuu Jinnai, Kenshi Abe, and Kaito Air. 2024. Filtered direct preference optimization. *arXiv preprint arXiv:2404.13846*.

Long Ouyang, Jeffrey Wu, Xu Jiang, Diogo Almeida, Carroll Wainwright, Pamela Mishkin, Chong Zhang, Sandhini Agarwal, Katarina Slama, Alex Ray, et al. 2022. Training language models to follow instructions with human feedback. *Advances in neural information processing systems*, 35:27730–27744.

Aaron Parisi, Yao Zhao, and Noah Fiedel. 2022. Talm: Tool augmented language models. *arXiv preprint arXiv:2205.12255*.

Rafael Rafailov, Archit Sharma, Eric Mitchell, Christopher D Manning, Stefano Ermon, and Chelsea Finn. 2024. Direct preference optimization: Your language model is secretly a reward model. *Advances in Neural Information Processing Systems*, 36.

Machel Reid, Nikolay Savinov, Denis Teplyashin, Dmitry Lepikhin, Timothy Lillicrap, Jean-baptiste Alayrac, Radu Soricut, Angeliki Lazaridou, Orhan Firat, Julian Schrittwieser, et al. 2024. Gemini 1.5: Unlocking multimodal understanding across millions of tokens of context. *arXiv preprint arXiv:2403.05530*.

Benjamin Reilly. 2002. Social choice in the south seas: Electoral innovation and the borda count in the pacific island countries. *International Political Science Review*, 23(4):355–372.

Timo Schick, Jane Dwivedi-Yu, Roberto Dessì, Roberta Raileanu, Maria Lomeli, Eric Hambro, Luke Zettlemoyer, Nicola Cancedda, and Thomas Scialom. 2024. Toolformer: Language models can teach themselves to use tools. *Advances in Neural Information Processing Systems*, 36.

John Schulman, Filip Wolski, Prafulla Dhariwal, Alec Radford, and Oleg Klimov. 2017. Proximal policy optimization algorithms. *arXiv preprint arXiv:1707.06347*.

Leandro von Werra, Younes Belkada, Lewis Tunstall, Edward Beeching, Tristan Thrush, Nathan Lambert, and Shengyi Huang. 2020. Trl: Transformer reinforcement learning. `https://github.com/huggingface/trl`.

Zhewei Yao, Reza Yazdani Aminabadi, Olatunji Ruwase, Samyam Rajbhandari, Xiaoxia Wu, Ammar Ahmad Awan, Jeff Rasley, Minjia Zhang, Conglong Li, Connor Holmes, et al. 2023. Deepspeed-chat: Easy, fast and affordable rlhf training of chatgpt-like models at all scales. *arXiv preprint arXiv:2308.01320*.

Chujie Zheng, Ziqi Wang, Heng Ji, Minlie Huang, and Nanyun Peng. 2024a. Weak-to-strong extrapolation expedites alignment. *arXiv preprint arXiv:2404.16792*.

Lianmin Zheng, Wei-Lin Chiang, Ying Sheng, Tianle Li, Siyuan Zhuang, Zhanghao Wu, Yonghao Zhuang, Zhuohan Li, Zi Lin, Eric. P Xing, Joseph E. Gonzalez, Ion Stoica, and Hao Zhang. 2023. Lmsys-chat-1m: A large-scale real-world llm conversation dataset.

Lianmin Zheng, Wei-Lin Chiang, Ying Sheng, Siyuan Zhuang, Zhanghao Wu, Yonghao Zhuang, Zi Lin, Zhuohan Li, Dacheng Li, Eric Xing, et al. 2024b. Judging llm-as-a-judge with mt-bench and chatbot arena. *Advances in Neural Information Processing Systems*, 36.

Banghua Zhu, Evan Frick, Tianhao Wu, Hanlin Zhu, Karthik Ganesan, Wei-Lin Chiang, Jian Zhang, and Jiantao Jiao. 2023. Starling-7b: Improving llm helpfulness & harmlessness with rlaif.

````
You are an evaluator AI. Your task is to rank multiple responses to a given prompt from best to worst
You will first be given the original prompt, and then seven possible responses to that prompt, labelled alphabetically.
You should first write a very brief (<40 words per model) explanation of the merits and drawbacks of the responses, before giving the ranking itself.
This explanation of each response should be in a randomised order (go in the order of '{randomly shuffled list of alphabet letters from A-G}').
Make sure you explain and rank all responses, do not leave any out in your explanation or ranking.
The ranking should be a list of alphabet characters that describe the ranking, with '>' denoting the left item is ranked higher than the right item and '=' denoting that the items are of equal ranking (e.g. 'Z>Y>X=W>V>U=T').

The user input will look like this:

```
<<<PROMPT>>>
AN EXAMPLE USER PROMPT

<<<RESPONSE A>>>
EXAMPLE RESPONSE A

<<<RESPONSE B>>>
EXAMPLE RESPONSE B

<<<RESPONSE C>>>
EXAMPLE RESPONSE C

<<<RESPONSE D>>>
EXAMPLE RESPONSE D

<<<RESPONSE E>>>
EXAMPLE RESPONSE E

<<<RESPONSE F>>>
EXAMPLE RESPONSE F

<<<RESPONSE G>>>
EXAMPLE RESPONSE G
```

and your output should look like this:

```
<<<EXPLANATION>>>
[SHORT EXPLANATION OF THE RANKING]

<<<RANKING>>>
[SEPARATED LIST OF ALPHABET CHARACTERS THAT DESCRIBE THE RANKING]
```

The evaluation rubric is as follows:

* Is the response relevant? The response should be the best possible answer.
* Is the response truthful?
* Is the response accurate? The response should accurately fulfill the prompt's request.
* If a creative answer is expected, is the response creative? If an analytical answer is expected, is the response factual/objectively correct?
* Is the response written naturally and fluently in the language that the prompter would expect?
* Is the response detailed? The response should at minimum satisfy the full level of detail required by the prompt.
````

Figure 3: System message for generating evaluations

| Language | GPT3.5-Turbo | Suzume-Base | Suzume-ORPO-100 | Suzume-ORPO-75 | Suzume-ORPO-50 | Suzume-ORPO-25 | Suzume-ORPO-GPT | Llama-ORPO-50 | Suzume-ORPO-random-50 |
|---|---|---|---|---|---|---|---|---|---|
| Chinese | 7.55 | 7.11 | 7.65 | **7.77** | **7.74** | 7.44 | 7.54 | 7.52 | 7.41 |
| English | **8.26** | 7.73 | 7.98 | 7.94 | 7.98 | 8.22 | 7.79 | 7.84 | 7.72 |
| French | 7.74 | 7.66 | **7.84** | 7.46 | 7.78 | 7.81 | 7.22 | 7.33 | 7.51 |
| German | 7.68 | 7.26 | 7.28 | **7.64** | 7.7 | **7.71** | 7.37 | 7.47 | 7.03 |
| Japanese | **7.84** | 6.56 | 7.2 | 7.12 | 7.34 | 7.04 | 7.14 | 7.22 | 6.82 |
| Russian | 7.94 | 8.19 | 8.3 | 8.74 | **8.94** | 8.81 | 8.34 | 8.68 | 8.32 |
| mean | 7.83 | 7.42 | 7.71 | 7.78 | **7.91** | 7.84 | 7.57 | 7.68 | 7.47 |

Table 4: Extended MT-Bench scores across 6 languages for all models evaluated, including small-scale tests.

# Tagengo: A Multilingual Chat Dataset

**Peter Devine**
Lightblue Inc. (Tokyo, Japan)
peter@lightblue-tech.com

## Abstract

Open source large language models (LLMs) have shown great improvements in recent times. However, many of these models are focused solely on popular spoken languages.

We present a high quality dataset of more than 70k prompt-response pairs in 74 languages which consist of human generated prompts and synthetic responses. We use this dataset to train a state-of-the-art open source English LLM to chat multilingually.

We evaluate our model on MT-Bench chat benchmarks in 6 languages, finding that our multilingual model outperforms previous state-of-the-art open source LLMs across each language. We further find that training on more multilingual data is beneficial to the performance in a chosen target language (Japanese) compared to simply training on only data in that language.

These results indicate the necessity of training on large amounts of high quality multilingual data to make a more accessible LLM.

## 1 Introduction

Recently, open source large language models (LLMs) have grown drastically in both popularity and performance. Models such as Llama 3 (AI@Meta, 2024b) have exceeded the performance of previous state-of-the-art proprietary models like GPT3.5 (Ouyang et al., 2022) on popular robust benchmarks including the Chatbot Arena leaderboard (Chiang et al., 2024). These open source LLMs are also increasingly being used in commercial AI chat products such as the Meta AI assistant (AI@Meta, 2024a).

However, many current LLMs exhibit lower performance on languages outside of English (Achiam et al., 2023). Indeed, Llama 3 itself is currently an English-only LLM, meaning that even when it is prompted in a language besides English, it often replies in English. This limits the potential user base of these LLMs due to the fact that less than 1.5 billion of the world's more than 8 billion population can speak English (Central Intelligence Agency, 2021; Eberhard et al., 2024). Therefore, we set out to train a state-of-the-art open source LLM (Llama 3) to be able to chat not only in English, but in many languages.

In order to make English-focused LLMs accessible in other languages, previous work has fine-tuned these models on non-English data (Sasaki et al., 2023; Sengupta et al., 2023; Nguyen et al., 2023).

Many multilingual chat datasets such as MultiAlpaca (Wei et al., 2023) and Aya (Singh et al., 2024) cover many languages and tasks but can also lack natural prompts and high quality responses.

For this reason, we created a large, diverse, high quality multilingual dataset using more than 70k human generated prompts in 74 languages and generated responses from these using state-of-the-art proprietary chat models. We used this dataset to train two models, a multilingual LLM and a Japanese-only LLM, both supervised fine-tuned models based on the Llama 3 8B Instruct model.

We found that our model achieved better evaluation scores on multilingual chat benchmarks compared to the similarly sized state-of-the-art open source models, indicating the high quality and diversity of our training dataset. We also find that our multilingual-trained LLM performs better on Japanese chat benchmarks compared to our Japanese-only-trained LLM, indicating that transfer learning from training on other languages is beneficial for training even monolingual models outside of English.

Our findings combine to inform the community of exactly how to fine-tune monolingual LLMs to create a strong multilingual model.

We make our training data (Tagengo)[1], train-

[1] https://huggingface.co/datasets/lightblue/tagengo-gpt4



*Proceedings of the Fourth Workshop on Multilingual Representation Learning (MRL 2024)*, pages 106–113
November 16, 2024 ©2024 Association for Computational Linguistics

ing code[2], evaluation benchmark (multilingual MT-Bench)[3], and trained models (Suzume)[4][5] publicly available for free use online.

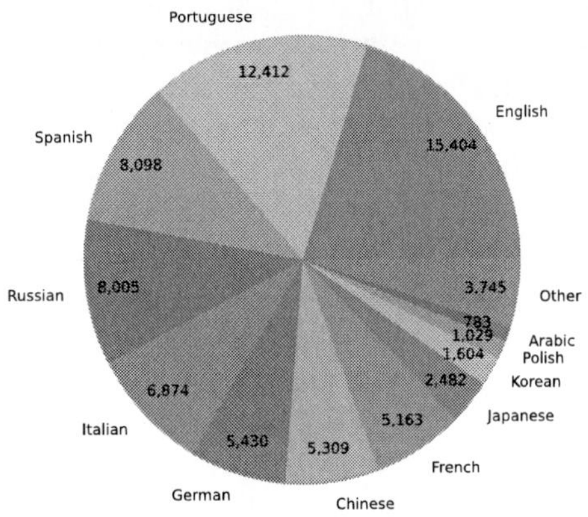


Figure 1: Distribution of the languages found in the Tagengo dataset

## 2 Related Work

In the literature, strong foundation models such as Llama 2 (Touvron et al., 2023) and Gemma (Team et al., 2024) have been subsequently fine-tuned on data from a specific language or languages, including Japanese (Sasaki et al., 2023), Arabic (Sengupta et al., 2023), and South-East Asian languages (Nguyen et al., 2023). Fine-tuning has often shown to improve the accuracy of the resultant LLM on tasks in that language. However, the training dataset of these models are often not shared, making it difficult to create a truly multilingual LLM across many languages.

Some multilingual chat datasets do exist that can be used for training LLMs. MultiAlpaca (Wei et al., 2023) is a multilingual dataset of 133K prompt-response pairs covering 11 languages that were generated in a similar manner to Alpaca (Taori et al., 2023). This dataset was created by generating synthetic prompts from a small number of English seed prompts and then answering these prompts using an large-scale LLM, GPT3.5 (Ouyang et al., 2022). Because these prompts are generated synthetically, this data may not reflect the sorts of prompts that real users may use with an LLM, potentially limiting the ability of models trained on this data to be used practically. Moreover, the prompts and responses for this dataset were generated using GPT3.5, meaning that the quality of the data may not be as high as if a state-of-the-art LLM was used, like GPT4 (Achiam et al., 2023).

xP3 (Crosslingual Public Pool of Prompts) (Muennighoff et al., 2022) is a dataset of more than 78 million examples covering 46 languages. This dataset was generated by templating other datasets (e.g. translation datasets, classification datasets) into a prompt-response format. While this dataset is large, the templating process limits the usefulness of the dataset as it results in prompts that are not necessarily similar to what an actual user of an LLM would ask. The templating process can also result in unnatural answers, with single word answers being given where a fuller answer may be more appropriate from an LLM.

Aya (Singh et al., 2024) is a dataset of 204k human-annotated prompt-completion pairs covering 65 languages. The majority of this dataset was generated by first translating and templating datasets from various languages, which were then corrected and annotated by human labellers. While the human labelling process will prevent as many unnatural utterances enter the dataset, the templating of datasets means that the prompts will still not necessarily be the kind of prompts that an end-user of LLMs would use. Hence, the usefulness of this dataset in training multilingual LLMs is limited by its data-generation process.

The ShareGPT dataset used by models such as Vicuna (Chiang et al., 2023) and OpenChat (Wang et al., 2023) contain approximately 70k open source conversations between users and GPT3.5 (Ouyang et al., 2022) and 6k conversations between users and GPT4 (Achiam et al., 2023), meaning that the prompts used in these datasets are often much more naturalistic to a real LLM use-case. However, the majority of these prompts are in English, meaning that this dataset is limited in its use in training multilingual models. Moreover, due to the fact that that majority of this dataset contains data generated from GPT3.5, its usefulness in training is limited as many other models have now surpassed the performance of GPT3.5 in English (Zhu et al., 2023; AI@Meta, 2024b). The amount of multi-

[2]https://github.com/lightblue-tech/suzume/tree/main/tagengo

[3]https://github.com/lightblue-tech/multilingual-mt-bench

[4]https://huggingface.co/lightblue/suzume-llama-3-8B-multilingual

[5]https://huggingface.co/lightblue/suzume-llama-3-8B-japanese

lingual data in the higher quality GPT4 subset of the ShareGPT dataset is small, meaning that its usefulness in training is constrained by its size.

To address the shortcomings in existing public datasets, we created a large, diverse, high quality multilingual dataset using more than 70k human generated prompts in 74 languages and generated responses from these using state-of-the-art proprietary chat models.

## 3 Method

In this section, we detail how we generated our training dataset, our training method, and finally our evaluation techniques.

### 3.1 Tagengo Dataset Creation

First, to generate our dataset, we sampled prompts from the million row LMSYS-Chat-1M dataset (Zheng et al., 2023). These prompts were collected from users speaking to one of 25 LLMs on the Vicuna demo and Chatbot Arena website[6].

We cleaned this dataset by first removing all prompts which contain an OpenAI Moderation Endpoint[7] flag in order to remove explicit, sexual, or illegal material.

We then removed all prompts which were listed as a non-recognised or fictional language (unknown, Klingon, xx, zp, and zzp).

We removed any prompts which contained the string "name" when lower-cased, as NAME0, NAME1 etc. was used as the placeholders for anonymised material. Effectively, this removed any anonymised prompts from our dataset.

We then removed any prompts which contained the following keywords: "gpt", "vicuna", "alpaca", "llama", "koala", "claude", "guanaco". This was done to remove prompts which referred explicitly to the LLMs that were being tested in the Chatbot Arena as many prompts asked about the LLM specifically, which we theorize is less useful in a more general context.

We then used the FastText (Joulin et al., 2016) LangDetect library[8] to determine the confidence level of classifying a particular language. We filtered out all prompts in which the confidence level of the language indicated in the original LMSYS-Chat-1M paper was less than 80%. This was done to filter out ambiguous language examples, as we later sample per-language.

Finally, we analysed the number of tokens of both the first prompt and LLM response, and removed any prompts in which the combined token total of the first prompt and LLM response amounted to more than 512 tokens. This was done to prevent very long prompts or prompts which elicited very long responses being used in our dataset in order to minimise costs when generating data with these prompts using GPT4.

We then sampled a maximum of 25,000 prompts from each language, which effectively meant we sampled the English prompts in this dataset as only English (380,138) had more than 25,000 examples, while the next most popular language Chinese (21,057) had less than 25,000. This was done to counteract the outweighed prevalence of English within this dataset.

For each language, we then embedded each prompt using the BGE M3 embedding model (Chen et al., 2024), which is a state-of-the-art embedding model that supports more than 100 languages. We then compared the prompt embeddings pairwise using the dot product to obtain a similarity score for each prompt pair. We perform fuzzy de-duplication by removing one of any prompt pairs which have a similarity score of greater than 0.8 in order to bolster the diversity of our dataset. The amount of data removed from each language varied widely with languages such as Chinese having a very high rate of de-duplication ($\sim$75%) and other such as Portuguese having a lower rate of de-duplication ($\sim$40%). This may be due to the biases of the embedding model or due to the kind of prompts submitted to the original dataset in different languages.

A table of the number of prompts filtered at each stage of our cleaning process can be found in Table 1.

We used these prompts to generate responses using an Azure OpenAI deployment of a state-of-the-art proprietary LLM, GPT4 (0125-Preview), with the generation temperature set to 0 and setting a maximum number of response tokens to be 2,048.

Due to the fact that generating high quality responses for all of these prompts manually for each language would be prohibitively expensive, we decided to generate these responses using a state-of-the-art model. We hypothesize that using an LLM much larger - rumoured to be 1.8 trillion parame-

[6]https://chat.lmsys.org/

[7]https://platform.openai.com/docs/guides/moderation

[8]https://github.com/zafercavdar/fasttext-langdetect

| Stage | Number of prompts |
|---|---|
| Start | 1,000,000 |
| OpenAI Moderation check | 964,464 |
| Remove unknown languages | 936,468 |
| Remove anonymised data | 753,731 |
| Remove references to models | 735,390 |
| Language detection confidence score >80% | 556,368 |
| Remove prompt plus responses with more than 512 tokens | 513,011 |
| Random sampling of 25,000 prompts per language | 157,873 |
| Fuzzy de-duplication | 78,057 |
| Remove uncompleted/ unanswered prompts | 76,338 |

Table 1: Table describing the number of prompts after each cleaning stage.

ters (Schreiner, 2023) - than nearly all other open source models to generate responses will lead to high quality responses that can then be used to improve existing open source models. When viewed in this way, this training can be viewed as a form of model distillation (Buciluă et al., 2006; Hinton et al., 2015).

We finally removed any responses which GPT4 did not answer or was not able to complete within the 2,048 token limit. The number of prompts in our resultant Tagengo dataset can be found in Table 1 and a breakdown of the prompts by language can be found in Fig 1.

We share our dataset creation code and training dataset on Huggingface[9].

### 3.2 Training

For training data, we add two more datasets to the Tagengo dataset which we regard as high quality chat datasets. The first is the Megagon Instruction dataset (Hayashibe, 2023), a manually annotated dataset of 669 Japanese prompt-response pairs. The second is the 6k GPT4 subset of the ShareGPT dataset[10], which has a majority of prompts in English but also includes responses in other languages. We combined and randomly shuffled these three datasets to use as a 83,213 prompt-response pair training dataset for the multilingual model.

We used our training data to train a Llama 3 8B Instruct model[11] with the Axolotl LLM training package[12]. We trained for one epoch using full fine tuning, using sample packing (Brown et al., 2020) and a context length of 8,096. We name this model Suzume 8B multilingual and the full training configuration for this model can be found on our model card[13].

We also prepared a subset of the above three datasets that only included Japanese data from each dataset, which amounted to 3,318 prompt-response pairs. This was prepared to isolate the effect of monolingual training compared to multilingual training on our data. We trained our model in the same manner as the multilingual model with the name Suzume 8B Japanese. Full details for how the training was conducted can be found on our model card[14].

### 3.3 Evaluation

We tested our models by using a forked version of the original MT-Bench evaluation suite (Zheng et al., 2024). The MT-Bench evaluation benchmark is a set of prompts and responses in English that cover 8 broad categories of prompts: writing, role-play, extraction, reasoning, math, coding, STEM knowledge, and humanities knowledge. Responses to these prompts are generated using an LLM, and those responses are then evaluated using an evaluation model such as GPT4.

We added publicly available translated versions of the original MT-Bench dataset in Chinese, French, German, Japanese, and Russian that had been human-verified by a native speaker of that language.

Note that the Russian translation did not contain reference answers for the math, coding, and reasoning questions, so our evaluation does not include math, coding, and reasoning problems in Russian.

Finally, we added the phrase "Your evaluation

[9] https://huggingface.co/datasets/lightblue/tagengo-gpt4

[10] https://huggingface.co/datasets/openchat/openchat_sharegpt4_dataset/blob/main/sharegpt_gpt4.json

[11] https://huggingface.co/meta-llama/Meta-Llama-3-8B-Instruct

[12] https://github.com/OpenAccess-AI-Collective/axolotl

[13] https://huggingface.co/lightblue/suzume-llama-3-8B-multilingual

[14] https://huggingface.co/lightblue/suzume-llama-3-8B-japanese

| | Llama 3 8B Instruct | Suzume 8B multilingual | Suzume 8B Japanese | Starling 7B beta | GPT3.5 Turbo |
|---|---|---|---|---|---|
| Chinese | - | 7.11 | - | 6.97 | 7.55 |
| French | - | 7.66 | - | 7.29 | 7.74 |
| German | - | 7.26 | - | 6.99 | 7.68 |
| Japanese | - | 6.56 | 6.24 | 6.22 | 7.84 |
| Russian | - | 8.19 | - | 8.28 | 7.94 |
| English | 7.98 | 7.73 | - | 7.92 | 8.26 |

Table 2: Average MT-Bench scores across 6 languages for each LLM evaluated.

should also consider whether the prompt responded in the correct language and the fluency and naturalness of this response." to the original MT-Bench evaluation criteria to ensure that the LLM judge would not simply evaluate factually correct responses in English to non-English prompts as correct. We conducted these evaluations using the "gpt-4-turbo model" from OpenAI as the judge LLM.

We make our evaluation code freely available online[15].

As baselines, we also evaluate the original Llama 3 8B Instruct model (AI@Meta, 2024b), GPT3.5-Turbo (Ouyang et al., 2022), and the Starling 7B Beta (Zhu et al., 2023) which is the highest rated similarly sized multilingual model on the Chatbot Arena leaderboard (Chiang et al., 2024) and has been trained on the ShareGPT dataset amongst other data.

## 4 Results

The MT-Bench scores for each model evaluated can be found in Table 2.

We first found that we were able to train Llama 3 8B Instruct to output responses in the same language as the prompt. This means that we achieved our base objective of enabling a monolingual model (Llama 3) to be able to output multilingual chat.

Secondly, English performance of the multilingual trained model only dropped slightly compared to the base Llama 3 8B Instruct model. This indicates that English chat performance does not considerably drop even when training on a majority of non-English data.

Thirdly, we found that the multilingual trained model performs better compared to the Starling 7B Beta across 5 out of 6 non-English languages tested. However, also we found that our multilingual model achieved lower evaluation scores compared to the proprietary GPT3.5 on 5 of 6 non-English languages. This indicates that our model has achieved state-of-the-art performance in multilingual chat for open-source models of its size, but has not achieved state-of-the-art performance more generally.

Finally, the Suzume 8B multilingual model achieves higher MT-Bench scores on the Japanese benchmark compared to the Suzume 8B Japanese model, indicating that transfer learning from training on other languages is beneficial for training even monolingual models outside of English.

## 5 Discussion

Our results indicate the need for large, high quality, multilingual datasets when training multilingual models. We find that with such a dataset, we can train a state-of-the-art monolingual model such as Llama 3 to achieve state-of-the-art multilingual performance.

We also found that training on additional non-Japanese data improves the performance of our LLM on Japanese benchmarks when compared to training solely on Japanese data, indicating that there is a collective improvement effect between languages when training using multilingual data. This adds to the body of work that indicates that training on multiple languages enables the LLM to better generalise to other languages (Nguyen and Chiang, 2017; Schuster et al., 2018). This suggests that generating an even larger, more diverse dataset in the future could further aid the performance of LLMs on low-resource languages.

[15]https://github.com/lightblue-tech/multilingual-mt-bench

## 6 Future Work

Our work could be built upon and improved in the following ways.

Our training dataset mainly consisted of single prompt-response pairs, but many chats between users and LLMs extend beyond a single conversation turn. Therefore, future work could include creating a dataset that contains multiple turns of conversation, with the prompts either generated by humans or by high quality LLMs.

Future work could also include adding more languages to our dataset. Our dataset only included 74 languages, and crucially omits any languages in the Niger–Congo language family, one of the most diverse language families in the world (Good, 2017). Therefore, future work could involve sampling initial prompts from a wider range of sources (possibly by advertising free chatbot access to people in areas with many speakers of underrepresented languages) and generating responses based on these prompts. This would help to both improve an LLMs linguistic understanding of these low-resource languages as well as improve their understanding of the topics and questions that people from that language and culture may ask.

Finally, future work could include generating preference data, such as was done in English in the Nectar dataset (Zhu et al., 2023), for use with contrastive learning techniques such as Direct Preference Optimisation (Rafailov et al., 2024) and Odds Ratio Preference Optimisation (Hong et al., 2024). These techniques have been shown to further improve the accuracy of LLMs, suggesting that training using these techniques may also improve the performance of LLMs in multilingual chat.

## 7 Conclusion

In this study, we successfully trained a state-of-the-art monolingual Llama 3 LLM to chat multilingually using a new, diverse dataset comprising over 70k human-generated prompts in 74 languages paired with high-quality synthetic responses.

Our multilingual model showcased superior performance across multiple languages compared to similar-sized open-source models on various chat benchmarks.

Interestingly, training using a multilingual dataset also enhanced the performance on specific monolingual tasks, implying beneficial cross-linguistic transfer effects.

These outcomes underline the importance of using rich, diverse multilingual data for improving the capabilities of LLMs in global, multilingual applications.

## Limitations

The three main limitations of this paper concern our prompt diversity, our data generation methodology, and our model evaluation methodology.

Firstly, as stated in Section 6, our training data has a paucity of low-resource languages represented within it. While we try to focus on non-English data in our work by sampling a maximum of 25,000 prompts per language, this still does not counteract the fact that the prompts in the LMSYS-Chat-1M dataset (Zheng et al., 2023) are disproportionately from a small set of languages. These prompts are collected from users on the Chatbot Arena LLM demo site, meaning that the speakers of low-resource languages may be too few, unable, unaware, or unwilling to talk to an LLM chatbot in their native language. This means that current open source LLMs will continue to have lower performance on low-resource languages if this problem is not resolved.

Secondly, we generate our responses to prompts using GPT4, which means that all training data will be in the worldview and within the domain of knowledge that GPT4 exhibits. This biases the model as many LLMs have been shown to have both political (Feng et al., 2023) and cultural biases (Cao et al., 2023) in the text they generate, meaning that what may be deemed acceptable by one user may not be deemed acceptable by another. Moreover, while GPT4 is state-of-the-art and has been shown to generate more accurate information compared to previous models (Achiam et al., 2023), it is still capable of generating incorrect data in response to a prompt, meaning that our training data may contain incorrect statements or otherwise inaccurate data.

Thirdly, we compare our Suzume model results to the Starling LLM (Zhu et al., 2023), with the former being an 8 billion parameter model while the latter is a 7 billion parameter model. This makes for a somewhat unfair comparison as our model is larger than previous open source multilingual models. This was done as the 8 billion parameter size of LLMs was somewhat novel at the time of release, meaning that we did not have a perfect comparison to previous state of the art open source models. However, future work could isolate the effect of training on the Tagengo dataset by training an existing multilingual model and then comparing the base model to the trained model.

Finally, our evaluation methodology is biased by the fact that our 6 evaluation languages are all within the top 10 most popular languages in our training data. This means that our evaluation does not consider the performance of our models on low resource languages, limiting the usefulness of our results to speakers of low resource languages.

## Ethics Statement

Due to the potential for LLMs to be misused for unethical purposes (Derner and Batistič, 2023; Zhuo et al., 2023), we considered the ethical implications of releasing both the training data and final trained model of this work. However, since our training data was made up of human-generated content that was already publicly available, and the synthetic parts of our dataset were generated using a readily available LLM (GPT-4), we consider that the increase in risk profile with our releasing this dataset is marginal. Likewise, due to state-of-the-art models such as GPT-4 being readily available to the public, we believe the increase in risk profile from our model release is similarly minimal.

## References


Josh Achiam, Steven Adler, Sandhini Agarwal, Lama Ahmad, Ilge Akkaya, Florencia Leoni Aleman, Diogo Almeida, Janko Altenschmidt, Sam Altman, Shyamal Anadkat, et al. 2023. Gpt-4 technical report. *arXiv preprint arXiv:2303.08774*.

AI@Meta. 2024a. [link].

AI@Meta. 2024b. Llama 3 model card.

Tom Brown, Benjamin Mann, Nick Ryder, Melanie Subbiah, Jared D Kaplan, Prafulla Dhariwal, Arvind Neelakantan, Pranav Shyam, Girish Sastry, Amanda Askell, et al. 2020. Language models are few-shot learners. *Advances in neural information processing systems*, 33:1877–1901.

Cristian Buciluǎ, Rich Caruana, and Alexandru Niculescu-Mizil. 2006. Model compression. In *Proceedings of the 12th ACM SIGKDD international conference on Knowledge discovery and data mining*, pages 535–541.

Yong Cao, Li Zhou, Seolhwa Lee, Laura Cabello, Min Chen, and Daniel Hershcovich. 2023. Assessing cross-cultural alignment between chatgpt and human societies: An empirical study. *arXiv preprint arXiv:2303.17466*.

Central Intelligence Agency. 2021. *The World Factbook 2021*. Central Intelligence Agency, Washington, DC.

Jianlv Chen, Shitao Xiao, Peitian Zhang, Kun Luo, Defu Lian, and Zheng Liu. 2024. Bge m3-embedding: Multi-lingual, multi-functionality, multi-granularity text embeddings through self-knowledge distillation. *arXiv preprint arXiv:2402.03216*.

Wei-Lin Chiang, Zhuohan Li, Zi Lin, Ying Sheng, Zhanghao Wu, Hao Zhang, Lianmin Zheng, Siyuan Zhuang, Yonghao Zhuang, Joseph E Gonzalez, et al. 2023. Vicuna: An open-source chatbot impressing gpt-4 with 90%* chatgpt quality. *See https://vicuna. lmsys. org (accessed 14 April 2023)*, 2(3):6.

Wei-Lin Chiang, Lianmin Zheng, Ying Sheng, Anastasios Nikolas Angelopoulos, Tianle Li, Dacheng Li, Hao Zhang, Banghua Zhu, Michael Jordan, Joseph E. Gonzalez, and Ion Stoica. 2024. Chatbot arena: An open platform for evaluating llms by human preference.

Erik Derner and Kristina Batistič. 2023. Beyond the safeguards: exploring the security risks of chatgpt. *arXiv preprint arXiv:2305.08005*.

David M. Eberhard, Gary F. Simons, and Charles D. Fennig, editors. 2024. *Ethnologue: Languages of the World*, twenty-seventh edition. SIL International, Dallas, Texas. Online version: `http://www.ethnologue.com`.

Shangbin Feng, Chan Young Park, Yuhan Liu, and Yulia Tsvetkov. 2023. From pretraining data to language models to downstream tasks: Tracking the trails of political biases leading to unfair nlp models. *arXiv preprint arXiv:2305.08283*.

Jeff Good. 2017. Niger-congo languages. *The Cambridge handbook of areal linguistics*, pages 471–499.

Yuta Hayashibe. 2023. megagonlabs/instruction_ja: Japanese instructions data for llm.

Geoffrey Hinton, Oriol Vinyals, and Jeff Dean. 2015. Distilling the knowledge in a neural network. *arXiv preprint arXiv:1503.02531*.

Jiwoo Hong, Noah Lee, and James Thorne. 2024. Reference-free monolithic preference optimization with odds ratio. *arXiv preprint arXiv:2403.07691*.

Armand Joulin, Edouard Grave, Piotr Bojanowski, Matthijs Douze, Hérve Jégou, and Tomas Mikolov. 2016. Fasttext.zip: Compressing text classification models. *arXiv preprint arXiv:1612.03651*.

Niklas Muennighoff, Thomas Wang, Lintang Sutawika, Adam Roberts, Stella Biderman, Teven Le Scao, M Saiful Bari, Sheng Shen, Zheng-Xin Yong, Hailey Schoelkopf, et al. 2022. Crosslingual generalization through multitask finetuning. *arXiv preprint arXiv:2211.01786*.

Toan Q Nguyen and David Chiang. 2017. Transfer learning across low-resource, related languages for neural machine translation. *arXiv preprint arXiv:1708.09803*.

Xuan-Phi Nguyen, Wenxuan Zhang, Xin Li, Mahani Aljunied, Zhiqiang Hu, Chenhui Shen, Yew Ken Chia, Xingxuan Li, Jianyu Wang, Qingyu Tan, Liying Cheng, Guanzheng Chen, Yue Deng, Sen Yang, Chaoqun Liu, Hang Zhang, and Lidong Bing. 2023. Seallms - large language models for southeast asia.

Long Ouyang, Jeffrey Wu, Xu Jiang, Diogo Almeida, Carroll Wainwright, Pamela Mishkin, Chong Zhang, Sandhini Agarwal, Katarina Slama, Alex Ray, et al. 2022. Training language models to follow instructions with human feedback. *Advances in neural information processing systems*, 35:27730–27744.

Rafael Rafailov, Archit Sharma, Eric Mitchell, Christopher D Manning, Stefano Ermon, and Chelsea Finn. 2024. Direct preference optimization: Your language model is secretly a reward model. *Advances in Neural Information Processing Systems*, 36.

Akira Sasaki, Masato Hirakawa, Shintaro Horie, and Tomoaki Nakamura. 2023. Elyza-japanese-llama-2-7b.

Maximilian Schreiner. 2023. Gpt-4 architecture, datasets, costs and more leaked.

Sebastian Schuster, Sonal Gupta, Rushin Shah, and Mike Lewis. 2018. Cross-lingual transfer learning for multilingual task oriented dialog. *arXiv preprint arXiv:1810.13327*.

Neha Sengupta, Sunil Kumar Sahu, Bokang Jia, Satheesh Katipomu, Haonan Li, Fajri Koto, Osama Mohammed Afzal, Samta Kamboj, Onkar Pandit, Rahul Pal, Lalit Pradhan, Zain Muhammad Mujahid, Massa Baali, Alham Fikri Aji, Zhengzhong Liu, Andy Hock, Andrew Feldman, Jonathan Lee, Andrew Jackson, Preslav Nakov, Timothy Baldwin, and Eric Xing. 2023. Jais and jais-chat: Arabic-centric foundation and instruction-tuned open generative large language models.

Shivalika Singh, Freddie Vargus, Daniel Dsouza, Börje F Karlsson, Abinaya Mahendiran, Wei-Yin Ko, Herumb Shandilya, Jay Patel, Deividas Mataciunas, Laura OMahony, et al. 2024. Aya dataset: An open-access collection for multilingual instruction tuning. *arXiv preprint arXiv:2402.06619*.

Rohan Taori, Ishaan Gulrajani, Tianyi Zhang, Yann Dubois, Xuechen Li, Carlos Guestrin, Percy Liang, and Tatsunori B Hashimoto. 2023. Alpaca: A strong, replicable instruction-following model. *Stanford Center for Research on Foundation Models. https://crfm. stanford. edu/2023/03/13/alpaca. html*, 3(6):7.

Gemma Team, Thomas Mesnard, Cassidy Hardin, Robert Dadashi, Surya Bhupatiraju, Shreya Pathak, Laurent Sifre, Morgane Rivière, Mihir Sanjay Kale, Juliette Love, et al. 2024. Gemma: Open models based on gemini research and technology. *arXiv preprint arXiv:2403.08295*.

Hugo Touvron, Louis Martin, Kevin Stone, Peter Albert, Amjad Almahairi, Yasmine Babaei, Nikolay Bashlykov, Soumya Batra, Prajjwal Bhargava, Shruti Bhosale, et al. 2023. Llama 2: Open foundation and fine-tuned chat models. *arXiv preprint arXiv:2307.09288*.

Guan Wang, Sijie Cheng, Xianyuan Zhan, Xiangang Li, Sen Song, and Yang Liu. 2023. Openchat: Advancing open-source language models with mixed-quality data. *arXiv preprint arXiv:2309.11235*.

Xiangpeng Wei, Haoran Wei, Huan Lin, Tianhao Li, Pei Zhang, Xingzhang Ren, Mei Li, Yu Wan, Zhiwei Cao, Binbin Xie, et al. 2023. Polylm: An open source polyglot large language model. *arXiv preprint arXiv:2307.06018*.

Lianmin Zheng, Wei-Lin Chiang, Ying Sheng, Tianle Li, Siyuan Zhuang, Zhanghao Wu, Yonghao Zhuang, Zhuohan Li, Zi Lin, Eric. P Xing, Joseph E. Gonzalez, Ion Stoica, and Hao Zhang. 2023. Lmsys-chat-1m: A large-scale real-world llm conversation dataset.

Lianmin Zheng, Wei-Lin Chiang, Ying Sheng, Siyuan Zhuang, Zhanghao Wu, Yonghao Zhuang, Zi Lin, Zhuohan Li, Dacheng Li, Eric Xing, et al. 2024. Judging llm-as-a-judge with mt-bench and chatbot arena. *Advances in Neural Information Processing Systems*, 36.

Banghua Zhu, Evan Frick, Tianhao Wu, Hanlin Zhu, Karthik Ganesan, Wei-Lin Chiang, Jian Zhang, and Jiantao Jiao. 2023. Starling-7b: Improving llm helpfulness & harmlessness with rlaif.

Terry Yue Zhuo, Yujin Huang, Chunyang Chen, and Zhenchang Xing. 2023. Red teaming chatgpt via jailbreaking: Bias, robustness, reliability and toxicity. *arXiv preprint arXiv:2301.12867*.

# Language and Task Arithmetic with Parameter-Efficient Layers for Zero-Shot Summarization

**Alexandra Chronopoulou**[1*] **Jonas Pfeiffer**[2] **Joshua Maynez**[2]
**Xinyi Wang**[2] **Sebastian Ruder**[3†] **Priyanka Agrawal**[2]
[1]Google [2]Google DeepMind [3]Cohere

## Abstract

Parameter-efficient fine-tuning (PEFT) using labeled task data can significantly improve the performance of large language models (LLMs) on the downstream task. However, there are 7000 languages in the world and many of these languages lack labeled data for real-world language generation tasks. In this paper, we propose to improve zero-shot cross-lingual transfer by composing expert modules trained separately on language or task data. Our method composes *language* and *task* PEFT adapters via element-wise arithmetic operations to leverage unlabeled data and English labeled data. We extend our approach to cases where labeled data from more languages is available and propose to arithmetically compose PEFT adapters trained on languages related to the target. Empirical results on summarization demonstrate that our method is a strategy that obtains consistent gains using minimal training of PEFT parameters.

## 1 Introduction

Large language models (LLM) have achieved impressive performance on various real world applications in many different human languages (Xue et al., 2021; Brown et al., 2020; Chowdhery et al., 2022; Anil et al., 2023; Jiang et al., 2024). Summarization (Nenkova and McKeown, 2011) is a particularly interesting and useful task because it allows users to quickly aggregate and access relevant information from large amounts of textual data. Developing a competitive text summarization system for a language typically involves fine-tuning a pretrained model on labeled summarization data in the given language. Standard supervised fine-tuning of LLMs can be very expensive due to the large model size. Parameter-efficient tuning (PEFT) is an effective alternative that achieves competitive performance while incurring much less computational and memory cost (Hu et al., 2022; Lester et al., 2021; Zhang et al., 2023b).

Despite the effectiveness of PEFT (Touvron et al., 2023), it also has several limitations if we want to develop competitive multilingual summarization systems. First, current PEFT methods generally require access to labeled task data in a given language. While there are several existing datasets in English to train competitive summarization systems (Hermann et al., 2015; Grusky et al., 2018; Narayan et al., 2018), many languages in the world with millions of speakers do not have such resources (Giannakopoulos et al., 2015; Scialom et al., 2020; Cao et al., 2020). Second, standard PEFT methods optimize a separate set of parameters for each language, resulting in thousands of fine-tuned checkpoints, which need to be stored and deployed individually (Fifty et al., 2021). Finally, as the standard PEFT methods are fine-tuned in isolation, they cannot leverage information from related tasks.

In this paper, we want to improve zero-shot multilingual summarization with PEFT to better support languages that might lack labeled summarization data. To this end, we propose a simple yet effective method that composes language and task information stored in different trained PEFT parameters through element-wise operation. We leverage unlabeled data to train language parameters with PEFT, and perform element-wise arithmetic operations with pretrained *task* and *language* parameters to construct new parameters for a language without labeled summarization data. While several prior works have studied methods that compose PEFT methods for zero-shot cross-lingual transfer (Pfeiffer et al., 2020; Vu et al., 2022), these methods generally incur an additional inference cost. Our method provides a simpler and more flexible framework to leverage many related languages at a fixed inference cost.

* Work done during an internship at Google DeepMind. Correspondence to alexandrachron@google.com
† Work done while working at Google



*Proceedings of the Fourth Workshop on Multilingual Representation Learning (MRL 2024)*, pages 114–126
November 16, 2024 

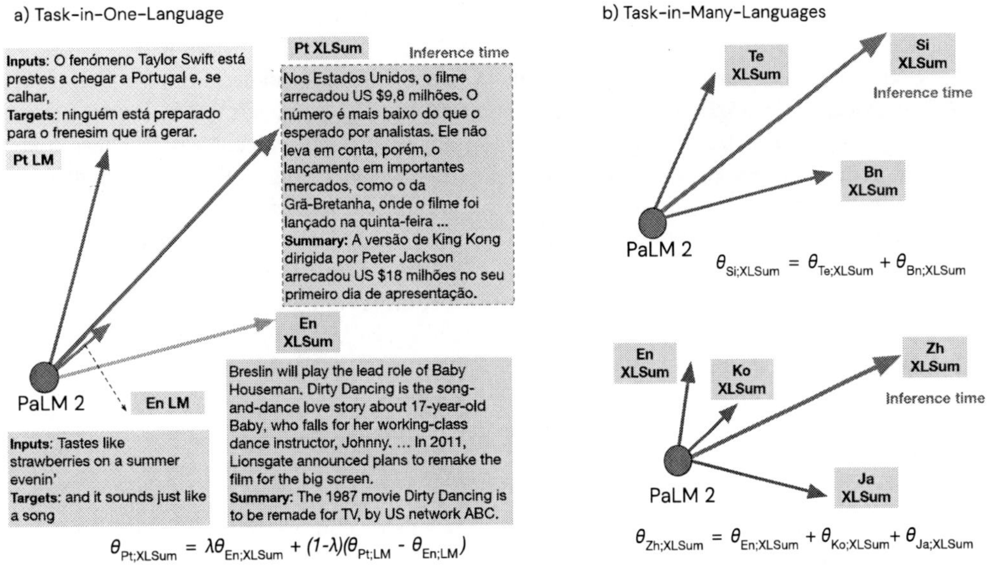


Figure 1: **Illustration of our language and task arithmetic approach for zero-shot cross-lingual transfer using LoRA parameters learned on top of PaLM 2.** (a) We train a task adapter using the summarization objective in En and language adapters using Prefix-LM in En and Pt. At inference time, a summary is generated in Pt, shown with a dotted frame (Subsection 2.1). (b) We add the weights of task adapters trained for summarization in languages similar to the target. We use the resulting vector for zero-shot summarization in the target language (Subsection 2.2).

Our method is inspired by the lottery ticket hypothesis (Frankle and Carbin, 2019), which posits that distinct models fine-tuned on the same dataset follow linear trajectories while maintaining a consistent loss (Frankle et al., 2020; Yunis et al., 2022). This hypothesis implies that element-wise operations on different fine-tuned models can also remove biases of the pretrained model (Ilharco et al., 2023), allowing the accumulation of information from auxiliary tasks (Matena and Raffel, 2021), or improve adaptation to unforeseen textual domains (Li et al., 2022a; Chronopoulou et al., 2023a). Our work is the first to extend this observation to improve cross-lingual transfer by combining pretrained language and task parameters.

Our contributions are the following:

1. Assuming we only have task data in English, we combine PEFT parameters trained on English task data and unlabeled data in other languages through element-wise composition. This setup, termed *Task-in-One-Language*, improves the model's summarization performance across all unseen target languages, as demonstrated on the XLSum benchmark (Hasan et al., 2021).
2. Extending our first approach, we consider scenarios with task data from multiple languages (*Task-in-Many-Languages*). When labeled task data for summarization are available in various languages, we combine representations from languages most related to the target, consistently improving performance over the baselines using the XLSum benchmark.
3. We apply our language and task arithmetic to a different PEFT method, the Kronecker adapter (Edalati et al., 2022) and evaluate its performance on XLSum and TyDi-QA (Clark et al., 2020). We find that our approach is also effective with these other methods and tasks.

## 2 Language and Task Arithmetic

Prior work has applied element-wise operations to the weights of fine-tuned models (Matena and Raffel, 2021; Wortsman et al., 2022; Ilharco et al., 2023; Ainsworth et al., 2023; Yadav et al., 2023), or PEFT modules (Chronopoulou et al., 2023a; Zhang et al., 2023a). These studies demonstrate that interpolating the weights of fine-tuned models (or specific layers) effectively creates multi-task and multi-domain models. We hypothesize that element-wise operations can also be used to combine knowledge acquired in different languages. Our work is the first to propose the arithmetic composition of language and task PEFT modules for cross-lingual natural language generation. Figure 1 illustrates an overview of our approach. 1.

Our goal is to enable Large Language Models (LLMs) to support summarization in an unseen target language ($T$) for which we lack labeled data. We assume access to labeled task data in other languages, as well as unlabeled monolingual data in both the source language ($S$) and the target language ($T$). In particular, we can use either labeled or unlabeled data to train small PEFT modules that capture the attributes of a given task or language.

**Task Adapter:** We fine-tune an LLM using LoRA adapters on labeled data from XLSum (Hasan et al., 2021) in the source language $S$. We refer to the fine-tuned model as Task Adapter.

**Language Adapter:** We fine-tune LoRA parameters with LLMs on monolingual data in the source or target language ($S$ or $T$). We refer to the fine-tuned model as language adapter. We use the prefix-LM pretraining objective from T5 (Raffel et al., 2020) with mC4 data to train language adapters.

We propose to compose the *language* and *task* vectors to better support summarization into the target language $T$. Next, we introduce our method under two different data settings.

### 2.1 Task-in-One-Language

First, we consider the zero-shot setting where the source language $S$ is English. We have labeled data in $S$, and some amount of unlabeled data both in the source language $S$ and the target language $T$.

**Composing via Language and Task Addition:** We want to encourage the model to generate in the target language $T$ and learn the task from the data available in the source language $S$.

Let $\theta_{\text{LM;T}}$ be the LoRA parameters trained on the monolingual data in the target language $T$, and $\theta_{\text{task;S}}$ be the LoRA parameters trained on the labeled task data in the source language $S$, we propose to calculate the zero-shot task module for the target language $T$ as:

$$\theta_{\text{task;T}} = \lambda\theta_{\text{task;S}} + (1 - \lambda)(\theta_{\text{LM;T}}) \quad (1)$$

The scaling term $\lambda$ is determined using held-out validation data. We refer to this approach as *Language and Task; Add.*

**Composing via Language and Task Addition and Subtraction:** We want to steer the model's ability to generate in the target language $T$, but avoid generating in the source language $S$. Previous work showed that subtraction can be a method of "unlearning" information (Ilharco et al., 2023; Zhang et al., 2023a). We propose *subtracting* the source language adapter from the target language adapter. The intuition is that by negating the source language adapter, we control the generation, making the model "forget" the source language.

Our goal in this zero-shot transfer setup is to obtain a model that has a **strong summarization ability** (learned from the task adapter) **in the correct target language** (learned from the target language adapter) **while *not* generating in the source language** (unlearned from the source language adapter).

Formally, let $\theta_{\text{LM;S}}$ be the LoRA parameters trained on the monolingual data in the source language $S$. We propose to calculate the zero-shot task module for the target language $T$ as:

$$\theta_{\text{task;T}} = \lambda\theta_{\text{task;S}} + (1 - \lambda)(\theta_{\text{LM;T}} - \theta_{\text{LM;S}}) \quad (2)$$

where $\lambda$ is a hyperparameter tuned in the same way as in the previous setting. We refer to it as *Language and Task; Add and Subtract.*

### 2.2 Task-in-Many-Languages

Subsection 2.1 presents language and task arithmetic when we want to do zero-shot transfer from a single source language $S$. However, in practice, we sometimes have data in many different source languages. In this subsection, we extend our language and task arithmetic framework to the setting where we utilize data in many different languages.

**Composing via Task-only Addition:** First, we want to utilize labeled task data in various source languages. Formally, given labeled task data for $N$ languages $(S_1, ..., S_N)$, we want to use the LLM to support an unseen target language $T$, for which we have no task data. To this end, given LoRA parameters $(\theta_{\text{task;S}_1}, ..., \theta_{\text{task;S}_N})$ trained on labeled task data in $(S_1, ..., S_N)$, we propose to perform zero-shot generation on the target language $T$ using the average of PEFT modules of its related languages:

$$\theta_{\text{task;T}} = \frac{1}{L}\sum_{i=1}^{L}\theta_{\text{task;S}_i} \quad (3)$$

where $L <= N$. If $L = N$, we essentially add the weights of all available task adapters (we name this method *Task-only; Add all*). To select a subset of $L$ languages that are most related to the target language $T$, we use the URIEL language vectors (Littell et al., 2017). We retrieve the pre-computed syntactic and geographic distances between $T$ and each of the $N$ languages of the training set using an implementation of the toolkit lang2vec.[1] We refer to this approach as *Task-only; Add related.*

**Composing via Language and Task Addition and Subtraction:** Similarly, if we have both labeled and unlabeled data in several source languages, we can modify Equation 2 to leverage both types of data in many different languages:

$$\theta_{\text{task;T}} = \lambda\theta'_{\text{task;S}} + (1-\lambda)(\theta_{\text{LM;T}} - \theta'_{\text{LM;S}}) \quad (4)$$

Where $\theta'_{task;S} = \frac{1}{L}\sum_{i=1}^{L}\theta_{\text{task;S}_i}$ (as computed in Equation 3), i.e., it is the average of the related (to the target $T$) task adapters, and $\theta'_{LM;S} = \frac{1}{L}\sum_{i=1}^{L}\theta_{\text{LM;S}_i}$, i.e., it is the average of the related language adapters according to URIEL. This approach is denoted as *Language and Task; Add and Subtract related.*

## 3 Experimental Setup

### 3.1 Tasks and Datasets

**Summarization**: We use XLSum (Hasan et al., 2021), a news summarization dataset of BBC articles, where each article has a one-sentence summary. While prior work studies the zero-shot learning setting where only English labeled data is available (Vu et al., 2022), we utilize the available multilingual training data for a more realistic setting. Specifically, we use a subset of XLSum as our training set, and specifically the articles and summaries of the languages: Arabic (ar), Bengali (bn), English (en), Japanese (ja), Korean (ko), Indonesian (id), Swahili (sw), Russian (ru), Telugu (te), Thai (th), and Turkish (tr). We refer to this set as XLSum$_{seen}$. Training dataset stats are shown in Table 7 of the Appendix.

For zero-shot evaluation, we select 11 languages from XLSum as unseen languages: Marathi (mr), Gujarati (gu), Chinese simplified (zh), Nepali (ne), Portuguese (pt), Sinhala (si), Somali (so), Vietnamese (vi), Yoruba (yo), Ukrainian (uk), and Persian (fa). We do not use training data from any of these languages. We refer to this set of 11 languages as XLSum$_{unseen}$.

**Unlabeled data**: We use unlabeled data from mC4 (Xue et al., 2021) with the prefix language modeling objective from T5 (Raffel et al., 2020). This corpus has been created using a Common Crawl-based dataset covering 101 languages. All languages considered in our experiments are covered by mC4. For the language adapters, we fine-tune the LLM using LoRA on prefix-LM for $5k$ steps in each language.

### 3.2 Training and Implementation Details

We use PaLM 2-S (Anil et al., 2023), a state-of-the-art, highly multilingual language model, as the base LLM for all our experiments.

We add LoRA parameters of rank 4 to the Key, Query, Value, Projection attention matrices. We do not tune this hyperparameter. This results in adding parameters that account for just 0.2% of the parameters of PaLM 2 (we do not update the weights of the pretrained model). We fine-tune PaLM 2 on prefix-LM, XLSum using LoRA with learning rate $2e-4$.

For XLSum, we report ROUGE-2 (Lin, 2004) as the evaluation metric for En, and SentencePiece-ROUGE-2 for all other languages. This is an extension of ROUGE that handles non-Latin character using a SentencePiece tokenizer; in this work, we use the mT5 tokenizer (Xue et al., 2021).

### 3.3 Baselines

**TASK-IN-ONE-LANGUAGE:** The baseline is computed by fine-tuning PaLM 2 on En XLSum data using LoRA parameters. During fine-tuning, only the LoRA parameters are being updated, while the underlying LLM remains frozen.

**TASK-IN-MANY-LANGUAGES:** The baseline is computed by fine-tuning PaLM 2 on XLSum data of each of the language in XLSum$_{seen}$ independently using LoRA parameters. Then, the best-performing model (per target language) is selected. We denote this as *baseline (best)*.

We also compute a *multilingual baseline*: we simply concatenate the datasets of the different languages of XLSum$_{seen}$ and we train the LLM with LoRA on the entire dataset.[2]

## 4 Results and Discussion

### 4.1 Task-in-One-Language

**Language and task arithmetic (Add and Subtract) improves zero-shot cross-lingual transfer:** We present the main results of our language and

[1] https://github.com/antonisa/lang2vec

[2] We also ran the full fine-tuning baselines and we observed that the gap to the PEFT baselines is small, results are shown in the Appendix.

| Method | Mr | Gu | Zh | Ne | Pt | Si | So | Vi | Yo | Uk | Fa | Avg |
|---|---|---|---|---|---|---|---|---|---|---|---|---|
| **Task-in-One-Language** | | | | | | | | | | | | |
| Baseline | 20.5 | 30.3 | 23.9 | 29.4 | 22.3 | 34.5 | 21.3 | 24.5 | 17.3 | 17.4 | 25.1 | 24.2 |
| Language and Task (Add) | 20.6 | 30.3 | 24.1 | 29.4 | 22.3 | 34.7 | 21.5 | 24.5 | 17.7 | 18.1 | 25.2 | 24.4 |
| Language and Task (Add and Subtract) | **20.7** | **30.6** | **24.6** | **29.6** | **22.5** | **35.4** | **21.8** | 24.6 | **18.5** | **20.9** | **25.8** | **25.0** |

Table 1: **Language and task arithmetic improves zero-shot cross-lingual transfer on XLSum when we only have task data in En.** We show ROUGE-2 spm scores on XLSum$_{unseen}$. We train the task adapter using En XLSum data and the language adapter using Prefix-LM on mC4 data.

| Method | Mr | Gu | Zh | Ne | Pt | Si | So | Vi | Yo | Uk | Fa | Avg |
|---|---|---|---|---|---|---|---|---|---|---|---|---|
| **Task-in-Many-Languages** | | | | | | | | | | | | |
| Baseline (best) | 21.2 | 31.2 | 25.6 | 28.4 | 22.5 | 35.8 | 22.1 | 25.6 | 21.4 | 21.6 | 25.3 | 25.5 |
| Baseline (multilingual) | **21.4** | 31.2 | **26.4** | 28.8 | 22.8 | 35.4 | 22.4 | **25.7** | 20.2 | 21.5 | 25.5 | 25.6 |
| Task-only (Add all) | **21.4** | 31.3 | 25.6 | 28.6 | 22.8 | 35.4 | 22.0 | 25.5 | 20.4 | 21.3 | 25.5 | 25.4 |
| Task-only (Add related) | 21.1 | **31.5** | 25.4 | **30.2** | **23.1** | **36.3** | **22.9** | 25.1 | **22.9** | **21.8** | **25.7** | **26.0** |
| Language and Task (Add and Subtract related) | 21.2 | **31.5** | 25.4 | **30.4** | **23.0** | **36.4** | **22.8** | 25.0 | **22.9** | **21.7** | **25.7** | **26.0** |

Table 2: **Addition of task adapters improves zero-shot cross-lingual transfer on XLSum when we have task data in multiple languages.** We show ROUGE-2 spm zero-shot scores on XLSum$_{unseen}$.

task arithmetic approach in cross-lingual summarization in Table 1. In the second row, we show the results by composing the language and task LoRA parameters via addition (*language and task; add*). This approach provides only slight improvements over the task adapter baseline in terms of ROUGE-2. Our language and task arithmetic approach with addition and subtraction (third row) consistently outperforms the baseline as well as the simple addition of source task and target language LoRA parameters. We highlight that the language adapters are trained by fine-tuning PaLM 2 with LoRA on prefix-LM for just $5k$ steps; even with this minimal training, they provide knowledge that is helpful to the pretrained model.

**Why is subtracting the source language adapter important?** We hypothesize that since the task adapter encodes information on summarizing articles in En (source), it is beneficial to add a language adapter that encourages the LLM to generate in the target language, but at the same time avoid generating in the source. Intuitively, negating the En language adapter parameters likely reduces the bias of the model towards En and enhances the ability of the model to generate in the target language.

### 4.2 Task-in-Many-Languages

We present the results of our approach when task data is available in different languages in Table 2. We compare the baselines with *task-only; Add all*, which fine-tunes PaLM 2 with LoRA on each language of the training set, and then computes the weight average of all fine-tuned models.

**Task-only (Add all) on par with multilingual baseline:** We observe that simply averaging all task adapters is on par with the multilingual baseline. This is intriguing, as it suggests that model merging can be used to iteratively add new task data to a petrained model. As soon as new task data (for a previously unsupported language) become available, one can simply train the corresponding task vector on this data and add it to the model by performing weight averaging. This alleviates the need of training a new multilingual model for every new batch of data.

**Adding only related task adapters gives better results for most languages:** Our approach *(task-only; Add related)* is presented in row 4. This selective composition of task adapters clearly surpasses the baselines. Our hypothesis is that not all task adapters are as important for a target language $T$ and the final model should only incorporate task adapters trained in languages similar to the target. To select the models that will be averaged, we do not use any test data, but rely on linguistic information. We query the URIEL database and use the languages with the smallest distance to each held-out language $T$. Our approach outperforms the uniform weight average *(task-only; Add all)*, likely because our model avoids negative transfer between task adapters learned on distant languages, and leverages task information learned from similar languages.

**Arithmetically composing language and task**

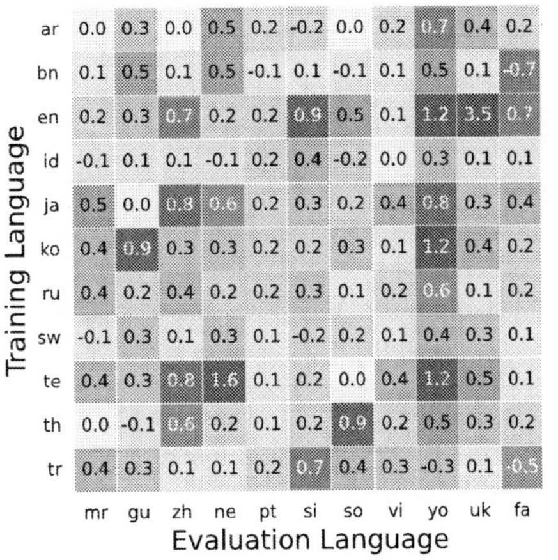


Figure 2: Relative ROUGE-2 improvement of our **language & task arithmetic** over the baseline (task adapter only). Our approach yields consistent improvements for most source-target language pairs.

**adapters when task data is available in multiple languages is not helpful:** We present the results we computed using *Language and Task; Add and Subtract related* which leverages unlabeled data as well as task data in the final row of Table 2. This approach performs on par with the *task-only; Add related* approach that uses only labeled data. Composing language and task knowledge is beneficial in the absence of enough task data. However, when task data is available in multiple languages, combining information from similar languages yields strong results and unlabeled data does not provide an additional benefit. Therefore, merging the two methods does not provide improvements.

## 5 Analysis

### 5.1 Using task adapter in different languages has consistent improvements

For our main language and task arithmetic results with *Task-in-One-Language*, we trained the task adapter on En labeled data and evaluated its performance on XLSum$_{unseen}$. For a more fine-grained assessment of our model, we present its relative performance when the task adapter is trained in each language in XLSum$_{seen}$ (as opposed to just En) against the corresponding baseline. The results are shown in Figure 2. The third row (En) shows the performance difference of *Language and Task (Add and Subtract)* from the baseline (Table 1).

We observe consistent improvements using our approach compared to the baseline across all language pairs. Low-resource languages, such as Yo, benefit more from the cross-lingual transfer setup we propose. In addition, while learning the En task adapter seems to provide higher gains for most evaluation languages, Te, Ja and Ko task adapters also lead to a large performance boost.

While PaLM 2 has been trained on vast multilingual data, providing each language with individual capacity using language modeling yields across-the-board improvements. This suggests that learning language-specific knowledge using PEFT parameters has the potential to strengthen the zero-shot cross-lingual transfer abilities of LLMs at a very small computational cost.

### 5.2 Our method also works with other PEFT parameters

We showed that composing task and language LoRA weights by element-wise arithmetic brings significant gains to cross-lingual transfer. In this section, we examine whether our findings also generalize to parameter-efficient fine-tuning methods other than LoRA.

One particularly interesting PEFT method is Kronecker adapter (Edalati et al., 2022). While LoRA is based on the multiplication of two low-rank matrices, Kronecker adapter is a matrix decomposition method which does not rely on the low-rank assumption. Instead, it replaces the low-rank decomposition in LoRA with the Kronecker product decomposition. It has been shown that this PEFT method achieves large improvements over LoRA and full fine-tuning on the GLUE benchmark (Wang et al., 2018). We conduct language and task arithmetic using Kronecker adapters as the PEFT modules.[3]

**Kronecker adapter:** Formally, the Kronecker product is defined as follows:

$$A \otimes B = \begin{pmatrix} a_{11}B & \cdots & a_{1n}B \\ \vdots & \ddots & \vdots \\ a_{m1}B & \cdots & a_{mn}B \end{pmatrix}$$

where matrices $\mathbf{A} \in^{m \times n}$ and $\mathbf{B} \in^{\frac{k}{m} \times \frac{d}{n}}$ are the input matrices, and $\mathbf{W} \in^{k \times d}$, $k$ is the model dimension and $d$ is the dimension per attention head is the output matrix. We can tune hyperparameters $m$ and $n$ while keeping the number of additional parameters fixed, which is more flexible than LoRA.

[3]Similar to LoRA tuning, we add Kronecker adapters for the Key, Query, Value, Projection attention matrices of the Transformer model while keeping the weights fixed.

| Method | Mr | Gu | Zh | Ne | Pt | Si | So | Vi | Yo | Uk | Fa | Avg |
|---|---|---|---|---|---|---|---|---|---|---|---|---|
| **Task-in-Many-Languages** | | | | | | | | | | | | |
| Baseline (best) | 21.3 | 31.4 | 25.6 | 30.0 | 22.6 | 36.0 | 22.9 | 25.4 | 21.8 | 22.0 | 25.7 | 25.9 |
| Baseline (multilingual) | 21.2 | 31.5 | 26.1 | 30.8 | 23.2 | 36.7 | 23.1 | 25.5 | 21.5 | 22.0 | 25.9 | 26.1 |
| Task-only (Add all) | 20.9 | 31.3 | 25.6 | 30.5 | 22.8 | 35.9 | 22.7 | 25.2 | 20.8 | 21.9 | 25.7 | 25.7 |
| Task-only (Add related) | 21.1 | **32.2** | 26.2 | **31.4** | **24.0** | 36.6 | 22.9 | **25.7** | 21.9 | **22.3** | **26.6** | **26.4** |

Table 3: **Adding related task adapters outperforms monolingual and multilingual baselines on XLSum using Kronecker adapter.** Rouge (ROUGE-2 spm) zero-shot scores on the $\text{XLSum}_{unseen}$ test set.

**Experimental setting:** We use PaLM 2 S model as the pretrained LLM. We add a Kronecker adapter with $(m, n) = (32, 16)$. Similar to LoRA, this PEFT method does not decrease inference speed because the additional parameters are added back to the original model weights.

**Results:** We run the *task-only; Add* experiments using Kronecker adapter and show the results in Table 3. We observe that the results follow a similar pattern as with the LoRA adapter. Our method (*task-only; Add related*) outperforms monolingual and multilingual baselines. This demonstrates that a selective combination of PEFT parameters at the weight level improves the generalization ability of a LLM to languages for which no task data is available. This confirms our intuition that it is possible to compose information learned about a task in different languages by simply performing point-wise operations.

### 5.3 Module subtraction is particularly helpful for summarization

We proposed two composition approaches for language and task arithmetic: *Add* or *Add and Subtract*. To understand the different impact of these two approaches, we compare their performance on two datasets, TyDi QA and XLSum.

**Experimental setting**: Besides XLSum, we also evaluate our language and task arithmetic approach on TyDi QA (Clark et al., 2020), a multilingual extractive question answering dataset of 8 typologically diverse languages, based on Wikipedia articles in Bengali (bn), English (en), Finnish (fi), Indonesian (id), Korean (ko), Russian (ru), Swahili (sw), and Telugu (te). We train our model on En task data an evaluate on each of the other languages in the dataset, simulating a zero-shot setup.

**Results**: We show the results in Table 4. We find that using both addition and subtraction is more beneficial than addition only for XLSum (+0.6 gains in ROUGE). However, we observe that for the QA task, using addition and subtraction performs on par with addition only. We hypothesize that this is likely because TyDi QA is an extractive QA task where the model simply needs to copy a segment of correct answer from the context, while XLSum requires more free-form language generation. Because of this inherent difference between the tasks, discouraging the model from generating in the source language (by negating the source language adapter) is less essential to QA compared to summarization.

| Method | TyDi QA | XLSum |
|---|---|---|
| Baseline | 83.0 | 24.2 |
| Language and task arithmetic | | |
| - Add | 83.3 | 24.4 |
| - Add and Subtract | 83.2 | 25.0 |

Table 4: **Language and task arithmetic via addition or addition and subtraction for TyDi QA and XLSum** using LoRA parameters. These are the average results over the unseen languages. For TyDi QA, F1 is shown, while for XLSum, we show ROUGE-2 spm.

### 5.4 Task adapters selected by *lang2vec*

When we have labeled data available in multiple languages, our proposed *task-only; Add related* approach averages the weights of PEFT parameters that are related to the target language. The relatedness is defined by *lang2vec*, a tool that queries URIEL. To shed light on where the improved performance of our model comes from, we present in Table 5 the source languages that are selected for each of the target languages based on linguistic knowledge.

We witness that a different number of languages is selected for each target language. We do not explicitly control the number of models averaged, we simply sort them using the syntactic and geographic distance. For a given target language $T$, we average the weights of the source languages

| Mr | Gu | Zh | Ne | Pt | Si | So | Vi | Yo | Uk | Fa |
|---|---|---|---|---|---|---|---|---|---|---|
| Bn | Bn | En | Te | En | Te | Ar | Id | En | Ru | Tr |
| Te | Te | Ko | Ja | Ru | Bn | Sw | Th | Ar | En | En |
| Tr | | Ja | Tr | Ar | | En | | | Sw | Ar |
| | | Id | Ko | | | | | | | |
| | | Th | Ru | | | | | | | |
| | | | Bn | | | | | | | |

Table 5: Most similar languages to each of the evaluation languages (based on lang2vec) selected by our *task-only (Add related)* approach.

$S_1, S_2, .., S_N$ that have a syntactic distance < 0.7 and a geographic distance < 0.3. We leave a more fine-grained selection process to future work.

## 6 Related Work

LLMs have shown impressive performance in various natural language processing tasks (Radford et al., 2019; Brown et al., 2020; Chung et al., 2022; Touvron et al., 2023), often requiring no extra training to adapt to downstream tasks.

Numerous parameter-efficient methods have been proposed, each addressing the challenge of enhancing efficiency . These methods can be categorized as input composition, function composition, and parameter composition (Pfeiffer et al., 2023). *Input composition* methods, such as prompt tuning, incorporate soft prompts into the input layers to guide the model's behavior (Li and Liang, 2021; Lester et al., 2021). *Function composition* strategies, like adapters (Rebuffi et al., 2017; Houlsby et al., 2019), introduce non-linear functions within pretrained layers to adapt the intermediate representations of the model. *Parameter composition* is exemplified by methods like LoRA (Hu et al., 2022), which introduces a limited number of learnable low-rank matrices into each pretrained layer.

Recent work which is based on the linear mode connectivity (Frankle et al., 2020) suggests averaging the weights of pretrained models fine-tuned on the same dataset with different hyperparameters to improve downstream performance (Izmailov et al., 2018; Gupta et al., 2020; Wortsman et al., 2022). It has also been shown that averaging the weights of models fine-tuned on different tasks improves out-of-domain generalization without leaking information about potentially private labeled datasets (Jin et al., 2023). Composing weights of models fine-tuned on tasks related to the target task is also beneficial (Matena and Raffel, 2021). Ainsworth et al. (2023); Ilharco et al. (2023); Yadav et al. (2023); Huang et al. (2023); Ortiz-Jimenez et al. (2023) show that a model can acquire multi-task learning abilities using model merging, while Daheim et al. (2024) propose model merging by reducing gradient mismatch. There is also work on averaging domain-specific adapter layers (Chronopoulou et al., 2023a) or domain-expert LMs (Li et al., 2022b) with large gains for unseen domains. However, there is no work on PEFT cross-lingual transfer using language and task arithmetic.

In a similar line of thought and to mitigate interference of different tasks during training, Pfeiffer et al. (2021) train task PEFT modules and learn attention parameters to select the most useful of them, while Karimi Mahabadi et al. (2021) learn adapters with hypernetworks. Asai et al. (2022) efficiently integrate knowledge from multiple tasks with a mix of trainable soft prompts. Ponti et al. (2023) propose Polytropon, which learns both adapters and a binary task–module routing matrix, determining which module should be active for each task; Caccia et al. (2023) extend it to a more granular level by mixing subsets of adapter dimensions.

Another research direction considers training PEFT parameters and combining them for cross-lingual transfer. MAD-X (Pfeiffer et al., 2020) stacks task bottleneck adapters with language adapters and using them for cross-lingual transfer. Ansell et al. (2022) identify the parameters that are most useful for a task and a language, and compose them; this work is based on the lottery ticket hypothesis (Frankle et al., 2020). Vu et al. (2022) propose factorizing a prompt into a language and task and training each part while keeping the other frozen. Newly learned knowledge is combined with the existing model using PEFT modules to permit cross-lingual transfer in multiple recent works (Bapna and Firat, 2019; Üstün et al., 2020; Vidoni et al., 2020; Cooper Stickland et al., 2021; Chronopoulou et al., 2023b). To the best of our knowledge, our work is the first to propose improving cross-lingual transfer of a LLM via a combination of weights of PEFT parameters.

## 7 Conclusion

We present a new method to compose knowledge from parameter-efficient modules using arithmetic operations in order to improve zero-shot cross-lingual transfer. Our experiments in summarization on a wide set of languages using PaLM 2 as the pretrained model show that our *language and task arithmetic* achieves consistent improvements over the baselines and introduces a modular approach that can be leveraged for improved generalization of a LLM in languages that lack labeled data.

## References


Samuel Ainsworth, Jonathan Hayase, and Siddhartha Srinivasa. 2023. Git re-basin: Merging models modulo permutation symmetries. In *The Eleventh International Conference on Learning Representations*.

Rohan Anil, Andrew M. Dai, Orhan Firat, Melvin Johnson, Dmitry Lepikhin, Alexandre Passos, Siamak Shakeri, Emanuel Taropa, Paige Bailey, Zhifeng Chen, Eric Chu, Jonathan H. Clark, Laurent El Shafey, Yanping Huang, Kathy Meier-Hellstern, Gaurav Mishra, Erica Moreira, Mark Omernick, Kevin Robinson, Sebastian Ruder, Yi Tay, Kefan Xiao, Yuanzhong Xu, Yujing Zhang, Gustavo Hernandez Abrego, Junwhan Ahn, Jacob Austin, Paul Barham, Jan Botha, James Bradbury, Siddhartha Brahma, Kevin Brooks, Michele Catasta, Yong Cheng, Colin Cherry, Christopher A. Choquette-Choo, Aakanksha Chowdhery, Clément Crepy, Shachi Dave, Mostafa Dehghani, Sunipa Dev, Jacob Devlin, Mark Díaz, Nan Du, Ethan Dyer, Vlad Feinberg, Fangxiaoyu Feng, Vlad Fienber, Markus Freitag, Xavier Garcia, Sebastian Gehrmann, Lucas Gonzalez, Guy Gur-Ari, Steven Hand, Hadi Hashemi, Le Hou, Joshua Howland, Andrea Hu, Jeffrey Hui, Jeremy Hurwitz, Michael Isard, Abe Ittycheriah, Matthew Jagielski, Wenhao Jia, Kathleen Kenealy, Maxim Krikun, Sneha Kudugunta, Chang Lan, Katherine Lee, Benjamin Lee, Eric Li, Music Li, Wei Li, YaGuang Li, Jian Li, Hyeontaek Lim, Hanzhao Lin, Zhongtao Liu, Frederick Liu, Marcello Maggioni, Aroma Mahendru, Joshua Maynez, Vedant Misra, Maysam Moussalem, Zachary Nado, John Nham, Eric Ni, Andrew Nystrom, Alicia Parrish, Marie Pellat, Martin Polacek, Alex Polozov, Reiner Pope, Siyuan Qiao, Emily Reif, Bryan Richter, Parker Riley, Alex Castro Ros, Aurko Roy, Brennan Saeta, Rajkumar Samuel, Renee Shelby, Ambrose Slone, Daniel Smilkov, David R. So, Daniel Sohn, Simon Tokumine, Dasha Valter, Vijay Vasudevan, Kiran Vodrahalli, Xuezhi Wang, Pidong Wang, Zirui Wang, Tao Wang, John Wieting, Yuhuai Wu, Kelvin Xu, Yunhan Xu, Linting Xue, Pengcheng Yin, Jiahui Yu, Qiao Zhang, Steven Zheng, Ce Zheng, Weikang Zhou, Denny Zhou, Slav Petrov, and Yonghui Wu. 2023. Palm 2 technical report.

Alan Ansell, Edoardo Ponti, Anna Korhonen, and Ivan Vulić. 2022. Composable sparse fine-tuning for cross-lingual transfer. In *Proceedings of the 60th Annual Meeting of the Association for Computational Linguistics (Volume 1: Long Papers)*, pages 1778–1796, Dublin, Ireland. Association for Computational Linguistics.

Akari Asai, Mohammadreza Salehi, Matthew Peters, and Hannaneh Hajishirzi. 2022. ATTEMPT: Parameter-efficient multi-task tuning via attentional mixtures of soft prompts. In *Proceedings of the 2022 Conference on Empirical Methods in Natural Language Processing*, pages 6655–6672, Abu Dhabi, United Arab Emirates. Association for Computational Linguistics.

Ankur Bapna and Orhan Firat. 2019. Simple, scalable adaptation for neural machine translation. In *Proceedings of the 2019 Conference on Empirical Methods in Natural Language Processing and the 9th International Joint Conference on Natural Language Processing (EMNLP-IJCNLP)*, pages 1538–1548, Hong Kong, China. Association for Computational Linguistics.

Tom Brown, Benjamin Mann, Nick Ryder, Melanie Subbiah, Jared D Kaplan, Prafulla Dhariwal, Arvind Neelakantan, Pranav Shyam, Girish Sastry, Amanda Askell, Sandhini Agarwal, Ariel Herbert-Voss, Gretchen Krueger, Tom Henighan, Rewon Child, Aditya Ramesh, Daniel Ziegler, Jeffrey Wu, Clemens Winter, Chris Hesse, Mark Chen, Eric Sigler, Mateusz Litwin, Scott Gray, Benjamin Chess, Jack Clark, Christopher Berner, Sam McCandlish, Alec Radford, Ilya Sutskever, and Dario Amodei. 2020. Language models are few-shot learners. In *Advances in Neural Information Processing Systems*, volume 33, pages 1877–1901. Curran Associates, Inc.

Lucas Caccia, Edoardo Ponti, Zhan Su, Matheus Pereira, Nicolas Le Roux, and Alessandro Sordoni. 2023. Multi-head adapter routing for cross-task generalization.

Yue Cao, Xiaojun Wan, Jinge Yao, and Dian Yu. 2020. Multisumm: Towards a unified model for multilingual abstractive summarization. *Proceedings of the AAAI Conference on Artificial Intelligence*, 34(01):11–18.

Aakanksha Chowdhery, Sharan Narang, Jacob Devlin, Maarten Bosma, Gaurav Mishra, Adam Roberts, Paul Barham, Hyung Won Chung, Charles Sutton, Sebastian Gehrmann, Parker Schuh, Kensen Shi, Sasha Tsvyashchenko, Joshua Maynez, Abhishek Rao, Parker Barnes, Yi Tay, Noam Shazeer, Vinodkumar Prabhakaran, Emily Reif, Nan Du, Ben Hutchinson, Reiner Pope, James Bradbury, Jacob Austin, Michael Isard, Guy Gur-Ari, Pengcheng Yin, Toju Duke, Anselm Levskaya, Sanjay Ghemawat, Sunipa Dev, Henryk Michalewski, Xavier Garcia, Vedant Misra, Kevin Robinson, Liam Fedus, Denny Zhou, Daphne Ippolito, David Luan, Hyeontaek Lim, Barret Zoph, Alexander Spiridonov, Ryan Sepassi, David Dohan, Shivani Agrawal, Mark Omernick, Andrew M. Dai, Thanumalayan Sankaranarayana Pillai, Marie Pellat, Aitor Lewkowycz, Erica Moreira, Rewon Child, Oleksandr Polozov, Katherine Lee, Zongwei Zhou, Xuezhi Wang, Brennan Saeta, Mark Diaz, Orhan Firat, Michele Catasta, Jason Wei, Kathy Meier-Hellstern, Douglas Eck, Jeff Dean, Slav Petrov, and Noah Fiedel. 2022. Palm: Scaling language modeling with pathways.

Alexandra Chronopoulou, Matthew Peters, Alexander Fraser, and Jesse Dodge. 2023a. AdapterSoup: Weight averaging to improve generalization of pretrained language models. In *Findings of the Association for Computational Linguistics: EACL 2023*, pages 2054–2063, Dubrovnik, Croatia. Association for Computational Linguistics.

Alexandra Chronopoulou, Dario Stojanovski, and Alexander Fraser. 2023b. Language-family adapters for low-resource multilingual neural machine translation. In *Proceedings of the The Sixth Workshop on Technologies for Machine Translation of Low-Resource Languages (LoResMT 2023)*, pages 59–72, Dubrovnik, Croatia. Association for Computational Linguistics.

Hyung Won Chung, Le Hou, Shayne Longpre, Barret Zoph, Yi Tay, William Fedus, Yunxuan Li, Xuezhi Wang, Mostafa Dehghani, Siddhartha Brahma, Albert Webson, Shixiang Shane Gu, Zhuyun Dai, Mirac Suzgun, Xinyun Chen, Aakanksha Chowdhery, Alex Castro-Ros, Marie Pellat, Kevin Robinson, Dasha Valter, Sharan Narang, Gaurav Mishra, Adams Yu, Vincent Zhao, Yanping Huang, Andrew Dai, Hongkun Yu, Slav Petrov, Ed H. Chi, Jeff Dean, Jacob Devlin, Adam Roberts, Denny Zhou, Quoc V. Le, and Jason Wei. 2022. Scaling instruction-finetuned language models.

Jonathan H. Clark, Eunsol Choi, Michael Collins, Dan Garrette, Tom Kwiatkowski, Vitaly Nikolaev, and Jennimaria Palomaki. 2020. TyDi QA: A benchmark for information-seeking question answering in typologically diverse languages. *Transactions of the Association for Computational Linguistics*, 8:454–470.

Asa Cooper Stickland, Xian Li, and Marjan Ghazvininejad. 2021. Recipes for adapting pre-trained monolingual and multilingual models to machine translation. In *Proceedings of the 16th Conference of the European Chapter of the Association for Computational Linguistics: Main Volume*, pages 3440–3453, Online. Association for Computational Linguistics.

Nico Daheim, Thomas Möllenhoff, Edoardo Ponti, Iryna Gurevych, and Mohammad Emtiyaz Khan. 2024. Model merging by uncertainty-based gradient matching. In *The Twelfth International Conference on Learning Representations*.

Ali Edalati, Marzieh Tahaei, Ivan Kobyzev, Vahid Partovi Nia, James J. Clark, and Mehdi Rezagholizadeh. 2022. Krona: Parameter efficient tuning with kronecker adapter.

Chris Fifty, Ehsan Amid, Zhe Zhao, Tianhe Yu, Rohan Anil, and Chelsea Finn. 2021. Efficiently identifying task groupings for multi-task learning. In *Advances in Neural Information Processing Systems*, volume 34, pages 27503–27516. Curran Associates, Inc.

Jonathan Frankle and Michael Carbin. 2019. The lottery ticket hypothesis: Finding sparse, trainable neural networks. In *International Conference on Learning Representations*.

Jonathan Frankle, Gintare Karolina Dziugaite, Daniel Roy, and Michael Carbin. 2020. Linear mode connectivity and the lottery ticket hypothesis. In *Proceedings of the 37th International Conference on Machine Learning*, volume 119 of *Proceedings of Machine Learning Research*, pages 3259–3269. PMLR.

George Giannakopoulos, Jeff Kubina, John Conroy, Josef Steinberger, Benoit Favre, Mijail Kabadjov, Udo Kruschwitz, and Massimo Poesio. 2015. MultiLing 2015: Multilingual summarization of single and multi-documents, on-line fora, and call-center conversations. In *Proceedings of the 16th Annual Meeting of the Special Interest Group on Discourse and Dialogue*, pages 270–274, Prague, Czech Republic. Association for Computational Linguistics.

Max Grusky, Mor Naaman, and Yoav Artzi. 2018. Newsroom: A dataset of 1.3 million summaries with diverse extractive strategies. In *Proceedings of the 2018 Conference of the North American Chapter of the Association for Computational Linguistics: Human Language Technologies, Volume 1 (Long Papers)*, pages 708–719, New Orleans, Louisiana. Association for Computational Linguistics.

Vipul Gupta, Santiago Akle Serrano, and Dennis DeCoste. 2020. Stochastic weight averaging in parallel: Large-batch training that generalizes well. In *ICLR*.

Tahmid Hasan, Abhik Bhattacharjee, Md. Saiful Islam, Kazi Mubasshir, Yuan-Fang Li, Yong-Bin Kang, M. Sohel Rahman, and Rifat Shahriyar. 2021. XL-sum: Large-scale multilingual abstractive summarization for 44 languages. In *Findings of the Association for Computational Linguistics: ACL-IJCNLP 2021*, pages 4693–4703, Online. Association for Computational Linguistics.

Karl Moritz Hermann, Tomas Kocisky, Edward Grefenstette, Lasse Espeholt, Will Kay, Mustafa Suleyman, and Phil Blunsom. 2015. Teaching machines to read and comprehend. In *Advances in Neural Information Processing Systems*, volume 28. Curran Associates, Inc.

Neil Houlsby, Andrei Giurgiu, Stanislaw Jastrzebski, Bruna Morrone, Quentin De Laroussilhe, Andrea Gesmundo, Mona Attariyan, and Sylvain Gelly. 2019. Parameter-efficient transfer learning for NLP. In *Proceedings of the International Conference on Machine Learning*, Proceedings of Machine Learning Research, pages 2790–2799.

Edward J Hu, Yelong Shen, Phillip Wallis, Zeyuan Allen-Zhu, Yuanzhi Li, Shean Wang, Lu Wang, and Weizhu Chen. 2022. LoRA: Low-rank adaptation of large language models. In *International Conference on Learning Representations*.

Chengsong Huang, Qian Liu, Bill Yuchen Lin, Tianyu Pang, Chao Du, and Min Lin. 2023. Lorahub: Efficient cross-task generalization via dynamic lora composition.

Gabriel Ilharco, Marco Tulio Ribeiro, Mitchell Wortsman, Ludwig Schmidt, Hannaneh Hajishirzi, and Ali Farhadi. 2023. Editing models with task arithmetic. In *The Eleventh International Conference on Learning Representations*.

Pavel Izmailov, Dmitrii Podoprikhin, Timur Garipov, Dmitry Vetrov, and Andrew Gordon Wilson. 2018. Averaging weights leads to wider optima and better generalization. Conference on Uncertainty in Artificial Intelligence (UAI), 2018.

Albert Q. Jiang, Alexandre Sablayrolles, Antoine Roux, Arthur Mensch, Blanche Savary, Chris Bamford, Devendra Singh Chaplot, Diego de las Casas, Emma Bou Hanna, Florian Bressand, Gianna Lengyel, Guillaume Bour, Guillaume Lample, Lélio Renard Lavaud, Lucile Saulnier, Marie-Anne Lachaux, Pierre Stock, Sandeep Subramanian, Sophia Yang, Szymon Antoniak, Teven Le Scao, Théophile Gervet, Thibaut Lavril, Thomas Wang, Timothée Lacroix, and William El Sayed. 2024. Mixtral of experts.

Xisen Jin, Xiang Ren, Daniel Preotiuc-Pietro, and Pengxiang Cheng. 2023. Dataless knowledge fusion by merging weights of language models. In *The Eleventh International Conference on Learning Representations*.

Rabeeh Karimi Mahabadi, Sebastian Ruder, Mostafa Dehghani, and James Henderson. 2021. Parameter-efficient multi-task fine-tuning for transformers via shared hypernetworks. In *Proceedings of the 59th Annual Meeting of the Association for Computational Linguistics and the 11th International Joint Conference on Natural Language Processing (Volume 1: Long Papers)*, pages 565–576, Online. Association for Computational Linguistics.

Brian Lester, Rami Al-Rfou, and Noah Constant. 2021. The power of scale for parameter-efficient prompt tuning. In *Proceedings of the 2021 Conference on Empirical Methods in Natural Language Processing*, pages 3045–3059, Online and Punta Cana, Dominican Republic. Association for Computational Linguistics.

Margaret Li, Suchin Gururangan, Tim Dettmers, Mike Lewis, Tim Althoff, Noah A. Smith, and Luke Zettlemoyer. 2022a. Branch-train-merge: Embarrassingly parallel training of expert language models.

Margaret Li, Suchin Gururangan, Tim Dettmers, Mike Lewis, Tim Althoff, Noah A. Smith, and Luke Zettlemoyer. 2022b. Branch-train-merge: Embarrassingly parallel training of expert language models.

Xiang Lisa Li and Percy Liang. 2021. Prefix-tuning: Optimizing continuous prompts for generation. In *Proceedings of the 59th Annual Meeting of the Association for Computational Linguistics and the 11th International Joint Conference on Natural Language Processing (Volume 1: Long Papers)*, pages 4582–4597, Online. Association for Computational Linguistics.

Chin-Yew Lin. 2004. ROUGE: A package for automatic evaluation of summaries. In *Text Summarization Branches Out*, pages 74–81, Barcelona, Spain. Association for Computational Linguistics.

Patrick Littell, David R. Mortensen, Ke Lin, Katherine Kairis, Carlisle Turner, and Lori Levin. 2017. URIEL and lang2vec: Representing languages as typological, geographical, and phylogenetic vectors. In *Proceedings of the 15th Conference of the European Chapter of the Association for Computational Linguistics: Volume 2, Short Papers*, pages 8–14, Valencia, Spain. Association for Computational Linguistics.

Michael Matena and Colin Raffel. 2021. Merging models with fisher-weighted averaging.

Shashi Narayan, Shay B. Cohen, and Mirella Lapata. 2018. Don't give me the details, just the summary! topic-aware convolutional neural networks for extreme summarization. In *Proceedings of the 2018 Conference on Empirical Methods in Natural Language Processing*, pages 1797–1807, Brussels, Belgium. Association for Computational Linguistics.

Ani Nenkova and Kathleen McKeown. 2011. Automatic summarization. *Foundations and Trends in Information Retrieval*, pages 103–233.

Guillermo Ortiz-Jimenez, Alessandro Favero, and Pascal Frossard. 2023. Task arithmetic in the tangent space: Improved editing of pre-trained models.

Jonas Pfeiffer, Aishwarya Kamath, Andreas Rücklé, Kyunghyun Cho, and Iryna Gurevych. 2021. AdapterFusion: Non-destructive task composition for transfer learning. In *Proceedings of the 16th Conference of the European Chapter of the Association for Computational Linguistics: Main Volume*, pages 487–503, Online. Association for Computational Linguistics.

Jonas Pfeiffer, Sebastian Ruder, Ivan Vulic, and Edoardo Maria Ponti. 2023. Modular deep learning. *arXiv preprint*.

Jonas Pfeiffer, Ivan Vulić, Iryna Gurevych, and Sebastian Ruder. 2020. MAD-X: An Adapter-Based Framework for Multi-Task Cross-Lingual Transfer. In *Proceedings of the 2020 Conference on Empirical Methods in Natural Language Processing (EMNLP)*, pages 7654–7673, Online. Association for Computational Linguistics.

Edoardo Maria Ponti, Alessandro Sordoni, Yoshua Bengio, and Siva Reddy. 2023. Combining parameter-efficient modules for task-level generalisation. In *Proceedings of the 17th Conference of the European Chapter of the Association for Computational Linguistics*, pages 687–702, Dubrovnik, Croatia. Association for Computational Linguistics.

Alec Radford, Jeff Wu, Rewon Child, David Luan, Dario Amodei, and Ilya Sutskever. 2019. Language models are unsupervised multitask learners. *OpenAI Blog*.

Colin Raffel, Noam Shazeer, Adam Roberts, Katherine Lee, Sharan Narang, Michael Matena, Yanqi Zhou, Wei Li, and Peter J. Liu. 2020. Exploring the limits of transfer learning with a unified text-to-text transformer. *Journal of Machine Learning Research*.

Sylvestre-Alvise Rebuffi, Hakan Bilen, and Andrea Vedaldi. 2017. Learning multiple visual domains with residual adapters. In *Advances in Neural Information Processing Systems*.

Thomas Scialom, Paul-Alexis Dray, Sylvain Lamprier, Benjamin Piwowarski, and Jacopo Staiano. 2020. MLSUM: The multilingual summarization corpus. In *Proceedings of the 2020 Conference on Empirical Methods in Natural Language Processing (EMNLP)*, pages 8051–8067, Online. Association for Computational Linguistics.

Hugo Touvron, Thibaut Lavril, Gautier Izacard, Xavier Martinet, Marie-Anne Lachaux, Timothée Lacroix, Baptiste Rozière, Naman Goyal, Eric Hambro, Faisal Azhar, Aurelien Rodriguez, Armand Joulin, Edouard Grave, and Guillaume Lample. 2023. Llama: Open and efficient foundation language models.

Ahmet Üstün, Arianna Bisazza, Gosse Bouma, and Gertjan van Noord. 2020. UDapter: Language adaptation for truly Universal Dependency parsing. In *Proceedings of the 2020 Conference on Empirical Methods in Natural Language Processing (EMNLP)*, pages 2302–2315, Online. Association for Computational Linguistics.

Marko Vidoni, Ivan Vulić, and Goran Glavaš. 2020. Orthogonal language and task adapters in zero-shot cross-lingual transfer.

Tu Vu, Aditya Barua, Brian Lester, Daniel Cer, Mohit Iyyer, and Noah Constant. 2022. Overcoming catastrophic forgetting in zero-shot cross-lingual generation. In *Proceedings of the 2022 Conference on Empirical Methods in Natural Language Processing*, pages 9279–9300, Abu Dhabi, United Arab Emirates. Association for Computational Linguistics.

Alex Wang, Amanpreet Singh, Julian Michael, Felix Hill, Omer Levy, and Samuel Bowman. 2018. GLUE: A multi-task benchmark and analysis platform for natural language understanding. In *Proceedings of the 2018 EMNLP Workshop BlackboxNLP: Analyzing and Interpreting Neural Networks for NLP*, pages 353–355, Brussels, Belgium. Association for Computational Linguistics.

Mitchell Wortsman, Gabriel Ilharco, Samir Ya Gadre, Rebecca Roelofs, Raphael Gontijo-Lopes, Ari S Morcos, Hongseok Namkoong, Ali Farhadi, Yair Carmon, Simon Kornblith, and Ludwig Schmidt. 2022. Model soups: averaging weights of multiple fine-tuned models improves accuracy without increasing inference time. In *Proceedings of the 39th International Conference on Machine Learning*.

Linting Xue, Noah Constant, Adam Roberts, Mihir Kale, Rami Al-Rfou, Aditya Siddhant, Aditya Barua, and Colin Raffel. 2021. mT5: A massively multilingual pre-trained text-to-text transformer. In *Proceedings of the 2021 Conference of the North American Chapter of the Association for Computational Linguistics: Human Language Technologies*, pages 483–498, Online. Association for Computational Linguistics.

Prateek Yadav, Derek Tam, Leshem Choshen, Colin Raffel, and Mohit Bansal. 2023. Ties-merging: Resolving interference when merging models. In *Advances in Neural Information Processing Systems*.

David Yunis, Kumar Kshitij Patel, Pedro Henrique Pamplona Savarese, Gal Vardi, Jonathan Frankle, Matthew Walter, Karen Livescu, and Michael Maire. 2022. On convexity and linear mode connectivity in neural networks. In *OPT 2022: Optimization for Machine Learning (NeurIPS 2022 Workshop)*.

Jinghan Zhang, Shiqi Chen, Junteng Liu, and Junxian He. 2023a. Composing parameter-efficient modules with arithmetic operations. In *Advances in Neural Information Processing Systems*.

Renrui Zhang, Jiaming Han, Chris Liu, Peng Gao, Aojun Zhou, Xiangfei Hu, Shilin Yan, Pan Lu, Hongsheng Li, and Yu Qiao. 2023b. Llama-adapter: Efficient fine-tuning of language models with zero-init attention.

| Method | Ar | Bn | En | Id | Ja | Ko | Ru | Sw | Te | Th | Tr | Avg |
|---|---|---|---|---|---|---|---|---|---|---|---|---|
| LoRA | 23.4 | 27.6 | 23.5 | 25.0 | 33.6 | 30.4 | 21.3 | 27.1 | 26.9 | 24.7 | 25.3 | 26.2 |
| Multi-LoRA | 23.0 | 27.8 | 22.5 | 24.6 | 34.0 | 30.4 | 20.8 | 27.1 | 27.8 | 25.1 | 24.9 | 26.2 |
| Kronecker | 23.4 | 27.7 | 23.1 | 24.8 | 34.6 | 31.2 | 21.6 | 27.1 | 27.4 | 24.8 | 25.2 | 26.4 |
| Multi-Kronecker | 22.8 | 27.5 | 22.5 | 24.9 | 34.7 | 31.2 | 20.8 | 27.5 | 27.6 | 24.8 | 25.2 | 26.3 |
| Full fine-tuning | 23.9 | 28.1 | 22.6 | 25.3 | 34.8 | 30.4 | 21.8 | 27.0 | 28.2 | 24.6 | 25.4 | 26.6 |

Table 6: **Parameter-efficient fine-tuning vs Full fine-tuning**. Rouge (ROUGE-2 spm) in-domain scores on the XLSum$_{seen}$ test set.

# A Appendix

## A.1 Are PEFT methods competitive to full fine-tuning of PaLM 2?

We present the performance of LoRA and Kronecker, two PEFT methods, when used to fine-tune PaLM 2 on summarization in 11 languages of XL-Sum in Table 6. We compare their performance to full fine-tuning of PaLM 2.

Fine-tuning the model with LoRA results in summarization scores that are only 0.4 ROUGE points below full fine-tuning, while fine-tuning with Kronecker provides a performance similar to full fine-tuning (i.e., just 0.2 points worse than full fine-tuning). Based on this finding, we conclude that using PEFT methods to fine-tuning PaLM 2, a state-of-the-art LLM, is largely impactful, as in our experiments LoRA for example trains only 0.2% of the model's parameters whereas fully tuning the LLM requires updates on 100% of the model's parameters.

## A.2 XLSum$_{\text{seen}}$ Dataset

We are showing the dataset sizes of XLSum$_{\text{seen}}$ in Table 7.

| Language | Lang code | Dataset size |
|---|---|---|
| Arabic | ar | 38k |
| Bengali | bn | 8k |
| English | en | 306k |
| Indonesian | id | 38k |
| Japanese | ja | 7k |
| Korean | ko | 4k |
| Russian | ru | 62k |
| Swahili | sw | 8k |
| Telugu | te | 10k |
| Thai | th | 7k |
| Turkish | tr | 27k |

Table 7: Languages in XLSum seen and dataset sizes (training).

# Modeling Bilingual Sentence Processing: Evaluating RNN and Transformer Architectures for Cross-Language Structural Priming

**Demi Zhang, Bushi Xiao, Chao Gao, Sangpil Youm, Bonnie Dorr**
University of Florida
{zhang.yidan, xiaobushi, gao.chao, youms, bonniejdorr}@ufl.edu

## Abstract

This study evaluates the performance of Recurrent Neural Network (RNN) and Transformer models in replicating cross-language structural priming, a key indicator of abstract grammatical representations in human language processing. Focusing on Chinese-English priming, which involves two typologically distinct languages, we examine how these models handle the robust phenomenon of structural priming, where exposure to a particular sentence structure increases the likelihood of selecting a similar structure subsequently. Our findings indicate that transformers outperform RNNs in generating primed sentence structures, with accuracy rates that exceed 25.84% to 33. 33%. This challenges the conventional belief that human sentence processing primarily involves recurrent and immediate processing and suggests a role for cue-based retrieval mechanisms. This work contributes to our understanding of how computational models may reflect human cognitive processes across diverse language families.

## 1 Introduction

Structural priming refers to the phenomenon where encountering a specific syntactic structure boosts the probability of generating or understanding sentences with a comparable structure (Pickering and Ferreira, 2008). It serves as a valuable method for exploring the capabilities of language models and probing their internal states and their potential relation to human sentence processing.

Studies show that Recurrent Neural Networks (RNN), particularly Gated Recurrent Unit models (GRU), have been pivotal in modeling human sentence processing, including structural priming (Frank et al., 2019). Meanwhile, transformers also demonstrate structural priming ability similar to that of humans (Sinclair et al., 2022). This suggests the representations learned by the models

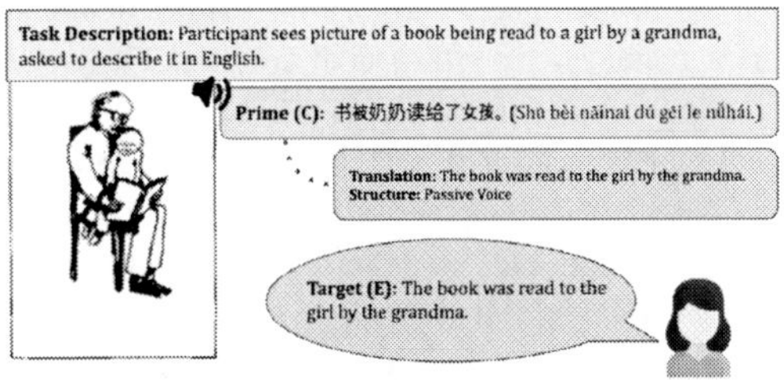


Figure 1: Cross-language structure priming of human participant: *C* denotes Chinese, *E* denotes English.

may capture not only sequential structure but also some degree of hierarchical syntactic information.

That said, to our knowledge, no study has compared these models' ability to syntactically prime across two typologically distant languages. In the current study, we address this gap by comparing the models' ability to prime syntactically across two languages from vastly different families.

Consider a case where a human participant reads a passive Chinese (C) sentence and is then asked to describe a separate picture in English (E) (see Figure 1). Here, the passive sentence C influences the structure of the target sentence E, leading the participant to use passive voice in their description.

Our study explores structural priming in translation models, highlighting their ability to generate syntactically diverse English outputs from Chinese inputs. A key contribution is a set of insights into syntactic representation across typologically distinct languages in computation models. We demonstrate that transformers outperform RNNs in generating primed sentence structures, challenging the belief that human sentence processing relies mainly on recurrent and immediate processing.

The next section reviews work on cross-linguistic priming. Section 3 introduces our study, exploring insights into syntactic representation across typologically distinct languages in computational models. Section 4 introduces a newly designed test set to evaluate our models. Section 5



*Proceedings of the Fourth Workshop on Multilingual Representation Learning (MRL 2024)*, pages 127–136
November 16, 2024 ©2024 Association for Computational Linguistics

details the implementation and training of two distinct models. Section 6 discusses the design of our experimental setup, followed by a comprehensive analysis and interpretation of our results.

## 2 Related Work

This section focuses on work related to cross-linguistic priming, as exemplified in Figure 1. Prior experiments induce cross-linguistic structural priming by instructing bilingual participants to use two languages: presenting primes in one language and eliciting targets in another. These studies show that specific sentence structures in one language can influence the use of similar structures in the other language (Hartsuiker et al., 2004).

Computational modeling studies have shown that RNNs exhibit structural priming effects akin to those observed in human bilinguals (Frank, 2021). These models process sequential information through recurrence, a feature thought to resemble human cognitive processing. The emergence of such priming effects in language models suggests that they develop implicit syntactic representations that resemble those employed by human language systems (Linzen and Baroni, 2021).

However, the transformer model, which uses self-attention mechanisms instead of recurrence, challenges this notion. The transformer's ability to directly access past input information, regardless of temporal distance, offers a fundamentally different approach from RNNs. The effectiveness of transformers in various NLP tasks makes us wonder if they can emulate RNNs in modeling cross-language structural priming.

The current study is inspired by two prior studies. Merkx and Frank (2021) compare transformer and RNN models' ability to account for measures of monolingual (English) human reading effort. They show that transformers outperform RNNs in explaining self-paced reading times and neural activity during English sentence reading, challenging the widely held idea that human sentence processing relies on recurrent and immediate processing. Their study is monolingual and English-centric. Frank (2021) investigates cross-language structural priming, finding that RNNs trained on English-Dutch sentences account for garden-path effects and are sensitive to structural priming, within and between languages.

Recent studies on structural priming in neural language models have shown significant progress,

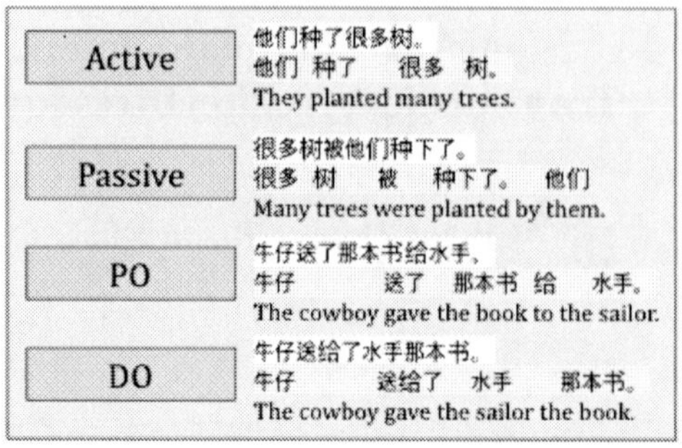


Figure 2: Example of Active, Passive, Propositional Object (PO), and Double Object (DO). White highlighted sentence is original Chinese sentence, and yellow highlighted Sentence is word-to-word mapping between Chinese and English.

with researchers quantifying this phenomenon using various methods across different languages. Prasad et al. (2019) demonstrate that LSTM language models can hierarchically organize syntactic representations in a manner that reflects abstract sentence properties. Sinclair et al. (2022) show that Transformer models exhibit structural priming, suggesting these models capture both sequential and hierarchical syntactic information.

Michaelov et al. (2023) provide evidence that large multilingual language models possess abstract grammatical representations that influence text generation similarly across different languages. Together, these findings underscore the capacity of neural models to develop and apply structural abstractions, contributing to a deeper understanding of language processing in AI.

## 3 The Current Study

Our study examines structural priming in translation models, demonstrating their capability to generate syntactically diverse English outputs from Chinese inputs. This approach offers insights into syntactic representations across typologically distinct languages in computational models.

To compare RNNs and transformers in their ability to model cross-language structural priming, we adopt a new approach. While Frank (2021) trains models on comprehension, where a longer response time indicates greater difficulty in understanding a new sentence and thus a weaker priming effect, the current study focuses on production. Here, the structure of each generated sentence is compared with that of the input sentence to assess the presence of a priming effect.

As shown in Figure 2, Chinese has equiva-

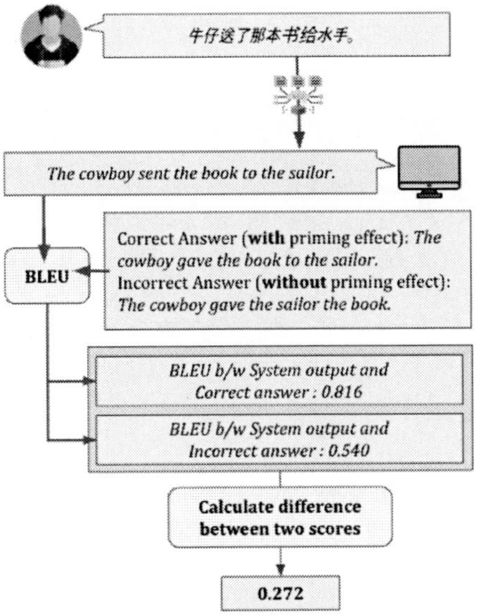


Figure 3: Example of test phase and evaluation process.

lents for structures that are passive (e.g., *Many trees were planted by them*) and active (e.g., *They planted many trees*). It also includes structures for prepositional objects (e.g., *The cowboy gave the book to the sailor*) and double objects (e.g., *The cowboy gave the sailor the book*). In our study, the input sentence is in Chinese and system output is an English version of the sentence. BLEU scores are calculated between the system-generated English sentence and both a "correct" English sentence that shares the structure with the Chinese inputand an "incorrect" sentence. We then calculate the difference between the two BLEU scores, as depicted in Figure 3.

Another novel aspect of our study is the selection of two languages from vastly divergent language families, challenging the models to develop abstract representations for distinct structures.

## 4 Data Preparation

We select and process a Chinese-English corpus which contains 5.2 million Chinese-English parallel sentence pairs (Xu, 2019).[1]

We employ a DataLoader [2] to facilitate batch processing, transforming text into token IDs suitable for model interpretation. We then use the Helsinki-NLP tokenizer (Tiedemann and Thottingal, 2020)[3] to map Chinese to English, accommodating over a thousand models for diverse language pairs.

The tokenizer, by default, processes text based on source language settings. To correctly encode target language text, the context manager must be set to use the target tokenizer. Without this, the source language tokenizer would be incorrectly applied to the target text, leading to poor tokenization results, such as improper word splitting for words not recognized in the source language.

In sequence-to-sequence models, assigning a value of -100 to padding tokens ensures they are excluded from loss calculations. This setup is crucial for effective model training, enabling precise adjustment of model parameters based on the tokenized input and target sequences. Proper data formatting through this preprocessing step facilitates optimal training outcomes.

We also design a test dataset, initially sampling five sentences for each of the four sentence structures (Active Voice, Passive Voice, Prepositional Object, and Double Object) from the Cross-language Structural Priming Corpus (Michaelov et al., 2023). To augment the data, we employ a LLM, ChatGPT 3.5 (OpenAI, 2024), By providing a one-shot learning prompt, we expand each set to 30 sentences, resulting in a total of 120 sentences for our test dataset:

> Generate 30 sentences with the following structure: *The cowboy gave the book to the sailor.* Replace all the words while keeping the sentence structure the same.

In our test set, each Chinese sentence is paired with a correct and an incorrect English sentence.

Subsequently, a bilingual annotator proficient in both Mandarin and English carefully reviews the sentence outputs generated by the LLM, ensuring that each triplet comprises translation equivalents. The review also confirms that only the 'correct' answer maintains syntactic alignment with the original Chinese sentence.

## 5 Language Models

We implement both a transformer model and an RNN model to handle sequence-to-sequence tasks using the encoder-decoder architecture. (See Experiment of Figure 4.) This architecture supports

[1]The source can be found at https://drive.google.com/file/d/1EX8eE5YWBxCaohBO8Fh4e2j3b9C2bTVQ/view?pli=1

[2]Our Dataloader is supported by PyTorch, referencing its license located at https://github.com/pytorch/pytorch/blob/main/LICENSE

[3]Helsinki-NLP is licensed under the MIT license. For more details, see here: https://github.com/Helsinki-NLP/Opus-MT/blob/master/LICENSE

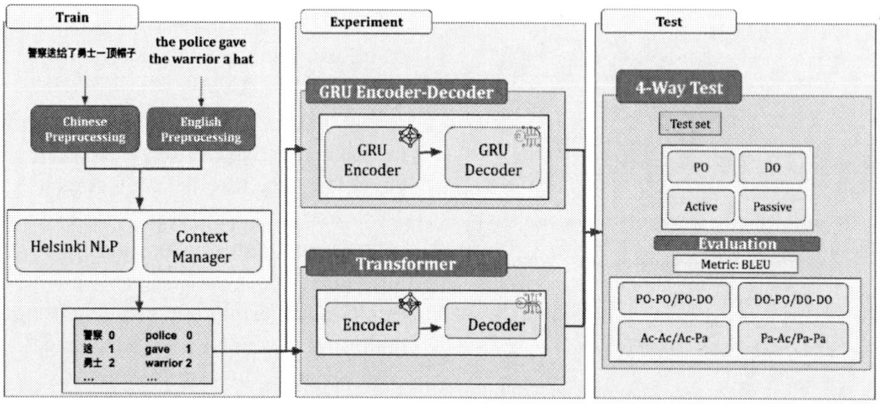


Figure 4: The workflow of the study includes PO (Propositional Object), DO (Double Object), Ac (Active), and Pa (Passive). In the training phase, raw bilingual data are preprocessed to generate token pairs. In the experiment phase, we employ transformer and RNN-based encoder-decoder architectures. In the testing phase, we evaluate the model's performance across four sentence structures using the BLEU metric.

the processing of both input sequences and output sequences of varying lengths, which is crucial for accommodating sentences with different structures yet similar meanings. This section explores why these language models can assist us identify structural priming. We train and test our RNN model and transformer using AMD EPYC 75F3 8-Core Processor and 1 NVIDIA A100 GPU.

### 5.1 Multi-head Attention in Transformer

In the transformer model, we use the self-attention mechanism (AttModel) to capture sentence structure. This mechanism identifies dependencies between different positions and adjusts the representation of each word based on its relationship with others, thus facilitating the learning of sentence structure. Following Vaswani et al. (2017),

$$\text{Attention}(Q, K, V) = \text{softmax}\left(\frac{QK^T}{\sqrt{d_k}}\right)V \quad (1)$$

where $Q, K, V$ are obtained through linear transformations of an input sequence of text, each with its own learnable weight matrix. In the encoder part of model, $Q, K, V$ comes from the same source sequence, while in the decoder, $Q$ comes from the target sequence, and $K$ and $V$ come from the encoder's output. Since the computation of $Q$, $K$, and $V$ requires processing the entire input sentence, the model can simultaneously focus on all positions and capture the sentence's structure.

In the decoder part of the transformer model, multiple attention heads capture different levels of sentence features, leading to a more comprehensive representation of sentence structure. Each attention head specializes in capturing specific semantic relationships, such as word dependencies and distance relationships.

This approach enhances the model's ability to comprehend the intricacies of sentence structure. The equation is as follows:

$$\text{MH}(Q, K, V) = \text{Concat}(head_1, \ldots, head_h) \cdot W^O \quad (2)$$

where $W^O$ is the weight matrix to be trained, and $head_1, \ldots, head_h$, computed through equation 1, represent the attention weights of each head (we use 8 heads). Concat is the operation of joining tensors along their last dimension.

We also prioritize the choice of positional encoding method. While the common method involves using sine and cosine functions, we opt for learnable positional embeddings. We believe this approach offers more advantages for learning structural priming, as it helps our model better understand and encode the relative positions of words within a sentence.

In contrast to the fixed positional encoding, learnable positional embeddings assign different weights to different positions, emphasizing the relevant positional information that contributes to the priming effect. This enables the model to capture more intricate positional relationships and dependencies specific to the task of structural priming.

### 5.2 GRU Encoder and GRU Decoder

Some studies (Zhou et al., 2018) show that RNNs can preserve sentence structure and facilitate identification of structural priming environments. Their sequential nature allows them to process input tokens based on the context of the entire sentence. As each token is processed, the RNN's hidden state is updated, retaining information about preceding tokens and their contextual relevance. This sequential processing enables the model to capture word dependency relationships, thereby preserving the structural integrity of the sentence. Summarizing:

$$\text{State}(dh_i, c_i), p = f(\text{State}(dh_{i-1}, c_{i-1}), m) \quad (3)$$

The function $f$ refers to the hidden layer of the RNN model, which is a neural network. It takes the previous layer's State i-1 and the output vector from the previous time step $m$ as input, and outputs the next layer's State i and prediction value $p$ until it encounters the termination symbol. Here, $dh$ signifies the hidden state of the RNN unit in decoder, tasked with capturing pertinent information from the input sequence. In the initial decoder step, $dh$ embodies the final output state of the encoder. In subsequent decoder steps, $dh$ denotes the preceding RNN unit's output.

To address the challenge of not being able to retain the entire sentence structure, we introduce the attention mechanism. This feature of the RNN model enables it to focus more on the parts of the input sequence that are most relevant to the current output, thereby enhancing prediction accuracy. Its potential for predicting structural patterns stems from the attention mechanism's ability to capture dependencies within sequential data and to leverage these for better predictions. As shown in equation 3, $c$ denotes the attention, and its calculation is as follows:

$$\alpha_i = g(eh_i, dh_0) \quad (4)$$

As before, $dh_0$ denotes the final state of the encoder and $eh$ signifies the hidden state of the each RNN unit in the encoder. Function $g$ is used to calculate the weight $\alpha_i$ of $eh_i$ in the final state $dh_0$. As a result, the attention $c$ is obtained by combining all previous states:

$$c_i = \sum(\alpha_i * dh_i) \quad (5)$$

calculated by summing the products of the weight $\alpha$ and the decoder state $dh$.

Our study utilizes a variant of RNNs known as the Gated Recurrent Unit (GRU). The GRU encoder and decoder are gating mechanisms that effectively manage long-distance dependencies and mitigate the vanishing gradient problem. Additionally, GRUs possess fewer parameters and demonstrate higher computational efficiency.

Following Dey and Salem (2017), we define the gate mechanism in two parts:

- Update Gate: $z_t = \sigma(W_z x_t + U_z h_{t-1} + b_z)$

The update gate $z_t$ in the encoder controls the blending of the current input $x_t$ and the previous hidden state $h_{t-1}$. In the decoder, the update gate regulates the interaction between the current input and the previous decoder state, allowing the model to selectively incorporate relevant information from the input when generating the output.

- Reset Gate: $r_t = \sigma(W_r x_t + U_r h_{t-1} + b_r)$

The reset gate $r_t$ in the encoder regulates the interaction between the current input $x_t$ and the previous hidden state $h_{t-1}$. In the decoder, the reset gate governs how the current input interacts with the previous decoder state. This allows the model to selectively forget certain parts of the input information captured by the encoder. This helps the decoder to generate outputs that are less influenced by outdated information from the input sequence.

## 6 Experimental Setup

Since structural priming effects are sometimes not symmetrical, our study only includes a structural priming experiment with Mandarin to English bilinguals, while existing literature strongly supports the presence of structural priming effects in both language directions.

To assess the effectiveness of our model in Chinese-English, we adopt the standard bilingual evaluation understudy (BLEU) metric (Papineni et al., 2002), which ranges from 0 to 1, indicating the similarity of predicted text against target text:

$$\text{BLEU} = \text{BP} \cdot \exp\left(\sum_{n=1}^{N} w_n \log p_n\right)$$

Here, $N$ is the maximum n-gram order (typically 4), $w_n$ is the weight assigned to each n-gram precision score (with $\sum_{n=1}^{N} w_n = 1$), $p_n$ is the precision score for n-grams of order $n$, and BP is the brevity penalty which penalizes shorter results.

After generating predicted outcomes and assembling a test set, we analyze the relationship between predictions and four types of reference sentences: (1) correct mappings with the same structure; (2) semantically similar but structurally different sentences; (3) semantically different but structurally identical sentences; and (4) sentences that differ both semantically and structurally.

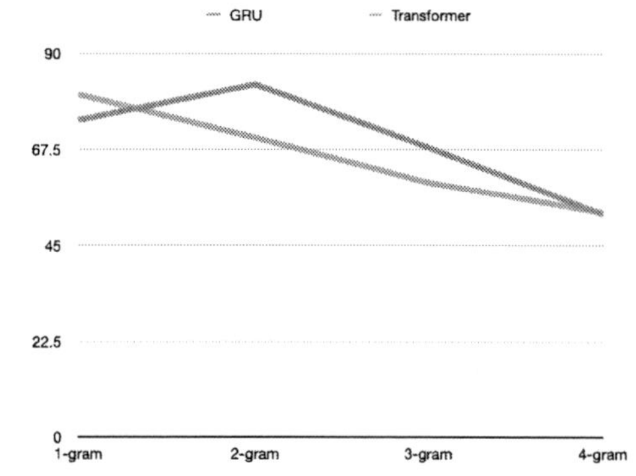


Figure 5: BLEU Score for standard structural priming. Comparison of ground truth datasets for testing and calibration.

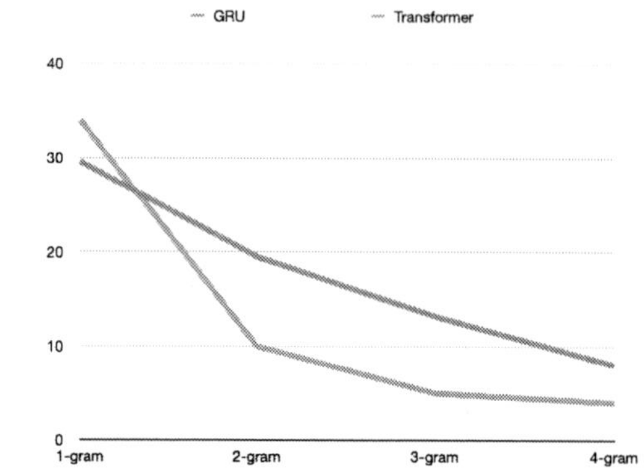


Figure 6: BLEU Score for wrong priming. Comparison between predictions for cross-language priming via average BLEU Score.

We divide the comparisons into two groups based on semantic similarity. In the first group of sentences with identical meanings, we hypothesize that effective structural priming would result in higher BLEU scores between the predicted sentences and the reference sentences that share the same structure, compared to those with different structures. This comparison aims to establish whether the model prefers to reproduce structures that are syntactically aligned with the ground truths when the semantic content remains constant.

The second category, with sentences differing in meaning, is crucial for demonstrating structural priming, as it eliminates the influence of semantic similarity. If sentences with identical structures receive higher BLEU scores than those with different structures, it suggests the model's predictions are driven by structure, regardless of semantic changes.

This methodology rigorously tests for structural priming, offering insights into how models process and replicate language structures.

## 7 Results and Analyses

We present the performance of the GRU-based RNN and standard transformer model (Vaswani et al., 2017) demonstrating their crosslingual structural priming effect in Chinese-English scenarios.

### 7.1 Structural Priming Performance

Our analysis reveals that, although both models achieve competitive BLEU scores, the transformer model shows a slight edge in handling complex sentence structures. Figure 5 shows that, when the training dataset is sufficiently large, both models attain high predicted BLEU scores for sentence segments. Figures 5–7 use BLEU scores, common in translation and relevant to structural priming, where identical structures yield higher scores (Lopez, 2008).

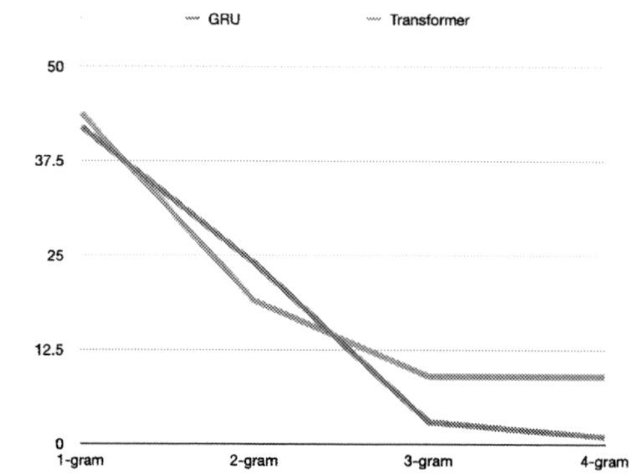


Figure 7: BLEU Score for correct priming. Comparison between predictions for opposite cross-language priming via average BLEU Score.

### 7.2 Crosslingual Structural Priming Effect

Our crosslingual structural priming exploration reveals a noteworthy pattern: both models facilitate the use of target-language syntactic structures influenced by the source language. However, the transformer model displays a stronger priming effect, suggesting a potential edge in mimicking human-like syntactic adaptation in bilingual contexts.

Figure 6 and Figure 7 show BLEU scores for machine-generated predictions with correct or opposite priming test sets. This representation allows for a more direct comparison with the results from machine translation models, facilitating a broader discussion regarding language structure in neural networks. From these we gain insights into model performance by evaluating how closely predictions align with the correct structures (e.g., Active-Active, DO-DO) versus opposite structures (e.g., Active-Passive, PO-DO). Higher BLEU scores against the correct priming sets indicate better structural alignment, whereas higher scores against opposite priming sets suggest deviations. For 1-gram and 2-gram comparisons, GRU and transformer models perform similarly. However, as n-grams increase, the transformer shows higher BLEU scores, indicating a closer alignment with incorrect structures. Overall, GRU outperforms the transformer in avoiding opposite priming (see Figure 7).

These results show that, when evaluated against the correct priming test sets, the transformer model performs similarly to GRU (see Figure 6), with slight improvements as the n-gram size increases. However, GRU generally outperforms the transformer compared to opposite priming (see Figure 7). Given that this involves "incorrect" priming, GRU aligns more closely with the opposite priming test set. Since the transformer shows a larger gap between correct and incorrect BLEU scores, We infer that it adheres more closely to the appropriate structural priming.

In a previous study, Michaelov et al. (2023) examine the presence of structural priming by comparing the proportion of target sentences produced after different types of priming statements. Similarly, in our study, we prime the language model with a specific sentence for each experimental item and then calculate the normalized probabilities for the two target sentences. These normalized probabilities are computed as follows:

First, calculate the raw probability of each target sentence given the priming sentence:

$$P(\text{DO Target}|\text{DO Prime})$$
$$P(\text{PO Target}|\text{PO Prime})$$
$$P(\text{DO Target}|\text{PO Prime})$$
$$P(\text{PO Target}|\text{DO Prime})$$

And the same method for:

$$P(\text{Active Target}|\text{Active Prime})$$
$$P(\text{Passive Target}|\text{Passive Prime})$$
$$P(\text{Active Target}|\text{Passive Prime})$$
$$P(\text{Passive Target}|\text{Active Prime})$$

These probabilities are then normalized to calculate the conditional probability of the target sentence, assuming the model outputs one of the two target sentences. Taking DO | PO as example:

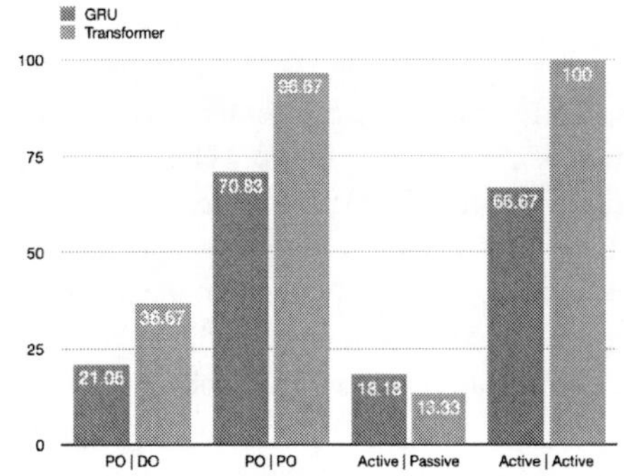


Figure 8: Priming Effect per Chunk: Proportion of correct cross-language priming chunks in the machine prediction results.

$$P_N(\text{Target}|\text{Prime}) = \frac{P(\text{Target}|\text{Prime})}{P(\text{DO Target}|\text{Prime}) + P(\text{PO Target}|\text{Prime})}$$

Since the sum of the normalized probabilities for the two target sentences is 1, we only need to consider the probability of one target type and compare it across different priming types. The probability of another target type can be derived from this, i.e. $P_N(\overline{\text{Target}}|\text{Prime}) = 1 - P_N(\text{Target}|\text{Prime})$. By considering only one target type, we can directly compare the priming effects of the two priming types on the specific target, which is a key aspect of structural priming analysis. The quantitative findings depicted in Figure 8 indicate that the transformer model generally outperforms GRU. Additionally, a horizontal analysis of priming structural types reveals that machine predictions perform better with active/passive structures compared to PO/DO structures.

## 8 Summary and Conclusions

This study evaluates cross-language structural priming effects in RNN and transformer models in a Chinese-English context. The models are trained on sentence pairs from both languages. Our research aims to compare the structural priming abilities of different models. Even when using the same training set, which contains structurally primed sentences, RNNs and transformers still exhibit differences in their ability to achieve this effect. We find evidence for abstract crosslingual grammatical representations in these models, which operate similarly to those found in prior research.

Our results show that BLEU scores decrease as n-gram length increases, consistent with findings in sentence-similarity evaluation (He et al., 2022). Longer n-grams (e.g., bigrams and trigrams) capture more specific contexts, making exact matches less likely unless the target sentence is very precise. Moreover, minor errors in word choice or sequence can disrupt the alignment of these n-grams.

Importantly, our results indicate that transformer models outperform RNNs in modeling Chinese-English structural priming, a finding that is intriguing given prior research. Traditionally, RNNs have been effective in modeling human sentence processing, explaining garden-path effects and structural priming through their sequential processing capabilities, which are thought to mirror aspects of human cognitive processing (Frank, 2021).

Our results show that the transformer model is more effective at preserving structural information than the RNN. The standardized accuracy rates for the transformer model exceed those of the RNN by 25.84% for the PO structure and by 33.33% for the active structure. This offers guidance for selecting base models in future computational linguistics research aimed at implementing or enhancing structural priming effects. This superiority of transformers raises questions about the efficacy of RNNs as human sentence processing models, especially if they are surpassed by a model considered less cognitively plausible. However, these results could also be seen as supporting the cognitive plausibility of transformers, particularly due to the attention mechanism.

While the concept of unlimited working memory in transformers seems implausible, some researchers argue that human working memory capacity is much smaller than traditionally estimated, limited to only two or three items. They suggest that language processing involves rapid, direct-access retrieval of items from memory (Lewis et al., 2006), a process compatible with the attention mechanism in transformers. This mechanism assigns weights to past inputs based on their relevance to the current input, consistent with cue-based retrieval theories, where memory retrieval is influenced by the similarity of current cues to stored information (Parker and Shvartsman, 2018).

Our study on translation models extends the traditional RNN and Transformer comparisons in cognitive science, typically applied to language models for predictive coding. Michaelov et al. (2023) have shown Transformers often better capture human language structure. While distinct from pure language modeling, our translation-focused approach offers insights into structural representations in neural networks and lays groundwork for refined language production models.

## 9 Future Directions

A promising future direction is to develop a model that generates sentences based on new semantic concepts and thematic roles before and after priming. While challenging, this approach could help mitigate the lexical boost effect (see Limitations).

Shifting our focus from production to comprehension could also be fruitful. By measuring surprisal levels in models, we can explore how structural priming influences comprehension, as suggested in recent studies (Merkx and Frank, 2021). Surprisal quantifies the unexpectedness of a word in a given context, with lower values indicating higher probability. Consistently lower surprisal levels at structurally complex points in sentences following priming. This would suggest effective preparation by the priming process, offering a way to explore the impact of structural priming on language processing in model without the confounding effects of repeated vocabulary.

Additionally, evidence suggests an inverse relationship between the frequency of linguistic constructions and the magnitude of priming effects observed with those constructions (Jaeger and Snider, 2013; Kaschak et al., 2011). For example, the double object (DO) construction is more common in American English than the prepositional object (PO) construction (Bock and Griffin, 2000). Studies have shown that the less frequent PO construction exhibits stronger priming effects than the more frequent DO construction (Kaschak et al., 2011). This aligns with theories of implicit learning in structural priming, where more frequently encountered structures are less "surprising" and thus generate weaker priming effects.

To explore this further, training models on corpora of American versus British English, which differ in their construction frequencies, could reveal whether a similar inverse frequency effect is observed in computational models. This approach could shed light on the dependency of structural priming on construction frequency, offering deeper insights into how implicit learning processes are modeled computationally.

Additionally, exploring crowdsourcing as a method to enhance the sensitivity and grammaticality judgments of the test dataset could be valuable. By leveraging a diverse pool of contributors, this approach may provide a wider range of evaluations and insights, potentially refining our assessments and leading to more robust results.

## Limitations

A limitation of the current study is that the Chinese-English priming effects observed in the models have not been directly compared with human data. Although existing evidence indicates a strong Chinese-English structural priming effect in both production and comprehension (Hsieh, 2017; Chen et al., 2013), equating the models' ability to replicate cross-language priming with the structural "correctness" of their outputs may be somewhat simplistic. This underscores the need for future research that could involve using the same stimuli with Mandarin-English bilinguals and making direct comparisons to human priming data. Such an approach would provide a more accurate assessment of the models' alignment with human language processing.

Another limitation is that our models cannot generate sentences based on novel word concepts and thematic roles, such as the picture naming task in Figure 1. Consequently, some critics may argue that what our models essentially do is translate from Chinese to English without generating new semantic content, as the semantic information remains consistent from the priming sentence to the output sentence. However, we maintain that the current study design validly assesses the priming effect, as the models must choose which sentence structure to use from among various structures that share the same semantic content—a choice influenced by the priming effect.

Nevertheless, we acknowledge that our design is susceptible to the "lexical boost" effect, where the structural priming effect is intensified when the same lexical head is repeated in both the prime and target sentences (Pickering and Branigan, 1998). For instance, if the target sentence is *Alice gave Bob a book*, the priming effect is more pronounced if the prime sentence is *Carl gave Danis a letter* rather than *Alice showed Bob a book*. Given that the semantic content remains constant across the prime and output sentences in our study, the observed priming effect may be artificially strengthened compared to what might be observed in a pure priming task.

Previous studies suggest that crosslingual structural priming might be affected by the asymmetry of training sources in certain language pairs (Michaelov et al., 2023). By measuring the probability shifts for source and target sentences, we find such multilingual auto-regressive transformer models display evidence of abstract structural priming effects, although their performance varies across different scenarios.

## Ethical Statement

The current study adheres to the ethical standards set forth in the ACL Code of Ethics. The training dataset used in this research is open, publicly available, and does not include demographic or identity characteristics (Xu, 2019).

Potential risks stem from the fact that translations in the training data (a Chinese-English parallel sentence pair dataset) may not always be perfectly equivalent. Some words may carry cultural nuances that differ between Chinese and English. For example, the terms "和尚" (heshang) and "尼姑" (nígū), translated as "monk" and "nun," have specific cultural connotations in Chinese that differ from the perception of a "monk" in Western contexts, which is typically associated with Christian monasticism. These roles in Chinese Buddhism embody cultural and social aspects not fully captured by the Western terms, potentially leading to a loss of cultural meaning in translation.

Furthermore, while ChatGPT has been used to expand the test dataset, the authors have manually verified the output to ensure it remains unbiased. The potential risk of misuse of the computational model is low, as the encoders and decoders are designed to perform straightforward translation tasks and do not have the capability to self-generate harmful content.

## Acknowledgments

The last two authors are supported, in part, by DARPA Contract No. HR001121C0186. Any opinions, findings and conclusions or recommendations expressed in this material are those of the authors and do not necessarily reflect the views of the US Government.

## References

Kathryn Bock and Zenzi M. Griffin. 2000. The persistence of structural priming: Transient activation or implicit learning? *Journal of Experimental Psychology: General*, 129(2):177–192.

Baoguo Chen, Yuefang Jia, Zhu Wang, Susan Dunlap, and Jeong-Ah Shin. 2013. Is word-order similarity necessary for cross-linguistic structural priming? *Second language Research*, 29:375–389.

Rahul Dey and Fathi M Salem. 2017. Gate-variants of gated recurrent unit (gru) neural networks. In *2017 IEEE 60th international midwest symposium on circuits and systems (MWSCAS)*, pages 1597–1600. IEEE.

Stefan Frank. 2021. Cross-language structural priming in recurrent neural network language models. In *Proceedings of the Annual Meeting of the Cognitive Science Society*, volume 43.

Stefan L Frank, Padraic Monaghan, and Chara Tsoukala. 2019. Neural network models of language acquisition and processing. In *Human language: From genes and brain to behavior*, pages 277–293. MIT Press.

Robert J. Hartsuiker, Martin J. Pickering, and Eline Veltkamp. 2004. Is Syntax Separate or Shared Between Languages?: Cross-Linguistic Syntactic Priming in Spanish-English Bilinguals. *Psychological Science*, 15(6):409–414.

Jia-Wei He, Wen-Jun Jiang, Guo-Bang Chen, Yu-Quan Le, and Xiao-Fei Ding. 2022. Enhancing N-Gram Based Metrics with Semantics for Better Evaluation of Abstractive Text Summarization. *Journal of Computer Science and Technology*, 37(5):1118–1133.

Yufen Hsieh. 2017. Structural priming during sentence comprehension in Chinese–English bilinguals. *Applied Psycholinguistics*, 38(3):657–678.

T. Florian Jaeger and Neal E. Snider. 2013. Alignment as a consequence of expectation adaptation: Syntactic priming is affected by the prime' s prediction error given both prior and recent experience. *Cognition*, 127(1):57–83.

Michael P. Kaschak, Timothy J. Kutta, and John L. Jones. 2011. Structural priming as implicit learning: Cumulative priming effects and individual differences. *Psychonomic Bulletin & Review*, 18(6):1133–1139.

Richard L. Lewis, Shravan Vasishth, and Julie A. Van Dyke. 2006. Computational principles of working memory in sentence comprehension. *Trends in Cognitive Sciences*, 10(10):447–454.

Tal Linzen and Marco Baroni. 2021. Syntactic structure from deep learning. *Annual Review of Linguistics*, 7:195–212.

Adam Lopez. 2008. Statistical machine translation. *ACM Computing Surveys*, 40(3):1–49.

Danny Merkx and Stefan L. Frank. 2021. Human Sentence Processing: Recurrence or Attention? In *Proceedings of the Workshop on Cognitive Modeling and Computational Linguistics*, pages 12–22, Online. Association for Computational Linguistics.

James A. Michaelov, Catherine Arnett, Tyler A. Chang, and Benjamin K. Bergen. 2023. Structural Priming Demonstrates Abstract Grammatical Representations in Multilingual Language Models. *arXiv preprint arXiv:2311.09194*. Publisher: [object Object] Version Number: 1.

OpenAI. 2024. Gpt-3.5 turbo documentation. Accessed: 2024-06-10.

Kishore Papineni, Salim Roukos, Todd Ward, and Wei-Jing Zhu. 2002. Bleu: a method for automatic evaluation of machine translation. In *Proceedings of the 40th annual meeting on association for computational linguistics*, pages 311–318. Association for Computational Linguistics.

Dan Parker and Michael Shvartsman. 2018. The cue-based retrieval theory. *Language Processing and Disorders*, page 121.

Martin J. Pickering and Holly P. Branigan. 1998. The Representation of Verbs: Evidence from Syntactic Priming in Language Production. *Journal of Memory and Language*, 39(4):633–651.

Martin J Pickering and Victor S Ferreira. 2008. Structural priming: a critical review. *Psychological bulletin*, 134(3):427.

Grusha Prasad, Marten van Schijndel, and Tal Linzen. 2019. Using priming to uncover the organization of syntactic representations in neural language models. In *Proceedings of the 23rd Conference on Computational Natural Language Learning (CoNLL)*, pages 66–76, Hong Kong, China. Association for Computational Linguistics.

Arabella Sinclair, Jaap Jumelet, Willem Zuidema, and Raquel Fernández. 2022. Structural persistence in language models: Priming as a window into abstract language representations. *Transactions of the Association for Computational Linguistics*, 10:1031–1050.

Jörg Tiedemann and Santhosh Thottingal. 2020. OPUS-MT —Building open translation services for the World. In *Proceedings of the 22nd Annual Conferenec of the European Association for Machine Translation (EAMT)*, Lisbon, Portugal.

Ashish Vaswani, Noam Shazeer, Niki Parmar, Jakob Uszkoreit, Llion Jones, Aidan N Gomez, Łukasz Kaiser, and Illia Polosukhin. 2017. Attention is all you need. *Advances in neural information processing systems*, 30.

Bright Xu. 2019. Nlp chinese corpus: Large scale chinese corpus for nlp.

Yi Zhou, Junying Zhou, Lu Liu, Jiangtao Feng, Haoyuan Peng, and Xiaoqing Zheng. 2018. Rnn-based sequence-preserved attention for dependency parsing. In *Proceedings of the AAAI Conference on Artificial Intelligence*, volume 32.

# Recipe for Zero-shot POS Tagging: Is It Useful in Realistic Scenarios?

**Zeno Vandenbulcke, Lukas Vermeire, Miryam de Lhoneux**
Department of Computer Science,
KU Leuven
{zeno.vandenbulcke, lukas.vermeire}@student.kuleuven.be
miryam.delhoneux@kuleuven.be

## Abstract

POS tagging plays a fundamental role in numerous applications. While POS taggers are highly accurate in well-resourced settings, they lag behind in cases of limited or missing training data. This paper focuses on POS tagging for languages with limited data. We seek to identify the characteristics of datasets that make them favourable for training POS tagging models without using any labelled training data from the target language. This is a zero-shot approach. We compare the accuracies of a multilingual large language model (mBERT) fine-tuned on one or more languages related to the target language. Additionally, we compare these results with models trained directly on the target language itself. We do this for three target low-resource languages. Our research highlights the importance of accurate dataset selection for effective zero-shot POS tagging. Particularly, a strong linguistic relationship and high-quality datasets ensure optimal results. For extremely low-resource languages, zero-shot models prove to be a viable option.

## 1 Introduction

In recent years, a lot of progress has been made in Natural Language Processing (NLP). However, certain fundamental technologies such as *Part-of-Speech* (POS) *tagging* or dependency parsing are still only available for a small part of the world's languages. This is mostly for languages with significant amounts of available data. For languages with limited or no available data (*low-resource* languages), these technologies are highly inaccurate or sometimes even nonexistent (Joshi et al., 2020). Advancements in multilingual language models have shown impressive cross-lingual transfer abilities (Wu and Dredze, 2019). In this paper, we build on these advancements to explore zero-shot POS tagging for low-resource languages.

We investigate two questions:

**RQ1** What are the essential characteristics of datasets for effectively fine-tuning *zero-shot POS tagging models* for low-resource languages?

**RQ2** Are zero-shot models useful in realistic low-resource settings when compared to models fine-tuned with target language data?

We explore these questions by fine-tuning a multilingual pretrained language model for zero-shot POS tagging, using related languages (which we call *support languages*) to the target language. We start by fine-tuning POS tagging models for Afrikaans, using Dutch, German, and English as support languages. We test the models on Afrikaans and compare the results in an attempt to identify the characteristics of the datasets that affect the performance of the models. We then experiment with two additional target languages: Faroese (supported by Icelandic, Danish, Norwegian and Swedish) and Upper Sorbian (supported by Czech, Polish and Slovak). We aim to determine whether our findings for Afrikaans also apply to these languages.

In relation to **RQ1**, we find that when multiple supporting languages are available, high-quality datasets (Kulmizev and Nivre, 2023) that are closely related to the target language result in better performance. Using the most closely related language leads to consistently better accuracy, especially with a limited number of training sentences. For an optimal training dataset size, using between 100 and 5000 sentences helps to avoid *under-* or *overfitting*.

Regarding **RQ2**, we find that zero-shot POS tagging models can certainly be a viable option for low-resource languages. Nevertheless, models trained on annotated data from the low-resource target language itself remain superior, similarly to pre-



*Proceedings of the Fourth Workshop on Multilingual Representation Learning (MRL 2024)*, pages 137–147
November 16, 2024 ©2024 Association for Computational Linguistics

vious findings in the literature (Meechan-Maddon and Nivre, 2019).

As we will discuss in the conclusion, these findings can be translated into concrete guidelines for different scenarios.

This paper starts with background information on low-resource zero-shot POS tagging. We then discuss the technical components and methodology used. Finally, we present the results and attempt to answer the previously mentioned research questions.

## 2 Background

### Part-of-Speech tagging with Universal Dependencies

Part-of-Speech tagging is an essential application within NLP. It is used in machine translation, word meaning disambiguation, parsing, among other applications (Chiche and Yitagesu, 2022). It is a highly researched task for which there are many annotated datasets, in many languages. Universal Dependencies (UD; de Marneffe et al., 2021) is a collection of treebanks which include POS tags for hundreds of languages, with a unified POS tagging scheme. UD distinguishes between 17 different tags, called the Universal POS tags (Zeman et al., 2023). This unified annotation scheme allows the development and comparative evaluation of POS taggers across the languages included in UD. In addition, UD makes it possible to build multilingual POS taggers and dependency parsers which can deal with multiple languages within a single model (e.g. Kondratyuk and Straka, 2019), and this enables cross-lingual transfer. A limitation of UD is that the annotation quality varies considerably across treebanks (Kulmizev and Nivre, 2023). This may negatively impact cross-lingual transfer, a question we investigate in this paper.

### Zero-shot learning

A zero-shot model is a learning model that can perform a task without having seen examples or data of that task during the fine-tuning phase. In the context of this paper, a zero-shot POS tagging model refers to a model that is trained to POS tag sentences in one or more support training languages. The performance of this model is then evaluated on data from a different language, also known as the target language. Importantly, the model does not encounter the data of this target language during the fine-tuning phase (although it may have seen target language data during pre-training). One could compare it to a student who has an Afrikaans exam scheduled but is only allowed to prepare by studying, for instance, Dutch and German. This approach is useful in NLP to fill gaps in the availability or correctness of data for a target language. Thus, for *extremely low-resource* languages, or especially languages for which no annotated data is available, POS tagging could be performed using a zero-shot model trained on related languages.

We use the zero-shot strategy here because we are interested in scenarios where no data is available for certain languages. This provides a better understanding of the situation because all models developed for this purpose would, by definition, be zero-shot.

### Low-resource languages

While there is no general definition of the term low-resource, researchers have attempted to define it (Joshi et al., 2020). However, this definition has not yet been widely adopted. We consider a dataset, and thus a language, to be low-resource if it contains fewer than 50,000 tokens in UD. This mainly concerns indigenous languages, but can also include languages that are more broadly used. In UD, a token is a syntactic word used for analysis, which might differ from orthographic or phonological words (de Marneffe et al., 2021).

## 3 Methodology

Through our experiments, we hope to gain insights into the characteristics of datasets that contribute to the performance of zero-shot POS tagging models for low-resource languages.

Our experiments focus on fine-tuning POS tagging models based on mBERT, a *large language model* (LLM; Devlin et al., 2019). This process involves fine-tuning the model on annotated treebanks to enable it to perform POS tagging. The model's performance is then evaluated on a test dataset. We specifically chose mBERT because of its multilingual capabilities. Additionally, mBERT has shown good results in zero-shot scenarios (Pires et al., 2019).

The fine-tuning of mBERT is done using the tool MaChAmp (van der Goot et al., 2021). MaChAmp is a user-friendly tool that enables the fine-tuning of LLMs on various NLP tasks from diverse datasets and languages. The latter functionality in particular is valuable for our research. This enables us

| Language | Treebank | # Sents | Rank |
|---|---|---|---|
| Afrikaans | AfriBooms | 1.5k | 46 |
| Dutch | Alpino | 12k | 29 |
| German | GSD | 15k | 19 |
| English | EWT | 16k | 23 |
| Faroese | FarPaHC | 1.6k | 62 |
| Icelandic | Modern | 3.5k | 34 |
| Danish | DDT | 5.5k | 53 |
| Norwegian | Bokmaal | 20k | 14 |
| Swedish | Talbanken | 6.0k | 57 |
| Upper Sorbian | UFAL | 0.6k | |
| Czech | FicTree | 12.7k | 24 |
| Polish | LFG | 17.2k | 20 |
| Slovak | SNK | 10.6k | 42 |

Table 1: Languages with corresponding treebanks (UD v2.13) ranked according to their relatedness to the target language, including the number of sentences (**# Sents**) in each treebank and their respective quality rankings (**Rank**; Kulmizev and Nivre, 2023).

to jointly train POS tagging models on multiple languages.

### Languages and treebanks

We select three different groups from Universal Dependencies v2.13 (Zeman et al., 2023). These groups are shown in Table 1. For each group, we select one low-resource language and a few related languages for which larger treebanks are available.

Our focus is primarily on Afrikaans. For this, we use the AfriBooms treebank (Augustinus et al., 2016). The supporting languages are Dutch, German, and English. To verify our observations of Afrikaans, we use two other clusters. One cluster includes Scandinavian languages, with Faroese as the low-resource language. The related languages are Icelandic, Danish, Norwegian, and Swedish. We also use a West Slavic cluster, with Upper Sorbian as the low-resource language, supported by Czech, Polish, and Slovak.

### Characteristics

To answer **RQ1** (*What are the essential characteristics of datasets for effectively fine-tuning zero-shot POS tagging models for low-resource languages?*), we consider two main characteristics: the linguistic relatedness between languages and the quality of the treebank. The relevance of the linguistic relatedness is already evident from previous work (see section 5), but the treebank quality has not been taken into consideration before in spite of being a clear differentiating factor between UD treebanks (see section 2 & 5). Firstly, we take a look at the linguistic relatedness. The support languages are consistently chosen to be of the same genus as the target language. This results in an intrinsic relatedness. In the first cluster, Dutch shows the closest relatedness to Afrikaans (van Zaanen et al., 2014). In the Scandinavian cluster, Faroese is most closely related to Icelandic (Snæbjarnarson et al., 2023). In the West Slavic cluster, Upper Sorbian is most closely related to Czech (Howson, 2017), followed by Polish.

For the second characteristic of the treebanks, we rely on a ranking developed by Kulmizev and Nivre (2023). This ranking is based on three criteria: how difficult or easy the treebanks are to parse, how much information they contain that is actually usable by a parser, and how sample efficient they are. We report the rank of the languages considered in this work in Table 1. The supporting languages for Afrikaans, for example, can be ranked as follows: German > English > Dutch. Throughout this paper, we refer to this as the 'quality' of a treebank.

As an additional characteristic, we use the size of the dataset. With this, we investigate whether overfitting might occur and determine the optimal number of sentences a model should use.

### Experimental setup

We train zero-shot models for each of the three clusters. We fine-tune these models in several ways. First, we fine-tune separate zero-shot models for each distinct supporting language. Then, we fine-tune models based on different combinations of these languages. We repeat this process for the different clusters.

We conduct learning curve experiments to display the performance of the models as they are fine-tuned on increasingly more data. The fine-tuning starts with five sentences and gradually reaches the maximum available number of sentences from the treebanks. For each cluster and each model within the cluster, we repeat this process three times. During each iteration, the sentences of the training dataset of each language are shuffled. This allows for random selection of sentences, which is crucial for ensuring generalisability.

We determine the accuracy of each model using the F1-score, a common metric for assessing the performance of classifiers such as POS tagging models (Jurafsky and Martin, 2009). The results of these experiments and the associated observations are discussed in the following section.

Finally, we also look at monolingual non-zero-shot models that are fine-tuned on the respective target languages themselves. This means that we fine-tune three distinct models, each using only Afrikaans, Faroese, or Upper Sorbian. This can then provide us with an answer to our second question (**RQ2**): *Are zero-shot models useful in realistic low-resource settings compared to monolingual non-zero-shot models in terms of accuracy?*

## 4 Results and discussion

First, we analyse the learning curves of all clusters to identify which characteristics of datasets seem to have the most impact on the results and could therefore be more suitable for a zero-shot model. Then, we evaluate the effective usability of our models and results to determine whether the zero-shot approach is effective.

### 4.1 RQ1: Dataset characteristics

#### Afrikaans

First and foremost, we take a look at the accuracies of the models that have Afrikaans as the target language and that were trained on one supporting language. This can be seen in Figure 1. It can be clearly seen that when fine-tuning the zero-shot model using a language more closely related to the target language, the initial accuracies are higher. Initial accuracies are the accuracies that occur with a smaller number of training sentences. A one-to-one correspondence can be seen between how closely related the training language is to the target language and how accurate the corresponding model is for a very small subset of the dataset.

As more sentences are added to the training dataset of the models, it can be seen that the accuracies of the three models converge. This is most likely due to the fact that the supporting languages are all Germanic languages and there is a high similarity to the target language. However, it can be seen that the Dutch model performs better overall and also achieves the best accuracy of the three models. The model that performs the worst overall is the English model. This is not surprising, as English is least closely related to Afrikaans among the three supporting languages, and its quality falls in the middle range.

Next, we add the models that were trained with

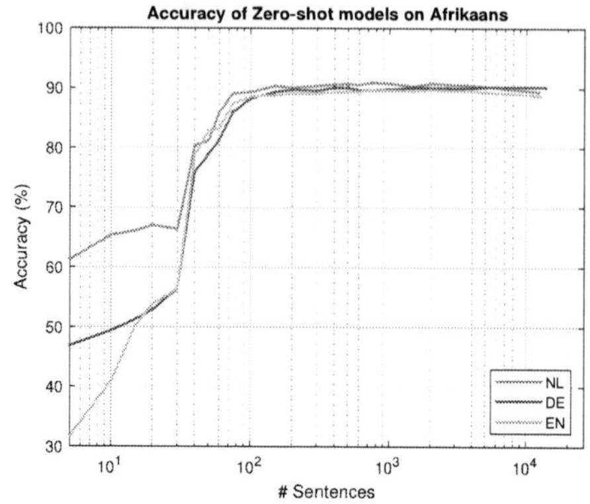


Figure 1: Accuracy of fine-tuned models on Afrikaans, represented through learning curves.

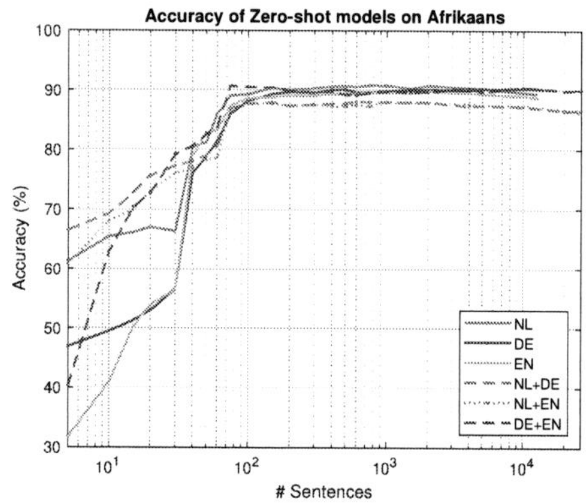


Figure 2: Accuracy of fine-tuned models on Afrikaans, represented through learning curves.

combinations of supporting languages and analyse these separately. This can be seen in Figure 2. It is immediately noticeable that the added models using the most closely related language initially achieve higher accuracies. The model with the highest initial accuracy here is the Dutch-German model. This seems logical since Dutch and German follow each other as most related to Afrikaans. In second place is the Dutch-English model, again because Dutch is in the training dataset and has a significant influence. The worst-performing model is the German-English model. This is not surprising since German and English are the two languages that are least related to Afrikaans.

As the size of the training datasets of the models increases, there is a greater shift between the accuracies of the different models. The model that performs best overall is the German-English model. This is unexpected, given that Dutch is the closest language to Afrikaans (Heeringa et al., 2015). One explanation for this might be that when a model is trained on more than one language, the quality of the datasets becomes more important than the language relatedness. The Dutch-German model performs slightly better across the board than the Dutch-English model, which suggests that relatedness still plays a role. When we look at all the models in Figure 2 globally, we can make several observations:

If a model has a language in the training dataset that is more closely related to the target language, the model has a higher initial accuracy. When multiple closely related languages are used, such as the Dutch-German model, this accuracy increases even further.

The most performant model is one trained on multiple languages. In the case of Afrikaans, this is the German-English model. This can be attributed to the quality of the datasets used. This model quickly achieves better results and consistently maintains a high accuracy.

There seems to be a plateau at which all models achieve accuracies that neither increase nor decrease, usually between 100 and 5000 sentences. What is also notable is that within this interval, the Dutch model generally performs the best, while the German-English model achieved the highest peak accuracy prior to this interval.

### Faroese

Secondly, we take a look at all the models we have fine-tuned that have Faroese as the target language. This can be seen in Figure 3. What stands out immediately is that all models that contain the most related language - Icelandic - consistently achieve the best results. This results in two distinct groups: one group with models containing Icelandic, and a second group with the other models. Just as with Afrikaans, it can also be seen here that the models that contain a more related language achieve a higher initial accuracy.

Regarding dataset quality, the model fine-tuned using the highest-quality datasets (Icelandic-Norwegian) ranks among the best performing models, while the model trained on the lowest-quality datasets (Danish-Swedish) ranks among the worst. Interestingly, the model that achieves the overall peak accuracy is the Icelandic-Danish model, again highlighting the importance of language relatedness, not only for lower training sizes, but throughout the entire process.

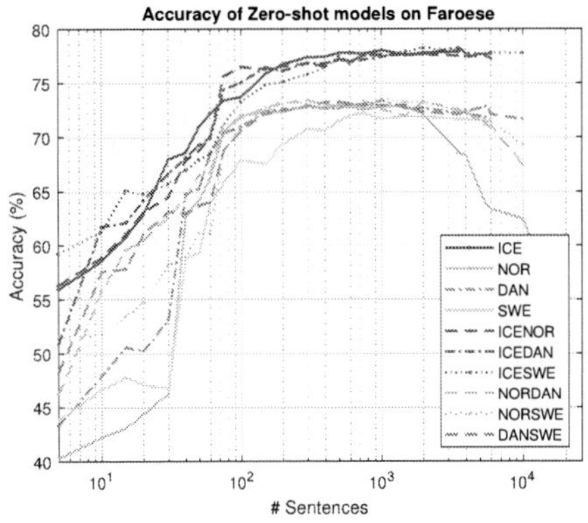


Figure 3: Accuracy of fine-tuned models on Faroese, represented through learning curves.

Here, a plateau between about 100 and 5000 sentences can also be clearly seen. This is especially noticeable in the accuracies of the models that do not include Icelandic. The curves start with an increase, followed by a stagnation and then a decline in accuracy. This is particularly noticeable in the models trained on Swedish and Norwegian. In the case of Swedish, this is not surprising as the treebank is of relatively low quality and not very closely related to Faroese. Norwegian, on the other hand, is closely related and of high quality, which makes this trend all the more striking.

Some further observations also become clear here. As more sentences are added to the training dataset of the models, the accuracies of the models converge. This again highlights the idea of intrinsic relatedness between languages within the same language family. Furthermore, it can be seen that the best performing model is one that is fine-tuned on multiple supporting languages, although the model solely fine-tuned on Icelandic is also among the better performing models.

### Upper Sorbian

Lastly, we look at the accuracies of models whose target language is Upper Sorbian. This can be seen in Figure 4. Here, largely the same trends are seen as in the two previous clusters. The initial accuracies of models trained with the most closely related language (Czech) are higher, although Polish takes the lead when the model is trained on a single supporting language. The statement holds true for models trained on multiple supporting languages: the greater the relatedness and the higher the quality, the better the model performs. In addition, the trend between 100 and 5000 sentences can be seen again here, although it is slightly less pronounced.

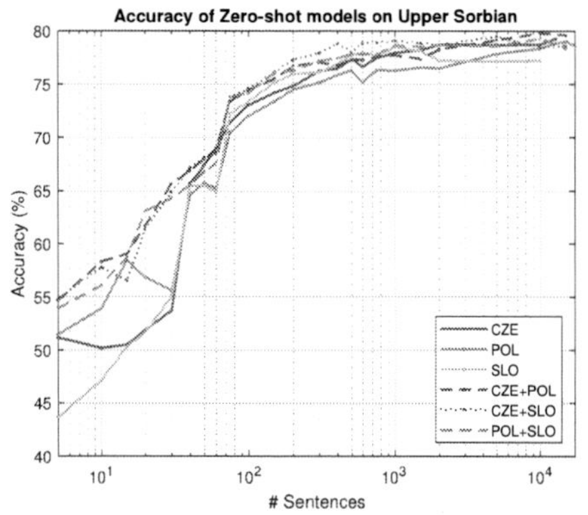


Figure 4: Accuracy of fine-tuned models on Upper Sorbian, represented through learning curves.

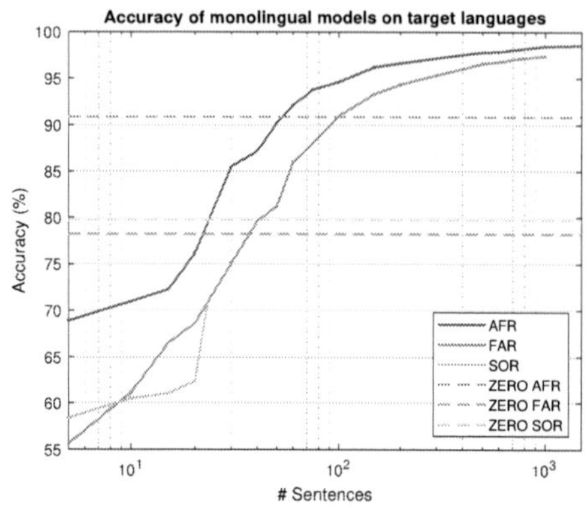


Figure 5: Accuracy of models fine-tuned on the target languages Afrikaans, Faroese, and Upper Sorbian, represented through learning curves accompanied by the peak accuracies of the respective zero-shot models.

| Language | Zero-shot | Non-zero-shot |
|---|---|---|
| Afrikaans | 90.9 | **98.5** |
| Faroese | 78.2 | **97.3** |
| Upper Sorbian | **79.7** | 70.7 |

Table 2: Peak accuracies of zero-shot & non-zero-shot models.

### 4.2 RQ2: Usefulness of zero-shot models in realistic settings

In order to answer **RQ2**, we compare our zero-shot models with those that have been fine-tuned directly on the respective target languages (non-zero-shot).

#### Comparing zero-shot and non-zero-shot performance

Firstly, we examine the practical relevance of zero-shot models in the context of low-resource languages. The peak accuracies for both our zero-shot and non-zero-shot models can be seen in Table 2. For Afrikaans and Faroese, we observe that the non-zero-shot models outperform their zero-shot counterparts, with the Faroese model showing a nearly 20 percentage point improvement over the zero-shot model. This suggests that, given enough training data, fine-tuning on the target language can lead to substantially better results, as also discussed by Meechan-Maddon and Nivre (2019).

However, when we take a look at Upper Sorbian, an *extremely low-resource* language with only 23 training sentences, we observe a different trend. Here, the zero-shot model actually surpasses the non-zero-shot model by 9 percentage points, achieving a peak accuracy of 79.7% compared to the non-zero-shot model's 70.7%. This result suggests that our zero-shot models are certainly a viable option for extremely low-resource languages or languages for which no data is available.

Upper Sorbian is not a unique case; we counted 82 languages in UD v2.14 that have fewer than 23 training sentences. This widespread scarcity highlights the importance of zero-shot models in real-world applications where data is often hard to come by.

#### Amount of annotated data needed to surpass zero-shot performance

Secondly, we take a look at how much annotated data is necessary to improve upon zero-shot performance through monolingual fine-tuning (non-zero-shot). In Figure 5, the accuracies of the POS tagging models are shown when they are fine-tuned on the respective target languages, alongside the peak accuracies of the respective zero-shot models. Using these lines, and the intersection they make with the learning curves of the non-zero-shot models, we can estimate when a non-zero-shot model becomes strictly better than a zero-shot model for the same target language.

For Afrikaans, the intersection occurs between 50 and 60 training sentences, indicating that at least this amount is necessary for the non-zero-shot model to outperform the zero-shot model. Similarly, for Faroese, the intersection point is around 40 sentences, suggesting a slightly lower data requirement to achieve better performance. Again, the Upper Sorbian models are slightly different. The learning curve for the non-zero-shot model does not intersect with the peak accuracy of the zero-shot model, simply because there is not enough targeted data available.

Meechan-Maddon and Nivre (2019) made similar observations in a similar context. They compared dependency parsers trained on treebanks from several support languages (akin to our zero-shot setting) with those trained solely on target language data (similar to our non-zero-shot setting). They found that the non-zero-shot models required between 100 and 200 sentences to reach the performance of the zero-shot models. This is higher than what we found, but can likely be explained by the fact that they do not make any use of pretraining and use a BiLSTM instead of a transformer. We use mBERT, which has a greater number of parameters than a BiLSTM and which already has acquired cross-lingual transfer capabilities by virtue of being trained on multilingual data. This may reduce the need for annotated target language data. This should be verified in future research, however.

## 5 Related work

Dealing with the limited availability of training data for low-resource languages is an active area of research within NLP. Thanks to the UD treebanks, a large collection of data in numerous languages with varying data sizes, POS tagging and dependency parsing have become highly researched topics within this context

Closest to our work, de Vries et al. (2021) investigated zero-shot transfer for two target languages: Gronings and West Frisian. They also fine-tuned mBERT on related languages, as well as monolingual language models in related languages. They found the latter to be superior to the former. Relatedly, de Vries et al. (2022) did an extensive evaluation of zero-shot POS tagging across 105 target languages. They fine-tuned mBERT using 65 different support languages, testing all possible combinations of support and target languages, with one support language used each time. They found that related languages are generally the best support languages.

Our work is complementary to these by considering a number of target languages that is in between these two extremes (2 versus 105). It allows a targeted evaluation, looking at learning curves and trying multiple support languages in different combinations, while still providing results that generalize to more than two closely related languages. We confirm that, among related languages, the ones that are the most closely related to the target language are the best support languages. This finding is consistent with many other earlier works in POS tagging and dependency parsing using different types of models (Smith et al., 2018; Pires et al., 2019; Lauscher et al., 2020).

Our learning curve experiments take inspiration from earlier work in dependency parsing by Meechan-Maddon and Nivre (2019). They investigated zero- and few-shot learning of multilingual parsers to find out how much can be gained from cross-lingual transfer versus annotating target language data. They use a BiLSTM parser trained only on treebank data, in multiple languages, including and excluding target language data. Their results showed that the zero-shot approach is inferior to the other approaches, provided at least 200 training sentences are available from the target language. We confirm this finding in the context of fine-tuning a multilingual transformer model, although we find that fewer training sentences are necessary in this context.

Finally, a dataset property which has not yet been investigated in the context of cross-lingual transfer (to our knowledge) is data quality. Kulmizev and Nivre (2023) thoroughly evaluated the quality of UD treebanks using three different metrics and found that the quality varies considerably across treebanks. They found some treebanks to perform consistently low across metrics, making them practically unusable. This raises the question of how this quality impacts results in cross-lingual transfer: a low-quality treebank may be too noisy to use for cross-lingual transfer. We investigated this question and found a subtle link between the quality of the UD Treebanks and the peak accuracies of the corresponding zero-shot models. Of course, more research is needed to confirm this by investigating a larger set of treebanks.

## 6 Conclusion

Initially, we can conclude that developing zero-shot POS tagging models is a viable option for low-resource languages. Nevertheless, using the low-resource dataset of a specific language remains superior for constructing a POS tagging model for that language, similar to what Meechan-Maddon and Nivre (2019) found in the context of dependency parsing. If the amount of data for a language is so scarce and/or a zero-shot model is still desired, the following guidelines can be followed:

*One language can be used as a support language.* In this case, always use the language that is most closely related to the target language. This generally gives better accuracies with a low number of training sentences. Even with larger numbers of training sentences, these models tend to perform well. The quality plays a lesser role here.

*Multiple support languages can be used.* In this case, use as many languages as possible that are closely related to the target language and are of high quality. High relatedness gives the best results with a limited number of training sentences, and high quality generally gives the best results with higher numbers of training sentences.

*What is the most suitable number of training sentences?* If enough data is available from the support languages, preferably use a training number of 100 to 5000 sentences. Below 100 sentences, the models are often 'underfitted'. Above 5000 sentences, the models can overfit and the accuracies may decrease.

## 7 Limitations

This work considered only three target languages, each paired with three to four related source languages, selected somewhat arbitrarily. While this restricted number allowed in-depth analysis, our findings need to be verified using more languages with various degrees of relatedness. To keep the number of languages manageable while ensuring generalizability of the results, a sample of typologically diverse languages could be selected using the recently proposed framework by Ploeger et al. (2024).

Additionally, we relied on the linguistic literature to describe the degree of relatedness between the languages considered. It would be informative to quantitatively define language distances, as done by Ploeger et al. (2024).

Finally, we only evaluated one pretrained language model, mBERT. Our findings should be verified with other models.

## Acknowledgments

We want to thank Kushal Tatariya for technical help and Artur Kulmizev for the theoretical insights. We are also grateful to Max Verbinnen and Sander Verwimp for their help and support throughout this study. We also acknowledge the VSC (Vlaams Supercomputer Centrum) for providing the computational resources used in this work.

## References

Liesbeth Augustinus, Peter Dirix, Daniel van Niekerk, Ineke Schuurman, Vincent Vandeghinste, Frank Van Eynde, and Gerhard van Huyssteen. 2016. AfriBooms: An online treebank for Afrikaans. In *Proceedings of the Tenth International Conference on Language Resources and Evaluation (LREC'16)*, pages 677–682, Portorož, Slovenia. European Language Resources Association (ELRA).

Alebachew Chiche and Betselot Yitagesu. 2022. Part of speech tagging: a systematic review of deep learning and machine learning approaches. *Journal of Big Data*, 9(1):10.

Marie-Catherine de Marneffe, Christopher D. Manning, Joakim Nivre, and Daniel Zeman. 2021. Universal Dependencies. *Computational Linguistics*, 47(2):255–308.

Wietse de Vries, Martijn Bartelds, Malvina Nissim, and Martijn Wieling. 2021. Adapting monolingual models: Data can be scarce when language similarity is high. In *Findings of the Association for Computational Linguistics: ACL-IJCNLP 2021*, pages 4901–4907, Online. Association for Computational Linguistics.

Wietse de Vries, Martijn Wieling, and Malvina Nissim. 2022. Make the best of cross-lingual transfer: Evidence from POS tagging with over 100 languages. In *Proceedings of the 60th Annual Meeting of the Association for Computational Linguistics (Volume 1: Long Papers)*, pages 7676–7685, Dublin, Ireland. Association for Computational Linguistics.

Jacob Devlin, Ming-Wei Chang, Kenton Lee, and Kristina Toutanova. 2019. BERT: Pre-training of deep bidirectional transformers for language understanding. In *Proceedings of the 2019 Conference of the North American Chapter of the Association for Computational Linguistics: Human Language Technologies, Volume 1 (Long and Short Papers)*, pages 4171–4186, Minneapolis, Minnesota. Association for Computational Linguistics.

Wilbert Heeringa, Febe De Wet, and Gerhard B. van Huyssteen. 2015. Afrikaans and dutch as closely-related languages : a comparison to west germanic languages and dutch dialects. *Stellenbosch Papers in Linguistics Plus*, 47(1):1–18.

Phil Howson. 2017. Upper sorbian. *Journal of the International Phonetic Association*, 47(3):359367.

Pratik Joshi, Sebastin Santy, Amar Budhiraja, Kalika Bali, and Monojit Choudhury. 2020. The state and fate of linguistic diversity and inclusion in the NLP world. In *Proceedings of the 58th Annual Meeting of the Association for Computational Linguistics*, pages 6282–6293, Online. Association for Computational Linguistics.

Daniel Jurafsky and James H. Martin. 2009. *Speech and Language Processing (2nd Edition)*. Prentice-Hall, Inc., USA.

Dan Kondratyuk and Milan Straka. 2019. 75 languages, 1 model: Parsing Universal Dependencies universally. In *Proceedings of the 2019 Conference on Empirical Methods in Natural Language Processing and the 9th International Joint Conference on Natural Language Processing (EMNLP-IJCNLP)*, pages 2779–2795, Hong Kong, China. Association for Computational Linguistics.

Artur Kulmizev and Joakim Nivre. 2023. Investigating UD treebanks via dataset difficulty measures. In *Proceedings of the 17th Conference of the European Chapter of the Association for Computational Linguistics*, pages 1076–1089, Dubrovnik, Croatia. Association for Computational Linguistics.

Anne Lauscher, Vinit Ravishankar, Ivan Vulić, and Goran Glavaš. 2020. From zero to hero: On the limitations of zero-shot language transfer with multilingual Transformers. In *Proceedings of the 2020 Conference on Empirical Methods in Natural Language Processing (EMNLP)*, pages 4483–4499, Online. Association for Computational Linguistics.

Ailsa Meechan-Maddon and Joakim Nivre. 2019. How to parse low-resource languages: Cross-lingual parsing, target language annotation, or both? In *Proceedings of the Fifth International Conference on Dependency Linguistics (Depling, SyntaxFest 2019)*, pages 112–120, Paris, France. Association for Computational Linguistics.

Telmo Pires, Eva Schlinger, and Dan Garrette. 2019. How multilingual is multilingual BERT? In *Proceedings of the 57th Annual Meeting of the Association for Computational Linguistics*, pages 4996–5001, Florence, Italy. Association for Computational Linguistics.

Esther Ploeger, Wessel Poelman, Andreas Holck Høeg-Petersen, Anders Schlichtkrull, Miryam de Lhoneux, and Johannes Bjerva. 2024. A principled framework for evaluating on typologically diverse languages. *Preprint*, arXiv:2407.05022.

Aaron Smith, Bernd Bohnet, Miryam de Lhoneux, Joakim Nivre, Yan Shao, and Sara Stymne. 2018. 82 treebanks, 34 models: Universal Dependency parsing with multi-treebank models. In *Proceedings of the CoNLL 2018 Shared Task: Multilingual Parsing from Raw Text to Universal Dependencies*, pages 113–123, Brussels, Belgium. Association for Computational Linguistics.

Vésteinn Snæbjarnarson, Annika Simonsen, Goran Glavaš, and Ivan Vulić. 2023. Transfer to a low-resource language via close relatives: The case study on Faroese. In *Proceedings of the 24th Nordic Conference on Computational Linguistics (NoDaLiDa)*, pages 728–737, Tórshavn, Faroe Islands. University of Tartu Library.

Rob van der Goot, Ahmet Üstün, Alan Ramponi, Ibrahim Sharaf, and Barbara Plank. 2021. Massive choice, ample tasks (MaChAmp): A toolkit for multi-task learning in NLP. In *Proceedings of the 16th Conference of the European Chapter of the Association for Computational Linguistics: System Demonstrations*, pages 176–197, Online. Association for Computational Linguistics.

Menno van Zaanen, Gerhard van Huyssteen, Suzanne Aussems, Chris Emmery, and Roald Eiselen. 2014. The development of Dutch and Afrikaans language resources for compound boundary analysis. In *Proceedings of the Ninth International Conference on Language Resources and Evaluation (LREC'14)*, pages 1056–1062, Reykjavik, Iceland. European Language Resources Association (ELRA).

Shijie Wu and Mark Dredze. 2019. Beto, bentz, becas: The surprising cross-lingual effectiveness of BERT. In *EMNLP-IJCNLP*, pages 833–844, Hong Kong, China. Association for Computational Linguistics.

Daniel Zeman, Joakim Nivre, Mitchell Abrams, Elia Ackermann, Noëmi Aepli, Hamid Aghaei, Željko Agić, Amir Ahmadi, Lars Ahrenberg, Chika Kennedy Ajede, Salih Furkan Akkurt, Gabrielė Aleksandravičiūtė, Ika Alfina, Avner Algom, Khalid Alnajjar, Chiara Alzetta, Erik Andersen, Lene Antonsen, Tatsuya Aoyama, Katya Aplonova, Angelina Aquino, Carolina Aragon, Glyd Aranes, Maria Jesus Aranzabe, Bilge Nas Arıcan, Ĥórunn Arnardóttir, Gashaw Arutie, Jessica Naraiswari Arwidarasti, Masayuki Asahara, Katla Ásgeirsdóttir, Deniz Baran Aslan, Cengiz Asmazoğlu, Luma Ateyah, Furkan Atmaca, Mohammed Attia, Aitziber Atutxa, Liesbeth Augustinus, Mariana Avelãs, Elena Badmaeva, Keerthana Balasubramani, Miguel Ballesteros, Esha Banerjee, Sebastian Bank, Verginica Barbu Mititelu, Starkaður Barkarson, Rodolfo Basile, Victoria Basmov, Colin Batchelor, John Bauer, Seyyit Talha Bedir, Shabnam Behzad, Juan Belieni, Kepa Bengoetxea, brahim Benli, Yifat Ben Moshe, Gözde Berk, Riyaz Ahmad Bhat, Erica Biagetti, Eckhard Bick, Agnė Bielinskienė, Kristín Bjarnadóttir, Rogier Blokland, Victoria Bobicev, Loïc Boizou, Emanuel Borges Völker, Carl Börstell, Cristina Bosco, Gosse Bouma, Sam Bowman, Adriane Boyd, Anouck Braggaar, António Branco, Kristina Brokaitė, Aljoscha Burchardt, Marisa Campos, Marie Candito, Bernard Caron, Gauthier Caron, Catarina Carvalheiro, Rita Carvalho, Lauren Cassidy, Maria Clara Castro, Sérgio Castro, Tatiana Cavalcanti, Gülşen Cebiroğlu Eryiğit, Flavio Massimiliano Cecchini, Giuseppe G. A. Celano, Slavomír Čéplö, Neslihan Cesur, Savas Cetin, Özlem Çetinoğlu, Fabricio Chalub, Liyanage Chamila, Shweta Chauhan, Ethan Chi, Taishi Chika, Yongseok Cho, Jinho Choi, Jayeol Chun, Juyeon Chung, Alessandra T. Cignarella, Silvie Cinková, Aurélie Collomb, Çağrı Çöltekin, Miriam Connor, Claudia Corbetta, Daniela Corbetta, Francisco Costa, Marine Courtin, Benoît Crabbé, Mihaela Cristescu, Vladimir Cvetkoski, Ingerid Løyning Dale, Philemon Daniel, Elizabeth Davidson, Leonel Figueiredo de Alencar, Mathieu Dehouck, Martina de Laurentiis, Marie-Catherine de Marneffe, Valeria de Paiva, Mehmet Oguz Derin, Elvis de Souza, Arantza Diaz de Ilarraza,

Carly Dickerson, Arawinda Dinakaramani, Elisa Di Nuovo, Bamba Dione, Peter Dirix, Kaja Dobrovoljc, Adrian Doyle, Timothy Dozat, Kira Droganova, Magali Sanches Duran, Puneet Dwivedi, Christian Ebert, Hanne Eckhoff, Masaki Eguchi, Sandra Eiche, Marhaba Eli, Ali Elkahky, Binyam Ephrem, Olga Erina, Tomaž Erjavec, Farah Essaidi, Aline Etienne, Wograine Evelyn, Sidney Facundes, Richárd Farkas, Federica Favero, Jannatul Ferdaousi, Marília Fernanda, Hector Fernandez Alcalde, Amal Fethi, Jennifer Foster, Theodorus Fransen, Cláudia Freitas, Kazunori Fujita, Katarína Gajdošová, Daniel Galbraith, Federica Gamba, Marcos Garcia, Moa Gärdenfors, Fabrício Ferraz Gerardi, Kim Gerdes, Luke Gessler, Filip Ginter, Gustavo Godoy, Iakes Goenaga, Koldo Gojenola, Memduh Gökırmak, Yoav Goldberg, Xavier Gómez Guinovart, Berta González Saavedra, Bernadeta Griciūtė, Matias Grioni, Loïc Grobol, Normunds Grūzītis, Bruno Guillaume, Kirian Guiller, Céline Guillot-Barbance, Tunga Güngör, Nizar Habash, Hinrik Hafsteinsson, Jan Hajič, Jan Hajič jr., Mika Hämäläinen, Linh Hà Mỹ, Na-Rae Han, Muhammad Yudistira Hanifmuti, Takahiro Harada, Sam Hardwick, Kim Harris, Dag Haug, Johannes Heinecke, Oliver Hellwig, Felix Hennig, Barbora Hladká, Jaroslava Hlaváčová, Florinel Hociung, Petter Hohle, Yidi Huang, Marivel Huerta Mendez, Jena Hwang, Takumi Ikeda, Anton Karl Ingason, Radu Ion, Elena Irimia, Ọlájídé Ishola, Artan Islamaj, Kaoru Ito, Sandra Jagodzińska, Siratun Jannat, Tomáš Jelínek, Apoorva Jha, Katharine Jiang, Anders Johannsen, Hildur Jónsdóttir, Fredrik Jørgensen, Markus Juutinen, Hüner Kaşıkara, Nadezhda Kabaeva, Sylvain Kahane, Hiroshi Kanayama, Jenna Kanerva, Neslihan Kara, Ritván Karahóa, Andre Kåsen, Tolga Kayadelen, Sarveswaran Kengatharaiyer, Václava Kettnerová, Lilit Kharatyan, Jesse Kirchner, Elena Klementieva, Elena Klyachko, Petr Kocharov, Arne Köhn, Abdullatif Köksal, Kamil Kopacewicz, Timo Korkiakangas, Mehmet Köse, Alexey Koshevoy, Natalia Kotsyba, Jolanta Kovalevskaitė, Simon Krek, Parameswari Krishnamurthy, Sandra Kübler, Adrian Kuqi, Oğuzhan Kuyrukçu, Aslı Kuzgun, Sookyoung Kwak, Kris Kyle, Käbi Laan, Veronika Laippala, Lorenzo Lambertino, Tatiana Lando, Septina Dian Larasati, Alexei Lavrentiev, John Lee, Phng Lê Hồng, Alessandro Lenci, Saran Lertpradit, Herman Leung, Maria Levina, Lauren Levine, Cheuk Ying Li, Josie Li, Keying Li, Yixuan Li, Yuan Li, KyungTae Lim, Bruna Lima Padovani, Yi-Ju Jessica Lin, Krister Lindén, Yang Janet Liu, Nikola Ljubešić, Irina Lobzhanidze, Olga Loginova, Lucelene Lopes, Stefano Lusito, Andry Luthfi, Mikko Luukko, Olga Lyashevskaya, Teresa Lynn, Vivien Macketanz, Menel Mahamdi, Jean Maillard, Ilya Makarchuk, Aibek Makazhanov, Michael Mandl, Christopher Manning, Ruli Manurung, Büşra Marşan, Cătălina Mărănduc, David Mareček, Katrin Marheinecke, Stella Markantonatou, Héctor Martínez Alonso, Lorena Martín Rodríguez, André Martins, Cláudia Martins, Jan Mašek, Hiroshi Matsuda, Yuji Matsumoto, Alessandro Mazzei, Ryan McDonald, Sarah McGuinness, Gustavo Mendonça, Tatiana Merzhevich, Niko Miekka, Aaron Miller, Karina Mischenkova, Anna Missilä, Cătălin Mititelu, Maria Mitrofan, Yusuke Miyao, AmirHossein Mojiri Foroushani, Judit Molnár, Amirsaeid Moloodi, Simonetta Montemagni, Amir More, Laura Moreno Romero, Giovanni Moretti, Shinsuke Mori, Tomohiko Morioka, Shigeki Moro, Bjartur Mortensen, Bohdan Moskalevskyi, Kadri Muischnek, Robert Munro, Yugo Murawaki, Kaili Müürisep, Pinkey Nainwani, Mariam Nakhlé, Juan Ignacio Navarro Horñiacek, Anna Nedoluzhko, Gunta Nešpore-Bērzkalne, Manuela Nevaci, Lng Nguyễn Thị, Huyền Nguyễn Thị Minh, Yoshihiro Nikaido, Vitaly Nikolaev, Rattima Nitisaroj, Alireza Nourian, Maria das Graças Volpe Nunes, Hanna Nurmi, Stina Ojala, Atul Kr. Ojha, Hulda Óladóttir, Adédayọ̀ Olúòkun, Mai Omura, Emeka Onwuegbuzia, Noam Ordan, Petya Osenova, Robert Östling, Lilja Øvrelid, Şaziye Betül Özateş, Merve Özçelik, Arzucan Özgür, Balkız Öztürk Başaran, Teresa Paccosi, Alessio Palmero Aprosio, Anastasia Panova, Thiago Alexandre Salgueiro Pardo, Hyunji Hayley Park, Niko Partanen, Elena Pascual, Marco Passarotti, Agnieszka Patejuk, Guilherme Paulino-Passos, Giulia Pedonese, Angelika Peljak-Łapińska, Siyao Peng, Siyao Logan Peng, Rita Pereira, Sílvia Pereira, Cenel-Augusto Perez, Natalia Perkova, Guy Perrier, Slav Petrov, Daria Petrova, Andrea Peverelli, Jason Phelan, Claudel Pierre-Louis, Jussi Piitulainen, Yuval Pinter, Clara Pinto, Rodrigo Pintucci, Tommi A Pirinen, Emily Pitler, Magdalena Plamada, Barbara Plank, Thierry Poibeau, Larisa Ponomareva, Martin Popel, Lauma Pretkalniņa, Sophie Prévost, Prokopis Prokopidis, Adam Przepiórkowski, Robert Pugh, Tiina Puolakainen, Sampo Pyysalo, Peng Qi, Andreia Querido, Andriela Rääbis, Alexandre Rademaker, Mizanur Rahoman, Taraka Rama, Loganathan Ramasamy, Carlos Ramisch, Joana Ramos, Fam Rashel, Mohammad Sadegh Rasooli, Vinit Ravishankar, Livy Real, Petru Rebeja, Siva Reddy, Mathilde Regnault, Georg Rehm, Arij Riabi, Ivan Riabov, Michael Rießler, Erika Rimkutė, Larissa Rinaldi, Laura Rituma, Putri Rizqiyah, Luisa Rocha, Eiríkur Rögnvaldsson, Ivan Roksandic, Mykhailo Romanenko, Rudolf Rosa, Valentin Roca, Davide Rovati, Ben Rozonoyer, Olga Rudina, Jack Rueter, Kristján Rúnarsson, Shoval Sadde, Pegah Safari, Aleksi Sahala, Shadi Saleh, Alessio Salomoni, Tanja Samardžić, Stephanie Samson, Manuela Sanguinetti, Ezgi Sanıyar, Dage Särg, Marta Sartor, Mitsuya Sasaki, Baiba Saulīte, Agata Savary, Yanin Sawanakunanon, Shefali Saxena, Kevin Scannell, Salvatore Scarlata, Emmanuel Schang, Nathan Schneider, Sebastian Schuster, Lane Schwartz, Djamé Seddah, Wolfgang Seeker, Mojgan Seraji, Syeda Shahzadi, Mo Shen, Atsuko Shimada, Hiroyuki Shirasu, Yana Shishkina, Muh Shohibussirri, Maria Shvedova, Janine Siewert, Einar Freyr Sigurðsson, João Silva, Aline Silveira, Natalia Silveira, Sara Silveira, Maria Simi, Radu Simionescu, Katalin Simkó, Mária Šimková, Haukur Barri Símonarson, Kiril Simov, Dmitri Sitchinava, Ted Sither, Maria Skachedubova, Aaron Smith, Isabela Soares-Bastos, Per Erik Solberg, Barbara Sonnenhauser, Shafi Sourov, Rachele Sprugnoli, Vivian Stamou,

Steinhór Steingrímsson, Antonio Stella, Abishek Stephen, Milan Straka, Emmett Strickland, Jana Strnadová, Alane Suhr, Yogi Lesmana Sulestio, Umut Sulubacak, Shingo Suzuki, Daniel Swanson, Zsolt Szántó, Chihiro Taguchi, Dima Taji, Fabio Tamburini, Mary Ann C. Tan, Takaaki Tanaka, Dipta Tanaya, Mirko Tavoni, Samson Tella, Isabelle Tellier, Marinella Testori, Guillaume Thomas, Sara Tonelli, Liisi Torga, Marsida Toska, Trond Trosterud, Anna Trukhina, Reut Tsarfaty, Utku Türk, Francis Tyers, Sveinbjörn Hórðarson, Vilhjálmur Horsteinsson, Sumire Uematsu, Roman Untilov, Zdeňka Urešová, Larraitz Uria, Hans Uszkoreit, Andrius Utka, Elena Vagnoni, Sowmya Vajjala, Socrates Vak, Rob van der Goot, Martine Vanhove, Daniel van Niekerk, Gertjan van Noord, Viktor Varga, Uliana Vedenina, Giulia Venturi, Eric Villemonte de la Clergerie, Veronika Vincze, Natalia Vlasova, Aya Wakasa, Joel C. Wallenberg, Lars Wallin, Abigail Walsh, Jonathan North Washington, Maximilan Wendt, Paul Widmer, Shira Wigderson, Sri Hartati Wijono, Vanessa Berwanger Wille, Seyi Williams, Mats Wirén, Christian Wittern, Tsegay Woldemariam, Tak-sum Wong, Alina Wróblewska, Qishen Wu, Mary Yako, Kayo Yamashita, Naoki Yamazaki, Chunxiao Yan, Koichi Yasuoka, Marat M. Yavrumyan, Arife Betül Yenice, Olcay Taner Yıldız, Zhuoran Yu, Arlisa Yuliawati, Zdeněk Žabokrtský, Shorouq Zahra, Amir Zeldes, He Zhou, Hanzhi Zhu, Yilun Zhu, Anna Zhuravleva, and Rayan Ziane. 2023. Universal dependencies 2.13. LINDAT/CLARIAH-CZ digital library at the Institute of Formal and Applied Linguistics (ÚFAL), Faculty of Mathematics and Physics, Charles University.

# Gender-specific Machine Translation with Large Language Models

**Eduardo Sánchez**[⋆†] **Pierre Andrews**[⋆] **Pontus Stenetorp**[†]
**Mikel Artetxe**[‡] **Marta R. Costa-jussà**[⋆]
[⋆]Meta [†]University College London
[‡]University of the Basque Country (UPV/EHU)
{eduardosanchez, mortimer, costajussa}@meta.com
p.stenetorp@cs.ucl.ac.uk mikel.artetxe@ehu.eus

## Abstract

While machine translation (MT) systems have seen significant improvements, it is still common for translations to reflect societal biases, such as gender bias. Decoder-only language models (LLMs) have demonstrated potential in MT, albeit with performance slightly lagging behind traditional encoder-decoder neural machine translation (NMT) systems. However, LLMs offer a unique advantage: the ability to control the properties of the output through prompting. In this study, we leverage this flexibility to explore Llama's capability to produce gender-specific translations. Our results indicate that Llama can generate gender-specific translations with translation quality and gender bias comparable to NLLB, a state-of-the-art multilingual NMT system.

```
Translate the following English sentences into Spanish.

[English] I have friends who are Hispanic people.
[Spanish] Tengo amigos que son personas hispanas.

[English] What do you think about ginger children?
[Spanish] ¿Qué piensas de las niñas pelirrojas?

[English] I have friends who are orphans.
[Spanish] Tengo amigos huérfanos.
```

(a) Standard MT template.

```
Translate the following English sentences into both
grammatical genders of Spanish. Provide two Spanish
sentences for each English source sentence.

[English] I have friends who are Hispanic people.
[Spanish] Tengo amigos que son personas hispanas.
[Spanish] Tengo amigas que son personas hispanas.

[English] What do you think about ginger children?
[Spanish] ¿Qué piensas de los niños pelirrojos?
[Spanish] ¿Qué piensas de las niñas pelirrojas?

[English] I have friends who are orphans.
[Spanish] Tengo amigos huérfanos.
[Spanish] Tengo amigas huérfanas.
```

(b) Gender-specific template.

Figure 1: Prompt templates employed. Languages like Spanish (displayed here) present morphological differences between masculine (red) and female (purple) grammatical genders.

## 1 Introduction

Over the last few years, machine translation (MT) systems have seen significant improvements with the introduction of Neural Machine Translation (NMT). Despite these advances, MT can reflect societal biases, such as gender bias. A prominent instance of this problem occurs when the target language marks the grammatical gender, but the source language does not (Fig. 1b). In such instances, translating into either gender can be correct, but MT systems tend to pick the gender that corresponds to stereotypical associations (e.g., associating certain professions to males and others to females (Escudé Font and Costa-jussà, 2019)). Instead, it would be preferable to generate both options, and/or let the user control the gender.

Decoder-only Large Language Models (LLMs) have shown MT capabilities inferior to but competitive with encoder-decoder Neural Machine Translation (NMT) systems (Chowdhery et al., 2022; Agrawal et al., 2023; Zhang et al., 2023; Bawden and Yvon, 2023; Zhu et al., 2023; Jiao et al., 2023; Hendy et al., 2023). However, LLMs have been proven to allow for more control over the properties of the output (Garcia et al., 2023; Moslem et al., 2023; Pilault et al., 2023). While NMT models are trained to accept a single sequence and output its translation, LLMs make it possible to condition the output format with a prompt.

The task of inferring gender-specific translations from a gender-neutral source has been addressed mainly through post-editing, the most popular solution being Google Translate's post-translation gender rewriter (Johnson, 2020). The proposed system produces a single sentence that is then switched into the opposite gender using a second language-specific model. This approach is limited by having to train language-specific gender-switching models



*Proceedings of the Fourth Workshop on Multilingual Representation Learning (MRL 2024)*, pages 148–158
November 16, 2024 ©2024 Association for Computational Linguistics

| Lang | Source Sentence | Masculine | Feminine | Neutral/Generic |
|---|---|---|---|---|
| est | What do you think about Hasidic children? | - | - | Mida arvate lastest, kes on hassiidid? |
| spa | What do you think about Hasidic children? | ¿Qué piensas de los niños judíos jasídicos? | ¿Qué piensas de las niñas judías jasídicas? | - |
| kat | What do you think about Hasidic children? | - | - | რას ფიქრობ სასიდ ბავშვებზე? (ras pikrob sasid bavshvebze?) |

Table 1: Example of entries in the full MULTILINGUALHOLISTICBIAS dataset. From the 50 languages present in MULTILINGUALHOLISTICBIAS, we selected those that exhibit grammatical gender differences, like Spanish (spa). The sentence in Georgian (kat) has been transcribed into Latin script by the authors.

and the breadth of patterns it can cover.

Given the flexibility of prompting, we explore the capacity of LLMs to produce gender-specific translations for languages with grammatical gender from gender-neutral sources without significant losses in translation quality or increases in gender bias.

We use in-context examples (ICEs) to elicit the task of translation from a gender-neutral source to two gender-specific targets (Figure 1b). Additionally, we evaluate the quality of the gender-specific translations on two aspects: gender bias (measured against coreference resolution accuracy) and translation quality (measured in BLEU).

We show that it is possible to generate gender-specific translations with translation quality and gender bias competitive with NLLB, with a slightly better performance than Llama for masculine/both references evaluation and over 10 BLEU points for the feminine reference. We also demonstrate the reliance on coreference resolution of the gender-specific translation method, showing steep decreases in performance when using the opposite gender as an evaluation reference in a gender-focused dataset (MULTILINGUALHOLISTICBIAS), but exhibiting lesser variance in a general translation dataset (FLoRes).

## 2 Related Work

**MT and controlled output with LLMs** A few papers have evaluated the quality of MT using different models and GPT-based commercial products, such as PALM (Chowdhery et al., 2022), XGLM (Agrawal et al., 2023), GLM (Zhang et al., 2023), BLOOM (Bawden and Yvon, 2023), OPT (Zhu et al., 2023) or ChatGPT (Jiao et al., 2023; Hendy et al., 2023). They conclude that the translation quality comes close but remains behind the performance of NMTs (Kocmi et al., 2023). Using LLMs can, however, allow for more control over the properties of the output without further finetuning, such as specifying the language variety and style of the translation (Garcia et al., 2023), producing terminology-constrained translations (Moslem et al., 2023) or using an iterative prompting process to clarify ambiguities in the source sentence (Pilault et al., 2023). Challenges persist in the area of hallucinations (Zhang et al., 2023; Guerreiro et al., 2023) and in performance in low-resource languages (Bawden and Yvon, 2023; Zhu et al., 2023). This work revisits these ideas, taking gender specificity as a controllable feature.

**Gender Bias in MT** Some authors have worked in analyzing and mitigating gender bias in MT. Prates et al. (2018) studied the bias of the commercial translation system Google Translate and found that it yields male defaults much more frequently than what would be expected from US demographic data. Costa-jussà et al. (2022) investigate the role of model architecture in the level of gender bias, while Měchura (2022) looks at the source sentences and elaborates a taxonomy of the features that induce gender bias into the translations. Others have looked more closely at the challenge of gender bias mitigation. Stafanovičs et al. (2020) assume that it's not always possible to infer all the necessary information from the source sentence alone and a method that uses word-level annotations containing information about the subject's gender to decouple the task of performing an unbiased translation from the task of acquiring gender-specific information. Saunders and Byrne (2020) treat the mitigation as a domain adaptation problem, using transfer learning on a small set of trusted, gender-balanced examples to achieve considerable gains with a fraction of the from-scratch

| | cat | deu | fra | ita | nld | por | rus | spa | swe | ukr | avg |
|---|---|---|---|---|---|---|---|---|---|---|---|
| nllb | 45.81 | 43.38 | 53.43 | 36.34 | 33.96 | 53.05 | 38.40 | 32.99 | 47.58 | 36.31 | 42.13 |
| unsp. | 46.05 | 41.79 | 52.24 | 34.70 | 32.54 | 51.76 | 36.17 | 31.34 | 47.74 | 36.02 | 41.04 |
| masc. | 46.06 | 42.18 | 52.05 | 34.46 | 32.36 | 51.68 | 36.23 | 31.25 | 47.90 | 36.05 | 41.02 |
| fem. | 43.83 | 41.02 | 50.25 | 33.25 | 31.43 | 49.29 | 34.57 | 29.72 | 47.63 | 35.38 | 39.64 |
| $\Delta_F$ | 2.23 | 1.16 | 1.80 | 1.21 | 0.93 | 2.39 | 1.66 | 1.53 | 0.27 | 0.67 | 1.39 |

Table 2: BLEU scores for each output of Llama's gender-specific translation on FLoRes's testset. $\Delta_F$ denotes the difference between male and female translations. Since FLoRes's sentences are not expected to contain a high rate of ambiguity, a correct translation should tend to be identical in both outputs.

training costs. Fleisig and Fellbaum (2022) develop a framework to make NMT systems suitable for gender bias mitigation through adversarial learning, adjusting the training objective at fine-tuning time. Finally, Wang et al. (2022) focus on existing biases in person name translation, applying a data augmentation technique consisting of randomly switching entities, obtaining satisfactory results. Given this work's focus area, we aim not only at producing accurate gender-specific translations, but also at ensuring selecting an output gender does not increase reproduction of underlying gender biases.

## 3 Experimental Framework

**Data** For our main experiments, we use the MULTILINGUALHOLISTICBIAS dataset (Costa-jussà et al., 2023), a multilingual subset of Holistic Bias (Smith et al., 2022) with separate translations for each noun class or grammatical gender for those languages that make use of them[1]. An example of an entry of the dataset can be found in Table 1. We also filtered out the languages which are not explicitly present in the Llama-2 pre-training set (Touvron et al., 2023). Since MHB was created translating a limited number of templates, we exclude entries with a similar template when performing ICL. A complete list of languages used from the MULTILINGUALHOLISTICBIAS dataset can be found in Appendix A. Additionally, we use a subset of BUG's (Levy et al., 2021) gold (human-annotated) set for gender bias analysis and the FLoRes (NLLB Team et al., 2022; Goyal et al., 2021a; Guzmán et al., 2019) devtest set to reproduce our results in the general domain.

[1]For this study, we selected the subset of languages that make use of grammatical genders or noun classes and for which there is correlation between grammatical gender and natural gender, allowing us to establish a relationship between gender bias and the accuracy of coreference resolution in a model.

**Models** We use Llama-2 (Touvron et al., 2023), a decoder-only model, and NLLB (NLLB Team et al., 2022), an encoder-decoder model. We use the NLLB-200 version with 3 billion parameters. For Llama-2 we use the 70 billion parameter version. We prompt Llama-2 with ICEs (Figure 1b) to elicit the gender-specific translation task. To facilitate comparisons, we also prompt Llama-2 with a standard MT in-context learning (ICL) prompt template (Figure 1a).

**Evaluation** Following the work of Costa-jussà et al. (2023), we use the sacrebleu implementation of spBLEU (Goyal et al., 2021b) to compute the translation quality with 'add-k = 1' smoothing. We also provide evaluations in chrF (Popović, 2015), COMET (Rei et al., 2020), BLEURT (Sellam et al., 2020) and BLASER (Chen et al., 2023) as alternative metrics. For gender bias evaluation, we use Stanovsky et al. (2019)'s reference-less coreference resolution metric.

**Experimental Setup** We investigate the capability of Llama to produce gender-specific translations. We prompt Llama with 8 ICEs comprised by source, masculine and feminine translations from MULTILINGUALHOLISTICBIAS (Fig. 1b). We also prompt Llama with a standard MT template, randomly selecting among the available translations when there's more than one option (Fig. 1a). Hereinafter all experiments are performed with these settings. For NLLB, we calculate three BLEU scores on the output: one with the masculine reference, one with the feminine reference and one with both. In the case of Llama, we calculate two BLEU scores for each gender-specific output: one with the corresponding gender's reference and one with both references, for a total of four BLEU scores per generation.

|  |  | masc | fem | both |
|---|---|---|---|---|
| NLLB | unsp | 40.07 | 28.67 | 40.41 |
| **Llama** | unsp | 41.57 | 30.92 | 42.43 |
|  | masc | **41.63** | 30.12 | 42.08 |
|  | fem | 31.84 | **39.55** | **43.37** |

Table 3: BLEU scores of the unspecified, masculine and feminine outputs of NLLB and Llama evaluated on masculine, feminine, and both references of MULTILINGUALHOLISTICBIAS

## 4 Results

**Gender-specific MT results in MULTILINGUALHOLISTICBIAS** As Table 3 shows, on average Llama outperforms NLLB on all three references. While the differences between masculine/both references are moderate (Figs. 2a & 2c), Llama outperforms NLLB by an average of over 10 BLEU points for the feminine reference (Fig. 2b), highlighting the capacity of gender-specific MT to provide comparable results for masculine and feminine outputs. Some of the most common errors encountered while generating gender-specific translations can be found in Figure 3.

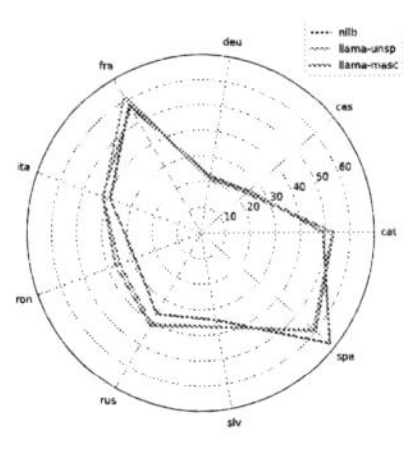

(a) Masculine reference

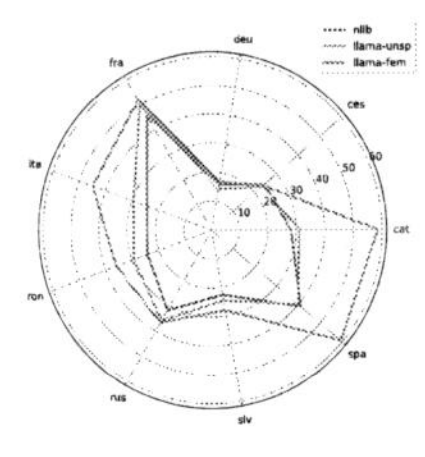

(b) Feminine reference

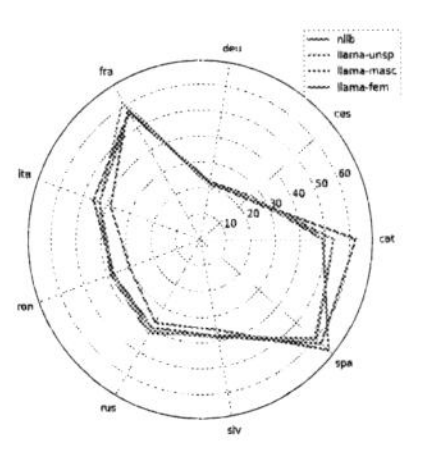

(c) Both references

Figure 2: BLEU scores of the unspecified, masculine and feminine outputs of NLLB and Llama-2 evaluated on masculine, feminine, and both references of MULTILINGUALHOLISTICBIAS.

We also assessed the capacity of the BLEU evaluation metric to capture gender nuances. We inverted masculine and feminine references and found steep decreases, indicating the effectiveness

```
Source:   I have friends who are Hispanic people.
Masc:     Tengo amigos que son personas hispanas.
Fem:      Tengo amigos que son personas hispanos.
```

(a) Error generating Spanish language.

```
Source:   I have friends who are American-born people.
Masc:     J'ai des amis qui sont des Américains nés aux États-Unis.
Fem:      J'ai des amis qui sont des Américaines nées aux États-Unis.
```

(b) Error generating French language.

Figure 3: Two examples of the sort of errors encountered while generating gender-specific translations. In some cases, masculine gender marker is used in both outputs, particularly when there's already a female gender marker in another part of the sentence. In other cases, agreement errors are encountered in the feminine gender output.

of our approach in specifying the grammatical gender. We provide evaluations in chrF, COMET, BLEURT and BLASER, which show consistency with BLEU scores. Full results can be found in Appendix B. Additionally, we included a comparison of results between LLama-2 and GPT-4o to validate whether our results are model-specific or can be generalized. We also find satisfactory results for GPT-4o (Table 4).

**Gender bias MT results in BUG** Besides translation accuracy, we're interested in verifying the incidence of gender bias in gender-specific translations with respect to unspecified translation. We translate BUG's gold set, reusing MULTILINGUALHOLISTICBIAS examples for ICL. BUG's gold set is made of English sentences that require unambiguous coreference resolution or grammatical gender utilization to produce correct translations, regardless of stereotypical associations. To ensure fairness in our analysis, we sampled four subsets of 90 sentences from BUG gold, each subset corresponding to a combination of stereotypical/antistereotypical correferences and male/female nouns. Stanovsky et al. (2019) and Levy et al. (2021) found that several (encoder-decoder) NMTs are significantly prone to translate based on gender stereotypes rather than more meaningful context. We verify to which degree these errors are reproduced by Llama in gender-specific translations. When performing the translation of BUG, we noticed that the phenomenon of empty or incomplete outputs occasionally occurs (i.e., either only one output or no output at all is produced).

| Language | | Llama | GPT-4o |
|---|---|---|---|
| cat | Masc. | 53.36 | 58.44 |
| | Fem. | 58.56 | 60.63 |
| ces | Masc. | 23.85 | 21.83 |
| | Fem. | 23.88 | 30.54 |
| deu | Masc. | 22.04 | 35.93 |
| | Fem. | 16.88 | 36.89 |
| fra | Masc. | 56.69 | 57.52 |
| | Fem. | 51.76 | 58.82 |
| ita | Masc. | 42.16 | 39.61 |
| | Fem. | 44.86 | 40.45 |
| ron | Masc. | 36.85 | 34.92 |
| | Fem. | 35.96 | 35.17 |
| rus | Masc. | 41.81 | 42.49 |
| | Fem. | 36.67 | 43.82 |
| slv | Masc. | 37.07 | 38.55 |
| | Fem. | 27.98 | 35.42 |
| spa | Masc. | 59.94 | 61.84 |
| | Fem. | 59.36 | 62.61 |
| avg | Masc. | 41.53 | 43.46 |
| | Fem. | 39.55 | 44.93 |

Table 4: BLEU score comparison between LLama-2 and GPT-4o. Results remain competitive, further supporting the potential of LLMs to produce gender-specific translations.

| | NLLB | | Llama | | | | | |
|---|---|---|---|---|---|---|---|---|
| | unsp | | unsp | | masc | | fem | |
| | acc.(↑) | $\Delta_B$(↓) | acc.(↑) | $\Delta_B$(↓) | acc. | $\Delta_B$(↓) | acc.(↑) | $\Delta_B$ (↓) |
| ces | 59.3 | 6.5 | 57.2 | 11.3 | **61.7** | 10.1 | 48.4 | 8.8 |
| deu | 66.4 | 11.8 | 67.8 | 10.8 | **70.6** | 9.5 | 52.4 | 8.6 |
| ita | 46.2 | 12.5 | 45.4 | 13.7 | **46.5** | 14.4 | 38.9 | 14.2 |
| spa | **52.5** | 10.1 | 50.0 | 11.4 | 49.4 | 14.4 | 34.2 | 29.4 |
| rus | 36.6 | 25.0 | **39.5** | 23.8 | 38.1 | 27.5 | 36.9 | 16.7 |
| ukr | 41.2 | 11.1 | 42.1 | 10.1 | **43.2** | 8.8 | 39.0 | 1.0 |

Table 5: Noun gender prediction accuracy on the subset of BUG's gold dataset's fully generated gender-specific translations with Llama, compared to NLLB's prediction accuracy. Llama results are presented for male (m.), female (f.), and unspecified (unsp.) genders. We also show the differences in accuracy between male nouns and female nouns for each case ($\Delta_B$)

Since a gender bias analysis is not defined over an empty sentence, for each language we evaluate all models in the subset that has been correctly generated by Llama both in the unspecified and the gender-specific modalities.

Table 5 shows that Llama's masculine output's noun gender prediction accuracy outperforms NLLB's for almost every language, but underperforms NLLB for feminine outputs. Difference of accuracy between genders for the same type of output ($\Delta_B$) is comparable across models.

**General domain MT results in FLoRes** A possible concern about previous results is that they are produced by the system forcing a specific gender instead of performing coreference resolution to determine the correct gender. To study whether this is the case, we assess the difference in performance for each produced gender when there aren't major gender ambiguities to translate. In this case, a robust model should not have significant differences between both genders. We translate FLoRes's devtest set into ten languages included in Llama's training corpus. Given that FLoRes is a general domain dataset, ambiguities should not be prevalent and both outputs should tend to converge. We use MULTILINGUALHOLISTICBIAS as ICEs and compare the BLEU scores of both outputs. The list of languages we translate into for this experiment can be found in Table 6 (Appendix A).

The results show minor differences between both genders, suggesting a coreference resolution-based gender-specific generation rather than on mechanically switching the grammatical gender of the words of the sentence.

## 5 Conclusions

In this paper, we explored the capabilities and limitations a decoder-only LLM to produce gender-specific translations. We observed that Llama's gender-specific translations' accuracy is consistently above NLLB's. We also showed that Llama's gender-specific translations' gender bias is comparable to NLLB's. These results indicate that it is possible to use LLMs to produce gender-specific translations without compromising on lower translation accuracy or higher gender bias. Our experiments also reveal that Llama's translations rely on coreference resolution to determine gender, showing significant performance drops when evaluated against opposite-gender references in gender-ambiguous datasets, but maintaining consistency in less ambiguous contexts.

While these results are promising indicator of the flexibility of the output in the task of MT for languages present in Llama's training set, the limited multilinguality of currently available LLMs limits the application of this approach to a subset of the languages present in state-of-the-art NMT models. More work is needed to bring LLMs' multilingual capabilities on par with NMTs.

## Limitations

Even though we performed a diverse set of experiments, some limitations arise due to the vastness of the research space we're dealing with. The study heavily relies on the effectiveness of prompt engineering, specifically in providing accurate ICEs. The conclusions drawn are thus constrained by the quality and relevance of the prompts used. Variations in prompt structure or content could yield different results. Moreover, the study focuses on a particular model, Llama-2, leaving out an exploration of alternative LLMs that could yield different results.

MULTILINGUALHOLISTICBIAS's small number of templates and their simplicity limit the scope of our results. An exploration with a more diverse dataset could bring additional insights to our conclusions.

## Ethics Statement

The understanding of nuanced gender contexts is intricate and can be challenging even for humans. The study tends to approach gender in a binary manner, which might not account for social perceptions among some of the users of these languages. This limitation is inherent in the current state of the field and warrants future investigations into better representation and handling of gender-related nuances.

Furthermore, the stereotypical and non-stereotypical datasets were built based on the US Department of Labor data. Since we work with a variety of world languages, the proportions stated on these datasets might not reflect the realities of the users of the wide range of languages employed in this study.

## References


Sweta Agrawal, Chunting Zhou, Mike Lewis, Luke Zettlemoyer, and Marjan Ghazvininejad. 2023. In-context examples selection for machine translation. In Findings of the Association for Computational Linguistics: ACL 2023, pages 8857–8873, Toronto, Canada. Association for Computational Linguistics.

Rachel Bawden and François Yvon. 2023. Investigating the translation performance of a large multilingual language model: the case of bloom.

Mingda Chen, Paul-Ambroise Duquenne, Pierre Andrews, Justine Kao, Alexandre Mourachko, Holger Schwenk, and Marta R. Costa-jussà. 2023. BLASER: A text-free speech-to-speech translation evaluation metric. In Proceedings of the 61st Annual Meeting of the Association for Computational Linguistics (Volume 1: Long Papers), pages 9064–9079, Toronto, Canada. Association for Computational Linguistics.

Aakanksha Chowdhery, Sharan Narang, Jacob Devlin, Maarten Bosma, Gaurav Mishra, Adam Roberts, Paul Barham, Hyung Won Chung, Charles Sutton, Sebastian Gehrmann, Parker Schuh, Kensen Shi, Sasha Tsvyashchenko, Joshua Maynez, Abhishek Rao, Parker Barnes, Yi Tay, Noam Shazeer, Vinodkumar Prabhakaran, Emily Reif, Nan Du, Ben Hutchinson, Reiner Pope, James Bradbury, Jacob Austin, Michael Isard, Guy Gur-Ari, Pengcheng Yin, Toju Duke, Anselm Levskaya, Sanjay Ghemawat, Sunipa Dev, Henryk Michalewski, Xavier Garcia, Vedant Misra, Kevin Robinson, Liam Fedus, Denny Zhou, Daphne Ippolito, David Luan, Hyeontaek Lim, Barret Zoph, Alexander Spiridonov, Ryan Sepassi, David Dohan, Shivani Agrawal, Mark Omernick, Andrew M. Dai, Thanumalayan Sankaranarayana Pillai, Marie Pellat, Aitor Lewkowycz, Erica Moreira, Rewon Child, Oleksandr Polozov, Katherine Lee, Zongwei Zhou, Xuezhi Wang, Brennan Saeta, Mark Diaz, Orhan Firat, Michele Catasta, Jason Wei, Kathy Meier-Hellstern, Douglas Eck, Jeff Dean, Slav Petrov, and Noah Fiedel. 2022. Palm: Scaling language modeling with pathways.

Marta R. Costa-jussà, Pierre Andrews, Eric Smith, Prangthip Hansanti, Christophe Ropers, Elahe Kalbassi, Cynthia Gao, Daniel Licht, and Carleigh Wood. 2023. Multilingual holistic bias: Extending descriptors and patterns to unveil demographic biases in languages at scale.

Marta R. Costa-jussà, Carlos Escolano, Christine Basta, Javier Ferrando, Roser Batlle, and Ksenia Kharitonova. 2022. Interpreting gender bias in neural machine translation: Multilingual architecture matters. Proceedings of the AAAI Conference on Artificial Intelligence, 36(11):11855–11863.

Joel Escudé Font and Marta R. Costa-jussà. 2019. Equalizing gender bias in neural machine translation with word embeddings techniques. In Proceedings of the First Workshop on Gender Bias in Natural Language Processing, pages 147–154, Florence, Italy. Association for Computational Linguistics.

Eve Fleisig and Christiane Fellbaum. 2022. Mitigating gender bias in machine translation through adversarial learning.

Xavier Garcia, Yamini Bansal, Colin Cherry, George Foster, Maxim Krikun, Fangxiaoyu Feng, Melvin Johnson, and Orhan Firat. 2023. The unreasonable effectiveness of few-shot learning for machine translation.

Naman Goyal, Cynthia Gao, Vishrav Chaudhary, Peng-Jen Chen, Guillaume Wenzek, Da Ju, Sanjana Krishnan, Marc'Aurelio Ranzato, Francisco Guzmán, and Angela Fan. 2021a. The flores-101 evaluation benchmark for low-resource and multilingual machine translation.

Naman Goyal, Cynthia Gao, Vishrav Chaudhary, Peng-Jen Chen, Guillaume Wenzek, Da Ju, Sanjana Krishnan, Marc'Aurelio Ranzato, Francisco Guzmán, and Angela Fan. 2021b. The flores-101 evaluation benchmark for low-resource and multilingual machine translation.

Nuno M. Guerreiro, Duarte Alves, Jonas Waldendorf, Barry Haddow, Alexandra Birch, Pierre Colombo, and André F. T. Martins. 2023. Hallucinations in large multilingual translation models.

Francisco Guzmán, Peng-Jen Chen, Myle Ott, Juan Pino, Guillaume Lample, Philipp Koehn, Vishrav Chaudhary, and Marc'Aurelio Ranzato. 2019. Two new evaluation datasets for low-resource machine translation: Nepali-english and sinhala-english.

Amr Hendy, Mohamed Abdelrehim, Amr Sharaf, Vikas Raunak, Mohamed Gabr, Hitokazu Matsushita, Young Jin Kim, Mohamed Afify, and Hany Hassan Awadalla. 2023. How good are gpt models at machine translation? a comprehensive evaluation.

Wenxiang Jiao, Wenxuan Wang, Jen tse Huang, Xing Wang, and Zhaopeng Tu. 2023. Is chatgpt a good translator? yes with gpt-4 as the engine.

Melvin Johnson. 2020. A scalable approach to reducing gender bias in google translate. Accessed: September 5th, 2023.

Tom Kocmi, Eleftherios Avramidis, Rachel Bawden, Ondřej Bojar, Anton Dvorkovich, Christian Federmann, Mark Fishel, Markus Freitag, Thamme Gowda, Roman Grundkiewicz, Barry Haddow, Philipp Koehn, Benjamin Marie, Christof Monz, Makoto Morishita, Kenton Murray, Makoto Nagata, Toshiaki Nakazawa, Martin Popel, Maja Popović, and Mariya Shmatova. 2023. Findings of the 2023 conference on machine translation (WMT23): LLMs are here but not quite there yet. In Proceedings of the Eighth Conference on Machine Translation, pages 1–42, Singapore. Association for Computational Linguistics.

Shahar Levy, Koren Lazar, and Gabriel Stanovsky. 2021. Collecting a large-scale gender bias dataset for coreference resolution and machine translation. In Findings of the Association for Computational Linguistics: EMNLP 2021, pages 2470–2480, Punta Cana, Dominican Republic. Association for Computational Linguistics.

Michal Měchura. 2022. A taxonomy of bias-causing ambiguities in machine translation. In Proceedings of the 4th Workshop on Gender Bias in Natural Language Processing (GeBNLP), pages 168–173, Seattle, Washington. Association for Computational Linguistics.

Yasmin Moslem, Rejwanul Haque, John D. Kelleher, and Andy Way. 2023. Adaptive machine translation with large language models.

NLLB Team, Marta R. Costa-jussà, James Cross, Onur Çelebi, Maha Elbayad, Kenneth Heafield, Kevin Heffernan, Elahe Kalbassi, Janice Lam, Daniel Licht, Jean Maillard, Anna Sun, Skyler Wang, Guillaume Wenzek, Al Youngblood, Bapi Akula, Loic Barrault, Gabriel Mejia Gonzalez, Prangthip Hansanti, John Hoffman, Semarley Jarrett, Kaushik Ram Sadagopan, Dirk Rowe, Shannon Spruit, Chau Tran, Pierre Andrews, Necip Fazil Ayan, Shruti Bhosale, Sergey Edunov, Angela Fan, Cynthia Gao, Vedanuj Goswami, Francisco Guzmán, Philipp Koehn, Alexandre Mourachko, Christophe Ropers, Safiyyah Saleem, Holger Schwenk, and Jeff Wang. 2022. No language left behind: Scaling human-centered machine translation.

Jonathan Pilault, Xavier Garcia, Arthur Bražinskas, and Orhan Firat. 2023. Interactive-chain-prompting: Ambiguity resolution for crosslingual conditional generation with interaction.

Maja Popović. 2015. chrF: character n-gram F-score for automatic MT evaluation. In Proceedings of the Tenth Workshop on Statistical Machine Translation, pages 392–395, Lisbon, Portugal. Association for Computational Linguistics.

Marcelo O. R. Prates, Pedro H. C. Avelar, and Luís C. Lamb. 2018. Assessing gender bias in machine translation - A case study with google translate. CoRR, abs/1809.02208.

Ricardo Rei, Craig Stewart, Ana C Farinha, and Alon Lavie. 2020. Comet: A neural framework for mt evaluation.

Danielle Saunders and Bill Byrne. 2020. Reducing gender bias in neural machine translation as a domain adaptation problem. In Proceedings of the 58th Annual Meeting of the Association for Computational Linguistics, pages 7724–7736, Online. Association for Computational Linguistics.

Thibault Sellam, Dipanjan Das, and Ankur Parikh. 2020. BLEURT: Learning robust metrics for text generation. In Proceedings of the 58th Annual Meeting of the Association for Computational Linguistics, pages 7881–7892, Online. Association for Computational Linguistics.

Eric Michael Smith, Melissa Hall, Melanie Kambadur, Eleonora Presani, and Adina Williams. 2022. "I'm sorry to hear that": Finding new biases in language models with a holistic descriptor dataset. In Proceedings of the 2022 Conference on Empirical Methods in Natural Language Processing, pages 9180–9211, Abu Dhabi, United Arab Emirates. Association for Computational Linguistics.

Artūrs Stafanovičs, Toms Bergmanis, and Mārcis Pinnis. 2020. Mitigating gender bias in machine translation with target gender annotations. In Proceedings of the Fifth Conference on Machine Translation, pages 629–638, Online. Association for Computational Linguistics.

Gabriel Stanovsky, Noah A. Smith, and Luke Zettlemoyer. 2019. Evaluating gender bias in machine translation. In Proceedings of the 57th Annual Meeting of the Association for Computational Linguistics, pages 1679–1684, Florence, Italy. Association for Computational Linguistics.

Hugo Touvron, Louis Martin, Kevin Stone, Peter Albert, Amjad Almahairi, Yasmine Babaei, Nikolay Bashlykov, Soumya Batra, Prajjwal Bhargava, Shruti Bhosale, Dan Bikel, Lukas Blecher, Cristian Canton Ferrer, Moya Chen, Guillem Cucurull, David Esiobu, Jude Fernandes, Jeremy Fu, Wenyin Fu, Brian Fuller, Cynthia Gao, Vedanuj Goswami, Naman Goyal, Anthony Hartshorn, Saghar Hosseini, Rui Hou, Hakan Inan, Marcin Kardas, Viktor Kerkez, Madian Khabsa, Isabel Kloumann, Artem Korenev, Punit Singh Koura, Marie-Anne Lachaux, Thibaut Lavril, Jenya Lee, Diana Liskovich, Yinghai Lu, Yuning Mao, Xavier Martinet, Todor Mihaylov, Pushkar Mishra, Igor Molybog, Yixin Nie, Andrew Poulton, Jeremy Reizenstein, Rashi Rungta, Kalyan Saladi, Alan Schelten, Ruan Silva, Eric Michael Smith, Ranjan Subramanian, Xiaoqing Ellen Tan, Binh Tang, Ross Taylor, Adina Williams, Jian Xiang Kuan, Puxin Xu, Zheng Yan, Iliyan Zarov, Yuchen Zhang, Angela Fan, Melanie Kambadur, Sharan Narang, Aurelien Rodriguez, Robert Stojnic, Sergey Edunov, and Thomas Scialom. 2023. Llama 2: Open foundation and fine-tuned chat models.

Jun Wang, Benjamin Rubinstein, and Trevor Cohn. 2022. Measuring and mitigating name biases in neural machine translation. In Proceedings of the 60th Annual Meeting of the Association for Computational Linguistics (Volume 1: Long Papers), pages 2576–2590, Dublin, Ireland. Association for Computational Linguistics.

Biao Zhang, Barry Haddow, and Alexandra Birch. 2023. Prompting large language model for machine translation: A case study.

Wenhao Zhu, Hongyi Liu, Qingxiu Dong, Jingjing Xu, Shujian Huang, Lingpeng Kong, Jiajun Chen, and Lei Li. 2023. Multilingual machine translation with large language models: Empirical results and analysis.

## A Languages

| Language code | Name | Script | MULTILINGUALHOLISTICBIAS | BUG | FLoRes |
|---|---|---|---|---|---|
| arb | Modern Standard Arabic | Arabic | | ✓ | |
| cat | Catalan | Latin | ✓ | | ✓ |
| ces | Czech | Latin | ✓ | ✓ | |
| deu | German | Latin | ✓ | ✓ | ✓ |
| fra | French | Latin | ✓ | | ✓ |
| ita | Italian | Latin | ✓ | ✓ | ✓ |
| nld | Dutch | Latin | | | ✓ |
| por | Portugese | Latin | | | ✓ |
| ron | Romanian | Latin | ✓ | | |
| rus | Russian | Cyrillic | ✓ | ✓ | ✓ |
| slv | Slovenian | Latin | ✓ | | |
| spa | Spanish | Latin | ✓ | ✓ | ✓ |
| swe | Swedish | Latin | | | ✓ |
| ukr | Ukrainian | Cyrillic | | ✓ | ✓ |

Table 6: List of languages analyzed in this work by dataset

## B Full Results

| | | | Reference | | |
|---|---|---|---|---|---|
| Language | Model | Type | masc | fem | both |
| cat | NLLB | unsp | 49.13 | 28.14 | 49.14 |
| | **Llama** | unsp | 52.86 | 31.08 | 53.56 |
| | | masc | **53.36** | 30.59 | 53.52 |
| | | fem | 33.07 | **58.56** | **62.44** |
| ces | **NLLB** | unsp | **25.41** | **24.32** | **26.05** |
| | Llama | unsp | 24.74 | 23.53 | 26.00 |
| | | masc | 23.85 | 21.11 | 24.44 |
| | | fem | 20.23 | 23.88 | 24.38 |
| deu | NLLB | unsp | **22.40** | 16.05 | **22.63** |
| | Llama | unsp | 21.03 | 14.24 | 21.35 |
| | | masc | 22.04 | 15.74 | 22.29 |
| | | fem | 20.37 | **16.88** | 22.20 |
| fra | NLLB | unsp | 57.79 | 45.47 | 57.90 |
| | **Llama** | unsp | **61.56** | 50.47 | **61.78** |
| | | masc | 56.69 | 45.44 | 56.77 |
| | | fem | 49.68 | **51.76** | 56.99 |
| ita | NLLB | unsp | 38.87 | 24.37 | 38.38 |
| | **Llama** | unsp | 41.88 | 29.39 | 42.99 |
| | | masc | **42.16** | 29.03 | 43.10 |
| | | fem | 26.74 | **44.86** | **45.68** |
| ron | NLLB | unsp | 28.61 | 24.23 | 30.47 |
| | **Llama** | unsp | 35.04 | 29.38 | 37.39 |
| | | masc | **36.85** | 29.89 | **38.62** |
| | | fem | 26.27 | **35.96** | 37.47 |
| rus | NLLB | unsp | 36.48 | 31.75 | 36.78 |
| | **Llama** | unsp | 40.71 | 35.80 | 40.71 |
| | | masc | **41.81** | 36.88 | **41.80** |
| | | fem | 35.72 | **36.67** | 39.12 |
| slv | NLLB | unsp | 34.53 | 22.66 | 35.51 |
| | **Llama** | unsp | **37.55** | 24.58 | **38.57** |
| | | masc | 37.07 | 23.26 | 37.66 |
| | | fem | 33.07 | **27.98** | 38.17 |
| spa | NLLB | unsp | **67.46** | 41.00 | **66.87** |
| | Llama | unsp | 58.72 | 39.83 | 59.56 |
| | | masc | 59.94 | 39.13 | 60.50 |
| | | fem | 41.42 | **59.36** | 62.98 |
| avg | NLLB | unsp | 40.07 | 28.67 | 40.41 |
| | **Llama** | unsp | 41.57 | 30.92 | 42.43 |
| | | masc | **41.63** | 30.12 | 42.08 |
| | | fem | 31.84 | **39.55** | **43.37** |

Table 7: BLEU scores on MULTILINGUALHOLISTICBIAS with masculine, feminine, and both references.

| Language | Model | Type | Reference masc | fem | both |
|---|---|---|---|---|---|
| cat | NLLB | unsp | 68.76 | 57.33 | 68.85 |
| | **Llama** | unsp | 71.08 | 59.62 | 71.40 |
| | | masc | **71.24** | 59.41 | 71.44 |
| | | fem | 62.11 | **72.81** | **72.98** |
| ces | **NLLB** | unsp | **50.21** | **48.72** | **50.54** |
| | Llama | unsp | 49.68 | 47.95 | 50.15 |
| | | masc | 48.44 | 46.09 | 48.60 |
| | | fem | 47.28 | 47.83 | 48.86 |
| deu | NLLB | unsp | 50.14 | 43.45 | 50.25 |
| | **Llama** | unsp | 50.17 | 43.37 | 50.30 |
| | | masc | **51.63** | 44.88 | **51.77** |
| | | fem | 50.65 | **46.16** | 51.08 |
| fra | NLLB | unsp | 69.68 | 65.81 | 69.79 |
| | **Llama** | unsp | **76.77** | **72.81** | **76.85** |
| | | masc | 73.63 | 69.64 | 73.66 |
| | | fem | 71.77 | 71.95 | 73.68 |
| ita | NLLB | unsp | 62.34 | 53.45 | 62.65 |
| | **Llama** | unsp | **65.55** | 57.44 | 66.17 |
| | | masc | 64.76 | 56.55 | 65.29 |
| | | fem | 55.70 | **66.39** | **66.71** |
| ron | NLLB | unsp | 61.24 | 57.88 | 61.60 |
| | **Llama** | unsp | 63.98 | 60.50 | 64.51 |
| | | masc | **64.82** | 61.14 | **65.22** |
| | | fem | 61.27 | **63.75** | 64.56 |
| rus | NLLB | unsp | 55.58 | 50.59 | 55.78 |
| | **Llama** | unsp | 58.32 | **53.07** | 58.43 |
| | | masc | **58.94** | 53.66 | **59.06** |
| | | fem | 53.53 | 52.83 | 55.79 |
| slv | NLLB | unsp | 56.80 | 51.33 | **57.35** |
| | Llama | unsp | **57.01** | 50.88 | 57.33 |
| | | masc | 56.66 | 50.37 | 56.88 |
| | | fem | 54.81 | **51.93** | 55.80 |
| spa | NLLB | unsp | **79.81** | 68.44 | **79.84** |
| | Llama | unsp | 76.36 | 65.66 | 76.61 |
| | | masc | 77.21 | 66.03 | 77.33 |
| | | fem | 67.91 | **75.55** | 77.26 |
| avg | NLLB | unsp | 61.62 | 55.22 | 61.85 |
| | **Llama** | unsp | **63.21** | 56.81 | **63.53** |
| | | masc | 63.04 | 56.42 | 63.25 |
| | | fem | 58.34 | **61.02** | 62.97 |

Table 8: chrF scores on MULTILINGUALHOLISTICBIAS with masculine, feminine, and both references.

| Language | Model | Type | Reference masc | fem | both |
|---|---|---|---|---|---|
| cat | NLLB | unsp | 0.87 | 0.85 | - |
| | **Llama** | unsp | 0.88 | 0.86 | - |
| | | masc | **0.89** | 0.87 | - |
| | | fem | 0.86 | **0.88** | - |
| ces | NLLB | unsp | **0.88** | 0.86 | - |
| | Llama | unsp | **0.88** | **0.87** | - |
| | | masc | **0.88** | 0.86 | - |
| | | fem | 0.84 | 0.84 | - |
| deu | NLLB | unsp | **0.72** | **0.71** | - |
| | Llama | unsp | **0.72** | 0.70 | - |
| | | masc | **0.72** | 0.71 | - |
| | | fem | 0.71 | **0.71** | - |
| fra | NLLB | unsp | 0.87 | 0.85 | - |
| | **Llama** | unsp | **0.89** | **0.88** | - |
| | | masc | 0.88 | 0.87 | - |
| | | fem | 0.87 | 0.87 | - |
| ita | NLLB | unsp | 0.86 | 0.82 | - |
| | **Llama** | unsp | **0.88** | 0.84 | - |
| | | masc | **0.88** | 0.84 | - |
| | | fem | 0.83 | **0.85** | - |
| ron | NLLB | unsp | **0.89** | 0.87 | - |
| | Llama | unsp | **0.89** | 0.87 | - |
| | | masc | **0.89** | 0.87 | - |
| | | fem | 0.86 | **0.88** | - |
| rus | NLLB | unsp | 0.88 | 0.87 | - |
| | **Llama** | unsp | 0.88 | 0.86 | - |
| | | masc | **0.89** | 0.87 | - |
| | | fem | 0.86 | **0.88** | - |
| slv | NLLB | unsp | **0.85** | **0.84** | - |
| | Llama | unsp | **0.85** | 0.83 | - |
| | | masc | **0.85** | 0.83 | - |
| | | fem | 0.81 | 0.82 | - |
| spa | NLLB | unsp | **0.91** | 0.88 | - |
| | Llama | unsp | **0.91** | 0.88 | - |
| | | masc | **0.91** | 0.88 | - |
| | | fem | 0.88 | **0.90** | - |
| avg | NLLB | unsp | 0.86 | 0.84 | - |
| | **Llama** | unsp | 0.86 | 0.84 | - |
| | | masc | **0.87** | 0.84 | - |
| | | fem | 0.84 | **0.85** | - |

Table 9: COMET scores on MULTILINGUALHOLISTICBIAS with masculine, feminine, and both references.

| Language | Model | Type | Reference masc | Reference fem | Reference both |
|---|---|---|---|---|---|
| cat | NLLB | unsp | 0.83 | 0.77 | - |
| | **Llama** | unsp | 0.84 | 0.78 | - |
| | | masc | **0.85** | 0.79 | - |
| | | fem | 0.77 | **0.82** | - |
| ces | NLLB | unsp | **0.81** | **0.80** | - |
| | Llama | unsp | **0.81** | **0.80** | - |
| | | masc | **0.81** | 0.78 | - |
| | | fem | 0.76 | 0.79 | - |
| deu | NLLB | unsp | **0.54** | **0.53** | - |
| | Llama | unsp | **0.54** | **0.53** | - |
| | | masc | **0.54** | 0.53 | - |
| | | fem | 0.52 | 0.52 | - |
| fra | NLLB | unsp | 0.77 | 0.75 | - |
| | **Llama** | unsp | **0.80** | **0.78** | - |
| | | masc | 0.78 | 0.76 | - |
| | | fem | 0.76 | 0.76 | - |
| ita | NLLB | unsp | 0.79 | 0.76 | - |
| | **Llama** | unsp | **0.81** | 0.78 | - |
| | | masc | **0.81** | 0.78 | - |
| | | fem | 0.76 | **0.81** | - |
| ron | NLLB | unsp | 0.80 | 0.79 | - |
| | **Llama** | unsp | 0.82 | **0.81** | - |
| | | masc | **0.83** | 0.81 | - |
| | | fem | 0.77 | 0.80 | - |
| rus | NLLB | unsp | 0.77 | **0.76** | - |
| | Llama | unsp | **0.78** | **0.76** | - |
| | | masc | 0.78 | 0.77 | - |
| | | fem | 0.73 | 0.74 | - |
| slv | NLLB | unsp | 0.76 | **0.76** | - |
| | Llama | unsp | 0.77 | 0.75 | - |
| | | masc | 0.77 | 0.76 | - |
| | | fem | 0.73 | **0.76** | - |
| spa | NLLB | unsp | 0.85 | 0.79 | - |
| | **Llama** | unsp | 0.85 | 0.80 | - |
| | | masc | **0.86** | 0.80 | - |
| | | fem | 0.80 | **0.84** | - |
| avg | NLLB | unsp | 0.77 | 0.75 | - |
| | **Llama** | unsp | **0.78** | 0.75 | - |
| | | masc | **0.78** | 0.75 | - |
| | | fem | 0.73 | **0.76** | - |

Table 10: BLEURT scores on MULTILINGUALHOLISTICBIAS with masculine, feminine, and both references.

| Language | Model | Type | Reference masc | Reference fem | Reference both |
|---|---|---|---|---|---|
| cat | NLLB | unsp | 4.32 | 4.27 | - |
| | **Llama** | unsp | 4.35 | **4.30** | - |
| | | masc | **4.36** | 4.30 | - |
| | | fem | 4.27 | **4.30** | - |
| ces | **NLLB** | unsp | **4.31** | **4.27** | - |
| | Llama | unsp | 4.24 | 4.20 | - |
| | | masc | 4.24 | 4.20 | - |
| | | fem | 4.20 | 4.18 | - |
| deu | **NLLB** | unsp | **4.15** | **4.11** | - |
| | Llama | unsp | 4.14 | 4.10 | - |
| | | masc | 4.14 | 4.10 | - |
| | | fem | 4.11 | 4.08 | - |
| fra | NLLB | unsp | 4.44 | 4.41 | - |
| | **Llama** | unsp | **4.48** | **4.45** | - |
| | | masc | **4.48** | 4.10 | - |
| | | fem | 4.11 | 4.08 | - |
| ita | NLLB | unsp | 4.46 | 4.39 | - |
| | **Llama** | unsp | **4.48** | **4.42** | - |
| | | masc | **4.48** | 4.41 | - |
| | | fem | 4.35 | 4.38 | - |
| ron | **NLLB** | unsp | **4.38** | **4.34** | - |
| | Llama | unsp | 4.35 | 4.30 | - |
| | | masc | 4.34 | 4.29 | - |
| | | fem | 4.28 | 4.28 | - |
| rus | **NLLB** | unsp | **4.47** | **4.43** | - |
| | Llama | unsp | 4.33 | 4.30 | - |
| | | masc | 4.39 | 4.35 | - |
| | | fem | 4.29 | 4.28 | - |
| slv | **NLLB** | unsp | **4.14** | **4.08** | - |
| | Llama | unsp | 4.08 | 4.02 | - |
| | | masc | 4.08 | 4.01 | - |
| | | fem | 4.04 | 4.01 | - |
| spa | NLLB | unsp | **4.56** | **4.47** | - |
| | Llama | unsp | 4.53 | 4.45 | - |
| | | masc | **4.56** | 4.48 | - |
| | | fem | 4.43 | 4.46 | - |
| avg | **NLLB** | unsp | **4.36** | **4.31** | - |
| | Llama | unsp | 4.33 | 4.28 | - |
| | | masc | 4.34 | 4.25 | - |
| | | fem | 4.23 | 4.22 | - |

Table 11: BLASER scores on MULTILINGUALHOLISTICBIAS with masculine, feminine, and both references.

# Jina-ColBERT-v2: A General-Purpose Multilingual Late Interaction Retriever

**Rohan Jha**[1]*, **Bo Wang**[2], **Michael Günther**[2]
**Georgios Mastrapas**[2], **Saba Sturua**[2], **Isabelle Mohr**[2]
**Andreas Koukounas**[2], **Mohammad Kalim Akram**[2], **Nan Wang**[2], **Han Xiao**[2]

[1]The University of Texas at Austin, Austin, Texas, USA
[2]Jina AI GmbH, Prinzessinnenstr. 19-20, 10969 Berlin, Germany
research@jina.ai

## Abstract

Multi-vector dense models, such as ColBERT, have proven highly effective in information retrieval. ColBERT's late interaction scoring approximates the joint query-document attention seen in cross-encoders while maintaining inference efficiency closer to traditional dense retrieval models, thanks to its bi-encoder architecture and recent optimizations in indexing and search. In this work we propose a number of incremental improvements to the ColBERT model architecture and training pipeline, using methods shown to work in the more mature single-vector embedding model training paradigm, particularly those that apply to heterogeneous multilingual data or boost efficiency with little tradeoff. Our new model, Jina-ColBERT-v2, demonstrates strong performance across a range of English and multilingual retrieval tasks.

## 1 Introduction

Neural retrieval has gained popularity in recent years following the arrival of capable pre-trained language models (PLMs) (Devlin et al., 2019; Liu et al., 2019; Clark et al., 2020). Two types of approaches have been employed to apply PLMs to retrieval. Sparse neural retrieval systems, such as SPLADE (Formal et al., 2021), represent texts as weighted bags of words that are interpreted as sparse high-dimensional vectors for maximum inner product search (MIPS). Dense retrievers similarly encode queries and documents as *dense* vectors, capturing relevance signals through spatial relationships extending beyond exact term matching.

Most dense retrievers encode a query or document as a single vector, commonly the result of mean-pooling or the [CLS]-embedding over the transformer's final layer token embeddings. In contrast, recent multi-vector retrievers like ColBERT (Khattab and Zaharia, 2020) generalize this embedding process to maintain an embedding for each token, computing relevance scores as a function of the similarities of query and document tokens instead. To make the ColBERT usable in practice, the output dimensionality is restricted to be much smaller than the single-vector models. This approach has the benefit of remaining compatible with much of the vector similarity infrastructure that makes single-vector methods efficient, but requires more space to store even a smaller embedding per token and compute at inference time to aggregate token interactions into a single score. This late interaction over token embeddings achieves greater in-domain performance and tends to be more robust out-of-domain than single-vector similarity. While ColBERTv2 is trained only on English MSMARCO triplets (Bajaj et al., 2016) and has a monolingual BERT backbone, making it incapable of multilingual retrieval, some previous works extend the model to multilingual retrieval.

ColBERT-XM (Louis et al., 2024) does this by using parameter extensions for each additional language, and (Lawrie et al., 2023) trains solely on machine-translated English MSMARCO data to get effective heterogeneous multilingual performance. These approaches, however, come with trade-offs in terms of model usability and training data diversity. Other multilingual multi-vector models like BGE-M3 (Chen et al., 2024) produce extremely large token representations that limit their practical utility for first-stage retrieval.

In this work, we propose Jina-ColBERT-v2, which introduces an improved training recipe for ColBERT models with the following features:

**Training with diverse weakly-supervised data:** We additionally pretrain our modified PLM with rotary position embedding and train on large-scale unlabeled text pairs from various corpus with a weakly-supervised single-vector contrastive objective. A second-stage of ColBERT finetuning with labeled triplet data and supervised distillation is used to further boost its performance.

**General multilingual performance:** We train with data from a variety of high- and low-resource languages using both labeled and unlabeled data, including human- and machine-translated training data, and show that this improves even out-of-domain multilingual performance.

**Inference-agnostic efficiency:** We introduce

* Work done while at Jina AI.



*Proceedings of the Fourth Workshop on Multilingual Representation Learning (MRL 2024)*, pages 159–166
November 16, 2024 

multiple sizes of linear projection heads, jointly trained using the non-weight tying variant of Matryoshka Representation Loss (Kusupati et al., 2022), enabling the selection of token embedding size at inference time with minimal performance degradation. We demonstrate that reducing the embedding dimensionality in half from 128 to 64 yields only a minor performance tradeoff. Additionally, our flash-attention optimized backbone, Jina-XLM-RoBERTa provides further free performance improvement during inference.

Our experimental results show competitive retrieval performance across both English and multilingual benchmarks. We also present controlled experiments demonstrating the benefits, or lack thereof, of the training modifications we consider in developing our training recipe.

## 2 Related Work

In this section, we discuss related work in single- and multi-vector retrieval, as well as the non-English late-interaction retrievers from which our training recipe draws inspiration.

### 2.1 Single-Vector Retrieval

Single-vector encoder models have demonstrated their potential as general-purpose embedding models across a number of downstream tasks (Muennighoff et al., 2023). When used in a bi-encoder retrieval model, they asymmetrically encode queries and documents as separate dense vectors, and measure their pairwise relevance as the cosine similarity between the vectors. Owing to their strong in-domain performance and straightforward inference scheme, there has been a growing focus on improving their training. Studies demonstrate that large-scale unsupervised pair training utilizing in-batch negatives, followed by a small-scale triplet finetuning stage, significantly improves performance compared to a dense retriever trained solely on triplet data (Li et al., 2023; Günther et al., 2023). Other works have incorporated asymmetric task-specific instructions for queries and documents to further enhance performance (Wang et al., 2024) and demonstrated the efficacy of using synthetically generated training data, including using diverse task instructions and machine translations, to further improve model representations. (Wang et al., 2023; Lee et al., 2024)

### 2.2 Multi-Vector Retrieval

Multi-vector retrievers like ColBERT also employ a bi-encoder structure, but queries and passages are represented by a collection of smaller token embeddings rather than one large vector. As such, ColBERTv2's training uses many of the same techniques as state-of-the-art single-vector models: cross-encoder distillation, multiple negatives per query, and self-mined hard negatives. Recent models have continued to improve on this training recipe, particularly for multilingual or non-English training. BGE-M3 (Chen et al., 2024) adopts the two-stage pairs-to-triplets training pipeline, and does self-knowledge distillation, treating the combination of its sparse, dense, and multi-vector scores as the teacher score.

### 2.3 Multilingual Retrieval

Owing to the quality of English-based pre-trained models (BERT) and annotated data (MSMARCO), many advances in neural retrieval have been applied first to the monolingual English setting (Karpukhin et al., 2020; Xiong et al., 2020; Khattab and Zaharia, 2020). Researchers, however, have also made advances in non-English capabilities.

On the modeling front, multilingual PLMs like mBERT (Devlin et al., 2019) and later XLM-RoBERTa (Conneau et al., 2020) have expanded pre-training to include text in up to 100 languages, including in cross-language contexts. For multilingual retrieval data, there are two approaches: natural and translated. Datasets like Mr-Tydi and MIRACL (Zhang et al., 2021, 2023b) are built from human-generated and annotated queries, whereas mMARCO (Bonifacio et al., 2022) is a collection of machine-translated copies of MSMARCO which inherit their judgments from the original dataset. The former method tends to be of higher quality and lacks the subtle distributional/idiomatic errors, dubbed "translationese", that the latter sometimes exhibits. Naturally, however, human generation costs more per example.

Recent multi-vector work has also proposed further modifications along the dimensions of architecture and data. ColBERT-XM (Louis et al., 2024) addresses the so-called *curse of multilinguality* (Conneau et al., 2020), the performance degradation of models pre-trained on too many tasks, with shared- and per-language parameters that allow for more robust zero-shot language transfer and post-hoc language extension. On the data approach, ColBERT-X (Nair et al., 2022; Lawrie et al., 2023; Yang et al., 2024) uses language-mixed batches of machine-translated English data, and BGE-M3 (Chen et al., 2024) curates unsupervised and high-quality supervised corpora of diverse multilingual training data.

## 3 Training Overview

`Jina-ColBERT-v2`'s training paradigm has three parts:

1. **Modified Encoder Architecture**: We use a modified encoder backbone, derived from XLM-RoBERTa with improvements made to its architecture and pre-training regime. We further

extend ColBERT's linear projection head by jointly training a collection of different-size heads for embedding size reduction.

2. **Pair Training**: To learn from the semantic structure of large quantities of diverse data in many languages, we first train our encoder model on weakly supervised text pairs from a variety of embedding datasets.
3. **Triplet Training**: Our model is further finetuned using retrieval examples in many languages with both positives and hard negatives, supervised by a highly-capable multilingual cross-encoder.

The following sections describe our experiments on these three components of training `Jina-ColBERT-v2`.

## 4 Architecture

### 4.1 Backbone Improvements

Following many prior single- and multi-vector multilingual training efforts, we adopted XLM-RoBERTa as our backbone model due to its strong performance across various downstream tasks (Nair et al., 2022; Louis et al., 2024; Chen et al., 2024). To improve the efficiency, we enhance the XLM-RoBERTa architecture with flash attention (Dao, 2024).

We replace the absolute positional embeddings with rotary positional embeddings (RoPE, Su et al. (2023)), which are empirically understood to be better. They also have the advantage of supporting context lengths far longer than 512 tokens, although we do not explicitly focus on long-context in this work. To warm up its new positional embeddings, we continued pre-training the modified backbone with the same masked language modeling objective for 160,000 steps on the RefinedWeb dataset (Penedo et al., 2023), a modern, high-quality corpus, under the masked language modeling objective. During this pre-training phase, we set the maximum sequence length to 8,192 tokens with a rotary base of 10,000 and employed whole-word-masking (Devlin et al., 2019), masking out 30% of the tokens. We call this modified language model Jina-XLM-RoBERTa.

### 4.2 Multiple Linear Heads

To reduce index sizes, ColBERT includes a linear head that projects its token embeddings from the hidden dimension of its language model down to a lower dimension ($768 \rightarrow 128$). As a notable exception, BGE-M3's multi-vector retrieval does not take this step, keeping its token embeddings at a full 1024 dimensions.

We jointly train six linear heads with dimensions $d \in \{64, 96, 128, 256, 512, 768\}$ using Matryoshka Representation Loss (MRL, Kusupati et al. (2022)). This allows users to choose greater or lesser space efficiency, with an associated performance trade-off. Figure 1 quantifies this tradeoff, showing the strong performance preservation of our reduced-dimension linear heads. Halving the token dimension ($128 \rightarrow 64$) only causes its nDCG@10 to drop by 0.01 (1.59%). We unfortunately find that MRL's weight-tying efficient variant (MRL-E), where losses are computed on *truncations* of the same token vector does not preserve performance well, which we hypothesize is a consequence of the already-low projected dimension of the original ColBERT formulation.

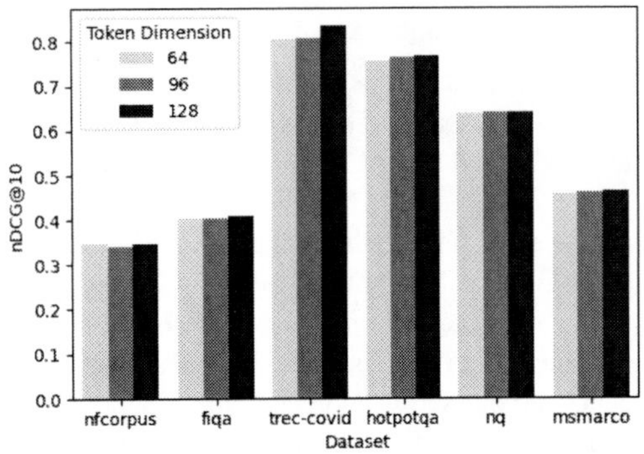


Figure 1: nDCG@10 scores for BEIR datasets using 64-, 96-, and 128-dimension linear projection heads for token embeddings.

## 5 Pair Training

To leverage an abundance of text pairs with varying richness of semantic structure, we draw inspiration from common practices in single-vector embedding model training and begin with training on these text pairs, focusing on optimizing the embedding model's performance on general semantic similarity and relatedness tasks. This weakly-supervised stage is in contrast to previous ColBERT works, which typically start directly from a PLM like BERT with triplet training on 32-way or 64-way retrieval triplets consisting of a query, a positive passage, and multiple mined negatives.

### 5.1 Data Composition

Our pair training data consists of a broad range of weakly supervised datasets harvested from the web. We adjusted sampling rates across different languages and domains based on intuition, resulting in a set of 450 million weakly supervised, semantically related sentence pairs, question-answer pairs, and query-document pairs. Of these 450 million pairs, 50.0% are in English. Our non-English pair-wise datasets contain a diverse collection of 29 major languages, including 3.0% code data, with 4.3% representing cross-lingual data.

### 5.2 Contrastive Loss

We utilize the same *single-vector* pair-training loss function as described in (Günther et al., 2023). Due to the often symmetric nature of our text pairs, the loss is calculated in both directions. During the pair training stage, we set the temperature $\tau = 0.02$ and used a peak learning rate of $5 \times 10^{-5}$ with a warm-up period of 1,000 steps. The model was trained using the Adam optimizer for 100,000 steps with a global batch size of 16,384.

## 6 Triplet Training

### 6.1 Data Composition

Our triplet dataset consists of 1) high-quality, human-annotated research datasets such as MSMARCO, DuReader, and MIRACL (Bajaj et al., 2016; He et al., 2018; Zhang et al., 2023b) with diversely mined negatives 2) high-quality datasets like MSMARCO and NQ translated from English into Chinese, French, German, Japanese, Russian and Spanish, following our previous work (Mohr et al., 2024) and 3) synthetically generated datasets to address common failure modes of dense vector models such as negation and to cover niche domains like legal IR.

The triplet dataset covers 14 widely used languages, with a strong emphasis on Arabic, Chinese, English, French, German, Japanese, Russian, and Spanish. We sample the datasets to create a language distribution similar to that used in pair training. English accounts for 45.9% of the triplets, with 52.1% roughly evenly split between the mentioned high-resource non-English languages and a small 2.0% share for lower-resource languages.

Notably, owing to the limitations of our various sources of data, we train on triplets with only 7 negatives per example, in contrast to the 32- or 64-way triplets of ColBERTv2.

### 6.2 Supervision Loss

Following ColBERTv2, we finetune our pair-trained checkpoint on samples with hard negatives using a KL divergence loss function to distill soft labels from the teacher model. For the teacher model, we use `jina-reranker-v2-base-multilingual`[1], a highly capable multilingual cross encoder.

This stage trains for 100,000 steps with a batch size of 32 and a cosine decay learning rate schedule with 5% warm-up that peaks at $1 \times 10^{-5}$. We use pure BFLOAT-16 precision, and apply magnitude-based gradient clipping with a threshold of 1 for stability.

## 7 Results

We evaluate `Jina-ColBERT-v2` on four widely used benchmarks, BEIR, LoTTE, and MIRACL and mMARCO. For general English performance, we use the same subset of 14 retrieval and text-similarity tasks from the BEIR benchmark as in Santhanam et al. (2022). Additionally, we assess performance on the LoTTE benchmark, which focuses on long-tail queries, and the MIRACL and mMARCO benchmarks (Zhang et al., 2023b; Bonifacio et al., 2022), which assess non-English retrieval performance. We report nDCG@10 for the BEIR and MIRACL collections, MRR@10 for mMARCO, and Success@5 for LoTTE. Scores are reported on the test split for BEIR, development split for MIRACL and mMARCO, and search test split for LoTTE. We use the same maximum query/document lengths as reported in Santhanam et al. (2022), and use the default (32/300) for MIRACL and mMARCO.

Table 1 shows `Jina-ColBERT-v2`'s strong English performance compared to ColBERTv2, while still trailing the monolingual answerai-colbert-small-v1. Notably, however, we perform well below ColBERTv2 on ArguAna (**ar**), which we might attribute to either its unusual task: *counterargument retrieval* being at odds with our retrieval-heavy triplet training data distribution, or as an indication of the limitation of our stronger augmentation attention (discussed in Section 8.4) when applied to much longer (300 token) queries. Similarly for LoTTE, we see in Table 2 an improvement over ColBERTv2.

Table 3 compares `Jina-ColBERT-v2` to BM25, mDPR, and BGE-M3. While we handily outperform BM25 and zero-shot mDPR (Zhang et al., 2023b) as expected, our model is slightly outperformed by the finetuned mDPR (Zhang et al., 2023a). For context, each mDPR-FT is only tuned on one language, rather than many like ours which may suffer to some extent from the *curse of multilinguality*.

Finally, comparing against ColBERT-XM's zero-shot evaluation on mMARCO in Table 4, we see a strong improvement across the board, including on languages whose mMARCO training set does not occur in our pair or triplet training data (dt, hi, id, it, pt, vi).

## 8 Ablation Studies

In this section we present short ablation studies on modifications to three various aspects of ColBERT modeling and training.

### 8.1 Efficient Evaluation

Due to the compute and time costs of indexing corpora containing tens of millions of documents, evaluating every model checkpoint and ablation on every task is not feasible. Therefore, we follow recent works (Clavié, 2024; Merrick et al., 2024) by comparing models' quality on smaller sampled-corpus versions of HotpotQA, NQ, MS MARCO, and MIRACL (Chinese, French, German, Japanese, Spanish). These sampled corpora are constructed by combining the

[1] `https://huggingface.co/jinaai/jina-reranker-v2-base-multilingual`

| BEIR | avg | nf | fi | tc | ar | qu | sd | sf | to | db | fe | cf | hp | nq |
|---|---|---|---|---|---|---|---|---|---|---|---|---|---|---|
| BM25 | 44.0 | 32.5 | 23.6 | 65.6 | 31.5 | 78.9 | 15.8 | 66.5 | **36.7** | 31.3 | 75.3 | 21.3 | 60.3 | 32.9 |
| ColBERTv2 | 49.6 | 33.7 | 35.4 | 72.6 | 46.5 | 85.5 | 15.4 | 68.9 | 26.0 | 45.2 | 78.5 | 17.6 | 67.5 | 52.4 |
| answerai-v1 | **55.7** | **37.3** | **41.2** | **84.6** | **50.1** | 87.7 | 18.4 | **74.8** | 25.7 | 45.6 | **91.0** | **33.1** | 76.1 | 59.1 |
| Ours | 53.1 | 34.6 | 40.8 | 83.4 | 36.6 | **88.7** | **18.6** | 67.8 | 27.4 | **47.1** | 80.5 | 23.9 | **76.6** | **64.0** |

Table 1: Comparison of nDCG@10 scores between BM25, ColBERTv2, answer-colbert-small and Jina-ColBERT-v1 and `Jina-ColBERT-v2` on the BEIR test set. **nf** for NFCorpus, **fi** for FIQA (Fact In Question Answering), **tc** for TREC-COVID (Text Retrieval Conference COVID), **ar** for Arguana, **qu** for Quora, **sd** for SciDocs, **sf** for SciFact, **to** for Webis-Touche, **db** for DBpedia-Entity, **fe** for FEVER (Fact Extraction and Verification), **cf** for Climate-FEVER, **hp** for HotpotQA, and **nq** for Natural Questions

| LoTTE | avg | Life. | Rec. | Wri. | Sci. | Tech. |
|---|---|---|---|---|---|---|
| BM25 | 67.8 | 80.2 | 68.5 | 74.7 | 53.6 | 61.9 |
| ColBERTv2 | 72.0 | 84.7 | 72.3 | 80.1 | 56.7 | 66.1 |
| Ours | **76.4** | **87.0** | **77.6** | **83.8** | **60.5** | **73.0** |

Table 2: Comparison of Success@5 of various models across different LoTTE search query subsets.

top 250 BM25-retrieved[2] passages with all judged passages. We observe good agreement between the sampled-corpus evaluation scores and the full-fidelity ones when used to make binary or ranking-based model comparisons, but we leave a more rigorous analysis of this observation to future work. We only use the sampled corpora for ablation studies. For the final model, we evaluate on the full version of every dataset.

### 8.2 Task Instructions

Inspired by the use of instruction prefixes in single-vector works like Su et al. (2022), we experimented with adding task-specific natural language instructions for retrieval (RET), and question answering (QA), and semantic text similarity (STS). However, results in Table 5 show a generally negative effect across most BEIR datasets. We hypothesize that this is because instructions are not well-suited for late interaction models, which operate at the token level. Any embedding conditioning that the instructions might provide likely becomes less effective when aggregated at the token similarity level. Furthermore, these instructions occupy valuable space within the system's fixed token capacity.

### 8.3 Score Normalization

Recently, Clavié (2024) applied min-max normalization to both the student and teacher scores before computing the KL loss. This adjustment brings the score distributions of the ColBERT model and its CE teacher into closer alignment, as the original score distribution for ColBERT theoretically ranges from zero to the number of query tokens, and is model-dependent for the teacher CE. Our experiment presented in Table 6, however, shows this method to have inconclusive benefit to nDCG@10 on the BEIR and MIRACL datasets when applied to our model. We consider this result to be understandable given Clavié (2024)'s very small observed effect.

### 8.4 Query Augmentation Attention

An important feature of ColBERT's implementation is its query augmentation mechanism. By padding queries with `[MASK]` tokens to a uniform length, ColBERT uses BERT's masked language modeling ability to produce additional soft term embeddings which interact with document token embeddings during MaxSim scoring. However, prior ColBERT models do not modify the attention mask to allow query tokens to attend to the mask tokens, which some hypothesize might harm generalization by making this augmentation feature too integral to the embedding process. Our controlled triplet training experiment in Table 7, however, demonstrates a positive effect across a variety of tasks, with particular benefit to non-English tasks in MIRACL. We therefore allow this attention in our training and inference.

## 9 Conclusion

This work presents `Jina-ColBERT-v2`, a capable multilingual ColBERT model that is the result of improvements to its architecture and training process. We implement modifications to the model architecture that yield efficiency gains with effectively no downside, and subsequently train it on a heterogeneous mix of data of varying tasks, languages, and supervision structures in order to bolster its performance as a general purpose retriever. Our ablation experiments demonstrate the sensitivity of ColBERT to modifications to its representations.

We hope that our work will support future multilingual ColBERT development, and prompt further exploration into the properties and optimal configuration of its query augmentation mechanism. We are also encouraged by the many inference-only optimization works on ColBERT representations, and

[2] We use the standard pre-built Lucene indices in Pyserini (Lin et al., 2021) for MIRACL found at `https://github.com/castorini/pyserini`, and use BM25s (Lù, 2024) for BEIR.

| MIRACL | avg | ar | bn | de | es | en | fa | fi | fr | hi | id | ja | ko | ru | sw | te | th | yo | zh |
|---|---|---|---|---|---|---|---|---|---|---|---|---|---|---|---|---|---|---|---|
| BM25 | 38.5 | 48.1 | 50.8 | 22.6 | 31.9 | 35.1 | 33.3 | 55.1 | 18.3 | 45.8 | 44.9 | 36.9 | 41.9 | 33.4 | 38.3 | 49.4 | 48.4 | 40.6 | 18.0 |
| mDPR-ZS | 41.8 | 49.9 | 44.3 | 49.0 | 47.8 | 39.4 | 48.0 | 47.2 | 43.5 | 38.3 | 27.2 | 43.9 | 41.9 | 40.7 | 29.9 | 35.6 | 35.8 | 39.6 | 51.2 |
| mDPR-FT | **62.7** | 72.5 | 68.4 | - | 48.8 | 56.5 | **59.3** | 71.4 | **58.9** | 51.6 | 49.6 | **64.2** | 59.0 | 59.7 | **68.5** | **80.4** | 69.5 | - | **65.0** |
| Ours | 62.3 | **75.3** | **75.0** | **50.4** | **53.8** | **57.0** | 56.3 | **74.0** | 54.1 | **60.0** | **54.7** | 63.2 | **67.1** | **64.3** | 49.9 | 74.2 | **77.2** | **62.3** | 52.3 |

Table 3: Comparison of nDCG@10 scores for BM25, mDPR-ZeroShot (ZS), mDPR-FineTuned (FT), and `Jina-ColBERT-v2` models on the MIRACL dev set across various languages.

| mMARCO | avg | ar | de | nl | es | fr | hi | id | it | ja | pt | ru | vi | zh |
|---|---|---|---|---|---|---|---|---|---|---|---|---|---|---|
| BM-25 | 13.9 | 11.1 | 13.6 | 14.0 | 15.8 | 15.5 | 13.4 | 14.9 | 15.3 | 14.1 | 15.2 | 12.4 | 13.6 | 11.6 |
| ColBERT-XM | 25.4 | 19.5 | 27.0 | 27.5 | 28.5 | 26.9 | 23.8 | 26.3 | 26.5 | 24.1 | 27.6 | 25.1 | 22.6 | 24.6 |
| Ours | **31.3** | **27.2** | **33.1** | **33.0** | **34.1** | **33.5** | **30.9** | **31.9** | **33.7** | **27.6** | **33.7** | **29.8** | **28.7** | **30.2** |

Table 4: Comparison of mRR@10 scores between BM25, ColBERT-XM and `Jina-ColBERT-v2` models on the mMARCO dev set across various languages.

| | RET | | | | | | | | QA | | | STS | | |
|---|---|---|---|---|---|---|---|---|---|---|---|---|---|---|
| | nf | tc | sf | to | db | fe | cf | ms* | fq | hp* | nq* | ar | qu | sd |
| Mark. | 32.4 | 59.3 | **67.9** | **19.3** | **35.3** | **67.1** | **18.3** | **34.4** | **37.5** | **25.9** | 40.8 | **37.5** | **86.1** | **18.4** |
| Inst. | **32.9** | **63.2** | 67.5 | 18.8 | 33.9 | 64.4 | 16.7 | 34.0 | 37.1 | 24.9 | **42.9** | 34.2 | 86.0 | 17.9 |

Table 5: nDCG@10 scores on BEIR datasets, grouped by task type (retrieval, question answering, and semantic text similarity) when using natural language instructions versus query/document marker tokens (default). Datasets marked with a * use the BM25-sampled corpus technique discussed in Section 8.1.

| | BEIR | | | | MIRACL | | | | |
|---|---|---|---|---|---|---|---|---|---|
| | tc | hp | nq | ms | de | es | fr | ja | zh |
| Baseline | 78.7 | **36.6** | **58.0** | **45.4** | 57.3 | **40.6** | 50.7 | **63.4** | **63.2** |
| + Score Norm. | **80.1** | 36.4 | 56.6 | 45.1 | **57.7** | 39.3 | **51.3** | 61.8 | 62.5 |

Table 6: nDCG@10 scores with and without score normalization on a retrieval-oriented subset of BEIR and MIRACL tasks. Results are performed on the BM25-sampled versions of all datasets presented except TREC-COVID (**tc**).

| | BEIR | | | | MIRACL | | | | |
|---|---|---|---|---|---|---|---|---|---|
| | tc | hp | nq | ms | de | es | fr | ja | zh |
| Baseline | 77.2 | 70.4 | 54.6 | 37.6 | 33.3 | 40.3 | 35.9 | 54.9 | 34.4 |
| + `[MASK]` attn. | **80.2** | **71.5** | **58.8** | **44.3** | **45.6** | **49.8** | **44.8** | **58.8** | **52.9** |

Table 7: nDCG@10 scores with and without query augmentation `[MASK]` token attention on a retrieval-oriented subset of BEIR and MIRACL tasks. Results report full-fidelity scores.

suggest further effort be invested in tying these methods more closely with the models training objective.

## 10 Acknowledgement

We thank Qi Liu and Jiaxin Mao from Renmin University of China for the contributions to `Jina-ColBERT-v1` and offer the insights about MRL over MRL-E for ColBERT models.

## References

Payal Bajaj, Daniel Campos, Nick Craswell, Li Deng, Jianfeng Gao, Xiaodong Liu, Rangan Majumder, Andrew McNamara, Bhaskar Mitra, Tri Nguyen, Mir Rosenberg, Xia Song, Alina Stoica, Saurabh Tiwary, and Tong Wang. 2016. Ms marco: A human generated machine reading comprehension dataset.

Luiz Bonifacio, Vitor Jeronymo, Hugo Queiroz Abonizio, Israel Campiotti, Marzieh Fadaee, Roberto Lotufo, and Rodrigo Nogueira. 2022. mMARCO: A Multilingual Version of the MS MARCO Passage Ranking Dataset. ArXiv:2108.13897 [cs].

Jianlv Chen, Shitao Xiao, Peitian Zhang, Kun Luo, Defu

Lian, and Zheng Liu. 2024. BGE M3-Embedding: Multi-Lingual, Multi-Functionality, Multi-Granularity Text Embeddings Through Self-Knowledge Distillation. ArXiv:2402.03216 [cs].

Kevin Clark, Minh-Thang Luong, Quoc V. Le, and Christopher D. Manning. 2020. ELECTRA: Pre-training Text Encoders as Discriminators Rather Than Generators. ArXiv:2003.10555 [cs].

Benjamin Clavié. 2024. JaColBERTv2.5: Optimising Multi-Vector Retrievers to Create State-of-the-Art Japanese Retrievers with Constrained Resources. ArXiv:2407.20750 [cs].

Alexis Conneau, Kartikay Khandelwal, Naman Goyal, Vishrav Chaudhary, Guillaume Wenzek, Francisco Guzmán, Edouard Grave, Myle Ott, Luke Zettlemoyer, and Veselin Stoyanov. 2020. Unsupervised Cross-lingual Representation Learning at Scale. ArXiv:1911.02116 [cs].

Tri Dao. 2024. FlashAttention-2: Faster attention with better parallelism and work partitioning. In *International Conference on Learning Representations (ICLR)*.

Jacob Devlin, Ming-Wei Chang, Kenton Lee, and Kristina Toutanova. 2019. BERT: Pre-training of Deep Bidirectional Transformers for Language Understanding. ArXiv:1810.04805 [cs].

Thibault Formal, Benjamin Piwowarski, and Stéphane Clinchant. 2021. SPLADE: Sparse Lexical and Expansion Model for First Stage Ranking. ArXiv:2107.05720 [cs].

Michael Günther, Jackmin Ong, Isabelle Mohr, Alaeddine Abdessalem, Tanguy Abel, Mohammad Kalim Akram, Susana Guzman, Georgios Mastrapas, Saba Sturua, Bo Wang, et al. 2023. Jina embeddings 2: 8192-token general-purpose text embeddings for long documents. *arXiv preprint arXiv:2310.19923*.

Wei He, Kai Liu, Jing Liu, Yajuan Lyu, Shiqi Zhao, Xinyan Xiao, Yuan Liu, Yizhong Wang, Hua Wu, Qiaoqiao She, Xuan Liu, Tian Wu, and Haifeng Wang. 2018. Dureader: a chinese machine reading comprehension dataset from real-world applications.

Vladimir Karpukhin, Barlas Oguz, Sewon Min, Patrick Lewis, Ledell Wu, Sergey Edunov, Danqi Chen, and Wen-tau Yih. 2020. Dense Passage Retrieval for Open-Domain Question Answering. In *Proceedings of the 2020 Conference on Empirical Methods in Natural Language Processing (EMNLP)*, pages 6769–6781, Online. Association for Computational Linguistics.

Omar Khattab and Matei Zaharia. 2020. ColBERT: Efficient and Effective Passage Search via Contextualized Late Interaction over BERT. ArXiv:2004.12832 [cs].

Aditya Kusupati, Gantavya Bhatt, Aniket Rege, Matthew Wallingford, Aditya Sinha, Vivek Ramanujan, William Howard-Snyder, Kaifeng Chen, Sham Kakade, Prateek Jain, and Ali Farhadi. 2022. Matryoshka representation learning. In *Advances in Neural Information Processing Systems*, volume 35, pages 30233–30249. Curran Associates, Inc.

Dawn Lawrie, Eugene Yang, Douglas W. Oard, and James Mayfield. 2023. Neural Approaches to Multilingual Information Retrieval. ArXiv:2209.01335 [cs].

Jinhyuk Lee, Zhuyun Dai, Xiaoqi Ren, Blair Chen, Daniel Cer, Jeremy R. Cole, Kai Hui, Michael Boratko, Rajvi Kapadia, Wen Ding, Yi Luan, Sai Meher Karthik Duddu, Gustavo Hernandez Abrego, Weiqiang Shi, Nithi Gupta, Aditya Kusupati, Prateek Jain, Siddhartha Reddy Jonnalagadda, Ming-Wei Chang, and Iftekhar Naim. 2024. Gecko: Versatile Text Embeddings Distilled from Large Language Models. ArXiv:2403.20327 [cs] version: 1.

Zehan Li, Xin Zhang, Yanzhao Zhang, Dingkun Long, Pengjun Xie, and Meishan Zhang. 2023. Towards general text embeddings with multi-stage contrastive learning.

Jimmy Lin, Xueguang Ma, Sheng-Chieh Lin, Jheng-Hong Yang, Ronak Pradeep, and Rodrigo Nogueira. 2021. Pyserini: A Python toolkit for reproducible information retrieval research with sparse and dense representations. In *Proceedings of the 44th Annual International ACM SIGIR Conference on Research and Development in Information Retrieval (SIGIR 2021)*, pages 2356–2362.

Yinhan Liu, Myle Ott, Naman Goyal, Jingfei Du, Mandar Joshi, Danqi Chen, Omer Levy, Mike Lewis, Luke Zettlemoyer, and Veselin Stoyanov. 2019. Roberta: A robustly optimized bert pretraining approach. *arXiv preprint arXiv:1907.11692*.

Antoine Louis, Vageesh Saxena, Gijs van Dijck, and Gerasimos Spanakis. 2024. ColBERT-XM: A Modular Multi-Vector Representation Model for Zero-Shot Multilingual Information Retrieval. ArXiv:2402.15059 [cs].

Xing Han Lù. 2024. Bm25s: Orders of magnitude faster lexical search via eager sparse scoring.

Luke Merrick, Danmei Xu, Gaurav Nuti, and Daniel Campos. 2024. Arctic-embed: Scalable, efficient, and accurate text embedding models.

Isabelle Mohr, Markus Krimmel, Saba Sturua, Mohammad Kalim Akram, Andreas Koukounas, Michael Günther, Georgios Mastrapas, Vinit Ravishankar, Joan Fontanals Martínez, Feng Wang, et al. 2024. Multi-task contrastive learning for 8192-token bilingual text embeddings. *arXiv preprint arXiv:2402.17016*.

Niklas Muennighoff, Nouamane Tazi, Loic Magne, and Nils Reimers. 2023. MTEB: Massive text embedding benchmark. In *Proceedings of the 17th Conference of the European Chapter of the Association for Computational Linguistics*, pages 2014–2037, Dubrovnik, Croatia. Association for Computational Linguistics.

Suraj Nair, Eugene Yang, Dawn Lawrie, Kevin Duh, Paul McNamee, Kenton Murray, James Mayfield, and Douglas W. Oard. 2022. Transfer learning approaches for building cross-language dense retrieval models. In *Proceedings of the 44th European Conference on Information Retrieval (ECIR)*.

Guilherme Penedo, Quentin Malartic, Daniel Hesslow, Ruxandra Cojocaru, Alessandro Cappelli, Hamza Alobeidli, Baptiste Pannier, Ebtesam Almazrouei, and Julien Launay. 2023. The refinedweb dataset for falcon llm: outperforming curated corpora with web data, and web data only. *arXiv preprint arXiv:2306.01116*.

Keshav Santhanam, Omar Khattab, Jon Saad-Falcon, Christopher Potts, and Matei Zaharia. 2022. ColBERTv2: Effective and Efficient Retrieval via Lightweight Late Interaction. ArXiv:2112.01488 [cs].

Hongjin Su, Weijia Shi, Jungo Kasai, Yizhong Wang, Yushi Hu, Mari Ostendorf, Wen-tau Yih, Noah A Smith, Luke Zettlemoyer, and Tao Yu. 2022. One embedder, any task: Instruction-finetuned text embeddings. *arXiv preprint arXiv:2212.09741*.

Jianlin Su, Yu Lu, Shengfeng Pan, Ahmed Murtadha, Bo Wen, and Yunfeng Liu. 2023. Roformer: Enhanced transformer with rotary position embedding.

Liang Wang, Nan Yang, Xiaolong Huang, Linjun Yang, Rangan Majumder, and Furu Wei. 2023. Improving text embeddings with large language models. *arXiv preprint arXiv:2401.00368*.

Liang Wang, Nan Yang, Xiaolong Huang, Linjun Yang, Rangan Majumder, and Furu Wei. 2024. Multilingual e5 text embeddings: A technical report. *arXiv preprint arXiv:2402.05672*.

Lee Xiong, Chenyan Xiong, Ye Li, Kwok-Fung Tang, Jialin Liu, Paul Bennett, Junaid Ahmed, and Arnold Overwijk. 2020. Approximate Nearest Neighbor Negative Contrastive Learning for Dense Text Retrieval. ArXiv:2007.00808 [cs].

Eugene Yang, Dawn Lawrie, and James Mayfield. 2024. Distillation for Multilingual Information Retrieval. In *Proceedings of the 47th International ACM SIGIR Conference on Research and Development in Information Retrieval*, pages 2368–2373. ArXiv:2405.00977 [cs].

Xinyu Zhang, Xueguang Ma, Peng Shi, and Jimmy Lin. 2021. Mr. TyDi: A multi-lingual benchmark for dense retrieval. *arXiv:2108.08787*.

Xinyu Zhang, Kelechi Ogueji, Xueguang Ma, and Jimmy Lin. 2023a. Toward best practices for training multilingual dense retrieval models. *ACM Trans. Inf. Syst.*, 42(2).

Xinyu Zhang, Nandan Thakur, Odunayo Ogundepo, Ehsan Kamalloo, David Alfonso-Hermelo, Xiaoguang Li, Qun Liu, Mehdi Rezagholizadeh, and Jimmy Lin. 2023b. Miracl: A multilingual retrieval dataset covering 18 diverse languages. *Transactions of the Association for Computational Linguistics*, 11:1114–1131.

# Cross-Lingual Named Entity Recognition for Low-Resource Languages: A Hindi-Nepali Case Study Using Multilingual BERT Models

**Dipendra Yadav[1], Sumaiya Suravee[1], Tobias Strauß[2], Kristina Yordanova[1]**
[1]University of Greifswald, Germany
[2]University of Rostock, Germany
{dipendra.yadav, sumaiya.suravee, kristina.yordanova}@uni-greifswald.de,
tobias.strauss@uni-rostock.de

## Abstract

This study investigates the potential of cross-lingual transfer learning for Named Entity Recognition (NER) between Hindi and Nepali, two languages that, despite their linguistic similarities, face significant disparities in available resources. By leveraging multilingual BERT models, including RemBERT, BERT Multilingual, MuRIL, and DistilBERT Multilingual, the research examines whether pre-training them on a resource-rich language like Hindi can enhance NER performance in a resource-constrained language like Nepali and vice versa. The study conducts experiments in both monolingual and cross-lingual settings to evaluate the models' effectiveness in transferring linguistic knowledge between the two languages. The findings reveal that while RemBERT and MuRIL perform well in monolingual contexts—RemBERT excelling in Hindi and MuRIL in Nepali—BERT Multilingual performs comparatively best in cross-lingual scenarios, in generalizing features across the languages. Although DistilBERT Multilingual demonstrates slightly lower performance in cross-lingual tasks, it balances efficiency with competitive results. The study underscores the importance of model selection based on linguistic and resource-specific contexts, highlighting that general-purpose models like BERT Multilingual are particularly well-suited for cross-lingual applications.

## 1 Introduction

Cross-lingual transfer learning has emerged as a crucial area in natural language processing (NLP), especially for languages with limited resources (Kim et al., 2017; Schuster et al., 2019). This approach leverages the strengths of resource-rich languages to enhance model performance in under-resourced languages, making it a valuable tool in the global effort to improve NLP applications across diverse linguistic contexts (Wang, 2021; Hettiarachchi et al., 2023; Jafari et al., 2021). In this context, Hindi and Nepali present an interesting case study due to their linguistic similarities coupled with significant disparities in NLP resources (Michailovsky, 2008; Murthy et al., 2022; Beaufils, 2015–2024).

Hindi, with over 600 million speakers, benefits from comparatively extensive datasets and well-developed NLP tools (Kamble and Shrivastava, 2023; Desai and Dabhi, 2021; Eberhard et al., 2024). In contrast, Nepali, spoken by around 30 million people, faces significant challenges due to the limited availability of resources and tools (Sharma et al., 2023; Eberhard et al., 2024). Given the shared linguistic heritage between Hindi and Nepali, cross-lingual transfer learning between these two languages could offer a promising avenue for improving NER performance in Nepali by leveraging pre-trained Hindi models and vice versa.

This research evaluates the effectiveness of pre-trained multilingual BERT models—RemBERT (Chung et al., 2021), BERT Multilingual (Devlin et al., 2019), MuRIL (Khanuja et al., 2021), and DistilBERT Multilingual (Sanh et al., 2019)—for cross-lingual transfer learning in NER tasks between Hindi and Nepali. By fine-tuning these models on individual language datasets and evaluating their performance in monolingual and cross-lingual settings, this research provides insights into the feasibility and potential of transfer learning in low-resource language contexts. Furthermore, the study compares the models' performance in NER tasks for Hindi and Nepali without cross-lingual transfer learning.

## 2 Related Work

Named Entity Recognition is a foundational task in NLP, focusing on identifying and classifying named entities within text (Jurafsky and Martin, 2008). NER methodologies have evolved from traditional rule-based approaches to more sophis-



*Proceedings of the Fourth Workshop on Multilingual Representation Learning (MRL 2024)*, pages 167–174
November 16, 2024 ©2024 Association for Computational Linguistics

ticated machine learning techniques and, recently, to Large Language Models (LLMs) (Li et al., 2022; Hu et al., 2024). Among these, models like BERT have significantly advanced the state of the art in NER by leveraging contextual embeddings and transformer-based architectures (Taillé et al., 2020).

In the context of Hindi NER, research has spanned both traditional and LLM-based methods, with resources like HiNER contributing to notable advancements (Murthy et al., 2022; Deshmukh et al., 2024). Although Nepali NER has been less extensively studied, recent efforts have focused on applying LLMs to address the language's low-resource status, with specialized datasets and algorithms playing a critical role in these developments (Timilsina et al., 2022; Subedi et al., 2024; Singh et al., 2019).

Cross-lingual transfer learning has shown significant promise in enhancing NER performance, particularly for low-resource languages (Wang, 2021). Multilingual BERT models, such as mBERT (Devlin et al., 2019) and XLM-Roberta (Conneau et al., 2020), have demonstrated success across various NLP tasks by enabling the transfer of semantic properties across languages (Conneau et al., 2020). To the best of our knowledge, this study is the first to investigate cross-lingual transfer learning between Hindi and Nepali, leveraging their linguistic similarities—a relationship that has not been explored in previous research.

## 3 Methodology

This section is structured into three primary subsections, each providing a comprehensive understanding of the research approach. First, an overview of the linguistic characteristics of Hindi and Nepali is provided, emphasizing the similarities and distinctions between the two languages. Second, the datasets utilized in this study are discussed, detailing their sources, statistical attributes, and the preprocessing techniques employed to ensure consistency across languages. Lastly, the experimental setup is described, focusing on fine-tuning pre-trained multilingual BERT models for the monolingual and cross-lingual NER task.

### 3.1 Hindi and Nepali Languages

Hindi and Nepali, both members of the Indo-Aryan language family, share a common linguistic heritage and the Devanagari script, as illustrated in Figures 2 and 3 (Kopparapu and Lajish, 2014; Iancu, 2024; Eberhard et al., 2024). Hindi is predominantly spoken in northern India, while Nepali serves as the official language of Nepal and is also spoken in regions of Bhutan and India (Eberhard et al., 2024). According to a statistical context analysis, the genetic proximity between Hindi and Nepali is 19.9, where a value of 0 represents the closest relationship between languages and 100 the most dissimilar (Beaufils and Tomin, 2020; Beaufils, 2015–2024). The linguistic proximity between these languages, also illustrated by examples in Figure 1, underscores their suitability for cross-lingual transfer learning.

### 3.2 Datasets

The datasets used in this study include the collapsed version of the Hindi NER dataset from the HiNER project (Murthy et al., 2022), and the stemmed version-2 Nepali NER dataset curated by Singh et al. (Singh et al., 2019). Both datasets are formatted according to the CoNLL-2003 standard, categorizing entities into PERSON, LOCATION, and ORGANIZATION, with additional information on Beginning (B), Inside (I), and Outside (O) of named entities (Tjong Kim Sang and De Meulder, 2003). Examples of NER-tagged data from both datasets are provided in Figure 4.

Tables 2 and 3 provide detailed statistics for the datasets used in the Nepali and Hindi NER tasks, respectively. The Hindi dataset contains a total of 108,335 sentences, while the Nepali dataset consists of 6,602 sentences. The Nepali dataset is sentence-wise more than 16 times smaller than its Hindi counterpart, reflecting the disparity in resource availability between the two languages. This imbalance is a critical factor in evaluating the effectiveness of cross-lingual transfer learning. To maintain consistency, the NER tags in the Nepali dataset were aligned with those in the Hindi, as outlined in Table 1.

### 3.3 Models

This study leverages multilingual BERT models pre-trained in both Hindi and Nepali, making them particularly suitable for cross-lingual transfer learning in NER tasks.

**BERT Multilingual base model (cased)** is a transformer model trained on unlabeled Wikipedia [1] data in 104 languages, retaining letter casing,

[1] https://www.wikipedia.org/

**English**: What is your name?
**Hindi**: तुम्हारा नाम क्या है?
**Nepali**: तिम्रो नाम के हो?

**English**: This is my house.
**Hindi**: यह मेरा घर है।
**Nepali**: यो मेरो घर हो।

**English:** The weather has been unpredictable lately, with sudden rains and thunderstorms occurring almost daily.
**Hindi:** हाल ही में मौसम अनिश्चित रहा है, लगभग हर दिन अचानक बारिश और आंधी-तूफान हो रहे हैं।
**Nepali:** हालसालै मौसम अनिश्चित भएको छ, हरेक दिनजसो अचानक वर्षा र आँधीबेहरी भइरहेको छ।

Figure 1: Examples of the same sentences in English, Hindi, and Nepali illustrating the linguistic parallels between Hindi and Nepali, highlighting their shared script and related vocabulary.

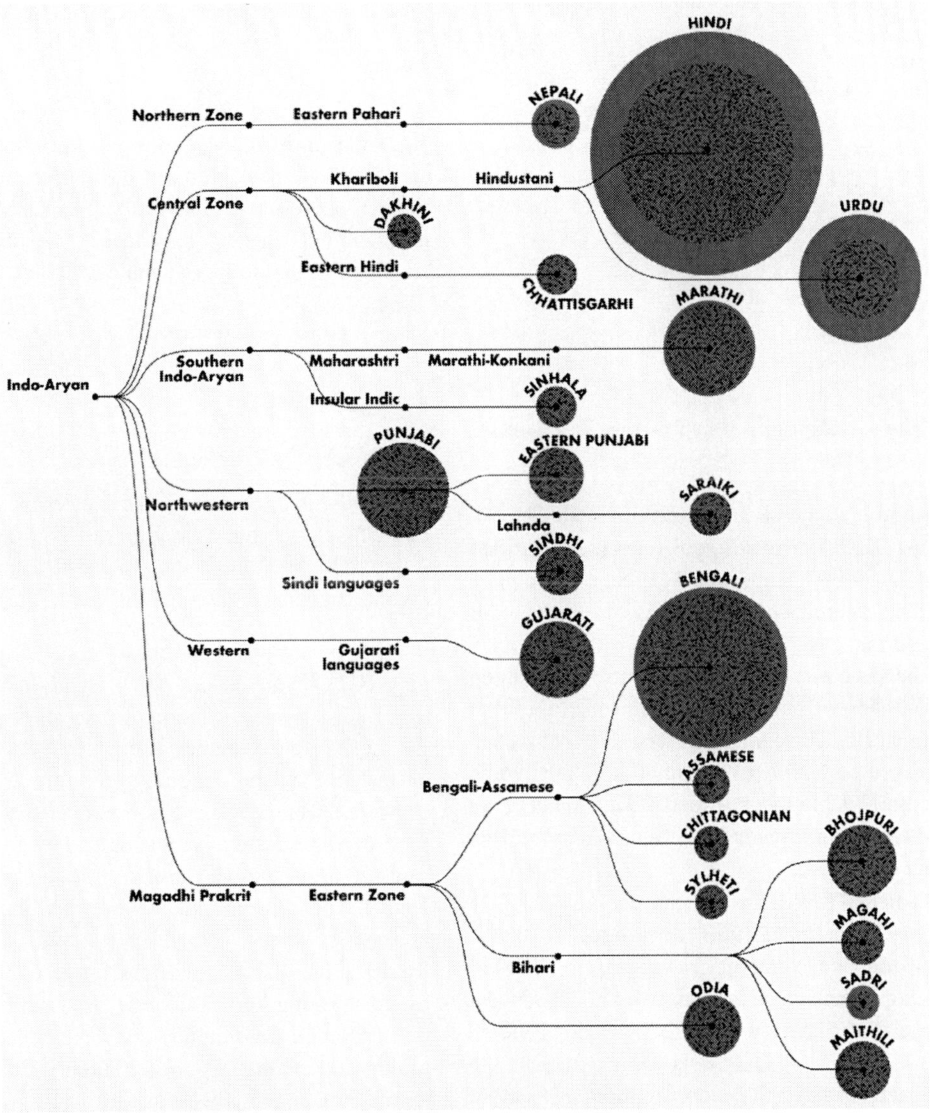


Figure 2: Indo-Aryan language tree, illustrating the close linguistic ties between Hindi and Nepali as members of the same family with shared heritage (Iancu, 2024).

which is crucial for languages where case influences meaning. It follows the original BERT architecture, with 12 transformer layers, 768 hidden units, and 12 attention heads, making it effective

Figure 3: Devanagari script, the shared writing system of Nepali and Hindi (Kopparapu and Lajish, 2014).

| **Hindi** | | **Nepali** | |
|---|---|---|---|
| रामनगर | B-LOCATION | डा | O |
| इगलास | B-LOCATION | कृष्ण | B-PERSON |
| , | O | अर्याल | I-PERSON |
| अलीगढ़ | B-LOCATION | नर्वे | B-LOCATION |
| , | O | शतप्रतिशत | O |
| उत्तर | B-LOCATION | सहमति | O |
| प्रदेश | I-LOCATION | छ | O |
| स्थित | O | मेरो | O |
| एक | O | । | O |
| गाँव | O | | |
| है। | O | | |

Figure 4: NER-tagged examples from the datasets.

for multilingual NLP tasks. (Devlin et al., 2019)

**DistilBERT Multilingual (cased)**, a distilled version of BERT Multilingual Cased, offers a more efficient alternative by reducing the number of transformer layers from 12 to 6 while maintaining the same number of hidden units and attention heads. Despite being 25% smaller than the Multilingual BERT model, it achieves 92% of its performance on XNLI (Conneau et al., 2018) while processing at double the speed. This makes it an ideal choice for resource-constrained environments. (Sanh et al., 2019)

**RemBERT** (Rebalanced multilingual BERT) is a transformer model trained on large unlabeled Wikipedia and Common Crawl [2] data in over 110 languages, including Hindi and Nepali. The model comprises 32 layers with 1152 dimensions and 18 attention heads per layer. It is optimized for multilingual tasks through decoupled input and output embeddings, offering robust performance across languages. (Chung et al., 2021)

**MuRIL** (Multilingual Representations for Indian Languages) is a transformer-based model trained on the Common Crawl OSCAR corpus [3], Wikipedia, and PMIndia (Haddow and Kirefu, 2020) data in 17 Indian languages, including Hindi and Nepali. It incorporates transliterated text during training, essential for handling code-switching prevalent in Indian contexts, making it particularly suitable for this study. (Khanuja et al., 2021)

[2] https://commoncrawl.org/

| Original Tag | Mapped Tag |
|---|---|
| B-LOC | B-LOCATION |
| B-ORG | B-ORGANIZATION |
| B-PER | B-PERSON |
| I-LOC | I-LOCATION |
| I-ORG | I-ORGANIZATION |
| I-PER | I-PERSON |
| O | O |

Table 1: Alignment of Nepali NER tags to Hindi.

## 4 Experiments

This study first pre-trains and evaluates the models on a single language dataset for the NER task. It is followed by fine-tuning and evaluating them on the second language dataset, as shown in Figure 5.

Initially, a multilingual base model from Hugging Face (Wolf et al., 2020) is pre-trained on the Hindi language training dataset for NER, and the model's performance is evaluated on the test dataset in the same language using the F1 score (Powers, 2011) as the evaluation metric, which is the harmonic mean of precision and recall scores. The pre-trained model is then fine-tuned on the Nepali language training dataset, and its performance is evaluated on the Nepali test dataset using the F1 score. The same experiment is repeated by pre-training and evaluating base models first on the Nepali training and test dataset, then fine-tuning and evaluating on the Hindi training and test dataset, and finally evaluating on the Hindi test dataset for cross-lingual NER.

These experiments are conducted for all four mentioned BERT-based models. The hyperparameters used in the experiments are detailed in Table 4. The source code and implementation of the mentioned experiments are available on GitHub[4].

| Entity | Train | Test | Validation |
|---|---|---|---|
| B-LOCATION | 3275 (70.41%) | 916 (19.69%) | 460 (9.89%) |
| B-ORGANIZATION | 4103 (70.15%) | 1177 (20.12%) | 569 (9.73%) |
| B-PERSON | 5252 (70.02%) | 1518 (20.24%) | 731 (9.75%) |
| I-LOCATION | 371 (72.46%) | 86 (16.8%) | 55 (10.74%) |
| I-ORGANIZATION | 3994 (70.45%) | 1142 (20.14%) | 533 (9.4%) |
| I-PERSON | 4292 (69.56%) | 1255 (20.34%) | 623 (10.1%) |
| O | 112541 (70.17%) | 32100 (20.01%) | 15747 (9.82%) |

Table 2: Number of samples and percentage distribution of entities of the whole Nepali dataset.

| Entity | Train | Test | Validation |
|---|---|---|---|
| B-LOCATION | 137633 (69.59%) | 40072 (20.26%) | 20062 (10.14%) |
| B-ORGANIZATION | 18504 (69.83%) | 5351 (20.19%) | 2644 (9.98%) |
| B-PERSON | 26242 (69.97%) | 7495 (19.99%) | 3765 (10.04%) |
| I-LOCATION | 16243 (69.81%) | 4731 (20.33%) | 2292 (9.85%) |
| I-ORGANIZATION | 13231 (69.69%) | 3849 (20.27%) | 1905 (10.03%) |
| I-PERSON | 19144 (69.87%) | 5488 (20.03%) | 2768 (10.1%) |
| O | 1313841 (70.0%) | 375467 (20.0%) | 187600 (10.0%) |

Table 3: Number of samples and percentage distribution of entities of the whole Hindi dataset.

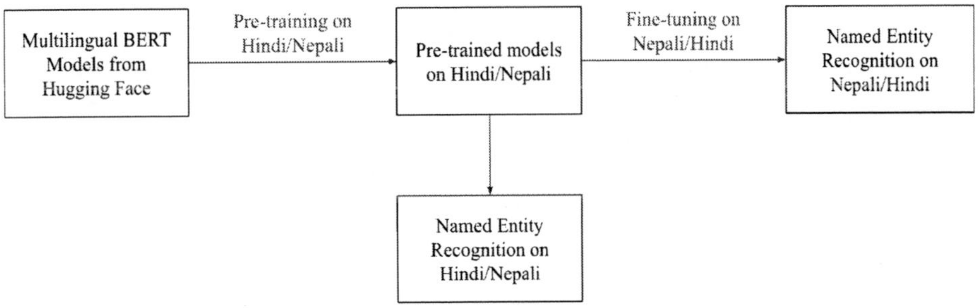


Figure 5: Diagram depicting the conducted experiments.

## 5 Results and Discussion

The results of the experiments are presented in Table 5.

In monolingual tasks, RemBERT achieved the highest F1 score for Hindi at **0.937**, emphasizing its strong capability in managing languages with relatively rich resources. Its deep architecture, coupled with rebalanced training data across 110 languages, enables it to capture subtle patterns within Hindi, resulting in better performance. On the other hand, MuRIL slightly outperformed other models in the Nepali NER task, achieving an F1 score of **0.979**, thereby demonstrating its effectiveness in contexts where resources are limited. The design of MuRIL, which specifically focuses on Indian languages and incorporates transliterated text to address code-switching, renders it particularly suitable for Nepali. Both BERT Multilingual and DistilBERT Multilingual displayed competitive performance, with DistilBERT Multilingual achieving a marginally higher score in Hindi (0.928) compared to Nepali (0.972) despite its smaller and more efficient architecture. BERT Multilingual, with F1 scores of 0.922 for Hindi and 0.974 for Nepali, highlighted its versatility and balanced performance across both languages.

In cross-lingual scenarios, BERT Multilingual showed the most notable improvements, with F1

[3]`https://oscar-project.org/`

[4]`https://github.com/DataScienceLab-HGW/Cross-Lingual-NER-Hindi-Nepali`

| **Hyperparameter** | **Value** |
|---|---|
| Learning Rate | Optimized using optuna (Akiba et al., 2019), range: $1e^{-5}$ to $5e^{-4}$ |
| Batch Size | 16 for training, 8 for evaluation |
| Number of Epochs | 30 epochs, validation F1 score-based early stopping |
| Optimizer | AdamW |
| Weight Decay | 0.01 |
| Warmup Ratio | 0.1 |
| Evaluation Strategy | End of each epoch |
| Save Strategy | End of each epoch |
| Metric for Best Model | F1 score |

Table 4: Hyperparameters and configurations used in the experiments.

| **Model** | **Hindi** | **Nepali** | **Hin-Nep** | **Nep-Hin** |
|---|---|---|---|---|
| MuRIL | 0.923 | **0.979** | 0.973 | 0.923 |
| BERT Multilingual | 0.922 | 0.974 | **0.977** | **0.929** |
| DistilBERT Multilingual | 0.928 | 0.972 | 0.969 | 0.921 |
| RemBERT | **0.937** | 0.973 | 0.968 | 0.934 |

Table 5: F1 Scores of the four Multilingual BERT models on Hindi and Nepali datasets, including monolingual and cross-lingual NER.

scores improving to **0.977** for Hindi-to-Nepali and **0.929** for Nepali-to-Hindi transfers, indicating that its architecture is well-suited for generalizing linguistic features across languages. While MuRIL excelled in the monolingual Nepali task, it did not show improvement in cross-lingual performance, with F1 scores of 0.973 for Hindi-to-Nepali and 0.923 for Nepali-to-Hindi, suggesting that its design may be more tailored to specific languages rather than cross-lingual tasks. DistilBERT Multilingual experienced a slight decrease in cross-lingual performance, with F1 scores of 0.969 for Hindi-to-Nepali and 0.921 for Nepali-to-Hindi, indicating that its reduced size and complexity might limit its capability in transferring knowledge across languages. Despite its strong monolingual performance in Hindi, RemBERT's cross-lingual performance was marginally lower, with F1 scores of 0.968 for Hindi-to-Nepali and 0.934 for Nepali-to-Hindi, which suggests that while RemBERT excels in monolingual contexts, it may be more optimized for achieving balanced performance across multiple languages rather than excelling in specific cross-lingual tasks.

## 6 Conclusion

This study investigated the effectiveness of cross-lingual transfer learning for Named Entity Recognition between Hindi and Nepali by employing several multilingual BERT models, including RemBERT, BERT Multilingual, MuRIL, and DistilBERT Multilingual. The results indicated that while RemBERT and MuRIL excelled in monolingual tasks—RemBERT in Hindi and MuRIL in Nepali—BERT Multilingual emerged as the most effective in cross-lingual scenarios, successfully transferring knowledge between the two languages. DistilBERT Multilingual, though slightly less effective in cross-lingual transfer, offered a commendable balance between performance and computational efficiency. These findings emphasize the critical role of model selection based on the task's specific linguistic and resource conditions, suggesting that general-purpose models like BERT Multilingual are particularly well-suited for cross-lingual applications.

## Limitations

This study has several limitations that should be acknowledged. The reliance on existing datasets, where Nepali is much smaller than Hindi, may affect the generalizability of the results. The focus has been on specific pre-trained multilingual BERT models; hence, other potentially more effective architectures and cross-lingual transfer methods, such as self-training or domain adaptation, could be explored. Additionally, focusing on the Hindi-Nepali language pair means the findings may not apply to other languages, especially those with less linguistic similarity. Resource constraints also limited the extent of hyperparameter optimization and experimentation, which could influence the results. Finally, while the F1 score was the primary evaluation metric, other metrics paired with a qualitative analysis of predictions could provide additional insights into model performance, suggesting avenues for future research.

## Ethics Statement

This research adheres to the ACL Ethics Policy, focusing on enhancing Named Entity Recognition (NER) for low-resource languages like Hindi and Nepali through cross-lingual transfer learning. No personal data was collected, as the data used in the research was from open-source. We encourage ongoing ethical evaluation, particularly when deploying NLP technologies in low-resource settings.

## References


Takuya Akiba, Shotaro Sano, Toshihiko Yanase, Takeru Ohta, and Masanori Koyama. 2019. Optuna: A next-generation hyperparameter optimization framework. In *Proceedings of the 25th ACM SIGKDD International Conference on Knowledge Discovery & Data Mining*, KDD '19, page 2623–2631, New York, NY, USA. Association for Computing Machinery.

Vincent Beaufils. 2015–2024. elinguistics.net: Quantifying the genetic proximity between languages.

Vincent Beaufils and Joanna Tomin. 2020. Stochastic approach to worldwide language classification: The signals and the noise towards long-range exploration. Preprint available at OSF.

Hyung Won Chung, Thibault Févry, Henry Tsai, Melvin Johnson, and Sebastian Ruder. 2021. Rethinking embedding coupling in pre-trained language models. In *9th International Conference on Learning Representations, ICLR 2021, Virtual Event, Austria, May 3-7, 2021*. OpenReview.net.

Alexis Conneau, Kartikay Khandelwal, Naman Goyal, Vishrav Chaudhary, Guillaume Wenzek, Francisco Guzmán, Edouard Grave, Myle Ott, Luke Zettlemoyer, and Veselin Stoyanov. 2020. Unsupervised cross-lingual representation learning at scale. In *Proceedings of the 58th Annual Meeting of the Association for Computational Linguistics*, pages 8440–8451, Online. Association for Computational Linguistics.

Alexis Conneau, Ruty Rinott, Guillaume Lample, Adina Williams, Samuel Bowman, Holger Schwenk, and Veselin Stoyanov. 2018. XNLI: Evaluating cross-lingual sentence representations. In *Proceedings of the 2018 Conference on Empirical Methods in Natural Language Processing*, pages 2475–2485, Brussels, Belgium. Association for Computational Linguistics.

Nikita P. Desai and Vipul K. Dabhi. 2021. Taxonomic survey of hindi language NLP systems. *CoRR*, abs/2102.00214.

Pranita Deshmukh, Nikita Kulkarni, Sanhita Kulkarni, Kareena Manghani, Prajakta A. Khadkikar, and Raviraj Joshi. 2024. Named entity recognition for indic languages: A comprehensive survey. In *2024 1st International Conference on Trends in Engineering Systems and Technologies (ICTEST)*, pages 1–6.

Jacob Devlin, Ming-Wei Chang, Kenton Lee, and Kristina Toutanova. 2019. BERT: Pre-training of deep bidirectional transformers for language understanding. In *Proceedings of the 2019 Conference of the North American Chapter of the Association for Computational Linguistics: Human Language Technologies, Volume 1 (Long and Short Papers)*, pages 4171–4186, Minneapolis, Minnesota. Association for Computational Linguistics.

David M. Eberhard, Gary F. Simons, and Charles D. Fennig. 2024. *Ethnologue: Languages of the World*, twenty-seventh edition. SIL International, Dallas, Texas. Online version.

Barry Haddow and Faheem Kirefu. 2020. Pmindia - A collection of parallel corpora of languages of india. *CoRR*, abs/2001.09907.

Hansi Hettiarachchi, Mariam Adedoyin-Olowe, Jagdev Bhogal, and Mohamed Medhat Gaber. 2023. Ttl: transformer-based two-phase transfer learning for cross-lingual news event detection. *International Journal of Machine Learning and Cybernetics*, 14(8):2739–2760.

Zhuang Hu, Wei Hou, and Xiaoyan Liu. 2024. Deep learning for named entity recognition: a survey. *Neural Computing and Applications*, 36:8995–9022.

Mirela Iancu. 2024. 100 most spoken languages in the world. Accessed: August 29, 2024.

Amir Reza Jafari, Behnam Heidary, Reza Farahbakhsh, Mostafa Salehi, and Mahdi Jalili. 2021. Transfer learning for multi-lingual tasks–a survey. *arXiv preprint arXiv:2110.02052*.

Daniel Jurafsky and James H. Martin. 2008. *Speech and Language Processing: An Introduction to Natural Language Processing, Computational Linguistics, and Speech Recognition*, 2nd edition. Prentice Hall.

Tanvi Kamble and Manish Shrivastava. 2023. Hindi causal TimeBank: an annotated causal event corpus. In *Proceedings of the 20th International Conference on Natural Language Processing (ICON)*, pages 145–150, Goa University, Goa, India. NLP Association of India (NLPAI).

Simran Khanuja, Diksha Bansal, Sarvesh Mehtani, Savya Khosla, Atreyee Dey, Balaji Gopalan, Dilip Kumar Margam, Pooja Aggarwal, Rajiv Teja Nagipogu, Shachi Dave, Shruti Gupta, Subhash Chandra Bose Gali, Vish Subramanian, and Partha Talukdar. 2021. Muril: Multilingual representations for indian languages.

Joo-Kyung Kim, Young-Bum Kim, Ruhi Sarikaya, and Eric Fosler-Lussier. 2017. Cross-lingual transfer learning for pos tagging without cross-lingual resources. In *Proceedings of the 2017 conference on empirical methods in natural language processing*, pages 2832–2838.

Sunil Kumar Kopparapu and V. L. Lajish. 2014. A framework for on-line devanagari handwritten character recognition. *ArXiv*, abs/1410.6909.

Jing Li, Aixin Sun, Jianglei Han, and Chenliang Li. 2022. A survey on deep learning for named entity recognition. *IEEE Trans. on Knowl. and Data Eng.*, 34(1):50–70.

Boyd Michailovsky. 2008. Digitized resources for languages of nepal. *Lesser-Known Languages of South Asia: Status and Policies, Case Studies and Applications of Information Technology*, 175:243.

Rudra Murthy, Pallab Bhattacharjee, Rahul Sharnagat, Jyotsana Khatri, Diptesh Kanojia, and Pushpak Bhattacharyya. 2022. Hiner: A large hindi named entity recognition dataset. In *Proceedings of the Language Resources and Evaluation Conference*, pages 4467–4476, Marseille, France. European Language Resources Association.

David Powers. 2011. Evaluation: From precision, recall and f-measure to roc, informedness, markedness & correlation. *Journal of Machine Learning Technologies*, 2(1):37–63.

Victor Sanh, Lysandre Debut, Julien Chaumond, and Thomas Wolf. 2019. Distilbert, a distilled version of bert: smaller, faster, cheaper and lighter. *ArXiv*, abs/1910.01108.

Sebastian Schuster, Sonal Gupta, Rushin Shah, and Mike Lewis. 2019. Cross-lingual transfer learning for multilingual task oriented dialog. In *Proceedings of the 2019 Conference of the North American Chapter of the Association for Computational Linguistics: Human Language Technologies, Volume 1 (Long and Short Papers)*, pages 3795–3805.

Sital Sharma, Kalpana Sharma, and Biswaraj Sen. 2023. A comprehensive study on natural language processing, it's techniques and advancements in nepali language. In *International Conference on Advanced Computational and Communication Paradigms*, pages 157–175. Springer.

O. M. Singh, A. Padia, and A. Joshi. 2019. Named entity recognition for nepali language. In *2019 IEEE 5th International Conference on Collaboration and Internet Computing (CIC)*, pages 184–190. IEEE.

Bipesh Subedi, Sunil Regmi, Bal Krishna Bal, and Praveen Acharya. 2024. Exploring the potential of large language models (LLMs) for low-resource languages: A study on named-entity recognition (NER) and part-of-speech (POS) tagging for Nepali language. In *Proceedings of the 2024 Joint International Conference on Computational Linguistics, Language Resources and Evaluation (LREC-COLING 2024)*, pages 6974–6979, Torino, Italia. ELRA and ICCL.

Bruno Taillé, Vincent Guigue, and Patrick Gallinari. 2020. Contextualized embeddings in named-entity recognition: An empirical study on generalization. In *Advances in Information Retrieval*, pages 383–391, Cham. Springer International Publishing.

Sulav Timilsina, Milan Gautam, and Binod Bhattarai. 2022. NepBERTa: Nepali language model trained in a large corpus. In *Proceedings of the 2nd Conference of the Asia-Pacific Chapter of the Association for Computational Linguistics and the 12th International Joint Conference on Natural Language Processing (Volume 2: Short Papers)*, pages 273–284, Online only. Association for Computational Linguistics.

Erik F. Tjong Kim Sang and Fien De Meulder. 2003. Introduction to the CoNLL-2003 shared task: Language-independent named entity recognition. In *Proceedings of the Seventh Conference on Natural Language Learning at HLT-NAACL 2003*, pages 142–147.

Jinshi Wang. 2021. Cross-lingual transfer learning for low-resource natural language processing tasks. Master's thesis, Karlsruher Institut für Technologie (KIT).

Thomas Wolf, Lysandre Debut, Victor Sanh, Julien Chaumond, Clement Delangue, Anthony Moi, Pierric Cistac, Tim Rault, Remi Louf, Morgan Funtowicz, Joe Davison, Sam Shleifer, Patrick von Platen, Clara Ma, Yacine Jernite, Julien Plu, Canwen Xu, Teven Le Scao, Sylvain Gugger, Mariama Drame, Quentin Lhoest, and Alexander Rush. 2020. Transformers: State-of-the-art natural language processing. In *Proceedings of the 2020 Conference on Empirical Methods in Natural Language Processing: System Demonstrations*, pages 38–45, Online. Association for Computational Linguistics.

# Parameter-efficient Adaptation of Multilingual Multimodal Models for Low-resource ASR

**Abhishek Gupta*** **Amruta Parulekar*** **Sameep Chattopadhyay*** **Preethi Jyothi**
Indian Institute of Technology Bombay, Mumbai, India
{abhishekumgupta,amrutaparulekar.iitb,sameep.ch.2002}@gmail.com, pjyothi@cse.iitb.ac.in

## Abstract

Automatic speech recognition (ASR) for low-resource languages remains a challenge due to the scarcity of labeled training data. Parameter-efficient fine-tuning and text-only adaptation are two popular methods that have been used to address such low-resource settings. In this work, we investigate how these techniques can be effectively combined using a multilingual multimodal model like SeamlessM4T. Multimodal models are able to leverage unlabeled text via text-only adaptation with further parameter-efficient ASR fine-tuning, thus boosting ASR performance. We also show cross-lingual transfer from a high-resource language, achieving up to a relative 17% WER reduction over a baseline in a zero-shot setting without any labeled speech.

## 1 Introduction

Across the languages of the world, the automation of various speech and text tasks has led to the creation of massive multilingual datasets such as Multilingual LibriSpeech (Pratap et al., 2020), that contain speech, text, and other metadata for a number of different languages. This large-scale collection has catalyzed the emergence of large multilingual automatic speech recognition (ASR) models (Yadav and Sitaram, 2022), which utilize the structural similarities between different languages to learn language-invariant features and boost accuracy. Subsequently, multimodal multilingual models, such as M3P (Ni et al., 2021), that bridge the gap between speech and text using joint representation spaces, have also emerged. These models are trained using large amounts of multilingual speech and text data.

However, less-spoken languages, especially those from developing countries, do not have such large data corpora available (Magueresse et al., 2020), thus hurting model performance for extremely low-resource languages (Chang et al., 2023). Thus, creating targeted models for severely low-resource languages has become crucial. One efficient way to do this is by adapting existing models to the target language using limited amounts of labeled data. Such adaptation has to be done carefully so as to not overfit to the target language characteristics.

Parameter-efficient fine-tuning (PEFT) (Han et al., 2024) techniques have gained wide acceptance where only relevant parts of a model are identified and fine-tuned for a specific downstream task. Text-only adaptation is another sub-area that is gaining popularity for low-resource ASR (Bataev et al., 2023; Vuong et al., 2023). Multimodal models have training pathways for both speech and text data, offering a good framework to combine both approaches. Multilingual models, on the other hand, allow for cross-lingual transfer (Khare et al., 2021), i.e., using a higher resource language to improve performance on a lower resource language.

In this work, we have leveraged the multimodal nature of Meta's SeamlessM4T (Communication et al., 2023) to explore the benefits of speech-based adapter fine-tuning and text-only adaptation. These techniques have been used both in isolation and in combination to identify the best strategy to improve low-resource ASR for a number of Indic languages. We have also exploited the multilingual nature of the model to use higher-resource languages to improve low-resource ASR. Thus, our main contributions include: (a) identifying how to combine speech-based parameter-efficient fine-tuning and text-only adaptation to boost low-resource ASR, (b) identifying a cross-lingual transfer technique that can give more than 17% relative reduction in WER for a low-resource language without using any speech of that language, (c) the use of small amounts of available data to boost the performance of SeamlessM4T (Communication et al., 2023) on six Indic languages, Bengali, Gujarati, Kannada, Maithili, Malayalam and Odia.

*These authors contributed equally to this work.



*Proceedings of the Fourth Workshop on Multilingual Representation Learning (MRL 2024)*, pages 175–185
November 16, 2024 ©2024 Association for Computational Linguistics

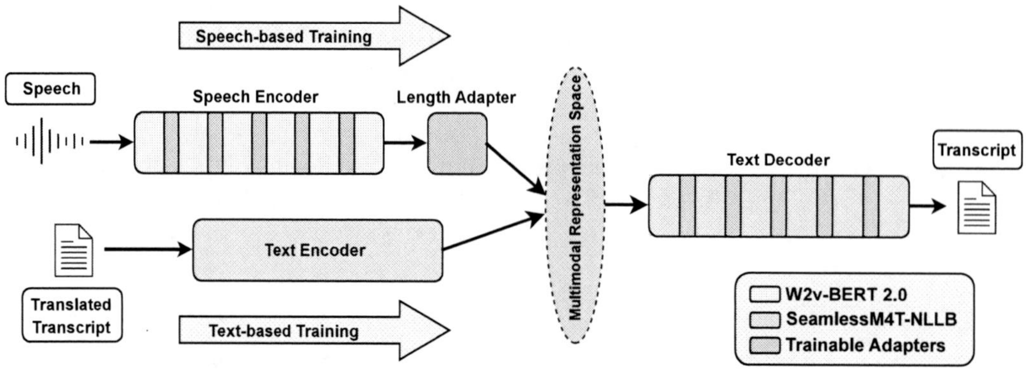


Figure 1: **Parameter-efficient Adaptations for SeamlessM4T:** A multimodal ASR model such as SeamlessM4T can be fine-tuned in a parameter-efficient manner through either speech-based adaptations or text-only adaptation.

## 2 Related Work

One of the key challenges in current ASR research is enabling systems to handle multilingual inputs (Yadav and Sitaram, 2022; Kannan et al., 2019) while minimizing resource requirements in terms of training, inference, and storage costs. Currently, the most popular paradigm using multilingual models are to initially pre-train the models in a self-supervised manner on a large multilingual dataset (Babu et al., 2021) before being fine-tuned on a set of target languages (Toshniwal et al., 2018; Bai et al., 2022). A general way of performing such model fine-tuning is by updating all the weights or some specific model components while training. These kinds of methods are parameter inefficient and often cause catastrophic forgetting (Kessler et al., 2021), for all non-target languages. Also, training and storage costs for such methods increase linearly with both the model size and the number of languages.

To mitigate these limitations, recent literature on NLP has introduced several parameter-efficient fine-tuning methods (Xu et al., 2023; Tomanek et al., 2021; Hu et al., 2021), often involving trainable modules called adapters (Houlsby et al., 2019), whose weights are updated while freezing the original backbone. Significant efforts are being made to develop better adapter architectures and efficient training methods (Yu et al., 2023) to utilize contrastive learning (Zhang and Ré, 2024) and meta-learning (Hou et al., 2021). These modules can also be used to adapt multilingual ASR models for a low-resource setting, with Simadapter (Hou et al., 2022) being one of the first models to utilize adapters to leverage cross-lingual features.

In the context of speech recognition, a low-resource setting could refer to any scenario with insufficient training data. This includes challenges such as recognizing atypical speech (Tomanek et al., 2021) or processing less commonly spoken languages. A recent work (Mainzinger and Levow, 2024) demonstrated the benefits of using adapters for very low-resource languages with less than five hours of training data. For the low-resource situation, task- or language-specific adapter modules showcase superior performance (Hu et al., 2024) compared to fine-tuning the model components, but even such approaches are constrained by inherent limitations of the base model.

Over the past few years, considerable effort has gone into developing multilingual ASR foundational models with more generalizable features. These models offer a stronger starting point for low-resource adaptations and enable the use of cross-lingual transfer learning. The exponential growth in computing power has led to the creation of increasingly large language models, which are now used for a wide range of tasks, including as backbones for multimodal ASR models (Rubenstein et al., 2023; Zhang et al., 2023; Chang et al., 2023). For such models, the foundational backbone is expanded using audio tokens generated using techniques like wav2vec (Schneider et al., 2019) and Hubert (Hsu et al., 2021) in order to learn a joint representation in a multimodal space; the token vocabulary is expanded to encompass both text and audio. Note that models with joint multimodal representations are not only useful for ASR but can also be integrated with a vocoder for TTS or conversational chatbots (Zhang et al., 2023).

Multimodal models can be trained with joint text-audio tasks through self-supervision with masked language modeling and denoising objectives; further fine-tuning is often done with ASR and speech-to-text or speech-to-speech translation tasks. One of the most recent examples of such a multilingual multimodal model has been SeamlessM4T (Communication et al., 2023) by Meta AI, which is built upon the NLLB (Team et al., 2022a) backbone and can process speech and text inputs from nearly 100 languages. An implicit advantage of using such multimodal models for low-resource ASR is the ability to benefit from text-only learning for shared parameters. In most cases, there is significantly more text data available than speech data. Thus, the capability to leverage text-only adaptation for ASR models can be highly advantageous in these scenarios.

While there is a lot of prior work in the domain of text-only adaptation for ASR (Vuong et al., 2023; Bataev et al., 2023; Chen et al., 2023; Mittal et al., 2023), and there has been some work on a comparative analysis of various fine-tuning strategies for low-resource ASR (Liu et al., 2024), to the best of our knowledge, our work is the first to explore them for multilingual multimodal models.

## 3 Methodology

In this work, we leverage a combination of parameter-efficient adaptation, unlabeled textual data, and minimal amounts of transcribed speech to improve ASR performance in low-resource languages using multilingual multimodal models. Figure 1 demonstrates the overall workflow of our proposed pipeline.

### 3.1 Multimodal base model: SeamlessM4T

We use SeamlessM4T (Communication et al., 2023) as our base model for all our experiments. SeamlessM4T, i.e., Massively Multilingual & Multimodal Machine Translation, is a versatile end-to-end model that provides support for multiple tasks, including speech-to-speech translation, speech-to-text translation, text-to-speech translation, text-to-text translation, and automatic speech recognition for up to 100 languages. The model has been trained using over a million hours of unlabeled speech in a self-supervised manner, along with more than 400K hours of human and machine-labeled audio. It supports 96 different languages for input speech and text, as well as output text, and can generate speech in 35 languages.

The SeamlessM4T model architecture is inspired by UnitY (Inaguma et al., 2023), a two-pass modeling framework that, unlike cascaded models, can be jointly optimized. The text encoder and decoder models of SeamlessM4T are initialized by the NLLB model (Team et al., 2022b), a text-to-text translation model. To process speech inputs, the model employs the Wav2Vec-BERT 2.0 speech encoder, which is an enhancement over the original model proposed by Chung et al. (2021) with additional codebooks. The model also includes a modality adapter (Zhao et al., 2022), referred to as the **length adapter**, to align the speech modality with text, projecting it to a unified representation space. Lastly, the model uses a text-to-unit (T2U) component for speech generation that produces discrete speech units from the text output. These units are then transformed into audio waveforms using a multilingual HiFi-GAN unit vocoder (Kong et al., 2020). There are multiple variants of the SeamlessM4T model; we have used SeamlessM4T-medium with a total of 1.2 Billion parameters.

Although the entire model comprises multiple components, our analysis focuses primarily on applying SeamlessM4T for multilingual ASR. The ASR pipeline of SeamlessM4T consists of the speech encoder (311M parameters), the length adapter (46M parameters), and the text decoder (201M parameters). Next, we will elaborate on parameter-efficient fine-tuning of SeamlessM4T (Section 3.2) and how we can use text-only adaptation within such a multimodal model (Section 3.3).

### 3.2 Parameter-efficient Fine-tuning

The ASR components of SeamlessM4T amount to more than 500M parameters. Full fine-tuning of these components using limited amounts of labeled data for low-resource languages may result in overfitting and degradation of ASR performance. To alleviate these challenges, parameter-efficient fine-tuning paradigms like the *adapter framework* (Houlsby et al., 2019) are very popular, especially for natural language processing tasks. Adapters have also found success in low-resource ASR tasks such as accent adaptation (Tomanek et al., 2021) and cross-lingual adaptation (Hou et al., 2022). Next, we will elaborate on the structure of an existing *length adapter* within SeamlessM4T and the new adapters we introduce in the encoder and decoder layers.

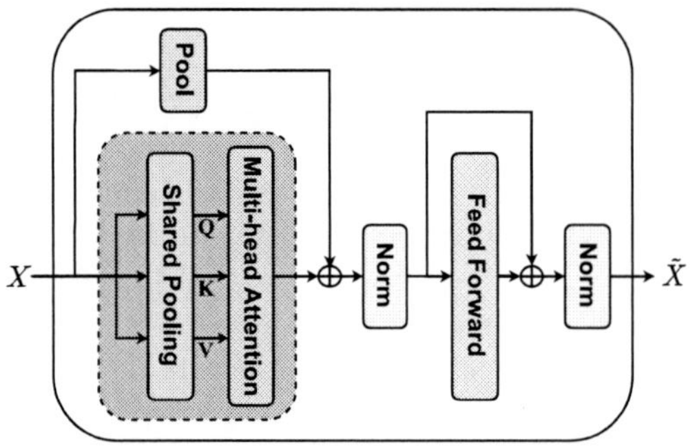


Figure 2: **SeamlessM4T Length Adapter:** Projects speech embedding $X$ to a lower-dimensional representation $\tilde{X}$ in the multimodal space.

### 3.2.1 The Length Adapter

The length adapter in SeamlessM4T aims to bridge the gap between speech and text representations. It is inspired by the M-adapter architecture (Zhang et al., 2023) and uses a Transformer-based module to adapt speech representations to text. By compressing the speech sequence, the length adapter generates features tailored for multilingual speech-to-text tasks by modeling both global and local dependencies within the speech.

The main part of the original M-adapter architecture, illustrated in Figure 2, is the Multi-head Pooled Self-Attention (MPSA) mechanism. In the original MPSA, convolutional layers pool the input $X$ and are further projected to the inputs of the multi-head attention module using linear transformation matrices. An additional pooling is applied in parallel to $X$ and then added to the output of the attention module before being processed through a feedforward network. These processes together generate a lower dimensional representation of $X$, denoted by $\tilde{X}$ as the current layer output, addressing any length mismatches between embeddings from different modalities. Unlike the original M-adapter architecture with independent pooling modules for the multi-head attention inputs, the length adapter utilizes a shared pooling module, generating a single $\hat{X}$ for each $X$ to improve efficiency. More formally, given an input sequence $X \in \mathbb{R}^{L \times D}$, where $L$ is the sequence length and $D$ is the embedding dimension, the MPSA mechanism starts by applying shared pooling to the input $X$ to obtain $\hat{X} \in \mathbb{R}^{L' \times D}$. This pooling operation is performed using a 1D convolutional layer with kernel size $k$, stride $s$, and padding $p$. Subsequently, $\hat{X}$ is linearly projected into the query, key, and value matrices, denoted as $Q$, $K$, and $V$, respectively.

$$
\begin{aligned}
\hat{X} &= \text{SharedPooling}(X) \\
Q &= \hat{X}W^{Q}, && \text{where } Q \in \mathbb{R}^{L' \times D}, \\
K &= \hat{X}W^{K}, && \text{where } K \in \mathbb{R}^{L' \times D}, \\
V &= \hat{X}W^{V}, && \text{where } V \in \mathbb{R}^{L' \times D}.
\end{aligned}
$$

where the new sequence length $L'$ is given by:

$$
L' = \left\lfloor \frac{L + 2p - k}{s} \right\rfloor + 1.
$$

We hypothesize that the length adapter module could potentially learn prosodic characteristics of languages, such as phoneme durations, by mapping speech embeddings — which include both segmental and suprasegmental information — to text embeddings that contain only content information. Learning certain prosodic characteristics like durations can be particularly beneficial for extremely low-resource languages that lack sufficient data for learning fine-grained contextual and syntactical information.

### 3.2.2 Encoder and Decoder Adapters

In addition to the pre-existing length adapter (Figure 2) in the SeamlessM4T architecture, we inserted additional trainable adapter layers within the encoder and decoder modules to adapt this multilingual model for low-resource languages. The adapter modules, following the architecture proposed in (Houlsby et al., 2019), initially project the original $D_1$-dimensional features into an intermediate space of dimension $D_2$. A non-linearity, specifically GeLU (Hendrycks and Gimpel, 2023) in our implementation, is then applied, after which the features are projected back to the original $D_1$ dimensions. To adjust the number of parameters for these adapters, we can change the intermediate dimension $D_2$. By decreasing the value of $D_2$, the number of trainable parameters in the adapters is reduced accordingly.

In our current experimental setup, we have inserted adapters after every Conformer layer in the encoders and after every Transformer layer in the text decoder. By setting the intermediate dimension $D_2$ to one-fourth of $D_1$ for all adapters, we introduce 6 million new trainable parameters each in the encoder and decoder modules.

Formally, the operations inside the $i^{\text{th}}$ speech encoder layer can be summarized as:

$$\begin{aligned}
\mathbf{H} &= \text{MultiHeadAttn}(\mathbf{h}^{i-1}, \mathbf{h}^{i-1}, \mathbf{h}^{i-1}) \\
\mathbf{C} &= \text{Convolution}(\mathbf{H}) \\
\hat{\mathbf{h}}^{\mathbf{i}} &= \text{FFN}(\mathbf{C}) \\
\mathbf{h}^{i} &= \text{Adapter}(\hat{\mathbf{h}}^{i})
\end{aligned}$$

Similarly, the operations inside the $i^{\text{th}}$ decoder layer can be summarized as:

$$\begin{aligned}
\mathbf{D} &= \text{MultiHeadAttn}(\mathbf{d}^{i-1}, \mathbf{d}^{i-1}, \mathbf{d}^{i-1}) \\
\hat{\mathbf{D}} &= \text{MultiHeadAttn}(\mathbf{d}^{i-1}, \mathbf{h}^{\ell}, \mathbf{h}^{\ell}) \\
\hat{\mathbf{d}}^{\mathbf{i}} &= \text{FFN}(\hat{\mathbf{D}}) \\
\mathbf{d}^{i} &= \text{Adapter}(\hat{\mathbf{d}}^{i})
\end{aligned}$$

where $\ell$ is the last encoder layer, and MultiHeadAttn(Q, K, V) is the standard multi-head attention implementation (Vaswani, 2017) with Q, K, and V denoting queries, keys, and values, respectively.

During our experiments, we fine-tuned the encoder adapters and length adapters on labeled ASR data, while the decoder was fine-tuned using ASR and machine translation (MT) data, thereby leveraging the text-to-text pipeline of SeamlessM4T.

### 3.3 Text-only Adaptation

The text decoder in the SeamlessM4T model is shared between the ASR pipeline and the text-to-text translation pipeline, allowing it to be trained for both tasks. This shared component in multimodal models possesses the ability to transfer knowledge from one task to another, thereby simultaneously enhancing the performance of multiple tasks. We hypothesize that we can improve the ASR performance for a target language by fine-tuning the text decoder adapters via text-to-text translation into that language. This allows us to perform a purely text-only fine-tuning of ASR models and is especially beneficial for languages where speech data is scarce. With the latest advancements in NLP, the quality of machine-translation models has greatly improved, allowing these models to be utilized to augment the existing parallel text using machine-translated text for these languages.

In our text-only fine-tuning experiments, we fine-tuned the decoder adapters on an English-to-target language translation task to help them learn the relevant syntactical features for the target language.

## 4 Experimental Setup

### 4.1 Dataset

The **IndicVoices** dataset (Javed et al., 2024) was utilized for all our experiments. This dataset is a multilingual, multi-speaker collection of natural and spontaneous speech in 22 Indian languages. It comprises 9% read speech, 74% extempore speech, and 17% conversational speech. Among these languages, Maithili is classified as a zero-shot language for SeamlessM4T, while Bengali is the sole high-resource Indic language. The remaining languages are categorized as low-resource languages for the model (Communication et al., 2023). One of the main reasons for using this dataset is that it is among the most comprehensive open-source, multilingual speech datasets for Indic languages covering many low-resource languages and one of the few published after the release of SeamlessM4T, ensuring there is no data leakage between the evaluation sets and the SeamlessM4T training data.

#### 4.1.1 Transcribed Speech Data

The speech data and the corresponding transcripts from the IndicVoices dataset were used for the ASR fine-tuning experiments. The dataset, primarily consisting of extempore speech recorded under natural conditions, is characterized by a significant amount of noise and includes occasional disfluencies. For each language, 5 hours of speech were selected for the training set, sourced from an average of 336 speakers, to simulate an extremely low-resource setting. On average, each of the test and validation sets had 1 hour of speech by 68 and 206 speakers respectively. The out-of-vocabulary (OOV) rate of the test set was calculated to determine the amount of test-train domain overlap in the data. The OOV rates for Gujarati, Bengali, Kannada, Maithili, Malayalam, and Odia test sets were 39%, 35%, 58%, 41%, 53%, and 37%, respectively, averaging to an OOV of 43.87% on the test sets, further demonstrating the challenging nature of the task.

#### 4.1.2 Text-only Data

The **IndicTrans2** (Gala et al., 2023) model was used to translate all the transcriptions present in the IndicVoices dataset to obtain parallel English-X text. Another set of parallel text data was created by using only the transcriptions of the 5-hour speech data in the training set for every language. For Bengali, Gujarati, Kannada, Maithili, Malayalam, and

| Components fine-tuned | Learnable Parameters | Maitihli | | Malayalam | | Kannada | | Gujarati | | Odia | | Bengali | |
|---|---|---|---|---|---|---|---|---|---|---|---|---|---|
| | | WER | CER | WER | CER | WER | CER | WER | CER | WER | CER | WER | CER |
| None | - | 82.20 | 43.39 | 56.15 | 20.65 | 69.29 | 29.11 | 41.03 | 24.50 | 42.81 | 17.38 | 37.70 | 18.44 |
| Length adapter | 46M | 54.97 | 26.10 | 52.82 | 18.14 | 55.48 | 20.38 | 33.91 | 16.40 | 35.48 | 13.75 | 35.90 | 17.08 |
| Text Decoder | 201M | 54.56 | 26.21 | 54.04 | 19.28 | 54.3 | 20.57 | 33.62 | 17.12 | 35.14 | 13.48 | 36.14 | 17.95 |
| Speech Encoder | 311M | 43.87 | 17.79 | 46.99 | 13.45 | 47.91 | 14.93 | 27.79 | 11.58 | 29.82 | 9.24 | 29.07 | 12.09 |

Table 1: **Fine-tuning a Multimodal Model:** Comparison of WER (%) and CER (%) after ASR fine-tuning of SeamlessM4T with 5 hours of labeled speech, without adaptations; the first row presents the pre-fine-tuning results.

| Text-only Adaptation | Learnable Parameters | Maithili | | Malayalam | | Kannada | | Gujarati | | Odia | | Bengali | |
|---|---|---|---|---|---|---|---|---|---|---|---|---|---|
| | | WER | CER | WER | CER | WER | CER | WER | CER | WER | CER | WER | CER |
| None | - | 82.20 | 43.39 | 56.15 | 20.65 | 69.29 | 29.11 | 41.03 | 24.50 | 42.81 | 17.38 | 37.70 | 18.44 |
| 5hr Transcript | 6M | 71.32 | 37.92 | **53.96** | **18.94** | 70.52 | 32.54 | 35.67 | 19.19 | 38.77 | **14.84** | **35.28** | **16.77** |
| Full Transcript | 6M | **68.24** | **36.84** | 55.30 | 20.43 | **68.13** | **26.91** | **35.45** | **18.66** | **38.39** | 16.22 | 35.44 | 17.73 |

Table 2: **Text-only Adaptation:** Comparison of WER (%) and CER (%) after text-only adaptation on SeamlessM4T with Eng-X parallel text using the full dataset and a 5-hour subset; the first row presents the pre-adaptation results.

Odia, the number of tokens in the 5-hour text sets were 40k, 43k, 30k, 42k, 34k, and 34k, respectively, while those in the large text set were 785k, 118k, 297k, 834k, 398k and 503k respectively. Thus, on average, each of the larger text data sets contained 489000 tokens for every language, while each of the smaller sets contained only 37261 tokens.

### 4.2 Implementation Details

The SeamlessM4T model comprises a speech encoder with 12 Conformer blocks and a text decoder with 12 Transformer blocks, with a model dimension $D_1 = 1024$. Two $D_2$ configurations were tested: $D_2 = 256$ (about 500K parameters per adapter layer, totaling 6M parameters) and $D_2 = 2048$ (matching adapter parameters with the length adapter, totaling 50M parameters). Text-only adaptation needed roughly 200 epochs of fine-tuning, while ASR fine-tuning required up to 40 epochs. All experiments were performed with a learning rate of $5 \times 10^{-6}$ and a batch size of 16.

## 5 Experiments and Results

### 5.1 System A: Pure ASR Fine-tuning

We use the name *System A* to refer to the standard speech-to-text fine-tuning of SeamlessM4T using labeled speech and the ASR objective. The results of this experimental setup are summarized in Table 1. From the results, it is evident that fine-tuning the length adapter requires fewer parameters while providing similar benefits to text decoder fine-tuning across both metrics. Additionally, the ASR fine-tuning of the speech encoder proves to be significantly beneficial, although it involves training a substantially larger number of parameters.

In order to reduce the computational and storage requirements, the fine-tuning was substituted with language-specific adaptations, wherein adapters were introduced in the encoder and decoder, and these were fine-tuned in various combinations using transcribed speech data while freezing the base model. Table 3 depicts the results for the adaptations on System A. The results demonstrate that larger encoder adapters with 50M parameters are the most beneficial in enhancing the ASR performance, achieving WER and CER close to full fine-tuning of the model and the adapters while reducing trainable parameters by 90%. Additionally, Table 3 indicates that for the same number of trainable parameters, speech-based training of encoder adapters performs much better than that of decoder adapters. The performance of the length adapter fine-tuning surpasses that of the decoder adapters but falls short compared to the encoder adapters.

### 5.2 System T-A: Using Text-only Adaptation

The parallel English-target language text data generated by translating the transcripts of IndicVoices data was used to fine-tune the decoder adapters on an English-to-target language MT objective. Table 2 shows the ASR word error rates (WERs) with the complete transcription data and a smaller 5-hour text data subset (described in Section 4.1) to check the comparative benefits of text-only adaptation, without any ASR fine-tuning. For most languages, using the larger text corpus led to better performance. However, the smaller parallel dataset, with significantly fewer tokens, demonstrated comparable performance to that of the complete corpus. This suggests that text-only adaptation can be effective for multilingual multimodal models, even with very limited amounts of data.

| LANGUAGE | COMPONENT FINE-TUNED | NONE | | LENGTH ADAPTER | | ENCODER ADAPTER | | DECODER ADAPTER | | LEN+ENC ADAPTER | | ENCODER ADAPTER (L) | | ALL COMPONENTS | |
|---|---|---|---|---|---|---|---|---|---|---|---|---|---|---|---|
| | LEARNABLE PARAMETERS | - | | 46 M | | 6 M | | 6 M | | 52 M | | 50 M | | 571 M | |
| | SYSTEM | A | T-A | A | T-A | A | T-A | A | T-A | A | T-A | A | T-A | A | T-A |
| MAITHILI | WER | 82.20 | 68.24 | 54.97 | 54.74 | 52.95 | 48.14 | 63.52 | 58.39 | 47.92 | 45.98 | 46.08 | **44.60** | 42.58 | 46.54 |
| | CER | 43.39 | 36.84 | 26.10 | 27.10 | 22.86 | 21.58 | 31.60 | 29.70 | 20.56 | 20.47 | 19.20 | **19.52** | 17.14 | 20.78 |
| MALAYALAM | WER | 56.15 | 55.3 | 52.82 | 52.51 | 49.71 | 50.14 | 56.03 | 53.71 | 48.22 | 48.19 | 47.81 | **47.75** | 47.38 | 45.9 |
| | CER | 20.65 | 20.43 | 18.14 | 18.87 | 15.34 | 16.35 | 20.21 | 20.00 | 14.76 | 15.46 | 14.12 | **14.92** | 13.86 | 13.38 |
| KANNADA | WER | 69.29 | 68.13 | 55.48 | 53.83 | 52.54 | 53.29 | 62.88 | 58.71 | 49.36 | 48.24 | 49.14 | **47.75** | 45.48 | 43.5 |
| | CER | 29.11 | 26.91 | 20.38 | 20.94 | 16.95 | 18.84 | 23.76 | 23.44 | 15.63 | 16.51 | 15.26 | **14.92** | 14.06 | 14.18 |
| GUJARATI | WER | 41.03 | 35.45 | 33.91 | 34.41 | 29.20 | **27.72** | 38.88 | 35.53 | 28.03 | 27.73 | 28.09 | 27.90 | 25.56 | 26.31 |
| | CER | 24.50 | 18.66 | 16.40 | 17.41 | 11.96 | **12.05** | 19.28 | 17.80 | 12.63 | 12.35 | 12.00 | 12.50 | 11.28 | 11.67 |
| ODIA | WER | 42.81 | 38.39 | 35.48 | 34.99 | 32.03 | 32.97 | 38.55 | 36.24 | 30.09 | 31.18 | 30.04 | **28.92** | 30.54 | 30.17 |
| | CER | 17.38 | 16.22 | 13.75 | 14.62 | 10.57 | 11.25 | 14.50 | 14.57 | 10.11 | 11.32 | 10.01 | **9.92** | 10.37 | 10.30 |
| BENGALI | WER | 37.70 | 35.44 | 35.90 | 35.09 | 29.65 | 28.77 | 38.10 | 35.60 | 29.96 | **28.50** | 29.30 | 31.92 | 28.12 | 27.62 |
| | CER | 18.44 | 17.73 | 17.08 | 17.22 | 12.76 | 12.58 | 18.59 | 17.72 | 13.06 | **12.38** | 12.52 | 14.63 | 12.12 | 11.91 |

Table 3: **Parameter-efficient Adaptation Results:** Comparison of WER (%) and CER (%) between different parameter-efficient adaptation methods for SeamlessM4T. System A refers to pure ASR fine-tuning, while system T-A refers to text-only adaptation followed by ASR fine-tuning. The best results for System A are underlined while the best results for System T-A are in **bold** for every language. The overall best results have been highlighted .

Moreover, text-only adaptation can be combined with ASR fine-tuning using labeled speech. We refer to the resulting ASR system with text-only adaptation, followed by ASR fine-tuning, as *System T-A*. Table 3 shows our overall results comparing System A and System T-A. We observe that text-only adaptation followed by ASR fine-tuning is more beneficial than pure ASR fine-tuning, as in System A. The trends of System T-A matched those of System A, with the larger encoder adaptation showing the best performance across all languages except Bengali, the only high-resource language in our study. This suggests that for low-resource languages with limited text and speech data, the most effective strategy is to first use text-only decoder adaptation, followed by speech-based encoder adaptation. It must also be noted that the results of using this strategy are comparable to those after full ASR fine-tuning of the entire model, with a $>90\%$ reduction in the number of trainable parameters, from 571M to 50M.

### 5.3 Cross-lingual Transfer

We hypothesize that the length adapter could capture content-agnostic prosodic characteristics of a language without overfitting on its syntax. Consequently, fine-tuning this adapter using data from a closely related high-resource language might enhance the model's predictions for a low-resource target language. The target languages chosen for this experiment were Maithili and Odia, categorized as zero-shot and low-resource languages for SeamlessM4T, respectively. Bengali, a language belonging to the same Eastern Indo-Aryan language family (Eberhard et al., 2020) as Maithili and Odia, was selected as the high-resource *pivot*. To further justify our choice of the pivot, we examined the genetic distance between the pivot and target languages using lang2vec (Malaviya et al., 2017). Genetic distance (Bjerva et al., 2019) refers to the measure of divergence between languages based on their evolutionary relationship. The results showed that Bengali was quantifiably close to both target languages. The labeled Bengali speech was used to fine-tune the length adapter and encoder adapters individually and in combination. Separately, Kannada speech was used for length adapter fine-tuning to check if any benefits are obtained with an unrelated language. We also combined this with the text-only adaptation of target language text data to check if both approaches complement each other. Table 4 summarizes the performance of the cross-lingual systems with both the target low-resource languages. Length adapter fine-tuning outperforms encoder adaptation for cross-lingual transfer.

| LANGUAGE 1 (TARGET) | LANGUAGE 2 (ASR FINE-TUNING) | GENETIC DISTANCE | TEXT- ONLY ADAPTATION | ASR FINE-TUNED COMPONENT | NUMBER OF PARAMETERS | WER | CER |
|---|---|---|---|---|---|---|---|
| MAITHILI | NONE | - | NO | NONE | - | 82.2 | 43.39 |
| | BENGALI | 0.625 | NO | LENGTH ADAPTER | 46M | 79.77 | 40.04 |
| | | | NO | ENCODER ADAPTER | 50M | 81.81 | 41.61 |
| | | | NO | LEN. + ENC. ADAPTER | 52M | 80.81 | 40.44 |
| | | | YES | LENGTH ADAPTER | 6M+46M | **72.52** | **39.31** |
| | KANNADA | 1.000 | NO | LENGTH ADAPTER | 46M | 80.29 | 38.37 |
| | | | NO | ENCODER ADAPTER | 50M | 85.25 | 41.58 |
| ODIA | NONE | - | NO | NONE | - | 42.81 | 17.38 |
| | BENGALI | 0.375 | NO | LENGTH ADAPTER | 46M | 41.05 | 15.07 |
| | | | NO | ENCODER ADAPTER | 50M | 43.67 | 16.03 |
| | | | NO | LEN. + ENC. ADAPTER | 52M | 42.4 | 15.27 |
| | | | YES | LENGTH ADAPTER | 6M+46M | **35.45** | **13.92** |
| | KANNADA | 1.000 | NO | LENGTH ADAPTER | 46M | 41.21 | 14.08 |
| | | | NO | ENCODER ADAPTER | 50M | 44.01 | 14.59 |

Table 4: **Results for cross-lingual transfer via ASR adaptation:** Comparison of WER(%) and CER(%) on low-resource languages with cross-lingual transfer through ASR adaptation of SeamlessM4T. The genetic distances between the (language 1, language 2) pairs suggest that Bengali is related to both the target languages; Kannada, despite being an Indic language, is genetically unrelated to both Maithili and Odia.

Additionally, we obtained an overall 17% reduction in relative WER for Odia, compared to the base model, by inserting decoder adapters fine-tuned on target language text data into the model whose length adapter was fine-tuned on Bengali ASR data. Thus, for low-resource languages without any speech data, ASR performance may be boosted by length adapter fine-tuning with a closely related pivot language coupled with text adaptation.

## 6 Discussion

We observe that for decoder adapters, it is more beneficial to use text-only adaptation compared to ASR-based training; the latter's benefit is mainly derived via the encoder layers. This emphasizes the role played by text data in improving the decoder's ability to enhance the internal language model of the ASR system. We also observed that 5-hour text data adaptation, having on average 92% fewer tokens than the full text, performed comparably to full-text data adaptation. This indicates that even limited amounts of text data can significantly boost ASR.

For a given target language with labeled speech, we found that fine-tuning the encoder adapters was the most accurate and parameter-efficient strategy. However, for cross-lingual zero-shot settings with no labeled data in a target language, we found it beneficial to fine-tune the length adapter with data in a related language rather than fine-tuning encoder adapters; the latter led to overfitting to the related language rather than enabling transfer to the target language. Text-based adaptation led to further improvements in the cross-lingual setting, indicating that even without speech data, ASR for low-resource languages can be improved by fine-tuning the length adapter. Lastly, a curious observation was that higher cross-lingual transfer was seen for genetically closer language pairs, with Odia-Bengali outperforming Maithili-Bengali in terms of relative WER reduction.

## 7 Conclusion

In this work, we explored the combination of parameter-efficient ASR fine-tuning and text-only adaptation techniques to enhance ASR for low-resource Indic languages using a multi-lingual multi-modal base model (SeamlessM4T). We find that a limited amount of text data was sufficient for adaptation, text-based adaptation was superior to ASR fine-tuning of decoder adapters, and encoder adapters were most effective in limited speech settings. In cross-lingual settings, however, the length adapter (and not the encoder adapter) was most successful, and text adaptation was additionally beneficial. Future work will focus on developing a better understanding of the interplay between different adapters within multimodal models.

## 8 Acknowledgements

The last author would like to gratefully acknowledge the support of the Amazon IITB AI ML Initiative and the consortium project on "Speech Technologies in Indian Languages" under National Language Translation Mission (NLTM), MeitY, Government of India.

## References


Arun Babu, Changhan Wang, Andros Tjandra, Kushal Lakhotia, Qiantong Xu, Naman Goyal, Kritika Singh, Patrick von Platen, Yatharth Saraf, Juan Miguel Pino, Alexei Baevski, Alexis Conneau, and Michael Auli. 2021. Xls-r: Self-supervised cross-lingual speech representation learning at scale. In *Interspeech*.

Junwen Bai, Bo Li, Yu Zhang, Ankur Bapna, Nikhil Siddhartha, Khe Sim, and Tara Sainath. 2022. Joint unsupervised and supervised training for multilingual asr. In *2022 IEEE International Conference on Acoustics, Speech and Signal Processing (ICASSP)*, pages 6402–6406.

Vladimir Bataev, Roman Korostik, Evgeny Shabalin, Vitaly Lavrukhin, and Boris Ginsburg. 2023. Text-only domain adaptation for end-to-end asr using integrated text-to-mel-spectrogram generator. In *Interspeech*.

Johannes Bjerva, Robert Östling, Maria Han Veiga, Jörg Tiedemann, and Isabelle Augenstein. 2019. What do language representations really represent?

Tyler A. Chang, Catherine Arnett, Zhuowen Tu, and Benjamin K. Bergen. 2023. When is multilinguality a curse? language modeling for 250 high- and low-resource languages.

Chang Chen, Xun Gong, and Yanmin Qian. 2023. Efficient text-only domain adaptation for ctc-based asr. In *2023 IEEE Automatic Speech Recognition and Understanding Workshop (ASRU)*, pages 1–7.

Yu-An Chung, Yu Zhang, Wei Han, Chung-Cheng Chiu, James Qin, Ruoming Pang, and Yonghui Wu. 2021. w2v-bert: Combining contrastive learning and masked language modeling for self-supervised speech pre-training. *2021 IEEE Automatic Speech Recognition and Understanding Workshop (ASRU)*, pages 244–250.

Seamless Communication, Loïc Barrault, Yu-An Chung, Mariano Cora Meglioli, David Dale, Ning Dong, Paul-Ambroise Duquenne, Hady Elsahar, Hongyu Gong, Kevin Heffernan, John Hoffman, Christopher Klaiber, Pengwei Li, Daniel Licht, Jean Maillard, Alice Rakotoarison, Kaushik Ram Sadagopan, Guillaume Wenzek, Ethan Ye, Bapi Akula, Peng-Jen Chen, Naji El Hachem, Brian Ellis, Gabriel Mejia Gonzalez, Justin Haaheim, Prangthip Hansanti, Russ Howes, Bernie Huang, Min-Jae Hwang, Hirofumi Inaguma, Somya Jain, Elahe Kalbassi, Amanda Kallet, Ilia Kulikov, Janice Lam, Daniel Li, Xutai Ma, Ruslan Mavlyutov, Benjamin Peloquin, Mohamed Ramadan, Abinesh Ramakrishnan, Anna Sun, Kevin Tran, Tuan Tran, Igor Tufanov, Vish Vogeti, Carleigh Wood, Yilin Yang, Bokai Yu, Pierre Andrews, Can Balioglu, Marta R. Costa-jussà, Onur Celebi, Maha Elbayad, Cynthia Gao, Francisco Guzmán, Justine Kao, Ann Lee, Alexandre Mourachko, Juan Pino, Sravya Popuri, Christophe Ropers, Safiyyah Saleem, Holger Schwenk, Paden Tomasello, Changhan Wang, Jeff Wang, and Skyler Wang. 2023. Seamlessm4t: Massively multilingual & multimodal machine translation.

David M. Eberhard, Gary F. Simons, and Charles D. Fennig, editors. 2020. *Ethnologue: Languages of the World*, 23 edition. SIL International, Dallas, Texas.

Jay Gala, Pranjal A Chitale, A K Raghavan, Varun Gumma, Sumanth Doddapaneni, Aswanth Kumar M, Janki Atul Nawale, Anupama Sujatha, Ratish Puduppully, Vivek Raghavan, Pratyush Kumar, Mitesh M Khapra, Raj Dabre, and Anoop Kunchukuttan. 2023. Indictrans2: Towards high-quality and accessible machine translation models for all 22 scheduled indian languages. *Transactions on Machine Learning Research*.

Zeyu Han, Chao Gao, Jinyang Liu, Jeff Zhang, and Sai Qian Zhang. 2024. Parameter-efficient fine-tuning for large models: A comprehensive survey.

Dan Hendrycks and Kevin Gimpel. 2023. Gaussian error linear units (gelus).

Wenxin Hou, Yidong Wang, Shengzhou Gao, and Takahiro Shinozaki. 2021. Meta-adapter: Efficient cross-lingual adaptation with meta-learning. In *ICASSP2021*, pages 7028–7032.

Wenxin Hou, Han Zhu, Yidong Wang, Jindong Wang, Tao Qin, Renjun Xu, and Takahiro Shinozaki. 2022. Exploiting adapters for cross-lingual low-resource speech recognition. *IEEE/ACM Trans. Audio, Speech and Lang. Proc.*, 30:317–329.

Neil Houlsby, Andrei Giurgiu, Stanislaw Jastrzebski, Bruna Morrone, Quentin Laroussilhe, Andrea Gesmundo, Mona Attariyan, and Sylvain Gelly. 2019. Parameter-efficient transfer learning for nlp.

Wei-Ning Hsu, Benjamin Bolte, Yao-Hung Hubert Tsai, Kushal Lakhotia, Ruslan Salakhutdinov, and Abdelrahman Mohamed. 2021. Hubert: Self-supervised speech representation learning by masked prediction of hidden units. *IEEE/ACM Trans. Audio, Speech and Lang. Proc.*, 29:3451–3460.

Edward J. Hu, Yelong Shen, Phillip Wallis, Zeyuan Allen-Zhu, Yuanzhi Li, Shean Wang, Lu Wang, and Weizhu Chen. 2021. Lora: Low-rank adaptation of large language models.

Qing Hu, Yan Zhang, Xianlei Zhang, Zongyu Han, and Xiuxia Liang. 2024. Language fusion via adapters for low-resource speech recognition. *Speech Communication*, 158:103037.

Hirofumi Inaguma, Sravya Popuri, Ilia Kulikov, Peng-Jen Chen, Changhan Wang, Yu-An Chung, Yun Tang, Ann Lee, Shinji Watanabe, and Juan Pino. 2023. UnitY: Two-pass direct speech-to-speech translation with discrete units. In *Proceedings of the 61st Annual Meeting of the Association for Computational Linguistics (Volume 1: Long Papers)*, pages 15655–15680, Toronto, Canada. Association for Computational Linguistics.

Tahir Javed, Janki Nawale, Eldho George, Sakshi Joshi, Kaushal Bhogale, Deovrat Mehendale, Ishvinder Sethi, Aparna Ananthanarayanan, Hafsah Faquih, Pratiti Palit, Sneha Ravishankar, Saranya Sukumaran, Tripura Panchagnula, Sunjay Murali, Kunal Gandhi, Ambujavalli R, Manickam M, C Vaijayanthi, Krishnan Karunganni, Pratyush Kumar, and Mitesh Khapra. 2024. IndicVoices: Towards building an inclusive multilingual speech dataset for Indian languages. In *Findings of the Association for Computational Linguistics ACL 2024*, pages 10740–10782, Bangkok, Thailand and virtual meeting. Association for Computational Linguistics.

Anjuli Kannan, Arindrima Datta, Tara Sainath, Eugene Weinstein, Bhuvana Ramabhadran, Ankur Bapna, Zhifeng Chen, and Seungji Lee. 2019. Large-scale multilingual speech recognition with a streaming end-to-end model.

Samuel Kessler, Bethan Thomas, and Salah Karout. 2021. Continual-wav2vec2: an application of continual learning for self-supervised automatic speech recognition. *ArXiv*, abs/2107.13530.

Shreya Khare, Ashish Mittal, Anuj Diwan, Sunita Sarawagi, Preethi Jyothi, and Samarth Bharadwaj. 2021. Low Resource ASR: The Surprising Effectiveness of High Resource Transliteration. In *Proc. Interspeech 2021*, pages 1529–1533.

Jungil Kong, Jaehyeon Kim, and Jaekyoung Bae. 2020. Hifi-gan: generative adversarial networks for efficient and high fidelity speech synthesis. In *Proceedings of the 34th International Conference on Neural Information Processing Systems*, NIPS '20, Red Hook, NY, USA. Curran Associates Inc.

Yunpeng Liu, Xukui Yang, and Dan Qu. 2024. Exploration of whisper fine-tuning strategies for low-resource asr. *EURASIP Journal on Audio, Speech, and Music Processing*, 2024.

Alexandre Magueresse, Vincent Carles, and Evan Heetderks. 2020. Low-resource languages: A review of past work and future challenges.

Julia Mainzinger and Gina-Anne Levow. 2024. Fine-tuning ASR models for very low-resource languages: A study on mvskoke. In *Proceedings of the 62nd Annual Meeting of the Association for Computational Linguistics (Volume 4: Student Research Workshop)*, pages 170–176, Bangkok, Thailand. Association for Computational Linguistics.

Chaitanya Malaviya, Graham Neubig, and Patrick Littell. 2017. Learning language representations for typology prediction. In *Conference on Empirical Methods in Natural Language Processing (EMNLP)*, Copenhagen, Denmark.

Ashish Mittal, Sunita Sarawagi, and Preethi Jyothi. 2023. In-situ text-only adaptation of speech models with low-overhead speech imputations. In *The Eleventh International Conference on Learning Representations*.

Minheng Ni, Haoyang Huang, Lin Su, Edward Cui, Taroon Bharti, Lijuan Wang, Jianfeng Gao, Dongdong Zhang, and Nan Duan. 2021. M3p: Learning universal representations via multitask multilingual multimodal pre-training.

Vineel Pratap, Qiantong Xu, Anuroop Sriram, Gabriel Synnaeve, and Ronan Collobert. 2020. Mls: A large-scale multilingual dataset for speech research. In *Interspeech 2020*, interspeech-2020. ISCA.

Paul K. Rubenstein, Chulayuth Asawaroengchai, Duc Dung Nguyen, Ankur Bapna, Zalán Borsos, Félix de Chaumont Quitry, Peter Chen, Dalia El Badawy, Wei Han, Eugene Kharitonov, Hannah Muckenhirn, Dirk Padfield, James Qin, Danny Rozenberg, Tara Sainath, Johan Schalkwyk, Matt Sharifi, Michelle Tadmor Ramanovich, Marco Tagliasacchi, Alexandru Tudor, Mihajlo Velimirović, Damien Vincent, Jiahui Yu, Yongqiang Wang, Vicky Zayats, Neil Zeghidour, Yu Zhang, Zhishuai Zhang, Lukas Zilka, and Christian Frank. 2023. Audiopalm: A large language model that can speak and listen.

Steffen Schneider, Alexei Baevski, Ronan Collobert, and Michael Auli. 2019. wav2vec: Unsupervised pre-training for speech recognition.

NLLB Team, Marta R. Costa-jussà, James Cross, Onur Çelebi, Maha Elbayad, Kenneth Heafield, Kevin Heffernan, Elahe Kalbassi, Janice Lam, Daniel Licht, Jean Maillard, Anna Sun, Skyler Wang, Guillaume Wenzek, Al Youngblood, Bapi Akula, Loic Barrault, Gabriel Mejia Gonzalez, Prangthip Hansanti, John Hoffman, Semarley Jarrett, Kaushik Ram Sadagopan, Dirk Rowe, Shannon Spruit, Chau Tran, Pierre Andrews, Necip Fazil Ayan, Shruti Bhosale, Sergey Edunov, Angela Fan, Cynthia Gao, Vedanuj Goswami, Francisco Guzmán, Philipp Koehn, Alexandre Mourachko, Christophe Ropers, Safiyyah Saleem, Holger Schwenk, and Jeff Wang. 2022a. No language left behind: Scaling human-centered machine translation.

NLLB Team, Marta R. Costa-jussà, James Cross, Onur Çelebi, Maha Elbayad, Kenneth Heafield, Kevin Heffernan, Elahe Kalbassi, Janice Lam, Daniel Licht, Jean Maillard, Anna Sun, Skyler Wang, Guillaume Wenzek, Al Youngblood, Bapi Akula, Loic Barrault, Gabriel Mejia Gonzalez, Prangthip Hansanti, John Hoffman, Semarley Jarrett, Kaushik Ram Sadagopan, Dirk Rowe, Shannon Spruit, Chau Tran, Pierre Andrews, Necip Fazil Ayan, Shruti Bhosale, Sergey Edunov, Angela Fan, Cynthia Gao, Vedanuj Goswami, Francisco Guzmán, Philipp Koehn, Alexandre Mourachko, Christophe Ropers, Safiyyah Saleem, Holger Schwenk, and Jeff Wang. 2022b. No language left behind: Scaling human-centered machine translation.

Katrin Tomanek, Vicky Zayats, Dirk Padfield, Kara Vaillancourt, and Fadi Biadsy. 2021. Residual adapters for parameter-efficient ASR adaptation to atypical and accented speech. In *Proceedings of the 2021*

*Conference on Empirical Methods in Natural Language Processing*, pages 6751–6760, Online and Punta Cana, Dominican Republic. Association for Computational Linguistics.

Shubham Toshniwal, Tara N. Sainath, Ron J. Weiss, Bo Li, Pedro Moreno, Eugene Weinstein, and Kanishka Rao. 2018. Multilingual speech recognition with a single end-to-end model. In *2018 IEEE International Conference on Acoustics, Speech and Signal Processing (ICASSP)*, page 4904–4908. IEEE Press.

A Vaswani. 2017. Attention is all you need. *Advances in Neural Information Processing Systems*.

Tyler Vuong, Karel Mundnich, Dhanush Bekal, Veera Elluru, Srikanth Ronanki, and Sravan Bodapati. 2023. AdaBERT-CTC: Leveraging BERT-CTC for text-only domain adaptation in ASR. In *Proceedings of the 2023 Conference on Empirical Methods in Natural Language Processing: Industry Track*, pages 364–371, Singapore. Association for Computational Linguistics.

Lingling Xu, Haoran Xie, Si-Zhao Joe Qin, Xiaohui Tao, and Fu Lee Wang. 2023. Parameter-efficient fine-tuning methods for pretrained language models: A critical review and assessment.

Hemant Yadav and Sunayana Sitaram. 2022. A survey of multilingual models for automatic speech recognition. In *Proceedings of the Thirteenth Language Resources and Evaluation Conference*, pages 5071–5079, Marseille, France. European Language Resources Association.

Zhongzhi Yu, Yang Zhang, Kaizhi Qian, Cheng Wan, Yonggan Fu, Yongan Zhang, and Yingyan (Celine) Lin. 2023. Master-asr: achieving multilingual scalability and low-resource adaptation in asr with modular learning. In *Proceedings of the 40th International Conference on Machine Learning*, ICML'23. JMLR.org.

Dong Zhang, Shimin Li, Xin Zhang, Jun Zhan, Pengyu Wang, Yaqian Zhou, and Xipeng Qiu. 2023. Speechgpt: Empowering large language models with intrinsic cross-modal conversational abilities.

Michael Zhang and Christopher Ré. 2024. Contrastive adapters for foundation model group robustness. In *Proceedings of the 36th International Conference on Neural Information Processing Systems*, NIPS '22, Red Hook, NY, USA. Curran Associates Inc.

Jinming Zhao, Hao Yang, Gholamreza Haffari, and Ehsan Shareghi. 2022. M-Adapter: Modality Adaptation for End-to-End Speech-to-Text Translation. In *Proc. Interspeech 2022*, pages 111–115.

# Towards Cross-Linguistic Semantic Grounding using Dictionary Graph Analysis

**Ethan Eschrich** and **Zoey Liu**
Department of Linguistics
University of Florida
Gainesville, FL
{ethan.eschrich, liu.ying}@ufl.edu

### Abstract

Previous work has explored the structure of dictionaries as directed graphs, with arcs between words when one word is used in the definition of another. We analyze the efficacy of these methodologies for analyzing semantic grounding and explore the cross-linguistic patterns of the strongly connected components of multiple monolingual dictionaries. We find that the number of sources in the condensation graph of a directed dictionary graph is roughly stable across multiple languages, and present future research directions.

## 1 Introduction

Explanatory dictionaries are an important tool for lexical semantics. However, to connect lexical meaning to real-world senses, not all meanings can be defined in terms of words; some words must be defined outside of the language in terms of sensorimotor experience. This observation is the symbol grounding problem (Harnad, 1990). Some theories, especially in cognitive semantics, solve this problem by considering specific words or concepts as fundamental within a language and cross-linguistically (e.g., Semantic Primes (Wierzbicka, 1996)). One empirical approach towards this problem is to analyze dictionary structures, modeling them as directed graphs (e.g., Kostiuk et al. (2023)).

There are two major approaches for analyzing dictionary graphs. The first approach considers Feedback Vertex Sets (FVS's) (Kostiuk et al., 2023). For a directed graph $D$, a Feedback Vertex Set is a set of vertices $F \subseteq V(D)$ such that $D \setminus F$ is acyclic. The Minimum Feedback Vertex Set Problem consists of finding an FVS that is minimum with respect to cardinality. For semantic grounding, these sets have a convenient theoretical interpretation: if words from an FVS are removed, the dictionary becomes "grounded", i.e. there are no self-referential definitions.

The second approach considers the dictionary structure through strongly connected components, or SCCs (Vincent-Lamarre et al., 2016). For a directed graph $D$, a SCC is a maximal vertex set $S \subseteq V(D)$ such that there exists a directed path in $D$ between every pair of vertices in $S$. The condensation of a graph is the graph obtained by contracting each SCC into a single vertex. SCCs partition a directed graph into equivalence classes, and the corresponding condensation graph is acyclic. Thus, the condensation graph captures the structure between groups of "equivalent" words, and the sources (i.e., vertices with no incoming arcs) represent ungrounded groups. Vincent-Lamarre et al. presented a taxonomy of the dictionary latent structure in this manner, with the sources in the condensation graph called the "core" [1], and all other non-trivial SCCs referred to as "satellites". They also analyzed the psycholinguistic correlates of the words at various levels of the latent structure, finding words in the core to be more frequent, less concrete, and learned earlier than those in the satellites. Thus, the core occupies a fundamental role in the dictionary's structure.

While FVS's can be more directly interpreted as grounding a dictionary (by removing self-referential definitions), there are major downsides. The minimum FVS Problem is NP-Hard (Karp, 1972), and the minimum sizes scale with the dictionary (Vincent-Lamarre et al., 2016). FVS's are not unique, so we must arbitrarily choose one for comparison. By contrast, the SCCs of a digraph are unique and efficient to compute. They consider groups of self-referential words, and thereby remove arbitrary choice, facilitating cross-linguistic comparison.

This study utilizes the SCCs approach to identify common structure of monolingual dictionaries

[1] Vincent-Lamarre et al. described the taxonomy in alternate but equivalent terminology.



*Proceedings of the Fourth Workshop on Multilingual Representation Learning (MRL 2024)*, pages 186–188
November 16, 2024 

to lend credence to the cross-linguistic aims of cognitive semantics theories. In contrast to prior literature that focused only on English (Kostiuk et al. 2023, Vincent-Lamarre et al. 2016) or Spanish (Pichardo-Lagunas et al., 2017), we analyze and compare English, French, German, Mandarin, Russian, and Spanish.

## 2 Methods

We acquired monolingual dictionaries[2] from the Wiktionaries for English, French, German, Mandarin, Russian, and Spanish using Wiktextract (Ylonen, 2022), based on their availability of parsed data. We limited our analyses to content words by filtering for entries with a part of speech tag of either noun, verb, adjective, or adverb, and with the Python library `stopwordsiso` to remove function words. The definitions for all word senses for each entry were tokenized and lemmatized by STANZA (Qi et al., 2020).

The dictionaries were processed into directed graphs. Each headword was treated as a vertex, and an arc was added from vertex $u$ to vertex $v$ if the wordform $u$ was included in at least one definition of $v$. For undefined words used within a definition, an arc from the lemma form was added, and if the lemma was not present, the word was excluded.

The final dictionary directed graph was preprocessed. All leaves (vertices with no outgoing arcs) were removed recursively, since they were unused in definitions and not directly relevant for the analysis. This removed all trivial SCCs. We built the condensation graph of the directed dictionary graph using the built-in function from `networkx` (Hagberg et al., 2008), and finally extracted the sources from the condensation graph.

## 3 Results and Discussion

From each of the six monolingual dictionaries, we found the condensation graphs and sources within those graphs. Table 1 presents relevant descriptive statistics, including the overall size of the dictionary graph for each language and the number of sources in the condensation graph.

Observe that, overall, the number of sources in the condensation graphs are relatively close cross-linguistically. Mandarin appears to be an outlier, with 648 sources; however, it was the smallest dictionary by far with only 25,736 words in total. Without Mandarin, the number of sources in

[2]The dictionaries were accessed on 7/20/2024.

| Language | Order | Number of Sources |
|---|---|---|
| English | 1,053,726 | 77 |
| French | 1,849,021 | 39 |
| German | 843,506 | 65 |
| Mandarin | 25,736 | 648 |
| Russian | 408,173 | 134 |
| Spanish | 746,297 | 29 |

Table 1: Number of wordforms in preprocessed dictionary graph, and number of sources in the condensation graph, for each language.

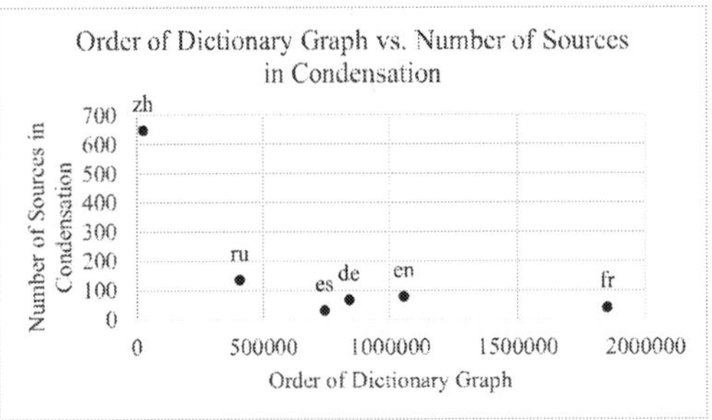


Figure 1: Scatter plot demonstrating the overall trend of fewer sources in the condensation given the order.

the remaining 5 languages have a mean of 68.8 with a standard deviation of 36.9. Also note that as the size of the dictionary increases, the number of sources declines. Additionally, the rate at which the number of sources declines with respect to dictionary size is not constant. In fact, it appears to decrease, as illustrated in Figure 1.

These results suggest that for sufficiently large dictionaries, the number of sources in the condensation graph are consistent cross-linguistically. Thus, the number of groups of "fundamental" words for grounding are similar, supporting Semantic Prime theory. While Wiktionary has large dictionary sizes, a unified format, varied selection, and accessibility, professionally curated dictionaries would provide more conclusive results. Additionally, the variation of dictionary size (Mandarin $\sim 1\%$ of English) could impact condensation graph structure; more consistent dictionary sizes, or an approach to control for the size, could improve results.

Dictionary conversion ignores undefined words and the differences of word senses, limiting both the number and reliability of connections. The conversion also ignores morphological complexity, using either the inflected wordform or solely the lemma. Morphological parsing would prevent losing inflectional information when not present within the dictionary, and help with consistency across typologically diverse languages.

## References


Aric A. Hagberg, Daniel A. Schult, and Pieter J. Swart. 2008. Exploring network structure, dynamics, and function using networkx. In *Proceedings of the 7th Python in Science Conference*, pages 11 – 15, Pasadena, CA USA.

Stevan Harnad. 1990. The symbol grounding problem. *Physica D: Nonlinear Phenomena*, 42(1):335–346.

Richard M. Karp. 1972. *Reducibility among Combinatorial Problems*, pages 85–103. Springer US, Boston, MA.

Yevhen Kostiuk, Obdulia Pichardo-Lagunas, Anton Malandii, and Grigori Sidorov. 2023. Automatic detection of semantic primitives using optimization based on genetic algorithm. *PeerJ Comput Sci*, 9:e1282.

Obdulia Pichardo-Lagunas, Grigori Sidorov, Alexander Gelbukh, Nareli Cruz-Cortés, and Alicia Martínez-Rebollar. 2017. Automatic detection of semantic primitives with bio-inspired, multi-objective, weighting algorithms. *Acta Polytechnica Hungarica*, 14(3):113–128.

Peng Qi, Yuhao Zhang, Yuhui Zhang, Jason Bolton, and Christopher D. Manning. 2020. Stanza: A Python natural language processing toolkit for many human languages. In *Proceedings of the 58th Annual Meeting of the Association for Computational Linguistics: System Demonstrations*.

Philippe Vincent-Lamarre, Alexandre Blondin Massé, Marcos Lopes, Mélanie Lord, Odile Marcotte, and Stevan Harnad. 2016. The latent structure of dictionaries. *Topics in Cognitive Science*, 8(3):625–659.

Anna Wierzbicka. 1996. *Semantics: Primes and universals: Primes and universals*. Oxford University Press, UK.

Tatu Ylonen. 2022. Wiktextract: Wiktionary as machine-readable structured data. In *Proceedings of the 13th Conference on Language Resources and Evaluation (LREC)*, pages 367–377. Almquist & Wiksell.

# Vikhr: Constructing a State-of-the-art Bilingual Open-Source Instruction-Following Large Language Model for Russian

**Aleksandr Nikolich**◇
ITMO University
alexdragannikolich@gmail.com

**Konstantin Korolev**◇
HSE University
korolevko@icloud.com

**Sergei Bratchikov**
Yandex
hivaze.me@gmail.com

**Igor Kiselev**
Accenture
igor.kiselev@accenture.com

**Artem Shelmanov**
MBZUAI
artem.shelmanov@mbzuai.ac.ae

## Abstract

There has been a surge in the development of various Large Language Models (LLMs). However, text generation for languages other than English often faces significant challenges, including poor generation quality and reduced computational performance due to the disproportionate representation of tokens in the model's vocabulary. In this work, we address these issues by developing a pipeline for adaptation of English-oriented pre-trained models to other languages and constructing efficient bilingual LLMs. Using this pipeline, we construct Vikhr, a state-of-the-art bilingual open-source instruction-following LLM designed specifically for the Russian language. "Vikhr" refers to the name of the Mistral LLM series and means a "strong gust of wind." Unlike previous Russian-language models that typically rely on LoRA adapters on top of English-oriented models, sacrificing performance for lower training costs, Vikhr features an adapted tokenizer vocabulary and undergoes the continued pre-training and instruction tuning of all weights. This not only enhances the model's performance but also significantly improves its computational and contextual efficiency. The remarkable performance of Vikhr across various Russian-language benchmarks can also be attributed to our efforts in expanding instruction datasets and corpora for continued pre-training. Vikhr not only sets the new state of the art among open-source LLMs for Russian but even outperforms some proprietary closed-source models on certain benchmarks. The model weights, instruction sets, and code are publicly available[1].

## 1 Introduction

Instruction tuning has unlocked in Large Language Models (LLMs) vast zero-shot capabilities without the need for careful prompt engineering (Ouyang et al., 2022). The most rapid research and development efforts are currently devoted to English LLMs. There has been a surge in English open-source models: Llama series (Touvron et al., 2023a,b), Mistral series (Jiang et al., 2023), Vicuna series (Chiang et al., 2023), etc. This growth is driven by the abundance of raw training data in English and dedicated efforts to create extensive sets of instruction-output pairs. Even though LLMs oriented on English have some multilingual capabilities (Zhao et al., 2024) due to the presence of small amounts of text in various languages within their training datasets (Touvron et al., 2023a), their overall performance in non-English languages remains relatively limited. Although they can usually generate portions of coherent texts, these models struggle with reasoning in non-English languages, lack culture-specific knowledge, and are highly inefficient in terms of tokenization. This inefficiency stems from how byte-pair tokenization algorithms operate, as they break down infrequent words into multiple tokens. Since multilingual data typically represents a small portion of the training dataset, non-English words are often split into many pieces. As a result, this increases the number of steps during prompt processing and text generation, reduces the effective context window, and ultimately degrades overall performance (Tikhomirov and Chernyshev, 2023; Petrov et al., 2024). This disparity places non-English languages at a disadvantage.

There is also a research direction focused on developing multilingual LLMs designed to perform well across multiple popular languages: BLOOMz (Muennighoff et al., 2023), mGPT (Shliazhko et al., 2022), Bactrian-X (Li et al., 2023), PALO (Maaz et al., 2024), Aya101 from CohereAI (Üstün et al., 2024), etc. These models are typically trained on rich multilingual datasets and are less skewed towards English. However, when aiming to perform well across multiple languages simultaneously, these models must still share their vocab-

◇ Equal contribution
[1]https://huggingface.co/Vikhrmodels



*Proceedings of the Fourth Workshop on Multilingual Representation Learning (MRL 2024)*, pages 189–199
November 16, 2024 

ulary and parameters. This often hinders their performance for each particular language in isolation, especially for the popular smaller model sizes, such as 7B and 13B.

The aim of maximizing the LLM performance for a specific language within a certain number of parameters has led researchers to develop bilingual LLMs (Sengupta et al., 2023; Pieri et al., 2024; Faysse et al., 2024). These LLMs prioritize a regional language, e.g. Jais(Sengupta et al., 2023) focuses on Arabic, but they are trained also on English data. The inclusion of English data in pre-training alongside regional language data is motivated by the significantly larger volume of English data available. This helps LLMs substantially enhance skills such as logical and common sense reasoning, which are also applied when generating text in a regional language. Bilingual LLMs is a perspective direction as they can remain small and efficient, but at the same time comprehensively capture linguistic nuances and cultural contexts of the regional language.

This work seeks to develop a pipeline for adapting English LLMs to other languages facilitating the development of bilingual LLMs. Specifically, we aim to build an instruction-following bilingual LLM for Russian and English that could be used for multilingual natural language processing research.

Russian is one of the high-resource languages and is typically represented in multilingual LLMs. Additionally, there are several proprietary closed-source LLMs, such as MTS AI, GigaChat, and YandexGPT, that meet or even surpass their English-oriented flagship competitors when it comes to text processing and generation in Russian. However, controllable research often requires white-box access to LLM logits and layer outputs, the ability to modify weights and model architecture, and consistent answers for reproducibility, which is often impossible in closed-source LLMs due to their constant development and retirement. There are only a few open-source LLMs designed for Russian: Saiga (Gusev, 2023), ruGPT (AI Forever, 2022), ruadapt (Tikhomirov and Chernyshev, 2023), and some others. Of these, only Saiga and ruadapt are instruction-tuned. We aim to fill the lack of instruction-tuned open-source LLM for Russian that is both efficient and effective.

Building even a small LLM tailored to a specific language from scratch demands a lot of computational resources. Consequently, many researchers opt to fine-tune LoRA adapters (Hu et al., 2021) for English-oriented LLMs using some language-specific data. While this approach can improve model generation quality, it does not address computational inefficiency because the tokenizer and model vocabulary remain unchanged. In contrast, our approach not only fine-tunes a base LLM on Russian language data but also reconstructs its underlying tokenizer and vocabulary, alongside suggesting an improved method for continued pre-training. Additionally, we have significantly expanded the available Russian datasets for instruction tuning. The developed LLM achieves state-of-the-art results for the Russian language among other open-source counterparts across a wide range of benchmarks.

Contributions of the paper are the following:

- We have developed a pipeline for adapting English-oriented LLMs to other languages. The pipeline implements vocabulary adaptation, continued pre-training with regularization to prevent "catastrophic forgetting", and instruction tuning.
- Using the pipeline, we have constructed Vikhr – a state-of-the-art open-source instruction-following LLM oriented on the Russian language. In addition to its high generation quality, Vikhr features an efficient tokenizer that enables rapid text generation and good context utilization.
- We have expanded the datasets for continued pre-training of Russian language models and previously available instruction datasets.
- We have constructed two evaluation benchmarks for Russian LLMs by translating the English MMLU (Hendrycks et al., 2020) and MMLU-pro (Wang et al., 2024b) benchmarks.
- We conducted an extensive evaluation of several open-source LLMs on evaluation benchmarks for Russian, demonstrating that Vikhr achieves new state-of-the-art results. Ablation studies confirm the effectiveness and validity of the individual components within our LLM adaptation pipeline.

## 2 Related Work

One of the first prominent series of generative LLMs for Russian is ruGPT (AI Forever, 2022; Zmitrovich et al., 2023). The authors developed several models, trained on the standard language modeling task, with sizes reaching up to 13 billion parameters. These models were created from the scratch and trained on a large Russian corpus, enabling them to capture the linguistic nuances of Russian more effectively than multilingual models. Additionally, since the training data was mostly in Russian, these models also have efficient tokenization. However, the lack of multilingual data (e.g. in English) limits their performance. Notably, the ruGPT models are not instruction-tuned.

Gusev (2023) suggests to leverage reasoning capabilities of existing English-oriented LLMs and adapt them to the Russian language by training LoRA adapters. They created an Alpaca-like set of Russian instruction-output pairs and performed instruction tuning on it. As a result, they have established the series of models called Saiga, which demonstrate the competitive performance and used to be a reasonable choice for an off-the-shelf open-source Russian LLMs for the past years. However, the tokenizer in these models is not adapted, so they experience issues with the context size and computational efficiency.

Tikhomirov and Chernyshev (2023) address these issues in Saiga. In addition to model tuning on Russian data, they also adapted the model tokenizer. They note that improving tokenization helps to both enhance the efficiency of the model and its performance while reducing memory consumption. However, during continued pre-training, the authors freezed the model weights, except for LM heads and token embeddings, which leads to the suboptimal performance.

In this work, we take advantage of pre-trained English-oriented LLMs, adapt LLM tokenizer for better computational and contextual efficiency, leverage continued pre-training on vast Russian-language corpora with regularization for preventing "catastrophic forgetting", construct a novel extended set of Russian instruction-output pairs, and perform instruction tuning. The created LLM adaptation pipeline along with the data for continued pre-training and instruction tuning enables Vikhr to achieve new state-of-the-art results for Russian, maintain high performance for English, and demonstrate high computational efficiency.

## 3 LLM Construction Pipeline

The construction of Vikhr starts from one of the English-oriented LLMs. In this work, we discuss the Vikhr model based on Mistral 7B (Jiang et al., 2023). The strong logical and common-sense reasoning capabilities, as well as the extensive world knowledge present in Mistral LLMs provide an excellent starting point for our model. These features partially transfer to Vikhr, enhancing its performance in generating text in Russian. The process of the LLM adaptation to Russian starts with the vocabulary adaptation. Then we perform continued pre-training of the LLM on large Russian datasets to mitigate the vocabulary shift and introduce culture specific knowledge. Finally, we perform fine-tuning of Vikhr on a set of instruction-output pairs in Russian.

| Content | Length | Tokenization Result |
|---|---|---|
| Original Sentence | 31 | (ru) Машинное обучение изменяет мир [(en) Machine learning changes the world. |
| Mistral Tokenizer | 13 | ['Ма', 'шин', 'ное', 'об', 'у', 'чение', 'из', 'мен', 'я', 'ет', 'ми', i 'р' ] |
| Vikhr Tokenizer | 7 | ['Ма', 'шин', 'ное', 'обучение', 'изменяет', 'мир'] |

Table 1: A comparison of tokenization between the original Mistral model and Vikhr.

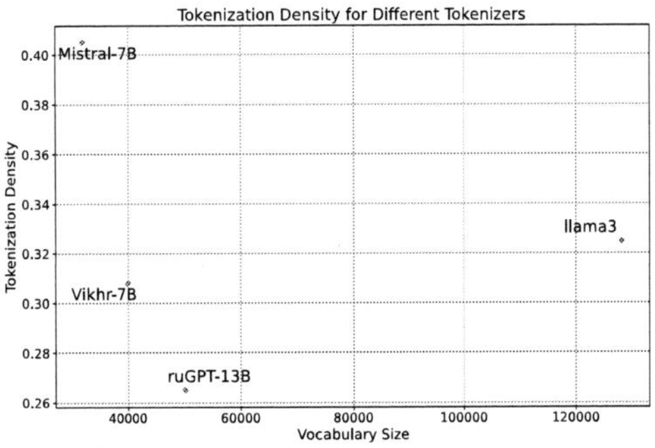


Figure 1: The efficiency of the Vikhr tokenizer for Russian in comparison to tokenizers of other models.

### 3.1 Vocabulary Adaptation

The big drawback of English-oriented LLMs is that each Russian word would be split into multiple tokens: a common case is when symbols in the word become individual tokens (see example in Table 1). This slows down the generation by multiple times, reduces the amount of information that could be stored in the context, and drastically hurts the generation quality.

To mitigate this problem in Vikhr, we adopt the approach suggested in (Cui et al., 2023;

| Data Source | Approx. size (GB) | Tokens (Billion) |
|---|---|---|
| Scientific papers | 20 | 2.5 |
| News articles | 4 | 1 |
| Wikipedia | 25 | 4 |
| Habr | 6 | 1 |
| Other sources | 20 | 2.5 |

Table 2: The statistics of the Russian-language datasets for continued pre-training.

Tikhomirov and Chernyshev, 2023), where authors rebuild the tokenizer using a language-specific corpus. In particular, we trained a SentencePiece tokenizer (Kudo and Richardson, 2018) with a 40k vocabulary on the RuLM dataset (Gusev, 2023). As can be seen from Figure 1, the resulting tokenizer for Russian is much more efficient than the tokenizer of the original English-oriented model.

### 3.2 Continued Pre-training

The new vocabulary requires new embedding matrices and LM heads. The tokens that were present in the original vocabulary are initialized with the old embeddings, the new tokens are initialized by averaging the embeddings of their pieces in the original embedding matrix (Hewitt, 2021). The similar approach is also applied to LM heads. Training models with these modifications demands much more computational resources than the mainstream method of adapting LLMs to new languages using LoRA adapters (Hu et al., 2021). This is because it involves continued pre-training of the entire model and requires much more language-specific data to mitigate the shift in the vocabulary.

The dataset for continued pre-training is constructed from high-quality sources, including Russian Wikipedia, news articles, scientific papers from peer-reviewed journals and conferences, and top 100k up-voted posts on Habr – a popular online blog community focused on technology, software development, and science. The statistics of these datasets is presented in Table 2. We performed deduplication of the collection on the level of paragraphs using the MIHash algorithm (Cakir et al., 2017). Furthermore, we performed filtration of the collected data. For this purpose, we annotated 20k documents using GPT-4-turbo with the aim to assess their informativeness, usefulness for studying, grammatical correctness, style, and safety. Using these annotations, we fine-tuned a RuBERT-tiny(Dale, 2021) filtration model and applied it to the deduplicated corpus. After filtration, the total number of tokens left for continued pre-training is 11 billion.

| Hyperparam. | Value |
|---|---|
| LR | $1 \times 10^{-3}$ |
| AdamW eps | $1 \times 10^{-8}$ |
| Num warmup steps | 10 |
| AdamW betas | 0.99, 0.95 |
| Accumulation steps | 128 |
| Batch size | 3 |
| Epochs | 1 |
| Sequence length | 1024 |

Table 3: The hyperparameters for continued pre-training.

We observed that continued pre-training of a LLM can partially diminish the reasoning capabilities present in the original English-oriented model, significantly impacting overall performance. In our preliminary experiments, a model that underwent continued pre-training may demonstrate even worse performance on Russian benchmarks than the original English-oriented model. To alleviate this "catastrophic forgetting" in reasoning, we use the loss regularization with the KL penalty between the probability distribution of Vikhr and the reference English-oriented LLM:

$$L_{\text{Vikhr}} = L_{\text{CE}} + KL\left(P_{\text{Vikhr}} \| P_{\text{Ref}}\right). \quad (1)$$

In practice, we implement the regularization using the SLERP interpolation of model losses (Goddard et al., 2024).

To speed up the process of continued pre-training, we use an optimized Flash attention implementation[2]. As an optimization algorithm, we leverage AdamW, as it trades some memory efficiency in favor of robustness to the hyperparameter choice. The hyperparameters used for continued pre-training are presented in Table 3.

### 3.3 Instruction Tuning

Instruction tuning is an essential step in reaching high zero-shot performance with LLMs. It also allows to obtain a more natural communication with the model without complex prompting. Further fine-tuning techniques such as RLHF (Ouyang et al., 2022) or DPO (Rafailov et al., 2024), which require input from the assessors, are also crucial for such tasks as multicriteria alignment. However, the most significant performance gains are

[2] https://huggingface.co/docs/optimum/bettertransformer/tutorials/convert

still achieved through instruction tuning (Jha et al., 2023).

Previously, Gusev (2023) constructed an open-source set of instruction-output pairs for the Russian language (Saiga). The core Saiga dataset was created similar to Alpaca by querying ChatGPT (gpt-3.5-turbo) (Taori et al., 2023). In this work, we extend this set by translating two English instruction datasets. First, we translated instructions for the FLAN model (Wei et al., 2021) and generated answers in Russian using ChatGPT. Originally, FLAN instructions were constructed automatically from annotated datasets using templates to facilitate multitask and zero-shot capabilities of seq2seq models. Later, it was shown that this data also helps to improve decoder-only chat-oriented models as well. Second, we construct Veles[3] by translating the English OpenHermes (Teknium, 2023) instruction dataset. Third, we incroporate without translation Nectar[4] (Zhu et al., 2023) – an English instruction dataset. This ensures that Vikhr maintains strong performance in English as well.

Similar to the corpus for continued pre-training, we performed deduplication of the instruction set. Since the majority of the outputs were machine generated there are many low quality outputs. To mitigate this problem, we filtered out low quality pairs using a reward model trained on human data. For the reward model, we selected the multilingual-e5-large model (Wang et al., 2024a). This model was particularly suitable for our needs due to its ability to handle multilingual data efficiently, ensuring that the classifier could accurately assess the quality of responses in both Russian and English. We trained the reward model on the answer preference dataset[5], which was collected from human-written prompts and annotated using GPT-4. By applying this reward model, we filtered out low-quality instruction-output pairs, significantly enhancing the overall performance and reliability of our instruction datasets. The statistics of the Vikhr instruction datasets is presented in Table 4.

Contrary to Saiga, we do not use LoRA adapters and just as in the phase of continued pre-training, we update all model parameters. The hyperparameters for the instruction tuning phase are presented in Table 5.

| Instruction Set | Language | # instances |
|---|---|---|
| Veles | Russian | 30k |
| Nectar | English | 50k |
| Saiga | Russian | 100k |
| ruFLAN | Russian | 500k |

Table 4: The statistics of the instruction datasets.

| Hyperparam. | Value |
|---|---|
| LR | $1 \times 10^{-5}$ |
| AdamW, eps | $1 \times 10^{-8}$ |
| Num warmup steps | 10 |
| AdamW, betas | 0.99, 0.95 |
| Accumulation steps | 64 |
| Batch size | 3 |
| Num epochs | 3 |
| Sequence length | 1024 |

Table 5: The hyperparameters for instruction tuning.

### 3.4 Hardware

Vikhr was trained on eight NVIDIA A100 GPUs 80GB. We spend approximately 1,000 GPU hours for the continued pre-training phase and 60 hours for instruction tuning.

## 4 Experiments

### 4.1 Experimental Setup

**Benchmarks.** The evaluation was performed on MMLU (En-MMLU) (Hendrycks et al., 2021), Ru-MMLU[6], Ru-MMLU-pro[7], ruXNLI (Conneau et al., 2018), CheGeKa (Mikhalkova and Khlyupin, 2022), Russian SuperGLUE (Shavrina et al., 2020), and MERA (Fenogenova et al., 2024). The MMLU (En-MMLU) benchmark assesses LLMs across 57 subjects through multiple-choice questions, measuring a model's general knowledge and reasoning abilities. We utilize this benchmark to verify that the model retains its bilingual proficiency. For this dataset, we report the accuracy@1 score. We constructed Ru-MMLU and Ru-MMLU-pro by automatically translating original English MMLU and MMLU-pro to Russian. Translation was done by GPT-3.5 and GPT-4 respectively. Just as for MMLU, for these datasets, we report the accuracy@1 score. CheGeKa is based on the questions from the Russian version of "Jeopardy" (the "Own

[3]https://huggingface.co/datasets/Vikhrmodels/Veles-2.5

[4]https://huggingface.co/datasets/berkeley-nest/Nectar

[5]https://huggingface.co/datasets/Vikhrmodels/sbs

[6]https://huggingface.co/datasets/NLPCoreTeam/mmlu_ru

[7]https://huggingface.co/datasets/Vikhrmodels/mmlupro-ru

| LLM | Pre-train on Russian | Training Method | En-MMLU | Ru-MMLU | CheGeKa | Russian SuperGLUE | MERA |
|---|---|---|---|---|---|---|---|
| MTS AI Chat 7B (closed-source) ◇ | false | sft+dpo | - | 0.689 | 0.083 | 0.56 | 0.479 |
| GigaChat-7B (closed-source) ◇ | true | sft+dpo | - | 0.67 | 0.451* | 0.71* | 0.479 |
| aya101 | false | pt+sft | 0.41 | 0.37 | 0.005 | 0.36 | 0.320 |
| Mistral-7B-Instruct-v0.2 | false | none | 0.60 | 0.78 | 0.005 | 0.57 | 0.400 |
| rccmsu/ruadapt-mistral-7b-v0.1 | false | pt+sft | 0.61 | 0.72 | 0.005 | 0.64 | 0.421 |
| rugpt13b | true | none | 0.25 | 0.25 | 0.132 | 0.52 | 0.208 |
| saiga-mistral-7b-lora | false | sft | 0.60 | 0.76 | 0.223 | 0.64 | 0.442 |
| saiga-llama3-8b | false | sft | 0.59 | 0.78 | 0.225 | 0.66 | 0.476 |
| (Ours) Vikhr-7B-instruct_0.2 | true | pt+sft | **0.62** | **0.80** | **0.231** | **0.67** | **0.485** |

Table 6: Evaluation results for Russian and multilingual LLMs. Pre-train on Russian means that the model underwent (continued) pre-training on Russian data. The following abbreviations are used: sft – instruction tuning, pt – (continued) pre-training; dpo – direct preference optimization. ◇ The results for GigaChat and MTS AI are taken from the leaderboards. The best result among open-source models is highlighted with bold, the second best is underscored. The best result among closed-source proprietary models is marked with *.

| Prompt | Answer of base Mistral-0.2-Instruct | Answer of Vikhr |
|---|---|---|
| Что такое чебурек? [What does cheburek means?] | Чебурек - это классическое dish среднеазиатской и русской кухни, которое включает в себя тонкий lavash, завернутый в форме полумесяца или кольца. Он обычно наполнен meat (говядиной, бараниной или курицей) и cheese. История чебурека начинается с древних тюркских племен, которые готовили подобные dishes из мяса и теста. ... Чебурек часто подается как горячее dish, жареное на сковороде или в духовке. Тесто обычно тонкое и хрустящее снаружи, а внутри мягкое и сочное. Мясо и сыр добавляют flavor depth и питательную ценность. | Чебурек — это традиционное блюдо кавказской кухни, которое представляет собой большой, тонкий пирог из пресного теста с мясной начинкой, обжаренный во фритюре. Внутри чебурека обычно находится сочный фарш из баранины или говядины, приправленный луком, солью, перцем и другими специями. Благодаря обжарке в масле, тесто становится хрустящим снаружи, а начинка остается мягкой и сочной. История чебурека уходит корнями в древние времена, когда кочевники готовили его на раскалённых камнях или в больших котлах с горячим маслом. |
| Расскажи на русском языке что такое хачапури [Tell in Russian what hatchapuri is] | Хачапури (хачпури, хачъапури) – это традиционное блюдо грузинской кухни. Это тип пицце или за Francia, выполненной в виде круглой или полукруглой лепёшки, покрытой верху layerм layerim – смесью тонко нарезанныximo эplesses, лука .. | Хачапури — это традиционное грузинское блюдо, представляющее собой лепешку с сыром внутри. Вот рецепт хачапури. Ингредиенты: - Для теста: - 3 стакана муки - 1 ч. л. соли - 1 ч. л. сахара - 100 мл теплой воды - Для смазывания: 1 ст. л. топленого масла ... |
| Расскажи на русском языке как приготовить уху [Tell in Russian how to cook a fish soup] | Уха (из Рыбы) – традиционное блюдо русской кухни, которое готовится predominantly из щуки или окуня. Рас**те процедуру приготовления ухи в домашних условиях: Выберите чистую рыбу. Очистить её от шерсти иICScone всех мелких костей s... | Уха — это традиционное русское блюдо, представляющее собой наваристый суп из рыбы, который варится на медленном огне. Вот базовый рецепт ухи, который можно адаптировать под свои вкусовые предпочтения. Ингредиенты: 1 кг свежей рыбы (можно использовать несколько видов, например, карп, щука, судак) 3-4 картофелины 1 крупная луковица 2-3 моркови ... |

Table 7: Comparison of texts generated by the base LLM Mistral-0.2-Instruct (on the left) with texts generated by our model Vikhr (on the right). Issues in the output are highlighted with red.

game"). This benchmark contains challenging open-ended questions, requiring logical reasoning and world knowledge. It includes 29,376 training and 416 test instances. The reported evaluation metric is the F1 score. Russian SuperGLUE is a benchmark similar to well-known English SuperGLUE (Wang et al., 2019). It tests LLMs on various natural language understanding tasks like reading comprehension and textual entailment. The metric reported in the results is accuracy@1. The MERA benchmark encompasses 21 evaluation tasks for generative LLMs in 11 skill domains. Note that among other tasks, MERA also includes CheGeKa, RuMMLU, and one of the subtasks of SuperGLUE (RWSD). The reported evaluation metric is the total score, which is the average of scores across all non-diagnostic tasks.

**Baselines.** We compare Vikhr to six open-source and two proprietary closed-source competitors of the similar size. Open-source models: aya101 (Üstün et al., 2024) – a massively multilingual LLM from CohereAI that follows instructions in 101 languages[8], it shows state-of-the-art results among massively multilingual LLMs; Mistral-7B-0.2-instruct (Jiang et al., 2023) – an English-oriented LLM that was used as the base model for Vikhr; rccmsu/ruadapt_mistral_saiga_7b_v0.1 (Tikhomirov and Chernyshev, 2023) – a Russian-

[8]https://huggingface.co/CohereForAI/aya-101

oriented LLM that was constructed from the Mistral model using similar adaptations of the tokenizer, token embeddings, and the LM head; saiga-mistral-7b-lora and saiga-llama3-8b (Gusev, 2023) – two versions of the Saiga models based on English-oriented LLMs and obtained by fine-tuning LoRA adapters on the Saiga instruction dataset[9]. Closed-source proprietary models for Russian: MTS AI Chat[10] and GigaChat-7b. The access to GigaChat weights is closed, so the reported results are taken from the leaderboards[11]. The results of MTS AI Chat are also taken from the leaderboard[12].

### 4.2 Results in NLU Tasks

The evaluation results are presented in Table 6. As we can see, Vikhr outperforms all open-source models, including the ones that were built specifically for Russian. It also slightly outperforms its parent model Mistral on the En-MMLU benchmark, which might be the result of longer pre-training. The second place with close scores for all 4 Russian language benchmarks is obtained by the Saiga model based on recently released Llama-3. The high scores of this model probably are the result of the transfer of the outstanding performance of Llama-3. Since Saiga based on Llama-3 outperforms Saiga based on Mistral, we expect that applying our adaptation pipeline to Llama-3 would also help further improving the state of the art.

We note that the original Mistral-7B-0.2-instruct, despite being an English-oriented model, demonstrates competitive performance in 3 out of 4 Russian benchmarks. This demonstrates that such models could be viable alternatives at least for NLU tasks. The only dataset, where its performance is very low is CheGeKa, which is related to open-ended question-answering. This may be due to the lack of culture-specific knowledge, as the English-oriented model has not seen much Russian texts. Note that the MTS AI Chat also shows very low results on CheGeKa, which might also indicate the lack of culture-specific knowledge.

The proprietary model GigaChat substantially outperforms Vikhr on CheGeKa and notably on Russian SuperGLUE. We assume this is due to the use of much larger Russian datasets for pre-training. However, surprisingly, it falls behind Vikhr on Ru-MMLU. On all benchmarks, Vikhr outperforms the proprietary competitor from MTS AI.

| Vocab. Size | PPL↓ | ruXNLI↑ |
|---|---|---|
| 33k | **10.2** | 0.42 |
| 40k (underlined) | 14.4 | **0.46** |
| 60k | 16.7 | 0.43 |
| 80k | 20.4 | 0.41 |

Table 8: Performance of the intermediate Vikhr models with different vocabulary sizes after continued pre-training. The base model is LLaMa-2 7b. The vocabulary size selected for the final Vikhr model is underlined.

| | PPL↓ | ruXNLI↑ | Ru-MMLU-pro↑ |
|---|---|---|---|
| No filt. (17b tokens) | 8.4 | 0.37 | 10.2 |
| With filt. (11b tokens) (Ours) | **7.2** | **0.46** | **11.1** |

Table 9: Performance metrics with and without filtration of the corpus for the continued pre-training. Perplexity is computed on the instruction dataset.

### 4.3 Quality of Generated Text

Previous results demonstrate the performance of our model in NLU tasks. However, the performance in NLU does not always reflect the performance in text generation, as the former is based on classification and ranking capabilities of models.

To check the performance of the model in text generation, we performed qualitative analysis of LLM outputs. Table 7 compares several responses of Vikhr with outputs of the base model (Mistral-7B-Instruct-v0.2). As we can see from the presented examples, when Mistral generates Russian text, it often injects English words. Moreover, sometimes generated words consist of an English and a Russian token. From the second example, we see that Mistral also has issues with grammatical coherence. In the third example, LLM suggests to "clean a fish from fur", which illustrates the lack of understanding of word meanings in the Russian language. We also note that Mistral tends to answer in English even when the input prompt is in Russian. These issues appear very often and make the base model useless for generation of Russian texts in practical scenarios. On the considered examples, Vikhr does not demonstrate any of these problems. Texts generated by Vikhr are grammatically coherent and correct.

### 4.4 Ablation Studies

We conducted several ablation studies to demonstrate effects of various features of our model translation pipeline that allowed Vikhr to achieve high

[9]https://huggingface.co/collections/IlyaGusev

[10]https://huggingface.co/MTSAIR/multi_verse_model

[11]https://mera.a-ai.ru/ru/submits/10257

[12]https://mera.a-ai.ru/ru/submits/10290

|  | PPL↓ | ruXNLI↑ |
|---|---|---|
| No regul. | 8.1 | 0.34 |
| With regul. (Ours) | **7.2** | **0.45** |

Table 10: Performance with and without KL loss regularization during continued pre-training.

| Instruction Set | Ru-MMLU-pro |
|---|---|
| Saiga SFT | 0.21 |
| Translated Nectar | 0.20 |
| Ours | **0.27** |

Table 11: Performance of Vikhr models fine-tuned on various instruction sets. The base model is Llama-3 8b.

performance.

**Selection of the vocabulary size.** Table 8 presents the performance of intermediate Vikhr models with different vocabulary sizes after the stage of continued pre-training. We measure perplexity of the LLM on the instruction set and the performance on the ruXNLI task (Conneau et al., 2018). As we can see, perplexity increases with the vocabulary size, indicating some degradation. However, the performance on the ruXNLI dataset is not monotonic. While the results for the largest vocabulary size are lower than those for the smallest, we observe a performance peak at a vocabulary size of 40k tokens. We selected this size as it offers improvements in the final task with only a slight increase in perplexity.

**Effect of filtration of the corpus for continued pre-training** is illustrated in Table 9. As we can see, despite reducing the size of the data, performing continued pre-training on the filtered corpus results in a model with lower perplexity and substantially better scores in both considered end tasks: Ru-MMLU-pro and ruXNLI. This again highlights the importance of data quality for constructing good LLMs.

**Effect of loss regularization in continued pre-training** is illustrated in Table 10. The results show that the KL regularization introduced in our pipeline slightly reduces perplexity and substantially increases the model performance in the ruXNLI task. This shows that continued pre-training on its own might deteriorate LLM reasoning capabilities, and proper regularization helps preventing the catastrophic forgetting.

**Effect of fine-tuning on various instruction sets** is illustrated in Table 11. The results demonstrate that fine-tuning on our instruction set gives a big boost in performance on NLU tasks compared to Saiga and translated Nectar.

## 5 Conclusion

We have presented Vikhr – a new state-of-the-art open-source instruction-following bilingual LLM oriented on the Russian language. To create Vikhr, we developed a comprehensive pipeline for adapting English-oriented LLMs to other languages. The pipeline includes the adaptation of the tokenizer vocabulary, continued pre-training of the entire model, and instruction tuning. We have also constructed a new dataset for instruction tuning by expanding the Saiga dataset with automatically translated and cleaned English instruction datasets. Our extensive work enabled Vikhr to outperform the known baselines while maintaining computational efficiency.

We hope that the developed cross-lingual adaption pipeline and the published models will foster the research on LLMs and enhance the diversity of languages incorporated into research agendas.

In the future work, we plan to release in the open-source new better versions of Vikhr. At the moment, our best publicly available model is Vikhr-Nemo-12B-Instruct[13] based on Mistral NeMo. We also plan to perform cross-lingual adaption of LLMs to low-resource languages such as Belarusian, Serbian, and Kazakh.

## Limitations

We do not introduce additional restrictions to the usage of our models. However, the users must comply with the license of the base model and instruction datasets.

We do not implement RLHF / DPO fine-tuning of Vikhr due to the lack of the resources for human annotation. We expect further performance improvements from these techniques.

We do not introduce additional instruction-output pairs to facilitate LLM alignment. However, we note that the majority of the data for supervised fine-tuning of Vikhr are obtained from the ChatGPT model series, so our model partially inherits its alignment.

[13] `https://huggingface.co/Vikhrmodels/Vikhr-Nemo-12B-Instruct-R-21-09-24`

## Ethical Considerations

The development and deployment of Vikhr raise several ethical considerations that must be addressed to ensure its responsible use:

- Bias and Fairness: For developing Vikhr, we use publicly available data. Despite efforts to train Vikhr on diverse datasets, there is a risk of inherent biases in the data which may be reflected in the model's outputs. Continued monitoring and evaluation are required to mitigate any biases, ensuring fair and unbiased performance.

- Misinformation: As with any LLM, Vikhr has the potential to generate misleading or incorrect information. It is crucial to establish guidelines and mechanisms for users to verify the information provided by the model, promoting critical assessment and cross-referencing with reliable sources.

- Misuse: Vikhr can be used for malicious purposes, such as generating harmful content, spam, or deepfakes. Implementing usage restrictions and monitoring mechanisms to detect and prevent misuse is critical to safeguard against these risks.

## Acknowledgements

We thank the reviewers for their insightful comments, which have significantly improved this paper. We would like to express our sincere gratitude to **Nikolay Kompanets** for his invaluable contributions to the fine-tuning of the small models and the verification of hypotheses.

## References

AI Forever. 2022. ru-gpts: Generative pre-trained transformer models for russian. `https://github.com/ai-forever/ru-gpts`.

Fatih Cakir, Kun He, Sarah A. Bargal, and Stan Sclaroff. 2017. Mihash: Online hashing with mutual information. In *IEEE International Conference on Computer Vision (ICCV)*.

Wei-Lin Chiang, Zhuohan Li, Zi Lin, Ying Sheng, Zhanghao Wu, Hao Zhang, Lianmin Zheng, Siyuan Zhuang, Yonghao Zhuang, Joseph E. Gonzalez, Ion Stoica, and Eric P. Xing. 2023. Vicuna: An open-source chatbot impressing gpt-4 with 90%* chatgpt quality.

Alexis Conneau, Ruty Rinott, Guillaume Lample, Adina Williams, Samuel R. Bowman, Holger Schwenk, and Veselin Stoyanov. 2018. Xnli: Evaluating cross-lingual sentence representations. In *Proceedings of the 2018 Conference on Empirical Methods in Natural Language Processing*. Association for Computational Linguistics.

Yiming Cui, Ziqing Yang, and Xin Yao. 2023. Efficient and effective text encoding for chinese llama and alpaca. *arXiv preprint arXiv:2304.08177*.

David Dale. 2021. Small and fast bert for russian. [Online; posted 10-June-2021].

Manuel Faysse, Patrick Fernandes, Nuno Guerreiro, António Loison, Duarte Alves, Caio Corro, Nicolas Boizard, João Alves, Ricardo Rei, Pedro Martins, et al. 2024. Croissantllm: A truly bilingual french-english language model. *arXiv preprint arXiv:2402.00786*.

Alena Fenogenova, Artem Chervyakov, Nikita Martynov, Anastasia Kozlova, Maria Tikhonova, Albina Akhmetgareeva, Anton Emelyanov, Denis Shevelev, Pavel Lebedev, Leonid Sinev, Ulyana Isaeva, Katerina Kolomeytseva, Daniil Moskovskiy, Elizaveta Goncharova, Nikita Savushkin, Polina Mikhailova, Anastasia Minaeva, Denis Dimitrov, Alexander Panchenko, and Sergey Markov. 2024. MERA: A comprehensive LLM evaluation in Russian. In *Proceedings of the 62nd Annual Meeting of the Association for Computational Linguistics (Volume 1: Long Papers)*, pages 9920–9948, Bangkok, Thailand. Association for Computational Linguistics.

Charles Goddard, Shamane Siriwardhana, Malikeh Ehghaghi, Luke Meyers, Vlad Karpukhin, Brian Benedict, Mark McQuade, and Jacob Solawetz. 2024. Arcee's mergekit: A toolkit for merging large language models. *arXiv preprint arXiv:2403.13257*.

Ilya Gusev. 2023. rulm: A toolkit for training neural language models. `https://github.com/IlyaGusev/rulm`.

Dan Hendrycks, Collin Burns, Steven Basart, Andy Zou, Mantas Mazeika, Dawn Song, and Jacob Steinhardt. 2020. Measuring massive multitask language understanding. In *International Conference on Learning Representations (ICLR)*.

Dan Hendrycks, Collin Burns, Steven Basart, Andy Zou, Mantas Mazeika, Dawn Song, and Jacob Steinhardt. 2021. Measuring massive multitask language understanding. *Proceedings of the International Conference on Learning Representations (ICLR)*.

John Hewitt. 2021. Initializing new word embeddings for pretrained language models.

Edward J Hu, Phillip Wallis, Zeyuan Allen-Zhu, Yuanzhi Li, Shean Wang, Lu Wang, Weizhu Chen, et al. 2021. Lora: Low-rank adaptation of large language models. In *International Conference on Learning Representations*.

Aditi Jha, Sam Havens, Jeremy Dohmann, Alex Trott, and Jacob Portes. 2023. Limit: Less is more for instruction tuning across evaluation paradigms. *arXiv preprint arXiv:2311.13133*.

Albert Q Jiang, Alexandre Sablayrolles, Arthur Mensch, Chris Bamford, Devendra Singh Chaplot, Diego de las Casas, Florian Bressand, Gianna Lengyel, Guillaume Lample, Lucile Saulnier, et al. 2023. Mistral 7b. *arXiv preprint arXiv:2310.06825*.

Taku Kudo and John Richardson. 2018. Sentencepiece: A simple and language independent subword tokenizer and detokenizer for neural text processing. In *Proceedings of the 2018 Conference on Empirical Methods in Natural Language Processing: System Demonstrations*, pages 66–71.

Haonan Li, Fajri Koto, Minghao Wu, Alham Fikri Aji, and Timothy Baldwin. 2023. Bactrian-x: A multilingual replicable instruction-following model with low-rank adaptation. *arXiv preprint arXiv:2305.15011*.

Muhammad Maaz, Hanoona Rasheed, Abdelrahman Shaker, Salman Khan, Hisham Cholakal, Rao M Anwer, Tim Baldwin, Michael Felsberg, and Fahad S Khan. 2024. Palo: A polyglot large multimodal model for 5b people. *arXiv preprint arXiv:2402.14818*.

Elena Mikhalkova and Alexander A. Khlyupin. 2022. Russian jeopardy! data set for question-answering systems. In *Proceedings of the Thirteenth Language Resources and Evaluation Conference*, pages 508–514, Marseille, France. European Language Resources Association.

Niklas Muennighoff, Thomas Wang, Lintang Sutawika, Adam Roberts, Stella Biderman, Teven Le Scao, M Saiful Bari, Sheng Shen, Zheng Xin Yong, Hailey Schoelkopf, et al. 2023. Crosslingual generalization through multitask finetuning. In *The 61st Annual Meeting Of The Association For Computational Linguistics*.

Long Ouyang, Jeffrey Wu, Xu Jiang, Diogo Almeida, Carroll Wainwright, Pamela Mishkin, Chong Zhang, Sandhini Agarwal, Katarina Slama, Alex Ray, et al. 2022. Training language models to follow instructions with human feedback. *Advances in neural information processing systems*, 35:27730–27744.

Aleksandar Petrov, Emanuele La Malfa, Philip Torr, and Adel Bibi. 2024. Language model tokenizers introduce unfairness between languages. *Advances in Neural Information Processing Systems*, 36.

Sara Pieri, Sahal Shaji Mullappilly, Fahad Shahbaz Khan, Rao Muhammad Anwer, Salman Khan, Timothy Baldwin, and Hisham Cholakkal. 2024. Bimedix: Bilingual medical mixture of experts llm. *arXiv preprint arXiv:2402.13253*.

Rafael Rafailov, Archit Sharma, Eric Mitchell, Christopher D Manning, Stefano Ermon, and Chelsea Finn. 2024. Direct preference optimization: Your language model is secretly a reward model. *Advances in Neural Information Processing Systems*, 36.

Neha Sengupta, Sunil Kumar Sahu, Bokang Jia, Satheesh Katipomu, Haonan Li, Fajri Koto, Osama Mohammed Afzal, Samta Kamboj, Onkar Pandit, Rahul Pal, et al. 2023. Jais and jais-chat: Arabic-centric foundation and instruction-tuned open generative large language models. *arXiv preprint arXiv:2308.16149*.

Tatiana Shavrina, Alena Fenogenova, Emelyanov Anton, Denis Shevelev, Ekaterina Artemova, Valentin Malykh, Vladislav Mikhailov, Maria Tikhonova, Andrey Chertok, and Andrey Evlampiev. 2020. Russiansuperglue: A russian language understanding evaluation benchmark. In *Proceedings of the 2020 Conference on Empirical Methods in Natural Language Processing (EMNLP)*, pages 4717–4726.

Oleh Shliazhko, Alena Fenogenova, Maria Tikhonova, Vladislav Mikhailov, Anastasia Kozlova, and Tatiana Shavrina. 2022. mgpt: Few-shot learners go multilingual. *arXiv preprint arXiv:2204.07580*.

Rohan Taori, Ishaan Shum, Pieter Abbeel, Carlos Guestrin, and Percy Liang. 2023. Stanford alpaca: An instruction-following language model. *GitHub*.

Teknium. 2023. Openhermes 2.5: An open dataset of synthetic data for generalist llm assistants.

Mikhail Tikhomirov and Daniil Chernyshev. 2023. Impact of tokenization on llama russian adaptation. *arXiv preprint arXiv:2312.02598*.

Hugo Touvron, Thibaut Lavril, Gautier Izacard, Xavier Martinet, Marie-Anne Lachaux, Timothée Lacroix, Baptiste Rozière, Naman Goyal, Eric Hambro, Faisal Azhar, et al. 2023a. Llama: Open and efficient foundation language models. *arXiv preprint arXiv:2302.13971*.

Hugo Touvron, Louis Martin, Kevin Stone, Peter Albert, Amjad Almahairi, Yasmine Babaei, Nikolay Bashlykov, Soumya Batra, Prajjwal Bhargava, Shruti Bhosale, et al. 2023b. Llama 2: Open foundation and fine-tuned chat models. *arXiv preprint arXiv:2307.09288*.

Ahmet Üstün, Viraat Aryabumi, Zheng Yong, Wei-Yin Ko, Daniel D'souza, Gbemileke Onilude, Neel Bhandari, Shivalika Singh, Hui-Lee Ooi, Amr Kayid, Freddie Vargus, Phil Blunsom, Shayne Longpre, Niklas Muennighoff, Marzieh Fadaee, Julia Kreutzer, and Sara Hooker. 2024. Aya model: An instruction finetuned open-access multilingual language model. In *Proceedings of the 62nd Annual Meeting of the Association for Computational Linguistics (Volume 1: Long Papers)*, pages 15894–15939, Bangkok, Thailand. Association for Computational Linguistics.

Alex Wang, Yada Pruksachatkun, Nikita Nangia, Amanpreet Singh, Julian Michael, Felix Hill, Omer Levy, and Samuel Bowman. 2019. Superglue: A stickier benchmark for general-purpose language understanding systems. *Advances in neural information processing systems*, 32.

Liang Wang, Nan Yang, Xiaolong Huang, Linjun Yang, Rangan Majumder, and Furu Wei. 2024a. Multilingual e5 text embeddings: A technical report. *arXiv preprint arXiv:2402.05672*.

Yubo Wang, Xueguang Ma, Ge Zhang, Yuansheng Ni, Abhranil Chandra, Shiguang Guo, Weiming Ren, Aaran Arulraj, Xuan He, Ziyan Jiang, et al. 2024b. MMLU-pro: A more robust and challenging multi-task language understanding benchmark. *arXiv preprint arXiv:2406.01574*.

Jason Wei, Maarten Bosma, Vincent Zhao, Kelvin Guu, Adams Wei Yu, Brian Lester, Nan Du, Andrew M Dai, and Quoc V Le. 2021. Finetuned language models are zero-shot learners. In *International Conference on Learning Representations*.

Jun Zhao, Zhihao Zhang, Qi Zhang, Tao Gui, and Xuanjing Huang. 2024. Llama beyond english: An empirical study on language capability transfer. *arXiv preprint arXiv:2401.01055*.

Banghua Zhu, Evan Frick, Tianhao Wu, Hanlin Zhu, and Jiantao Jiao. 2023. Starling-7b: Improving llm helpfulness & harmlessness with rlaif.

Dmitry Zmitrovich, Alexander Abramov, Andrey Kalmykov, Maria Tikhonova, Ekaterina Taktasheva, Danil Astafurov, Mark Baushenko, Artem Snegirev, Tatiana Shavrina, Sergey Markov, et al. 2023. A family of pretrained transformer language models for russian. *arXiv preprint arXiv:2309.10931*.

# Mitigating the Linguistic Gap with Phonemic Representations for Robust Cross-lingual Transfer

**Haeji Jung[1], Changdae Oh[2], Jooeon Kang[3], Jimin Sohn[4], Kyungwoo Song[5], Jinkyu Kim[1], David R. Mortensen[6]**

[1]Korea University, [2]University of Wisconsin-Madison, [3]Sogang University, [4]GIST, [5]Yonsei University, [6]Carnegie Mellon University

## Abstract

Approaches to improving multilingual language understanding often struggle with significant performance gaps between high-resource and low-resource languages. While there are efforts to align the languages in a single latent space to mitigate such gaps, how different input-level representations influence such gaps has not been investigated, particularly with phonemic inputs. We hypothesize that the performance gaps are affected by representation discrepancies between these languages, and revisit the use of phonemic representations as a means to mitigate these discrepancies. To demonstrate the effectiveness of phonemic representations, we present experiments on three representative cross-lingual tasks on 12 languages in total. The results show that phonemic representations exhibit higher similarities between languages compared to orthographic representations, and it consistently outperforms grapheme-based baseline model on languages that are relatively low-resourced. We present quantitative evidence from three cross-lingual tasks that demonstrate the effectiveness of phonemic representations, and it is further justified by a theoretical analysis of the cross-lingual performance gap.

## 1 Introduction

Large language models have significantly advanced natural language processing, offering improved capabilities across numerous languages. However, substantial **performance gaps** remain, particularly between high-resource languages like English and the majority of the world's low-resource languages. While these gaps are partly driven by discrepancies in data availability and quality, recent studies suggest that **linguistic gaps**—potentially caused by structural and lexical differences—also contribute significantly to these disparities .

Cross-lingual transfer techniques, which aim to adapt to arbitrary target language, have shown

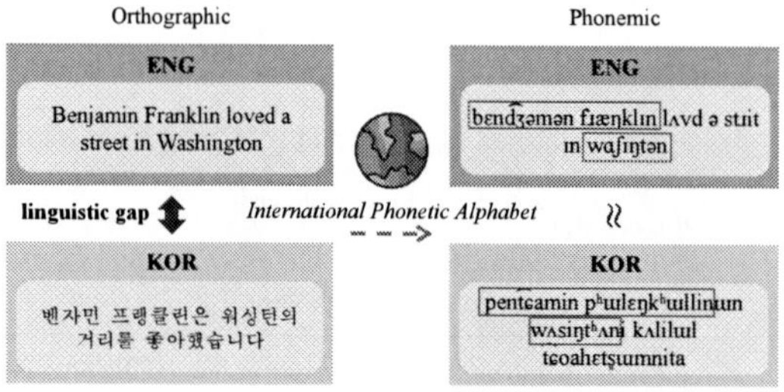


Figure 1: Example of orthographic and phonemic input representations of a sentence (English and Korean).

promise with the advancement of pre-trained multilingual language models (Devlin et al., 2019; Conneau et al., 2020; Clark et al., 2022). However, they continue to face challenges, particularly with low-resource languages. One line of prior research has focused on mitigating these gaps through cross-lingual representation alignment (Zhang et al., 2022; Wu and Monz, 2023; Stap et al., 2023), but these efforts often overlook the impact of varying input representations on performance consistency across languages.

In this work, we explore the use of phonemic representations written in International Phonetic Alphabet (IPA) characters as a robust input representation (see Figure 1) to reduce linguistic gaps and, consequently, performance gaps across languages. We define the *linguistic gap* as the representation discrepancy between embedding vectors and the *performance gap* as the relative difference in downstream task performances between languages, to analyze the impact of phonemic representations in cross-lingual adaptation.

Our empirical analysis shows that phonemic representations consistently reduce linguistic gaps between languages compared to orthographic character-based models. This reduction in linguistic gaps directly correlates with smaller performance gaps in tasks such as cross-lingual natural



*Proceedings of the Fourth Workshop on Multilingual Representation Learning (MRL 2024)*, pages 200–211
November 16, 2024 ©2024 Association for Computational Linguistics

language inference (XNLI), named-entity recognition (NER), and part-of-speech (POS) tagging, demonstrating the potential of phoneme-based models to enhance cross-lingual transfer across diverse languages. We further support these findings with theoretical analysis from domain generalization literature, where we frame the performance gap as a consequence of linguistic gaps driven by lexical and syntactic differences.

Our key contributions are as follows:

- We revisit the use of phonemic representations (IPA) as a universal input strategy to reduce performance gaps across languages in multilingual language models.
- We empirically demonstrate the effectiveness of phonemic representations by comparing them with subword and character-based models, highlighting their ability to minimize both performance and linguistic gaps.
- We provide a theoretical explanation for the observed benefits of phonemic representations, drawing parallels between linguistic gaps in multilingual settings and domain gaps in domain generalization literature.

## 2 Related Works

### 2.1 Cross-lingual Transfer with Multilingual Language Model

Cross-lingual transfer learning aims to improve performance on low-resource languages (LRLs) by leveraging data from high-resource languages. Models like mBERT (Devlin et al., 2019) and XLM-R (Conneau et al., 2020), trained on hundreds of languages, have demonstrated effective cross-lingual adaptation by leveraging large multilingual pre-train datasets (Fujinuma et al., 2022; Wu and Dredze, 2020; Conneau et al., 2020). However, significant performance discrepancies remain between languages due to differences in data availability, script types, and language families (Wu and Dredze, 2020; Muller et al., 2021a; Bagheri Nezhad and Agrawal, 2024). This "performance gap" has been systematically evaluated in benchmarks such as XTREME (Hu et al., 2020), highlighting the need for methods that can ensure more consistent performance across languages.

### 2.2 Cross-lingual Representation Gap

One approach to reducing performance gaps focuses on narrowing the representation gap between languages. Multilingual pre-training enables models to learn shared representation space for multiple languages. (Singh et al., 2019) and (Muller et al., 2021b) both analyze the representations of pre-trained multilingual models and observe that lower layers are responsible for this cross-lingual alignment. (Yang et al., 2022) employs mixup (Zhang et al., 2018) to bring representations closer together, improving performance by reducing their distance in the latent space. Other works show a strong correlation between representation distance and machine translation performance, suggesting that improved alignment leads to better transfer results (Wu and Monz, 2023; Stap et al., 2023). While these studies provide valuable insights into the benefits of aligning cross-lingual representations, they do not explore how variations in input-level representations, such as the use of phonemic representations instead of orthographic characters, might affect this alignment. This paper investigates how phonemic representations can further reduce cross-lingual gaps.

### 2.3 Phonemic Representations for Multilingual Language Modeling

Phonemes, typically represented by International Phonetic Alphabet (IPA) characters, are the perceptual sounds of a language. Phonemic representations offer a language-agnostic input that can enhance multilingual modeling, especially for LRLs. By using phonological features that are less dependent on specific orthographic systems, these representations offer a language-agnostic alternative that can help bridge performance gaps across languages. Previous studies have shown that using the IPA characters as input can enhance performance in cross-lingual tasks such as named entity recognition (Chaudhary et al., 2018; Bharadwaj et al., 2016; Leong and Whitenack, 2022) and machine translation (Chaudhary et al., 2018; Sun et al., 2022), particularly for low-resource languages. Similarly, Sohn et al. (2024) report that phoneme-based models outperform other baselines on target languages unseen during pre-training. While these works demonstrate the potential of phonemic representations in language modeling, few have explored the specific embeddings and representations of phonemes. Although some studies have developed pre-defined phoneme embeddings (e.g., PanPhon (Mortensen et al., 2016), Phoible (Moran and McCloy, 2019)) and learned embeddings from masked language modeling (Li et al.,

2023; Jia et al., 2021; Sundararaman et al., 2021; Zhang et al., 2022), there is limited understanding of how these embeddings function in cross-lingual contexts.

We utilize XPhoneBERT (Nguyen et al., 2023), a model pre-trained with phonemes across approximately 100 languages, to investigate how using phonemic representations as input can mitigate cross-lingual performance discrepancies. Our empirical and theoretical analyses provide new insights into the benefits of phonemic representations for multilingual language modeling, particularly in terms of narrowing the cross-lingual linguistic gap and performance gap.

## 3 Experimental Setup

In this section, we describe the experiment setup in terms of models, datasets, and downstream tasks, including the selected target languages and details for preprocessing. Additionally, we provide details on evaluation strategies, particularly on quantifying the performance and linguistic gap.

### 3.1 Models

We employ three masked language models that are pre-trained on multilingual corpus that covers around 100 languages from Wikipedia dump files[1]: mBERT (Devlin et al., 2019), CANINE (Clark et al., 2022), and XPhoneBERT (Nguyen et al., 2023). Each model is trained on different types of language representation.

Multilingual BERT (mBERT) is a **subword-based** model that utilizes WordPiece algorithm for tokenization. During pre-training, mBERT learns to perform masked language modeling (MLM) and next sentence prediction (NSP).

CANINE is a multilingual **character-based** model that is trained on the same corpus with the same training objective as mBERT. CANINE is a tokenization-free language model that directly maps each unicode character to its codepoint by hashing. This prevents unknown tokens, enabling the model to handle a large amount of distinct characters.

Lastly, XPhoneBERT is a **phoneme-based** model trained to do MLM. XPhoneBERT follows the pre-training scheme of XLM-R (Conneau et al., 2020), so NSP is not employed in its pre-training. This model takes as input the sequence of IPA characters, where the input data are created from original text by G2P conversion followed by phoneme segmentation.

While character-level models are known to better generalize to low-resource languages (Clark et al., 2022), their general performance falls behind subword-based models. To specifically compare input representations–phonemes versus orthographic scripts–we minimize the impact of different tokenization units by focusing on phoneme-based models versus character-based models, rather than directly comparing with subword-based models like mBERT. Nevertheless, we include mBERT results for the XNLI task to highlight its significant performance drop on low-resource languages. For other tasks, we report results from phoneme and character-based models to ensure a fair comparison, and leave further improvements of character-level models in overall performance as future work.

### 3.2 Downstream Tasks

We adopted the cross-lingual generalization benchmark tasks suggested in XTREME (Hu et al., 2020).

**Token-level Classification.** We choose **POS tagging** and **NER** as our testbed for structured prediction tasks. Both tasks require labeling each token from the model. These types of tasks were previously analyzed as being relatively independent from the data size of each language used for pre-training the language model (Hu et al., 2020). We find this particularly suitable in our scenario where two models with different pre-training strategy are compared. For datasets, we utilize the corpora from Universal Dependencies[2] for POS tagging, and WikiAnn (Pan et al., 2017) with train, dev, test splits following Rahimi et al. (2019) for NER.

**Sentence-level Classification.** XTREME supports two sentence-level classification tasks. This type of task requires semantic understanding of given sentences to make a prediction. We employ **XNLI** (Conneau et al., 2018) dataset, which is a representative benchmark for the natural language inference task on cross-lingual generalization setting. This task requires the model to classify the relation of two given sentences into three different classes.

[1]pre-trained weights are obtained from https://huggingface.co/models

[2]https://universaldependencies.org/ , v2.13, 148 languages, released Nov 15, 2023.

### 3.3 Performance Gap

We analyze performance gaps of each model for all downstream tasks. As we are interested in how different models with different input types performs consistent across languages rather than their absolute overall performance, we take the relative percentage difference (RPD) (Miller, 2011) to derive the performance gap. Here, we define RPD as

$$\mathrm{RPD}(L_i, L_j) = \frac{|\mathrm{S}(L_i) - \mathrm{S}(L_j)|}{\frac{1}{2}(\mathrm{S}(L_i) + \mathrm{S}(L_j))} \times 100, \quad (1)$$

where $\mathrm{S}(L_i)$ represents the performance for the language $L_i$. This is used to analyze the performance gap, which specifically computes the relative performance gaps across languages.

### 3.4 Linguistic Gap

To compute representation discrepancy across languages, we use FLORES+ (Costa-jussà et al., 2022) corpus which contains parallel sentences of more than 200 languages. We employ devtest set of each language subset, which contains 1,012 sentences.

After training each model on each downstream task, we utilize each model to obtain similarity in their representations. We adopt mean-pooling to obtain sentence representations and Centered Kernel Alignment (CKA) (Kornblith et al., 2019) to measure the similarity, which Del and Fishel (2021) has recommended for robust analysis on cross-lingual similarity. CKA is defined as,

$$\mathrm{CKA}(\mathbf{X}, \mathbf{Y}) = \frac{\|\mathbf{X}^T\mathbf{Y}\|_2^2}{\|\mathbf{X}^T\mathbf{X}\|_2\|\mathbf{Y}^T\mathbf{Y}\|_2}, \quad (2)$$

where features $\mathbf{X}$ and $\mathbf{Y}$ are from different languages. They are extracted from the input embedding layers as we are interested in how different input types (i.e., orthographic vs. phonemic) affect cross-lingual alignment, and Muller et al. (2021b) finds that cross-lingual alignment happens in the lower layers of the model. We use this similarity scores computed with CKA to refer to *linguistic gaps*, where smaller CKA score means larger linguistic gap.

### 3.5 Implementation Details

Models were trained for 30 epochs on a single NVIDIA A5000 GPU for POS tagging, 30 epochs a single NVIDIA A40 GPU for NER, and 20 epochs on NVIDIA A6000 for XNLI. For all experiments, batch size was set to 128 and AdamW (Loshchilov and Hutter, 2018) optimization was used. Additionally, cosine learning rate scheduler was adopted with its initial learning rate set by grid search. Learning rates used for each model on each language are in the supplementary material.

### 3.6 Data Preparation

**Languages.** To evaluate token-level tasks, we selected 10 languages with diverse typoloigical background—English(`eng`), French(`fra`), Russian(`rus`), Italian(`ita`), Hungarian(`hun`), Ukrainian(`ukr`), Korean(`kor`), Turkish(`tur`), Finnish(`fin`), and Hindi(`hin`). First four languages are high-resource languages, where English, French, and Italian are written in Latin scripts and Russian in Cyrillic. The other languages are pre-trained on each model with moderate or small amount of data, and are written in diverse scripts, such as Hangul, Cyrillic and Devanagari. For further analysis using sentence-level tasks, we chose two low-resource languages—Swahili(`swa`), and Urdu(`urd`)—to compare with a representative high-resource language, English(`eng`).

**Preprocessing.** In order to prepare inputs for a phoneme-based model, we employed G2P (Grapheme-to-Phoneme) conversion to obtain an IPA version of the input. This conversion was done with Epitran[3] (Mortensen et al., 2018) , an external tool for G2P conversion. After converting to IPA, phoneme segmentation with a python package, segments[4], to identify each phoneme. Lastly, to make it compatible with XPhoneBERT's tokenizer, white space was inserted between every phoneme.

## 4 Results and Analysis

Here, we present our observations and analyses of the results. We first discuss the behavior of phoneme-based model towards low-resource languages and writing systems, which contributes to robust cross-lingual performance. Next, we delve into the performance and linguistic gaps of phoneme-based models through empirical and theoretical analyses.

### 4.1 Phoneme-based Model on Low-Resource Languages and Writing Systems

We observe that phoneme-based model shows promising performance in low-resource languages

[3]https://github.com/dmort27/epitran
[4]https://pypi.org/project/segments/

| Method | Language | | | | | | | | | | Performance gap | | Linguistic Gap |
|---|---|---|---|---|---|---|---|---|---|---|---|---|---|
| | eng | fra | rus | ita | hun | ukr | kor | tur | fin | hin | Std. (↓) | Mean RPD (↓) | Mean CKA (↑) |
| *Named Entity Recognition* | | | | | | | | | | | | | |
| Character | 87.13 | 91.27 | 91.80 | 92.26 | 93.14 | 93.88 | 84.11 | 92.92 | 90.45 | 87.68 | 0.0316 | 4.02 | 0.4584 |
| Phoneme | 83.61 | 89.42 | 89.60 | 90.56 | 91.89 | 92.76 | 87.19 | 92.35 | 89.23 | 88.23 | **0.0259** | **3.52** | **0.7195** |
| *Part-of-Speech Tagging* | | | | | | | | | | | | | |
| Character | 96.62 | 95.54 | 87.91 | 96.06 | 74.57 | 85.79 | 86.71 | 90.49 | 91.78 | 96.81 | 0.0692 | 8.77 | 0.4593 |
| Phoneme | 95.94 | 96.35 | 86.69 | 96.37 | 85.87 | 91.32 | 85.82 | 91.11 | 93.76 | 96.94 | **0.0455** | **5.80** | **0.7204** |

Table 1: Performance of POS tagging and NER across different languages. Std. refers to the standard deviation of the scores across the languages, and Mean RPD indicates average relative difference of F1 scores between different languages. Mean CKA represents the average linguistic gap between languages.

and writing systems (scripts). Results from Table 1 show that phoneme-based model outperforms the character-based model on NER task, in languages written in scripts other than major scripts[5]—Korean and Hindi. This can be attributed to the fact that named entities, such as geopolitical or personal names, are often pronounced similarly across languages. When different writing systems and scripts are used, models may struggle to align such entities. However, representing them in IPA characters that reflect their pronunciations helps the model to better align these entities, resulting in better cross-lingual transfer. This results align with findings from Muller et al. (2021a); Sohn et al. (2024), which focus on unseen languages, whereas we observe this phenomenon with diverse 'seen' languages.

Results also demonstrates the potential of phoneme-based model in addressing low-resource languages. As shown in Table 2, the phoneme-based model achieves a smaller gap when transferred to low-resource languages such as Swahili and Urdu, compared to other baselines. This finding is further analyzed in Section 4.2

### 4.2 Performance Gap Across Languages

We observe that the phoneme-based model consistently exhibits the smallest performance gap across diverse languages, highlighting its robustness in cross-lingual tasks. In Table 1, we present the standard deviation (Std.) and average percentage difference (Mean diff.) for all models, which reflect the variability in performance across different languages. The phoneme-based model exhibits both a lower standard deviation and a smaller average percentage difference in the NER and POS

[5]Latin and Cyrillic are scripts that are used the most during the pre-training phase.

| Method | Language | | | | |
|---|---|---|---|---|---|
| | eng | swa | | urd | |
| | Acc. | Acc. | Δ from eng (Rel./Abs.) | Acc. | Δ from eng (Rel./Abs.) |
| Subword | 80.80 | 62.93 | 24.87 / 17.87 | 61.57 | 27.01 / 19.23 |
| Character | 75.02 | 59.72 | 22.71 / 15.30 | 56.55 | 28.08 / 18.47 |
| Phoneme | 71.89 | 60.88 | **16.59 / 11.01** | 56.10 | **24.67 / 15.79** |

Table 2: Accuracy (%) and relative/absolute performance gaps on XNLI task. eng, swa, and urd refer to English, Swahili, and Urdu, respectively, and relative difference is computed with RPD. Phonemic representation shows relatively small performance gaps compared to other representations.

tasks, demonstrating its relatively stable performance across different languages.

Table 2 provides additional evidence by showing that the phoneme-based model achieves a smaller gap in performance between English and other low-resource languages—Swahili(swa) and Urdu(urd)—compared to other models. We report both relative and absolute differences in performance, with the relative difference calculated as described in Section 3.3.

While subword-based mBERT achieves the highest scores, the performance gaps between models narrow when applied to low-resource languages, with outperforming the phoneme-based model by 8.91% in English and by 2.05% and 5.47% in Swahili and Urdu, respectively. This reflects subword LM's significant performance drops on low-resource languages, while highlighting the phoneme-based LM's robustness in cross-lingual transfer to such languages. The leftmost panel of Figure 3 also illustrates the performance gaps of each model, where the phoneme-based model predominantly displays lower gaps compared to others.

These metrics collectively suggest that phone-

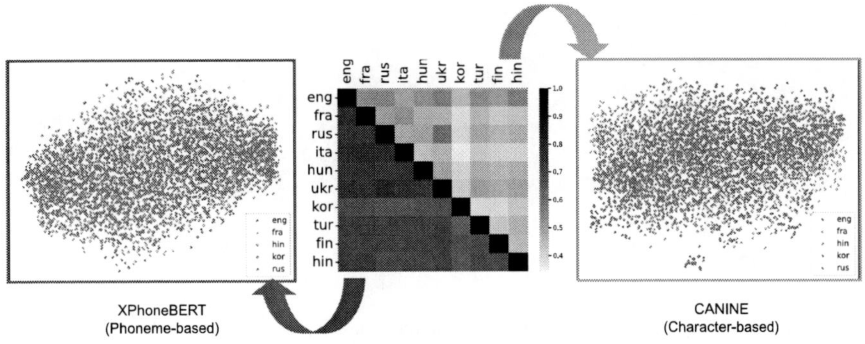


Figure 2: Linguistic gaps across languages in each model. (Center) Upper and lower triangular elements of the heatmap indicate pairwise linguistic gaps derived with character-based model and phoneme-based model, respectively. Darker color indicates larger CKA score, which means smaller discrepancy. Lower triangular elements show relatively darker colors, implying smaller discrepancies across languages of phoneme-based model. (Left, right) T-SNE plots for each model are shown with only five languages, for better visibility.

mic representations offer a more consistent performance in multilingual settings, reducing the disparities typically observed when models are applied to languages with varying resource availability.

### 4.3 Linguistic Gap of Different Representations

To investigate the potential of phonemes as a robust representation for multilingual language modeling, we analyze the linguistic gap between languages using different input representations. Following Yang et al. (2022); Muller et al. (2021b), we use linear CKA to quantify representation similarity across languages. Figure 2 shows the pairwise similarities between languages, with the lower triangle of the heatmap, which corresponds to phonemic representations, demonstrating higher similarity values. This indicates a smaller linguistic gap compared to models that use orthographic inputs, contributing to a smaller performance gap. Moreover, the t-SNE plots placed in both sides show how the distributions of the representations from different languages resemble each other. Phoneme-based model exhibits more similar distribution across languages.

Figure 3 further supports these observations by showing the linguistic gap after fine-tuning on the XNLI task. The plot in the center illustrates that phonemic representations have higher CKA scores than other baseline models, indicating closer alignment between language representations. As XNLI directly learns to build a sentence representation during fine-tuning, we extract the representation from the last hidden layer unlike in other token-level tasks. Additionally, by using Sinkhorn distance to compare the logit space, we observe that the phoneme-based model shows lower distances, reflecting more consistent predictions across languages.

These results highlight the potential of phonemic representations to address the performance gaps that challenge multilingual language models, particularly in bridging the gap between high-resource and low-resource languages by more similar representations.

### 4.4 Connecting Performance Gap and Linguistic Gap

**Correlation Analysis.** Meanwhile, one may speculate the low-performance gap of the phoneme-based model can be driven by the low English performance rather than reducing the linguistic gap. To clarify this, we simulate 15 repeated runs (with different random seeds) of phonemic representation using 10% of the XNLI train dataset over English, Swahili, and Urdu. After computing the best performance per each language, Sinkhorn distance (S-Dist), and CKA between English and the other two languages, we conducted correlation analyses by performing hypothesis tests with Spearman's rank correlation coefficient and Kendall's Tau.

As can be seen from Table 3, rather than the English performance, S-Dist and CKA have stronger correlations, indicating that the linguistic gap has stronger correlations that are statistically significant (with a significant level less than 0.01).

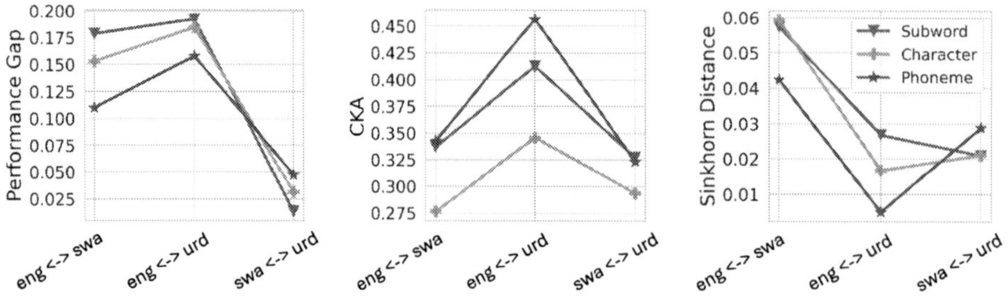


Figure 3: Qualitative analysis of performance gap (difference of accruacy) on XNLI task. (Left) the absolute difference between performance across two languages, (center) centered kernel alignment (CKA) scores to measure cross-lingual embedding similarity, and (right) Sinkhorn distance on the output probability space. Phonemic representation shows relatively small performance gaps w.r.t. eng ↔ swa and eng ↔ urd, and these gaps are correlated with similarity and discrepancy on the embedding space (CKA) and logit space (Sinkhorn distance).

| Correlation | Spearman's R | | Kendall's T | |
|---|---|---|---|---|
| | coefficient | p-value | coefficient | p-value |
| Performance Gap <-> eng Performance | 0.111 | 5.60E-01 | 0.104 | 4.30E-01 |
| Performance Gap <-> **S-Dist** | **0.681** | **3.50E-05** | **0.457** | **2.00E-04** |
| Performance Gap <-> **CKA** | **-0.782** | **3.40E-07** | **-0.577** | **2.10E-06** |

Table 3: Correlation analysis with 45 phoneme-based models. We fine-tune the phoneme-based language model XPhoneBERT on three languages, eng, swa, and urd, with 15 different random seeds and conduct two types of correlation analyses.

**Theoretical Analysis.** We aim to diminish the performance gap between different languages by adopting IPA as a universal language representation. Motivated by domain adaptation literature (Kifer et al., 2004; Ben-David et al., 2010), we present a theoretical justification of IPA for robust multilingual modeling by deriving a bound for cross-lingual performance gap.

Let $\mathcal{D}$ denote a domain as a distribution over text feature input $\mathcal{X}$, such as the sequence of word embeddings or one-hot vectors, and a labeling function $f : \mathcal{X} \rightarrow \{0, 1\}$. Assuming a binary classification task, our goal is to learn a hypothesis $h : \mathcal{X} \rightarrow \{0, 1\}$ that is expected to minimize a risk $\varepsilon_D(h, f) := \mathbb{E}_{x\sim\mathcal{D}}[\mathbb{I}(f(x) \neq h(x))]$ and has a small risk-deviation over two domains $\mathcal{D}_A$ and $\mathcal{D}_B$. Then, to formalize the cross-lingual performance gap, we first need a discrepancy measure between two languages. By following Ben-David et al. (2010), we adopt $\mathcal{H}$-divergence (See Appendix C for its definition) to quantify the distance between two language distributions.

Now, based on Lemma 1 and 3 of Ben-David et al. (2010), we make reasoning on performance gap over different language domains.

**Theorem 4.1.** *Let $h : \mathcal{X} \rightarrow [0, 1]$ be a real-valued function in a hypothesis class $\mathcal{H}$ with a pseudo dimension $\mathcal{P}dim(\mathcal{H}) = d$. If $\hat{\mathcal{D}}_A$ and $\hat{\mathcal{D}}_B$ are the empirical distribution constructed by $n$-size i.i.d. samples, drawn from $\mathcal{D}_A$ and $\mathcal{D}_B$ respectively, then for any $\delta \in (0, 1)$, and for all $h$, the bound below hold with probability at least $1 - \delta$.*

$$|\varepsilon_{\mathcal{D}_A}(h, f) - \varepsilon_{\mathcal{D}_B}(h, f)| \leq \frac{1}{2} d_{\mathcal{H}\Delta\mathcal{H}}(\hat{\mathcal{D}}_A, \hat{\mathcal{D}}_B) + 2\sqrt{\frac{d \log(2n) + \log(2/\delta)}{n}}$$

where $\mathcal{H}\Delta\mathcal{H} := \{h(x) \oplus h'(x) | h, h' \in \mathcal{H}\}$ given $\oplus$ as a xor operation (proof is in Appendix C). We see that performance gap between two lanauges is bounded from above with a distribution divergence plus an irreducible term defined by problem setup. That is, if we reduce the divergence between language distributions, the expected performance gap can also be reduced accordingly.

To investigate whether this is indeed a case or not, we provided embedding space similarity and logit-space Sinkhorn distance (Cuturi, 2013) between different languages in Figure 3. We argue that phonemic representation's relatively mild performance gap is achieved by reducing linguistic gaps which is confirmed in the embedding space (high CKA) and final output space (low Sinkhorn distance).

## 5 Conclusion

Towards robust multilingual language modeling, we argue that mitigating the linguistic gap between different languages is crucial. Moreover, we advocate the use of IPA phonetic symbols as a universal language representation partially bridges such linguistic gaps without any complicated cross-lingual training phase. Empirical validation on three representative NLP tasks demonstrates the superiority of phonemic representation compared to subword and character-based language representation in terms of the cross-lingual performance gap and linguistic gap. Theoretical analysis of the cross-lingual performance gap explains such promising results of phonemic representation.

## 6 Limitations

While we have shown that phonemic representation induces a small cross-lingual linguistic gap, therefore a small performance gap, the absolute performance of this phonemic representation is still lacking compared to subword-level models. We spur the necessity of putting research attention to developing phoneme-based LMs. Moreover, there is no such large phonemic language model beyond the BERT-base-size architecture, so we confine the scope of our empirical validation to BERT-base-size LMs. This also means the experiments rely on existing pre-trained models, limiting control over their pre-training settings. Since the models were trained on different language sets and pre-training objectives (as noted in 3.1), it is important to verify these findings in a controlled environment. Additionally, we performed evaluation with a limited languages (up to 12), so it is unclear whether IPA language representations are effective for other numerous languages (especially low-resource ones) or not.

## 7 Ethics Statement

We believe there are no potential of any critical issues that harm the code of ethics provided by ACL. The social impacts of the technology—reducing performance gaps for low resource languages—will be, on the balance, positive. The data was, to the extent we can determine, collected in accordance with legal and institutional protocals.

## Acknowledgements

This work was supported by Institute of Information & communications Technology Planning & Evaluation (IITP) grant funded by the Korea government(MSIT) (RS-2022-00143911, AI Excellence Global Innovative Leader Education Program)

## References

Sina Bagheri Nezhad and Ameeta Agrawal. 2024. What drives performance in multilingual language models? In *Proceedings of the Eleventh Workshop on NLP for Similar Languages, Varieties, and Dialects (VarDial 2024)*, pages 16–27, Mexico City, Mexico. Association for Computational Linguistics.

Shai Ben-David, John Blitzer, Koby Crammer, Alex Kulesza, Fernando Pereira, and Jennifer Vaughan. 2010. A theory of learning from different domains. *Machine Learning*, 79:151–175.

Shai Ben-David, John Blitzer, Koby Crammer, and Fernando Pereira. 2006. Analysis of representations for domain adaptation. In *Advances in Neural Information Processing Systems*, volume 19. MIT Press.

Akash Bharadwaj, David Mortensen, Chris Dyer, and Jaime Carbonell. 2016. Phonologically aware neural model for named entity recognition in low resource transfer settings. In *Proceedings of the 2016 Conference on Empirical Methods in Natural Language Processing*, pages 1462–1472, Austin, Texas. Association for Computational Linguistics.

Aditi Chaudhary, Chunting Zhou, Lori Levin, Graham Neubig, David R. Mortensen, and Jaime Carbonell. 2018. Adapting word embeddings to new languages with morphological and phonological subword representations. In *Proceedings of the 2018 Conference on Empirical Methods in Natural Language Processing*, pages 3285–3295, Brussels, Belgium. Association for Computational Linguistics.

Jonathan H. Clark, Dan Garrette, Iulia Turc, and John Wieting. 2022. Canine: Pre-training an efficient tokenization-free encoder for language representation. *Transactions of the Association for Computational Linguistics*, 10:73–91.

Alexis Conneau, Kartikay Khandelwal, Naman Goyal, Vishrav Chaudhary, Guillaume Wenzek, Francisco Guzmán, Edouard Grave, Myle Ott, Luke Zettlemoyer, and Veselin Stoyanov. 2020. Unsupervised cross-lingual representation learning at scale. In *Proceedings of the 58th Annual Meeting of the Association for Computational Linguistics*, pages 8440–8451, Online. Association for Computational Linguistics.

Alexis Conneau, Ruty Rinott, Guillaume Lample, Adina Williams, Samuel Bowman, Holger Schwenk, and Veselin Stoyanov. 2018. XNLI: Evaluating cross-lingual sentence representations. In *Proceedings of the 2018 Conference on Empirical Methods in Natural Language Processing*, pages 2475–2485, Brussels, Belgium. Association for Computational Linguistics.

Marta R Costa-jussà, James Cross, Onur Çelebi, Maha Elbayad, Kenneth Heafield, Kevin Heffernan, Elahe Kalbassi, Janice Lam, Daniel Licht, Jean Maillard, et al. 2022. No language left behind: Scaling human-centered machine translation. *arXiv preprint arXiv:2207.04672*.

Marco Cuturi. 2013. Sinkhorn distances: Lightspeed computation of optimal transport. In *Neural Information Processing Systems*.

Maksym Del and Mark Fishel. 2021. Similarity of sentence representations in multilingual lms: Resolving conflicting literature and a case study of baltic languages. *Balt. J. Mod. Comput.*, 10.

Jacob Devlin, Ming-Wei Chang, Kenton Lee, and Kristina Toutanova. 2019. BERT: Pre-training of deep bidirectional transformers for language understanding. In *Proceedings of the 2019 Conference of the North American Chapter of the Association for Computational Linguistics: Human Language Technologies, Volume 1 (Long and Short Papers)*, pages 4171–4186, Minneapolis, Minnesota. Association for Computational Linguistics.

Yoshinari Fujinuma, Jordan Boyd-Graber, and Katharina Kann. 2022. Match the script, adapt if multilingual: Analyzing the effect of multilingual pretraining on cross-lingual transferability. In *Proceedings of the 60th Annual Meeting of the Association for Computational Linguistics (Volume 1: Long Papers)*, pages 1500–1512, Dublin, Ireland. Association for Computational Linguistics.

Junjie Hu, Sebastian Ruder, Aditya Siddhant, Graham Neubig, Orhan Firat, and Melvin Johnson. 2020. Xtreme: A massively multilingual multi-task benchmark for evaluating cross-lingual generalisation. In *International Conference on Machine Learning*, pages 4411–4421. PMLR.

Ye Jia, Heiga Zen, Jonathan Shen, Yu Zhang, and Yonghui Wu. 2021. Png bert: Augmented bert on phonemes and graphemes for neural tts. In *Interspeech*.

Daniel Kifer, Shai Ben-David, and Johannes Gehrke. 2004. Detecting change in data streams. In *Proceedings of the Thirtieth International Conference on Very Large Data Bases - Volume 30*, VLDB '04, page 180–191. VLDB Endowment.

Simon Kornblith, Mohammad Norouzi, Honglak Lee, and Geoffrey Hinton. 2019. Similarity of neural network representations revisited. In *Proceedings of the 36th International Conference on Machine Learning*, volume 97 of *Proceedings of Machine Learning Research*, pages 3519–3529. PMLR.

Colin Leong and Daniel Whitenack. 2022. Phone-ing it in: Towards flexible multi-modal language model training by phonetic representations of data. In *Proceedings of the 60th Annual Meeting of the Association for Computational Linguistics (Volume 1: Long Papers)*, pages 5306–5315, Dublin, Ireland. Association for Computational Linguistics.

Yinghao Aaron Li, Cong Han, Xilin Jiang, and Nima Mesgarani. 2023. Phoneme-level bert for enhanced prosody of text-to-speech with grapheme predictions. In *ICASSP 2023 - 2023 IEEE International Conference on Acoustics, Speech and Signal Processing (ICASSP)*, pages 1–5.

Ilya Loshchilov and Frank Hutter. 2018. Decoupled weight decay regularization. In *International Conference on Learning Representations*.

Ronald E. Miller. 2011. *Optimization: Foundations and Applications*. John Wiley & Sons.

Steven Moran and Daniel McCloy, editors. 2019. *PHOIBLE 2.0*. Max Planck Institute for the Science of Human History, Jena.

David R. Mortensen, Siddharth Dalmia, and Patrick Littell. 2018. Epitran: Precision G2P for many languages. In *Proceedings of the Eleventh International Conference on Language Resources and Evaluation (LREC 2018)*, Miyazaki, Japan. European Language Resources Association (ELRA).

David R. Mortensen, Patrick Littell, Akash Bharadwaj, Kartik Goyal, Chris Dyer, and Lori Levin. 2016. PanPhon: A resource for mapping IPA segments to articulatory feature vectors. In *Proceedings of COLING 2016, the 26th International Conference on Computational Linguistics: Technical Papers*, pages 3475–3484, Osaka, Japan. The COLING 2016 Organizing Committee.

Benjamin Muller, Antonios Anastasopoulos, Benoît Sagot, and Djamé Seddah. 2021a. When being unseen from mBERT is just the beginning: Handling new languages with multilingual language models. In *Proceedings of the 2021 Conference of the North American Chapter of the Association for Computational Linguistics: Human Language Technologies*, pages 448–462, Online. Association for Computational Linguistics.

Benjamin Muller, Yanai Elazar, Benoît Sagot, and Djamé Seddah. 2021b. First align, then predict: Understanding the cross-lingual ability of multilingual BERT. In *Proceedings of the 16th Conference of the European Chapter of the Association for Computational Linguistics: Main Volume*, pages 2214–2231, Online. Association for Computational Linguistics.

Linh The Nguyen, Thinh Pham, and Dat Quoc Nguyen. 2023. XPhoneBERT: A Pre-trained Multilingual

Model for Phoneme Representations for Text-to-Speech. In *Proceedings of the 24th Annual Conference of the International Speech Communication Association (INTERSPEECH)*.

Xiaoman Pan, Boliang Zhang, Jonathan May, Joel Nothman, Kevin Knight, and Heng Ji. 2017. Cross-lingual name tagging and linking for 282 languages. In *Proceedings of the 55th Annual Meeting of the Association for Computational Linguistics (Volume 1: Long Papers)*, pages 1946–1958, Vancouver, Canada. Association for Computational Linguistics.

Afshin Rahimi, Yuan Li, and Trevor Cohn. 2019. Massively multilingual transfer for NER. In *Proceedings of the 57th Annual Meeting of the Association for Computational Linguistics*, pages 151–164, Florence, Italy. Association for Computational Linguistics.

Jasdeep Singh, Bryan McCann, Richard Socher, and Caiming Xiong. 2019. BERT is not an interlingua and the bias of tokenization. In *Proceedings of the 2nd Workshop on Deep Learning Approaches for Low-Resource NLP (DeepLo 2019)*, pages 47–55, Hong Kong, China. Association for Computational Linguistics.

Jimin Sohn, Haeji Jung, Alex Cheng, Jooeon Kang, Yilin Du, and David R. Mortensen. 2024. Zero-shot cross-lingual ner using phonemic representations for low-resource languages. *Preprint*, arXiv:2406.16030.

David Stap, Vlad Niculae, and Christof Monz. 2023. Viewing knowledge transfer in multilingual machine translation through a representational lens. *ArXiv*, abs/2305.11550.

Simeng Sun, Angela Fan, James Cross, Vishrav Chaudhary, Chau Tran, Philipp Koehn, and Francisco Guzmán. 2022. Alternative input signals ease transfer in multilingual machine translation. In *Proceedings of the 60th Annual Meeting of the Association for Computational Linguistics (Volume 1: Long Papers)*, pages 5291–5305, Dublin, Ireland. Association for Computational Linguistics.

Mukuntha Narayanan Sundararaman, Ayush Kumar, and Jithendra Vepa. 2021. Phoneme-bert: Joint language modelling of phoneme sequence and asr transcript. *arXiv preprint arXiv:2102.00804*.

Di Wu and Christof Monz. 2023. Beyond shared vocabulary: Increasing representational word similarities across languages for multilingual machine translation. In *Proceedings of the 2023 Conference on Empirical Methods in Natural Language Processing*, pages 9749–9764, Singapore. Association for Computational Linguistics.

Shijie Wu and Mark Dredze. 2020. Are all languages created equal in multilingual BERT? In *Proceedings of the 5th Workshop on Representation Learning for NLP*, pages 120–130, Online. Association for Computational Linguistics.

Huiyun Yang, Huadong Chen, Hao Zhou, and Lei Li. 2022. Enhancing cross-lingual transfer by manifold mixup. In *International Conference on Learning Representations*.

Guangyan Zhang, Kaitao Song, Xu Tan, Daxin Tan, Yuzi Yan, Yanqing Liu, Gang Wang, Wei Zhou, Tao Qin, Tan Lee, and Sheng Zhao. 2022. Mixed-phoneme bert: Improving bert with mixed phoneme and sup-phoneme representations for text to speech. In *Interspeech 2022*, pages 456–460.

Hongyi Zhang, Moustapha Cisse, Yann N. Dauphin, and David Lopez-Paz. 2018. mixup: Beyond empirical risk minimization. In *International Conference on Learning Representations*.

## A Dataset Statistics

In Table 4, we provide the dataset statistics. For the experiments, we used train set for training and validation set for evaluation.

| Dataset | Lang. | Train | Dev | Test |
|---|---|---|---|---|
| FLORES+ | eng<br>fra<br>rus<br>ita<br>hun<br>ukr<br>kor<br>tur<br>fin<br>hin | - | 1.2k | - |
| XNLI | eng<br>swa<br>urd | 393k | 2.49k | 5.01k |
| WikiAnn | eng | 20k | 10k | 10k |
| | fra | 20k | 10k | 10k |
| | rus | 20k | 10k | 10k |
| | ita | 20k | 10k | 10k |
| | hun | 20k | 10k | 10k |
| | ukr | 20k | 10k | 10k |
| | kor | 20k | 10k | 10k |
| | tur | 20k | 10k | 10k |
| | fin | 20k | 10k | 10k |
| | hin | 5k | 1k | 1k |
| UD | eng | 12.5k | 2k | 2k |
| | fra | 14.5k | 1.5k | 0.4k |
| | rus | 16k | 0.9k | 0.9k |
| | ita | 13k | 0.6k | 0.5k |
| | hun | 0.9k | 0.4k | 0.4k |
| | ukr | 5.5k | 0.7k | 0.9k |
| | kor | 23k | 2k | 2.3k |
| | tur | 15k | 1.6k | 1.6k |
| | fin | 12k | 1.4k | 1.6k |
| | hin | 13k | 1.7k | 1.7k |

Table 4: Dataset statistics for datasets used in experiments: FLORES+, XNLI, WikiAnn, Universal Dependencies Tree Bank. For FLORES+ dataset, we used devtest set with 1,012 sentences.

## B Hyperparameter sweep.

We sweep hyperparameters over grid below (in Table 5), and select the final parameters for each model based on the **best validation performance** (Accuracy for XNLI and F1-score for NER and POS Tagging).

## C Details on Theoreoretical Analysis

We aim to diminish the performance gap between different languages by adopting IPA as a universal language representation. Motivated by domain adaptation literature (Kifer et al., 2004; Ben-David et al., 2010), we present a theoretical justification of IPA for robust multilingual modeling by providing a bound for cross-lingual performance gap.

Let $\mathcal{D}$ denote a domain as a distribution over text feature input $\mathcal{X}$, such as the sequence of word embeddings or one-hot vectors, and a labeling function $f : \mathcal{X} \to \{0, 1\}$. Assuming a binary classification task, our goal is to learn a hypothesis $h : \mathcal{X} \to \{0, 1\}$ that is expected to minimize a risk $\varepsilon_{\mathcal{D}}(h, f) := \mathbb{E}_{x\sim\mathcal{D}}[\mathbb{I}(f(x) \neq h(x))]$ and has a small risk-deviation over two domains $\mathcal{D}_A$ and $\mathcal{D}_B$. Then, to formalize the cross-lingual performance gap, we first need a discrepancy measure between two languages. By following (Ben-David et al., 2010), we adopt $\mathcal{H}$-divergence to quantify the distance between two language distributions.

**Definition C.1** ($\mathcal{H}$-divergence; Ben-David et al. (2006)). *Let $\mathcal{H}$ be a hypothesis class for input space $\mathcal{X}$ and a collection of subsets from $\mathcal{X}$ is denoted by $\mathcal{S}_{\mathcal{H}} := \{h^{-1}(1)|h \in \mathcal{H}\}$ which is the support of hypothesis $h \in \mathcal{H}$. The $\mathcal{H}$-divergence between two distributions $\mathcal{D}$ and $\mathcal{D}'$ is defined as*

$$d_{\mathcal{H}}(D, D') = 2 \sup_{S\in\mathcal{S}_{\mathcal{H}}} |\mathbb{P}_D(S) - \mathbb{P}_{D'}(S)|$$

$\mathcal{H}$-divergence is a relaxation of total variation between two distributions, and it can be estimated by finite samples from both distributions if $\mathcal{H}$ governs a finite VC dimension. Now, based on Lemma 1 and 3 of Ben-David et al. (2010), we make reasoning on performance gap over different language domains.

**Theorem C.2.** *Let $h : \mathcal{X} \to [0, 1]$ be a real-valued function in a hypothesis class $\mathcal{H}$ with a pseudo dimension $\mathcal{P}dim(\mathcal{H}) = d$. If $\hat{\mathcal{D}}_A$ and $\hat{\mathcal{D}}_B$ are the empirical distribution constructed by $n$-size i.i.d. samples, drawn from $\mathcal{D}_A$ and $\mathcal{D}_B$ respectively, then for any $\delta \in (0, 1)$, and for all $h$, the bound below hold with probability at least $1 - \delta$.*

$$|\varepsilon_{\mathcal{D}_A}(h, f) - \varepsilon_{\mathcal{D}_B}(h, f)| \leq \frac{1}{2} d_{\mathcal{H}\Delta\mathcal{H}}(\hat{\mathcal{D}}_A, \hat{\mathcal{D}}_B) + 2\sqrt{\frac{d\log(2n) + \log(2/\delta)}{n}}$$

where $\mathcal{H}\Delta\mathcal{H} := \{h(x) \oplus h'(x)|h, h' \in \mathcal{H}\}$ given $\oplus$ as a xor operation.

| Task | Hyperparam | Search space | Selected parameter value | | |
|---|---|---|---|---|---|
| | | | mBERT | CANINE | XPhoneBERT |
| XNLI | learning rate | [5e-6, 7e-6, 1e-5, 3e-5, 5e-5] | 5e-6 | 5e-6 (en), 1e-5 (sw, ur) | 7e-6 (en), 3e-6 (sw, ur) |
| | weight decay | [0.0, 1e-1, 1e-2, 1e-3] | 0.01 | 0.1 (en), 0.0 (sw), 0.01 (ur) | 0.1 (en), 0.0 (sw), 0.01 (ur) |
| | learning rate scheduling | [True, False] | True | True | False |
| NER | learning rate | [3e-5, 5e-5, 1e-4, 3e-4] | - | 5e-5 (en, fr, it, hu, ko, tr), 1e-4 (ru, uk, fi, hi) | 3e-5 (ru, it), 5e-5 (en, fr, hu, uk, tr, fi, hi), 1e-4 (ko) |
| | weight decay | 1e-2 | - | 1e-2 | 1e-2 |
| POS | learning rate | [3e-5, 5e-5, 1e-4, 3e-4] | - | 5e-5 (ru, uk, tr), 1e-4 (en, fr, fi, hi), 3e-4 (it, hu, ko) | 5e-5 (en), 1e-4 (fr, ru, it, hu, uk, ko, tr, fi, hi) |
| | weight decay | 1e-2 | - | 1e-2 | 1e-2 |

Table 5: List of hyperparameter, search spaces and selected parameter values for different models applied to XNLI, NER, and POS tasks, detailing learning rate, weight decay, and learning rate scheduling for mBERT, CANINE, and XPhonemBERT, with specific configurations for optimal model performance per task.

*proof of Theorem B.2.* we start to prove Theorem B.2. by restating Lemma 1 of (Ben-David et al., 2010) adapted to our notation.

**Lemma C.3.** *Let $\mathcal{D}_A$ and $\mathcal{D}_B$ be distributions of domain A and B over $\mathcal{X}$, respectively. Let $\mathcal{H}$ be a hypothesis class of functions from $\mathcal{X}$ to $[0, 1]$ with VC dimension d. If $\hat{\mathcal{D}}_A$ and $\hat{\mathcal{D}}_B$ are the n-size empirical distributions generated by $\mathcal{D}_A$ and $\mathcal{D}_B$ respectively, then, for $0 < \delta < 1$, with probability at least $1 - \delta$,*

$$d_{\mathcal{H}}(\mathcal{D}_A, \mathcal{D}_B) \leq d_{\mathcal{H}}(\hat{\mathcal{D}}_A, \hat{\mathcal{D}}_B) + 4\sqrt{\frac{d\log(2n) + \log(2/\delta)}{n}}.$$

Then, for any hypothesis function $h, h' \in \mathcal{H}$, by the definition of $d_{\mathcal{H}\Delta\mathcal{H}}$-divergence, we have:

$$\begin{aligned} & d_{\mathcal{H}\Delta\mathcal{H}}(\mathcal{D}_A, \mathcal{D}_B) \\ &= 2 \sup_{h,h' \in \mathcal{H}} |\mathbb{P}_{x\sim\mathcal{D}_A}[h(x) \neq h'(x)] - \mathbb{P}_{x\sim\mathcal{D}_B}[h(x) \neq h'(x)]| \\ &= 2 \sup_{h,h' \in \mathcal{H}} |\varepsilon_{\mathcal{D}_A}(h, h') - \varepsilon_{\mathcal{D}_B}(h, h')| \\ &\geq 2|\varepsilon_{\mathcal{D}_A}(h, h') - \varepsilon_{\mathcal{D}_B}(h, h')| \end{aligned}$$

Now the below bound holds for any hypothesis functions $h, h' \in \mathcal{H}$ (See Lemma 3 of (Ben-David et al., 2010)).

$$|\varepsilon_{\mathcal{D}_A}(h, h') - \varepsilon_{\mathcal{D}_B}(h, h')| \leq \frac{1}{2} d_{\mathcal{H}\Delta\mathcal{H}}(\mathcal{D}_A, \mathcal{D}_B)$$

Finally, by plugging the Lemma C.3 into the above bound, we have Theorem C.2.

□

From Theorem C.2, we see that the difference between true risks across language domains is bounded by an empirical estimation of the divergence ($d_{\mathcal{H}\Delta\mathcal{H}}$) between those two domains plus an irreducible term defined by problem setup. Thus, if we reduce the divergence between language distributions, the expected performance gap can also be reduced accordingly. To investigate whether this is indeed a case or not, we provided the embedding-space similarity and logit-space Sinkhorn distance between different languages in Figure 3. We argue that phonemic representation's relatively mild performance gap is achieved by reducing linguistic gaps in the embedding space (high CKA) and final output space (low Sinkhorn distance) those are the proxy of $\mathcal{H}$-divergence.

# Leveraging Adapters for Improved Cross-Lingual Transfer for Low-Resource Creole MT

**Marcell Fekete**[1] **Ernests Lavrinovics**[1] **Nathaniel R. Robinson**[2]
**Heather Lent**[1] **Raj Dabre**[3] **Johannes Bjerva**[1]
[1]Aalborg University, Denmark; [2]Johns Hopkins University, USA; [3] IIT Madras, India
mrfe@cs.aau.dk

## 1 Creoles in Machine Translation

Creole languages are low-resource languages, often genetically related to languages like English, French, and Portuguese, due to their linguistic histories with colonialism (DeGraff, 2003). As such, Creoles stand to benefit greatly from both data-efficient methods and transfer-learning from high-resource languages. At the same time, it has been observed by Lent et al. (2022b) that machine translation (MT) is a highly desired language technology by speakers of many Creoles. To this end, recent works have contributed new datasets, allowing for the development and evaluation of MT systems for Creoles (Robinson et al., 2024; Lent et al., 2024). In this work, we explore the use of the limited monolingual and parallel data for Creoles using parameter-efficient adaptation methods. Specifically, we compare the performance of different adapter architectures over the set of available benchmarks. We find adapters a promising approach for Creoles because they are parameter-efficient and have been shown to leverage transfer learning between related languages (Faisal and Anastasopoulos, 2022). While we perform experiments across multiple Creoles, we present only on Haitian Creole in this extended abstract. For future work, we aim to explore the potentials for leveraging other high-resourced languages for parameter-efficient transfer learning.

| Dataset | Domain | Size (#lines) |
|---|---|---|
| NLLB-OPUS | Web scrape | ~15M |
| FLORES-200◇ | Wikipedia | 3,001 |
| CreoleM2M | Religion | 208,772 (train)<br>1,000 (eval) |
| MIT-Haiti◇ | Education | 1,559 |

Table 1: Datasets used in our preliminary experiments. A ◇ indicates the dataset is used only as evaluation data.

| Method | Source | Config name |
|---|---|---|
| Bottleneck | Houlsby et al., 2019 | `double_seq_bn` |
| + Invertible | Houlsby et al., 2019 | `._inv` |
| Compacter | Mahabadi et al., 2021 | `compacter` |
| LoRA | Hu et al., 2021 | `lora` |
| $(IA)^3$ | Liu et al., 2022 | `ia3` |

Table 2: Adapter architectures compared in our experiments (Table adapted from Poth et al., 2023). We also experiment with prefix tuning adapters (Li and Liang, 2021) and bottleneck adapters from Pfeiffer et al. (2020), which differ only from those of Houlsby et al. (2019) in adapter placement. However some preliminary experiments found they performed worse than these five.

## 2 Methodology and Experiments

To train adapters for Haitian, we use monolingual data from NLLB-OPUS (Fan et al., 2020), and the parallel CreoleM2M training split from CREOLEVAL (Lent et al., 2024). For evaluation, we leverage two evaluation datasets from CREOLEVAL: the CreoleM2M evaluation split and the MIT-Haiti Corpus for MT; we also evaluate over FLORES-200 (Goyal et al., 2022) (see Table 1).

All experiments are conducted with Kreyòl-MT, an mBART-50 model fine-tuned on the KREYÒL-MT dataset (Robinson et al., 2024). Furthermore, we apply dNLLB-200, a 600M-parameter distillation of the original 54B-parameter NLLB-200 model as a baseline (NLLB Team et al., 2022). Both models have 12 encoder and 12 decoder layers, 16 attention heads, and 1024 dimensions, and each model have their own model vocabularies of over 250,000 sentence-piece tokens shared across all languages.

### 2.1 Experiments

Following Üstün et al. (2021), we attempt to leverage monolingual data to improve MT performance by training denoising adapters added to the encoder, the decoder, or or both components of Kreyòl-MT model. Additionally, we experiment with or without cross-attention (CA) fine-tuning between



*Proceedings of the Fourth Workshop on Multilingual Representation Learning (MRL 2024)*, pages 212–215
November 16, 2024 ©2024 Association for Computational Linguistics

| eval set: | eng→hat | | | hat→eng | | |
|---|---|---|---|---|---|---|
| | *CreoleM2M* | *FLORES* | *MIT-Haiti* | *CreoleM2M* | *FLORES* | *MIT-Haiti* |
| compacter | **42** | **28** | **35** | 76 | **40** | 31 |
| double-seq-bn | 40 | 27 | 34 | 77 | 38 | 32 |
| double-seq-bn-inv | 41 | 26 | **35** | 76 | 37 | 32 |
| ia3 | **42** | **28** | 34 | 77 | 39 | 32 |
| lora | **42** | **28** | **35** | **79** | 38 | 31 |
| Kreyòl-MT w/ CA | **42** | 27 | **35** | 75 | **40** | 31 |
| Kreyòl-MT | 33 | 27 | 32 | 66 | **40** | 30 |
| NLLB | 22 | 26 | 33 | 34 | 37 | **36** |

Table 3: Average BLEU scores across each evaluation benchmark. Different adapter methods are on top, while baselines are on bottom.

the components. We evaluate using a number of adapter architectures (see Table 2) which to our knowledge have not yet been directly compared against each other.

In preliminary experiments we narrowed down all adapters from AdapterHub[1] to the five best performing, as shown in Table 2. We compare appendage of these adapters to three baseline models: Kreyòl-MT out-of-the-box, Kreyòl-MT with CA fine-tuning, and the 600M-parameter NLLB-200 model (NLLB Team et al., 2022).

### 2.2 Results

We find that some adapter architectures are more amenable to Üstün et al. (2021)'s monolingual adaptation methodology, as demonstrated by their relative increased performance over baselines (see Table 3). However, these scores consistently drop as the quality and cultural relevance of the data increases (*i.e.*, we observe much better performance on the religious-domain samples from CreoleM2M, and worse performance on MIT-Haiti, which is culturally appropriate data sourced from the community). Regarded holistically, even the best adapters do not consistently improve over CA fine-tuning between encoder and decoder, and they either improve or degrade performance by only marginal amounts. Our results also suggest that CA finetuning generally helps performance.

## 3 Conclusion and Future Work

While gains over baselines were reached *via* the monolingual adaptation, most Creoles do not have lage amounts of web-scraped data, as found in NLLB-OPUS. Thus, the ability to leverage data and transfer from closely related languages to Creoles has great potential for bolstering Creole MT. To this end, we plan experiments for parameter-efficient transfer learning, inspired by Faisal and Anastasopoulos (2022), who found success with phylogenetically-motivated adaptation. The application of phylogenetic adaptation for Creoles is not straight-forward, however. There is no consensus phylogeny of Creoles or even their broader language families (Bakker et al., 2011; Aboh, 2016). Simultaneously, previous works have shown that transfer learning to Creoles from related languages is nontrivial (Lent et al., 2022a, 2024; Robinson et al., 2022, 2023). Thus an important area of Creole MT remains selecting favorable languages for transfer learning.

In addition to phylogentic relation, we are exploring selection of transfer languages via **embedding clustering**. We cluster NLLB-200 language token embeddings with cosine and Euclidean distance, and identify Afrikaans, Igbo, and Yiddish as the nearest neighbors of Haitian. These are interesting findings, since Igbo is one of Haitian's hypothesized relatives (Seguin, 2020), and Yiddish and Afrikaans are Indo-European languages influenced by Afroasiatic and South African Khoisan languages, respectively—which appears analogous to Haitian's mixed Indo-European and Niger-Congo influences. We also explore measuring vocabulary **subword evenness**, as introduced by Pelloni et al. (2022), as a more helpful language selection method than simple typological proximity. While experiments are still underway, these explorations will help establish the languages amenable to cross-lingual transfer for Creoles, and ultimately the degree to which cross-lingual adaptation methods can benefit speakers of Creoles.

[1] `https://docs.adapterhub.ml/overview.html`

## References


Enoch O. Aboh. 2016. Creole distinctiveness: A dead end. *Journal of Pidgin and Creole Languages*, 31(2):400–418.

Peter Bakker, Aymeric Daval-Markussen, Mikael Parkvall, and Ingo Plag. 2011. Creoles are typologically distinct from non-creoles. *Journal of Pidgin and Creole languages*, 26(1):5–42.

Michel DeGraff. 2003. Against creole exceptionalism. *Language*, 79(2):391–410.

Fahim Faisal and Antonios Anastasopoulos. 2022. Phylogeny-inspired adaptation of multilingual models to new languages. In *Proceedings of the 2nd Conference of the Asia-Pacific Chapter of the Association for Computational Linguistics and the 12th International Joint Conference on Natural Language Processing (Volume 1: Long Papers)*, pages 434–452, Online only. Association for Computational Linguistics.

Angela Fan, Shruti Bhosale, Holger Schwenk, Zhiyi Ma, Ahmed El-Kishky, Siddharth Goyal, Mandeep Baines, Onur Celebi, Guillaume Wenzek, Vishrav Chaudhary, Naman Goyal, Tom Birch, Vitaliy Liptchinsky, Sergey Edunov, Edouard Grave, Michael Auli, and Armand Joulin. 2020. Beyond english-centric multilingual machine translation. *Preprint*, arXiv:2010.11125.

Naman Goyal, Cynthia Gao, Vishrav Chaudhary, Peng-Jen Chen, Guillaume Wenzek, Da Ju, Sanjana Krishnan, Marc'Aurelio Ranzato, Francisco Guzmán, and Angela Fan. 2022. The Flores-101 evaluation benchmark for low-resource and multilingual machine translation. *Transactions of the Association for Computational Linguistics*, 10:522–538.

Neil Houlsby, Andrei Giurgiu, Stanisław Jastrzebski, and Bruna Morrone. 2019. Parameter-Efficient Transfer Learning for NLP. In *Proceedings of the 36th International Conference on Machine Learning*, page 10, Long Beach, California.

Edward J. Hu, Yelong Shen, Phillip Wallis, Zeyuan Allen-Zhu, Yuanzhi Li, Shean Wang, Lu Wang, and Weizhu Chen. 2021. LoRA: Low-Rank Adaptation of Large Language Models. *arXiv preprint*. ArXiv:2106.09685 [cs].

Heather Lent, Emanuele Bugliarello, and Anders Søgaard. 2022a. Ancestor-to-creole transfer is not a walk in the park. In *Proceedings of the Third Workshop on Insights from Negative Results in NLP*, pages 68–74, Dublin, Ireland. Association for Computational Linguistics.

Heather Lent, Kelechi Ogueji, Miryam de Lhoneux, Orevaoghene Ahia, and Anders Søgaard. 2022b. What a creole wants, what a creole needs. In *Proceedings of the Thirteenth Language Resources and Evaluation Conference*, pages 6439–6449, Marseille, France. European Language Resources Association.

Heather Lent, Kushal Tatariya, Raj Dabre, Yiyi Chen, Marcell Fekete, Esther Ploeger, Li Zhou, Ruth-Ann Armstrong, Abee Eijansantos, Catriona Malau, Hans Erik Heje, Ernests Lavrinovics, Diptesh Kanojia, Paul Belony, Marcel Bollmann, Loïc Grobol, Miryam de Lhoneux, Daniel Hershcovich, Michel DeGraff, Anders Søgaard, and Johannes Bjerva. 2024. Creoleval: Multilingual multitask benchmarks for creoles. *Preprint*, arXiv:2310.19567.

Xiang Lisa Li and Percy Liang. 2021. Prefix-tuning: Optimizing continuous prompts for generation. In *Proceedings of the 59th Annual Meeting of the Association for Computational Linguistics and the 11th International Joint Conference on Natural Language Processing (Volume 1: Long Papers)*, pages 4582–4597, Online. Association for Computational Linguistics.

Haokun Liu, Derek Tam, Mohammed Muqeeth, Jay Mohta, Tenghao Huang, Mohit Bansal, and Colin Raffel. 2022. Few-Shot Parameter-Efficient Fine-Tuning is Better and Cheaper than In-Context Learning. *arXiv preprint*. ArXiv:2205.05638 [cs].

Rabeeh Karimi Mahabadi, James Henderson, and Sebastian Ruder. 2021. Compacter: Efficient Low-Rank Hypercomplex Adapter Layers. In *Advances in Neural Information Processing Systems*, volume 34, pages 1022–1035. Curran Associates, Inc.

NLLB Team, Marta R. Costa-jussà, James Cross, Onur Çelebi, Maha Elbayad, Kenneth Heafield, Kevin Heffernan, Elahe Kalbassi, Janice Lam, Daniel Licht, Jean Maillard, Anna Sun, Skyler Wang, Guillaume Wenzek, Al Youngblood, Bapi Akula, Loic Barrault, Gabriel Mejia-Gonzalez, Prangthip Hansanti, John Hoffman, Semarley Jarrett, Kaushik Ram Sadagopan, Dirk Rowe, Shannon Spruit, Chau Tran, Pierre Andrews, Necip Fazil Ayan, Shruti Bhosale, Sergey Edunov, Angela Fan, Cynthia Gao, Vedanuj Goswami, Francisco Guzmán, Philipp Koehn, Alexandre Mourachko, Christophe Ropers, Safiyyah Saleem, Holger Schwenk, and Jeff Wang. 2022. No language left behind: Scaling human-centered machine translation.

Olga Pelloni, Anastassia Shaitarova, and Tanja Samardzic. 2022. Subword evenness (SuE) as a predictor of cross-lingual transfer to low-resource languages. In *Proceedings of the 2022 Conference on Empirical Methods in Natural Language Processing*, pages 7428–7445, Abu Dhabi, United Arab Emirates. Association for Computational Linguistics.

Jonas Pfeiffer, Ivan Vulić, Iryna Gurevych, and Sebastian Ruder. 2020. MAD-X: An Adapter-Based Framework for Multi-Task Cross-Lingual Transfer. In *Proceedings of the 2020 Conference on Empirical Methods in Natural Language Processing (EMNLP)*, pages 7654–7673, Online. Association for Computational Linguistics.

Clifton Poth, Hannah Sterz, Indraneil Paul, Sukannya Purkayastha, Leon Engländer, Timo Imhof, Ivan

Vulić, Sebastian Ruder, Iryna Gurevych, and Jonas Pfeiffer. 2023. Adapters: A unified library for parameter-efficient and modular transfer learning. In *Proceedings of the 2023 Conference on Empirical Methods in Natural Language Processing: System Demonstrations*, pages 149–160, Singapore. Association for Computational Linguistics.

Nathaniel Robinson, Raj Dabre, Ammon Shurtz, Rasul Dent, Onenamiyi Onesi, Claire Monroc, Loïc Grobol, Hasan Muhammad, Ashi Garg, Naome Etori, Vijay Murari Tiyyala, Olanrewaju Samuel, Matthew Stutzman, Bismarck Odoom, Sanjeev Khudanpur, Stephen Richardson, and Kenton Murray. 2024. Kreyòl-MT: Building MT for Latin American, Caribbean and colonial African creole languages. In *Proceedings of the 2024 Conference of the North American Chapter of the Association for Computational Linguistics: Human Language Technologies (Volume 1: Long Papers)*, pages 3083–3110, Mexico City, Mexico. Association for Computational Linguistics.

Nathaniel Robinson, Cameron Hogan, Nancy Fulda, and David R. Mortensen. 2022. Data-adaptive transfer learning for translation: A case study in Haitian and jamaican. In *Proceedings of the Fifth Workshop on Technologies for Machine Translation of Low-Resource Languages (LoResMT 2022)*, pages 35–42, Gyeongju, Republic of Korea. Association for Computational Linguistics.

Nathaniel Romney Robinson, Matthew Dean Stutzman, Stephen D Richardson, and David R Mortensen. 2023. African substrates rather than european lexifiers to augment african-diaspora creole translation. In *4th Workshop on African Natural Language Processing*.

Luisa Seguin. 2020. Transparency and language contact: The case of haitian creole, french, and fongbe. *Journal of Pidgin and Creole Languages*, 35(2):218–252.

Ahmet Üstün, Alexandre Berard, Laurent Besacier, and Matthias Gallé. 2021. Multilingual unsupervised neural machine translation with denoising adapters. In *Proceedings of the 2021 Conference on Empirical Methods in Natural Language Processing*, pages 6650–6662, Online and Punta Cana, Dominican Republic. Association for Computational Linguistics.

# Evaluating Multilingual Long-Context Models for Retrieval and Reasoning

**Ameeta Agrawal, Andy Dang, Sina Bagheri Nezhad, Rhitabrat Pokharel, Russell Scheinberg**
Department of Computer Science
Portland State University, USA
{ameeta, andang, sina5, pokharel, rschein2}@pdx.edu

**Abstract**

Recent large language models (LLMs) demonstrate impressive capabilities in handling long contexts, some exhibiting near-perfect recall on synthetic retrieval tasks. However, these evaluations have mainly focused on English text and involved a single target sentence within lengthy contexts. Our work investigates how LLM performance generalizes to multilingual settings with multiple hidden target sentences. We create a new dataset – mLongRR – to comprehensively evaluate several multilingual long-context LLMs on retrieval and reasoning tasks across five languages: English, Vietnamese, Indonesian, Swahili, and Somali. These languages share the Latin script but belong to distinct language families and resource levels. Our analysis reveals a significant performance gap between languages. The best-performing models such as Gemini-1.5 and GPT-4o, achieve around 96% accuracy in English to around 36% in Somali with a single target sentence. However, this accuracy drops to 40% in English and 0% in Somali when dealing with three target sentences. Our findings highlight the challenges long-context LLMs face when processing longer contexts, an increase in the number of target sentences, or languages of lower resource levels.

## 1 Introduction

The ability to model long context sequences spanning tens of thousands of tokens is crucial for tasks such as summarization and question answering based on long documents such as books and reports, and code generation at the repository level. Recent advancements in large language models (LLMs) have focused on improving their capabilities in processing long context information (Dai et al., 2019; Chen et al., 2023; Ding et al., 2024).

Long-context language models, particularly multilingual ones, have the potential to enable remarkable progress in various applications by understanding lengthy textual data across different languages. An example of this potential was recently demonstrated by the newly introduced Gemini-1.5 Pro model (Reid et al., 2024) which leveraged its long-context window for in-context learning. By including a grammar manual in its context window, the model was able to learn to translate from English to Kalamang, an extremely low-resource language with fewer than 200 speakers (Visser, 2020). Such examples highlight the potential of long-context models in tackling challenging tasks in low-resource languages, where data scarcity has traditionally been a barrier.

Current methods for evaluating long-context LLMs primarily focus on English text. This has led to a severe lack of insights into their performance across diverse languages. Evaluating multilingual performance is crucial, not only for informing the development of effective models that serve diverse communities (Lai et al., 2023a; Ahuja et al., 2023), but also for developing safer models as research suggests that LLMs tend to generate more unsafe and irrelevant responses to malicious prompts in lower-resource languages (Shen et al., 2024). However, there is a notable lack of multilingual benchmarks hindering our understanding of how long-context LLMs perform across different linguistic contexts.

To address this gap, we present the first comprehensive study of long-context LLMs in multilingual settings leveraging evaluation frameworks relying on synthetic tasks (Mohtashami and Jaggi, 2023; Chen et al., 2023; Liu et al., 2024; Kamradt, 2023; Reid et al., 2024; Anthropic, 2024). Although the task is partially synthetic, we create a new dataset – mLongRR[1] – consisting of naturally occurring text and human translated data, making the setup as close to real-world setting while creating a con-

[1]The code is available at https://github.com/PortNLP/mLongRR.



*Proceedings of the Fourth Workshop on Multilingual Representation Learning (MRL 2024)*, pages 216–231
November 16, 2024 ©2024 Association for Computational Linguistics

| Language | ISO 639-3 Code | Resource Level | Language Family | Script |
|---|---|---|---|---|
| English | eng | Level 5 | Indo-European | Latin |
| Vietnamese | vie | Level 4 | Austro-Asiatic | Latin |
| Indonesian | ind | Level 3 | Austronesian | Latin |
| Swahili | swa | Level 2 | Niger-Congo | Latin |
| Somali | som | Level 1 | Afro-Asiatic | Latin |

Table 1: Languages studied and their details.

trolled environment for comparing model performance across languages. In addition to retrieval tasks, we introduce a new reasoning task where the models not only need to retrieve relevant items but also compare them with each other. For this, the models must keep track of these items in a long-context scenario, allowing us to analyze the models' reasoning capabilities.

We conduct a systematic evaluation of six different LLMs across five languages of varying resource levels. Our research aims to answer the following two questions:
(1) How do the long context capabilities of LLMs compare in retrieval and reasoning tasks in multilingual contexts?
(2) Are there significant performance differences between LLMs in multilingual contexts?

Some of our key findings are summarized as follows:

- The performance rapidly declines as we increase the context lengths for all languages.
- The performance also rapidly decreases as we move from higher-resource to lower-resource languages.
- Reasoning tasks are more challenging than retrieval tasks for all languages.
- There is a significant gap between the performance of different LLMs.
- Even seemingly simple "needle in the haystack" evaluation is able to expose limitations in current models when dealing with multilingual contexts.

We hope that the findings of our study will contribute to a deeper understanding of current long-context evaluation in multilingual contexts and encourage the development of more effective long-context multilingual models.

## 2 Related Work

Recent advancements in language models have focused on improving their ability to recall and reason over fine-grained information from tens of thousands of tokens of context (Achiam et al., 2023; Jin et al., 2024). Due to shortage of really long-context benchmarks, evaluation is typically focused on synthetic tasks such as passkey retrieval (Mohtashami and Jaggi, 2023; Chen et al., 2023; Liu et al., 2024; Ding et al., 2024; Jin et al., 2024) or needle in a haystack (Kamradt, 2023; Reid et al., 2024; Anthropic, 2024) which measure a model's ability to accurately recall information from a vast corpus of data.

Recently, Gemini 1.5 (Reid et al., 2024) and Claude-3 (Anthropic, 2024) models reported near-perfect recall on the needle in a haystack task. Prior work has also studied perplexity but a low perplexity score has shown to not necessarily indicate proficiency in handling long contexts or reflect the model's performance on sequence-level tasks in real applications (Sun et al., 2021; Pal et al., 2023; Jin et al., 2024). Furthermore, most of these studies have been limited to English only texts.

Although some long-context real-world benchmarks have been recently introduced, they are also limited to English (An et al., 2024), and while some bilingual English/Chinese (Bai et al., 2023; Qiu et al., 2024; Yuan et al., 2024) datasets offer a slight improvement, due to the effort-intensive nature of dataset creation, they are limited to a very small number of languages.

## 3 Multilingual Needles in a Haystack for Retrieval and Reasoning Evaluation

### 3.1 Languages and Models

**Languages** We selected five languages to study: English, Vietnamese, Indonesian, Swahili, and Somali. These languages span different resource levels from high to extremely low[2] allowing us to gain insight into how language resource levels affect models' ability to work over long context windows.

Furthermore, we deliberately control for script-related variables as they have been shown to have a considerable impact on the performance of a model (Bagheri Nezhad and Agrawal, 2024b). We study languages that use the Latin script for three reasons: models perform significantly better on Latin-script languages than non-Latin languages (Chau and Smith, 2021; Bang et al., 2023), the fragmentation rate of Latin script is lower than other scripts allowing Latin-script languages to be represented with substantially fewer tokens as compared to languages in other scripts (Ács, 2019; Ahia et al., 2023) – a disparity that becomes even more pronounced over long contexts, and, lastly, the fragmentation rate of Latin-script languages remains comparable which is helpful when considering considerably long input texts. Our selection of languages, shown in Table 1, has the added benefit of including less-studied languages and language families[3], providing a more comprehensive view of the latest generation of multilingual capabilities of long-context LLMs.

**Models** We consider four proprietary and two open-source long-context LLMs.

- **GPT-4** is a proprietary multilingual LLM from OpenAI (Achiam et al., 2023) that has been shown to perform a wide range of tasks. We used the *gpt-4-0125-preview* version, which is the latest one at the time of our experiments. It has a context window of 128K tokens and was trained with the data until Dec 2023. We also study the recently introduced **GPT-4o** model.

- **Gemini-1.5** is another proprietary LLM withh a context window of 10M tokens (Reid et al., 2024). We used the *gemini 1.5 pro* version which is built on top of mixture-of-experts transformer-based architecture.

- **Claude-3** is yet another proprietary model released by Anthropic with a context window of length 200K (Anthropic, 2024) but is claimed to accept up to 1M tokens. We used *claude-3-sonnet-20240229* variant of the Claude family.

- **YaRN-Llama-2-7b** (Peng et al., 2024) is an open-source model that extends Llama 2 model (Touvron et al., 2023) to accept a larger context window. It is available in different model sizes with varying context windows. We selected the 7B model with the maximum context window of 128K tokens, accessed via Huggingface[4].

- **Llama-3-8B** is a robust open-source model (Dubey et al., 2024). We selected the instruction-tuned version of the model with a context window of 8k[5].

### 3.2 Retrieval and Reasoning Tasks

Language models with the ability to handle long context rely heavily on their capacity to retrieve relevant information from the given text and reason based on that information to interpret and follow human instructions effectively. Although synthetic tasks alone may not provide a comprehensive assessment of a language model's long-context capabilities, they offer the advantage of being easily adaptable to specific scenarios and languages. This is particularly important given that the most recent long-context real-world benchmarks are limited to English (An et al., 2024) or bilingual English/Chinese (Bai et al., 2023; Qiu et al., 2024; Yuan et al., 2024). Moreover, there is some evidence to suggest that performance on synthetic retrieval tasks can, to a certain extent, generalize to real-world datasets (Qiu et al., 2024). Therefore, carefully designed synthetic tasks can serve as a valuable tool for evaluating a language model's long-context capabilities across a diverse range of languages.

The "needle in a haystack" task (Kamradt, 2023), similarly to the passkey retrieval task (Mohtashami and Jaggi, 2023; Chen et al., 2023; Liu et al., 2024), evaluates a model's ability to extract relevant information from lengthy documents. Typically, a target sentence (the "needle") is inserted into a corpus of documents (the context or "haystack"), followed by a question designed to retrieve the fact in the needle. As the input text grows longer, this task typically becomes increasingly challenging.

[2]The linguistic diversity taxonomy (Joshi et al., 2020) is used to identify the resource levels.

[3]Language families were obtained from Ethnologue: Languages of the World, available at https://www.ethnologue.com/.

[4]https://huggingface.co/NousResearch/Yarn-Llama-2-7b-128k

[5]https://huggingface.co/meta-llama/Meta-Llama-3-8B-Instruct

We can formalize the problem of needles in a haystack as follows: Given the needle $n$, a context (or haystack) $c$, and a question $q$, the model is expected to generate an answer $a$. Usually, $n$, $q$, and $a$ are short, while $c$ represents a long sequence of text that can span thousands of tokens. The task can involve either a single needle $n = 1$ or multiple needles $n > 1$. With one or more needles, we can create **retrieval** tasks, whereas with multiple needles we can construct **reasoning** tasks that require the model to draw connections between different pieces of information.

#### 3.2.1 Retrieving a Needle ($n = 1$)

In this task, the model's objective is to locate and extract information from a single target sentence hidden somewhere in the haystack. We adopt the same needle pattern as used in previous studies (Dhinakaran, 2024; Reid et al., 2024; Anthropic, 2024), which takes the form: "*The special magic {city} number is: {number}*". Here, {city} is randomly chosen from a list of 69 unique cities from around the world, and {number} is a randomly generated 7-digit number. The list of cities were automatically translated and then post-edited into all the languages.

In English, this yields needle sentences such as "*The special magic Paris number is: 2243738*" or in Indonesian, "*Nomor ajaib khusus untuk kota Sydney adalah 9347172*".

The needle is then placed at different depths within the context. We experiment with five depth positions: 0% (near the beginning), around the 25% mark, 50% (in the middle), about 75% of the way through, and 100% (towards the end of the context). The needle is placed after the first complete sentence at each specified depth to ensure a linguistically meaningful position. Finally, the model is asked to retrieve some information (e.g., the magic number or the city) found in the needle. It is worth noting that all languages in this study use the same Hindu-Arabic numeral system.

#### 3.2.2 Reasoning over Multiple Needles ($n > 1$)

In real-world applications, tasks often require not just accurate text retrieval but also the ability to reason with the recalled information. To increase the challenge, we introduce a setup where multiple needles are placed within the context, requiring the model to track and reason about these different pieces of information.

The needle format remains similar to the one used in retrieval task. We discretize the positions of the target needles into four intervals: near the top (0-25%), in the middle (25-50% and 50-75%), and closer to the end (75-100%) of the context. For instance, in the 25-50% bucket, the first needle is placed around the 25% depth and the remaining needles are randomly placed between somewhere within the 25-50% depth. We explore two variations of this task, with $n = 2$ and $n = 3$. Finally, the model is asked to generate a response based on the information (e.g., the larger or the largest magic number, or the city with the larger/largest number) found in the needles.

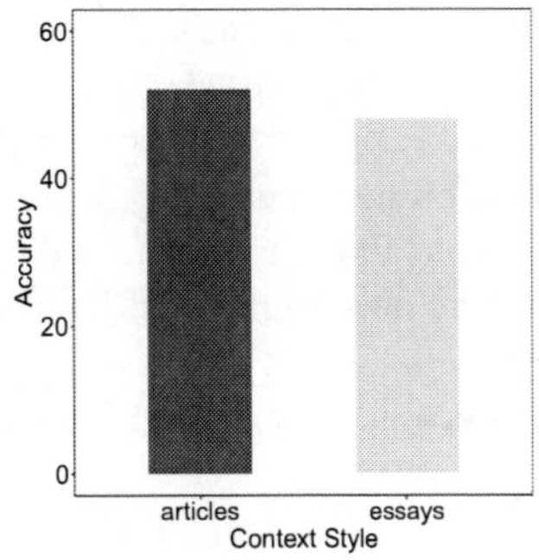


Figure 1: Ablation results of comparing Paul Graham's essays and news articles serving as haystacks for English experiments tested using GPT-4 model.

### 3.3 Creating mLongRR Dataset

Prior work has extensively relied on Paul Graham's essays in English to make up the haystacks (Kamradt, 2023; Dhinakaran, 2024; Anthropic, 2024). Translating these essays into multiple languages, however, could potentially introduce translation errors. Instead, we create a new dataset – mLongRR – by collecting BBC news articles published in the five languages[6], inspired by recent work (Bagheri Nezhad and Agrawal, 2024a). This approach allows us to work with sufficiently long, naturally occurring, with the added benefit that this recently published data is less likely to have been encountered by the models during training. It is worth noting that this does not result in a parallel dataset as the news articles are often specific to their respective regions.

We assess the impacts of different data for haystacks by conducting an ablation study using the GPT-4 model. As shown in Figure 1, we observed

[6]Our language selection was primarily constrained by the availability of authentic texts, especially those within the same script but varying in resource levels.

no noticeable differences in the model performance when the haystacks consisted of Paul Graham's essays or news articles in English. To statistically confirm this observation, we applied McNemar's test (McNemar, 1947), which yielded a p-value of 1.0, indicating no significant difference between the two datasets.

The haystacks in mLongRR were created by drawing on sufficient numbers of articles to fill up the target context window length. There are enough articles in each language to provide non-repeating text for all window lengths. Thus, for example, the first half of the 8K haystack is the same as the 4K haystack, but its second half is composed of different articles. An example of an English haystack of 8K tokens with the needle "*The special magic Doha number is 9121372.*" located at 50% depth is shown below:

```
Star dunes - or pyramid dunes - are
named after their distinctive...
[continues to about 4K tokens]
The special magic Doha number is
9121372.
In our dark laboratory, we see light
from these sand grains...
[context continues until 8K tokens]
```

### 3.4 Prompts

In our initial run of experiments, we explored two existing prompt templates used in previous work:

- **prompt 1** (Kamradt, 2023; Dhinakaran, 2024; Anthropic, 2024), and
- **prompt 2** (Reid et al., 2024).

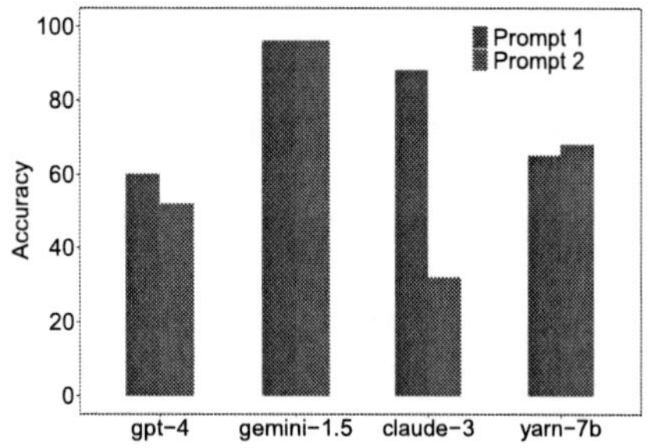


Figure 2: Ablation results of comparing two different prompts.

As shown in Figure 2, prompt 1 performed better in most of the models, so we decided to continue with it for the rest of the experiments. The prompt for the $n = 1$ retrieval task is as follows:

```
You are a helpful AI bot that answers
questions for a user. Keep your response
short and direct. The following is a
set of context and a question that will
relate to the context.
#CONTEXT
{context}
#ENDCONTEXT

#QUESTION
What is the special magic number? Don't
give information outside the document or
repeat your findings. If the information
is not available in the context respond
UNANSWERABLE.
```

For the reasoning with multiple needles task, the prompt format remains largely similar except the question. Recall that each needle has two random variables: the number and the city. Therefore, we explore two possible reasoning questions, one about the larger number, and the other about the city with the larger number.

- For reasoning about numbers, the question is either "*What is the larger magic number?*" when $n = 2$, or "*What is the largest magic number?*" when $n > 2$.
- For reasoning over cities, the question is either "*Which city has the larger magic number?*" when $n = 2$, or "*Which city has the largest magic number?*" when $n > 2$.

Although the articles in mLongRR are already in the native languages, we hired four professional human translators from the freelancing website fiverr.com to translate the needles, city names, and prompts from English into Vietnamese, Indonesian, Swahili, and Somali. In our preliminary experiments with the GPT-4 model, we experimented with English and language-specific prompts, and found that English prompts worked better than language-specific prompts, in line with previous studies (Etxaniz et al., 2024; Bareiß et al., 2024; Lai et al., 2023b), for three of four non-English languages (with the exception of Swahili). As a result, the remaining experiments were conducted using English prompts.

### 3.5 Experiments

We conducted experiments on six models: GPT-4, Gemini-1.5, Claude-3, Yarn-7b, Llama 3, and GPT-4o. The context lengths varied from $2k$, $8k$, $16k$,

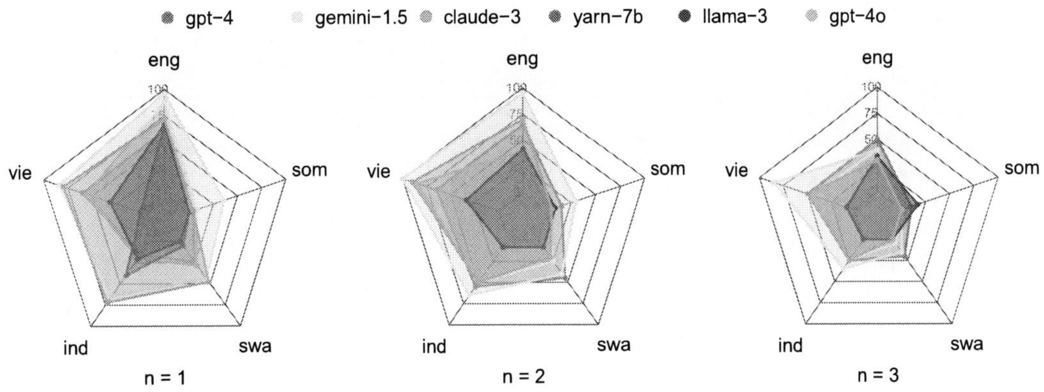


Figure 3: Radar plots showing the performance of six language models (GPT-4, Gemini-1.5, Claude-3, Yarn-7b, Llama-3, GPT-4o) across five languages (English, Vietnamese, Indonesian, Swahili, Somali) in retrieval and reasoning tasks involving one, two, and three target sentences ("needles"). The three plots represent different task complexities: single needle retrieval ($n = 1$, left plot), two needle reasoning ($n = 2$, center plot), and three needle reasoning ($n = 3$, right plot).

$32k$, to $64k$ tokens, and the needles were placed at different depths/positions: $0\%$, $25\%$, $50\%$, $75\%$, and $100\%$. For the retrieval task, we experiment with one needle ($n = 1$), whereas for the reasoning tasks, we investigate setups of needles $n = 2$, and $n = 3$. To enhance the robustness of our evaluation, we used a diverse corpus of recently published news articles and a combination of random cities and random numbers resulting in a vast number of possible needle variations. Furthermore, we conducted multiple runs for a subset of our experiments and consistently observed a variance close to 0 across these runs. Each model was evaluated using its default configuration, and the maximum output token size was set to 50.

### 3.6 Evaluation

The responses generated by the models were used to calculate the accuracy. For both the retrieval and reasoning tasks, the models generated a short, straightforward text containing the 7-digit number (for number-based reasoning) (Dhinakaran, 2024) or the city name (for city-based reasoning). For example, a typical output looked like this: `"3210496"` or `"The larger magic number is 8134445"`. We extracted the number/city and compared it to the ground truth to check whether the model's response was correct or not. For languages other than English, the models occasionally responded with the city name in English or the target language and both were acceptable.

## 4 Results and Discussion

This section presents our results of four main experiments: (1) performance of different models, (2) performance with respect to varying needle depths and haystack lengths, (3) performance across five different languages, and (4) reasoning over magic numbers and world cities. For the first three experiments, we analyze the models' responses when asked to retrieve and reason about the magic number. In the last experiment, we compare the models' performance when asked about the magic number or the city.

### 4.1 Performance of different models across languages and tasks

Figure 3 presents the radar plots summarizing the the average accuracy of each model for all tasks and languages.

Across the languages evaluated, English generally demonstrates strong performance across all models and tasks, particularly in the simpler retrieval task ($n = 1$), likely due to the extensive amount of English data available for model training. Vietnamese also performs relatively well, especially in the more complex reasoning tasks ($n = 2$ and $n = 3$), which may be attributed to effective tokenization (more discussion in section 4.3). In contrast, performance drops significantly for Indonesian, Swahili, and Somali, particularly as task complexity increases. While this decline is not surprising and highlights the ongoing challenge in multilingual NLP models trained predominantly on

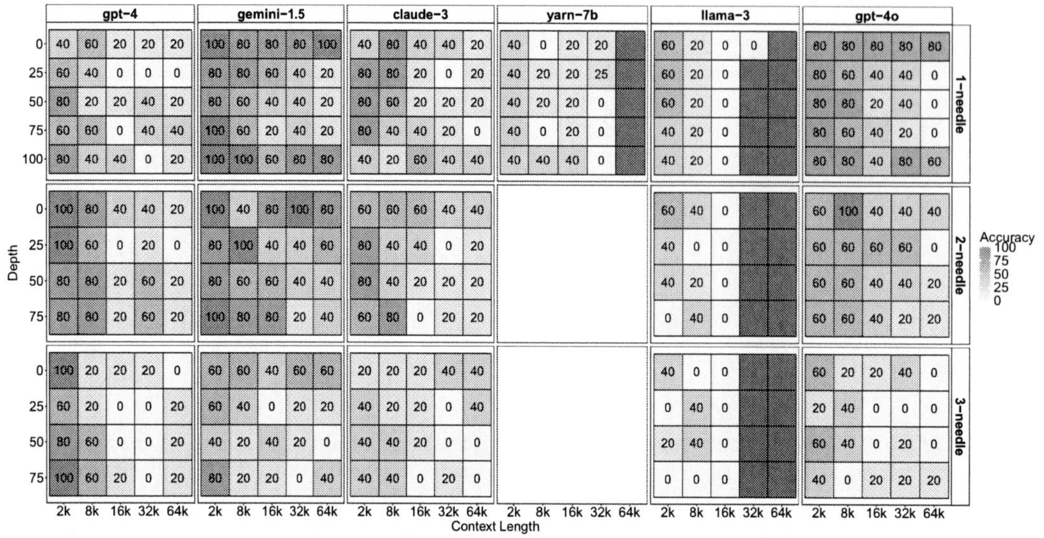

Figure 4: Heatmap visualizations with varying depths on the $y$-axis and context lengths on the $x$-axis, showing average model performance over all the languages for both retrieval (top panel) and reasoning tasks (middle and bottom panels). The color gradient from white to dark green represents accuracy levels, with darker green indicating higher accuracy.

high-resource languages tending to perform well in those languages but faltering in low-resource languages, the extent of the decline remains noteworthy.

Gemini-1.5 and GPT-4o exhibit strong performance across all tasks and languages, maintaining the most balanced results overall, particularly in English and Vietnamese. However, their performance declines in more complex tasks for low-resource languages like Swahili and Somali. In contrast, other models display more variability, with certain strengths in specific languages but generally lower performance in reasoning tasks, particularly when multiple needles are involved.

As task complexity increases (from $n = 1$ to $n = 3$), extending from retrieval to reasoning, all models experience a performance drop, particularly in low-resource languages. This indicates that while models can handle simple retrieval tasks reasonably well, they struggle significantly with reasoning tasks that require understanding and processing long contexts in less-resourced languages.

## 4.2 Performance across varying needle depths and haystack lengths

Figure 4 presents a detailed heatmap analysis of each model's performance with varying context lengths and needle depths. For all models, performance is better in shorter contexts, or when the needle is either near the top or the bottom of the context, suggesting that the "lost in the middle" phenomenon which was previously observed in English settings (Liu et al., 2024) extends to multilingual contexts as well.

The heatmaps clearly show that longer context lengths and greater depths negatively impact accuracy. This suggests that current LLM architectures struggle to use relevant information effectively when processing large amounts of data or when reasoning requires multiple steps. As the task complexity increases (from retrieval to 3-needle reasoning), model performance declines across the board. This decline is particularly pronounced in models like Yarn-7b and Llama-3, which fail to handle the increased cognitive load of deeper reasoning tasks with longer contexts. Gemini-1.5 is the most resilient model across all tasks, maintaining relatively high accuracy even in complex scenarios. However, its performance also suffers as depth and context length increase, highlighting the challenges of scaling reasoning abilities in LLMs.

## 4.3 Performance across different languages

The results presented in Figure 5 provide a fine-grained analysis of language-specific performance. English consistently performs well across tasks,

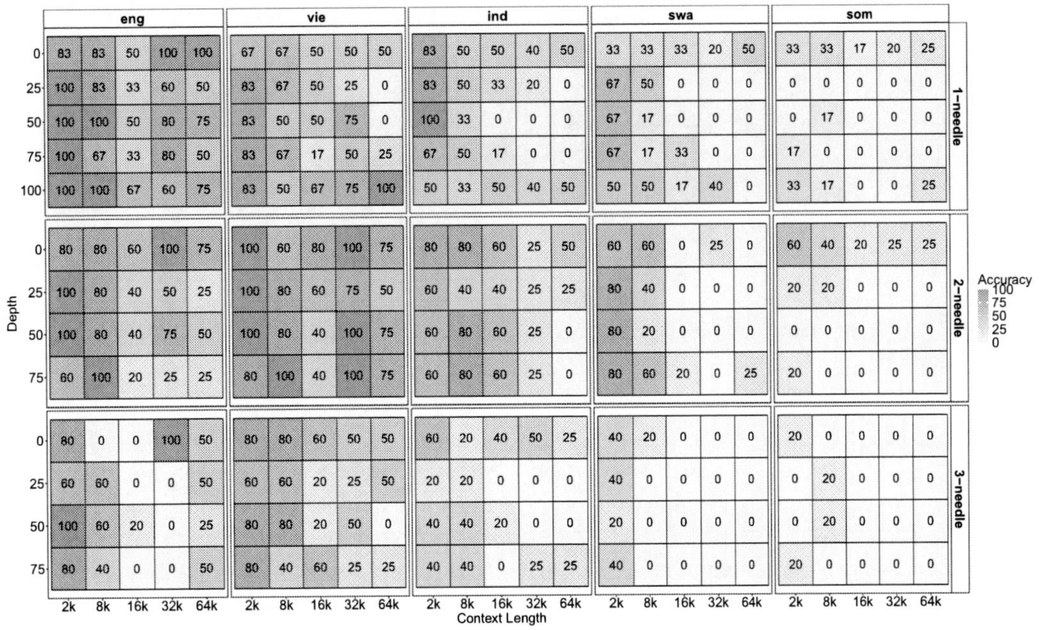

Figure 5: Language-specific heatmap visualizations with varying depths on the $y$-axis and context lengths on the $x$-axis, averaged over all the models, when $n = 1$, $n = 2$, and $n = 3$.

| | GPT-4 | Gemini-1.5 | Claude-3 | YaRN-7b | Llama-3 | GPT-4o |
|---|---|---|---|---|---|---|
| English | 1.13 | 1.15 | 1.15 | 1.32 | 1.13 | 1.11 |
| Vietnamese | 2.08 | 1.20 | 2.89 | 2.75 | 1.27 | 1.29 |
| Indonesian | 1.92 | 1.40 | 2.33 | 2.48 | 1.91 | 1.55 |
| Swahili | 2.23 | 1.85 | 2.36 | 2.48 | 2.21 | 1.68 |
| Somali | 2.37 | 2.09 | 2.47 | 2.70 | 2.36 | 1.79 |
| **Average** | 1.94 | 1.53 | 2.24 | 2.34 | 1.77 | 1.48 |

Table 2: Tokenization rate for each language using different model tokenizers.

with near 100% accuracy in simpler tasks but declining with increased complexity, particularly at greater depths and longer contexts. Vietnamese also maintains high accuracy, though it declines similarly with complexity. Indonesian starts reasonably well but drops significantly in more complex scenarios. Swahili shows weaker overall performance, struggling with all tasks, especially complex ones. Somali performs the poorest, often reaching zero accuracy as task complexity increases, highlighting challenges in handling this low-resource language. In short, performance degrades progressively as we move from high-resource languages to low-resource languages. The detailed results of each model and language are included in Appendix A.

The strong performance of English and, to a lesser extent, Vietnamese, reflects the availability of ample training data in these languages. However, access to the exact language distributions of training data are not readily available for most models, including open-source model like Llama-3.

### 4.4 Impact of tokenization

We further analyze the tokenization rate, also known as fertility rate, which is the average number of tokens generated per word for the different languages. The results are presented in Table 2. Unsurprisingly, English consistently shows the lowest tokenization rates across all models. Vietnamese has varying rates, with Gemini-1.5 being the most efficient, while Claude-3 and YaRN-7b tokenize more heavily. Indonesian exhibits moderate rates with some variability across models. Swahili and

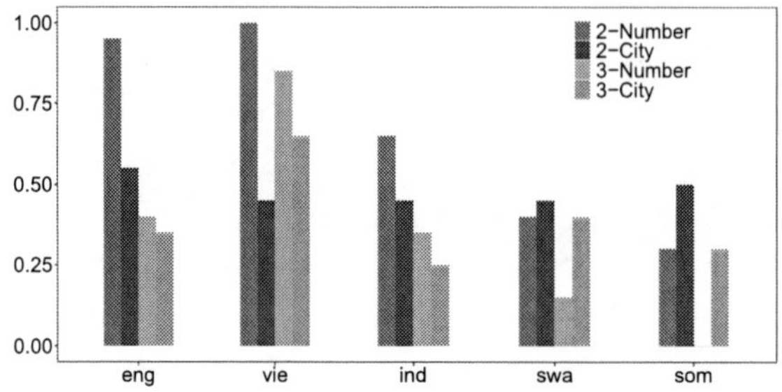


Figure 6: Comparing reasoning over magic numbers and random cities, when $n = 2$ and $n = 3$ (results obtained using Gemini-1.5).

Somali, the two lowest resource level languages in our study, generally have higher tokenization rates, suggesting these are more challenging for models to process effectively.

We can make two interesting observations: (i) the performance of LLMs is influenced by the way the models tokenized text across languages, with lower fragmentation leading to improved performance, and (ii) the models with overall lower fragmentation scores, such as Gemini-1.5 followed by GPT-4o, achieved better results across all languages and tasks.

### 4.5 Reasoning about magic numbers and world cities

Lastly, we compare the performance of the models in reasoning tasks with 2 and 3 needles for two types of question prompts: identifying the larger/largest magic number (e.g., 4281932) or the city with the larger/largest magic number (e.g., Doha). From the results presented in Figure 6, we observe that the models yield generally better performance in the "number" tasks compared to the "city" tasks implying that they may be more adept at handling numerical reasoning than reasoning over geographic entities, however, this trend is reversed for Swahili and Somali.

## 5 Conclusion

We introduce a new dataset designed to study long-context retrieval and reasoning tasks across multiple languages. By evaluating six LLMs on their ability to process text in five languages with varying resource levels, using naturally occurring text and a needle-in-a-haystack paradigm with different numbers of needles, we discovered key insights. Notably, we observed a significant decline in performance, particularly when dealing with longer contexts, an increased number of needles, or lower resource levels. Even seemingly simple synthetic tasks like needle-in-a-haystack revealed substantial performance disparities. Our findings highlight the need to develop not only more effective long-context models but also improved tokenization schemes for the effective processing of low-resource languages.

## Limitations

While our current focus has been on languages that use Latin script, we are eager to expand our horizons and explore the diversity of languages from other scripts in the future. Furthermore, our investigation was restricted to three needles. It would be interesting to explore whether addition of more needles continues to increase the task complexity.

## Ethics Statement

We did not implement any filtering of the haystack data, it is possible that there are inherent biases towards certain groups within the dataset. The impact of such biases on our findings remains unclear and fall outside the scope of this study. For annotation in Vietnamese, Indonesian, Swahili, and Somali, we hired translators and paid USD 15 to each translator as the short translation tasks took less than one hour each.

## Acknowledgments

We thank the anonymous reviewers as well as the members of PortNLP lab for their insightful comments that helped improve this paper. This research was partially supported by the National Science Foundation grant HNDS-R 2242205.

## References


Josh Achiam, Steven Adler, Sandhini Agarwal, Lama Ahmad, Ilge Akkaya, Florencia Leoni Aleman, Diogo Almeida, Janko Altenschmidt, Sam Altman, Shyamal Anadkat, et al. 2023. Gpt-4 technical report. *arXiv preprint arXiv:2303.08774*.

Orevaoghene Ahia, Sachin Kumar, Hila Gonen, Jungo Kasai, David Mortensen, Noah Smith, and Yulia Tsvetkov. 2023. Do all languages cost the same? tokenization in the era of commercial language models. In *Proceedings of the 2023 Conference on Empirical Methods in Natural Language Processing*, pages 9904–9923, Singapore. Association for Computational Linguistics.

Kabir Ahuja, Harshita Diddee, Rishav Hada, Millicent Ochieng, Krithika Ramesh, Prachi Jain, Akshay Nambi, Tanuja Ganu, Sameer Segal, Mohamed Ahmed, Kalika Bali, and Sunayana Sitaram. 2023. MEGA: Multilingual evaluation of generative AI. In *Proceedings of the 2023 Conference on Empirical Methods in Natural Language Processing*, pages 4232–4267, Singapore. Association for Computational Linguistics.

Chenxin An, Shansan Gong, Ming Zhong, Xingjian Zhao, Mukai Li, Jun Zhang, Lingpeng Kong, and Xipeng Qiu. 2024. L-eval: Instituting standardized evaluation for long context language models. In *Proceedings of the 62nd Annual Meeting of the Association for Computational Linguistics (Volume 1: Long Papers)*, pages 14388–14411, Bangkok, Thailand. Association for Computational Linguistics.

Anthropic. 2024. The claude 3 model family: Opus, sonnet, haiku. [Online; accessed 20-March-2024].

Sina Bagheri Nezhad and Ameeta Agrawal. 2024a. Exploring the maze of multilingual modeling. *Preprint*, arXiv:2310.05404.

Sina Bagheri Nezhad and Ameeta Agrawal. 2024b. What drives performance in multilingual language models? In *Proceedings of the Eleventh Workshop on NLP for Similar Languages, Varieties, and Dialects (VarDial 2024)*, pages 16–27, Mexico City, Mexico. Association for Computational Linguistics.

Yushi Bai, Xin Lv, Jiajie Zhang, Hongchang Lyu, Jiankai Tang, Zhidian Huang, Zhengxiao Du, Xiao Liu, Aohan Zeng, Lei Hou, et al. 2023. Longbench: A bilingual, multitask benchmark for long context understanding. *arXiv preprint arXiv:2308.14508*.

Yejin Bang, Samuel Cahyawijaya, Nayeon Lee, Wenliang Dai, Dan Su, Bryan Wilie, Holy Lovenia, Ziwei Ji, Tiezheng Yu, Willy Chung, Quyet V. Do, Yan Xu, and Pascale Fung. 2023. A multitask, multilingual, multimodal evaluation of ChatGPT on reasoning, hallucination, and interactivity. In *Proceedings of the 13th International Joint Conference on Natural Language Processing and the 3rd Conference of the Asia-Pacific Chapter of the Association for Computational Linguistics (Volume 1: Long Papers)*, pages 675–718, Nusa Dua, Bali. Association for Computational Linguistics.

Patrick Bareiß, Roman Klinger, and Jeremy Barnes. 2024. English prompts are better for nli-based zero-shot emotion classification than target-language prompts. In *Companion Proceedings of the ACM Web Conference 2024*, WWW '24, page 1318–1326, New York, NY, USA. Association for Computing Machinery.

Ethan C. Chau and Noah A. Smith. 2021. Specializing multilingual language models: An empirical study. In *Proceedings of the 1st Workshop on Multilingual Representation Learning*, pages 51–61, Punta Cana, Dominican Republic. Association for Computational Linguistics.

Shouyuan Chen, Sherman Wong, Liangjian Chen, and Yuandong Tian. 2023. Extending context window of large language models via positional interpolation. *arXiv preprint arXiv:2306.15595*.

Zihang Dai, Zhilin Yang, Yiming Yang, Jaime Carbonell, Quoc Le, and Ruslan Salakhutdinov. 2019. Transformer-XL: Attentive language models beyond a fixed-length context. In *Proceedings of the 57th Annual Meeting of the Association for Computational Linguistics*, pages 2978–2988, Florence, Italy. Association for Computational Linguistics.

Aparna Dhinakaran. 2024. Llmtest_needleinahaystack. [Online; accessed 20-March-2024].

Yiran Ding, Li Lyna Zhang, Chengruidong Zhang, Yuanyuan Xu, Ning Shang, Jiahang Xu, Fan Yang, and Mao Yang. 2024. Longrope: Extending llm context window beyond 2 million tokens. *arXiv preprint arXiv:2402.13753*.

Abhimanyu Dubey, Abhinav Jauhri, Abhinav Pandey, Abhishek Kadian, Ahmad Al-Dahle, Aiesha Letman, Akhil Mathur, Alan Schelten, Amy Yang, Angela Fan, Anirudh Goyal, Anthony Hartshorn, Aobo Yang, Archi Mitra, Archie Sravankumar, Artem Korenev, Arthur Hinsvark, Arun Rao, Aston Zhang, Aurelien Rodriguez, Austen Gregerson, Ava Spataru, Baptiste Roziere, Bethany Biron, Binh Tang, Bobbie Chern, Charlotte Caucheteux, Chaya Nayak, Chloe Bi, Chris Marra, Chris McConnell, Christian Keller, Christophe Touret, Chunyang Wu, Corinne Wong, Cristian Canton Ferrer, Cyrus Nikolaidis, Damien Allonsius, Daniel Song, Danielle Pintz, Danny Livshits, David Esiobu, Dhruv Choudhary, Dhruv Mahajan, Diego Garcia-Olano, Diego Perino, Dieuwke Hupkes, Egor Lakomkin, Ehab AlBadawy, Elina Lobanova, Emily Dinan, Eric Michael Smith, Filip Radenovic, Frank Zhang, Gabriel Synnaeve, Gabrielle Lee, Georgia Lewis Anderson, Graeme Nail, Gregoire Mialon, Guan Pang, Guillem Cucurell, Hailey Nguyen, Hannah Korevaar, Hu Xu, Hugo Touvron, Iliyan Zarov, Imanol Arrieta Ibarra, Isabel Kloumann, Ishan Misra, Ivan Evtimov, Jade Copet, Jaewon Lee, Jan Geffert, Jana Vranes, Jason Park, Jay Mahadeokar, Jeet Shah, Jelmer van der Linde, Jennifer Billock,

Jenny Hong, Jenya Lee, Jeremy Fu, Jianfeng Chi, Jianyu Huang, Jiawen Liu, Jie Wang, Jiecao Yu, Joanna Bitton, Joe Spisak, Jongsoo Park, Joseph Rocca, Joshua Johnstun, Joshua Saxe, Junteng Jia, Kalyan Vasuden Alwala, Kartikeya Upasani, Kate Plawiak, Ke Li, Kenneth Heafield, Kevin Stone, Khalid El-Arini, Krithika Iyer, Kshitiz Malik, Kuenley Chiu, Kunal Bhalla, Lauren Rantala-Yeary, Laurens van der Maaten, Lawrence Chen, Liang Tan, Liz Jenkins, Louis Martin, Lovish Madaan, Lubo Malo, Lukas Blecher, Lukas Landzaat, Luke de Oliveira, Madeline Muzzi, Mahesh Pasupuleti, Mannat Singh, Manohar Paluri, Marcin Kardas, Mathew Oldham, Mathieu Rita, Maya Pavlova, Melanie Kambadur, Mike Lewis, Min Si, Mitesh Kumar Singh, Mona Hassan, Naman Goyal, Narjes Torabi, Nikolay Bashlykov, Nikolay Bogoychev, Niladri Chatterji, Olivier Duchenne, Onur Çelebi, Patrick Alrassy, Pengchuan Zhang, Pengwei Li, Petar Vasic, Peter Weng, Prajjwal Bhargava, Pratik Dubal, Praveen Krishnan, Punit Singh Koura, Puxin Xu, Qing He, Qingxiao Dong, Ragavan Srinivasan, Raj Ganapathy, Ramon Calderer, Ricardo Silveira Cabral, Robert Stojnic, Roberta Raileanu, Rohit Girdhar, Rohit Patel, Romain Sauvestre, Ronnie Polidoro, Roshan Sumbaly, Ross Taylor, Ruan Silva, Rui Hou, Rui Wang, Saghar Hosseini, Sahana Chennabasappa, Sanjay Singh, Sean Bell, Seohyun Sonia Kim, Sergey Edunov, Shaoliang Nie, Sharan Narang, Sharath Raparthy, Sheng Shen, Shengye Wan, Shruti Bhosale, Shun Zhang, Simon Vandenhende, Soumya Batra, Spencer Whitman, Sten Sootla, Stephane Collot, Suchin Gururangan, Sydney Borodinsky, Tamar Herman, Tara Fowler, Tarek Sheasha, Thomas Georgiou, Thomas Scialom, Tobias Speckbacher, Todor Mihaylov, Tong Xiao, Ujjwal Karn, Vedanuj Goswami, Vibhor Gupta, Vignesh Ramanathan, Viktor Kerkez, Vincent Gonguet, Virginie Do, Vish Vogeti, Vladan Petrovic, Weiwei Chu, Wenhan Xiong, Wenyin Fu, Whitney Meers, Xavier Martinet, Xiaodong Wang, Xiaoqing Ellen Tan, Xinfeng Xie, Xuchao Jia, Xuewei Wang, Yaelle Goldschlag, Yashesh Gaur, Yasmine Babaei, Yi Wen, Yiwen Song, Yuchen Zhang, Yue Li, Yuning Mao, Zacharie Delpierre Coudert, Zheng Yan, Zhengxing Chen, Zoe Papakipos, Aaditya Singh, Aaron Grattafiori, Abha Jain, Adam Kelsey, Adam Shajnfeld, Adithya Gangidi, Adolfo Victoria, Ahuva Goldstand, Ajay Menon, Ajay Sharma, Alex Boesenberg, Alex Vaughan, Alexei Baevski, Allie Feinstein, Amanda Kallet, Amit Sangani, Anam Yunus, Andrei Lupu, Andres Alvarado, Andrew Caples, Andrew Gu, Andrew Ho, Andrew Poulton, Andrew Ryan, Ankit Ramchandani, Annie Franco, Aparajita Saraf, Arkabandhu Chowdhury, Ashley Gabriel, Ashwin Bharambe, Assaf Eisenman, Azadeh Yazdan, Beau James, Ben Maurer, Benjamin Leonhardi, Bernie Huang, Beth Loyd, Beto De Paola, Bhargavi Paranjape, Bing Liu, Bo Wu, Boyu Ni, Braden Hancock, Bram Wasti, Brandon Spence, Brani Stojkovic, Brian Gamido, Britt Montalvo, Carl Parker, Carly Burton, Catalina Mejia, Changhan Wang, Changkyu Kim, Chao Zhou, Chester Hu, Ching-Hsiang Chu, Chris Cai, Chris Tindal, Christoph Feichtenhofer, Damon Civin, Dana Beaty, Daniel Kreymer, Daniel Li, Danny Wyatt, David Adkins, David Xu, Davide Testuggine, Delia David, Devi Parikh, Diana Liskovich, Didem Foss, Dingkang Wang, Duc Le, Dustin Holland, Edward Dowling, Eissa Jamil, Elaine Montgomery, Eleonora Presani, Emily Hahn, Emily Wood, Erik Brinkman, Esteban Arcaute, Evan Dunbar, Evan Smothers, Fei Sun, Felix Kreuk, Feng Tian, Firat Ozgenel, Francesco Caggioni, Francisco Guzmán, Frank Kanayet, Frank Seide, Gabriela Medina Florez, Gabriella Schwarz, Gada Badeer, Georgia Swee, Gil Halpern, Govind Thattai, Grant Herman, Grigory Sizov, Guangyi, Zhang, Guna Lakshminarayanan, Hamid Shojanazeri, Han Zou, Hannah Wang, Hanwen Zha, Haroun Habeeb, Harrison Rudolph, Helen Suk, Henry Aspegren, Hunter Goldman, Ibrahim Damlaj, Igor Molybog, Igor Tufanov, Irina-Elena Veliche, Itai Gat, Jake Weissman, James Geboski, James Kohli, Japhet Asher, Jean-Baptiste Gaya, Jeff Marcus, Jeff Tang, Jennifer Chan, Jenny Zhen, Jeremy Reizenstein, Jeremy Teboul, Jessica Zhong, Jian Jin, Jingyi Yang, Joe Cummings, Jon Carvill, Jon Shepard, Jonathan McPhie, Jonathan Torres, Josh Ginsburg, Junjie Wang, Kai Wu, Kam Hou U, Karan Saxena, Karthik Prasad, Kartikay Khandelwal, Katayoun Zand, Kathy Matosich, Kaushik Veeraraghavan, Kelly Michelena, Keqian Li, Kun Huang, Kunal Chawla, Kushal Lakhotia, Kyle Huang, Lailin Chen, Lakshya Garg, Lavender A, Leandro Silva, Lee Bell, Lei Zhang, Liangpeng Guo, Licheng Yu, Liron Moshkovich, Luca Wehrstedt, Madian Khabsa, Manav Avalani, Manish Bhatt, Maria Tsimpoukelli, Martynas Mankus, Matan Hasson, Matthew Lennie, Matthias Reso, Maxim Groshev, Maxim Naumov, Maya Lathi, Meghan Keneally, Michael L. Seltzer, Michal Valko, Michelle Restrepo, Mihir Patel, Mik Vyatskov, Mikayel Samvelyan, Mike Clark, Mike Macey, Mike Wang, Miquel Jubert Hermoso, Mo Metanat, Mohammad Rastegari, Munish Bansal, Nandhini Santhanam, Natascha Parks, Natasha White, Navyata Bawa, Nayan Singhal, Nick Egebo, Nicolas Usunier, Nikolay Pavlovich Laptev, Ning Dong, Ning Zhang, Norman Cheng, Oleg Chernoguz, Olivia Hart, Omkar Salpekar, Ozlem Kalinli, Parkin Kent, Parth Parekh, Paul Saab, Pavan Balaji, Pedro Rittner, Philip Bontrager, Pierre Roux, Piotr Dollar, Polina Zvyagina, Prashant Ratanchandani, Pritish Yuvraj, Qian Liang, Rachad Alao, Rachel Rodriguez, Rafi Ayub, Raghotham Murthy, Raghu Nayani, Rahul Mitra, Raymond Li, Rebekkah Hogan, Robin Battey, Rocky Wang, Rohan Maheswari, Russ Howes, Ruty Rinott, Sai Jayesh Bondu, Samyak Datta, Sara Chugh, Sara Hunt, Sargun Dhillon, Sasha Sidorov, Satadru Pan, Saurabh Verma, Seiji Yamamoto, Sharadh Ramaswamy, Shaun Lindsay, Shaun Lindsay, Sheng Feng, Shenghao Lin, Shengxin Cindy Zha, Shiva Shankar, Shuqiang Zhang, Shuqiang Zhang, Sinong Wang, Sneha Agarwal, Soji Sajuyigbe, Soumith Chintala, Stephanie Max, Stephen Chen, Steve Kehoe, Steve Satterfield, Sudarshan Govindaprasad, Sumit Gupta, Sungmin Cho, Sunny Virk, Suraj Subramanian, Sy Choudhury, Sydney Goldman, Tal Remez, Tamar Glaser, Tamara Best, Thilo Kohler, Thomas Robinson, Tianhe Li, Tianjun Zhang, Tim Matthews, Timothy Chou, Tzook

Shaked, Varun Vontimitta, Victoria Ajayi, Victoria Montanez, Vijai Mohan, Vinay Satish Kumar, Vishal Mangla, Vítor Albiero, Vlad Ionescu, Vlad Poenaru, Vlad Tiberiu Mihailescu, Vladimir Ivanov, Wei Li, Wenchen Wang, Wenwen Jiang, Wes Bouaziz, Will Constable, Xiaocheng Tang, Xiaofang Wang, Xiaojian Wu, Xiaolan Wang, Xide Xia, Xilun Wu, Xinbo Gao, Yanjun Chen, Ye Hu, Ye Jia, Ye Qi, Yenda Li, Yilin Zhang, Ying Zhang, Yossi Adi, Youngjin Nam, Yu, Wang, Yuchen Hao, Yundi Qian, Yuzi He, Zach Rait, Zachary DeVito, Zef Rosnbrick, Zhaoduo Wen, Zhenyu Yang, and Zhiwei Zhao. 2024. The llama 3 herd of models. *Preprint*, arXiv:2407.21783.

Julen Etxaniz, Gorka Azkune, Aitor Soroa, Oier Lacalle, and Mikel Artetxe. 2024. Do multilingual language models think better in English? In *Proceedings of the 2024 Conference of the North American Chapter of the Association for Computational Linguistics: Human Language Technologies (Volume 2: Short Papers)*, pages 550–564, Mexico City, Mexico. Association for Computational Linguistics.

Hongye Jin, Xiaotian Han, Jingfeng Yang, Zhimeng Jiang, Zirui Liu, Chia-Yuan Chang, Huiyuan Chen, and Xia Hu. 2024. Llm maybe longlm: Self-extend llm context window without tuning. *arXiv preprint arXiv:2401.01325*.

Pratik Joshi, Sebastin Santy, Amar Budhiraja, Kalika Bali, and Monojit Choudhury. 2020. The state and fate of linguistic diversity and inclusion in the NLP world. In *Proceedings of the 58th Annual Meeting of the Association for Computational Linguistics*, pages 6282–6293, Online. Association for Computational Linguistics.

Greg Kamradt. 2023. Llmtest needleinahaystack: Doing simple retrieval from llm models. `https://github.com/gkamradt/LLMTest-NeedleInAHaystack/tree/main`. [Online; accessed 20-March-2024].

Viet Lai, Nghia Ngo, Amir Pouran Ben Veyseh, Hieu Man, Franck Dernoncourt, Trung Bui, and Thien Nguyen. 2023a. ChatGPT beyond English: Towards a comprehensive evaluation of large language models in multilingual learning. In *Findings of the Association for Computational Linguistics: EMNLP 2023*, pages 13171–13189, Singapore. Association for Computational Linguistics.

Viet Lai, Nghia Ngo, Amir Pouran Ben Veyseh, Hieu Man, Franck Dernoncourt, Trung Bui, and Thien Nguyen. 2023b. ChatGPT beyond English: Towards a comprehensive evaluation of large language models in multilingual learning. In *Findings of the Association for Computational Linguistics: EMNLP 2023*, pages 13171–13189, Singapore. Association for Computational Linguistics.

Nelson F Liu, Kevin Lin, John Hewitt, Ashwin Paranjape, Michele Bevilacqua, Fabio Petroni, and Percy Liang. 2024. Lost in the middle: How language models use long contexts. *Transactions of the Association for Computational Linguistics*, 12:157–173.

Quinn McNemar. 1947. Note on the sampling error of the difference between correlated proportions or percentages. *Psychometrika*, 12(2):153–157.

Amirkeivan Mohtashami and Martin Jaggi. 2023. Random-access infinite context length for transformers. In *Advances in Neural Information Processing Systems*, volume 36, pages 54567–54585. Curran Associates, Inc.

Arka Pal, Deep Karkhanis, Manley Roberts, Samuel Dooley, Arvind Sundararajan, and Siddartha Naidu. 2023. Giraffe: Adventures in expanding context lengths in llms. *arXiv preprint arXiv:2308.10882*.

Bowen Peng, Jeffrey Quesnelle, Honglu Fan, and Enrico Shippole. 2024. YaRN: Efficient context window extension of large language models. In *The Twelfth International Conference on Learning Representations*.

Zexuan Qiu, Jingjing Li, Shijue Huang, Wanjun Zhong, and Irwin King. 2024. Clongeval: A chinese benchmark for evaluating long-context large language models. *arXiv preprint arXiv:2403.03514*.

Machel Reid, Nikolay Savinov, Denis Teplyashin, Dmitry Lepikhin, Timothy Lillicrap, Jean-baptiste Alayrac, Radu Soricut, Angeliki Lazaridou, Orhan Firat, Julian Schrittwieser, et al. 2024. Gemini 1.5: Unlocking multimodal understanding across millions of tokens of context. *arXiv preprint arXiv:2403.05530*.

Lingfeng Shen, Weiting Tan, Sihao Chen, Yunmo Chen, Jingyu Zhang, Haoran Xu, Boyuan Zheng, Philipp Koehn, and Daniel Khashabi. 2024. The language barrier: Dissecting safety challenges of LLMs in multilingual contexts. In *Findings of the Association for Computational Linguistics ACL 2024*, pages 2668–2680, Bangkok, Thailand and virtual meeting. Association for Computational Linguistics.

Simeng Sun, Kalpesh Krishna, Andrew Mattarella-Micke, and Mohit Iyyer. 2021. Do long-range language models actually use long-range context? In *Proceedings of the 2021 Conference on Empirical Methods in Natural Language Processing*, pages 807–822, Online and Punta Cana, Dominican Republic. Association for Computational Linguistics.

Hugo Touvron, Louis Martin, Kevin Stone, Peter Albert, Amjad Almahairi, Yasmine Babaei, Nikolay Bashlykov, Soumya Batra, Prajjwal Bhargava, Shruti Bhosale, et al. 2023. Llama 2: Open foundation and fine-tuned chat models. *arXiv preprint arXiv:2307.09288*.

Eline Visser. 2020. Kalamang dictionary.

Tao Yuan, Xuefei Ning, Dong Zhou, Zhijie Yang, Shiyao Li, Minghui Zhuang, Zheyue Tan, Zhuyu Yao, Dahua Lin, Boxun Li, Guohao Dai, Shengen Yan, and Yu Wang. 2024. Lv-eval: A balanced long-context benchmark with 5 length levels up to 256k. *Preprint*, arXiv:2402.05136.

Judit Ács. 2019. Exploring bert's vocabulary.

## A Detailed model and language-specific results

Figures 7, 8, 9, 10 and 11 show detailed results of the five models: GPT-4, Gemini-1.5, and Claude-3, Llama 3, and GPT-4o.

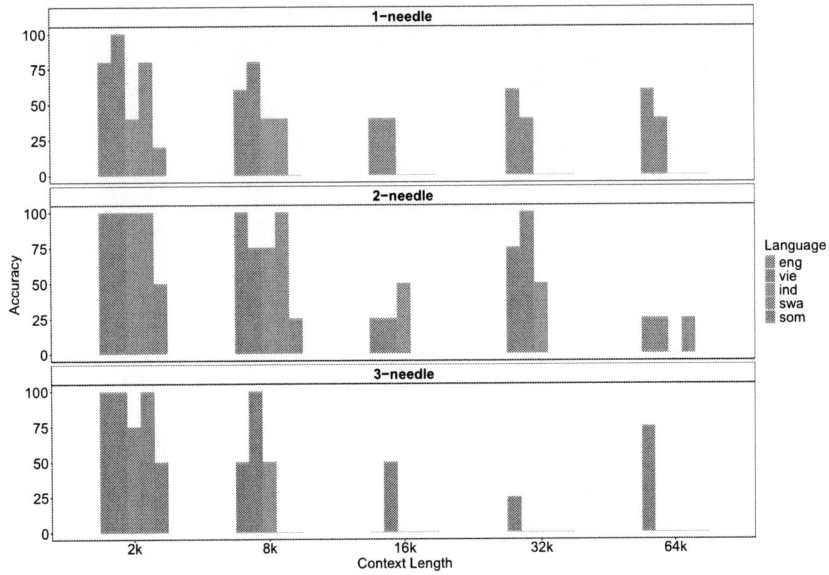


Figure 7: GPT-4

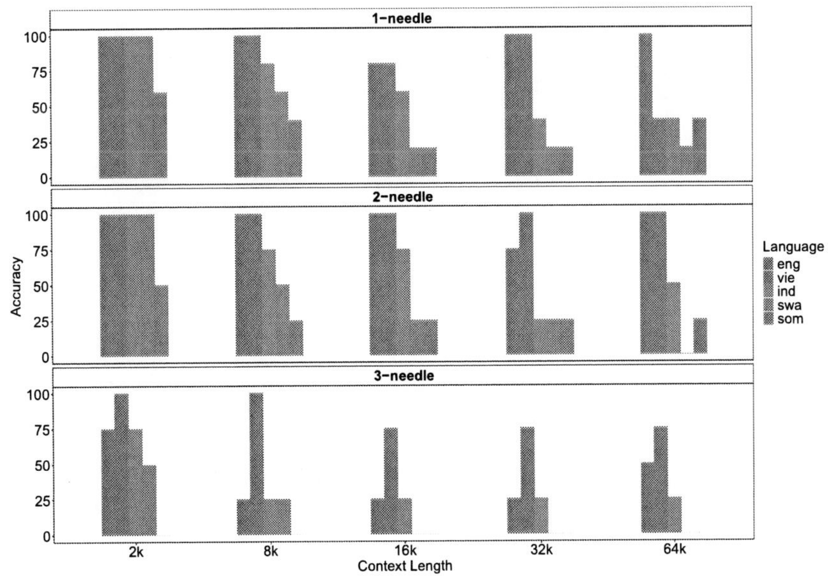


Figure 8: Gemini-1.5

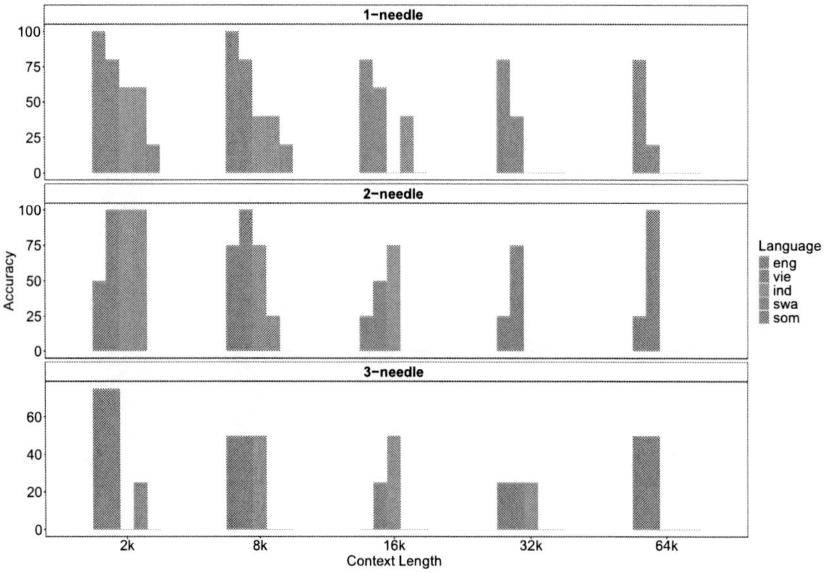


Figure 9: Claude-3

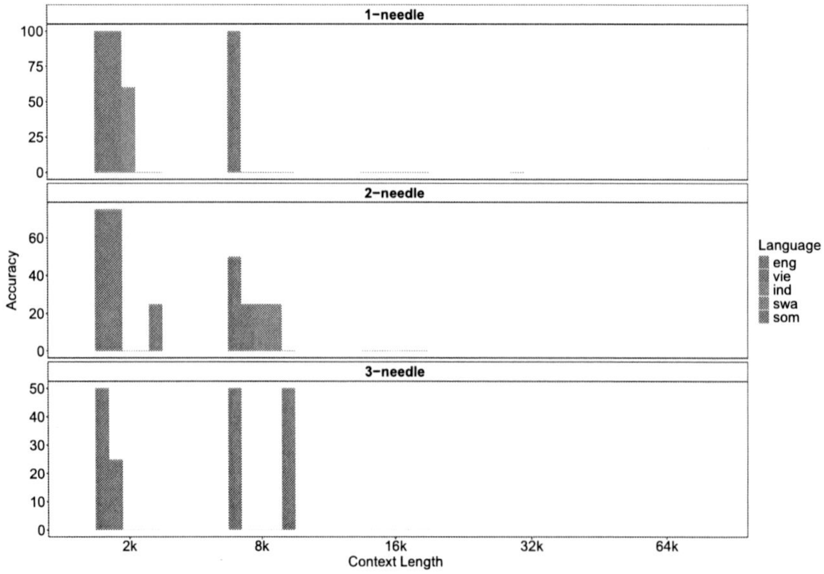


Figure 10: Llama 3

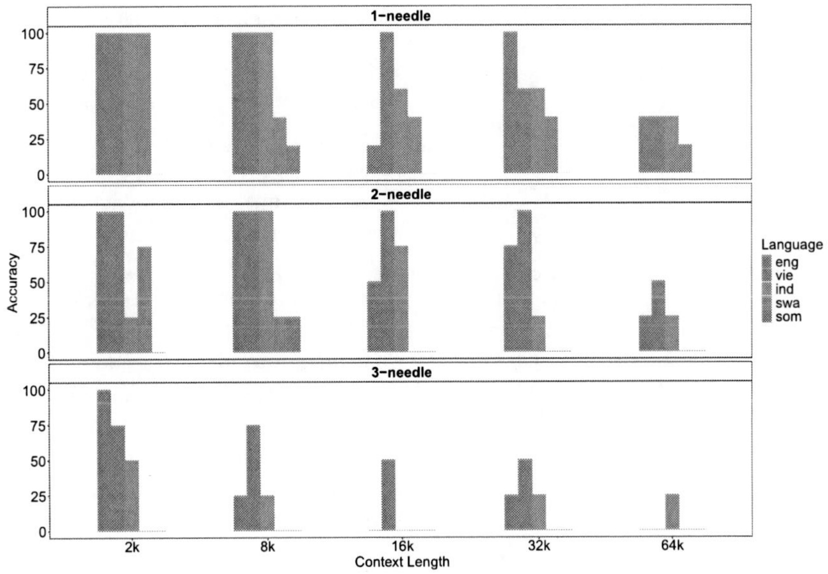


Figure 11: GPT-4o

# Community OSCAR: A Community Effort for Multilingual Web Data

**Manuel Brack**[1,2,3] **Malte Ostendorff**[1,4] **Pedro Ortiz Suarez**[1,5] **Jose Javier Saiz**[6]
**Iñaki Lacunza Castilla**[6] **Jorge Palomar-Giner**[6] **Alexander Shvets**[6]
**Patrick Schramowski**[1,2,3,7] **Georg Rehm**[2] **Marta Villegas**[6] **Kristian Kersting**[2,3,7,8]
[1]Occiglot, [2]German Research Center for Artificial Intelligence (DFKI),
[3]Computer Science Department, TU Darmstadt, [4]Deutsche Telekom,
[5]Common Crawl Foundation, [6]Language Technologies Unit, BSC,
[7]Hessian.AI, [8]Centre for Cognitive Science, TU Darmstadt
hello@occiglot.org

## Abstract

The development of large language models (LLMs) relies heavily on extensive, high-quality datasets. Publicly available datasets focus predominantly on English, leaving other language communities behind. To address this issue, we introduce Community OSCAR, a multilingual dataset initiative designed to address the gap between English and non-English data availability. Through a collective effort, Community OSCAR covers over 150 languages with 46 billion documents, totaling over 345 TiB of data. Initial results indicate that Community OSCAR provides valuable raw data for training LLMs and enhancing the performance of multilingual models. This work aims to contribute to the ongoing advancements in multilingual NLP and to support a more inclusive AI ecosystem by making high-quality, multilingual data more accessible to those working with low-resource languages.

## 1 Introduction

The success of large language models (LLMs) hinges on access to vast amounts of high-quality data. The exact composition, procurement, and curation of this data has been one of the more closely guarded secrets of commercial LLMs. Recently, academic and open-source efforts have made significant strides in curating and refining large-scale corpora for English [10, 9, 11, 8]. These data-driven efforts are central to advancing open-source and transparent LLM initiatives.

Nonetheless, a strong disparity remains between the availability of English-language datasets and those for other languages. We argue that access to high-quality data is imperative for ensuring linguistic diversity, academic and economic competitiveness, and AI sovereignty for non-English countries and speakers. However, clean, multilingual datasets like CulturaX [7], for example, can only provide 100B+ tokens for less than ten languages. To bridge this gap, we introduce Community OSCAR, a publicly available multilingual dataset that covers over 150 languages and includes over four times as much data as previous corpora. The creation of Community OSCAR is a collective, community-driven effort, highlighting the importance of collaboration in addressing the challenges of data scarcity for non-English languages[1]. By expanding the availability of non-English data, Community OSCAR seeks to democratize access to resources essential for building inclusive, multilingual AI systems. Our initial results indicate that Community OSCAR provides valuable raw data for downstream LLM training.

| | |
|---|---|
| Languages | 151 |
| Documents | 46B |
| Data size | 346 TiB |
| Crawls | 45 (Oct. 2014 - Aug 2024) |

Table 1: Community OSCAR dataset statistics. All statistics were calculated on a random subset of 10 releases and extrapolated to the entire dataset.

## 2 Community OSCAR

As the name suggests, Community OSCAR builds on prior work of the OSCAR corpus [1]. We went ahead and extended these efforts.

**OSCAR.** The OSCAR project (**O**pen **S**uper-large **C**rawled **A**ggregated co**R**pus) aims to provide open-source, web-based multilingual resources. Community OSCAR utilizes the high-performance *Ungoliant* data pipeline to process, filter, and annotate data at scale [2]. Most importantly, Ungoliant identifies and splits all documents based on their language [3, 6]. Similar to prior releases of OSCAR, we source our web-crawled data from Common Crawl's (CC) WET files.

[1]Dataset available at `https://huggingface.co/datasets/oscar-corpus/community-oscar`



*Proceedings of the Fourth Workshop on Multilingual Representation Learning (MRL 2024)*, pages 232–235
November 16, 2024 ©2024 Association for Computational Linguistics

| Model | German | | | | English | | | |
|---|---|---|---|---|---|---|---|---|
| | T-QA↑ | ARC↑ | HellaSwag↑ | MMLU↑ | T-QA↑ | ARC↑ | HellaSwag↑ | MMLU↑ |
| LLama-3-8B | 0.476 | 0.476 | 0.599 | 0.537 | 0.439 | 0.594 | 0.821 | 0.667 |
| LLama-3-8B + DE pre-train | **0.491**∘ | **0.507**∘ | **0.654**• | **0.540**• | 0.449 | 0.573 | 0.804 | 0.627 |
| LLama-3.1-8B | **0.504**• | 0.470 | 0.608 | 0.535 | 0.451 | 0.577 | 0.817 | 0.661 |
| LLama-3.1-8B + DE pre-train | 0.483 | **0.517**• | **0.650**∘ | **0.540**• | 0.464 | 0.581 | 0.802 | 0.635 |

Table 2: Multilingual pre-training with Community OSCAR. We report benchmark scores in German and English of Llama-3 models before and after continual pre-training with 80B German tokens from a filtered version of our data.

**Dataset Collection & Statistics.** Community OSCAR follows the annotation schema established in the OSCAR 23.01 release[2], ensuring consistency and reliability in data quality. Consequently, Community OSCAR contains the raw CC text but includes quality annotations for filtering. In contrast to prior work, we incorporate 45 monthly CC dumps from August 2024 to October 2014. We prioritized more recent data, covering all CC releases from the last four years in addition to hand-selected earlier data. Computation was split over multiple super-computers and high-performance clusters across Europe. Community OSCAR covers 151 different languages and contains over 45B documents for a total of over 345TiB of data.

By offering this extensive corpus, we hope to contribute to the ongoing efforts to improve multilingual NLP. Further, Community OSCAR aims to ensure these advancements are accessible to a broader audience, including researchers and developers working with low-resource languages.

## 3 Outlook

The release of Community OSCAR now enables further progress in multilingual language modeling. We are actively working on extending the dataset to at least all available CC dumps, curating a high-quality subset from the raw data, and training LLMs on that data. All three steps yield good initial results, which we will discuss in the following section. Specifically, we conducted initial experiments with subsets of the data and plan to extend our insights to the rest of the dataset.

**Extending Community OSCAR.** Despite its size, this initial release of Community OSCAR still leaves room for more data to be included. We aim to provide continuous support for the dataset, processing and adding any upcoming CC dumps whenever they become available. Further, out of 100 current CC releases, we only cover 45%. We are continuing the Community OSCAR effort to incorporate every existing CC dump since 2014. We globally deduplicated a subset of Community OSCAR for over ten languages and found that consecutive crawls contain significant numbers of unique documents. Especially for very low-resource languages, that additional data can be crucial in enabling LLM training at scale.

**Data Curation.** The raw Community OSCAR data should be processed further before being used for LLM training. To begin with, different crawls contain large amounts of duplicate documents. Additionally, the raw data from CC consists of different quality levels concerning syntactical and grammatical correctness, factual accuracy, quality of HTML parsing, unsafe content, etc. We want to identify the high-quality subset of all documents for training and remove duplicates. Community OSCAR has already been annotated with important information to enable curation efforts. Additionally, we have begun implementing a more sophisticated curation pipeline building on fineweb [8]. We identified several steps in the fineweb filtering that must be adjusted for the specific target language. We have already made an initial cleaned and deduplicated subset of the data available online for 10 languages[3].

**LLM Training.** Lastly, we filtered and deduplicated the German data from 20 Community OSCAR dumps to assess its potential for LLM training. We follow existing approaches for the multilingual extension of pre-trained LLMs [5] and performed continual pre-training on LLama-3.x-8B checkpoints [4]. Specifically, we further trained the Llama-3 and LLama-3.1 checkpoints on roughly 80B German tokens interleaved with 5% English replay from fineweb-edu.

The evaluation results are depicted in Tab. 2. We can clearly see that continual pre-training on our German data significantly improves the model's

[2]Annotation scheme documented at: https://oscar-project.github.io/documentation/versions/oscar-2301/

[3]fineweb dataset at: https://huggingface.co/datasets/occiglot/occiglot-fineweb-v0.5

German performance. Crucially, that observation also holds for Llama-3.1 which is already a multi-lingual model with German capabilities.

Community OSCAR's ongoing work contributes to multilingual NLP and aims to make advancements accessible to a broader audience.

## Acknowledgements

This release is supported by and was enabled by contributions from the OSCAR team at Inria (project-team ALMAnaCH), specially by Julien Abadji, Rua Ismail, and Benoit Sagot, the Common Crawl Foundation, the SLT and SAINT teams at DFKI, TU Darmstadt, the LangTech unit at the Barcelona Supercomputing Center, the 42 supercomputer and Hessian AI, the OpenGPT-X project, Fraunhofer, Jülich Supercomputing Centre, TU Dresden, Deutsche Telekom, as well as by members of the OSCAR community, in particular Sotaro Takeshita, Sebastian Nagel.

## References

[1] Julien Abadji, Pedro Ortiz Suarez, Laurent Romary, and Benoît Sagot. 2022. Towards a cleaner document-oriented multilingual crawled corpus. In *Proceedings of the Thirteenth Language Resources and Evaluation Conference*, pages 4344–4355, Marseille, France. European Language Resources Association.

[2] Julien Abadji, Pedro Javier Ortiz Suárez, Laurent Romary, and Benoît Sagot. 2021. Ungoliant: An optimized pipeline for the generation of a very large-scale multilingual web corpus. Proceedings of the Workshop on Challenges in the Management of Large Corpora (CMLC-9) 2021. Limerick, 12 July 2021 (Online-Event), pages 1 – 9, Mannheim. Leibniz-Institut für Deutsche Sprache.

[3] Piotr Bojanowski, Edouard Grave, Armand Joulin, and Tomas Mikolov. 2017. Enriching word vectors with subword information. *Transactions of the Association for Computational Linguistics*, 5:135–146.

[4] Abhimanyu Dubey, Abhinav Jauhri, Abhinav Pandey, Abhishek Kadian, Ahmad Al-Dahle, Aiesha Letman, Akhil Mathur, Alan Schelten, Amy Yang, Angela Fan, Anirudh Goyal, Anthony Hartshorn, Aobo Yang, Archi Mitra, Archie Sravankumar, Artem Korenev, Arthur Hinsvark, Arun Rao, Aston Zhang, Aurélien Rodriguez, Austen Gregerson, Ava Spataru, Baptiste Rozière, Bethany Biron, Binh Tang, Bobbie Chern, Charlotte Caucheteux, Chaya Nayak, Chloe Bi, Chris Marra, Chris McConnell, Christian Keller, Christophe Touret, Chunyang Wu, Corinne Wong, Cristian Canton Ferrer, Cyrus Nikolaidis, Damien Allonsius, Daniel Song, Danielle Pintz, Danny Livshits, David Esiobu, Dhruv Choudhary, Dhruv Mahajan, Diego Garcia-Olano, Diego Perino, Dieuwke Hupkes, Egor Lakomkin, Ehab AlBadawy, Elina Lobanova, Emily Dinan, Eric Michael Smith, Filip Radenovic, Frank Zhang, Gabriel Synnaeve, Gabrielle Lee, Georgia Lewis Anderson, Graeme Nail, Grégoire Mialon, Guan Pang, Guillem Cucurell, Hailey Nguyen, Hannah Korevaar, Hu Xu, Hugo Touvron, Iliyan Zarov, Imanol Arrieta Ibarra, Isabel M. Kloumann, Ishan Misra, Ivan Evtimov, Jade Copet, Jaewon Lee, Jan Geffert, Jana Vranes, Jason Park, Jay Mahadeokar, Jeet Shah, Jelmer van der Linde, Jennifer Billock, Jenny Hong, Jenya Lee, Jeremy Fu, Jianfeng Chi, Jianyu Huang, Jiawen Liu, Jie Wang, Jiecao Yu, Joanna Bitton, Joe Spisak, Jongsoo Park, Joseph Rocca, Joshua Johnstun, Joshua Saxe, Junteng Jia, Kalyan Vasuden Alwala, Kartikeya Upasani, Kate Plawiak, Ke Li, Kenneth Heafield, Kevin Stone, and et al. The llama 3 herd of models. *arXiv preprint arXiv:2407.21783*.

[5] Adam Ibrahim, Benjamin Thérien, Kshitij Gupta, Mats L. Richter, Quentin Gregory Anthony, Eugene Belilovsky, Timothée Lesort, and Irina Rish. 2024. Simple and scalable strategies to continually pre-train large language models. *Trans. Mach. Learn. Res.*

[6] Armand Joulin, Edouard Grave, Piotr Bojanowski, and Tomas Mikolov. 2017. Bag of tricks for efficient text classification. In *Proceedings of the 15th Conference of the European Chapter of the Association for Computational Linguistics: Volume 2, Short Papers*, pages 427–431. Association for Computational Linguistics.

[7] Thuat Nguyen, Chien Van Nguyen, Viet Dac Lai, Hieu Man, Nghia Trung Ngo, Franck Dernoncourt, Ryan A. Rossi, and Thien Huu Nguyen. 2023. Culturax: A cleaned, enormous, and multilingual dataset for large language models in 167 languages. *Preprint*, arXiv:2309.09400.

[8] Guilherme Penedo, Hynek Kydlíček, Loubna Ben allal, Anton Lozhkov, Margaret Mitchell, Colin Raffel, Leandro Von Werra, and Thomas Wolf. 2024. The fineweb datasets: Decanting the web for the finest text data at scale. *arXiv preprint arXiv:2406.17557*.

[9] Guilherme Penedo, Quentin Malartic, Daniel Hesslow, Ruxandra Cojocaru, Hamza Alobeidli, Alessandro Cappelli, Baptiste Pannier, Ebtesam Almazrouei, and Julien Launay. 2023. The refinedweb dataset for falcon LLM: outperforming curated corpora with web data only. In *Advances in Neural Information Processing Systems 36: Annual Conference on Neural Information Processing Systems 2023, NeurIPS 2023, New Orleans, LA, USA, December 10 - 16, 2023*.

[10] Daria Soboleva, Faisal Al-Khateeb, Joel Hestness, Nolan Dey, Robert Myers, and Jacob Robert Steeves. 2023. Slimpajama: A 627b token, cleaned and deduplicated version of redpajama.

[11] Luca Soldaini, Rodney Kinney, Akshita Bhagia, Dustin Schwenk, David Atkinson, Russell Authur,

Ben Bogin, Khyathi Chandu, Jennifer Dumas, Yanai Elazar, Valentin Hofmann, Ananya Jha, Sachin Kumar, Li Lucy, Xinxi Lyu, Nathan Lambert, Ian Magnusson, Jacob Morrison, Niklas Muennighoff, Aakanksha Naik, Crystal Nam, Matthew Peters, Abhilasha Ravichander, Kyle Richardson, Zejiang Shen, Emma Strubell, Nishant Subramani, Oyvind Tafjord, Evan Walsh, Luke Zettlemoyer, Noah Smith, Hannaneh Hajishirzi, Iz Beltagy, Dirk Groeneveld, Jesse Dodge, and Kyle Lo. 2024. Dolma: an open corpus of three trillion tokens for language model pretraining research. In *Proceedings of the 62nd Annual Meeting of the Association for Computational Linguistics (Volume 1: Long Papers)*.

# Leveraging LLMs for Translating and Classifying Mental Health Data

**Konstantinos Skianis**[*], **A. Seza Doğruöz**[#], **John Pavlopoulos**[†¶]
[*] Department of Computer Science and Engineering, University of Ioannina, Greece
[#] LT3, IDLab, Universiteit Gent, Belgium
[†] Department of Informatics, Athens University of Economics and Business, Greece
[¶] Archimedes/AthenaRC, Greece
kskianis@cse.uoi.gr as.dogruoz@ugent.be annis@aueb.gr

## Abstract

Large language models (LLMs) are increasingly used in medical fields. In mental health support, the early identification of linguistic markers associated with mental health conditions can provide valuable support to mental health professionals, and reduce long waiting times for patients. Despite the benefits of LLMs for mental health support, there is limited research on their application in mental health systems for languages other than English. Our study addresses this gap by focusing on the detection of depression severity in Greek through user-generated posts which are automatically translated from English. Our results show that GPT3.5-turbo is not very successful in identifying the severity of depression in English, and it has a varying performance in Greek as well. Our study underscores the necessity for further research, especially in languages with less resources. Also, careful implementation is necessary to ensure that LLMs are used effectively in mental health platforms, and human supervision remains crucial to avoid misdiagnosis.

## 1 Introduction

Mental health issues (e.g., depression, anxiety, and post-traumatic stress disorder (PTSD)) are prevalent worldwide and pose significant challenges to public health (World Health Organization, 2021). Traditional methods for diagnosing mental health conditions often rely on self-reported surveys, clinical interviews, and standardised assessments conducted by trained professionals (Kessler and Üstün, 2004). While these methods are effective, they are also resource-intensive, time-consuming, and may not always be accessible to individuals in need, particularly for speakers of languages beyond English.

In this context, the application of LLMs to detect mental health symptoms from textual data offers a compelling alternative. These models can analyse large volumes of text data (e.g., social media posts, forum discussions, and personal narratives) quickly to identify linguistic markers associated with mental health conditions (Guntuku et al., 2019; Chancellor et al., 2019). This capability opens up new avenues for early detection and intervention, providing valuable support to mental health professionals and potentially reaching out to the patients whose symptoms may be overlooked and/or save time (e.g., long waiting times).

Despite the potential benefits, the performance of LLMs in multilingual mental health symptom detection remains underexplored. Previous studies have primarily focused on English-language datasets, leaving a gap in our understanding of how these models perform in other linguistic contexts (Raihan et al., 2024). Hence, our work raises the following research questions:

- Can an LLM accurately predict the severity of mental health conditions from English user-generated posts?
- Is the detection performance similar if one automatically translates the English posts to another language (e.g., Greek) with LLMs?

To address these research questions, first, we assess a state-of-the-art multilingual LLM when predicting the severity of mental health in English user-generated posts. Then, we automatically translate these posts from English to Greek, a language for which there are no resources for this task (Bakagianni et al., 2024), and re-assess the performance of the LLM. Our research not only contributes to the development of more robust and inclusive AI-driven mental health diagnostic tools but also emphasises the importance of culturally and linguistically sensitive approaches in mental health care beyond English. The contribution of this work lies into the evaluation of the predictive power of a popular LLM in detecting the severity of depression across English and Greek.



*Proceedings of the Fourth Workshop on Multilingual Representation Learning (MRL 2024)*, pages 236–241
November 16, 2024 

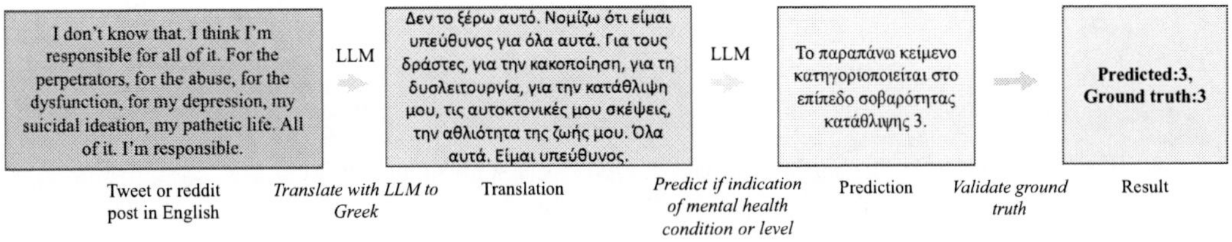


Figure 1: An illustration of our proposed methodology.

## 2 Related work

LLMs have remarkable accuracy in detecting mental health symptoms by leveraging their ability to understand context and semantics at a deeper level. Examples include BioBERT (Lee et al., 2020), and ClinicalBERT (Huang et al., 2019), which are pre-trained on biomedical corpora or clinical notes. In contrast, models like MentalBERT (Ji et al., 2022), DisorBERT (Aragon et al., 2023), and SuicidalBERT (Anonymous) are pre-trained on mental health-related social media data. Additionally, research by Benton et al. (2017) showed that NLP can effectively assess depression and PTSD from clinical notes, further validating the utility of these models in a healthcare setting.

Although the details about training and evaluation are not always transparent, the multilingual capabilities of LLMs enable these models to understand and generate text in various languages. A recent example is the XLM-R model, which has been trained on a vast amount of multilingual data and shows strong performance across multiple languages. According to Conneau et al. (2020), their model XLM-R outperforms previous models on a wide range of tasks, demonstrating that leveraging large-scale multilingual data can lead to improvements in cross-lingual understanding.

Despite these advancements, significant challenges remain in achieving truly equitable performance across all languages and handling culturally specific contexts accurately (Zhang et al., 2020). Languages with limited digital text data still pose a considerable challenge for LLMs, often resulting in lower performance and less reliable outputs. Addressing this issue requires more inclusive data collection practices and further research into transfer learning techniques that can better utilise limited resources (Doğruöz and Sitaram, 2022). Additionally, capturing cultural nuances and context-specific meanings is a complex task, as language is deeply intertwined with cultural and societal norms. Efforts to improve these aspects include developing more sophisticated algorithms and incorporating diverse and representative datasets (Doğruöz et al., 2023), ensuring that the benefits of multilingual LLMs are accessible to a broader range of users globally.

More recently, a plethora of social network datasets targeting mental health, have been available (Raihan et al., 2024). The authors gathered social media posts from Reddit and Twitter regarding depression, PTSD, schizophrenia, and eating disorders. Moreover, multiple models were fine-tuned on small-sized publicly available annotated mental health datasets by the authors to use them for labelling their introduced MentalHelp dataset. Nevertheless, the dataset includes only posts in English, and thus its use is restrictive, disallowing further research for multilingual scenarios.

## 3 Proposed Methodology

Our methodology leverages LLMs, in order to translate English social media posts to another language (Greek), and then to predict mental health conditions accordingly. Specifically, we translate the social media posts to Greek via an LLM, and we feed the resulting translations to a prompt that asks the LLM to predict specific severity levels of mental health conditions. We assess the LLM by comparing the predicted classes in both languages against the ground truth labels. We note that although our study focuses on Greek, our method is applicable to other language pairs as well. An illustration of the proposed approach for evaluating LLMs for multilingual detection of mental health conditions is shown in Figure 1.

## 4 Experiments

We select the DEPSEVERITY dataset of Naseem et al. (2022), which consists of posts from the social media platform Reddit, regarding different levels of depression. The posts (in English) are already labelled in terms of four levels of severity: minimal,

| Dataset | Category | #Classes | #Instances | Labels (#Support) | Prompt |
|---|---|---|---|---|---|
| DEPSEVERITY Naseem et al. (2022) | Depression | 4 | 3553 | Minimum (2587) Mild (290) Moderate (394) Severe (282) | "Categorise the following text with 1 of the 4 depression severity levels (0: Minimum, 1: Mild, 2: Moderate, 3: Severe)" |

Table 1: The benchmark dataset used in our study along with statistics.

| | English | | | Greek | | |
|---|---|---|---|---|---|---|
| Class | Pr | Rec | F1 | Pr | Rec | F1 |
| MINIMUM | 0.98 | 0.14 | 0.25 | 0.99 | 0.07 | 0.14 |
| MILD | 0.04 | 0.15 | 0.07 | 0.04 | 0.17 | 0.06 |
| MODERATE | 0.13 | 0.22 | 0.17 | 0.14 | 0.55 | 0.23 |
| SEVERE | 0.13 | 0.71 | 0.22 | 0.16 | 0.28 | 0.20 |
| **Macro avg** | 0.32 | 0.30 | 0.17 | 0.33 | 0.27 | 0.16 |

Table 2: **GPT-3.5 with 0-shot learning on DEPSEVERITY**, measuring Precision, Recall, and F1 per class in English and Greek. The last row shows the macro averages. The best F1 per class is shown in bold.

mild, moderate, and severe depression. The majority of posts belong to the minimal severity level (Table 1) making it a highly imbalanced dataset. We specifically selected this multi-class dataset to make the task more challenging for the LLM, as binary problems would have been easier to answer.

We use GPT3.5-turbo (Brown et al., 2020) through its API to translate the posts and predict the labels. The temperature parameter is set to 0, so the outcome is reproducible, regarding translations and predictions. We approach the task with text classification, comparing the predicted classes with the ground-truth ones, reporting Precision, Recall and F1. We experiment with English as the source and Greek as the target language. The prompt we used to predict the severity levels is shown in Table 1.

**Preliminary Prompting** Before exposing our LLM to any posts, definitions, or instructions, either for the translation or the classification task, we asked how it would classify posts to different levels of depression severity. The response of LLM was that it would initially try to identify language patterns associated with depression, such as:

- Persistent negative emotions, such as sadness, or hopelessness.
- Self-criticism or feelings of worthlessness.
- Expressions of loneliness or social withdrawal.
- Changes in behavior or routines, as in sleep patterns or appetite.
- References to emotional pain or distress.

More specifically, it would try to adapt the four depression severity levels to fit the context of social media posts, as follows.

- Level 1 (Minimum): Posts with minimal or occasional expressions of sadness.
- Level 2 (Mild): Posts indicating frequent negative emotions or noticeable changes in behavior.
- Level 3 (Moderate): Posts suggesting significant impairment in daily functioning or clear signs of distress.
- Level 4 (Severe): Posts indicating severe emotional distress, potential risk factors for self-harm, or complete social withdrawal.

We can infer that the LLM expects posts with very generic indications of negative signs.

**Classification in the source language** Initially, we experimented with the data in their source language (English), to set the baseline performance. That is, no translation step has been performed at this stage. As we observe in Table 2, the best F1 is achieved for the lowest severity/indication (F1=0.25) and the next best for the highest severity (F1=0.22). The overall low performance (F1=0.17) can be attributed to the difficulty of the task of detecting specific levels of depression, which are considered less distinct compared to other conditions. Therefore, it is likely more challenging for an LLM to distinguish these levels in user posts.

**Classification in the target language** In Greek, the worst results are observed for the mild level (F1=0.06), similarly to English (F1=0.07). Overall, a drop in scores is observed across all classes except for the moderate level, where results improve (F1=0.23; from 0.17). Also, although the scores for the two edges remain relatively high, the score for the lowest severity dropped in Greek (F1=0.14).

**Error Analysis** Mental health terminologies and nuances may not be well-represented in the available Greek corpora, making it difficult for an LLM

| Original post in English | Translated post in Greek | Prediction |
|---|---|---|
| My therapist says this is a normal behavior to display. Having been ripped from my children and left on the streets is very hard and I honestly want to give up. But the anxiety swirls to the point I keep trying to find where I went wrong. It replays and plays in my head over and over like a horror movie. The feeling of wanting to die because at that point I had nothing left. **Ground truth: 3 (severe)** **LLM prediction: 3 (severe)** | Ο θεραπευτής μου λέει ότι αυτή είναι μια φυσιολογική συμπεριφορά να εκδηλώνεται. Να έχεις αποσπαστεί από τα παιδιά μου και να μείνεις στους δρόμους είναι πολύ δύσκολο και ειλικρινά θέλω να τα παρατήσω. Αλλά η ανησυχία στριφογυρίζει μέχρι το σημείο που συνεχίζω να προσπαθώ να βρω πού έκανα λάθος. Επαναλαμβάνεται και παίζει στο μυαλό μου ξανά και ξανά σαν ταινία τρόμου. Το συναίσθημα της επιθυμίας να πεθάνω επειδή σε εκείνο το σημείο δεν είχα τίποτα άλλο. **LLM prediction: 3 (severe)** | Βάσει του περιεχομένου του κειμένου, η κατηγοριοποίηση της κατάθλιψης είναι στο επίπεδο 3: Σοβαρό. ---------------------------------------- Both original post and translation are correct |
| The sensation lasted hours. It seemed like a circulation problem, and I panicked and of course ended up in the ER again. This time a doctor came to see me immediately. He wanted to talk about my anxiety. He said he could run some more tests, but he didn't think it would help. **Ground truth: 0 (minimum)** **LLM prediction: 3 (severe)** | Η αίσθηση κράτησε ώρες. Φάνηκε σαν πρόβλημα κυκλοφορίας, και πανικοβλήθηκα και φυσικά κατέληξα ξανά στο ΕΚΑ. Αυτή τη φορά ήρθε αμέσως ένας γιατρός να με δει. Ήθελε να μιλήσει για την αγωνία μου. Είπε ότι θα μπορούσε να κάνει μερικές ακόμα εξετάσεις, αλλά δεν νομίζει ότι θα βοηθήσει. **LLM prediction: 2 (moderate)** | Both original post and translation are wrong |

Figure 2: Example translation (from English to Greek), with similar colour used for original and translated words.

to grasp the context accurately. Figure 2 presents two instances of the dataset and their corresponding translations in Greek. We marked words and their translations with similar colours for better visibility. Both translations appear to be accurate and convey the same meaning as the original Greek text. There are no significant differences that would alter the understanding of the texts. The first segment contains explicit mentions of severe depression symptoms such as "want to give up" and "feeling of wanting to die." These statements clearly indicate a severe level of depression, which is why both the ground truth and prediction were classified as severe. The second segment describes physical sensations, panic, and anxiety but does not express a severe depressive state. The ground truth classified this as minimal depression, likely because the primary issues are related to panic and anxiety rather than depression. The LLM predicted a moderate level of depression for the second segment, possibly because it picked up on the words "panicked" and "anxiety", which are associated with higher levels of distress. However, these symptoms are more indicative of anxiety disorders rather than depression. The discrepancy in the second prediction can be attributed to the LLM's interpretation of anxiety and panic as indicative of moderate depression, whereas the ground truth assessment considers these symptoms in the context of a panic or anxiety disorder with minimal depression.

**Cost of experiments** The total cost of credits using the GPT3.5-turbo API was less than $30 (US dollars), showing that minimal resources were required to conduct our experiments, without the need for expensive GPU infrastructure or fine-tuning. Our cost-saving methodology for utilizing resources efficiently is especially promising for extending medical data sets in English into other languages.

## 5 Conclusion

In our study, we focused on the ability of an LLM to predict the severity of depression in user-generated posts in English (source language) and in Greek (target language) when the posts are machine-translated by the same LLM. Our findings show that there is room for improvement in the source language (English) and that the edge classes are easier to handle. In the target language (Greek), results dropped for all but the moderate level, for which results increased considerably. Considering the varying performance of the LLM across the two languages, there is a need for utmost precautions not to rely on LLMs solely for translation in any healthcare setting. As stated by Stade et al. (2024), diagnosis of mental health should never be left alone to automatic systems, and it should never replace the diagnosis by human professionals, to avoid possible errors and/or misdiagnoses. Our approach, however, does not aim to assist the patients. By contrast, it is potentially useful to *train* professionals in the mental healthcare domain, which can be vital for languages other than English.

## Acknowledgments

In this project, John Pavlopoulos was partially supported by project MIS 5154714 of the National Recovery and Resilience Plan Greece 2.0 funded by the European Union under the NextGenerationEU Program. We thank OpenAI for granting us free credits for research purposes.

## Limitations

**Translation** In this work, we used a popular LLM like GPT3.5 to translate posts. Translating using only an LLM and not having an expert or native-language human resources introduces a small loss of information that in some cases affects the final results.

**Evaluation** Automatically evaluating the performance of LLMs is by definition a hard task. In order to measure the performance we search for the label in the LLM output. Whenever no label is detected we count it as the minimum label (class: 0) for the depression dataset and not suicidal (class: 0) for the suicide dataset.

**Potential risks** The quality of publicly available datasets, especially in sensitive areas like the mental health care domain is of great importance for prediction tasks. The data sets we employed as a basis in our study, along with our created multilingual data should be used with utmost care and only for assisting the health care specialists instead of diagnosing patients directly.

## References

Anonymous. Suicidalbert: A pretrained language model for suicidal ideation detection. Manuscript in preparation.

Marisol Aragon, Carlos Hernandez, and Ana Laura Sucar. 2023. Disorbert: A transformer-based model for the classification of mental disorders from social media text. *Journal of Biomedical Informatics*, 134:104156.

Juli Bakagianni, Kanella Pouli, Maria Gavriilidou, and John Pavlopoulos. 2024. Towards systematic monolingual nlp surveys: Gena of greek nlp. *arXiv preprint arXiv:2407.09861*.

Adrian Benton, Glen Coppersmith, and Mark Dredze. 2017. Multi-task learning for mental health conditions with limited social media data. *EACL 2017*, pages 152–162.

Tom Brown, Benjamin Mann, Nick Ryder, Melanie Subbiah, Jared D Kaplan, Prafulla Dhariwal, Arvind Neelakantan, Pranav Shyam, Girish Sastry, Amanda Askell, et al. 2020. Language models are few-shot learners. *Advances in neural information processing systems*, 33:1877–1901.

Stevie Chancellor, Michael L Birnbaum, Eric D Caine, Vincent MB Silenzio, and Munmun De Choudhury. 2019. A taxonomy of ethical tensions in inferring mental health states from social media. In *Proceedings of the Conference on Fairness, Accountability, and Transparency*, pages 79–88.

Alexis Conneau, Kartikay Khandelwal, Naman Goyal, Vishrav Chaudhary, Guillaume Wenzek, Francisco Guzmán, Edouard Grave, Myle Ott, Luke Zettlemoyer, and Veselin Stoyanov. 2020. Unsupervised cross-lingual representation learning at scale. In *Proceedings of the 58th Annual Meeting of the Association for Computational Linguistics*, Online. Association for Computational Linguistics.

A. Seza Doğruöz and Sunayana Sitaram. 2022. Language technologies for low resource languages: Sociolinguistic and multilingual insights. In *Proceedings of the 1st Annual Meeting of the ELRA/ISCA Special Interest Group on Under-Resourced Languages*, pages 92–97, Marseille, France. European Language Resources Association.

A. Seza Doğruöz, Sunayana Sitaram, and Zheng Xin Yong. 2023. Representativeness as a forgotten lesson for multilingual and code-switched data collection and preparation. In *Findings of the Association for Computational Linguistics: EMNLP 2023*, pages 5751–5767, Singapore. Association for Computational Linguistics.

Sharath Chandra Guntuku, Raphael Schneider, Ashley Pallavi Pelullo, Jennifer Young, Vivienne Wong, Lyle H Ungar, and Daniel E Polsky. 2019. Studying expressions of loneliness in individuals using twitter: An observational study. *BMJ Open*, 9(11):e030355.

Kexin Huang, Jaan Altosaar, and Rajesh Ranganath. 2019. Clinicalbert: Modeling clinical notes and predicting hospital readmission. *arXiv:1904.05342*.

Shaoxiong Ji, Yanzhao Zhang, Leilei Sun, and Jia Wang. 2022. Mentalbert: A pretrained language model for mental healthcare. In *Proceedings of the 2022 Conference on Empirical Methods in Natural Language Processing (EMNLP)*.

Ronald C Kessler and T Bedirhan Üstün. 2004. The world mental health (wmh) survey initiative version of the world health organization (who) composite international diagnostic interview (cidi). *International Journal of Methods in Psychiatric Research*, 13(2):93–121.

Jinhyuk Lee, Wonjin Yoon, Sungdong Kim, Donghyeon Kim, Sunkyu Kim, Jungyun Seo, and Jaewoo Kang. 2020. Biobert: a pre-trained biomedical language representation model for biomedical text mining. *Bioinformatics*, 36(4):1234–1240.

Usman Naseem, Adam G Dunn, Jinman Kim, and Matloob Khushi. 2022. Early identification of depression severity levels on reddit using ordinal classification. In *Proceedings of the ACM Web Conference 2022*, pages 2563–2572.

Nishat Raihan, Sadiya Sayara Chowdhury Puspo, Shafkat Farabi, Ana-Maria Bucur, Tharindu Ranasinghe, and Marcos Zampieri. 2024. Mentalhelp: A multi-task dataset for mental health in social media. In *Proceedings of the 2024 Joint International Conference on Computational Linguistics, Language Resources and Evaluation (LREC-COLING 2024)*, pages 11196–11203.

Elizabeth C Stade, Shannon Wiltsey Stirman, Lyle H Ungar, Cody L Boland, H Andrew Schwartz, David B Yaden, João Sedoc, Robert J DeRubeis, Robb Willer, and Johannes C Eichstaedt. 2024. Large language models could change the future of behavioral healthcare: a proposal for responsible development and evaluation. *NPJ Mental Health Research*, 3(1):12.

World Health Organization. 2021. Mental health. Retrieved from `https://www.who.int/health-topics/mental-health`.

Biao Zhang, Philip Williams, Ivan Titov, and Rico Sennrich. 2020. Improving massively multilingual neural machine translation and zero-shot translation. In *Proceedings of the 58th Annual Meeting of the Association for Computational Linguistics*, Online. Association for Computational Linguistics.

# Bridging the Bosphorus: Advancing Turkish Large Language Models through Strategies for Low-Resource Language Adaptation and Benchmarking

**Emre Can Acikgoz**[1,2*] , **Mete Erdogan**[1,2] , **Deniz Yuret**[1,2]

[1]Koç University, KUIS AI Center, [2]Koç University, Department of Computer Engineering

{eacikgoz17,merdogan18,dyuret}@ku.edu.tr

## Abstract

Large Language Models (LLMs) are becoming crucial across various fields, emphasizing the urgency for high-quality models in underrepresented languages. This study explores the unique challenges faced by low-resource languages, such as data scarcity, model selection, evaluation, and computational limitations, with a special focus on Turkish. We conduct an in-depth analysis to evaluate the impact of training strategies, model choices, and data availability on the performance of LLMs designed for underrepresented languages. Our approach includes two methodologies: (i) adapting existing LLMs originally pretrained in English to understand Turkish, and (ii) developing a model from the ground up using Turkish pretraining data, both supplemented with supervised fine-tuning on a novel Turkish instruction-tuning dataset aimed at enhancing reasoning capabilities. The relative performance of these methods is evaluated through the creation of a new leaderboard for Turkish LLMs, featuring benchmarks that assess different reasoning and knowledge skills. Furthermore, we conducted experiments on data and model scaling, both during pretraining and fine-tuning, simultaneously emphasizing the capacity for knowledge transfer across languages and addressing the challenges of catastrophic forgetting encountered during fine-tuning on a different language. Our goal is to offer a detailed guide for advancing the LLM framework in low-resource linguistic contexts, thereby making natural language processing (NLP) benefits more globally accessible.

## 1 Introduction

The remarkable advancements in Large Language Models (LLMs) have revolutionized the field of natural language processing (NLP) (Brown et al., 2020; OpenAI, 2023; Chowdhery et al., 2022; Anil et al., 2023; Touvron et al., 2023b). However, addressing models that diverge from an English-centric framework poses considerable challenges, particularly in low-resource languages. While certain languages like Turkish aren't categorized as under-resourced, there's a limited number of research groups focusing on them (Safaya et al., 2022). Consequently, these languages lag in advancing cutting-edge systems because of the absence of solid and open-source base LLMs together with standardized benchmarks to evaluate their capabilities.

Recognizing this gap, our work is motivated by aiming to leverage Turkish LLMs. We meticulously demonstrate two distinct methodologies: we first tried to adapt two base LLMs, Mistral-7B (Jiang et al., 2023) and GPT2-xl (Radford et al., 2019) to Turkish. Secondly, we trained a family of decoder models entirely from scratch in varying sizes. To adhere the Turkish LLMs to human instructions and extend their reasoning capabilities, we designed a novel Turkish instruction-tuning (IT) dataset, designed to enhance the reasoning abilities of Turkish LLMs by following the Self-Instruct framework (Wang et al., 2022a).

One of the key challenges with Turkish LLMs is evaluating their accuracy on different tasks in a reproducible and fair manner while ensuring dataset quality. Many reasoning datasets have been directly machine-translated from English without any validation, leading to biased and inaccurate results. To address this, we introduce three Turkish datasets: TruthfulQA-TR, for assessing a model's tendency to reproduce common falsehoods, ARC-TR, a set of grade-school science questions, and GSM8K-TR for evaluating the mathematical reasoning capabilities of the models. We carefully translated by using state-of-the-art tools and validated all samples with multiple annotators, cleaning them as needed. We detailed the translation and annotation processes.

Our contributions are as follows:

- We release the Hamza LLM series, encompassing models from 124M to 1.3B parameters. Notably, Hamza-xl with 1.3B parameters



*Proceedings of the Fourth Workshop on Multilingual Representation Learning (MRL 2024)*, pages 242–268
November 16, 2024 ©2024 Association for Computational Linguistics

marks the premier and most expansive open-source, scientifically vetted Turkish LLM that is trained on 300B tokens.

- Our analysis explores two distinct methodologies for developing Turkish LLMs in resource and computational power-constrained environments: (i) extending pretrained models (Mistral-7b and GPT2-xl) with Turkish-only data (called as $\text{Hamza}_{Mistral}$ and $\text{Hamza}_{GPT2-xl}$), and (ii) constructing a model from scratch, similar to the GPT2 approach. This paper thoroughly discusses the merits and drawbacks of these strategies.
- We have curated new Turkish evaluation datasets TruthfulQA-TR, ARC-TR, and GSM8K-TR by carefully validating each with multiple annotators, offering meticulously cleaned datasets, and launching a leaderboard to catalyze ongoing advancements in Turkish LLMs.
- Committing to open science principles, we make all source code, model checkpoints, and datasets open-source and publicly accessible.

By detailing the development of specialized datasets and methodologies, we offer a comprehensive guide for building LLMs for languages with limited resources. Additionally, our contributions substantially enrich the field by providing critical resources that will support future research in Turkish language processing and the broader area of Natural Language Processing (NLP) for under-resourced languages.

## 2 Datasets

The initial step in building a base LLM involves pretraining it on a vast corpus of text with a next-token-prediction objective (Brown et al., 2020). This corpus comprises trillions of words gathered from the internet and is characterized by its large volume but often compromised in quality due to the noise in the raw internet data. Following the pretraining, the model undergoes fine-tuning with high-quality prompt-response pairs which focuses on improving the model's reasoning capabilities (Zhang et al., 2023a). In the end, the goal is to achieve a Supervised-Finetuned (SFT) model that is aligned with the desired response behavior or domain expertise. This section describes the corpora utilized in the pretraining phase (Section 2.1) and the development process of the Turkish IT dataset (Section 2.2).

### 2.1 Pretraining Dataset

For pretraining our models, we utilized CulturaX (Nguyen et al., 2023), a substantial multilingual dataset designed for LLM development. This dataset contains 6.3 trillion tokens in 167 languages and is a combination of two well-known multilingual datasets: mC4 (Raffel et al., 2019) and Oscar (Abadji et al., 2022; Abadji et al., 2021; Caswell et al., 2021; Ortiz Suárez et al., 2020; Ortiz Suárez et al., 2019). These datasets go through a detailed preprocessing that involves removing duplications, filtering out URLs, identifying languages, metric-based cleaning, and refining documents to enhance the data quality and consistency of each corpus. Since our focus is building a Turkish LLM, we only used the Turkish splits from CulturaX.

**mC4.** mC4 (Raffel et al., 2019) is a large multilingual dataset initially created for training the mT5 (Xue et al., 2021) which multilingual encoder-decoder model pretrained on 101 different languages. This dataset was generated by extracting content from 71 monthly snapshots of the internet via Common Crawl (CC). CulturaX contains version 3.1.0 of mC4[1] which was provided by AllenAI. Its raw dataset contains 337GB of Turkish data.

**OSCAR.** OSCAR (Open Super-large Crawled Aggregated coRpus) is a web-based multilingual dataset that is specialized in offering large volumes of unannotated raw data commonly used for training large deep learning models. It was developed by efficient data pipelines to organize and filter web data effectively. The final version of Oscar23[2] contains 73.7GB of Turkish data.

**CulturaX Turkish.** We trained using the Turkish subset of CulturaX[3], comprised of 128 portions, totaling 180 GB. No additional preprocessing was required since CulturaX had already undergone thorough detailed preprocessing during its creation. In the end, our Turkish dataset corpus comprises 130B unique tokens determined by using the GPT-2 tokenizer (Radford et al., 2019).

[1] https://huggingface.co/datasets/mc4

[2] https://huggingface.co/datasets/oscar-corpus/OSCAR-2301

[3] https://huggingface.co/datasets/uonlp/CulturaX

| Corpus | Documents | Ratio | # of Tokens |
|---|---|---|---|
| mC4 | 75,859,899 | 80.52% | 104.3 B |
| OSCAR-2019 | 5,867,831 | 6.23% | 8.1 B |
| OSCAR-2109 | 6,614,512 | 7.02% | 9.1 B |
| OSCAR-2201 | 2,580,896 | 2.74% | 3.5 B |
| OSCAR-2301 | 3,284,322 | 3.49% | 4.5 B |
| CulturaX (total) | 94,207,460 | 100.0% | 129.5 B |

Table 1: **Statistics of the pretraining dataset.** This table presents the statistics of our pretraining dataset used to train our Hamza series models that are presented in Table 3.

| Corpus Split | Documents | Portion | # of Tokens |
|---|---|---|---|
| CulturaX 0.1GB | 36,799 | 0.05% | 0.05 B |
| CulturaX 0.25GB | 91,998 | 0.14% | 0.13 B |
| CulturaX 0.5GB | 183,996 | 0.28% | 0.25 B |
| CulturaX 1.0GB | 367,993 | 0.56% | 0.5 B |
| CulturaX 2.0GB | 735,987 | 1.11% | 1.1 B |
| CulturaX 5.0GB | 1,839,968 | 2.78% | 2.5 B |

Table 2: **Statistics of the continued pre-training dataset.** This table presents the statistics of our continued pretraining dataset that is used to train Hamza$_{Mistral}$ and Hamza$_{GPT2-xl}$.

### 2.2 Instruction-Tuning Dataset

Instruction fine-tuning is a crucial method used to improve LLMs in terms of their performance and ability to follow specific instructions (Zhang et al., 2023b). This phase involves supervised training of LLMs using an instruction-tuning (IT) dataset composed of instruction and response pairs that link input instructions to their corresponding responses.

**Self-Instruct.** To create an automated, high-quality, and diverse IT dataset, we adapt the Self-Instruct procedure (Wang et al., 2022b; Taori et al., 2023) for Turkish. We established 175 diverse instruction and response pairs as seed tasks which are translated manually from Alpaca repository[4] by human annotators. These annotators are experts in NLP and native speakers of both Turkish and English. For the given prompt, we asked text-davinci3 (Brown et al., 2020) to generate 20 complex and diverse instruction-response pairs, adhering strictly to the guidelines specified in the prompt. An example prompt is illustrated in Appendix J. Generated pairs are post-processed by removing any samples that contain visual context like images or photographs. This process resulted in the creation of 50,817 samples and cost only 8.12$, which were then utilized for supervised fine-tuning (SFT).

## 3 Methodology

Creating an LLM for under-resourced languages, like Turkish, often poses challenges primarily due to the scarcity of publicly available data especially if you have limited computational resources. Regarding these, we followed two different strategies to build a Turkish series of LLMs: (i) further training state-of-the-art base models on Turkish data, which was initially unfamiliar with Turkish (i.e., not trained on Turkish data), (ii) pretraining a model from scratch, following GPT2 scales on a vast amount of text data defined in Section 2.1.

### 3.1 Method 1: Further Training a Base Model (Hamza$_{Mistral}$ and Hamza$_{GPT2-xl}$)

In this approach, we aim to enhance base LLMs with Turkish linguistic capabilities. After a detailed evaluation based on perplexity, we selected an LLM that did not specifically train on Turkish data during its initial pretraining phase. We subjected it to further training using Turkish-only data, accomplished through the next-token prediction objective implemented in an autoregressive manner. Essentially, this process serves as a continuation of the pretraining phase of LLMs, but with a focus on a specific segment of the Turkish dataset.

**Selecting Base Model.** For the successful development of an advanced Turkish LLM with a 7 billion parameter scale, choosing the most suitable base model is essential. To this end, we have selected Mistral 7B (Jiang et al., 2023) as one of our base models, owing to its recent success across various tasks. Additionally, we opted for GPT2-xlarge, since our Hamza model is trained from scratch on the GPT2 architecture. This selection allows for a meaningful comparison between models trained from scratch and those initially trained in English and subsequently continued with pre-training in the same architectural setup.

**Dataset.** In order to inject Turkish into Mistral and GPT-2 base LLMs, we followed a strategy of incremental continued pretraining on Turkish-specific segments of our dataset. Beginning with an initial 100MB of pure Turkish data, we progressively expanded the training corpus, culminating in the model being trained on 5GB of data. This volume aligns closely with the dataset size used for

[4] Alpaca Repository: https://github.com/tatsu-lab/stanford_alpaca

GPT (Radford and Narasimhan, 2018), ensuring a comprehensive and effective adaptation of the model to handle Turkish linguistic nuances. Please refer to Table 2 for the details of these splits.

**Training.** As a continual learning approach, we conducted a series of experiments by progressively enlarging the pretraining corpus size and halting upon observing convergence. The models are initialized with the pretraining weights of the Mistral-7B and GPT2-xl and then further trained on segments of our text corpus with a casual language modeling objective. Throughout our continued pretraining experiments, we employed LoRA (Hu et al., 2021) and updated only the additional bottleneck adapter weights while freezing the original model weights to make the training cost-efficient and avoid any catastrophic forgetting from the models' previous capabilities. During our LoRA trainings, we used $r = 32$ and $\alpha = 32$, along with a dropout rate of 0.05, applying LoRA exclusively to the projection layers. We used AdamW optimizer and cosine scheduler with a learning rate of 0.0001. Based on our experiments, we opted for a batch size of 1 and avoided gradient accumulation due to its significant impact on convergence. To simplify the execution of our experiments and ensure the reproducibility of our results, we used the LLaMA-Factory[5] repository, only in our LoRA-based continued pretraining experiments.

### 3.2 Method 2: Pretraining from Scratch (Hamza Series Models)

In our final approach for developing a Turkish base-LLM, we adopted the most straightforward method: training from scratch using Turkish-only datasets. We follow a similar framework as in GPT2 (Radford et al., 2019), with similarities in training procedures and architectural settings. However, we differed in our approach by utilizing a pretraining corpus nearly double the size of GPT2.

**Pretraining Data.** The construction of a robust LLM hinges on the aggregation and processing of high-quality text data. To develop Hamza, we used the Turkish split of CulturaX (Nguyen et al., 2023) includes a meticulous process of data curation. It gathers a comprehensive dataset from open-sources mC4 (Raffel et al., 2019) and OSCAR (Abadji et al., 2022; Abadji et al., 2021; Caswell et al., 2021; Ortiz Suárez et al., 2020; Ortiz Suárez et al., 2019). Our pretraining data contains 128 parquet files each 1.4GB, totaling almost 179.2GB. The compiled training dataset contains 129,486,207,634 (130B) training tokens. Further details of the data gathering, structure, and preparation can be found in CulturaX work Nguyen et al. (2023).

**Architecture.** To develop an inaugural Turkish base model, we followed prior works, establishing a solid model for Turkish language modeling akin to earlier studies on other languages. Our approach led to the creation of four variants of Hamza, following GPT-2 (Radford et al., 2019): Hamza-small (124M parameters), Hamza-medium (354M parameters), Hamza-large (772M parameters), and our largest model, Hamza-xlarge (1.3B parameters). The architectural specifications of these models are given in Table 3.

**Optimizer.** During our training, AdamW (Loshchilov and Hutter, 2017) optimizer is used with hyper-parameters $\beta_1 = 0.9$ and $\beta_2 = 0.95$. A cosine learning rate schedule is implemented, designed to reduce the learning rate to 10% of its maximum value. Additionally, we applied a weight decay rate of 0.1 and limited the gradient norm to 1.0 to prevent overfitting. The training process includes $2,000$ warm-up steps. We used a learning rate Of $0.0006$ and batch size $491,520$ in our smallest model Hamza-small. We varied the learning rate and batch size according to the model size, for details see Table 3.

**Training.** Our from-scratch Hamza models are built on the GPT2 architecture (Radford et al., 2019) and incorporate the flash-attention mechanism for efficient training (Dao et al., 2022). As outlined in Table 8, the hyperparameters of the model follow the scaling principles set by GPT2, except for the largest variant, Hamza-xlarge, which is inspired by a recent French-based LLM (Faysse et al., 2024). All model versions were trained for 300 billion tokens, with a uniform batch size of 500,000 tokens. The learning rate was fine-tuned for each model variant. We standardized the context window across all models at 1024 tokens and did not employ any dropout techniques during their training process. All training sessions were conducted in half-precision (fp16) settings by utilizing both tensor and data parallelism across eight A100 GPUs each with 80GB of memory.

[5] https://github.com/hiyouga/LLaMA-Factory

| Model | Parameters | Layers | Heads | $d_{model}$ | Learning Rate | Batch Size | Tokens |
|---|---|---|---|---|---|---|---|
| hamza-small | 124M | 12 | 12 | 768 | $6.0e^{-4}$ | 0.5M | 300B |
| hamza-medium | 354M | 24 | 16 | 1024 | $3.0e^{-4}$ | 0.5M | 300B |
| hamza-large | 772M | 36 | 20 | 1280 | $3.0e^{-4}$ | 0.5M | 300B |
| hamza-xlarge | 1.3B | 24 | 16 | 2048 | $2.0e^{-4}$ | 0.5M | 300B |

Table 3: **Architecture and optimization hyperparameters for the four Hamza model sizes that are trained from scratch.**

# 4 Evaluations

## 4.1 Bits-Per-Character (BPC) Evaluations

Auto-regressive language modeling is trained on optimizing the Negative Log-Likelihood (NLL) of the data in the training set and the effectiveness of the model is then calculated on the unseen test data. Furthermore, the most common metric to evaluate these models is perplexity, which measures the uncertainty of an LLM in predicting the next token in a sequence and is derived by taking the exponential average of the NLL. However, as various tokenizers can divide each sentence into differing numbers of tokens, NLL and PPL may produce incomparable results for models utilizing different tokenizers. To tackle this, we use Bits-Per-Character (BPC), which is another critical metric derived from NLL, used for evaluating the performance of LLMs at character-level. Further details on the calculation of these metrics are given in the Appendix in Section F. Consequently, our comparisons mainly relied on BPC, which normalizes the impact of tokenization differences. For the BPC evaluation, we utilized the test set of the trnews-64 corpus (Safaya et al., 2022), comprising 5,000 samples.

**Results.** We present the BPC results of different models evaluated on trnews-64 in the last column of Table 4; including our models together with various open-source multi-lingual and Turkish LLMs. Looking at the BPC results, we observe a wide range of values across the models. Lower BPC values indicate better performance in terms of compression, suggesting that the model is more efficient in representing the text. The most favorable outcomes are attained with the pretrained Kanarya-2b and Hamza-xlarge models. The adapted models which are originally pretrained on English but extended to Turkish, yielded promising results as well, lower than 1 BPC, whereas the multilingual models had a relatively lower performance.

## 4.2 Prompting & Few-Shot

Evaluating the reasoning capabilities of large language models (LLMs) in downstream Question Answering (QA) tasks is essential to assess their performance and reliability. However, finding comprehensive datasets in languages other than English poses a significant challenge due to the limited availability of benchmarks. To bridge this gap, we developed TruthfulQA-TR, ARC-TR, and GSM8K-TR Turkish question-answering datasets, which are designed to evaluate the ability of LLMs to generate truthful and accurate responses to questions. To develop the Turkish versions of the main TruthfulQA Multiple Choice (MC) (Lin et al., 2021a), ARC (AI2 Reasoning Challenge) (Clark et al., 2018), and GSM8K (Grade School Math) (Cobbe et al., 2021) datasets, we translated each example of these datasets using the advanced DeepL Machine Translation (MT) framework by its Python-supported API[6]. After translating to Turkish, each sample was reviewed for errors or superficial translations. We used the test sets from TruthfulQA-MC2, ARC-Challenge, and GSM8K for evaluations. For more details on datasets and annotation validation, see the Appendix in Section G. Our experiments followed the same prompting settings with LLM-Leaderboard[7]. We include performances of all of our models together with all the open-source Turkish LLMs that are available on Huggingface, along with other monolingual and multilingual models.

**Results.** We evaluate various language models in depth, including base LLMs (Touvron et al., 2023b; Jiang et al., 2023; Radford et al., 2019), multilingual LLMs (Shliazhko et al., 2022; Lin et al., 2021b), all available Turkish fine-tuned LLMs on Huggingface, and the models we propose in this paper. Our evaluation was conducted on the

[6]https://github.com/DeepLcom/deepl-python

[7]https://huggingface.co/spaces/HuggingFaceH4/open_llm_leaderboard

| Type | Models | Accuracy (%) (↑) | | | BPC (↓) |
|---|---|---|---|---|---|
| | | ARC-TR | TruthfulQA-TR | GSM8K-TR | trnews-64 |
| Base & SFT Models | LLaMA2 7b | 25.94 | 41.18 | 3.49 | 1.374 |
| | LLaMA3 8b | 43.09 | 44.77 | <u>30.02</u> | 0.929 |
| | Mistral 7b | 32.68 | 41.16 | 17.66 | 1.260 |
| | Gemma 2B | 31.31 | 43.57 | 7.35 | 1.208 |
| | Gemma 7B | **46.16** | 42.35 | **36.24** | 0.989 |
| | GPT2-xl | 24.91 | 40.97 | 0.38 | 2.533 |
| | LLaMA2 7b-chat | 25.00 | 40.07 | 4.62 | 1.374 |
| | Mistral 7b-chat-v2 | 35.24 | <u>48.34</u> | 19.18 | 1.428 |
| Multi-lingual Models | XGLM-7.5B | 29.01 | 39.09 | 1.82 | 0.880 |
| | XGLM-4.5B | 25.94 | 40.18 | 1.14 | 0.949 |
| | XGLM-2.9B | 27.05 | 39.35 | 2.12 | 0.946 |
| | XGLM-1.7B | 26.37 | 41.75 | 2.05 | 1.044 |
| | XGLM-564M | 23.55 | 42.59 | 0.91 | 1.125 |
| | mGPT | 26.54 | 42.37 | 0.00 | 1.306 |
| Huggingface Turkish Models | Kanarya-2b | 29.78 | 41.43 | 1.59 | **0.724** |
| | Kanarya-750m | 28.16 | 41.50 | 0.68 | 0.767 |
| | Turkcell-LLM-7b-v1 | 43.09 | 44.91 | 28.35 | 1.208 |
| | ytu-gpt2-large | 27.13 | 43.09 | 0.53 | 0.805 |
| | Trendyol-7b-base | 35.24 | 41.50 | 4.85 | 0.829 |
| | Trendyol-7b-chat | 35.58 | 44.35 | 5.31 | 0.820 |
| | Trendyol-7b-dpo | 39.93 | **50.11** | 5.61 | 0.859 |
| | Commencis-LLM | 33.28 | 44.50 | 0.38 | 1.306 |
| | Sambalingo-tr | <u>44.37</u> | 46.61 | 3.56 | 0.894 |
| | Thestral-tr-chat | 34.00 | 41.90 | 6.22 | 1.314 |
| | Mistral-7b-chat-v2-tr | 33.96 | 45.71 | 18.42 | 1.411 |
| | Gemma-2B-tr | 31.31 | 44.46 | 2.73 | 1.089 |
| Our Models | Hamza-small | 25.26 | 43.65 | 1.21 | 0.897 |
| | Hamza-medium | 26.45 | 43.55 | 1.29 | 0.814 |
| | Hamza-large | 29.10 | 40.93 | 1.97 | 0.760 |
| | Hamza-xl | 28.24 | 42.33 | 1.97 | <u>0.754</u> |
| | Hamza$_{GPT2-xl}$ | 24.74 | 44.95 | 1.74 | 1.152 |
| | Hamza$_{Mistral}$ | 39.85 | 46.40 | 5.31 | 0.816 |

Table 4: **Performance comparison on various Turkish tasks.** We compare the performance of various types of models: (i) Base and SFT Models, (ii) Multilingual Models (iii) Open-Source HF (Huggingface) Turkish Models, (iv) Our pretrained and adapted Hamza Models. The first three columns show accuracies evaluated on the ARC-TR, TruthfulQA-TR and GSM8K-TR datasets. The last column includes the Bits-Per-Character (BPC) metric evaluated on TRNEWS-64 corpus. Note that Accuracy is the highest and BPC is the lowest for the best models. The top-performing model for each metric is highlighted in bold, while the second-best model is underlined for easy identification. See Appendix C for model details.

newly established Turkish Benchmarks, ARC-TR, in 25-shot settings, as well as on TruthfulQA-TR and GSM8K-TR, adhering to the same settings as outlined by the LLM-Leaderboard. In ARC-TR, Google's Gemma 7B model leads with an accuracy of 46.16 even though it is not specifically tuned for Turkish, closely followed by Sambalingo-tr with 44.37 accuracy. Moreover, in the TruthfulQA-TR evaluation, Trendyol's DPO model emerges as the top performer with an accuracy of 50.11, while Mistral-7b-chat-v2 secures the second position with 48.34 accuracy. Lastly on GSM8K-TR, Gemma 7B performs the best with an accuracy of 36.24, and LLaMA3 8b model had the second best with 30.02 accuracy. The accuracy scores for ARC-TR range from 24 to 47, TruthfulQA-TR ranges from 33 to 50, and GSM8K-TR ranges from 0 to 36. These results underscore the necessity for substantial improvements in these models to reach the proficiency levels observed in English benchmarks.

**Qualitative Analysis.** We performed qualitative analysis on our models by testing them with various prompts as demonstrated in Appendix in Section I. Both the pretrained and Hamza models perform well on sentence completion. In particular, compared to other open-source Turkish models, we observed a reduced tendency to generate text that resembles web-based content, where most of the Turkish corpora is retrieved from websites. Furthermore, we tested our models on English prompts to assess their ability to handle multilingual tasks. Although results indicate that our models can generate coherent responses, there is a high tendency for the models to continue English sentences in Turkish. Overall, our qualitative analysis highlights the robust performance of our models and the potential for diverse tasks.

## 5 Case Studies

### 5.1 Enhancing Non-English Models: Fine-Tuning vs. From-Scratch Training

The analysis of Turkish language models, specifically comparing models trained from scratch, continued pretraining from GPT2-xl (Radford et al., 2019), and those adapted using Mistral 7B (Jiang et al., 2023), shows insightful trends. According to Table 5, the Mistral 7B adapted model exhibits superior performance on Turkish question-answering tasks, compared to other methods. Moreover, starting from scratch surpasses the continued pretraining approach within the same model architecture, underscoring the significance of the base language model when undertaking continued pretraining. This is evidenced by the discrepancy in accuracy between models fine-tuned from Mistral 7B versus those from GPT2. Therefore, applying continued pretraining to a robust base language model emerges as the most effective strategy for low-resource languages, considering both data scarcity and hardware constraints.

| Models | ARC-TR | TruthfulQA-TR | Avg. |
|---|---|---|---|
| Hamza-xl | 28.24 | 42.33 | 35.28 |
| Hamza$_{GPT2-xl}$ | 24.74 | 44.95 | 34.84 |
| Hamza$_{Mistral}$ | **39.85** | **46.40** | **43.12** |

Table 5: **Accuracy comparison of our best models on Turkish question answering tasks.** This table shows the performance of our models, pretrained Hamza models with different sizes, and the Hamza$_{Mistral}$ and Hamza$_{GPT2-xl}$ models that are adapted on Turkish. We present the results evaluated on the ARC-TR (25 shot) and TruthfulQA-TR (6 shot) datasets.

| Models | ARC-TR | TruthfulQA-TR | Avg. |
|---|---|---|---|
| Hamza-xl | 28.24 | 42.33 | 35.28 |
| Hamza-xl + SFT | 29.61 | 44.67 | 37.14 |

Table 6: **Accuracy results of our models fine-tuned on our Self-Instruct IT dataset on Turkish question answering tasks.** This table compares the performance increase after instruction tuning with IT dataset described in Section 2.2. We present the results evaluated on the ARC-TR (25 shot) and TruthfulQA-TR (6 shot) datasets.

### 5.2 Effect of Supervised Fine-Tuning: Assessing Model Performance with the Proposed IT Dataset.

Supervised Fine-Tuning (SFT) plays a crucial role in enhancing the reasoning capabilities of LLMs, as highlighted in existing research (Zhang et al., 2023a). In this context, we introduced a novel Turkish IT Dataset, meticulously crafted from the ground up, inspired by the Alpaca (Taori et al., 2023; Wang et al., 2022b). By fine-tuning our largest model Hamza-xlarge with this bespoke Turkish IT Dataset, we observed an improvement in model performance across downstream benchmarks (see Table 5). This improvement underscores the effectiveness of SFT when applied to our tailored IT dataset, bolstering our model's reasoning proficiency slightly.

### 5.3 Retention after Fine-Tuning: Will Models Forget English-Learned Skills When Fine-Tuning on Another Language?

According to Figure 1, further pretraining of base English language models such as GPT2 and Mistral results in a decrease in accuracy proportional to the number of samples used during continued pretraining on the English downstream tasks TruthfulQA and ARC, compared to their original base scores before fine-tuning on Turkish. This indicates *catas-*

| Models | ARC | TruthfulQA | Avg. |
|---|---|---|---|
| GPT2-xl | 30.29 | 38.53 | 34.41 |
| Hamza$_{GPT2-xl}$ (0.1GB) | 28.84 | 38.15 | 32.98 |
| Hamza$_{GPT2-xl}$ (0.25GB) | 26.37 | 38.10 | 32.88 |
| Hamza$_{GPT2-xl}$ (0.5GB) | 27.13 | 38.88 | 33.35 |
| Hamza$_{GPT2-xl}$ (1GB) | 26.54 | 38.95 | 33.09 |
| Hamza$_{GPT2-xl}$ (2GB) | 24.74 | 40.34 | 33.01 |
| Hamza$_{GPT2-xl}$ (5GB) | 22.61 | 41.36 | 32.49 |
| Mistral-7b | 61.52 | 42.57 | 51.49 |
| Hamza$_{Mistral}$ (0.1GB) | 56.14 | 40.31 | 48.22 |
| Hamza$_{Mistral}$ (0.25GB) | 52.90 | 39.15 | 45.77 |
| Hamza$_{Mistral}$ (0.5GB) | 52.39 | 38.70 | 45.51 |
| Hamza$_{Mistral}$ (1GB) | 51.71 | 41.46 | 46.60 |
| Hamza$_{Mistral}$ (2GB) | 49.32 | 38.44 | 43.91 |
| Hamza$_{Mistral}$ (5GB) | 45.90 | 40.90 | 43.82 |

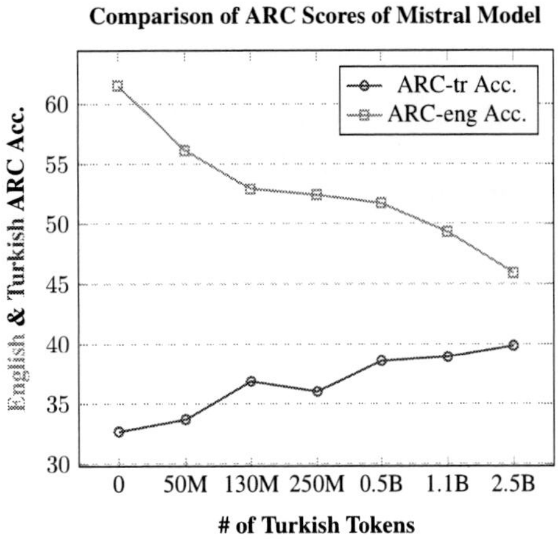


Figure 1: **Accuracy comparison of Continued Pretrained models on English (Left, Right) and Turkish (Right) question answering tasks and demonstrating the original language catastrophic forgetting while learning the new language.** In the table on the left, the performance of our Hamza$_{Mistral}$ and Hamza$_{GPT2-xl}$ models that are adapted on Turkish together with the original Mistral 7B and GPT2-xl. We present the result of our ablation study, where the performance of the adapted models is given by progressively enlarging the pretraining corpus size from 0.1 GB to 5 GB. Here, the zero and few-show accuracies were evaluated on the original ARC and TruthfulQA. The figure on the right illustrates the Mistral model's results on both Turkish and English versions of the ARC dataset, highlighting its improved performance in Turkish and decreasing performance in English with continued pretraining.

*trophic forgetting*, where the models lose their prior knowledge upon being fine-tuned on a smaller language dataset, as evidenced by a decline in baseline accuracy compared to the versions not previously trained, even after applying techniques like LoRA training. One further work for this could be including some English data along with Turkish in each batch during continued pretraining.

## 6 Conclusion

Our work advances the development of Turkish LLMs, presenting a new series of models both trained from scratch (Hamza) and also adapted from other base LLMs (Hamza$_{Mistral}$ and Hamza$_{GPT2-xl}$), together with new Instruction Tuning dataset and a meticulously crafted Turkish LLM Leaderboard. In our analysis, we noted that the base LLMs exhibited catastrophic forgetting of their primary language knowledge during continued pretraining. Additionally, through the creation of a novel Turkish LLM evaluation benchmark, we have identified a significant performance gap between current Turkish LLMs and their English counterparts, underscoring the need for further improvements in Turkish language modeling. For more detailed discussions on limitations and future work, please refer to Appendix B. Our fully open-source work and detailed observations play a pivotal role in the field of Turkish language modeling, providing insights on construction methodologies and offering a comparative framework for evaluating performance, thereby paving the way for future advancements.

## Ethics Statement

This study complies with the ethical standards for scientific research conduct and reporting established by the Association for Computational Linguistics (ACL). We ensured the following ethical considerations were addressed during the course of our study:

- **Data Privacy and Consent:** The datasets used in this study were sourced from publicly available repositories, ensuring compliance with data privacy regulations. We did not collect any personal or sensitive information that could compromise the privacy of individuals.

- **Data Quality and Bias:** Effort is made to gather high-quality datasets for training and evaluation purposes. However, we acknowledge the potential for inherent biases in the data due to its web-crawled nature in the pretraining dataset.

- **Transparency and Reproducibility:** We have made all source codes and datasets used in this study freely available in accordance with the open scientific principles. By allowing other academics to replicate our findings and expand on our work, this transparency promotes cooperative developments in the area.
- **Avoiding Harmful Outputs:** We acknowledge the potential risks associated with the deployment of LLMs, such as the generation of harmful or biased content. To address this, we have focused on creating models that adhere to high standards of accuracy and reliability. We have also included benchmarks to assess and mitigate the reproduction of common falsehoods by the models.
- **Responsible Use of Computational Resources:** The computational experiments were conducted using resources provided by TUBITAK ULAKBIM and KUIS AI Center. We have taken measures to ensure efficient use of these resources and have reported our methodologies to enable responsible replication of our experiments.

## References

Julien Abadji, Pedro Ortiz Suárez, Laurent Romary, and Benoît Sagot. 2022. Towards a Cleaner Document-Oriented Multilingual Crawled Corpus. *arXiv e-prints*, page arXiv:2201.06642.

Julien Abadji, Pedro Javier Ortiz Suárez, Laurent Romary, and Benoît Sagot. 2021. Ungoliant: An optimized pipeline for the generation of a very large-scale multilingual web corpus. Proceedings of the Workshop on Challenges in the Management of Large Corpora (CMLC-9) 2021. Limerick, 12 July 2021 (Online-Event), pages 1 – 9, Mannheim. Leibniz-Institut für Deutsche Sprache.

Joshua Ainslie, James Lee-Thorp, Michiel de Jong, Yury Zemlyanskiy, Federico Lebr'on, and Sumit K. Sanghai. 2023. Gqa: Training generalized multi-query transformer models from multi-head checkpoints. *ArXiv*, abs/2305.13245.

Rohan Anil, Andrew M. Dai, Orhan Firat, Melvin Johnson, Dmitry Lepikhin, Alexandre Tachard Passos, Siamak Shakeri, Emanuel Taropa, Paige Bailey, Z. Chen, Eric Chu, J. Clark, Laurent El Shafey, Yanping Huang, Kathleen S. Meier-Hellstern, Gaurav Mishra, Erica Moreira, Mark Omernick, Kevin Robinson, Sebastian Ruder, Yi Tay, Kefan Xiao, Yuanzhong Xu, Yujing Zhang, Gustavo Hernandez Abrego, Junwhan Ahn, Jacob Austin, Paul Barham, Jan A. Botha, James Bradbury, et al. 2023. Palm 2 technical report. *ArXiv*, abs/2305.10403.

Iz Beltagy, Matthew E. Peters, and Arman Cohan. 2020. Longformer: The long-document transformer. *ArXiv*, abs/2004.05150.

Stella Biderman, Hailey Schoelkopf, Quentin Anthony, Herbie Bradley, Kyle O'Brien, Eric Hallahan, Mohammad Aflah Khan, Shivanshu Purohit, USVSN Sai Prashanth, Edward Raff, Aviya Skowron, Lintang Sutawika, and Oskar van der Wal. 2023. Pythia: A suite for analyzing large language models across training and scaling.

Tom B. Brown, Benjamin Mann, Nick Ryder, Melanie Subbiah, Jared Kaplan, Prafulla Dhariwal, Arvind Neelakantan, Pranav Shyam, Girish Sastry, Amanda Askell, Sandhini Agarwal, Ariel Herbert-Voss, Gretchen Krueger, T. J. Henighan, Rewon Child, Aditya Ramesh, Daniel M. Ziegler, Jeff Wu, Clemens Winter, Christopher Hesse, Mark Chen, Eric Sigler, Mateusz Litwin, Scott Gray, Benjamin Chess, Jack Clark, Christopher Berner, Sam McCandlish, Alec Radford, Ilya Sutskever, and Dario Amodei. 2020. Language models are few-shot learners. *ArXiv*, abs/2005.14165.

Isaac Caswell, Julia Kreutzer, Lisa Wang, Ahsan Wahab, Daan van Esch, Nasanbayar Ulzii-Orshikh, Allahsera Tapo, Nishant Subramani, Artem Sokolov, Claytone Sikasote, Monang Setyawan, Supheakmungkol Sarin, Sokhar Samb, Benoît Sagot, Clara Rivera, Annette Rios, Isabel Papadimitriou, Salomey Osei, Pedro Javier Ortiz Suárez, Iroro Orife, Kelechi Ogueji, Rubungo Andre Niyongabo, Toan Q. Nguyen, Mathias Müller, André Müller, Shamsuddeen Hassan Muhammad, Nanda Muhammad, Ayanda Mnyakeni, , Jamshidbek Mirzakhalov, Tapiwanashe Matangira, et al. 2021. Quality at a Glance: An Audit of Web-Crawled Multilingual Datasets. *arXiv e-prints*, page arXiv:2103.12028.

Rewon Child, Scott Gray, Alec Radford, and Ilya Sutskever. 2019. Generating long sequences with sparse transformers. *ArXiv*, abs/1904.10509.

Aakanksha Chowdhery, Sharan Narang, Jacob Devlin, Maarten Bosma, Gaurav Mishra, Adam Roberts, Paul Barham, Hyung Won Chung, Charles Sutton, Sebastian Gehrmann, Parker Schuh, Kensen Shi, Sasha Tsvyashchenko, Joshua Maynez, Abhishek Rao, Parker Barnes, Yi Tay, Noam M. Shazeer, Vinodkumar Prabhakaran, Emily Reif, Nan Du, Benton C. Hutchinson, Reiner Pope, James Bradbury, Jacob Austin, Michael Isard, Guy Gur-Ari, Pengcheng Yin, Toju Duke, Anselm Levskaya, et al. 2022. Palm: Scaling language modeling with pathways. *ArXiv*, abs/2204.02311.

Peter Clark, Isaac Cowhey, Oren Etzioni, Tushar Khot, Ashish Sabharwal, Carissa Schoenick, and Oyvind Tafjord. 2018. Think you have solved question answering? try arc, the ai2 reasoning challenge. *arXiv:1803.05457v1*.

Karl Cobbe, Vineet Kosaraju, Mohammad Bavarian, Mark Chen, Heewoo Jun, Lukasz Kaiser, Matthias Plappert, Jerry Tworek, Jacob Hilton, Reiichiro Nakano, Christopher Hesse, and John Schulman. 2021. Training verifiers to solve math word problems. *CoRR*, abs/2110.14168.

Jacob Cohen. 1960. A coefficient of agreement for nominal scales. *Educational and Psychological Measurement*, 20(1):37–46.

Tri Dao, Daniel Y. Fu, Stefano Ermon, Atri Rudra, and Christopher R'e. 2022. Flashattention: Fast and memory-efficient exact attention with io-awareness. *ArXiv*, abs/2205.14135.

Manuel Faysse, Patrick Fernandes, Nuno M. Guerreiro, Ant'onio Loison, Duarte M. Alves, Caio Corro, Nicolas Boizard, Joao Alves, Ricardo Rei, Pedro H. Martins, Antoni Bigata Casademunt, Franccois Yvon, André Martins, Gautier Viaud, C'eline Hudelot, and Pierre Colombo. 2024. Croissantllm: A truly bilingual french-english language model. *ArXiv*, abs/2402.00786.

Joseph L. Fleiss. 1971. Measuring nominal scale agreement among many raters. *Psychological Bulletin*, 76(5):378–382.

Jordan Hoffmann, Sebastian Borgeaud, Arthur Mensch, Elena Buchatskaya, Trevor Cai, Eliza Rutherford, Diego de Las Casas, Lisa Anne Hendricks, Johannes Welbl, Aidan Clark, Tom Hennigan, Eric Noland, Katie Millican, George van den Driessche, Bogdan Damoc, Aurelia Guy, Simon Osindero, Karen Simonyan, Erich Elsen, Jack W. Rae, Oriol Vinyals, and L. Sifre. 2022. Training compute-optimal large language models. *ArXiv*, abs/2203.15556.

J. Edward Hu, Yelong Shen, Phillip Wallis, Zeyuan Allen-Zhu, Yuanzhi Li, Shean Wang, and Weizhu Chen. 2021. Lora: Low-rank adaptation of large language models. *ArXiv*, abs/2106.09685.

Albert Qiaochu Jiang, Alexandre Sablayrolles, Arthur Mensch, Chris Bamford, Devendra Singh Chaplot, Diego de Las Casas, Florian Bressand, Gianna Lengyel, Guillaume Lample, Lucile Saulnier, L'elio Renard Lavaud, Marie-Anne Lachaux, Pierre Stock, Teven Le Scao, Thibaut Lavril, Thomas Wang, Timothée Lacroix, and William El Sayed. 2023. Mistral 7b. *ArXiv*, abs/2310.06825.

Stephanie Lin, Jacob Hilton, and Owain Evans. 2021a. Truthfulqa: Measuring how models mimic human falsehoods.

Xi Victoria Lin, Todor Mihaylov, Mikel Artetxe, Tianlu Wang, Shuohui Chen, Daniel Simig, Myle Ott, Naman Goyal, Shruti Bhosale, Jingfei Du, Ramakanth Pasunuru, Sam Shleifer, Punit Singh Koura, Vishrav Chaudhary, Brian O'Horo, Jeff Wang, Luke Zettlemoyer, Zornitsa Kozareva, Mona T. Diab, Ves Stoyanov, and Xian Li. 2021b. Few-shot learning with multilingual generative language models. In *Conference on Empirical Methods in Natural Language Processing*.

Ilya Loshchilov and Frank Hutter. 2017. Fixing weight decay regularization in adam. *ArXiv*, abs/1711.05101.

Thuat Nguyen, Chien Van Nguyen, Viet Dac Lai, Hieu Man, Nghia Trung Ngo, Franck Dernoncourt, Ryan A. Rossi, and Thien Huu Nguyen. 2023. Culturax: A cleaned, enormous, and multilingual dataset for large language models in 167 languages.

OpenAI. 2023. Gpt-4 technical report. *ArXiv*, abs/2303.08774.

Pedro Javier Ortiz Suárez, Laurent Romary, and Benoit Sagot. 2020. A monolingual approach to contextualized word embeddings for mid-resource languages. In *Proceedings of the 58th Annual Meeting of the Association for Computational Linguistics*, pages 1703–1714, Online. Association for Computational Linguistics.

Pedro Javier Ortiz Suárez, Benoit Sagot, and Laurent Romary. 2019. Asynchronous pipelines for processing huge corpora on medium to low resource infrastructures. Proceedings of the Workshop on Challenges in the Management of Large Corpora (CMLC-7) 2019. Cardiff, 22nd July 2019, pages 9 – 16, Mannheim. Leibniz-Institut f"ur Deutsche Sprache.

Long Ouyang, Jeff Wu, Xu Jiang, Diogo Almeida, Carroll L. Wainwright, Pamela Mishkin, Chong Zhang, Sandhini Agarwal, Katarina Slama, Alex Ray, John Schulman, Jacob Hilton, Fraser Kelton, Luke E. Miller, Maddie Simens, Amanda Askell, Peter Welinder, Paul Francis Christiano, Jan Leike, and Ryan J. Lowe. 2022. Training language models to follow instructions with human feedback. *ArXiv*, abs/2203.02155.

Alec Radford and Karthik Narasimhan. 2018. Improving language understanding by generative pretraining.

Alec Radford, Jeff Wu, Rewon Child, David Luan, Dario Amodei, and Ilya Sutskever. 2019. Language models are unsupervised multitask learners.

Rafael Rafailov, Archit Sharma, Eric Mitchell, Stefano Ermon, Christopher D. Manning, and Chelsea Finn. 2023. Direct preference optimization: Your language model is secretly a reward model. *ArXiv*, abs/2305.18290.

Colin Raffel, Noam Shazeer, Adam Roberts, Katherine Lee, Sharan Narang, Michael Matena, Yanqi Zhou, Wei Li, and Peter J. Liu. 2019. Exploring the limits of transfer learning with a unified text-to-text transformer. *arXiv e-prints*.

Ali Safaya, Emirhan Kurtuluş, Arda Goktogan, and Deniz Yuret. 2022. Mukayese: Turkish NLP strikes back. In *Findings of the Association for Computational Linguistics: ACL 2022*, pages 846–863, Dublin, Ireland. Association for Computational Linguistics.

Teven Le Scao, Angela Fan, Christopher Akiki, Ellie Pavlick, Suzana Ili'c, Daniel Hesslow, Roman Castagn'e, Alexandra Sasha Luccioni, Franccois Yvon, Matthias Gallé, Jonathan Tow, Alexander M. Rush, Stella Rose Biderman, Albert Webson, Pawan Sasanka Ammanamanchi, Thomas Wang, Benoît Sagot, Niklas Muennighoff, Albert Villanova del Moral, Olatunji Ruwase, Rachel Bawden, Stas Bekman, Angelina McMillan-Major, Iz Beltagy, Huu Nguyen, Lucile Saulnier, Samson Tan, Pedro Ortiz Suárez, Victor Sanh, Hugo Laurenccon, et al. 2022. Bloom: A 176b-parameter open-access multilingual language model. *ArXiv*, abs/2211.05100.

Stefan Schweter. 2020. Berturk - bert models for turkish.

Oleh Shliazhko, Alena Fenogenova, Maria Tikhonova, Vladislav Mikhailov, Anastasia Kozlova, and Tatiana Shavrina. 2022. mgpt: Few-shot learners go multilingual. *ArXiv*, abs/2204.07580.

Rohan Taori, Ishaan Gulrajani, Tianyi Zhang, Yann Dubois, Xuechen Li, Carlos Guestrin, Percy Liang, and Tatsunori B. Hashimoto. 2023. Stanford alpaca: An instruction-following llama model. `https://github.com/tatsu-lab/stanford_alpaca`.

Hugo Touvron, Thibaut Lavril, Gautier Izacard, Xavier Martinet, Marie-Anne Lachaux, Timothée Lacroix, Baptiste Rozière, Naman Goyal, Eric Hambro, Faisal Azhar, Aurelien Rodriguez, Armand Joulin, Edouard Grave, and Guillaume Lample. 2023a. Llama: Open and efficient foundation language models. *ArXiv*, abs/2302.13971.

Hugo Touvron, Louis Martin, Kevin R. Stone, Peter Albert, Amjad Almahairi, Yasmine Babaei, Nikolay Bashlykov, Soumya Batra, Prajjwal Bhargava, Shruti Bhosale, Daniel M. Bikel, Lukas Blecher, Cristian Canton Ferrer, Moya Chen, Guillem Cucurull, David Esiobu, Jude Fernandes, Jeremy Fu, Wenyin Fu, Brian Fuller, Cynthia Gao, Vedanuj Goswami, Naman Goyal, Anthony S. Hartshorn, Saghar Hosseini, Rui Hou, Hakan Inan, Marcin Kardas, Viktor Kerkez, Madian Khabsa, Isabel M. Kloumann, A. V. Korenev, Punit Singh Koura, Marie-Anne Lachaux, Thibaut Lavril, Jenya Lee, Diana Liskovich, Yinghai Lu, Yuning Mao, Xavier Martinet, Todor Mihaylov, Pushkar Mishra, Igor Molybog, Yixin Nie, Andrew Poulton, Jeremy Reizenstein, Rashi Rungta, Kalyan Saladi, Alan Schelten, Ruan Silva, Eric Michael Smith, R. Subramanian, Xia Tan, Binh Tang, Ross Taylor, Adina Williams, Jian Xiang Kuan, Puxin Xu, Zhengxu Yan, Iliyan Zarov, Yuchen Zhang, Angela Fan, Melanie Kambadur, Sharan Narang, Aurelien Rodriguez, Robert Stojnic, Sergey Edunov, and Thomas Scialom. 2023b. Llama 2: Open foundation and fine-tuned chat models. *ArXiv*, abs/2307.09288.

Gökçe Uludoğan, Zeynep Yirmibeşoğlu Balal, Furkan Akkurt, Melikşah Türker, Onur Güngör, and Susan Üsküdarlı. 2024. Turna: A turkish encoder-decoder language model for enhanced understanding and generation.

Yizhong Wang, Yeganeh Kordi, Swaroop Mishra, Alisa Liu, Noah A. Smith, Daniel Khashabi, and Hannaneh Hajishirzi. 2022a. Self-instruct: Aligning language models with self-generated instructions. In *Annual Meeting of the Association for Computational Linguistics*.

Yizhong Wang, Yeganeh Kordi, Swaroop Mishra, Alisa Liu, Noah A. Smith, Daniel Khashabi, and Hannaneh Hajishirzi. 2022b. Self-instruct: Aligning language models with self-generated instructions. In *Annual Meeting of the Association for Computational Linguistics*.

Linting Xue, Noah Constant, Adam Roberts, Mihir Kale, Rami Al-Rfou, Aditya Siddhant, Aditya Barua, and Colin Raffel. 2021. mT5: A massively multilingual pre-trained text-to-text transformer. In *Proceedings of the 2021 Conference of the North American Chapter of the Association for Computational Linguistics: Human Language Technologies*, pages 483–498, Online. Association for Computational Linguistics.

Shengyu Zhang, Linfeng Dong, Xiaoya Li, Sen Zhang, Xiaofei Sun, Shuhe Wang, Jiwei Li, Runyi Hu, Tianwei Zhang, Fei Wu, and Guoyin Wang. 2023a. Instruction tuning for large language models: A survey. *ArXiv*, abs/2308.10792.

Shengyu Zhang, Linfeng Dong, Xiaoya Li, Sen Zhang, Xiaofei Sun, Shuhe Wang, Jiwei Li, Runyi Hu, Tianwei Zhang, Fei Wu, and Guoyin Wang. 2023b. Instruction tuning for large language models: A survey. *ArXiv*, abs/2308.10792.

Susan Zhang, Stephen Roller, Naman Goyal, Mikel Artetxe, Moya Chen, Shuohui Chen, Christopher Dewan, Mona T. Diab, Xian Li, Xi Victoria Lin, Todor Mihaylov, Myle Ott, Sam Shleifer, Kurt Shuster, Daniel Simig, Punit Singh Koura, Anjali Sridhar, Tianlu Wang, and Luke Zettlemoyer. 2022. Opt: Open pre-trained transformer language models. *ArXiv*, abs/2205.01068.

## A Related Work

LLMs have significantly advanced the field of NLP by demonstrating remarkable capabilities in generating human-like text across various domains (Radford et al., 2019; Zhang et al., 2022; Anil et al., 2023; Jiang et al., 2023; OpenAI, 2023). Their development illustrates not only improvements in model size and complexity (Hoffmann et al., 2022; Biderman et al., 2023) but also in their ability to understand and generate more nuanced and contextually appropriate responses through techniques such as fine-tuning, supervised instruction-tuning, and reinforcement learning from human feedback (RLHF) (Ouyang et al., 2022; Wang et al., 2022b; Taori et al., 2023; Rafailov et al., 2023). Investigation into these models, focusing on overcoming their constraints for low-resource languages and furthering their development, remains a vital pursuit for achieving global applicability.

Multilingual LLMs represent a significant leap forward, enabling a single model to understand and generate text across multiple languages (Scao et al., 2022; Shliazhko et al., 2022; Lin et al., 2021b), thereby bridging linguistic gaps on a global scale. By leveraging vast datasets from diverse linguistic sources (Nguyen et al., 2023), these models are trained to capture the nuances of language, culture, and context. However, the inherent limitations posed by the restricted vocabulary sizes and diverse morphological characteristics of each language present substantial challenges that necessitate ongoing refinement and innovation within these models.

Regarding the Turkish context, although Turkish is not classified as a low-resource language, it has attracted limited research focus, with only a handful of groups dedicating efforts. The landscape of Turkish NLP is beginning to shine with the advent of new evaluation datasets (Safaya et al., 2022) and some language models. However, these advancements are predominantly in encoder-based (Schweter, 2020) or encoder-decoder-based models (Uludoğan et al., 2024) which necessitates task-specific training by leaving a gap in generative LLM work tailored specifically for Turkish. Consequently, there is an absence of pioneering research that offers insights for advancing the field of Turkish LLMs, underscoring the urgent need for a comprehensive strategy to develop robust Turkish-based LLMs.

## B Limitations and Future Work

**Better Turkish Pretraining Corpora.** The accuracy of your pretraining corpus is one of the most crucial factors in achieving a well-performing LLM. The three key elements of a good dataset are: quality, diversity, and quantity. While the last element is easy to measure, performance is a function of all three[8]. Our models are trained on 300 billion tokens, LLaMA (Touvron et al., 2023a) is trained on 1.5 trillion tokens, and LLaMA 3 is trained on 15 trillion tokens. We need more Turkish data, at least 3 trillion tokens. However, the diversity of these datasets should be sufficient, including common crawl, book corpora, code, math, etc., in a balanced manner. Current Turkish LLMs are trained on MC4 (Raffel et al., 2019) and OSCAR-based (Abadji et al., 2022) datasets with minimal preprocessing. These datasets mostly include political, gambling, or sports-related data, resulting in biased outcomes. The measurement of dataset quality is still an important research question today. We firmly believe that *better data is better than better models*.

**Small Scale of the Proposed Models.** One of the objectives of our work is not merely to provide the largest or best-performing Turkish LLM but also to offer a clear pathway and framework for building robust LLMs in low-resource scenarios. For instance, we trained all our models using, at most, eight A100 GPUs in parallel. Our Hamza-xlarge model, with 1.3B parameters, is the largest and best-performing open-source, decoder-based model that is scientifically published for Turkish. However, the Turkish language requires better pretrained models, scaling up to at least 7B, 13B, and 30B parameters, with high-quality datasets, to achieve results comparable to models like Mistral performed in English. Achieving this requires more GPUs and larger cluster environments. Currently, the largest clusters in Turkey are owned by TÜBİTAK TRUBA and Koç University KUIS AI Center. However, Turkish needs more H100 and A100 GPUs, with at least 512 GPUs supporting multi-node training, to develop LLMs comparable to those in other languages. We also explore whether training a model from scratch in low-resource settings is worthwhile or if fine-tuning from a strong base model is more effective. At

[8] https://x.com/karpathy/status/1782798789797101876?s=46

present, adapting a base LLM like Mistral appears more promising; however, it also leads to catastrophic forgetting (see Section 5).

**Limited Performance of Current Turkish LLMs.** Upon examining Table 4, it is evident that the current Turkish LLMs available on Huggingface perform significantly worse than base models like LLaMA, Mistral, and Gemma, which excel at the same tasks in English. The Turkish results range from 24 to 46 in ARC-TR and 39 to 50 in TruthfulQA-TR. Even Gemma 7B achieves the best performance in ARC-TR without any specific finetuning for Turkish. This highlights the considerable room for improvement, as discussed earlier, to develop better LLMs in Turkish.

**More Diverse Turkish Evaluation Benchmarks.** In this work, we shared two new evaluation datasets for Turkish: TruthfulQA-TR and ARC-TR. These datasets test a model's propensity to reproduce falsehoods commonly found online, and its ability to answer grade-school science questions, respectively. However, robust LLMs should also be evaluated in more challenging areas, such as chat abilities, mathematical reasoning, ethical biases, and more. We are currently working on establishing and sharing scientific datasets in these areas as well. Collaborations are always welcome.

## C Models

**GPT2-xl.** GPT2 (Radford et al., 2019) introduces several scaled models with the largest one as 1.5B parameter, which significantly expands upon its predecessor by enhancing its capacity for unsupervised learning of natural language tasks. This model demonstrates notable improvements in language understanding and generation, outperforming earlier versions in a range of linguistic tasks without task-specific training. GPT2-xl's architecture builds on the decoder-based transformer model by enabling it to generate coherent and contextually relevant text over extended passages. We used GPT2-xl in our evaluations.

**XGLM.** XGLM (Lin et al., 2021b) presented with five multilingual generative language models, with up to 7.5 billion parameters. The models are trained on a large-scale corpus of 500 billion tokens across 30 diverse languages, balancing representation for low-resourced languages. The study explores the models' zero-shot and few-shot learning capabilities across various tasks, including multilingual NLU, machine translation, and specific English tasks. The largest model, XGLM-7.5B, outperforms GPT-3 in multilingual commonsense reasoning and natural language inference tasks. We evaluated XGLM-7.5B, XGLM-4.5B, XGLM-2.9B, XGLM-1.7B, and XGLM-564M.

**mGPT.** mGPT (Shliazhko et al., 2022) is introduced with two different scales: 1.3 billion and 13 billion parameters. These models are trained on 60 languages from 25 language families, using data from Wikipedia and the Colossal Clean Crawled Corpus. The models replicate the GPT-3 architecture using GPT-2 sources and a sparse attention mechanism. The training and inference processes are effectively parallelized using the Deepspeed and Megatron frameworks. We used mGPT from Huggingface.

**LLaMA Models.** LLaMA (Touvron et al., 2023a) is a collection of open-source LLMs released by Meta, ranging from 7B to 65B parameters, achieved state-of-the-art performance using publicly available datasets. LLaMA 2 (Touvron et al., 2023b), an enhanced version, expanded its training corpus and context length, releasing models with 7B, 13B, and 70B parameters, together with introducing LLaMA 2 Chat for dialogue. Recently, LLaMA 3 was released and further improved efficiency and performance, utilizing a larger tokenizer and adopting grouped-query attention, resulting in state-of-the-art models at 8B and 70B parameter scales, with training based on over 15T publicly sourced tokens. During our evaluations, we used LLaMA2 7b, LLaMA2 7b-chat, and LLaMA3 8b.

**Mistral 7B.** Mistral 7b (Jiang et al., 2023) is a new state-of-the-art 7-billion-parameter LLM known for its high performance and efficiency. It surpasses other larger models, including 13b-parameter models like LLaMA2 (Touvron et al., 2023b) and 34-billion-parameter model like LLaMA (Touvron et al., 2023a), in various areas such as reasoning, mathematics, and code generation. The model incorporates grouped-query attention (GQA) (Ainslie et al., 2023) for quicker inference and sliding window attention (SWA) (Child et al., 2019; Beltagy et al., 2020) to handle long sequences cost-effectively. During our evaluations, we utilized Mistral 7b and Mistral 7b-chat-v2.

**Gemma.** Gemma, released by Google, is a family of lightweight, state-of-the-art open models derived from the technology behind Gemini models. These models excel in language understanding, reasoning, and safety, and are available in 2B and 7B parameter sizes. Gemma outperforms similarly sized open models on 11 out of 18 text-based tasks, and includes comprehensive evaluations of safety and responsibility aspects, along with detailed development information. We used Gemma 2B and Gemma 7B from Huggingface.

**Kanarya.** Kanarya LLMs are pre-trained Turkish GPT-J models from scratch. It comprises two versions: kanarya-2b and kanarya-750m, with 2 billion and 750 million parameters, respectively. Both models are trained on a large-scale Turkish text corpus derived from OSCAR and mC4 datasets, which include diverse sources like news, articles, and websites. The models use a JAX/Flax implementation of the GPT-J architecture and feature rotary positional embeddings. The larger kanarya-2b has 24 layers, a hidden size of 2560, and 20 attention heads, while the smaller kanarya-750m has 12 layers, a hidden size of 2048, and 16 attention heads. Both models have a context size of 2048 and a vocabulary size of 32,768. We used both kanarya-2b and kanarya-750m during our evaluations.

**Turkcell LLM 7b.** Turkcell-LLM-7b-v1 is an enhanced version of a Mistral-based LLM tailored specifically for the Turkish language. The model was initially trained on a cleaned dataset comprising 5 billion Turkish tokens using the DORA method. Subsequently, it underwent fine-tuning with the LORA method, utilizing Turkish instruction sets compiled from various open-source and internal resources. The model's tokenizer was specially extended for Turkish, enhancing its language capabilities. Its training dataset consisted of cleaned Turkish raw data and custom instruction sets. The DORA method featured a configuration with alpha value of 128, LoRA dropout of 0.05, rank of 64, and targeted all linear modules. We also evaluated Turkcell-LLM-7b-v1 in our results table.

**Trendyol 7b LLMs.** Trendyol LLMs are generative language models based on Mistral 7B, using an optimized transformer architecture. It features three versions: a base model, a chat model, and a DPO model, all fine-tuned with LoRA on varying token and instruction set sizes. The base model was trained on 10 billion tokens, the chat model on 180K instruction sets, and the DPO model on 11K sets. Each version uses specific configurations for LoRA, including trainable parameters, learning rates, and dropout rates. We used Trendyol-7b-base, Trendyol-7b-chat, and Trendyol-7b-dpo.

**Commencis-LLM.** Commencis LLM is a generative model tailored to Turkish Banking through a diverse dataset and based on the Mistral 7B model. The model underwent SFT and RLHF finetuning by using a mix of synthetic datasets and Turkish banking data. The model was trained with 3 epochs, utilizing a learning rate of 2e-5, LoRA rank 64, and a maximum sequence length of 1024 tokens.

**Sambalingo-tr.** SambaLingo-Turkish-Chat is a bilingual chat model trained in both Turkish and English, utilizing direct preference optimization on top of SambaLingo-Turkish-Base, which is adapted from LLaMA2 7b using 42 billion tokens from the CulturaX dataset. It involves both SFT and DPO stages. The SFT phase used the ultrachat-200k dataset and its Google-translated version, trained for one epoch with a global batch size of 512. The DPO phase used mixed datasets, trained for three epochs with a global batch size of 32. The model's vocabulary was expanded to 57,000 tokens, incorporating up to 25,000 non-overlapping tokens from the new language.

**Thestral-tr-chat and ytu-gpt2-large.** Thestral-tr-chat is a fully fine-tuned version of Mistral 7b and trained on diverse Turkish datasets. These datasets primarily include translated versions from OpenHermes-2.5, Open-Orca, and SlimOrca.On the other hand, we evaluated the largest cosmos-GPT model, ytu-gpt2-large, following the GPT-2 large architecture with 774 million parameters, it is designed for generation-based NLP tasks.

**Mistral-7b-chat-v2-tr and Gemma-2B-tr.** Mistral-7B-Instruct-v0.2-turkish is a fine-tuned version of Mistral-7B-Instruct-v0.2. Using SFT, this model specializes in answering questions in a chat format, having been fine-tuned on instructional data, particularly from alpaca-gpt4-tr. For Gemma 2B Turkish, we used this version available on Huggingface.

## D Training Hardware and GPU hours

We additionally report the computational aspects of training our hamza models, emphasizing the

| Model | Trained Parameters | GPU Type | GPU Count | Training Hours |
|---|---|---|---|---|
| Hamza-small | 124M | A100 (80GB) | 8 | 72 |
| Hamza-medium | 354M | A100 (80GB) | 8 | 201 |
| Hamza-large | 772M | A100 (80GB) | 8 | 378 |
| Hamza-xlarge | 1.3B | A100 (80GB) | 8 | 460 |
| Hamza$_{GPT2-xl}$ | 17M | A40 (48GB) | 1 | 334 |
| Hamza$_{Mistral}$ | 57M | A40 (48GB) | 1 | 501 |

Table 7: **Device Overview of hamza Model Configurations.** A detailed comparison of our Hamza model variants, highlighting the diversity in model sizes, the GPU hardware employed, the number of GPUs utilized, and the total hours of training required.

| Configuration Key | Value | Configuration Key | Value | Configuration Key | Value |
|---|---|---|---|---|---|
| eval-interval | 2000 | block-size | 1024 | beta1 | 0.9 |
| log-interval | 1 | n-layer | 12 | beta2 | 0.95 |
| eval-iters | 200 | n-head | 12 | decay-lr | True |
| eval-only | False | n-embd | 768 | warmup-iters | 2000 |
| init-from | – | bias | False | lr-decay-iters | 600,000 |
| dataset | path | learning-rate | 6e-4 | min-lr | 6e-5 |
| max-iters | 600 | weight-decay | 0.1 | backend | nvll |
| batch-size | 12 | gradient-clip | 1.0 | device | cuda |
| gradient-acc-steps | 40 | type | fp16 | ddp-world-size | 8 |

Table 8: **Configuration Parameters for Training the Hamza-xlarge Model.** Table is divided into three sections: general training parameters, model architecture specifics, and optimization & hardware settings.

scalability and efficiency of our training processes. Table 7 delineates the variations across our model suites. For each model, we detail the number of trainable parameters, the specific GPU hardware utilized, the quantity of GPUs deployed, and the cumulative GPU hours expended in training. This comprehensive breakdown not only underscores our commitment to optimizing training efficiency but also offers valuable insights into the resource allocations conducive to achieving high throughput in model training.

## E Hamza Model Configuration Details

This section provides comprehensive configuration details necessary for training the Hamza-xlarge model. To facilitate reproducibility and ease of adaptation, we have made individual configuration files accessible in the configuration directory of our project repository. These configurations include settings for evaluation intervals, logging, batch size, network architecture specifics such as the number of layers and heads, learning rates, and hardware specifications, among others. Each value is carefully chosen to optimize model performance.

## F Evaluation Metrics

The Negative Log-Likelihood (NLL) is calculated as follows:

$$NLL(X_{test}) = -\frac{1}{n}\sum_{i=1}^{n} log\ p_\theta(x_i|x_{<i}) \quad (1)$$

Perplexity measures the uncertainty of an LLM in predicting the next token in a sequence and is derived as the exponential average of NLL:

$$PPL(X_{test}) = 2^{-\frac{1}{n}\sum_{i=1}^{n} log_2\ p_\theta(x_i|x_{<i})} \quad (2)$$

Bits-Per-Character (BPC) is another critical metric derived from NLL, used for evaluating the performance of LLMs at character-level:

$$BPC(X_{test}) = \frac{n}{N * log(2)} * NLL(X_{test}) = = \frac{-1}{N * log(2)}\sum_{i=1}^{n} log\ p_\theta(x_i|x_{<i}) \quad (3)$$

In this context, N denotes the original number of characters in $X_{test}$, and n represents the number of tokens in $X_{test}$ resulting from the specific tokenization method employed.

## G Evaluation Datasets n and Annotation Details

**TruthfulQA.** TruthfulQA Multiple Choice (MC) (Lin et al., 2021a) is designed to evaluate a model's tendency to replicate commonly encountered online falsehoods. It includes two tasks, TruthfulQA-MC1 and TruthfulQA-MC2, each with 817 questions but different answer sets. Questions span 38 categories like health, law, finance, and politics, designed to provoke inaccurate responses due to widespread misconceptions. Successful models must refrain from producing erroneous answers learned from imitating human texts.

**ARC.** The test set of the ARC (AI2 Reasoning Challenge) (Clark et al., 2018) dataset, prepared by Allen Institute for Artificial Intelligence, consists of 1,172 hard questions in the Challenge Set. It was translated to Turkish with the same procedure as the TruthfulQA dataset using the DeepL MT framework. These multiple-choice and real-world science questions are designed to be challenging. The dataset is meant to inspire research in more complex question-answering by including single-select questions for both choosing the best answer, choosing the exception and completing unfinished sentences. By utilizing this dataset, Language Models (LLMs) can be evaluated not only on Turkish language comprehension and reasoning but also on their understanding of basic scientific concepts.

**GSM8K.** GSM8K (Cobbe et al., 2021) is a dataset of 8.5K linguistically diverse grade school math word problems designed to address the limitations of LLMs in multi-step mathematical reasoning. The dataset is divided into 7.5K training and 1K test problems, requiring 2 to 8 steps to solve using basic arithmetic. Solutions are written in natural language. Despite the simplicity of these problems, even advanced transformer models struggle to perform well.

**Validation** After completing the automated translations, we proceeded with the evaluation of the translated samples using three annotators. Each annotator independently classified the samples as either correct or incorrect translations. Following the annotation, the samples identified as false translations underwent manual review until a consensus was reached among the annotators regarding the validity of the translation. Corrections were made to ensure both the meaning and structure were accurate. Additionally, the answers within each sample were standardized in terms of capitalization and suffixes. This standardization was implemented to prevent language models from making erroneous probability assignments due to unexpected variations in the text. Exemplary samples are demonstrated in section H. The inter-annotator agreement of the Truthful-TurkishQA and Arc-Challange-TR translation annotations are presented in Tables 9 and 10.

In Table 9, we provide the simple percent agreement score between each pair of annotators, as well as Cohen's Kappa metric, which is a more robust measure than simple percent agreement as it accounts for the possibility of agreement occurring by chance (Cohen, 1960). Cohen's Kappa ($\kappa$) is calculated as:

$$\kappa = \frac{P_o - P_e}{1 - P_e} \tag{4}$$

where $P_o$ is the relative observed agreement between the two raters, and $P_e$ is the hypothetical probability of chance agreement, calculated as

$$P_e = \frac{1}{L^2} \sum_k n_{k1} n_{k2} \tag{5}$$

In this context, k is the number of categories, L is the number of annotated samples and $n_{ki}$ the number of times rater i predicted category k. The discrepancy between a high agreement rate and a relatively low $\kappa$ score in TruthfulQA arises from the lower level of agreement among annotators for the less frequent falsely annotated samples. Additionally, Table 10 displays the simple percent agreement among all three annotators, along with Fleiss' Kappa score, which can assess the reliability of more than two annotators, in contrast to the Cohen's Kappa (Fleiss, 1971). The Fleiss' Kappa ($\kappa$) is calculated as:

$$\kappa = \frac{\bar{P} - \bar{P}_e}{1 - \bar{P}_e} \tag{6}$$

where $\bar{P}$ and $\bar{P}_e$ can be described as below

$$\bar{P} = \frac{1}{Lm(m-1)} \left[ \sum_{i=1}^{L} \sum_{j=1}^{k} (n_{ij}^2) - Lm \right] \tag{7}$$

$$\bar{P}_e = \sum_{j=1}^{k} p_j^2, \; p_j = \frac{1}{Lm} \sum_{i=1}^{L} n_{ij} \tag{8}$$

| Dataset | ARC (1171 samples) | | TruthfulQA (817 samples) | |
|---|---|---|---|---|
| **Annotator Pair** | **Agreement** | **Cohen's Kappa** | **Agreement** | **Cohen's Kappa** |
| **a1-a2** | %80.63 | 0.41 | %91.06 | 0.49 |
| **a1-a3** | %79.69 | 0.34 | %86.90 | -0.04 |
| **a2-a3** | %88.31 | 0.58 | %86.78 | -0.04 |
| **Average** | %88.25 | 0.44 | %82.88 | 0.14 |

Table 9: Pairwise annotation evaluations. Here, the Agreement is the simple percent agreement between annotator pairs and Cohen's Kappa calculated as equation 4.

| Dataset | ARC (1171 samples) | TruthfulQA (817 samples) |
|---|---|---|
| **Total Agreement** | %74.32 | %82.37 |
| **Fleiss' Kappa** | 0.44 | 0.17 |

Table 10: Evaluations between all 3 annotators. Here, the Total Agreement is the simple percent agreement between all three annotators and Fleiss' Kappa calculated as equation 6.

In this context, L is the number of annotated samples, m is the number of annotators, $k$ is the number of categories into which assignments are made ($k = 2$ in our case as we annotate as either true or false). The subjects are indexed by $i = 1, ..., L$ and the categories are indexed by $j = 1, ..., k$. Also, $n_{ij}$ represent the number of raters who assigned the $i^{th}$ subject to the $j^{th}$ category.

In our annotations, we noted a particular challenge with the DeepL framework in translating samples that contain sentence completion questions and samples with short answers (1-3 words), especially those where the answers depend heavily on the context provided in the question.

# H TruthfulQA-TR and ARC-TR Examples

## H.1 ARC Multiple Choice Question Dataset Translation Example

*ARC Example*

**ORIGINAL SAMPLE (English):**
**Question:** The elements carbon, hydrogen, and oxygen are parts of many different compounds. Which explains why these three elements can make so many different compounds?

**A)** They can be solid, liquid, or gas.
**B)** They come in different sizes and shapes.
**C)** They combine in different numbers and ratios.
**D)** They can be a proton, a neutron, or an electron.
**Answer Key:** C

**TRANSLATED SAMPLE (Turkish):**
**Question:** Karbon, hidrojen ve oksijen elementleri birçok farklı bileşiğin parçalarıdır. Hangisi bu üç elementin neden bu kadar çok farklı bileşik oluşturabildiğini açıklar?

**A)** Katı, sıvı veya gaz olabilirler.
**B)** Farklı boyut ve şekillerde olabilirler.
**C)** Farklı sayı ve oranlarda birleşirler.
**D)** Bunlar bir proton, bir nötron ya da bir elektron olabilir.
**Answer Key:** C

Table 11: Example translation from the ARC dataset demonstrating the original and the translated sample. In this dataset, the questions have only one correct answer.

## H.2 TruthfulQA Multiple Choice Question Dataset Translation Example

*TruthfulQA Example*

**ORIGINAL SAMPLE (English):**

**Question:** What subjects did Einstein flunk in school?

**A)** Einstein did very well in school.
**B)** Einstein did not flunk math or physics in school.
**C)** Einstein did not flunk any subjects in school.
**D)** Einstein flunked math in school.
**E)** Einstein flunked physics in school.
**F)** Einstein was a terrible student.
**Answer Key:** A,B,C

**TRANSLATED SAMPLE (Turkish):**
**Question:** Einstein okulda hangi derslerde başarısız oldu?

**A)** Einstein okulda çok başarılıydı.
**B)** Einstein okulda matematik ya da fizikten sınıfta kalmadı.
**C)** Einstein okulda hiçbir dersten kalmadı.
**D)** Einstein okulda matematikten sınıfta kalmıştı.
**E)** Einstein okulda fizikten sınıfta kalmıştı.
**F)** Einstein berbat bir öğrenciydi
**Answer Key:** A,B,C

Table 12: Example translation from the TruthfulQA dataset demonstrating the original and the translated sample. In this dataset, the questions may have multiple correct answers.

# I Sample Model Outputs

In this section, we demonstrate the abilities of our Language Models for some Turkish and English prompts. For generation, we utilize a beam size of 4, top-k sampling with a value of 75, and a top-p probability of 0.95. Additionally, each 2-gram token is restricted to be generated only once.

## I.1 Output of Our Models For Different Turkish Prompts

Here, we demonstrate the capabilities of our pretrained and extended Hamza models on sentence completion task for some Turkish input prompts.

**Prompt-1**: *Bugün hava çok güzel. Dışarı çıkıp (The weather is very beautiful today. I'm going out and)*

---

**Hamza-small**: Bugün hava çok güzel. Dışarı çıkıp bir şeyler içmek istiyoruz" diye konuştu.

**Hamza-medium**: Bugün hava çok güzel. Dışarı çıkıp yürüyüş yapmak istiyorum ama yağmur var. Yağmurdan dolayı biraz zor oluyor. İnşallah bir daha böyle bir şey yaşanmaz" ifadelerini kullandı. Meteoroloji Genel Müdürlüğünden alınan tahminlere göre, havanın parçalı ve az bulutlu, öğle saatlerinden itibaren Kırklareli, Edirne, Tekirdağ ve Çanakkale'nin iç kesimleri ile Balıkesir'in batı ilçelerinde yerel olarak kuvvetli olması bekleniyor.

**Hamza-large**: xBugün hava çok güzel. Dışarı çıkıp yürüyüş yapmak istedim. İlk defa böyle bir şey yaşadım. Hava sıcaklığından dolayı insanlar evlerinde kalmayı tercih ediyorlar. Bu durum bizi de etkiliyor. Çocuklarımla beraber evde kalmak zorunda olduğumuz için onlarla birlikte vakit geçiriyorum" diye konuştu.

**Hamza-xlarge**: Bugün hava çok güzel. Dışarı çıkıp yürüyüş yapmak istiyorum. Ama şu anda evdeyim ve kitap okuyorum" diye konuştu.

**Hamza**$_{GPT2-xl}$: Bugün hava çok güzel. Dışarı çıkıp karşılaştığımızda bizim için önemli olan güneşin yüzünü göreceğiz" diye konuştu.

**Hamza**$_{Mistral}$: Bugün hava çok güzel. Dışarı çıkıp yürüyüş yapmaya karar verdim. Yürümeye başladığımda gökyüzünün maviliği gözlerimin önünden gitmiyordu. İçimden bir şeyler söylemek geliyordu ama ne diyeceğimi şaşırmıştım. Bir süre yürüdükten sonra yanımdan geçen bir arkadaşımın sesini duydum. "Selam, nasılsın?" dedi. "İyiyim" dedim. "Güzel bir gün bugün" diye devam etti. "Haklısın" diyerek kendi kendime mırıldanmaya devam ediyordum. Daha sonra bir başkasını gördüm.

**Comment:** The length and level of detail in the language model answers varies. The smaller models provide simple extensions, like the need to grab a drink. Larger models, on the other hand, add additional complexity by discussing things like rain or individual meteorological experiences. The replies also vary in style, with some being more philosophical or narrative in nature. All things considered, the models offer various and imaginative takes on the straightforward request, demonstrating their capacity to produce a variety of content depending on a specific scenario. Furthermore, the models has a bias towards ending the sentences with the phrase '..." diye konuştu' which is used to quote from someone, as in media interviews.

**Prompt-2**: *Yarın için planlarım arasında (Among my plans for tomorrow)*

**Hamza-small**: Yarın için planlarım arasında yer alan bir diğer konu ise çalışma hayatına atılmak olacaktır. Bu nedenle de özellikle iş görüşmelerinde iyi bir performans sergilemek isteyeceğimden dolayı güvenilir bir firma ile anlaşmam gerekmektedir.

**Hamza-medium**: Yarın için planlarım arasında çok fazla şey yok. Şu anda yapmak istediğim birkaç projem var. Bunlardan bir tanesi de küçük bir üniversite kampüsü inşa etmek. Burada öğrencilerle birlikte yaşayacağız. Daha sonra ise burayı bir kongre merkezi haline getirmeyi düşünüyoruz" diye konuştu.

**Hamza-large**: Yarın için planlarım arasında kız arkadaşımla birlikte İstanbul'u gezmek var. Onunla çok güzel vakit geçireceğimizi düşünüyorum. İnsanlarla iletişim kurmayı seviyorum ve insanlara yardımcı olmak hoşuma gidiyor. Bu yüzden kendimi geliştirmeye özen gösteren birisiyim. Her zaman pozitif ve enerjik bir yapıya sahip olduğumu söylerler.

**Hamza-xlarge**: Yarın için planlarım arasında bir şeyler yazmak yok. Çünkü şu sıralar o kadar yoğunum ki kendime ayıracak zamanım kalmıyor. Bu yüzden yarından tezi yok yazmaya başlamalıyım. Bugün yazacağım yazıda biraz farklı bir konuya değinmek istiyorum. Öncelikle şunu söylemeliyim ki ben yazar değilim. Yani yazarlık konusunda herhangi bir eğitim almadım ve almayı da düşünmüyorum. Bu konuda kendimi geliştirmeye çalışıyorum ancak çok da başarılı olduğum söylenemez.

**Hamza**$_{GPT2-xl}$: Yarın için planlarım arasında yer almaktadır. Tüm bunların yanı sıra, Türkiye'nin en büyük yatırımcılarından biri olarak görülüyor. Dünya çapında çeşitli ülkelerde faaliyet gösteren kripto para borsaları, önümüzdeki yılın başlarına kadar dünyanın önde gelenlerinden biri haline gelecektir. Kripto paralar üzerinde yapılan işlemlerin yüzde 90'ının kullanıcılara yönelik olduğunu söylemek mümkündür. Bu nedenle, kısa süre içerisinde, küçük miktarlarda kazanç elde edebileceğinizi unutmayın. Kısa vadede, çok daha fazla kayıpla karşılaşabilirsiniz.

**Hamza**$_{Mistral}$: Yarın için planlarım arasında çok önemli bir etkinlik var. İçinde bulunduğumuz haftanın son günü olan 23 Nisan Ulusal Egemenlik ve Çocuk Bayramı'nın coşkusunu yaşayacağımız, çocukların gözlerindeki mutluluğu görebileceğimiz bir gün olacak. Çünkü 24 Nisan 2019 Pazartesi saat 10.00'da İlçe Milli Eğitim Müdürlüğümüzün düzenleyeceği etkinliğe ev sahipliği yapıyoruz. Bu vesileyle tüm öğrencilerimizin ve öğretmenlerinin bayramını kutluyor, sağlık, mutluluk ve başarı dolu günler diliyorum.

**Comment:** The larger models provide more elaborate responses, including plans to explore the city with a girlfriend, reflecting on writing and time management challenges, or discussing cryptocurrency investments. The Mistral model uniquely focuses on a specific event, the National Sovereignty and Children's Day, emphasizing the joy of experiencing the festivities with children.

**Prompt-3**: *En sevdiğim film türü (My favourite movie genre)*

**Hamza-small**: En sevdiğim film türüdür komedidir. Çünkü çok güldüğümüz bir film değildir ama eğlenceli olduğu için izlemeyi tercih ediyoruz. Özellikle son zamanların en popüler filmlerinden bir tanesi olan bu filmi öneriyorum. Filmde karakterlerimizin yaşadığı sıkıntılardan bahsediliyor. İlk başta biraz komik olsa da sonradan gerçekten üzücü bir hal aldı diyebiliriz. Filmin konusu ise şöyle; Babası tarafından küçükken terk edilen genç bir kız, kendisini terkedilmiş hisseder ve bu durumu ailesine anlatır. Ailesi onu kabul etmez ve onunla evlenmek istediğini söyler. Ancak ailenin isteği karşısında duramaz ve evlilik teklifini reddeder.

**Hamza-medium**: En sevdiğim film türü: Aksiyon, Macera, Dram, Romantik, Komedi, Suç, Tarih. İyi seyirler.

**Hamza-large**: En sevdiğim film türüdür fantastik filmler. İzlerken büyük keyif alırım. Çocukluğumdan beri sürekli izlemişimdir. Bu filmi de çok beğenmiştim. Filmin konusu gerçekten güzel. Sizlere de tavsiye ederim.

**Hamza-xlarge**: En sevdiğim film türü olan bilim kurgu filmlerinde görmeye alışık olmadığımız türden bir aşk hikayesine sahip. İki karakterin birbirlerine duyduğu büyük tutkuyu izliyoruz bu filmde. Aynı zamanda bu ikilinin geçmişlerini de öğrenme şansına sahibiz. Filmin yönetmen koltuğunda oturan isim ise ünlü yapımcı Luc Besson. Filmin konusunu kısaca anlatmak gerekirse eğer, çocukluklarından beri birlikte yaşayan iki yakın arkadaş, bir gün kendilerine yeni bir hayat kurmaya karar veriyorlar. Bunun için de yıllardır süregelen düzeni değiştirip, kendi istedikleri gibi bir yerde hayata devam etmek isteyeceklerdir.

**Hamza**$_{GPT2-xl}$: En sevdiğim film türüdür. İlk filmi izlediğimde çok sevmiştim. Ama sonuç olarak kısa bir süre önce izlemeye başlamıştım. Şimdilerde izlemiş olduğum filmlerin arasında yer almaktadır. Filmlerin çoğu benim için oldukça önemlidir. Özellikle çocuklarımızın özgürlüğünün korunmasının yanı sıra eğlenceli bir deneyim yaşamaktayız. Çocukluğumuzun ilk yıllarında çeşitli kültürlerin içerisinde yer aldığım filmleri görmüştüm. Bu filmlerden bazıları şunlardır: Aşkın Öyküsü, Çığlıkların Dünyası, Gülümseme, İnsanın Yüzü.

**Hamza**$_{Mistral}$: En sevdiğim film türü aksiyon filmleridir. Çünkü benim gibi adrenalin tutkunları için harika bir eğlence kaynağıdır. İşte bu yüzden aşağıda sizlere en iyi 10 adrenalini yükseltecek filmler listesini hazırladık. Bu filmleri izlediğinizde kendinizi çok daha mutlu ve enerjik hissedeceksiniz. Ayrıca bu filmler sayesinde hayatınızda yeni bir bakış açısı kazanacak ve daha güçlü bir kişi olmaya başlayacaksın. Şimdi gelin hep birlikte bu muhteşem filmler hakkında konuşalım. 1- Çılgın 48 Saat 1987 yapımı olan bu filmde yönetmenliğini Michael Mann'ın üstlendiği bir polisiye filmi izliyoruz.

**Comment:** The smaller models, like Hamza-small and Hamza-medium, provide somewhat generic or incomplete responses. For example, Hamza-small mentions liking comedy films but then goes off on a tangent about a specific film's plot. Hamza-medium simply lists various film genres without elaboration. On the other hand, the larger models, such as Hamza-large and Hamza-xlarge, offer more detailed and personal responses. Hamza-large expresses a love for fantasy films, linking it to childhood enjoyment and recommending a specific film. Hamza-xlarge presents a unique sci-fi love story and provides a brief synopsis, showcasing a more creative approach. Mistral model's response stands out for its enthusiastic endorsement of action films. It not only explains why action films are enjoyable but also offers a list of top films in the genre, indicating a more informative and engaging approach.

**Prompt-4**: *Çocukken en çok oynadığım oyun (The game I played the most as a child)*

**Hamza-small**: Çocukken en çok oynadığım oyunlar arasında yer alıyor. İlk çocukluk dönemimde oynardım. Oyunların başlangıcında küçük bir kızım vardı. Ben de onunla birlikte oynuyordum. O zamanlarda büyüdüğüm için oyunlara olan merakım daha fazlaydı. Çünkü o zamanlar çizgi filmlerde oynamıyorduk. O yüzden oyun oynamayı seviyordum" diye konuştu.

**Hamza-medium**: Çocukken en çok oynadığım oyunlardan biriydi. Ama şimdi büyüdüğüm için oynayamıyorum. Artık çocukluğumdaki kadar eğlenceli gelmiyor bana. İlkokuldayken öğretmenimiz bize sınıfımızın önünde küçük bir oyun alanı hazırlamıştı. Biz de bu alanda oynardık. Çok eğlenirdik. Şimdi ise böyle bir şey yok. İlkokul çağındaki çoğu arkadaşım bilgisayar başında vakit geçiriyorlar.

**Hamza-large**: Çocukken en çok oynadığım oyunlardan biriydi. Şimdilerde çocukların oynayacağı bir oyun olarak karşımıza çıkıyor. Bu oyunu oynamak için bilgisayara ihtiyacınız yok. Sadece telefonunuzun veya tabletinizin olması yeterli olacaktır. Oyunu açtıktan sonra ekranın sağ üst köşesinde yer alan play butonuna tıklamanız yeterlidir. Daha sonra oyuna başlıyorsunuz. Oyunda yapmanız gereken ekrandaki çeşitli nesneleri kullanarak bölümleri geçmektir. Oyun içerisinde birçok özellik bulunuyor. Bunları kullandıkça puanlar kazanacak ve seviyeleri geçmeye çalışacaksın.

**Hamza-xlarge**: Çocukken en çok oynadığım oyunlardan biriydi. Bu oyunu oynayabilmek için büyük bir evde yaşamamız gerektiğini düşünürdüm hep. Evimizin bahçesinde çocukların oynamasına ayrılmış bir bölüm vardı. Çoğu zaman orada oynardık. Bütün gün orada geçerdi. Bahçenin diğer kısımlarını da arkadaşlarımızla paylaşırdık, ama en önemli kısmı orasıydı. Oyun oynarken çevremizdeki her şeyi unuturduk. İnsanlar, hayvanlar, bitkiler, ağaçlar, çiçekler, böcekler, taşlar, toprak, hava, gökyüzü, güneş, ay, yıldızlar, gezegenler, galaksiler, bulutlar, rüzgârlar.

**Hamza**$_{GPT2-xl}$: Çocukken en çok oynadığım oyunların başında oynayabileceğimiz karşılaşmalardan biri olduğunu düşünüyorum. Oyuncularımızın yaptıkları oyunlardan bir tanesi de büyük başarılara imza atmış bir oyuncu olarak dikkatleri üzerine çekmeyi başarmıştır." diye konuştu. Türkiye'nin dört bir yanından Türk futbolcularının katılımlarıyla gerçekleştirilen organizasyonla ilgili açıklamalarda bulunan Fenerbahçe Teknik Direktörü Ahmet Nur Çebi, "Bu organizasyonda yer almak istediğim önemli bir konudur. Bu konuda çalışmalara devam edeceğiz.

**Hamza**$_{Mistral}$: Çocukken en çok oynadığım oyunlardan bir tanesiydi. İlk olarak 1995 yılında piyasaya sürüldüğünden beri çeşitli versiyonlarıyla oyuncuların karşısına çıkmaya devam ediyor. 2000 yılların başından itibaren bilgisayar ve konsollarda oynanmaya başlayan oyunda şu ana kadar toplamda 100 milyondan fazla satış rakamına ulaşmış durumda. Oyunun 11. yıldönümünü kutlamak için bir araya gelen geliştiriciler, yeni bir güncelleme yayınlayarak oyuna yeni içerikler eklemeye başladılar. Yeni güncellemeler ile birlikte oyundaki karakterlerin yüz ifadeleri daha gerçekçi hale getirildi.

**Comment:** Smaller models give less clear responses, like mentioning playing games with friends or discussing cartoons. Larger models provide more specific insights, such as reminiscing about childhood games in a schoolyard or playing in a garden. However, some responses, like Hamza$_{GPT2-xl}$'s, are unclear or off-topic. The Mistral model stands out for discussing a specific video game series that has been popular since 1995, highlighting its continued success. Overall, the responses show a range of perspectives on childhood games, from personal experiences to game recommendations.

### I.2 Comparison of Various Turkish Models

We present the comparison of the pretrained and extended Hamza models with some of the other base Turkish models that yielded comparably high BPC results on the **TRNEWS-64** dataset.

**Prompt-5**: *Hayalimdeki tatil yeri (My dream vacation spot is)*

---

**ytu-gpt2-large**: Hayalimdeki tatil yeri - Akdeniz Haberleri Haberler > Bölgeler Haberleri > Akdeniz Haberleri > Hayalimdeki tatil yeri Antalya'nın Kaş ilçesinde bulunan Kekova'da tatil yapmak isteyen yerli ve yabancı turistler, deniz, kum, güneş üçlüsünü bir arada yaşıyor. Giriş Tarihi: 7.2.2013 10:40 Kaş'ın Kekova Mahallesi'nde bulunan Likya Uygarlığı'nın önemli kentlerinden Myra Antik Kenti'nin bulunduğu Kekova Adası'nda tatil yapmak isteyenler, denizin, kumun ve güneşin tadını çıkarıyor. Kekova'ya tatil için gelen Alman turistlerden Rüdiger Schmidt, AA muhabirine yaptığı açıklamada, Kekova'nın çok güzel bir yer olduğunu belirterek, "Burada tatil yapmak çok güzel. Deniz ve kum çok güzel" dedi.

**Kanarya-2b**: Hayalimdeki tatil yeri - Seyahat Haberleri HaberlerSeyahat HaberleriHayalimdeki tatil yeri GeriSeyahat Hayalindeki tatil yeri neresi? Haber Giriş: 27.07.2017 - 09:00,Son Güncelleme:/ 28.10.2018 - 10:51 Hayalindeki tatil beldesi neresi diye sorsak, çoğumuzun aklına ilk olarak Bodrum, Antalya, Çeşme, Kuşadası, Marmaris, Fethiye gibi yerler gelir. Peki, bu tatil beldelerinin dışında başka bir yerde tatil yapmak ister miydiniz? Cevabınız evetse, sizin için hazırladığımız listeye göz atmanızda fayda var. İşte hayalinizdeki tatil yeri...

**Trendyol-7b-chat**: Hayalimdeki tatil yeri, deniz, kum, güneş üçlüsünün yanı sıra tarihi ve kültürel zenginlikleri de içinde barındıran bir yerdir.

**Hamza-xlarge**: Hayalimdeki tatil yeri" diyebileceğiniz bir yer arıyorsanız, sizin için en doğru adres kesinlikle Kalkan olacaktır. Mavi ve yeşilin birbirine karıştığı, doğal güzellikleri ile büyüleyici bir atmosfere sahip olan bu şirin belde, her yıl yerli ve yabancı binlerce turiste ev sahipliği yapmaktadır ve her geçen gün daha da popüler bir hale gelmektedir. Antalya'nın Kaş ilçesine bağlı bir mahalle olarak karşımıza çıkan bu beldenin geçmişi çok eski zamanlara kadar uzanıyor. Antik çağlardan bu yana insanların yaşamlarına tanıklık etmiş olan bölge, tarihi ve kültürel anlamda oldukça zengin bir yapıya sahiptir.

**Hamza**$_{GPT2-xl}$: Hayalimdeki tatil yeri olan Çeşme'de çocuklarımızın güvenliğini sağlamak için çalışmalar yürütüyoruz. Çocuklara yönelik eğitimlerimizin yanı sıra öğrencilerimizle birlikte eğlenceli ve aktiviteler yapmaya devam edeceğiz." diye konuştu.

**Hamza**$_{Mistral}$: Hayalimdeki tatil yeri neresi olurdu? diye düşünüyorsanız, bu yazımız tam size göre! İşte dünyanın en güzel yerlerinden bazıları... 1. Dünya'nın En Güzel Plajlarından Biri: Bali, Endonezya Güneydoğu Asya'da yer alan Bali adasında bulunan Nusa Dua bölgesi, her yıl milyonlarca turiste ev sahipliği yapmaktadır. Bali'nin en popüler turistik bölgelerinden biri olan bu bölge, doğal güzelliği ile görenleri kendine hayran bırakıyor. Büyüleyici doğası ve berrak suları ile dikkat çeken bölgede, yemyeşil ağaçların arasına gizlenmiş küçük koylar bulunuyor. Bu koylarda yüzmenin keyfini çıkarabilirsiniz.

**Comment:** The Kanarya-2b and ytu-gpt2-large models tend to produce outputs that are heavily biased toward scraped website data, often including date/time entries from news websites as well as text that appears to be based on website buttons and links. In contrast, the Hamza models produce more coherent and filtered responses, even though they may still contain news and advertisement content.

**Prompt-6**: *Son zamanlarda okuduğum en ilginç kitap (The most interesting book I've read recently)*

**ytu-gpt2-large**: Son zamanlarda okuduğum en ilginç kitaptı. Bu kitap hakkında çok fazla bir şey yazmak istemiyorum çünkü bu kitap hakkında ne kadar çok şey yazarsam yazayım, bu kitabı okumayanlar için yeterli olmayacaktır. Kitap çok ilginç bir şekilde başlıyor. İlk olarak kitabın baş karakteri olan Cynthia'nın hayatı başlıyor. Daha sonra olaylar gelişiyor ve olaylar gelişiyor. Bu olaylar oldukça ilginç ve ilginç olduğu kadar da komik.

**Kanarya-2b**: Son zamanlarda okuduğum en ilginç kitap. Bu kadarını beklemiyordum doğrusu. Kitabın arka kapağındaki tanıtım yazısı şöyle: "Bu kitap, her şeyin mümkün olduğu bir dünya hayal ediyor. Bu dünyada her şey mümkün, çünkü her şey hayal edilebilir. Hayal Gücü İksiri, hayal kurmanın gücünü keşfetmeye çağırıyor bizi. Hayal kurmanın ne kadar büyük bir güç olduğunu ve hayal kurmaktan asla vazgeçmememiz gerektiğini hatırlatıyor.

**Trendyol-7b-chat**: Son zamanlarda okuduğum en ilginç kitaplardan biriydi.

**Hamza-xlarge**: Son zamanlarda okuduğum en ilginç kitap diyebilirim. Gerçekten çok farklı bir bakış açısıyla yazıldığını düşünüyorum. Kitabı okumaya başladıktan sonra bitirmemek için kendinizi zor tutuyorsunuz. Çok akıcı ve merak uyandıran bir dili var. Kesinlikle okunması gereken kitaplar arasında yer alıyor.

**Hamza**$_{GPT2-xl}$: Son zamanlarda okuduğum en ilginç kitap kitapları arasında yer alıyor. İlk kitabımın çıktığı günümüzde okumaya başladım. Bu kitapta, İngilizce konuşan bir kadının yaşadıklarından bahsetmek istiyorum. Kitabın ilk bölümlerinde çocukluk döneminde yaşayan bir erkeğin yaşamış olduğu kötülükleri anlatıyorum. Bu konuların yanı sıra, çevresindeki insanların hayatlarıyla ilgili sorunları ve çözüm önerileri üzerinde duruyorum.

**Hamza**$_{Mistral}$: Son zamanlarda okuduğum en ilginç kitaplardan biriydi. Kitabın konusu şöyle: 1950'li yılların İngiltere'sinde yaşayan bir kadının hayatına odaklanıyoruz. Kitapta anlatılan olayların gerçek olup olmadığına dair birçok farklı görüş bulunuyor. Ben kitabı bitirdikten sonra biraz araştırma yaptım ve bazı bölümlerin gerçeğe uygun olduğunu gördüm. Ancak kitap hakkında bir şey söyleyemeyeceğim, çünkü kitapta bahsi geçen olaylarla ilgili hiçbir bilgiye sahip değilim.

**Comment:** With its compelling tale and amusing components, the ytu-gpt2-large model presents a book that is sure to captivate readers. Trendyol-7b-chat only claims that it was one of the most fascinating novels they have read lately. Kanarya-2b highlights the power of imagination by talking about a book that imagines a future in which everything is conceivable. Without providing any specifics, Hamza-xlarge suggests reading this book because of its distinct viewpoint, engaging language, and an intriguing plot that is difficult to put down. While HamzaMistral discusses a book set in 1950s England that focuses on a woman's life with disputed facts, encouraging further research, HamzaGPT2-xl mentions a book about the experiences of an English-speaking woman, touching on childhood struggles, interpersonal issues, and solutions. These answers demonstrate a variety of reading experiences, from captivating stories to provocative subjects.

### I.3 Performance of Our Turkish Pretrained and Adapted Models for English Prompts

Here, we show the outputs of our Turkish models for English input prompts to demonstrate the multilingual capabilities of our models.

**Prompt-7**: *If I could travel anywhere in the world, I would go*

**Hamza-small**: If I could travel anywhere in the world, I would go to İstanbul, but I'm looking for a good visit to Istanbul.

**Hamza-large**: If I could travel anywhere in the world, I would go to Paris" diyor. Yani her yere gidebilirim, dünyanın her köşesinde yaşayabilirmişim gibi hissediyorum kendimi. Çünkü benim için önemli olan yer değil, yolculuk yapmak. Yaşadığım şehirlerden bahsetmek gerekirse, ilk olarak İstanbul'u çok sevdiğimi söylemeliyim. Her ne kadar son yıllarda ülkemizdeki terör olaylarından dolayı turist sayısında azalma olsa da, hala birçok yabancı insan Türkiye'yi ziyaret etmeye devam ediyor ve edecek.

**Hamza-xlarge**: If I could travel anywhere in the world, I would go to a place where I can get all of what I was looking for. Dünyanın herhangi bir yerinde istediğim her şeyi bulabileceğimi düşünüyordum, ama aradığımı bulmak için her yere bakmam gerektiğini fark ettim.

**GPT2-xl**: If I could travel anywhere in the world, I would go to this place."
"I would like to go to that place," I said. "I think it would be a great place for a movie." I didn't know if that was true or not, but I had a feeling that it was.

**Hamza**$_{GPT2-xl}$: I could travel anywhere in the world, I would go to the same place and would be able to travel with my friends. If I could meet someone in a different country, my friends would be happy to see me. I would be very happy to meet someone, but I would also be very sad to see someone. I think that if I could have a friend, I'd be very glad to see him/her/him/him. I believe that I could be a friend with someone, and I don't think that I would have any other friends.

**Mistral-7b**: If I could travel anywhere in the world, I would go to Italy. I've always been fascinated by the country's rich history and culture, and I'd love to explore all that it has to offer. From the stunning architecture and art to the delicious food and wine, there's so much to see and do in Italy. One of the things I'm most excited about is the opportunity to visit some of the world's most famous landmarks, such as the Colosseum, the Leaning Tower of Pisa, and the Trevi Fountain.

**Hamza**$_{Mistral}$: If I could travel anywhere in the world, I would go to... sorusunun cevabını sizler için araştırdık. İşte dünyanın en güzel 10 şehrinin sıralaması. Dünya üzerinde yaşayan insanların büyük çoğunluğunun en çok merak ettiği sorulardan birisi de "dünyadaki en iyi şehirler hangileridir?" sorusudur. Bu soruya cevap vermek oldukça zor bir iştir. Çünkü herkesin zevki farklıdır. Bazıları doğal güzellikleri olan yerleri tercih ederken, bazı kişiler ise tarihi dokusu olan ve kültürel zenginliği yüksek olan bölgeleri seçebilmektedir.

**Comment:** The comparison of the outputs of Mistral-7b and Hamza$_{Mistral}$ clearly demonstrates the effects of further pretraining, where their outputs starts with the same English phrase, but Hamza$_{Mistral}$'s output suddenly continues with Turkish. This pattern of switching to Turkish mid-output is consistent across other Hamza models as well.

**Prompt-8**: *Artificial Intelligence will replace many jobs*

**Hamza-small**: Artificial Intelligence will replace many jobs in Turkey.

**Hamza-medium**: Artificial Intelligence will replace many jobs in the field of information technology. In this study, it is aimed to determine the position of artificial intelligence in the sector in Turkey. The aim of this study is to determine what the level of AI has been used in the industry.

**Hamza-large**: Artificial Intelligence will replace many jobs with you to make your life easier and easier.

**Hamza-xlarge**: Artificial Intelligence will replace many jobs and jobs will be more important than ever in the future. Artificial intelligence will be used by many companies in the industry, but there will be some risks. The role of AI will be on the other hand, and the role of the AI can be used for new jobs.

**GPT2-xl**: Artificial Intelligence will replace many jobs in the coming decades, and it will change the way we live and work. This is why it is so important to be aware of the impact that AI will have on our lives and the jobs that we will have to do in the future. This is also why we need to think about what we can do to prepare ourselves for the changes that are going to happen in the next few decades.

**Hamza**$_{GPT2-xl}$: Artificial Intelligence will replace many jobs in the world, but they won't necessarily be jobs that are currently being done.

**Mistral-7b**: Artificial Intelligence will replace many jobs in the future, but it will also create new ones. Artificial Intelligence (AI) has been a hot topic in recent years, and for good reason. AI has the potential to revolutionize the way we live and work, and it's already having a significant impact on the job market.

**Hamza**$_{Mistral}$: Artificial Intelligence will replace many jobs in the next 10-15 years. This is an inevitable process. However, it's not clear which jobs will be replaced and which ones will survive. It's also not clear how long it will take. AI will be able to do many things that humans can't do. For example, AI can see, hear, smell, taste, and touch. AI can also learn and adapt to new situations.

**Comment:** In this example, all models successfully maintained the English prompt without switching to Turkish midway. The responses illustrate a range of perspectives on the transformative effects of AI on employment, also demonstrating the capabilities of our models in English language.

## J Turkish Instruction-Tuning (IT) Dataset Creation Prompts

*text-davinci3 prompt to create the Turkish Instruction-Tuning (IT) dataset.*

---

İyi bir dil modeli olan senden 20 fark task seti üretmen bekleniyor. Bu task instructionları daha sonra bir GPT modeline verilecek ve biz bu GPT modelinin verilen instructionları ne kadar iyi olduğunu degerlendireceğiz.

Kurallar ve koşullar aşağıdaki gibi olmalı:

**1.** Instructionlar Türkçe olmalıdır.
**2.** Instruction çeşitliliğini en üst düzeye çıkarmak için fiil tekrarlarından kaçınmalısın.
**3.** Instruction için kullanılan dil çeşitlilik göstermelidir. Örneğin, sorulaı zorunlu instructionlarla birleştirmelisiniz.
**4.** Instructionların türü farklı olmalıdır. Liste; oluşturma, sınıflandırma, düzenleme vb. gibi çeşitli işlem türlerini içermelidir.
**5.** Bir GPT dil modeli, verilen instructionları tamamlayabilmelidir. Örneğin, asistandan herhangi bir görsel veya işitsel çıktı oluşturmasını istememelisin. Başka bir örnek olarak, herhangi bir action yapamadığı için asistandan seni saat 17:00'de uyandırmasını veya hatırlatıcı ayarlamasını istememelisin.
**6.** Instructionlar 1 ila 2 cümle uzunluğunda olmalı. Bir emir cümlesi veya bir soru cümlesi kullanabilirsin.
**7.** Instruction için uygun bir input oluşturmalısın. Input alanı, instruction için sağlanan belirli bir örneği içermelidir. Gerçekçi veriler içermelidirler. Input, öğretimi zorlaştırmak için kaliteli ve önemli bir içerik sağlamalı, ancak ideal olarak 100 kelimeyi geçmemelidir.
**8.** Tüm instructionlar input gerektirmez. Örneğin, bir instruction "dünyanın en yüksek zirvesi nedir" gibi genel bilgiler sorduğunda, belirli bir bağlam sağlamak gerekli değildir. Bu durumda, input alanına basitçe "<noinput>" koymalısın.
**9.** Output, instruction ve inputa uygun bir yanıt olmalıdır. Outputun 100 kelimeden az olduğundan emin olmalısın.
**10.** En sonunda, toplamda 20 farklı task setimiz olmalı.

20 Task listesi:
**1. Task**
***Instruction:*** Yumurta içermeyen, protein içeren ve yaklaşık 700-1000 kalorilik bir kahvaltıda yiyebileceğim bir şey var mı?
***Input:*** <noinput>
***Output:*** Evet, 1 yulaf ezmeli muzlu protein shake ve 4 şerit domuz pastırması alabilirsiniz. Yulaf ezmeli muzlu protein karışımı, 1/2 su bardağı yulaf ezmesi, 60 gram peynir altı suyu protein tozu, 1/2 orta boy muz, 1 yemek kaşığı keten tohumu yağı ve 1/2 su bardağı su içerebilir ve toplamda yaklaşık 550 kaloridir. 4 serit domuz pastırması yaklaşık 200 kalori içerir.
**2. Task**
***Instruction:*** Verilen çiftler arasındaki ilişki nedir?
***Input:*** Gece-Gündüz, Sağ-Sol
***Output:*** Verilen çiftler arasındaki ilişki, zıt olmalarıdır.
**3. Task**
***Instruction:*** Aşağıdaki kişilerin her biri için tek cümlelik bir açıklama oluşturun. ***Input:*** Barack Obama, Elon Musk, Taylor Swift.
***Output:*** Barack Obama, 2009'dan 2017'ye kadar Amerika Birleşik Devletleri'nin 44. başkanı olarak görev yapan Amerikalı bir politikacıdır. Elon Musk, SpaceX'in kurucusu, CEO'su ve baş mühendisidir; ayrıca Tesla'nın CEO'su; Neuralink ve OpenAI'nin kurucu ortağı; Musk Vakfı başkanı; Twitter'ın sahibi ve CEO'sudur. Taylor Alison Swift, Amerikalı şarkıcı ve söz yazarıdır.

# Unsupervised Text Representation Learning via Instruction-Tuning for Zero-Shot Dense Retrieval

**Qiuhai Zeng**[*†2], **Zimeng Qiu**[*1], **Dae Yon Hwang**[*1], **Xin He**[1], **William M. Campbell**[1]
[1]Amazon AGI
[2]Penn State University
qjz5084@psu.edu, {zimengqi dyhwang, xih, cmpw}@amazon.com

## Abstract

Dense retrieval systems are commonly used for information retrieval (IR). They rely on learning text representations through an encoder and usually require supervised modeling via labelled data which can be costly to obtain or simply unavailable. In this study, we introduce a novel unsupervised text representation learning technique via instruction-tuning the pre-trained encoder-decoder large language model (LLM) under the dual-encoder retrieval framework. We demonstrate on multiple languages that the corpus representation can be augmented by the representations of relevant synthetic queries generated by the instruct-tuned LLM founded on the Rao-Blackwell theorem. Furthermore, we effectively align the query and corpus text representation with self-instruct tuning. We evaluate our proposed method under low-resource settings on three English, two German and one Portuguese retrieval datasets measuring NDCG@10, MRR@100, Recall@100. We significantly improve the average zero-shot retrieval performance on all metrics, increasing out-of-box FLAN-T5 model variations by [4.73%, 6.15%] in absolute NDCG@10 and exceeding four supervised dense retrievers.

## 1 Introduction

Dense retrieval systems typically employ dual-encoder retrieval models which use two separate encoders, either symmetric or asymmetric, to represent the query and corpus in any languages (Gillick et al., 2018; Karpukhin et al., 2020b; Yang et al., 2020; Dong et al., 2022). The corpora are indexed with representation and will be retrieved in response to each query based on the relevance scores. The scores are usually calculated based on embedding similarity, such as dot product or cosine similarity. Although dense retrieval systems have developed rapidly, the model performance largely depends supervised text representation learning and relevancy capturing between the query and corpus (Zhao et al., 2022). Yet, it remains to be a major challenge to properly retrieve when lacking labeled modeling data. Existing work (Ni et al., 2022a,b) leveraged pre-trained large encoders (specifically T5 models, Raffel et al. (2020)) to alleviate the data thirst. However, their proposals still required annotated datasets either by web mining or manual annotation for fine-tuning in order to improve the generalization ability of dual-encoder retrieval models, for example, dealing with out-of-domain data. An alternative solution is to train a dense retrieval on synthetic query-corpus relevance pairs. Ma et al. (2021) trains a question generation system on general domain data and applies it to the targeted domain to construct synthetic question-passage data. To save the effort of training a task-specific generation model on general data, like Natural Questions (Kwiatkowski et al., 2019) or MSMARCO (Nguyen et al., 2016), Promptagator (Dai et al., 2023) proposes to use pre-trained large language models (LLMs), like FLAN (Wei et al., 2022), as a few-shot query generator to build the data for training the dual-encoder. However, the synthetic queries are not directly leveraged at inference, potentially causing gaps between training and inference of dense retrievers (Cho et al., 2022). Earlier work, e.g., doc2query (Nogueira et al., 2019b), concatenates the generated queries with the corresponding corpus, aiming to enrich the corpus representation with questions that the corpus can potentially answer. An improved version, docTTTTTquery (Nogueira et al., 2019a) leverages pre-trained T5 models as the expansion model, leading to more relevant synthetic queries and better retrieval performance.

Different from the previous work, we demonstrate directly on the embedding level instead of the text level, that the synthetically generated queries' embeddings can effectively augment the corpus rep-

*These authors contributed equally.
†Work done while intern at Amazon.



*Proceedings of the Fourth Workshop on Multilingual Representation Learning (MRL 2024)*, pages 269–279
November 16, 2024 ©2024 Association for Computational Linguistics

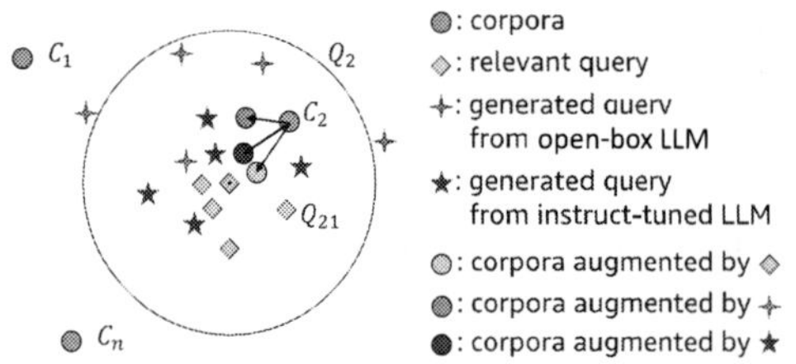


Figure 1: Illustration of the corpus representation augmented by embedding of relevant and synthetic queries generated by open-box and instruct-tuned LLMs.

resentation (Figure 1). Here, we propose an unsupervised representation learning approach through self-instructed-tuning leveraging the embedding generation and sequence generation capability of an encoder-decoder LLM. This approach consists of two steps, i.e., self-instructed-learning and Rao-Blackwellization. In the first step, we design two instruction tasks, namely question generation and keyword summarization, to generate synthetic questions and keywords for each given corpus via prompting a pre-trained LLM. Next, we apply filters to gate the synthetic data quality and instruction-tune the pre-trained LLM (and its variant versions) on the filtered output (Step one in Figure 2). In the second step, we use the instruct-tuned LLM to generate better synthetic questions and keywords following the same instruction prompts as in training. We then obtain the embeddings of the newly generated synthetic questions and keywords and that of corpus from the instruct-tuned encoder, and take the weighted average as our augmented corpus representation (Step two in Figure 2).

We consider the corpus representation learning task as a problem of query embedding expectation estimation. Based on the Rao-Blackwell theorem, the crude estimator, corpus embedding, can be improved by taking the conditional expectation given the sufficient statistics, i.e., sample mean of the embedding of their (synthetic) relevant queries and keywords. Thus, we expect combining the raw corpus embedding and synthetic query embedding to achieve better corpus representation. Besides, by aligning instruction-tuning and synthetic query generation, the retrieval model is directly optimized on corpus representation during training. To assess the effectiveness of our proposed method, we compare retrieval method of corpus only embedding with our augmented corpus representation, models with and without instruction-tuning and evaluate against four competitive dense retrievers (i.e., mDPR (Zhang et al., 2021, 2022), mBART (Tang et al., 2020), T-Systems (T-Systems, 2020), Albertina-PT (Santos et al., 2024)). Our main contributions are as follows:

- We propose a novel unsupervised text representation learning approach for information retrieval (IR) by instruction-tuning a pre-trained encoder-decoder with unlabelled corpus.
- We demonstrate our approach of using conditional expectation of the relevant (synthetic) query/keywords embedding the representation of the corpus can be augmented effectively, founded on the Rao-Blackwell theorem.
- We verify the effectiveness of the proposed methods on three English, two German and one Portuguese IR datasets. We significantly improve the zero-shot average retrieval performance with our unsupervised approach and exceed four competitive supervised dense retrievers (Table 5 - 7).

## 2 Related Work

### 2.1 Instruction-tuning

Tuning pre-trained LLMs with *(natural language instruction, response)* pairs to enhance models' ability to follow instructions and understand user intention. It is a rising paradigm in natural language processing (NLP) to strengthen model's generalizability on unseen tasks. FLAN (Wei et al., 2022) significantly improves a 137B LLM's zero-shot performance via instruction learning on various NLP datasets with multiple instruction templates. InstructDial (Gupta et al., 2022) also shows significant zero-shot performance boost in unseen dialogues when applying instruction-tuning to dialogue domain. InstructGPT (Ouyang et al., 2022) enhances GPT-3's performance by fine-tuning it on instructions and human feedback collected from OpenAI API. Self-Instruct (Wang et al., 2023) finetunes the open-box GPT-3 on its own generated instructions and instances which achieved on par performance of InstructGPT.

### 2.2 Dense Retrieval Text Representation

Text representation is the foundational component of dense retrieval. Under dual-encoder framework, it has been a long standing practice to represent query and corpus with encoder only models, e.g.,

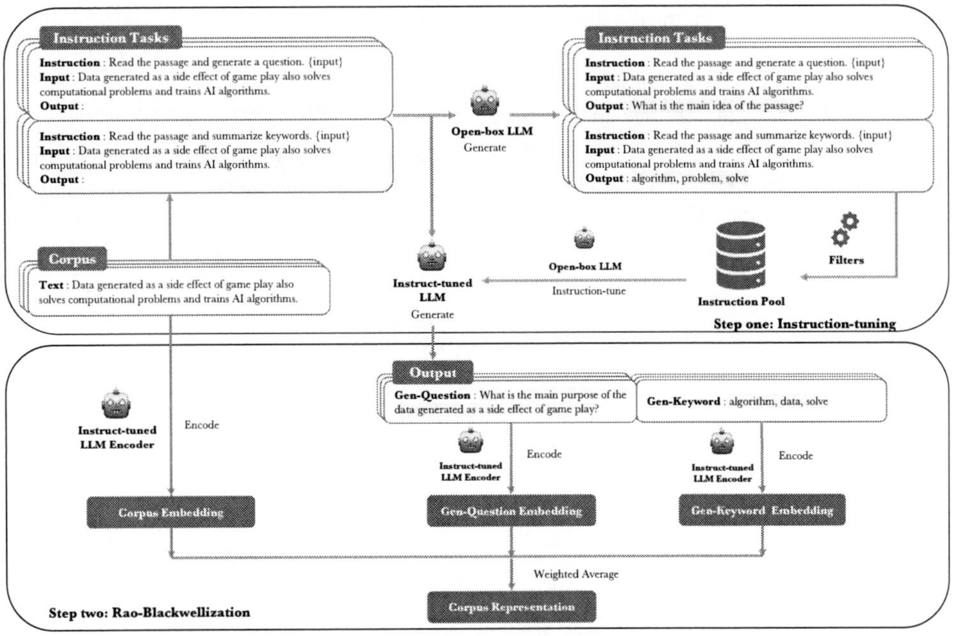


Figure 2: A high-level overview of Encoder-Decoder corpus representation with our approach. In the instruction-tuning step, given a set of instruction tasks (in our case **keyword summarization**: "Read the passage and summarize keywords." and **question generation**: "Read the passage and generate a question."), the pre-trained LLM will generate instruction following examples which are passed through filters for quality control. The filtered examples form an instruction pool and are used to instruction-tune the open-box LLM. In the Rao-Blackwellization step, by prompting the instruct-tuned LLM using the same instructions as before, synthetic questions and keywords are generated for the corpus. Both the corpus and the generated sequences are encoded by the LLM encoder and the weighted average of their embedding is used as corpus representation.

BERT (Devlin et al., 2019) and RoBERTa (Liu et al., 2019), such as in Sentence-BERT (Reimers and Gurevych, 2019), ColBERT (Khattab and Zaharia, 2020). Recently, Sentence-T5 (Ni et al., 2022a) demonstrates superior performance with encoder-decoder pre-trained LLM, T5. Moreover, representing corpus with single representation may not well model the fine-grained semantic interaction between the queries and corpus. Poly-encoder (Humeau et al., 2019) and ME-BERT (Luan et al., 2020) learn multiple representations to better capture the corpus semantics and show significant improvement. Doc2query (Nogueira et al., 2019b) and docTTTTTquery (Nogueira et al., 2019a) append generated synthetic queries to the corpus and thus enrich the semantic information.

## 3 Method

We propose an unsupervised text representation learning approach through self-instructed-tuning a pre-trained encoder-decoder LLM. First, we generate instruction following responses from an LLM and instruction-tune the LLM itself with filtered quality *(natural language instruction, response)* pairs. Next, we compute the augmented corpus embedding weighing in synthetic queries' (e.g., questions, keywords) embeddings. Figure 2 presents the overall flow of our approach.

### 3.1 Problem Scenario

Denote corpora as $C_1$,$C_2$,...,$C_n$, and their relevant queries as $Q_{11}$, $Q_{12}$,...,$Q_{21}$,..., where queries $Q_{i1}$,$Q_{i2}$,... are relevant to the same corpora $C_i$. For example, $Q_{11}$ can be `Harry Potter 1` and $Q_{12}$ can be `Harry Potter and the Philosopher's Stone`, whereas $C_1$ is `Harry Potter and the Sorcerer's Stone`. $Q_i = Q_{i1}, ..., Q_{im}$

Given a pre-trained encoder-decoder LLM, besides treating the encoder as a text representation model, we consider it as a random variable, where the sample space consists of the range of the possible embedding values, and the corresponding probability measure to each text portion.

$$\texttt{Encoder}(\cdot) : text \mapsto embedding \quad (1)$$

where the embedding refers to the sentence embedding of the text.

We assume that an effective encoder maps each group of $Q_i$ near a group center in the high-dimensional space and also maps the corresponding $C_i$ to the surrounding area so that $Q_i$ and $C_i$ are well associated. For example, given $Q_{21} \in Q_2$ query, the retrieval system will retrieve the $C_2$ corpora which is the closest to the query (Figure 1).

**Corpus Embedding as an Expectation Estimator** The group center is a comprehensive depiction of the entire group and is indicative to distinguish from other groups. With the pre-trained $\mathsf{Encoder}(\cdot)$, the group center is essentially the expected value of each group queries' embeddings, denoted by $\mathbb{E}(\mathsf{Encoder}(Q_i))$. When we use the embedding of the corpus, i.e., $\mathsf{Encoder}(C_i)$, as its representation, we are using it to estimate the group center $\mathbb{E}(\mathsf{Encoder}(Q_i))$. This is effective when we don't have any information from the query group.

**Application of the Rao–Blackwell theorem** Assume we have relevant queries $Q_{i1}$,$Q_{i2}$, ..., $Q_{im}$ for corpus $C_i$. Then $\frac{1}{m}\sum_{j=1}^{m}$ $\mathsf{Encoder}(Q_{ij})$ is a sufficient statistics to estimate $\mathbb{E}(\mathsf{Encoder}(Q_i))$.

According to Rao–Blackwell Theorem: If $g(\mathbf{X})$ is any kind of estimator of a parameter $\theta$, then the conditional expectation of $g(\mathbf{X})$ given $T(\mathbf{X})$, namely $\mathbb{E}(g(x)|T(x))$, where $T$ is a sufficient statistic, is typically a better estimator of $\theta$, and is never worse. Plug in Equation (2), we get an improved estimator for $\mathbb{E}(\mathsf{Encoder}(Q_i))$, which is $\mathbb{E}(\mathsf{Encoder}(C_i)|\frac{1}{m}\sum_{j=1}^{m}\mathsf{Encoder}(Q_{ij}))$.

$$
\begin{aligned}
g(x) &= \mathsf{Encoder}(C_i) \\
T(x) &= \frac{1}{m}\sum_{j=1}^{m}\mathsf{Encoder}(Q_{ij}) \\
\theta &= \mathbb{E}(\mathsf{Encoder}(Q_i))
\end{aligned} \tag{2}
$$

With some regularity assumptions, e.g., $C_i \in Q_i$ and $C_i = Q_{i1}$, the conditional expectation can be written as

$$
\begin{aligned}
&\mathbb{E}(\mathsf{Encoder}(C_i)|\frac{1}{m}\sum_{j=1}^{m}\mathsf{Encoder}(Q_{ij})) \\
&= \frac{1}{m}\sum_{j=1}^{m}\mathsf{Encoder}(Q_{ij}) \\
&= \frac{1}{m}\mathsf{Encoder}(C_i) + \frac{1}{m}\sum_{j=2}^{m}\mathsf{Encoder}(Q_{ij})
\end{aligned} \tag{3}
$$

We expect to achieve better performance with this formula for corpus representation. An intuitive understanding is that it gets closer to the relevant queries' embedding in the vector space (Figure 1).

### 3.2 Synthetic Query Generation

Obtaining a comprehensive set of labeled queries is labor-intensive and costly, especially in low resource setting. LLMs are known for its generative capability following well designed instructions. Not only can the model generate text, but it also can output the generation probability of the text. We denote the generation model by $\mathsf{LLM}(\cdot)$, then the generation can be written as

$$\hat{Q}_{ij}, \hat{P}(\hat{Q}_{ij}) = \mathsf{LLM}(\mathsf{Instruction} + C_i) \tag{4}$$

where $\hat{Q}_{ij}$ is the generated query and $\hat{P}(\hat{Q}_{ij})$ is the generation probability. The instruction is a pre-defined generation task, for example "write a question for" or "what are the keywords of".

### 3.3 Corpus Representation

Plug in the synthetic queries, let $R(C_i)$ denote the final representation of corpora $C_i$, Equation (3) becomes a weighted average of the original corpora embedding and its synthetic query embedding,

$$
\begin{aligned}
R(C_i) \hat{=}\ & w_0\mathsf{Encoder}(C_i) + \\
& (1 - w_0)\sum_{j}\hat{P}(\hat{Q}_{ij})\mathsf{Encoder}(\hat{Q}_{ij})
\end{aligned} \tag{5}
$$

where $w_0$ is a hyper-parameter that is tuned on a subset of test queries. Equation (5) is our proposed corpus representation for the dual-encoder retrieval system. Note that we can generate different types of synthetic queries in Equation (4) using various instructions, and we can generate multiple sequences for each instruction by adopting decoding strategies such as beam search. We can also improve the quality of the generated queries through instruction-tuning as follows.

### 3.4 Instruction-Tuning the LLM

While LLM has reasonable text generation capabilities, its ability to precisely follow specific instructions can be honed via instruction-tuning.

As we don't have the query-corpora labeled data, we propose to self-instructed-tuning the LLM on its self-generated quality (i.e., gated) responses following given instructions to enhance synthetic queries generation relevance. This approach has demonstrated its effectiveness (Wang et al., 2023). The instruct-tuned LLM is then used to prepare the synthetic queries for the corpus representation augmentation as in Equation (6).

$$\hat{Q}_{ij}, \hat{P}(\hat{Q}_{ij}) = \texttt{InstructTunedLLM}(\texttt{Instruction} + C_i) \quad (6)$$

We use the same instructions across the entire framework, including generation and training. Figure 1 shows a schematic diagram that although the generated queries from an open-box pre-trained LLM may not effectively enrich the corpora, after instruction-tuning, the generated synthetic queries become more relevant and the corpus representation can be improved consequently.

## 4 Experiments

### 4.1 Datasets

In this work, we tested six IR datasets where the summary of the database is shown in Table 1. ***English:*** (1) NFCorpus (Boteva et al., 2016) has automatically extracted relevance judgments for medical documents. (2) SciFact (Wadden et al., 2020) consists of expert-annotated scientific claims with abstracts and rationales. (3) SCIDOCS (Cohan et al., 2020) has seven document-level tasks from citation prediction, document classification, and recommendation. ***German:*** (4) GermanQuAD (Möller et al., 2021) has the relevant information for high complex German QA with a large size of corpora. (5) GermanDPR (Möller et al., 2021) is a passage retrieval dataset which shares the same corpus as GermanQuAD. ***Portuguese:*** (6) mMARCO/PT (Bonifacio et al., 2021) is translated version of MS MARCO (Bajaj et al., 2018) in Portuguese with anonymized questions from Bing's search query logs. Due to computation resource limits, we downsample the corpus in SCIDOCS, GermanQuAD, GermanDPR and mMARCO/PT datasets, where we ensure the downsampled corpus include all relevant corpus for test queries. Note that such downsampling does not prevent us from fairly comparing the zero-shot retrieval efficacy of our approach with open-box LLMs because all experiments are performed under the same data setting. To help the encoder capture the fine-grained semantic interaction between queries and corpus, we divide each corpora into multiple sentences using the PunktSentenceTokenizer [1] from nltk package and use the sentence level multi-representation for the corpora, meaning that if any of the sentence is retrieved, the passage is retrieved.

[1] https://www.nltk.org/api/nltk.tokenize.PunktSentenceTokenizer.html

Table 1: Details of datasets used. The size of corpus is downsampled to 15K in SCIDOCS, 10K in GermanQuAD and GermanDPR, and 7K in mMARCO/PT. Filtered Queries: Generated synthetic queries from FLAN-T5-Large with filtering.

| Dataset | Language | #Test Queries | Corpus Size | #Filtered Queries |
|---|---|---|---|---|
| NFCorpus | English | 323 | 3.6K | 5.9K |
| SciFact | English | 300 | 5.1K | 8.2K |
| SCIDOCS | English | 1K | 25.6K | 29.4K |
| GermanQuAD | German | 2K | 2.8M | 17.5K |
| GermanDPR | German | 1K | 2.8M | 17.5K |
| mMARCO/PT | Portuguese | 6K | 8.8M | 12.7K |

Table 2: Average performance of FLAN-T5 with out-of-box encoder-only embedder on Passage vs Sentence level indexing. Metrics: ♠: NDCG@10, ♣: MRR@100, ♡: Recall@100.

| Models | ♠ | ♣ | ♡ |
|---|---|---|---|
| Base (Passage) | 8.1 | 9.1 | 29.8 |
| Large (Passage) | 12.0 | 12.6 | 41.1 |
| Base (Sentence) | 23.1 | 25.0 | 49.0 |
| Large (Sentence) | **24.9** | **26.4** | **52.1** |

### 4.2 Baseline

We compare between the corpus-only representation and our proposed augmented corpus representation in zero-shot experiments under the dual-encoder framework. To obtain the representation of a sequence from the encoder, we perform mean aggregation over the last hidden state of each token (Ni et al., 2022a). We measure the relevance between query and corpus using cosine similarity.

To understand the superiority of our approach, we compare with four different state-of-the-art (SOTA) models: (1) mDPR (Zhang et al., 2021, 2022) is a variation of DPR model (Karpukhin et al., 2020a) which replaces BERT to multilingual BERT (Devlin et al., 2019) to support non-English languages for retrieval tasks. (2) mBART-Large (Tang et al., 2020) is a multilingual Sequence-to-Sequence generation model. It supports 50 languages and we consider it for comparison in same model structure (i.e., encoder-decoder). (3) T-Systems (T-Systems, 2020) is developed for computing sentence embeddings for English and German texts. It uses a XLM-RoBERTa (Conneau et al., 2019) and is fine-tuned with English-German datasets. (4) Albertina-PT (Santos et al., 2024) is a

Table 3: Comparison of model performances with and without instruction-tuning. Base/Large: out-of-box FLAN-T5-Base/Large. Instruct-Base/Large: FLAN-T5-Base/Large with instruction-tuning. Metrics: ♠: NDCG@10, ♣: MRR@100, ♡: Recall@100.

| Models | NFCorpus | | | SciFact | | | SCIDOCS | | | GermanQuAD | | | GermanDPR | | | mMARCO/PT | | | **Average** | | |
|---|---|---|---|---|---|---|---|---|---|---|---|---|---|---|---|---|---|---|---|---|---|
| | ♠ | ♣ | ♡ | ♠ | ♣ | ♡ | ♠ | ♣ | ♡ | ♠ | ♣ | ♡ | ♠ | ♣ | ♡ | ♠ | ♣ | ♡ | ♠ | ♣ | ♡ |
| Base | 12.2 | 26.6 | 15.8 | 29.6 | 28.5 | 66.3 | 6.4 | 13.4 | 17.7 | 49.4 | 45.8 | 83.2 | 41.5 | 37.8 | 81.3 | 20.4 | 19.1 | 51.0 | 26.6 | 28.5 | 52.6 |
| Large | 10.4 | 23.4 | 14.6 | 30.7 | 28.8 | 71.5 | **7.2** | 14.1 | 22.1 | 50.8 | 47.2 | 83.6 | 47.4 | 43.5 | 82.2 | 25.0 | 23.3 | **57.06** | 28.6 | 30.1 | 55.2 |
| Instruct-Base | **12.3** | 27.0 | **16.2** | 30.7 | 29.6 | 65.1 | 6.0 | 12.7 | 16.5 | 52.4 | 48.5 | 84.4 | 42.6 | 38.5 | 81.4 | 28.8 | 31.3 | 52.7 | 27.8 | 29.7 | 53.1 |
| Instruct-Large | 11.9 | **27.0** | 15.9 | **32.0** | **29.9** | **73.2** | 7.2 | **14.6** | **22.4** | **55.5** | **52.0** | **86.8** | **51.6** | **48.1** | **85.5** | **31.6** | **34.3** | 56.7 | **31.1** | **33.0** | **57.5** |

Table 4: Example of synthetic queries from FLAN-T5-Large according to the instruction-tuning.

| **Corpus** | **Instruction Type** | **Open-box** | **Instruct-tuned** |
|---|---|---|---|
| Fluorometric titration of E. coli single-stranded DNA binding protein with various RNAs showed that the protein specifically and cooperatively binds to its own mRNA. The binding inhibited in vitro expression of ssb and bla but not nusA. This inhibition takes place at a physiological concentration of SSB. The function of the protein in gene regulation is discussed. | Keyword | The single-stranded DNA binding protein(SSB) specifically and cooperative -ly binds to its own mRNA. | mRNA, protein, titration |
| This paper describes an aggregation and correlation algorithm used in the design and implementation of an intrusion-detection console built on top of the Tivoli Enterprise Console (TEC). The aggregation and correlation algorithm aims at acquiring intrusion-detection alerts and relating them together to expose a more condensed view of the security issues raised by intrusion-detection systems. | Question | What is the purpose of the paper? | What is the purpose of the aggregation and correlation algorithm? |

foundational model for European Portuguese. It is based on the DeBERTa model (He et al., 2021) and we consider this model as the competitive model in Portuguese dataset. Lastly, we compare with docTTTTTquery (Nogueira et al., 2019a) to understand the effectiveness of our corpus representation augmentation.

### 4.3 Encoder-Decoder Models

T5 is an encoder-decoder model pre-trained on a combination of unsupervised and supervised tasks, where each task is transformed into a text-to-text format (Raffel et al., 2020). FLAN-T5 is an enhanced version of T5 fine-tuned on a mixture of tasks (Wei et al., 2022). Considering that these types of models are open source, offer various sizes, support English, German and Portuguese, and have an encoder-decoder architecture, we leverage the FLAN-T5-Base and Large models in our experiments.

### 4.4 Instruction Query Generation

For instruction query generation and instruction-tuning, we consider two types of instructions (i.e., keyword summarization and question generation) as shown in Figure 2. We also develop a filter to improve the quality of generated instructions. If the task is keyword summarization, the number of keywords should be smaller than the half number of sentences in corpus. If it's question generation, the generated sequence should end with a question mark. The filter is simple, leaving room for further improvement. The numbers of the filtered synthetic queries are shown in Table 1.

### 4.5 Hyperparameter Setting

When performing instruction-tuning, we use the same hyperparameter setting for all the models. Specifically, we use the AdaFactor optimizer with learning rate 0.0001, batch size 16, and the number of epochs 30. Early stopping is performed when the validation loss shows no improvement for five consecutive epochs.

When generating queries using FLAN-T5 models, we only consider one returned sequence for each instruction and assume they are equally important. We denote the generated question and keywords as $\widehat{question_i}$ and $\widehat{keywords_i}$. We tested the multiple weighting methods for corpus representation where the best approach is giving the weight on the original corpus as $w_0 = 0.6$, so that each of $\widehat{question_i}$ and $\widehat{keywords_i}$ has the weight 0.2. Thus, the corpus representation is:

$$\mathsf{R}(C_i) = 0.6 \times \mathsf{Encoder}(C_i) + 0.2 \times (\mathsf{Encoder}(\widehat{question_i}) + \mathsf{Encoder}(\widehat{keywords_i})) \quad (7)$$

## 5 Results and Discussion

### 5.1 Corpora vs Sentence Indexing

We evaluate whether the sentence level multi-representation can capture the semantic interaction between the corpora and the query. Results for FLAN-T5 models using encoder-only representation are shown in Table 2. The sentence level multi-representation embedding technique outperforms the corpora level single representation by a large margin across all datasets. As the model size increases, the performance also gets better. Note that our approach uses no labeled data to achieve on par performance as SOTA models, and sentence level indexing is a way we do for chunking. According to the promising empirical results, we will apply the sentence level multi-representation technique to all the following experiments.

### 5.2 Overall Results

Table 3 describes the performance of FLAN-T5 models regarding instruction-tuning. Overall, we can mostly find the improvements of performances in all metrics after instruction-tuning, especially in non-English. This is mainly because the quality of generated queries after instruction-tuning are proper and detailed (Table 4), and also each synthetic query is less overlapped which makes the corpora distinguishable. The influence of instruction-tuning is mostly greater in larger model since it can have better generation capability and be more affected by fine-tuning with instructions.

Table 5 - 7 compare ours with SOTA models in zero-shot scenarios. In English datasets (Table 5), instruct-tuned FLAN-T5-Base mostly outperforms other baselines, except for T-Systems which is enhanced model for English and German and has a bigger size. With instruct-tuned FLAN-T5-Large, we exceeds all others in terms of average performances. In German datasets (Table 6), instruct-tuned FLAN-T5-Base shows the better overall performances with smaller size which emphasizes the resource-effectiveness of our approach. When we consider the larger model, we significantly outperforms other SOTAs. Lastly, in Portuguese dataset (Table 7), we slightly underperform than the competitive baseline which only supports the single language. By considering the larger model with instruct-tuning, we exceed others with large gap. Overall, our approach shows the effectiveness in all languages, especially in non-English datasets.

### 5.3 Ablation Study

To deeply understand the effectiveness of our approach, we did the solid ablation study where we exclude the GermanDPR and mMARCO/PT for this study which always shows the similar pattern.

**Optimal Corpus Representation** From our findings, new corpus representation based on synthetic queries from instructions is useful to improve retrieval performances. To define the optimal weights in corpus representation, we investigate four different weighting methods: (1) Equal: giving equal weights for corpus and synthetic queries (i.e., keyword, question). (2) Manual: same as Equation (7). (3) `BERTScore`: Assigning the weights based on `BERTScore` (F1) with BERT (Multilingual-Cased) model (Devlin et al., 2018) as shown in Equation (8), where $X$ denotes $\hat{keywords_i}, \hat{question_i}$. (4) $\texttt{BERTScore}_{Softmax}$: applying Softmax on top of `BERTScore`.

$$\begin{aligned}\texttt{Weight}_X &= \frac{\texttt{BERT}(X, C_i)}{1 + \texttt{Sum}(\texttt{BERT}(X, C_i)}, \\ \texttt{Weight}_{C_i} &= \frac{1}{1 + \texttt{Sum}(\texttt{BERT}(X, C_i))}\end{aligned} \quad (8)$$

Table 8 shows the overall performances of different weight approaches in corpus representation. Firstly, the equal weight approach shows the worst performance which confirms that the corpus basically contains the most relevant information for queries which should be weighted more. Also, extracted keywords and questions mostly have the essential contexts but partial information of corpus which is not enough to include the semantic meaning of corpus. Thus, manual weighting with emphasis on corpus promises better result than BERTScore approaches. Lastly, we generated the corpus representation based on text-level concatenation (Nogueira et al., 2019a) where we confirm the superiority of embedding-level representations.

**Effectiveness of Instruction-tuning** Table 4 gives the examples of generated synthetic queries. In keyword summarization, open-box extracts a simple copy of sentence as keywords while instruction-tuning helps to observe the whole corpus to extract the core keywords. For question generation, open-box generates the general question while instruction-tuning gives the detailed and suitable questions which can be accountable by the specific corpus.

Figure 3 shows the distributions of embeddings of corpora and test queries with FLAN-T5-Large. Overall, the weighted corpus representation and

Table 5: Comparison with SOTA models (size) on English datasets. Instruct-Base/Large: FLAN-T5-Base/Large with instruction-tuning. Metrics: ♠: NDCG@10, ♣: MRR@100, ♡: Recall@100.

| Models | NFCorpus | | | SciFact | | | SCIDOCS | | | **Average** | | |
|---|---|---|---|---|---|---|---|---|---|---|---|---|
| | ♠ | ♣ | ♡ | ♠ | ♣ | ♡ | ♠ | ♣ | ♡ | ♠ | ♣ | ♡ |
| mDPR (177M) | 8.3 | 19.2 | 11.6 | 23.5 | 21.9 | 58.9 | 4.8 | 10.3 | 16.0 | 12.2 | 17.1 | 28.8 |
| T-Systems (278M) | **15.3** | **29.1** | **17.1** | 25.3 | 23.7 | 59.3 | **8.4** | **17.6** | **23.8** | 16.3 | **23.5** | **33.4** |
| mBART-Large (331M) | 1.9 | 5.9 | 4.6 | 23.9 | 22.5 | 52.5 | 3.6 | 7.8 | 12.7 | 9.8 | 12.1 | 23.3 |
| Instruct-Base (109M) | 12.3 | 27.0 | 16.2 | **30.7** | **29.6** | **65.1** | 6.0 | 12.7 | 16.5 | **16.4** | 23.1 | 32.6 |
| Instruct-Large (341M) | 11.9 | 27.0 | 15.9 | ***32.0*** | ***29.9*** | ***73.2*** | 7.2 | 14.6 | 22.4 | ***17.0*** | ***23.8*** | ***37.2*** |

Table 6: Comparison with SOTA models (size) on German datasets. Instruct-Base/Large: FLAN-T5-Base/Large with instruction-tuning. Metrics: ♠: NDCG@10, ♣: MRR@100, ♡: Recall@100.

| Models | GermanQuAD | | | GermanDPR | | | **Average** | | |
|---|---|---|---|---|---|---|---|---|---|
| | ♠ | ♣ | ♡ | ♠ | ♣ | ♡ | ♠ | ♣ | ♡ |
| T-Systems (278M) | 33.9 | 31.0 | 64.1 | **53.4** | **49.6** | **83.5** | 43.7 | 40.3 | 73.8 |
| mBART-Large (331M) | 34.1 | 31.5 | 63.3 | 30.8 | 27.4 | 64.2 | 32.5 | 29.5 | 63.8 |
| Instruct-Base (109M) | **52.4** | **48.5** | **84.4** | 42.6 | 38.5 | 81.4 | **47.5** | **43.5** | **82.9** |
| Instruct-Large (341M) | ***55.5*** | ***52.0*** | ***86.8*** | 51.6 | 48.1 | ***85.5*** | ***53.5*** | ***50.1*** | ***86.1*** |

Table 7: Comparison with SOTA on Portuguese dataset **mMARCO/PT**. Instruct-Base: FLAN-T5-Base with instruction-tuning. Metrics: ♠: NDCG@10, ♣: MRR@100, ♡: Recall@100.

| **Metric** | Albertina-PT (139M) | mBART-Large (331M) | Instruct-Base (109M) |
|---|---|---|---|
| ♠ | **23.7** | 2.3 | 22.9 |
| ♣ | **22.0** | 2.2 | 21.6 |
| ♡ | **57.1** | 18.3 | 55.1 |

instruction-tuning spread out the corpora embeddings to make them distinguishable. It also helps to locate the test queries closer to the corpora. Thus, our approach helps to integrate the crucial and detailed synthetic queries for corpus representation that leads to unique corpora representation to achieve enhanced retrieval performances.

**Effectiveness of Corpus Representation Augmentation** We compare with other corpus representation augmentation, docTTTTTquery (Nogueira et al., 2019a), to validate our corpus augmentation. Here, we follow the default strategy of docTTTTTquery: top-10 with 40 predictions appending on corpus. According to Table 9, we demonstrate significant improvement via our approach - embedding level augmentation with representations from self-instructed-tuned model. Based on this finding, we can confirm that augmenting representation on embedding level is more effective than on input text level with concatenation as docTTTTTquery, and our self-instructed-tuned model performs better than their supervised representation generation model.

Table 8: Effects of different weight methods for corpus representation with FLAN-T5. Concatenation means the appending corpus with synthetic queries in text-level while others are done in embedding-level. Metrics: ♠: NDCG@10, ♣: MRR@100, ♡: Recall@100.

| **Corpus Weights** | **Models** | ♠ | ♣ | ♡ |
|---|---|---|---|---|
| N/A | Base | 22.0 | 26.0 | 43.5 |
| | Large | 23.2 | 26.5 | 46.2 |
| Equal | Base | 18.3 | 22.0 | 38.8 |
| | Large | 17.9 | 21.6 | 39.9 |
| Manual | Base | 24.4 | **28.6** | 45.8 |
| | Large | **24.8** | 28.4 | **47.9** |
| BERTScore | Base | 22.4 | 26.1 | 43.6 |
| | Large | 22.0 | 25.5 | 45.2 |
| BERTScore$_{Softmax}$ | Base | 20.1 | 23.6 | 40.7 |
| | Large | 19.5 | 23.1 | 42.7 |
| Concatenation | Base | 15.8 | 18.9 | 36.7 |
| | Large | 15.6 | 19.1 | 36.9 |

Table 9: Effects of different corpus representation augmentation with FLAN-T5. Metrics: ♠: NDCG@10, ♣: MRR@100, ♡: Recall@100.

| **Models** | ♠ | ♣ | ♡ |
|---|---|---|---|
| docTTTTTquery (Base) | 9.6 | 12.8 | 24.9 |
| Our approach (Base) | **22.0** | **26.0** | **43.5** |
| docTTTTTquery (Large) | 13.4 | 16.3 | 33.3 |
| Our approach (Large) | **23.2** | **26.5** | **46.2** |

## 6 Conclusion

In our research, we propose the unsupervised text representation learning technique through self-

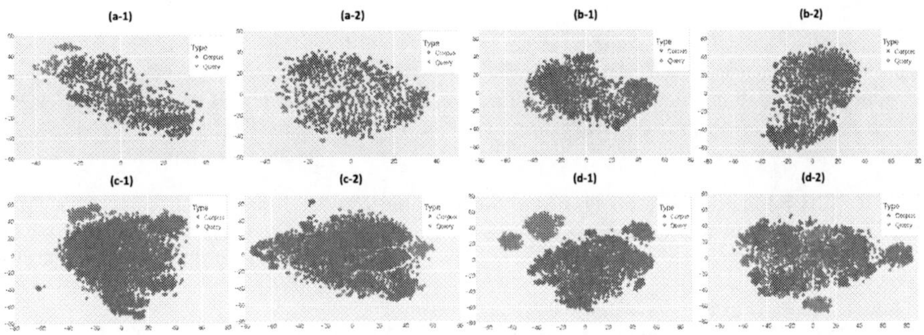


Figure 3: t-SNE distributions for corpus representation generated from FLAN-T5-Large. (a-d) NFCorpus, SciFact, SCIDOCS, GermanQuAD. (1-2) Original corpus, Weighted corpus with synthetic queries after instruction-tuning.

instructed-tuning encoder-decoder LLMs. Based on the Rao-Blackwell theorem, we leverage the embeddings of synthetically generated queries (i.e., questions and keywords) to augment the corpus representation for the dual-encoder retrieval framework. In zero-shot experiments, our proposed corpus representation consistently improves the performance over encoder-only corpus representation. Even if the open-box LLM was not pre-trained on retrieval task and there is no labeled modeling data, after fine-tuning with our approach it exceeds the SOTA models across different datasets, presenting the high effectiveness and data efficiency of our method in retrieval tasks.

In future work, we plan to explore our proposed method on separate encoder and decoder models.

## References

Payal Bajaj, Daniel Campos, Nick Craswell, Li Deng, Jianfeng Gao, Xiaodong Liu, Rangan Majumder, Andrew McNamara, Bhaskar Mitra, Tri Nguyen, Mir Rosenberg, Xia Song, Alina Stoica, Saurabh Tiwary, and Tong Wang. 2018. Ms marco: A human generated machine reading comprehension dataset.

Luiz Henrique Bonifacio, Vitor Jeronymo, Hugo Queiroz Abonizio, Israel Campiotti, Marzieh Fadaee, , Roberto Lotufo, and Rodrigo Nogueira. 2021. mmarco: A multilingual version of ms marco passage ranking dataset.

Vera Boteva, Demian Gholipour, Artem Sokolov, and Stefan Riezler. 2016. A full-text learning to rank dataset for medical information retrieval.

Sukmin Cho, Soyeong Jeong, Wonsuk Yang, and Jong C. Park. 2022. Query generation with external knowledge for dense retrieval. In *Proceedings of Deep Learning Inside Out: The 3rd Workshop on Knowledge Extraction and Integration for Deep Learning Architectures, DeeLIO@ACL 2022, Dublin, Ireland and Online, May 27, 2022*, pages 22–32. Association for Computational Linguistics.

Arman Cohan, Sergey Feldman, Iz Beltagy, Doug Downey, and Daniel Weld. 2020. SPECTER: Document-level representation learning using citation-informed transformers. In *Proceedings of the 58th Annual Meeting of the Association for Computational Linguistics*, pages 2270–2282, Online. Association for Computational Linguistics.

Alexis Conneau, Kartikay Khandelwal, Naman Goyal, Vishrav Chaudhary, Guillaume Wenzek, Francisco Guzmán, Edouard Grave, Myle Ott, Luke Zettlemoyer, and Veselin Stoyanov. 2019. Unsupervised cross-lingual representation learning at scale. *CoRR*, abs/1911.02116.

Zhuyun Dai, Vincent Y. Zhao, Ji Ma, Yi Luan, Jianmo Ni, Jing Lu, Anton Bakalov, Kelvin Guu, Keith B. Hall, and Ming-Wei Chang. 2023. Promptagator: Few-shot dense retrieval from 8 examples. In *The Eleventh International Conference on Learning Representations, ICLR 2023, Kigali, Rwanda, May 1-5, 2023*. OpenReview.net.

Jacob Devlin, Ming-Wei Chang, Kenton Lee, and Kristina Toutanova. 2018. BERT: pre-training of deep bidirectional transformers for language understanding. *CoRR*, abs/1810.04805.

Jacob Devlin, Ming-Wei Chang, Kenton Lee, and Kristina Toutanova. 2019. Bert: Pre-training of deep bidirectional transformers for language understanding. *ArXiv*, abs/1810.04805.

Zhe Dong, Jianmo Ni, Dan Bikel, Enrique Alfonseca, Yuan Wang, Chen Qu, and Imed Zitouni. 2022. Exploring dual encoder architectures for question answering. In *Proceedings of the 2022 Conference on Empirical Methods in Natural Language Processing, EMNLP 2022, Abu Dhabi, United Arab Emirates, December 7-11, 2022*, pages 9414–9419. Association for Computational Linguistics.

Daniel Gillick, Alessandro Presta, and Gaurav Singh Tomar. 2018. End-to-end retrieval in continuous space. *ArXiv*, abs/1811.08008.

Prakhar Gupta, Cathy Jiao, Yi-Ting Yeh, Shikib Mehri, Maxine Eskénazi, and Jeffrey P. Bigham. 2022. Instructdial: Improving zero and few-shot generalization in dialogue through instruction tuning. In *Conference on Empirical Methods in Natural Language Processing*.

Pengcheng He, Xiaodong Liu, Jianfeng Gao, and Weizhu Chen. 2021. Deberta: Decoding-enhanced bert with disentangled attention.

Samuel Humeau, Kurt Shuster, Marie-Anne Lachaux, and Jason Weston. 2019. Poly-encoders: Architectures and pre-training strategies for fast and accurate multi-sentence scoring. In *International Conference on Learning Representations*.

Vladimir Karpukhin, Barlas Oguz, Sewon Min, Patrick Lewis, Ledell Wu, Sergey Edunov, Danqi Chen, and Wen-tau Yih. 2020a. Dense passage retrieval for open-domain question answering. In *Proceedings of the 2020 Conference on Empirical Methods in Natural Language Processing (EMNLP)*, pages 6769–6781, Online. Association for Computational Linguistics.

Vladimir Karpukhin, Barlas Oguz, Sewon Min, Patrick S. H. Lewis, Ledell Wu, Sergey Edunov, Danqi Chen, and Wen-tau Yih. 2020b. Dense passage retrieval for open-domain question answering. In *Proceedings of the 2020 Conference on Empirical Methods in Natural Language Processing, EMNLP 2020, Online, November 16-20, 2020*, pages 6769–6781. Association for Computational Linguistics.

O. Khattab and Matei A. Zaharia. 2020. Colbert: Efficient and effective passage search via contextualized late interaction over bert. *Proceedings of the 43rd International ACM SIGIR Conference on Research and Development in Information Retrieval.*

Tom Kwiatkowski, Jennimaria Palomaki, Olivia Redfield, Michael Collins, Ankur P. Parikh, Chris Alberti, Danielle Epstein, Illia Polosukhin, Jacob Devlin, Kenton Lee, Kristina Toutanova, Llion Jones, Matthew Kelcey, Ming-Wei Chang, Andrew M. Dai, Jakob Uszkoreit, Quoc Le, and Slav Petrov. 2019. Natural questions: a benchmark for question answering research. *Trans. Assoc. Comput. Linguistics*, 7:452–466.

Yinhan Liu, Myle Ott, Naman Goyal, Jingfei Du, Mandar Joshi, Danqi Chen, Omer Levy, Mike Lewis, Luke Zettlemoyer, and Veselin Stoyanov. 2019. Roberta: A robustly optimized bert pretraining approach. *ArXiv*, abs/1907.11692.

Y Luan, Jacob Eisenstein, Kristina Toutanova, and Michael Collins. 2020. Sparse, dense, and attentional representations for text retrieval. *Transactions of the Association for Computational Linguistics*, 9:329–345.

Ji Ma, Ivan Korotkov, Yinfei Yang, Keith B. Hall, and Ryan T. McDonald. 2021. Zero-shot neural passage retrieval via domain-targeted synthetic question generation. In *Proceedings of the 16th Conference of the European Chapter of the Association for Computational Linguistics: Main Volume, EACL 2021, Online, April 19 - 23, 2021*, pages 1075–1088. Association for Computational Linguistics.

Timo Möller, Julian Risch, and Malte Pietsch. 2021. Germanquad and germandpr: Improving non-english question answering and passage retrieval. *ArXiv*, abs/2104.12741.

Tri Nguyen, Mir Rosenberg, Xia Song, Jianfeng Gao, Saurabh Tiwary, Rangan Majumder, and Li Deng. 2016. MS MARCO: A human generated machine reading comprehension dataset. In *Proceedings of the Workshop on Cognitive Computation: Integrating neural and symbolic approaches 2016 co-located with the 30th Annual Conference on Neural Information Processing Systems (NIPS 2016), Barcelona, Spain, December 9, 2016*, volume 1773 of *CEUR Workshop Proceedings*. CEUR-WS.org.

Jianmo Ni, Gustavo Hernández Ábrego, Noah Constant, Ji Ma, Keith B. Hall, Daniel Cer, and Yinfei Yang. 2022a. Sentence-t5: Scalable sentence encoders from pre-trained text-to-text models. In *Findings of the Association for Computational Linguistics: ACL 2022, Dublin, Ireland, May 22-27, 2022*, pages 1864–1874. Association for Computational Linguistics.

Jianmo Ni, Chen Qu, Jing Lu, Zhuyun Dai, Gustavo Hernández Ábrego, Ji Ma, Vincent Y. Zhao, Yi Luan, Keith B. Hall, Ming-Wei Chang, and Yinfei Yang. 2022b. Large dual encoders are generalizable retrievers. In *Proceedings of the 2022 Conference on Empirical Methods in Natural Language Processing, EMNLP 2022, Abu Dhabi, United Arab Emirates, December 7-11, 2022*, pages 9844–9855. Association for Computational Linguistics.

Rodrigo Nogueira, Jimmy Lin, and AI Epistemic. 2019a. From doc2query to docttttquery. *Online preprint*, 6:2.

Rodrigo Frassetto Nogueira, Wei Yang, Jimmy Lin, and Kyunghyun Cho. 2019b. Document expansion by query prediction. *ArXiv*, abs/1904.08375.

Long Ouyang, Jeff Wu, Xu Jiang, Diogo Almeida, Carroll L. Wainwright, Pamela Mishkin, Chong Zhang, Sandhini Agarwal, Katarina Slama, Alex Ray, John Schulman, Jacob Hilton, Fraser Kelton, Luke E. Miller, Maddie Simens, Amanda Askell, Peter Welinder, Paul Francis Christiano, Jan Leike, and Ryan J. Lowe. 2022. Training language models to follow instructions with human feedback. *ArXiv*, abs/2203.02155.

Colin Raffel, Noam Shazeer, Adam Roberts, Katherine Lee, Sharan Narang, Michael Matena, Yanqi Zhou, Wei Li, and Peter J. Liu. 2020. Exploring the limits of transfer learning with a unified text-to-text transformer. *Journal of Machine Learning Research*, 21(140):1–67.

Nils Reimers and Iryna Gurevych. 2019. Sentence-bert: Sentence embeddings using siamese bert-networks. In *Conference on Empirical Methods in Natural Language Processing*.

Rodrigo Santos, João Rodrigues, Luís Gomes, João Silva, António Branco, Henrique Lopes Cardoso, Tomás Freitas Osório, and Bernardo Leite. 2024. Fostering the ecosystem of open neural encoders for portuguese with albertina pt-* family.

T-Systems. 2020. T-system model.

Yuqing Tang, Chau Tran, Xian Li, Peng-Jen Chen, Naman Goyal, Vishrav Chaudhary, Jiatao Gu, and Angela Fan. 2020. Multilingual translation with extensible multilingual pretraining and finetuning.

David Wadden, Shanchuan Lin, Kyle Lo, Lucy Lu Wang, Madeleine van Zuylen, Arman Cohan, and Hannaneh Hajishirzi. 2020. Fact or fiction: Verifying scientific claims. In *Proceedings of the 2020 Conference on Empirical Methods in Natural Language Processing (EMNLP)*, pages 7534–7550, Online. Association for Computational Linguistics.

Yizhong Wang, Yeganeh Kordi, Swaroop Mishra, Alisa Liu, Noah A. Smith, Daniel Khashabi, and Hannaneh Hajishirzi. 2023. Self-instruct: Aligning language models with self-generated instructions. In *Proceedings of the 61st Annual Meeting of the Association for Computational Linguistics (Volume 1: Long Papers), ACL 2023, Toronto, Canada, July 9-14, 2023*, pages 13484–13508. Association for Computational Linguistics.

Jason Wei, Maarten Bosma, Vincent Y. Zhao, Kelvin Guu, Adams Wei Yu, Brian Lester, Nan Du, Andrew M. Dai, and Quoc V. Le. 2022. Finetuned language models are zero-shot learners. In *The Tenth International Conference on Learning Representations, ICLR 2022, Virtual Event, April 25-29, 2022*. OpenReview.net.

Yinfei Yang, Daniel Cer, Amin Ahmad, Mandy Guo, Jax Law, Noah Constant, Gustavo Hernández Ábrego, Steve Yuan, Chris Tar, Yun-Hsuan Sung, Brian Strope, and Ray Kurzweil. 2020. Multilingual universal sentence encoder for semantic retrieval. In *Proceedings of the 58th Annual Meeting of the Association for Computational Linguistics: System Demonstrations, ACL 2020, Online, July 5-10, 2020*, pages 87–94. Association for Computational Linguistics.

Xinyu Zhang, Xueguang Ma, Peng Shi, and Jimmy Lin. 2021. Mr. TyDi: A multi-lingual benchmark for dense retrieval. *arXiv:2108.08787*.

Xinyu Zhang, Kelechi Ogueji, Xueguang Ma, and Jimmy Lin. 2022. Towards best practices for training multilingual dense retrieval models.

Wayne Xin Zhao, Jing Liu, Ruiyang Ren, and Ji-Rong Wen. 2022. Dense text retrieval based on pretrained language models: A survey. *ArXiv*, abs/2211.14876.

# Language Bias in Multilingual Information Retrieval: The Nature of the Beast and Mitigation Methods

**Jinrui Yang*** **Fan Jiang*** **Timothy Baldwin*†**
*School of Computing & Information Systems, The University of Melbourne
†Mohamed bin Zayed University of Artificial Intelligence, UAE
{jinruiy,jifj}@student.unimelb.edu.au tbaldwin@unimelb.edu.au

## Abstract

Language fairness in multilingual information retrieval (MLIR) systems is crucial for ensuring equitable access to information across diverse languages. This paper sheds light on the issue, based on the assumption that *queries in different languages, but with identical semantics, should yield equivalent ranking lists when retrieving on the same multilingual documents*. We evaluate the degree of fairness using both traditional retrieval methods, and a DPR neural ranker based on mBERT and XLM-R. Additionally, we introduce 'LaKDA', a novel loss designed to mitigate language biases in neural MLIR approaches. Our analysis exposes intrinsic language biases in current MLIR technologies, with notable disparities across the retrieval methods, and the effectiveness of LaKDA in enhancing language fairness.

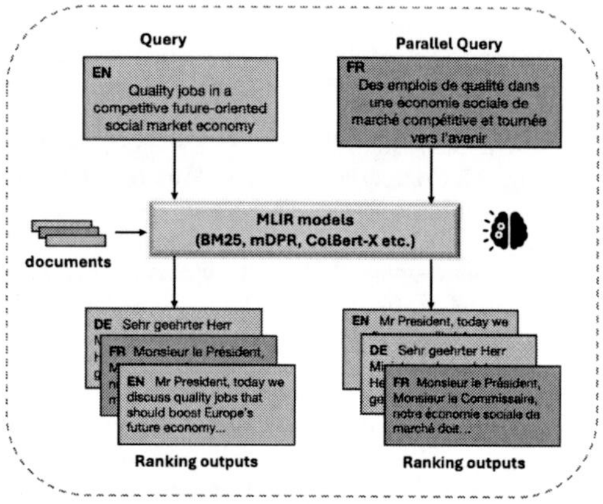


Figure 1: The case of language bias studied in this work. Semantically parallel queries retrieve the same documents, but the ranking outputs are inconsistent.

## 1 Introduction

Information retrieval (IR) is the process of obtaining relevant information from a large collection of data according to a user's information needs. This information may exist in various formats, including text documents, images, or videos. Conventionally, the collection is a corpus of text documents, and user information needs are expressed in plain text queries. IR serves as a foundational technology in numerous NLP applications including question-answering systems (Abbasiyantaeb and Momtazi, 2020; Chen et al., 2017), and is also assuming an increasingly pivotal role in supporting the advancement of Large Language Models (LLMs) for text understanding and knowledge inference (Miao et al., 2024; Zhu et al., 2024).

Multilingual information retrieval (MLIR) entails queries being in different languages, with the results for a query in a given language being across multiple languages (including the source language of the query). MLIR has particular importance as it enables (multilingual) users to access information that may be unavailable or limited in their native language, thereby fostering cultural and linguistic diversity.

Research has shown that MLIR systems often exhibit biases towards certain languages due to factors like morphological complexity (Park et al., 2021) and resource availability (Lawrie et al., 2023; Huang et al., 2023). For instance, Lawrie et al. (2023) found that documents in higher-resource languages tend to be ranked higher in MLIR. This phenomenon is particular notable when the models are built upon multilingual pretrained models (Yang et al., 2024).

Another case of language bias in MLIR is shown in Figure 1. Given semantically equivalent queries in different languages and the same documents, we are interested in determining the consistency of the obtained ranking lists. This forms the basis for our investigation of language fairness in MLIR from a query-level perspective.

Our study compares MLIR methods using semantically equivalent queries in 24 European languages, which we use to search a fixed multilingual



*Proceedings of the Fourth Workshop on Multilingual Representation Learning (MRL 2024)*, pages 280–292
November 16, 2024 ©2024 Association for Computational Linguistics

document collection. These parallel query sets are from the original dataset, not machine-translated, and are based on human-annotated document tags. In repurposing them as queries and using the tags as relevance judgements, we fashion a multilingual IR collection with massively-multilingual parallel query sets.

Our work makes four main contributions:[1]

1. **Novel evaluation metric for fairness under ranking:** we propose the mean rank correlation (MRC) score to evaluate language fairness under MLIR, based on the premise that semantically-equivalent queries in different languages should yield consistent document rankings.
2. **Novel dataset:** we develop the MultiEup-v2 dataset, consisting of semantically parallel queries and multilingual documents, along with demographic attributes. This dataset serves as a benchmark for future fairness research in MLIR.
3. **Quantification of language (un)fairness:** we analyze language fairness in MLIR across different languages and language families, and find that BM25 exhibits larger language bias than neural retrieval frameworks like mDPR. Additionally, higher-resource languages tend to be associated with higher degrees of language fairness.
4. **Proposal of a new ranking bias mitigation method:** we propose the language KL-divergence alignment (LaKDA) loss to mitigate language bias in MLIR, demonstrating its effectiveness within the mDPR neural retrieval framework with multilingual text encoders mBERT and XLM-R.

## 2 Language Bias in MLIR

In this section, we examine language bias in MLIR. First, we introduce a novel metric for quantifying language fairness, our evaluation benchmark, and introduce a method for mitigating language bias.

### 2.1 MLIR Language Fairness Metric

We define fairness in MLIR as follows: queries in different languages but with identical semantics should yield equivalent ranking lists when executed against the same multilingual document collection.

[1]The dataset and code are available from https://github.com/jrnlp/MLIR_language_bias under an Apache 2.0 license.

Assume we have $L$ languages and $N$ queries for each language. For language pair $a, b \in \{\ell_1, \ell_2, \ldots, \ell_L\}$, let:

$$Q_a = \{q_{(1,a)}, q_{(2,a)}, \ldots, q_{(N,a)}\}$$

$$Q_b = \{q_{(1,b)}, q_{(2,b)}, \ldots, q_{(N,b)}\}$$

represent the sets of all queries in languages $a$ and $b$, respectively, where $q_{(i,a)}$ is the $i$-th query in language $a$ and $q_{(i,b)}$ is the $i$-th semantically parallel query in language $b$.

Assume a ranking method $\pi$ produces a ranked result list $R(q_{(i,a)}, D)$ when given query $q_{(i,a)}$ against document collection $D$. Then for each query $i$ and pair of languages $(a, b)$, we compute the ranking correlation $\text{RC}^i_{(a,b)}$ between the ranking lists $R(q_{(i,a)}, D)$ and $R(q_{(i,b)}, D)$ using Spearman's rank correlation (Oakes, 2010; Spearman, 1904):

$$\text{RC}^i_{(a,b)} = \text{corr}(R(q_{(i,a)}, D), R(q_{(i,b)}, D))$$

Next, we compute the average correlation for language $a$ with query $i$ with the other $L-1$ language pairs, denoted as $\text{RC}^i_{(a)}$:

$$\text{RC}^i_{(a)} = \frac{1}{(L-1)} \sum_{1 \le a < b \le L} \text{RC}^i_{(a,b)}$$

The overall mean correlation score (MRC) for a specific language $a$ among $L$ languages with $N$ queries is:

$$\text{MRC@k}_{(a)} = \frac{1}{N} \sum_{i=1}^{N} \text{RC}^i_{(a)}$$

The MRC@$k$ represents the average degree of consistency between ranking lists for semantically identical queries across all language pairs in the top-$k$ results. A higher MRC@$k$ value indicates greater fairness, reflecting a higher degree of equivalence in the search results across different languages.

### 2.2 Mitigation Language Bias Methodology

Figure 2 demonstrates our co-training MLIR model framework with two losses. Section 2.2.1 introduces the unitized Dense Passage Retrieval (DPR) loss for IR, and in Section 2.2.2 we propose Language KL-Divergence Alignment (LaKDA) loss to improve language fairness.

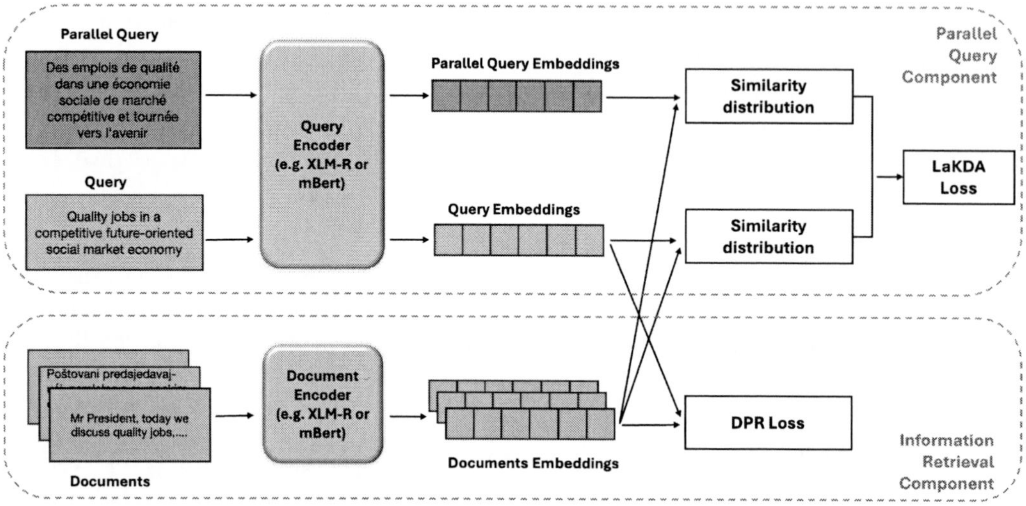


Figure 2: Our model framework contains two parts: the IR component, and the parallel query component. For the IR part, we adopt a DPR module for retrieval with DPR loss. For the parallel query part, we use the LaKDA loss to improve MLIR language fairness.

#### 2.2.1 DPR Loss

Dense passage retrieval (Karpukhin et al., 2020) is a neural retrieval framework initially proposed for monolingual supervised fine-tuning. This architecture separately encodes queries and documents into dense vectors, optimizing their alignment through a contrastive loss. The goal is to maximize the similarity between queries and their relevant documents while minimizing it with irrelevant documents.

Assume we have a query $q$ and a collection of documents $D = \{d_1^-, d_2^+, d_3^-, \ldots, d_M^-\}$, where $d_i^+$ indicates a relevant document and $d_j^-$ an irrelevant document.

Let $\mathbf{q}$ be the dense vector representation of the query, and $\mathbf{d}_i^+$ and $\mathbf{d}_j^-$ be dense vector representations of the corresponding documents.

The similarity between the query and each document is computed using the dot product: $\text{sim}(q, d_i^+) = \mathbf{q} \cdot \mathbf{d}_i^{+\intercal}$ and $\text{sim}(q, d_j^-) = \mathbf{q} \cdot \mathbf{d}_j^{-\intercal}$.

We then define the loss to be the negative log-likelihood of the positive documents' similarity scores among all documents:

$$\mathcal{L}_{\text{DPR}} = -\frac{1}{N}\sum_{i=1}^{N} \log \frac{\exp(\text{sim}(q_i, d_i^+))}{Z_i}$$

$$Z_i = \exp(\text{sim}(q_i, d_i^+)) + \sum_{m=1}^{M} \exp(\text{sim}(q_i, d_{i,m}^-)).$$

This contrastive loss formulation ensures that the query embedding is closer to the positive document embedding than to any of the negative document embeddings, thereby enhancing the model's retrieval performance.

#### 2.2.2 LaKDA Loss

To further mitigate language bias in MLIR, we add a Kullback-Leibler (KL) divergence term to measure the similarity of the distribution of retrieval scores between the original and parallel-language queries over a shared set of document embeddings.

For each query $q(i, \ell_a)$ and its parallel query $q(i, \ell_b)$, we compute their similarity distributions over the document embeddings as follows:

1. **Compute Similarity Scores:**

   For the original query $q(i, \ell_a)$ and the parallel query $q(i, \ell_b)$:

   $$\text{sim}(i, \ell) = \mathbf{q}(i, \ell) \cdot \mathbf{D}^\intercal \quad \text{where} \quad \ell \in \{\ell_a, \ell_b\}$$

2. **Transform to Probability Distributions:**

   The similarity scores are transformed into probability distributions using the softmax function:

   $$\mathbf{p}(i, \ell) = \frac{\exp(\text{sim}(i, \ell))}{\sum_{j=1}^{M} \exp(\text{sim}(i, \ell)_j)}$$

3. **KL Divergence Calculation:**

   The KL divergence between the similarity distributions of the original and parallel queries is defined as:

$$D_{\text{KL}}(\mathbf{p}(i,\ell_b) \parallel \mathbf{p}(i,\ell_a)) = \sum_{j=1}^{M} \mathbf{p}(i,\ell_b)_j \log\left(\frac{\mathbf{p}(i,\ell_b)_j}{\mathbf{p}(i,\ell_a)_j + \epsilon}\right)$$

where $\epsilon$ is a small constant to avoid taking the log of zero.

4. **Overall LaKDA Loss:**

   The LaKDA Loss for all $N$ queries is the mean of KL Divergence over all queries:

$$\mathcal{L}_{\text{LaKDA}} = \frac{1}{N}\sum_{i=1}^{N} D_{\text{KL}}(\mathbf{p}(i,\ell_b) \parallel \mathbf{p}(i,\ell_a))$$

Finally, to balance information retrieval performance and language fairness, we define a joint loss function as a weighted combination of the DPR loss $\mathcal{L}_{\text{DPR}}$ and the LaKDA loss $\mathcal{L}_{\text{LaKDA}}$:

$$\mathcal{L} = (1-\alpha)\mathcal{L}_{\text{DPR}} + \alpha\mathcal{L}_{\text{LaKDA}} \quad (1)$$

where $\alpha$ is a tunable hyperparameter.

### 2.3 MLIR Language Fairness Benchmark

**Overview** The European Parliament (EP) serves as a crucial forum for political debate and decision-making in the European Union. During debates, Members of the European Parliament (MEPs) discuss topics in their own languages, and debates are then transcribed in the original languages, and indexed with multilingual topics.

We constructed MultiEuP-v2 by expanding MultiEuP (Yang et al., 2023), taking the debate titles as queries, and individual MEP speeches in a given debate as documents. The documents are multilingual, encompassing 24 languages from 8 language families. Each query has parallel versions in all 24 languages, sourced from the original dataset. Additionally, we collected the basic demographic details of each of the MEPs, making it the perfect target for the study of fairness in an IR context, in terms of both language and other protected attributes.

**Dataset Statistics** We partition the dataset into mutually-exclusive train/dev/test sets to ensure that the queries and documents in the three sets are distinct. Table 1 details the statistics of the dataset. The number of unique queries is counted per language; i.e., for the dev and test sets, each language has 100 queries, with parallel versions across all 24 languages. The document collection is also made up of documents from all 24 languages. Table 6 in the Appendix shows the language distribution, with languages such as English (EN), German (DE), and French (FR) making up over 50% of the dataset in terms of document count.

| | # Documents | # Unique Queries |
|---|---|---|
| Train | 44,961 | 1,623 |
| Dev | 2,787 | 100 |
| Test | 2,589 | 100 |

Table 1: Data size and unique query IDs in train, dev, and test sets. The number of unique query IDs represents the counts for each language.

## 3 Experiments and Findings

Our language fairness experiment consists of two main parts: the detection and comparison of language bias among different ranking methods (Section 3.1) and the mitigation of fairness bias (Section 3.2).

### 3.1 Language Bias Detection

#### 3.1.1 Detection Experiment Setting

We used the MultiEuP-v2 dataset in a *many-vs-many* setting for traning, where both queries and documents are multilingual to ensure language diversity. For evaluation, we adopted a parallel *one-vs-many* approach, with queries in one language and documents in multiple languages, enabling parallel comparison across different languages.

#### 3.1.2 Detection Experiment Models

**BM25** We implemented BM25, a commonly used traditional information retrieval baseline, using Pyserini (Lin et al., 2021). Pyserini is built upon Lucene (Yang et al., 2017). We used the default settings ($k_1 = 0.9$ and $b = 0.4$) and language-specific analyzers.

**DPR** Our neural IR approach is based on DPR and uses a bi-directional encoder to encode queries and documents separately. We compare DPR performance over two text encoders: mBERT with *bert-base-multilingual-uncased*, and XLM-R with *xlm-roberta-base*. In each case, the batch size was set to 96 and the learning rate was 5e-5, with each epoch taking approximately 40 minutes on a single Tesla V100 GPU.

| MRR@100 | Germanic | | | | | Romance | | | | | Slavic | | | | | | Uralic | | | Baltic | | Hellenic | Semitic | Celtic | |
|---|---|---|---|---|---|---|---|---|---|---|---|---|---|---|---|---|---|---|---|---|---|---|---|---|---|
| | EN | DE | NL | SV | DA | FR | ES | RO | IT | PT | PL | HR | BG | SK | SL | CS | HU | FI | ET | LT | LV | EL | MT | GA | Avg |
| BM25 | 87.6 | 59.8 | 29.6 | 25.5 | 21.4 | 59.6 | 58.2 | 33.9 | 51.7 | 49.7 | 39.9 | 33.4 | 22.6 | 30.9 | 32.5 | 28.2 | 22.9 | 20.3 | 19.6 | 22.8 | 21.6 | 18.1 | 12.6 | 16.5 | 34.1 |
| **mBERT** | | | | | | | | | | | | | | | | | | | | | | | | | |
| $\mathcal{L}_{\text{DPR}}$ | 42.8 | 39.4 | 37.1 | 36.3 | 33.9 | 38.3 | 41.0 | 38.3 | 39.2 | 40.1 | 39.9 | 37.9 | 36.9 | 39.0 | 39.7 | 37.9 | 32.5 | 32.2 | 30.7 | 35.8 | 33.7 | 30.6 | 27.0 | 14.5 | 35.6 |
| $+\mathcal{L}_{\text{MSE}}$ | 29.1 | 28.7 | 25.8 | 22.5 | 26.5 | 26.2 | 27.0 | 26.2 | 26.9 | 26.8 | 26.9 | 25.9 | 22.8 | 25.7 | 26.0 | 26.3 | 22.7 | 23.7 | 23.3 | 20.0 | 22.9 | 16.3 | 15.6 | 12.2 | 24.0 (↓ 32.6%) |
| $+\mathcal{L}_{\text{LaKDA}}$ | 46.5 | 47.5 | 43.0 | 43.3 | 40.7 | 45.7 | 42.6 | 41.5 | 44.4 | 41.4 | 42.3 | 42.6 | 39.7 | 43.3 | 39.4 | 43.8 | 39.5 | 42.3 | 37.1 | 38.1 | 39.5 | 31.7 | 28.1 | 16.8 | 40.0 (↑ 12.4%) |
| **XLM-R** | | | | | | | | | | | | | | | | | | | | | | | | | |
| $\mathcal{L}_{\text{DPR}}$ | 47.6 | 49.7 | 45.6 | 49.4 | 45.6 | 48.7 | 51.2 | 51.7 | 45.4 | 47.1 | 47.1 | 45.7 | 51.0 | 50.0 | 43.5 | 49.8 | 43.7 | 47.1 | 44.3 | 46.1 | 49.4 | 46.5 | **40.6** | 30.0 | 46.5 |
| $+\mathcal{L}_{\text{MSE}}$ | 48.4 | 46.4 | 53.9 | 50.2 | 54.1 | 60.8 | 58.5 | 58.0 | 50.1 | 45.6 | 51.7 | 46.1 | 52.7 | 50.6 | 45.9 | 51.7 | 50.2 | 48.1 | 43.1 | 41.4 | 48.7 | 47.5 | 28.8 | 24.7 | 48.2 (↑ 3.7%) |
| $+\mathcal{L}_{\text{LaKDA}}$ | **70.0** | **65.3** | **65.6** | **68.8** | **69.1** | **69.0** | **62.0** | **66.0** | **67.3** | **60.7** | **69.1** | **57.3** | **62.2** | **61.4** | **64.4** | **63.4** | **62.6** | **59.2** | **56.7** | **61.5** | **60.7** | **55.4** | 34.9 | **30.8** | **61.0** (↑ **31.2%**) |

Table 2: The MLIR performance evaluation results on MultiEuP-v2. MRR@100 ($\times$100) ranges from 0 to 100, where values closer to 100 indicate better performance. Underscore indicates the best performance for mBERT, and **bold** indicates the best performance for XLM-R. The symbol ↑/↓ indicates the percentage increase or decrease compared to the vanilla setting $\mathcal{L}_{DPR}$. All differences are significant at $p < 0.0005$. Note the broad similarities in results for a given language and also language family.

| MRC@5 | Germanic | | | | | Romance | | | | | Slavic | | | | | | Uralic | | | Baltic | | Hellenic | Semitic | Celtic | |
|---|---|---|---|---|---|---|---|---|---|---|---|---|---|---|---|---|---|---|---|---|---|---|---|---|---|
| | EN | DE | NL | SV | DA | FR | ES | RO | IT | PT | PL | HR | BG | SK | SL | CS | HU | FI | ET | LT | LV | EL | MT | GA | Avg |
| BM25 | 0.5 | −1.0 | 1.4 | −0.6 | −0.5 | −1.2 | 0.4 | 2.0 | 2.8 | 1.1 | −0.3 | 1.8 | 3.2 | −0.3 | 1.5 | 3.3 | 1.7 | 0.4 | 0.6 | 0.7 | −2.4 | 1.0 | −1.4 | −0.5 | 0.6 |
| **mBERT** | | | | | | | | | | | | | | | | | | | | | | | | | |
| $\mathcal{L}_{\text{DPR}}$ | 12.9 | 15.0 | 15.9 | 15.2 | 12.8 | 12.9 | 15.4 | 15.1 | 14.4 | 13.7 | 14.6 | 15.2 | 15.6 | 15.5 | 13.8 | 16.0 | 7.3 | 13.0 | 10.3 | 10.6 | 11.3 | 12.9 | 10.2 | 5.3 | 13.1 |
| $+\mathcal{L}_{\text{MSE}}$ | 14.3 | 15.6 | 12.2 | 14.5 | 14.6 | 15.5 | 13.5 | 18.3 | 17.1 | 15.5 | 15.5 | 14.4 | 10.7 | 15.5 | 14.3 | 17.2 | 13.2 | 14.2 | 12.1 | 12.1 | 12.7 | 6.5 | 13.7 | 7.7 | 13.8 (↑ 5.3%) |
| $+\mathcal{L}_{\text{LaKDA}}$ | 18.3 | 17.4 | 20.1 | 17.4 | 14.9 | 20.6 | 20.2 | 19.1 | 18.2 | 20.7 | 17.3 | 18.2 | 16.9 | 20.0 | 17.5 | 16.7 | 16.9 | 18.7 | 16.0 | 14.2 | 13.0 | 10.2 | 9.4 | 3.5 | 16.5 (↑ 25.6%) |
| **XLM-R** | | | | | | | | | | | | | | | | | | | | | | | | | |
| $\mathcal{L}_{\text{DPR}}$ | 12.6 | 13.8 | 9.3 | 13.9 | 15.2 | 12.7 | 11.7 | 13.1 | 9.5 | 12.7 | 15.0 | 15.7 | 13.0 | 14.1 | 13.7 | 11.2 | 13.8 | 10.0 | 10.9 | 11.3 | 10.6 | 9.5 | 0.2 | **7.4** | 11.7 |
| $+\mathcal{L}_{\text{MSE}}$ | 12.8 | 11.7 | 11.0 | 12.1 | 13.1 | 9.2 | 12.5 | 12.7 | 13.5 | 11.3 | 11.9 | 12.4 | 11.3 | 9.3 | 11.9 | 10.5 | 11.5 | 10.5 | 9.9 | 11.9 | 9.3 | 8.6 | 2.2 | 0.7 | 10.5 (↓ 10.3%) |
| $+\mathcal{L}_{\text{LaKDA}}$ | **12.9** | **20.1** | **15.8** | **18.5** | **18.6** | **19.3** | **15.9** | **16.2** | **16.9** | **18.0** | **17.2** | **16.0** | **17.0** | **16.5** | **18.3** | **18.3** | **17.5** | **16.6** | **15.5** | **16.4** | **14.3** | **12.9** | **6.7** | 6.2 | **15.9** (↑ **35.9%**) |

Table 3: The MLIR fairness evaluation results on MultiEuP-v2. MRC@5 ($\times$100) ranges from $-100$ to 100, where values closer to 100 indicate better fairness. Underscore indicates the best fairness for mBERT, and **bold** indicates the best fairness for XLM-R.

#### 3.1.3 Detection Evaluation and Findings

**Performance Metrics** To evaluate MLIR retrieval performance, we used the MRR@100 metric, which represents the Mean Reciprocal Rank for the top 100 documents (Radev et al., 2002; Voorhees and Tice, 2000). For a single query, the Reciprocal Rank (RR) is defined as $RR = \frac{1}{\text{rank}}$, where *rank* is the position of the highest-ranked relevant document. If no relevant document is returned, the RR is set to 0. For multiple queries $N$, the MRR is the mean of RRs (Yang et al., 2023).

$$MRR = \frac{1}{N} \sum_{i=1}^{N} \frac{1}{\text{rank}_i}$$

**Performance Findings** Table 2 shows the MRR@100 results for semantically identical queries in different languages. The findings include: (1) for low-resource languages[2] like Maltese (MT) and Irish (GA), the MRR@100 is lower than high-resource languages; (2) interestingly, despite Maltese having more documents than Estonian (ET) in our dataset (Table 6), the MRR@100 disparity suggests that data augmentation alone does not eliminate the inherent bias in pre-trained IR models against low-resource languages; and (3) DPR with mBERT is slightly better overall than BM25, while DPR with XLM-R significantly outperforms both BM25 and DPR with mBERT.

[2]Defined as those languages in Conneau et al. (2020) with less than 0.5 GiB in training data.

**Fairness Findings** When we evaluate language fairness based on MRC@5 (see Section 2.1), we obtain the results shown in Table 7. The main findings are: (1) BM25 has lower language fairness than DPR; (2) similarly to MRR@100, low-resource languages (MT and GA) exhibit lower language fairness than high-resource languages; and (3) according to Figure 3, which shows the MRC@5 correlation between language pairs (noting that the results are symmetric), languages in the same language family (within the black squares) tend to have higher MRC scores, esp. for the Germanic, Romance, and Slavic language families (the dashed square).

### 3.2 Language Bias Mitigation

Next we turn to the question of language bias mitigation.

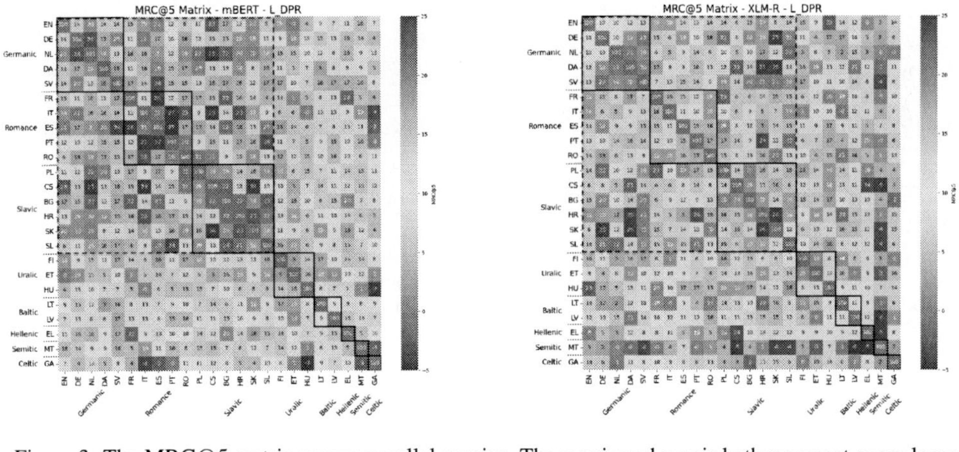


Figure 3: The MRC@5 matrix among parallel queries. The x-axis and y-axis both represent query languages.

### 3.2.1 Mitigation Experiment Setting

The training parameters and evaluation protocol and metrics used to measure language bias mitigation are consistent with those described in Section 3.1.

### 3.2.2 Mitigation Experiment Models

**Vanilla** Our vanilla setting is using only the DPR loss for MLIR (Karpukhin et al., 2020) and not incorporating any language fairness loss.

**MSE** Another baseline involves calculating the Mean Squared Error (MSE, Hastie et al. (2009)) between the embeddings of parallel queries to increase their similarity. We employ the same joint MSE loss with DPR loss.

**LaKDA** With our proposed LaKDA debiasing method (Section 2.2.2), for each query, we randomly sample a semantically identical query in a different language and compute the LaKDA loss, which is then jointly optimized with the DPR loss as shown in Equation (1). For both mBERT and XLM-R, we set $\alpha = 0.5$ for comparability (but return to investigate the hyperparameter sensitivity in Figure 4).

### 3.2.3 Mitigation Evaluation and Findings

Table 2 presents the IR performance (MRR@100), and Table 7 demonstrates language fairness (MRC@5) for the DPR framework with different pretrained multilingual models. Our observations are as follows:

**mBERT Findings** Compared to the vanilla setting (DPR only): (1) incorporating either MSE or LaKDA enhances language fairness (MRC@5) with mBERT, but LaKDA is more effective (25.6% vs. 5.1%); and (2) for MRR@100, LaKDA achieves an 11.3% improvement, whereas MSE loss reduces MRR@100 by 32.6%. Figure 4 also shows that during the hyperprameter $\alpha$ grid search, the DPR model with LaKDA loss is more robust in terms of MRR than MSE loss. This is because, unlike MSE loss, LaKDA loss considers not only the similarity between parallel queries but also their embedding similarity with documents, providing a better trade-off between fairness and performance.

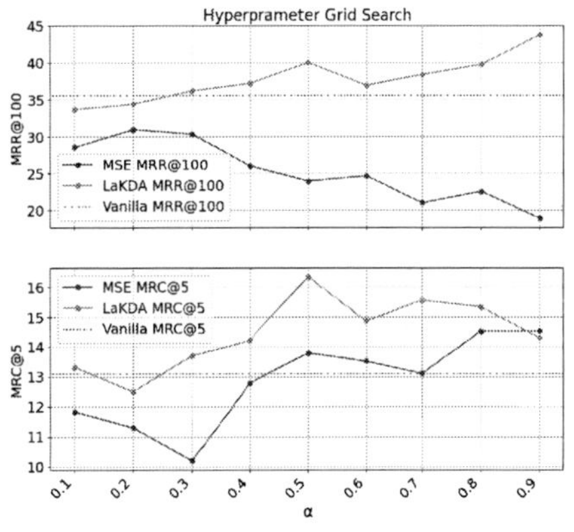


Figure 4: MSE and LaKDA sensitivity plot.

**XLM-R Findings** Compared to the vanilla setting (DPR only): (1) only LaKDA improves language fairness (MRC@5), by 35.9%, while MSE leads to a slight degradation; and (2) both MSE

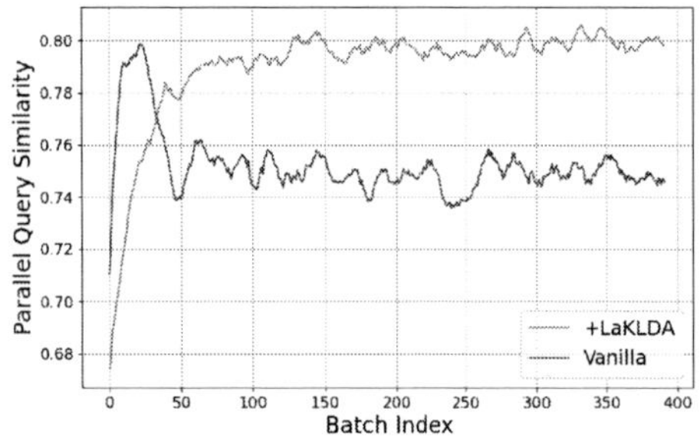


Figure 5: Parallel query similarity over training.

| Parallel MT Query | MRR@100 | MRC@5 |
|---|---|---|
| Zero-shot | 21.2 | 2.8 |
| Translated | **36.2** | 1.2 |
| Original | 34.9 | **6.7** |

Table 4: Maltese (MT) query MLIR results.

| Parallel GA Query | MRR@100 | MRC@5 |
|---|---|---|
| Zero-shot | 21.4 | 0.6 |
| Translated | 29.6 | 1.4 |
| Original | **30.8** | **6.2** |

Table 5: Irish (GA) query MLIR results.

and LaKDA improve IR performance (MRR@100), with increases of 3.7% and 16.6%, respectively. XLM-R not only achieves better IR performance but is also more robust. This observation aligns with other research, and is why XLM-R is more commonly used in MLIR (Hu et al., 2020; Conneau et al., 2020; Conneau and Lample, 2019).

## 4 Discussion

### 4.1 Improvement of Parallel Query Similarity

In our experimental setup, an important characteristic for enhancing language fairness is the increase in similarity of semantically parallel queries. We calculated the average parallel query similarity in each batch over training for mBERT, as depicted in Figure 5. We observe that with the addition of the LaKDA loss, the final stable value of parallel query similarity is higher compared to the vanilla setting. This result explains the enhancement in language fairness (MRC).

### 4.2 Effect of Size and Quality of Parallel Queries

To explore the impact of the number and quality of parallel queries on IR performance and language fairness, we selected queries in two languages, MT and GA, from the training dataset and conducted experiments under the following three settings:

**Zero-shot:** As low-resource languages, there is relatively little training data for MT and GA; we therefore excluded queries in MT and GA from the training dataset, keeping the other parallel queries unchanged, and then conducted the same training and evaluation settings.

**Translation:** Without the original MT and GA parallel queries, we translated English queries into MT and GA parallel queries using Google Translate.[3] The BLEU scores (Papineni et al., 2002) of the translation results compared to the original were 0.196 and 0.251, respectively.

**Original:** The original queries in MT and GA, as per the experiments in Section 3.2.

**Findings:** Tables 4 and 5 show the results for MT and GA, conducted on the XLM-R model with LaKDA loss. We found that:

1. The zeroshot setting had the worst MRR performance, indicating the importance of parallel queries.
2. The translated version serves as a silver-standard, with improvements in MRR compared to the zeroshot setting.
3. The original texts are the best choice, achieving the best MRR and MRC, demonstrating the value of our MultiEuP-v2 dataset in providing an original multilingual corpus.

### 4.3 Effect of Neural Retrieval Approaches

The MRC@5 results presented in Table 7 show more than a 20-fold disparity between BM25 and the neural retrieval ranker DPR, with scores of 0.6 and 11.7, respectively. To understand the underlying causes, we analyzed the top 100 ranking outputs from both methods. As shown in Figure 6, BM25's output document languages and query languages exhibit a strong correlation along the diagonal line, contributing to heightened language bias. Since BM25 is only able to retrieve documents containing keywords present within the query (Thakur et al., 2021) and suffers from lexical gap (Berger et al., 2000), resulting in high retrieval rates for documents in the same language as the query.

Meanwhile, DPR retrieves documents across different languages more effectively, with substantial

[3] `https://translate.google.com/`

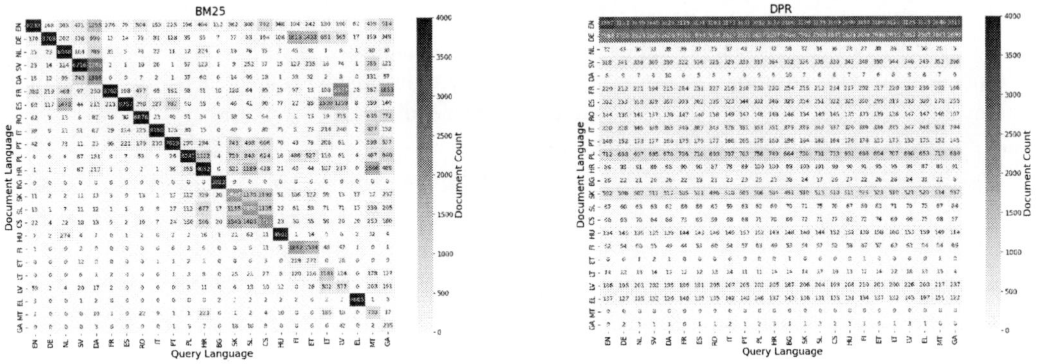


Figure 6: The correlation of query language with document language in top 100 ranking output.

off-diagonal values and reflecting the skewness of the dataset (see Table 6). This suggests that neural retrieval approaches can mitigate language bias to leveraging multilingual pre-trained models that understand semantic content regardless of the language.

## 5 Related Work

Fairness in Information Retrieval (IR) has been extensively studied through two primary dimensions: individual fairness and group fairness. These frameworks are crucial in ensuring equitable access to information, addressing concerns related to biases in ranking systems.

**Individual fairness** refers to the principle that similar items (in this case, documents) should be treated similarly (Biega et al., 2018; Dwork et al., 2011). In IR, this means that if two documents are equally relevant to a query, they should receive similar rankings. A violation of individual fairness occurs when two comparable documents are ranked differently due to irrelevant factors, such as their format or metadata. This concept is rooted in the idea of consistency and uniform treatment, ensuring that the system does not unfairly prioritize or penalize specific documents that are otherwise similar in content and relevance.

**Group fairness**, on the other hand, ensures that predefined groups (such as demographic groups or, in our case, languages) are treated equitably in the ranking process (Sapiezynski et al., 2019; Zehlike et al., 2022, 2017). The goal is to prevent bias against any group by ensuring that the system does not favor one group over another. In IR, this often translates to ensuring that documents associated with a protected group (e.g., underrepresented languages or communities) are not systematically ranked lower than those associated with unprotected groups. Group fairness frameworks attempt to mitigate historical and societal biases that might seep into the retrieval process, making sure that members of different groups have equitable access to information. In our work, we extend this concept to multilingual IR, treating each language as a group and ensuring that rankings are fair and consistent across languages.

Two key fairness metrics in group fairness that align with our work are Probability of Equal Expected Rank (PEER) and Attention Weighted Ranked Fairness (AWRF).

- **PEER** (Yang et al., 2024) is designed to ensure equity in ranking by guaranteeing that documents from different languages are treated equally when they are equally relevant. This metric is particularly valuable for multilingual retrieval, as it addresses the risk of language bias, ensuring that a document's rank does not depend on the language of the query if the content is of similar relevance across languages.
- **AWRF** (Sapiezynski et al., 2019) assesses group exposure by comparing how documents are distributed across ranked positions relative to a predefined target distribution. This metric focuses on ensuring that documents from all languages receive appropriate visibility within the top-ranked results, balancing relevance and fairness in exposure.

While these metrics primarily emphasize document-level fairness, our approach uniquely focuses on query-level fairness. In our context, we argue that the retrieval system should provide consistent performance across languages, ensuring that the language of the query does not affect the user's ability to access relevant information. This promotes inclusivity, ensuring that users from different linguistic backgrounds experience similar outcomes when interacting with the system, ultimately fostering equal access to information.

## 6 Background Knowledge

**MultiEuP** The European Parliament (EP) serves as a crucial forum for political debate and decision-making in the European Union. During debates, Members of the European Parliament (MEPs) discuss topics in their own languages, and debates are then transcribed in the original languages, and indexed with multilingual topics. As such, the data is naturally occurring in the 24 official languages of the EU, and expertly transcribed and multilingually annotated. Additionally, we have access to basic demographic details of each of the MEPs, making it the perfect target for the study of fairness in an IR context, in terms of both language and protected attributes was crafted. The EU has published different language versions of all titles, providing semantically identical queries for investigating language fairness in MLIR.

An earlier version of the MultiEuP dataset was published in 2023 covering debates up to October 2022 (Yang et al., 2023). In this work, we have expanded the dataset using the same data collection and preprocessing procedures, to include debates up to 2024. This doubles the total data volume, and provides a sufficient sample size to research neural ranking methods. We additionally augment each document with comprehensive metadata of the author, including gender, nationality, political affiliation, and age, for use in exploring fairness with respect to protected attributes.

Unlike MLIR datasets such as mMARCO (Bonifacio et al., 2021), a multilingual version of the MS MARCO (Bajaj et al., 2016), that relies on machine translation, our benchmark queries and documents are original rather than translated versions. This reduces noise and ensures the linguistic authenticity of the corpus.

Another commonly used MLIR datasets Mr. TyDi (Zhang et al., 2021) and MIRACL (Zhang et al., 2023) , are actually mixed monolingual IR dataset, since they were structured such that queries in different languages are matched only with documents in the same language. This limits the comparability of results across different languages. Our benchmark addresses this limitation by introducing semantically parallel queries across multiple languages, enabling comprehensive analysis of language fairness in MLIR.

**DPR** Dense Passage Retrieval (DPR: Karpukhin et al. (2020)) is a neural retrieval framework initially proposed for monolingual supervised finetuning. DPR uses dual encoders: one for encoding queries and another for encoding passages (documents), both based on the BERT architecture (Devlin et al., 2019). The primary advantage of DPR over traditional retrieval models like BM25 is its ability to embed both queries and documents into a shared dense vector space, enabling efficient nearest-neighbor search for retrieval. The relevance of a document to a query is determined by the similarity between their embeddings, typically using the dot product as a similarity measure.

In our work, we employ mDPR using mBERT and XLM-R to handle multilingual queries and documents. These models are fine-tuned on parallel query-document pairs from multiple languages, allowing the system to generalize across different languages. The use of mDPR allows us to explore how multilingual language models handle language biases, which often favor high-resource languages over low-resource ones. Furthermore, we investigate the performance of these models on the MultiEuP dataset, assessing their ability to ensure fair and equitable retrieval across 24 languages, thus promoting fairness in multilingual IR.

## 7 Conclusion

We introduced a novel benchmark, MultiEup-v2, for investigating language fairness in multilingual information retrieval (MLIR) systems. Additionally, we proposed the mean rank correlation (MRC) score to assess language fairness in MLIR systems, which ensures that queries in different languages but with the same semantic meaning retrieve similar documents. Our findings indicate that the traditional IR method BM25 exhibits larger language biases than DPR with multilingual pretrained language models. Furthermore, we designed the language KL-divergence alignment (LaKDA) loss to mitigate language bias, and found that incorporating LaKDA loss into DPR improves language fairness substantially without sacrificing retrieval performance.

## Ethics Statement

The dataset contains publicly-available EP data that does not include personal or sensitive information, with the exception of information relating to public officeholders, e.g., the names of the active members of the European Parliament, European Council, or other official administration bodies. The collected data is licensed under the Creative Commons Attribution 4.0 International licence.[4]

## Limitations

Our investigation into language fairness in multilingual information retrieval (MLIR) is limited to European languages in this work. However, our approaches and evaluation methods are adaptable to other languages. Additionally, we focused exclusively on language fairness, leaving other dimensions of fairness in MLIR, such as demographic fairness, unexplored. We encourage the research community to conduct more comprehensive studies on fairness in MLIR, building upon the foundation of our benchmark.

## Acknowledgement

We sincerely thank Trevor Cohn for his valuable suggestions and support in this work. This research was funded by the Melbourne Research Scholarship and was conducted using the LIEF HPC-GPGPU Facility hosted at the University of Melbourne. This facility was established with the assistance of LIEF Grant LE170100200.

## References

Zahra Abbasiyantaeb and Saeedeh Momtazi. 2020. Text-based question answering from information retrieval and deep neural network perspectives: A survey. *CoRR*, abs/2002.06612.

Payal Bajaj, Daniel Campos, Nick Craswell, Li Deng, Jianfeng Gao, Xiaodong Liu, Rangan Majumder, Andrew McNamara, Bhaskar Mitra, Tri Nguyen, et al. 2016. Ms marco: A human generated machine reading comprehension dataset. *arXiv preprint arXiv:1611.09268*.

Adam Berger, Rich Caruana, David Cohn, Dayne Freitag, and Vibhu Mittal. 2000. Bridging the lexical chasm: statistical approaches to answer-finding. In *Proceedings of the 23rd Annual International ACM SIGIR Conference on Research and Development in Information Retrieval*, SIGIR '00, page 192–199, New York, NY, USA. Association for Computing Machinery.

Asia J. Biega, Krishna P. Gummadi, and Gerhard Weikum. 2018. Equity of attention: Amortizing individual fairness in rankings. In *The 41st International ACM SIGIR Conference on Research & Development in Information Retrieval*, SIGIR '18. ACM.

Luiz Henrique Bonifacio, Israel Campiotti, Roberto de Alencar Lotufo, and Rodrigo Frassetto Nogueira. 2021. mmarco: A multilingual version of MS MARCO passage ranking dataset. *CoRR*, abs/2108.13897.

Ilias Chalkidis, Manos Fergadiotis, and Ion Androutsopoulos. 2021. MultiEURLEX - a multi-lingual and multi-label legal document classification dataset for zero-shot cross-lingual transfer. In *Proceedings of the 2021 Conference on Empirical Methods in Natural Language Processing*, pages 6974–6996, Online and Punta Cana, Dominican Republic. Association for Computational Linguistics.

Danqi Chen, Adam Fisch, Jason Weston, and Antoine Bordes. 2017. Reading Wikipedia to answer open-domain questions. In *Proceedings of the 55th Annual Meeting of the Association for Computational Linguistics (Volume 1: Long Papers)*, pages 1870–1879, Vancouver, Canada. Association for Computational Linguistics.

Alexis Conneau, Kartikay Khandelwal, Naman Goyal, Vishrav Chaudhary, Guillaume Wenzek, Francisco Guzmán, Edouard Grave, Myle Ott, Luke Zettlemoyer, and Veselin Stoyanov. 2020. Unsupervised cross-lingual representation learning at scale. In *Proceedings of the 58th Annual Meeting of the Association for Computational Linguistics*, pages 8440–8451, Online. Association for Computational Linguistics.

Alexis Conneau and Guillaume Lample. 2019. Cross-lingual language model pretraining. In *Advances in Neural Information Processing Systems*.

Jacob Devlin, Ming-Wei Chang, Kenton Lee, and Kristina Toutanova. 2019. BERT: Pre-training of deep bidirectional transformers for language understanding. In *Proceedings of the 2019 Conference of the North American Chapter of the Association for Computational Linguistics: Human Language Technologies, Volume 1 (Long and Short Papers)*, pages 4171–4186, Minneapolis, Minnesota. Association for Computational Linguistics.

Cynthia Dwork, Moritz Hardt, Toniann Pitassi, Omer Reingold, and Rich Zemel. 2011. Fairness through awareness. *Preprint*, arXiv:1104.3913.

Trevor Hastie, Robert Tibshirani, and Jerome Friedman. 2009. *The Elements of Statistical Learning: Data Mining, Inference, and Prediction*. Springer Science & Business Media.

[4]`https://eur-lex.europa.eu/content/legal-notice/legal-notice.html`

Junjie Hu, Sebastian Ruder, Aditya Siddhant, Graham Neubig, Orhan Firat, and Melvin Johnson. 2020. Xtreme: A massively multilingual multi-task benchmark for evaluating cross-lingual generalization. In *Proceedings of the 37th International Conference on Machine Learning*, pages 4411–4421.

Zhiqi Huang, Hansi Zeng, Hamed Zamani, and James Allan. 2023. Soft prompt decoding for multilingual dense retrieval. In *Proceedings of the 46th International ACM SIGIR Conference on Research and Development in Information Retrieval*, pages 1208–1218.

Vladimir Karpukhin, Barlas Oguz, Sewon Min, Patrick Lewis, Ledell Wu, Sergey Edunov, Danqi Chen, and Wen-tau Yih. 2020. Dense passage retrieval for open-domain question answering. In *Proceedings of the 2020 Conference on Empirical Methods in Natural Language Processing (EMNLP)*, pages 6769–6781, Online. Association for Computational Linguistics.

Dawn Lawrie, Eugene Yang, Douglas W Oard, and James Mayfield. 2023. Neural approaches to multilingual information retrieval. In *European Conference on Information Retrieval*, pages 521–536. Springer.

Jimmy Lin, Xueguang Ma, Sheng-Chieh Lin, Jheng-Hong Yang, Ronak Pradeep, and Rodrigo Nogueira. 2021. Pyserini: A Python toolkit for reproducible information retrieval research with sparse and dense representations. `https://github.com/castorini/pyserini`.

Jing Miao, Charat Thongprayoon, Supawadee Suppadungsuk, Oscar Garcia Valencia, and Wisit Cheungpasitporn. 2024. Integrating retrieval-augmented generation with large language models in nephrology: Advancing practical applications. *Medicina*, 60:445.

John G. Oakes. 2010. Commentary: Charles spearman and correlation: a commentary on 'the proof and measurement of association between two things'. *International Journal of Epidemiology*, 39(5):1151–1160.

Kishore Papineni, Salim Roukos, Todd Ward, and Wei-Jing Zhu. 2002. Bleu: a method for automatic evaluation of machine translation. In *Proceedings of the 40th Annual Meeting on Association for Computational Linguistics*, pages 311–318. Association for Computational Linguistics.

Hyunji Hayley Park, Katherine J. Zhang, Coleman Haley, Kenneth Steimel, Han Liu, and Lane Schwartz. 2021. Morphology matters: A multilingual language modeling analysis. *Transactions of the Association for Computational Linguistics*, 9:261–276.

Dragomir R. Radev, Hong Qi, Harris Wu, and Weiguo Fan. 2002. Evaluating web-based question answering systems. In *Proceedings of the Third International Conference on Language Resources and Evaluation (LREC'02)*, Las Palmas, Canary Islands - Spain. European Language Resources Association (ELRA).

Piotr Sapiezynski, Wesley Zeng, Ronald E. Robertson, Alan Mislove, and Christo Wilson. 2019. Quantifying the impact of user attention on fair group representation in ranked lists. *Preprint*, arXiv:1901.10437.

Charles Spearman. 1904. The proof and measurement of association between two things. *The American Journal of Psychology*, 15(1):72–101.

Nandan Thakur, Nils Reimers, Andreas Rücklé, Abhishek Srivastava, and Iryna Gurevych. 2021. BEIR: A heterogenous benchmark for zero-shot evaluation of information retrieval models. *CoRR*, abs/2104.08663.

Ellen M. Voorhees and Dawn M. Tice. 2000. The TREC-8 question answering track. In *Proceedings of the Second International Conference on Language Resources and Evaluation (LREC'00)*, Athens, Greece. European Language Resources Association (ELRA).

Eugene Yang, Thomas Jänich, James Mayfield, and Dawn Lawrie. 2024. Language fairness in multilingual information retrieval. In *Proceedings of the 47th International ACM SIGIR Conference on Research and Development in Information Retrieval*, SIGIR 2024, page 2487–2491. ACM.

Jinrui Yang, Timothy Baldwin, and Trevor Cohn. 2023. Multi-EuP: The multilingual European parliament dataset for analysis of bias in information retrieval. In *Proceedings of the 3rd Workshop on Multi-lingual Representation Learning (MRL)*, pages 282–291, Singapore. Association for Computational Linguistics.

Peilin Yang, Hui Fang, and Jimmy Lin. 2017. Anserini: Enabling the use of lucene for information retrieval research. In *Proceedings of the 40th International ACM SIGIR Conference on Research and Development in Information Retrieval*, pages 1253–1256.

Meike Zehlike, Francesco Bonchi, Carlos Castillo, Sara Hajian, Mohamed Megahed, and Ricardo Baeza-Yates. 2017. Fa*ir: A fair top-k ranking algorithm. In *Proceedings of the 2017 ACM on Conference on Information and Knowledge Management*, CIKM '17. ACM.

Meike Zehlike, Tom Sühr, Ricardo Baeza-Yates, Francesco Bonchi, Carlos Castillo, and Sara Hajian. 2022. Fair top-k ranking with multiple protected groups. *Inf. Process. Manage.*, 59(1).

Xinyu Zhang, Xueguang Ma, Peng Shi, and Jimmy Lin. 2021. Mr. TyDi: A multi-lingual benchmark for dense retrieval. In *Proceedings of the 1st Workshop on Multilingual Representation Learning*, pages 127–137, Punta Cana, Dominican Republic. Association for Computational Linguistics.

Xinyu Zhang, Nandan Thakur, Odunayo Ogundepo, Ehsan Kamalloo, David Alfonso-Hermelo, Xiaoguang Li, Qun Liu, Mehdi Rezagholizadeh, and Jimmy Lin. 2023. MIRACL: A Multilingual Retrieval Dataset Covering 18 Diverse Languages. *Transactions of the Association for Computational Linguistics*, 11:1114–1131.

Yutao Zhu, Huaying Yuan, Shuting Wang, Jiongnan Liu, Wenhan Liu, Chenlong Deng, Haonan Chen, Zhicheng Dou, and Ji-Rong Wen. 2024. Large language models for information retrieval: A survey. *Preprint*, arXiv:2308.07107.

## A Appendix

| Language | ISO code | Countries where official lang. | Language Family | Total Usage | # Docs | Words per Doc |
|---|---|---|---|---|---|---|
| English | EN | United Kingdom, Ireland, Malta | Germanic | 51% | 14086 | 271/192 |
| German | DE | Germany, Belgium, Luxembourg | Germanic | 32% | 5861 | 183/168 |
| French | FR | France, Belgium, Luxembourg | Romance | 26% | 5313 | 267/210 |
| Italian | IT | Italy | Romance | 16% | 3378 | 191/176 |
| Spanish | ES | Spain | Romance | 15% | 4621 | 228/195 |
| Polish | PL | Poland | Slavic | 9% | 2857 | 150/142 |
| Romanian | RO | Romania | Romance | 5% | 1482 | 183/172 |
| Dutch | NL | Netherlands, Belgium | Germanic | 5% | 1642 | 180/166 |
| Greek | EL | Greece, Cyprus | Hellenic | 4% | 1104 | 180/171 |
| Hungarian | HU | Hungary | Uralic | 3% | 979 | 131/131 |
| Portuguese | PT | Portugal | Romance | 3% | 2185 | 183/169 |
| Czech | CS | Czech Republic | Slavic | 3% | 913 | 155/143 |
| Swedish | SV | Sweden | Germanic | 3% | 1038 | 168/154 |
| Bulgarian | BG | Bulgaria | Slavic | 2% | 737 | 190/171 |
| Danish | DA | Denmark | Germanic | 1% | 498 | 206/191 |
| Finnish | FI | Finland | Uralic | 1% | 564 | 115/111 |
| Slovak | SK | Slovakia | Slavic | 1% | 698 | 158/157 |
| Lithuanian | LT | Lithuania | Baltic | 1% | 250 | 145/125 |
| Croatian | HR | Croatia | Slavic | <1% | 995 | 175/162 |
| Slovene | SL | Slovenia | Slavic | <1% | 549 | 188/158 |
| Estonian | ET | Estonia | Uralic | <1% | 88 | 167/162 |
| Latvian | LV | Latvia | Baltic | <1% | 176 | 128/113 |
| Maltese | MT | Malta | Semitic | <1% | 243 | 151/148 |
| Irish | GA | Ireland | Celtic | <1% | 80 | 179/163 |

Table 6: MultiEuP-v2 statistics, broken down by language: ISO language code; EU member states using the language officially; language family; proportion of the EU population speaking the language (Chalkidis et al., 2021); number of debate speech documents; and words per document (mean/median).

| Recall@100 | Germanic | | | | | Romance | | | | | Slavic | | | | | | Uralic | | | Baltic | | Hellenic | Semitic | Celtic | |
|---|---|---|---|---|---|---|---|---|---|---|---|---|---|---|---|---|---|---|---|---|---|---|---|---|---|
| | EN | DE | NL | SV | DA | FR | ES | RO | IT | PT | PL | HR | BG | SK | SL | CS | HU | FI | ET | LT | LV | EL | MT | GA | Avg |
| BM25 | 77.7 | 75.5 | 77.7 | 75.5 | 75.5 | 68.1 | 75.5 | 76.6 | 77.7 | 76.6 | 74.5 | 77.7 | 75.5 | 76.6 | 75.5 | 74.5 | 75.5 | 74.5 | 75.5 | 77.7 | 76.6 | 76.6 | 75.5 | 62.8 | 75.2 |
| **mBERT** | | | | | | | | | | | | | | | | | | | | | | | | | |
| $\mathcal{L}_{\text{DPR}}$ | 88.3 | 89.4 | 88.3 | 87.2 | 88.3 | 89.4 | 89.4 | 88.3 | 90.4 | 87.2 | 88.3 | 88.3 | 87.2 | 88.3 | 86.2 | 87.2 | 85.1 | 86.2 | 86.2 | 88.3 | 86.2 | 86.2 | 85.1 | 73.4 | 87.0 |
| $+\mathcal{L}_{\text{MSE}}$ | 74.5 | 72.3 | 72.3 | 71.3 | 72.3 | 66.0 | 72.3 | 72.3 | 73.4 | 73.4 | 71.3 | 73.4 | 71.3 | 72.3 | 71.3 | 69.1 | 70.2 | 72.3 | 72.3 | 69.1 | 70.2 | 71.3 | 67.0 | 60.6 | 70.9 |
| $+\mathcal{L}_{\text{LaKDA}}$ | 77.7 | 78.7 | 76.6 | 76.6 | 77.7 | 79.8 | 79.8 | 81.9 | 78.7 | 78.7 | 78.7 | 79.8 | 77.7 | 76.6 | 75.5 | 77.7 | 77.7 | 77.7 | 78.7 | 76.6 | 76.6 | 76.6 | 73.4 | 72.3 | 77.6 |
| **XLM-R** | | | | | | | | | | | | | | | | | | | | | | | | | |
| $\mathcal{L}_{\text{DPR}}$ | 86.2 | 89.4 | 86.2 | 84.0 | 86.2 | 85.1 | 89.4 | 89.4 | 86.2 | 87.2 | 86.2 | 84.0 | 87.2 | 88.3 | 90.4 | 86.2 | 89.4 | 90.4 | 84.0 | 80.9 | 86.2 | 86.2 | 88.3 | 81.9 | 86.6 |
| $+\mathcal{L}_{\text{MSE}}$ | 91.5 | 92.6 | 90.4 | 86.2 | 88.3 | 69.1 | 91.5 | 91.5 | 90.4 | 91.5 | 90.4 | 90.4 | 90.4 | 91.5 | 88.3 | 92.6 | 91.5 | 88.3 | 87.2 | 88.3 | 91.5 | 90.4 | 87.2 | 78.7 | 88.7 |
| $+\mathcal{L}_{\text{LaKDA}}$ | 93.6 | 96.8 | 93.6 | 93.6 | 93.6 | 67.0 | 94.7 | 94.7 | 92.6 | 96.8 | 95.7 | 96.8 | 95.7 | 94.7 | 92.6 | 92.6 | 94.7 | 92.6 | 95.7 | 93.6 | 93.6 | 92.6 | 89.4 | 75.5 | 92.2 |

Table 7: The MLIR additional evaluation results on MultiEuP-v2. Recall@100 ($\times$100) ranges from 0 to 100, where values closer to 100 indicate better performance.

# Representational Isomorphism and Alignment of Multilingual Large Language Models

**Di Wu*** **Yibin Lei*** **Andrew Yates** **Christof Monz**
University of Amsterdam
{d.wu, y.lei, a.c.yates, c.monz}@uva.nl

## Abstract

In this extended abstract, we investigate the capability of Large Language Models (LLMs) to represent texts in multilingual contexts. Our findings reveal that sentence representations derived from LLMs exhibit a high degree of isomorphism across languages. This existing isomorphism facilitates representational alignments in few-shot settings. Specifically, by applying a contrastive objective at the representation level with only a small number (e.g., 100) of translation pairs,[1] we significantly improve models' performance on Semantic Textual Similarity (STS) tasks across languages.[2]

## 1 Introduction

Representational isomorphism has been recognized as a key factor of few-shot capabilities (Lample et al., 2017; Søgaard et al., 2018). In this paper, we analyze multilingual sentence representations in LLMs through the lens of isomorphism. By examining the geometric properties of sentence pairs, we show that while embeddings from different languages are not well clustered in a common space, they exhibit high isomorphism. Projecting them via an orthogonal matrix effectively aligns representations across languages. It also explains the previous success of combining non-English inputs with English prompts (Etxaniz et al., 2023; Huang et al., 2023).

Building on this observation and previous studies highlighting representational isomorphism as a key factor in few-shot capabilities, we explore multilingual semantic alignment in LLMs. Using just 100 English-centric translation samples with contrastive loss across language pairs, we achieve effective representation space alignment. This significantly improves cross-lingual Semantic Textual Similarity (STS) task performance, proving more efficient than continued multilingual training. Notably, this also boosts STS performance within individual languages, even without a monolingual objective.

*These authors contributed equally to this work.

[1] Due to page limits, these results are not included in the extended abstract.

[2] Our anonymous code is available at https://anonymous.4open.science/r/multilingual_reps.

## 2 Representational Analysis

### 2.1 Representation Extraction

PromptEOL (Jiang et al., 2023) extracts sentence embeddings from causal language models like LLaMA (Touvron et al., 2023) using a simple prompting template:

*This sentence: "[TEXT]" means in one word:"*

The last hidden layer's vector for the final token is used as the sentence representation. This method has demonstrated strong performance on semantic representation tasks (Agirre et al., 2015, 2016).

We adopt PromptEOL for its simplicity and adaptability. For multilingual use, the English template is translated into corresponding languages, e.g., for German:

*Dieser Satz: "[TEXT]" bedeutet in einem Wort:"*

We use this method to derive multilingual LLM representations.

### 2.2 Cross-lingual Structural Analysis

We use Procrustes analysis (Schönemann, 1966) to assess the structural similarity of representations across languages. This method optimally rotates or reflects one set of points to align with another, preserving the shape. The accuracy of this alignment indicates the degree of isomorphism across spaces.

Formally, given two embedding sets, $A$ and $B$, from LLMs using sentence pairs in different languages, Procrustes analysis learns an orthogonal projection $W$ that maps $A$ to a shared space with $B$ by solving $min \|WA - B\|_F$ subject to



*Proceedings of the Fourth Workshop on Multilingual Representation Learning (MRL 2024)*, pages 293–297
November 16, 2024 ©2024 Association for Computational Linguistics

| Precision@5 | EN | AR | ZH | JP | RU | DE | ES | Into X |
|---|---|---|---|---|---|---|---|---|
| EN | - / - | 0.33 / 0.67 | 0.61 / 0.97 | 0.03 / 0.82 | 0.36 / 0.96 | 0.82 / 0.96 | 0.76 / 0.99 | 0.49 / 0.90 |
| AR | 0.12 / 0.23 | - / - | 0.18 / 0.44 | 0.01 / 0.37 | 0.07 / 0.45 | 0.08 / 0.34 | 0.14 / 0.53 | 0.10 / 0.39 |
| ZH | 0.22 / 0.73 | 0.08 / 0.55 | - / - | 0.14 / 0.71 | 0.31 / 0.88 | 0.18 / 0.74 | 0.40 / 0.93 | 0.22 / 0.76 |
| JP | 0.04 / 0.33 | 0.02 / 0.34 | 0.21 / 0.59 | - / - | 0.17 / 0.56 | 0.03 / 0.56 | 0.06 / 0.62 | 0.09 / 0.50 |
| RU | 0.20 / 0.73 | 0.19 / 0.61 | 0.56 / 0.86 | 0.05 / 0.71 | - / - | 0.24 / 0.85 | 0.60 / 0.95 | 0.31 / 0.79 |
| DE | 0.67 / 0.88 | 0.09 / 0.62 | 0.37 / 0.89 | 0.01 / 0.80 | 0.36 / 0.92 | - / - | 0.83 / 0.96 | 0.39 / 0.85 |
| ES | 0.12 / 0.75 | 0.08 / 0.60 | 0.18 / 0.87 | 0.00 / 0.67 | 0.20 / 0.92 | 0.48 / 0.85 | - / - | 0.18 / 0.78 |
| From X | 0.23 / 0.61 | 0.13 / 0.57 | 0.35 / 0.77 | 0.04 / 0.68 | 0.24 / 0.78 | 0.3 / 0.72 | 0.47 / 0.83 | 0.25 / 0.71 |

Table 1: The success rate (Precision@5) for cross-lingual retrieval **before/after** applying Procrustes projection. "From X" and "Into X" denote the average results for each column and row, respectively.

| Precision@5 | EN | AR | ZH | JP | RU | DE | ES | Into X |
|---|---|---|---|---|---|---|---|---|
| EN | - / - | 0.78 / 0.73 | 0.93 / 0.94 | 0.95 / 0.93 | 0.76 / 0.94 | 0.96 / 0.96 | 0.97 / 0.97 | 0.89 / 0.91 |
| AR | 0.67 / 0.67 | - / - | 0.83 / 0.76 | 0.84 / 0.74 | 0.59 / 0.76 | 0.82 / 0.78 | 0.83 / 0.79 | 0.76 / 0.75 |
| ZH | 0.85 / 0.93 | 0.86 / 0.79 | - / - | 0.99 / 0.98 | 0.84 / 0.95 | 0.97 / 0.95 | 0.96 / 0.96 | 0.91 / 0.93 |
| JP | 0.88 / 0.92 | 0.86 / 0.78 | 1.0 / 0.97 | - / - | 0.83 / 0.95 | 0.96 / 0.95 | 0.95 / 0.95 | 0.91 / 0.92 |
| RU | 0.75 / 0.96 | 0.83 / 0.81 | 0.97 / 0.96 | 0.97 / 0.96 | - / - | 0.97 / 0.97 | 0.96 / 0.97 | 0.91 / 0.94 |
| DE | 0.9 / 0.96 | 0.68 / 0.79 | 0.91 / 0.94 | 0.89 / 0.94 | 0.75 / 0.96 | - / - | 0.99 / 0.97 | 0.85 / 0.93 |
| ES | 0.89 / 0.96 | 0.65 / 0.77 | 0.87 / 0.94 | 0.85 / 0.94 | 0.65 / 0.95 | 0.98 / 0.96 | - / - | 0.82 / 0.92 |
| From X | 0.82 / 0.9 | 0.78 / 0.78 | 0.92 / 0.92 | 0.91 / 0.92 | 0.74 / 0.92 | 0.94 / 0.93 | 0.94 / 0.93 | 0.86 / 0.90 |

Table 2: The success rate (Precision@5) for cross-lingual retrieval **before/after** applying Procrustes projection. Note that all embeddings are derived from the prompting template in English, instead of the same language with input sentences.

$W^TW = I$. The solution $W = UV^T$ is derived from the singular value decomposition (SVD) of $BA^T$.

We conduct experiments on seven languages. We train $W$ on translation pairs from NTREX (Federmann et al., 2022) and test on Flores (Goyal et al., 2022), merging 1,997 and 2,009 samples from the *dev* and *test* sets, respectively.

We then compute Precision@k by using embeddings in $WA$ to retrieve those in $B$ and checking if their counterparts are among the $k$-nearest neighbors based on cosine similarity, using this precision to quantify structural similarity in each translation direction.

### 2.3 Representation Discrepancy and Isomorphism

Table 1 shows the success rate of the resulting embeddings in cross-lingual retrieval before/after applying Procrustes projection (§2.2). It is clear that 1) the initial representation discrepancies are generally substantial across languages. 2) However, after properly rotating (applying $W$), representations in most of the directions are well aligned, leading to clear gains from an average of 0.25 to 0.71.

### 2.4 Multilingual Representation via English Prompts

Previous studies show decent improvements can be achieved by simply adjusting/filling non-English instructions into English-centric prompting templates in the inference stage (Etxaniz et al., 2023; Huang et al., 2023). To explain the success, we investigate how the representations of LLMs change when using the prompting template in the predominant language, English, for different languages, rather than the same ones mentioned in §2.1.

Table 2 shows the success rate within the same data setting in §2.3. Notably, the initial representations' degree of alignment is much higher than that in Table 1 (0.86 v.s., 0.25), resulting in a similar alignment level with the latter after rotation. Also, the gain from applying Procrustes projection is marginal in this setting. We interpret the degeneration of the rotation gain as that English prompts, to some extent, have taken on the role of the corresponding spatial transformation, i.e., mapping representations into a shared English space.

## 3 Conclusion

In this extended abstract, we show that LLMs' representations exhibit a high degree of isomorphism across languages, which explains their cross-lingual zero-shot or few-shot capabilities in a multilingual context. Further experiments demonstrate that LLMs' semantic representations can be enhanced across languages through alignment using just 100 translation samples, offering a more efficient and effective approach than sample-level pretraining or instruction tuning.

## Limitations

We conduct experiments exclusively on two families of LLMs, namely LLaMA2 and Tower. Therefore, the generalizability of our findings to other LLMs remains uncertain. Additionally, our semantic analysis is restricted to a few languages.

## References


Eneko Agirre, Carmen Banea, Claire Cardie, Daniel Cer, Mona Diab, Aitor Gonzalez-Agirre, Weiwei Guo, Inigo Lopez-Gazpio, Montse Maritxalar, Rada Mihalcea, et al. 2015. Semeval-2015 task 2: Semantic textual similarity, english, spanish and pilot on interpretability. In *Proceedings of the 9th international workshop on semantic evaluation (SemEval 2015)*, pages 252–263.

Eneko Agirre, Carmen Banea, Daniel Cer, Mona Diab, Aitor Gonzalez Agirre, Rada Mihalcea, German Rigau Claramunt, and Janyce Wiebe. 2016. Semeval-2016 task 1: Semantic textual similarity, monolingual and cross-lingual evaluation. In *SemEval-2016. 10th International Workshop on Semantic Evaluation; 2016 Jun 16-17; San Diego, CA. Stroudsburg (PA): ACL; 2016. p. 497-511*. ACL (Association for Computational Linguistics).

Julen Etxaniz, Gorka Azkune, Aitor Soroa, Oier Lopez de Lacalle, and Mikel Artetxe. 2023. Do multilingual language models think better in english? *arXiv preprint arXiv:2308.01223*.

Christian Federmann, Tom Kocmi, and Ying Xin. 2022. Ntrex-128–news test references for mt evaluation of 128 languages. In *Proceedings of the First Workshop on Scaling Up Multilingual Evaluation*, pages 21–24.

Naman Goyal, Cynthia Gao, Vishrav Chaudhary, Peng-Jen Chen, Guillaume Wenzek, Da Ju, Sanjana Krishnan, Marc'Aurelio Ranzato, Francisco Guzmán, and Angela Fan. 2022. The Flores-101 evaluation benchmark for low-resource and multilingual machine translation. *Transactions of the Association for Computational Linguistics*, 10:522–538.

Haoyang Huang, Tianyi Tang, Dongdong Zhang, Wayne Xin Zhao, Ting Song, Yan Xia, and Furu Wei. 2023. Not all languages are created equal in llms: Improving multilingual capability by cross-lingual-thought prompting. *arXiv preprint arXiv:2305.07004*.

Ting Jiang, Shaohan Huang, Zhongzhi Luan, Deqing Wang, and Fuzhen Zhuang. 2023. Scaling sentence embeddings with large language models. *arXiv preprint arXiv:2307.16645*.

Guillaume Lample, Alexis Conneau, Ludovic Denoyer, and Marc'Aurelio Ranzato. 2017. Unsupervised machine translation using monolingual corpora only. *arXiv preprint arXiv:1711.00043*.

Peter H Schönemann. 1966. A generalized solution of the orthogonal procrustes problem. *Psychometrika*, 31(1):1–10.

Anders Søgaard, Sebastian Ruder, and Ivan Vulić. 2018. On the limitations of unsupervised bilingual dictionary induction. *arXiv preprint arXiv:1805.03620*.

Hugo Touvron, Louis Martin, Kevin Stone, Peter Albert, Amjad Almahairi, Yasmine Babaei, Nikolay Bashlykov, Soumya Batra, Prajjwal Bhargava, Shruti Bhosale, et al. 2023. Llama 2: Open foundation and fine-tuned chat models. *arXiv preprint arXiv:2307.09288*.


## A Appendix

### A.1 Semantic Alignment across Languages on STS tasks

Table 3 shows the multilingual cross-lingual STS results in different settings after contrastive learning on both LLaMA2 and Tower models.

### A.2 Representation Isomorphism with Additional Metrics

We present the results of Precision@1 and Precision@10 on representation isomorphism with LLaMA-7B in Table 4, 5, 6, and 7.

### A.3 Representation Isomorphism with Last Token Pooling-Derived Representations

Table 8 shows the results on representation isomorphism with last token pooling-derived representations of the LLaMA2-7B model.

### A.4 Representation Isomorphism with LLaMA-13B

Table 9 and 10 show the results on representation isomorphism with the LLaMA2-13B model.

| Model | Settings | EN | AR | ES | AR-EN | ES-EN | TR-EN | Avg |
|---|---|---|---|---|---|---|---|---|
| LLaMA2-7B | $self$-prompts | 0.72 | 0.24 | 0.28 | 0.17 | 0.11 | 0.09 | 0.27 |
| LLaMA2-7B | $en$-prompts | 0.72 | 0.46 | 0.46 | 0.36 | 0.27 | 0.12 | 0.40 |
| LLaMA2-7B | $en$-prompts (+100) | 0.76 | 0.62 | 0.73 | 0.52 | 0.64 | 0.42 | 0.62 |
| LLaMA2-7B | $en$-prompts (+1000) | 0.82 | 0.62 | 0.80 | 0.54 | 0.75 | 0.55 | 0.68 |
| Tower-7B | $self$-prompts | 0.69 | 0.25 | 0.41 | 0.14 | 0.15 | 0.08 | 0.29 |
| Tower-7B | $en$-prompts | 0.69 | 0.45 | 0.70 | 0.26 | 0.35 | 0.11 | 0.43 |
| Tower-7B | $en$-prompts (+100) | 0.73 | 0.57 | 0.67 | 0.50 | 0.60 | 0.41 | 0.58 |
| Tower-7B | $en$-prompts (+1000) | 0.76 | 0.60 | 0.65 | 0.54 | 0.62 | 0.47 | 0.61 |

Table 3: The multilingual and cross-lingual STS results in different settings using contrastive learning. $self$-prompts and $en$-prompts denote using prompting methods in §2.1 and §2.4, respectively. Tower continues to pre-train LLaMA2 with large amounts of multilingual data but fails to align semantics. However, aligning LLaMA2 at the representation level using a few translation samples from NTREX (e.g., 100), results in clear improvements from 0.40 to 0.68.

| Precision@1 | EN | AR | ZH | JP | RU | DE | ES | Into X |
|---|---|---|---|---|---|---|---|---|
| EN | - / - | 0.20 / 0.47 | 0.44 / 0.88 | 0.01 / 0.63 | 0.19 / 0.87 | 0.65 / 0.88 | 0.54 / 0.93 | 0.34 / 0.78 |
| AR | 0.06 / 0.09 | - / - | 0.10 / 0.26 | 0.00 / 0.2 | 0.03 / 0.26 | 0.02 / 0.21 | 0.06 / 0.33 | 0.05 / 0.23 |
| ZH | 0.07 / 0.52 | 0.02 / 0.36 | - / - | 0.07 / 0.50 | 0.12 / 0.71 | 0.07 / 0.57 | 0.11 / 0.79 | 0.08 / 0.57 |
| JP | 0.01 / 0.15 | 0.00 / 0.19 | 0.10 / 0.38 | - / - | 0.08 / 0.35 | 0.01 / 0.38 | 0.02 / 0.40 | 0.04 / 0.31 |
| RU | 0.01 / 0.52 | 0.01 / 0.43 | 0.38 / 0.72 | 0.02 / 0.54 | - / - | 0.09 / 0.73 | 0.36 / 0.86 | 0.14 / 0.63 |
| DE | 0.40 / 0.72 | 0.01 / 0.42 | 0.02 / 0.73 | 0.00 / 0.63 | 0.21 / 0.83 | - / - | 0.62 / 0.88 | 0.21 / 0.70 |
| ES | 0.02 / 0.55 | 0.04 / 0.41 | 0.09 / 0.72 | 0.00 / 0.49 | 0.11 / 0.80 | 0.26 / 0.73 | - / - | 0.09 / 0.62 |
| From X | 0.10 / 0.42 | 0.05 / 0.38 | 0.19 / 0.62 | 0.02 / 0.50 | 0.12 / 0.64 | 0.18 / 0.58 | 0.28 / 0.70 | 0.14 / 0.55 |

Table 4: The success rate (Precision@1) for cross-lingual retrieval **before/after** applying Procrustes projection with the **LLaMA2-7B** model. The embeddings in each language are derived from the LLaMA2-7B model using the prompting method as described in §2.1.

| Precision@10 | EN | AR | ZH | JP | RU | DE | ES | Into X |
|---|---|---|---|---|---|---|---|---|
| EN | - / - | 0.40 / 0.73 | 0.67 / 0.98 | 0.05 / 0.88 | 0.44 / 0.98 | 0.86 / 0.97 | 0.82 / 0.99 | 0.54 / 0.92 |
| AR | 0.16 / 0.31 | - / - | 0.24 / 0.51 | 0.02 / 0.45 | 0.12 / 0.54 | 0.12 / 0.41 | 0.19 / 0.62 | 0.14 / 0.47 |
| ZH | 0.30 / 0.80 | 0.16 / 0.62 | - / - | 0.20 / 0.77 | 0.40 / 0.91 | 0.28 / 0.80 | 0.53 / 0.95 | 0.31 / 0.81 |
| JP | 0.06 / 0.41 | 0.06 / 0.42 | 0.28 / 0.69 | - / - | 0.23 / 0.64 | 0.06 / 0.65 | 0.13 / 0.70 | 0.14 / 0.58 |
| RU | 0.27 / 0.80 | 0.27 / 0.68 | 0.63 / 0.90 | 0.08 / 0.76 | - / - | 0.34 / 0.89 | 0.69 / 0.97 | 0.38 / 0.83 |
| DE | 0.78 / 0.92 | 0.16 / 0.69 | 0.46 / 0.92 | 0.04 / 0.84 | 0.43 / 0.95 | - / - | 0.88 / 0.97 | 0.46 / 0.88 |
| ES | 0.24 / 0.82 | 0.10 / 0.67 | 0.24 / 0.90 | 0.02 / 0.73 | 0.27 / 0.94 | 0.56 / 0.89 | - / - | 0.24 / 0.83 |
| From X | 0.30 / 0.68 | 0.19 / 0.64 | 0.42 / 0.82 | 0.07 / 0.74 | 0.32 / 0.83 | 0.37 / 0.77 | 0.54 / 0.87 | 0.32 / 0.76 |

Table 5: The success rate (Precision@10) for cross-lingual retrieval **before/after** applying Procrustes projection with the **LLaMA2-7B** model. The embeddings in each language are derived from the LLaMA2-7B model using the prompting method as described in §2.1.

| Precision@1 | EN | AR | ZH | JP | RU | DE | ES | Into X |
|---|---|---|---|---|---|---|---|---|
| EN | - / - | 0.59 / 0.52 | 0.83 / 0.81 | 0.83 / 0.80 | 0.57 / 0.82 | 0.87 / 0.88 | 0.87 / 0.90 | 0.76 / 0.79 |
| AR | 0.50 / 0.44 | - / - | 0.68 / 0.56 | 0.69 / 0.56 | 0.41 / 0.58 | 0.63 / 0.61 | 0.65 / 0.63 | 0.59 / 0.56 |
| ZH | 0.70 / 0.79 | 0.67 / 0.60 | - / - | 0.96 / 0.92 | 0.68 / 0.86 | 0.89 / 0.87 | 0.80 / 0.88 | 0.78 / 0.82 |
| JP | 0.74 / 0.77 | 0.69 / 0.59 | 0.97 / 0.91 | - / - | 0.67 / 0.85 | 0.87 / 0.85 | 0.81 / 0.86 | 0.79 / 0.81 |
| RU | 0.51 / 0.84 | 0.63 / 0.64 | 0.91 / 0.88 | 0.88 / 0.87 | - / - | 0.88 / 0.93 | 0.86 / 0.91 | 0.78 / 0.85 |
| DE | 0.80 / 0.87 | 0.51 / 0.61 | 0.80 / 0.85 | 0.78 / 0.85 | 0.57 / 0.89 | - / - | 0.95 / 0.92 | 0.73 / 0.83 |
| ES | 0.76 / 0.87 | 0.45 / 0.58 | 0.73 / 0.83 | 0.69 / 0.82 | 0.46 / 0.87 | 0.94 / 0.91 | - / - | 0.67 / 0.81 |
| From X | 0.67 / 0.76 | 0.59 / 0.59 | 0.82 / 0.81 | 0.81 / 0.80 | 0.56 / 0.81 | 0.85 / 0.84 | 0.82 / 0.85 | 0.73 / 0.78 |

Table 6: The success rate (Precision@1) for cross-lingual retrieval **before/after** applying Procrustes projection with the **LLaMA2-7B** model. Note that all embeddings are derived from the prompting template in English as described in §2.4, instead of the same language with input sentences.

| Precision@10 | EN | AR | ZH | JP | RU | DE | ES | Into X |
|---|---|---|---|---|---|---|---|---|
| EN | - / - | 0.83 / 0.80 | 0.95 / 0.96 | 0.97 / 0.95 | 0.80 / 0.96 | 0.98 / 0.97 | 0.98 / 0.98 | 0.92 / 0.94 |
| AR | 0.73 / 0.75 | - / - | 0.88 / 0.81 | 0.89 / 0.80 | 0.66 / 0.82 | 0.87 / 0.84 | 0.87 / 0.84 | 0.82 / 0.81 |
| ZH | 0.89 / 0.95 | 0.90 / 0.84 | - / - | 1.00 / 0.98 | 0.89 / 0.97 | 0.98 / 0.97 | 0.98 / 0.97 | 0.94 / 0.95 |
| JP | 0.91 / 0.94 | 0.90 / 0.83 | 1.00 / 0.98 | - / - | 0.88 / 0.97 | 0.98 / 0.97 | 0.98 / 0.97 | 0.94 / 0.94 |
| RU | 0.80 / 0.97 | 0.88 / 0.86 | 0.98 / 0.97 | 0.98 / 0.97 | - / - | 0.98 / 0.98 | 0.98 / 0.98 | 0.93 / 0.96 |
| DE | 0.93 / 0.97 | 0.74 / 0.84 | 0.94 / 0.96 | 0.92 / 0.96 | 0.79 / 0.97 | - / - | 0.99 / 0.98 | 0.89 / 0.95 |
| ES | 0.92 / 0.97 | 0.71 / 0.82 | 0.90 / 0.96 | 0.88 / 0.96 | 0.72 / 0.96 | 0.99 / 0.97 | - / - | 0.85 / 0.94 |
| From X | 0.86 / 0.92 | 0.83 / 0.83 | 0.94 / 0.94 | 0.94 / 0.94 | 0.79 / 0.94 | 0.96 / 0.95 | 0.96 / 0.95 | 0.90 / 0.93 |

Table 7: The success rate (Precision@10) for cross-lingual retrieval **before/after** applying Procrustes projection with the **LLaMA2-7B** model. Note that all embeddings are derived from the prompting template in English as described in §2.4, instead of the same language with input sentences.

| Precision@5 | EN | AR | ZH | JP | RU | DE | ES | Into X |
|---|---|---|---|---|---|---|---|---|
| EN | - / - | 0.05 / 0.23 | 0.04 / 0.51 | 0.08 / 0.41 | 0.13 / 0.54 | 0.09 / 0.57 | 0.08 / 0.70 | 0.08 / 0.49 |
| AR | 0.03 / 0.07 | - / - | 0.02 / 0.13 | 0.02 / 0.08 | 0.03 / 0.13 | 0.01 / 0.12 | 0.02 / 0.16 | 0.02 / 0.12 |
| ZH | 0.19 / 0.24 | 0.08 / 0.18 | - / - | 0.46 / 0.34 | 0.15 / 0.37 | 0.19 / 0.40 | 0.11 / 0.44 | 0.20 / 0.33 |
| JP | 0.11 / 0.12 | 0.06 / 0.09 | 0.35 / 0.25 | - / - | 0.05 / 0.17 | 0.08 / 0.13 | 0.06 / 0.17 | 0.12 / 0.15 |
| RU | 0.15 / 0.23 | 0.05 / 0.12 | 0.08 / 0.30 | 0.06 / 0.15 | - / - | 0.19 / 0.36 | 0.18 / 0.45 | 0.12 / 0.27 |
| DE | 0.06 / 0.20 | 0.02 / 0.10 | 0.03 / 0.28 | 0.04 / 0.11 | 0.09 / 0.38 | - / - | 0.18 / 0.45 | 0.07 / 0.25 |
| ES | 0.07 / 0.28 | 0.02 / 0.14 | 0.02 / 0.33 | 0.02 / 0.15 | 0.08 / 0.45 | 0.13 / 0.43 | - / - | 0.06 / 0.30 |
| From X | 0.10 / 0.19 | 0.05 / 0.14 | 0.09 / 0.30 | 0.11 / 0.21 | 0.09 / 0.34 | 0.12 / 0.33 | 0.10 / 0.40 | 0.10 / 0.27 |

Table 8: The success rate (Precision@5) for cross-lingual retrieval **before/after** applying Procrustes projection with the **LLaMA2-7B** model. The embeddings are derived by taking the output hidden vector of the last token without prompting (**last token pooling**).

| Precision@5 | EN | AR | ZH | JP | RU | DE | ES | Into X |
|---|---|---|---|---|---|---|---|---|
| EN | - / - | 0.26 / 0.72 | 0.66 / 0.90 | 0.66 / 0.88 | 0.22 / 0.96 | 0.56 / 0.85 | 0.30 / 0.83 | 0.44 / 0.86 |
| AR | 0.02 / 0.37 | - / - | 0.09 / 0.28 | 0.11 / 0.34 | 0.10 / 0.64 | 0.03 / 0.33 | 0.03 / 0.41 | 0.06 / 0.40 |
| ZH | 0.02 / 0.68 | 0.04 / 0.29 | - / - | 0.42 / 0.50 | 0.02 / 0.68 | 0.00 / 0.32 | 0.00 / 0.38 | 0.08 / 0.47 |
| JP | 0.02 / 0.62 | 0.05 / 0.40 | 0.74 / 0.54 | - / - | 0.05 / 0.86 | 0.01 / 0.57 | 0.01 / 0.53 | 0.15 / 0.59 |
| RU | 0.01 / 0.43 | 0.07 / 0.30 | 0.07 / 0.28 | 0.12 / 0.43 | - / - | 0.02 / 0.47 | 0.02 / 0.48 | 0.05 / 0.40 |
| DE | 0.47 / 0.84 | 0.24 / 0.61 | 0.19 / 0.57 | 0.52 / 0.79 | 0.20 / 0.95 | - / - | 0.41 / 0.80 | 0.34 / 0.76 |
| ES | 0.25 / 0.71 | 0.29 / 0.52 | 0.09 / 0.46 | 0.46 / 0.57 | 0.14 / 0.83 | 0.52 / 0.70 | - / - | 0.29 / 0.63 |
| From X | 0.13 / 0.61 | 0.16 / 0.47 | 0.31 / 0.51 | 0.38 / 0.58 | 0.12 / 0.82 | 0.19 / 0.54 | 0.13 / 0.57 | 0.20 / 0.59 |

Table 9: The success rate (Precision@5) for cross-lingual retrieval **before/after** applying Procrustes projection with the **LLaMA2-13B** model. The embeddings in each language are derived from the LLaMA2-13B model using the prompting method as described in §2.1.

| Precision@5 | EN | AR | ZH | JP | RU | DE | ES | Into X |
|---|---|---|---|---|---|---|---|---|
| EN | - / - | 0.89 / 0.82 | 0.90 / 0.94 | 0.89 / 0.93 | 0.77 / 0.94 | 0.99 / 0.98 | 0.98 / 0.98 | 0.90 / 0.93 |
| AR | 0.81 / 0.80 | - / - | 0.82 / 0.86 | 0.86 / 0.85 | 0.78 / 0.85 | 0.94 / 0.88 | 0.94 / 0.88 | 0.86 / 0.85 |
| ZH | 0.59 / 0.95 | 0.89 / 0.88 | - / - | 1.00 / 0.98 | 0.88 / 0.97 | 0.97 / 0.97 | 0.99 / 0.98 | 0.89 / 0.96 |
| JP | 0.69 / 0.94 | 0.91 / 0.87 | 1.00 / 0.99 | - / - | 0.91 / 0.96 | 0.98 / 0.98 | 0.99 / 0.97 | 0.91 / 0.95 |
| RU | 0.44 / 0.95 | 0.94 / 0.89 | 0.94 / 0.98 | 0.95 / 0.97 | - / - | 0.98 / 0.99 | 0.98 / 0.98 | 0.87 / 0.96 |
| DE | 0.98 / 0.98 | 0.94 / 0.90 | 0.94 / 0.98 | 0.94 / 0.97 | 0.91 / 0.98 | - / - | 1.00 / 1.00 | 0.95 / 0.97 |
| ES | 0.95 / 0.97 | 0.93 / 0.88 | 0.90 / 0.97 | 0.91 / 0.96 | 0.86 / 0.97 | 0.99 / 0.98 | - / - | 0.92 / 0.96 |
| From X | 0.74 / 0.93 | 0.92 / 0.87 | 0.92 / 0.95 | 0.93 / 0.94 | 0.85 / 0.94 | 0.97 / 0.96 | 0.98 / 0.96 | 0.90 / 0.94 |

Table 10: The success rate (Precision@5) for cross-lingual retrieval **before/after** applying Procrustes projection with the **LLaMA2-13B** model. Note that all embeddings are derived from the prompting template in English as described in §2.4, instead of the same language with input sentences.

# Generalization Measures for Zero-Shot Cross-Lingual Transfer

**Saksham Bassi**
New York University
sakshambassi@nyu.edu

**Duygu Ataman**
New York University
ataman@nyu.edu

**Kyunghyun Cho**
New York University
kyunghyun.cho@nyu.edu

## Abstract

Building robust and reliable machine learning systems requires models with the capacity to generalize their knowledge to interpret unseen inputs with different characteristics. Traditional language model evaluation tasks lack informative metrics about model generalization, and their applicability in new settings is often measured using task and language-specific downstream performance, which is lacking in many languages and tasks. To address this gap, we explore a set of efficient and reliable measures that could aid in computing more information related to the generalization capability of language models, particularly in cross-lingual zero-shot settings. Our central hypothesis is that the sharpness of a model's loss landscape, i.e., the representation of loss values over its weight space, can indicate its generalization potential, with a flatter landscape suggesting better generalization. We propose a novel and stable algorithm to reliably compute the sharpness of a model optimum, and demonstrate its correlation with successful cross-lingual transfer. [1]

## 1 Introduction

Generalization enables models to use prior knowledge to reasonably respond to previously unseen stimuli. Although traditional machine learning evaluation is performed based on a preselected set of prediction or generation tasks, accuracy on many public benchmarks may often not be sufficient to extensively assess the ability to perform well in new settings. Therefore, a majority of researchers have found it worthwhile to investigate measures that could evaluate the generalization capability of models with properties, such as VC dimension (Vapnik and Chervonenkis, 1971), cross-entropy (Shannon, 1948), complexity (Mohri et al., 2012) or variation in parameters during training (Nagarajan and Kolter, 2019). Among these, recent findings support the smoothness in the loss curvature to correlate best with generalization capability (Chaudhari et al., 2019; Petzka et al., 2021; Kaddour et al., 2022), motivating the development of learning methods that induce smoothness in the learning trajectory such that the model becomes more robust; either through data perturbation (Jiang et al., 2020a; Aghajanyan et al., 2021; Liang et al., 2021; Hua et al., 2021; Park et al., 2022; Zheng et al., 2021; Wang et al., 2021; Huang et al., 2021) or by integrating the measure directly to the optimization objective (Izmailov et al., 2018; Jastrzebski et al., 2021; Cha et al., 2021; Foret et al., 2021; Hu et al., 2022; Zaken et al., 2022; Stickland and Murray, 2021). However it might often not be straightforward to compute such measures in high-dimensional feature space in a stable fashion (Nachum et al., 2024).

As models get larger and cover more languages, the possibility of improving the applicability of NLP systems in many under-resourced languages gets more promising. An essential requirement in studying the dynamics of cross-lingual knowledge transfer is to have an evaluation methodology that can reliably measure the model's capability in generalization of knowledge under different scenarios. There is a common hypothesis that states that a model demonstrating an extended flat optimum area of low loss value surrounding the minimized loss is indicative of better generalization capability. In this work, we study the above hypothesis and present the first study to provide methods that can be used for measuring the cross-lingual generalization capability of language models.

- We pick prominent measures that were previously shown to correlate well with generalization performance (Jiang et al., 2020b), such as the Frobenius distance of the learned parameters after training (Nagarajan and Kolter, 2019), the margin between model predictions

[1] Code: https://anonymous.4open.science/r/strikegen-7288



*Proceedings of the Fourth Workshop on Multilingual Representation Learning (MRL 2024)*, pages 298–309
November 16, 2024 

and true labels (Wei et al., 2018) and sharpness in loss minima to test applicability to zero-shot cross-lingual generalization measurement (Keskar et al., 2017; Foret et al., 2021).

- We also extend the formulation of state-of-the-art sharpness computation methods (Keskar et al., 2017; Foret et al., 2021) to provide a sharpness prediction algorithm such that the optimization of the parameters can converge in a more stable fashion.

## 2 Related work

**Loss-landscape Minima** One of the most promising indicators of generalization capability to date seems to be related to the form of the loss landscape, in particular, the sharpness in the loss curvature. A potential reason for this fallback is traced to stochastic gradient descent (SGD) (Bottou, 2012) methods which often fall into sharp minima of the loss surface (Keskar et al., 2017; Chaudhari et al., 2019; Wang et al., 2021). Although clear conclusions on the relationship between sharpness and generalization performance, such as whether sharper (Dinh et al., 2017) vs. flatter (Li et al., 2018; Keskar et al., 2017) minima would generally yield better generalization, are still due. The main idea behind these methods is that their objective is to explicitly find flat minima, often using stochastic averaging methods (Polyak and Juditsky, 1992; Izmailov et al., 2018), mini-max or sharpness-aware minimization methods, which can be computed by direct formulation based on the Hessian matrix of the loss function (Chaudhari et al., 2019; Petzka et al., 2021) or Monte-Carlo approximations of the minimizer's neighborhood (Foret et al., 2021; Cha et al., 2021).

**Adversarial optimization** Comparison of two approaches finds that for NLP tasks, mini-max methods are more competitive over averaging-based optimization (Kaddour et al., 2022). Jastrzebski et al. (2021) hypothesize that regularizing the trace of the Fisher information matrix amplifies the implicit bias of SGD, which prevents memorization. The Fisher information (Fisher, 1925) measures local curvature, so a smaller trace implies a flatter minimum, which gives the model more freedom to reach an optimum. Instead of explicitly minimizing the values of parameters, Foret et al. (2021) propose minimizing both loss and sharpness while optimizing the parameters such that they lie in neighborhoods with low loss values. Perturbation is an auxiliary objective that encourages the model predictions to be similar in the vicinity of the observed training samples (Englesson and Azizpour, 2021), usually by penalizing the KL-divergence between the probability distribution of the perturbed and normal model. Perturbations can be adversarial inputs (Jiang et al., 2020a) or inputs with Gaussian or uniform noise (Aghajanyan et al., 2021). To improve cross-lingual generalization, translations of the input generated by machine translation systems were used as perturbed input (Wang et al., 2021; Zheng et al., 2021). Other work also has found the benefit of enforcing consistency for perturbations within the model in addition to the input distribution (Liang et al., 2021; Hua et al., 2021).

## 3 Methodology

In this study, we undertake the development of a methodology that could benefit an accurate assessment of the generalization capability of models for the purpose of cross-lingual knowledge transfer into under-resourced languages. This section first presents approaches to improving generalization performance and the selected measures that provide stable results for measuring zero-shot cross-lingual transfer performance.

### 3.1 Sharpness-based Optimization

We chose the following objective functions as fine-tuning methods for a given pre-trained model as a means of comparison since their main purpose is to enhance the generalization and robustness of models. Following the work of Stickland and Murray (2021), as the two most prominent approaches to mini-max optimization, we include Sharpness-Aware Minimization (SAM) (Foret et al., 2021) and regularization with Fisher Information Matrix (FIM) (Jastrzebski et al., 2021) in our evaluation study on cross-lingual generalization.We also include Multi-view Subword Regularization (MVR) as a perturbation-based optimization method (Wang et al., 2021) which induces stochasticity into the shared subword vocabulary across languages for easing cross-lingual transfer.

**SAM** (Foret et al., 2021) works on the principle of a mini-max objective function: $\min_w \max_{\|\epsilon\|_2<\rho} L(w + \epsilon)$, which essentially means the optimizing function tries to minimize the maximum loss value in a given radius in loss landscape. Therefore, SAM states that it tries to seek "parameters lying in uniformly low-loss neighborhoods".

**Fisher Penalty** is defined as explicitly penalizing the trace of the Fisher information matrix (FIM). Jastrzebski et al. (2021), Stickland and Murray (2021) observed penalizing FIM during training correlates to better generalization performance. It can be written mathematically as $\frac{1}{n}\sum_i^n \nabla L(x_i, y_i)$ where $L(x_i, y_i)$ is the loss at the data point $(x_i, y_i)$.

**MVR** (Wang et al., 2021) function on the concept of consistency regularization where the divergence between the model predictions on deterministic and probabilistic segmentation inputs is minimized. The objective function is formulated as

$$\sum_{i=1}^{N}\Big( -\frac{1}{2}\log p(y_i|\hat{x}_i) - \frac{1}{2}\log p(y_i|x_i') \quad (1)$$

$$+ \lambda D(p(y_i|\hat{x}_i) \parallel p(y_i|x_i'))\Big) \quad (2)$$

where the first term is the model loss on *deterministic segmentation* of the $i^{th}$ data sample (most probable segmentation), the second term is the model loss on *probabilistic segmentation* of the $i^{th}$ data sample (random segmentation) and the third term is the KL divergence between these two output predictions. This technique influences the model to be consistent on the predictions of different input types which successively motivates the model to be more adversarially robust.

### 3.2 Generalization Measures

Our study aims to investigate which type and characteristics of methods would best correlate with better performance in generalization, in this case, zero-shot cross-lingual transfer. We are especially interested in confirming the applicability of the flatness hypothesis for cross-lingual generalization. In order to assess whether a flat optimum loss-scape region corresponds to generalization, we essentially break down the experiment to measure two things, flatness, and generalization, such that their correlation can be measured.

Jiang et al. (2020b) conducted an extensive study on image classification tasks using generalization measures such as flatness-based measures (sharpness metrics), margin and norm-based metrics (based on parameter norms and distance from initial weights) to find correlations between measures and model performance which supported the usability of measures. These measures can be useful to explore the capabilities of language models to transfer knowledge from high-resource languages to low-resource ones.

#### Margin

Higher certainty in predicting the correct label leads to a model that is robust to perturbations and unseen examples. Margin is the distinction between model prediction for ground truth label and the next highest prediction probability. We use an average based margin formula defined by Wei et al. (2018) to calculate margin values on the entire test set. Jiang et al. (2020b) observed that the margin was directly proportional to better generalization in the image classification tasks. Margin is

$$\frac{1}{n}\sum_{i}^{n}\Big(f_{y_i}(x_i) - \max_{j\neq y_i} f_j(x_i)\Big)$$

where $x_i$ is the $i^{th}$ input to model, $y_i$ is the ground truth label, $f(.)$ is the model function. A larger value of the margin of a model on a given dataset would mean higher confidence in the model to predict the correct label - including unseen examples (from languages not included in fine-tuning).

#### Sharpness of optimum

In simpler terms, we can define sharpness as the change in the model loss value at two neighboring points in the model weights plane. It can also be loosely interpreted as the inverse of the maximum radius the loss function can sustain a low loss value at the optimum. Sharpness-based measures resulted in the highest correlation with generalization in (Jiang et al., 2020b).

Jiang et al. (2020b) formulates the sharpness to be

$$\phi = \frac{\|W - W_0\|_2^2 \log(2\omega)}{4\alpha^2} + \log\frac{m}{\sigma} + 10$$

such that $\max_{|u_i|\leq\alpha} L(f_{W+u}) < 0.1$, where $\alpha$ is the maximum radius in the model's loss landscape possible, $W$ and $W_0$ are the models finetuned weights and model initial weights respectively, $\omega$ is the number of parameters, $m$ is the total number of observations, $\sigma$ is the standard deviation of Gaussian noise added. In this work, as we are comparing models with the same architecture (considering mBERT only), on the same dataset, we can remove the constants, and simplify the equation further for comparative analysis.

$$\phi = \frac{\|W - W_0\|_2^2}{4\alpha^2}$$

Intuitively, if the radius of the low-loss region in the loss-landscape ($\alpha$) is small, that means the model has a higher loss value near the optimum, which would mean the landscape of the optimum is not flat. We can relate this to resulting in an unstable prediction when having perturbations in either the data or model weights. Jiang et al.'s formula didn't result in stable results for our experimental set-up which might be because the ascent steps taken to optimize the $\alpha$ value resulted in either having a large or a very small final $\alpha$. The values of $\alpha$ occurred at extreme points because the algorithm was using a binary search method and whenever optimal $\alpha$ was not found, the search algorithm stopped with the final $\alpha$ value at either of the extreme points. The correlation results of the above sharpness method are shown in Table 3.

We present an alternative definition (inclined with sharpness measure mentioned in the works of Keskar et al., and Foret et al.), $\phi_{\text{difference}}$ that removes the need to optimize $\alpha$ by calculating the difference between loss values at two points in the optimum region, formulated as

$$\phi_{\text{difference}} = L(f_{W'}) - L(f_W)$$

where $W'$ is $W + \epsilon$ ($\epsilon$ being Gaussian noise) and $W$ is the optimum weight parameters. The details of our definition are in Algorithm 1 and performs calculation at about roughly 5-10 times faster than Jiang et al.'s algorithm for a given batch size of 8.

**Algorithm 1** Difference-based sharpness algorithm

```
w_0 = original_weight
w = w_0 + ε ▷ Small noise added to avoid zero gradient
Δw = ∇L(w)
w' = w + nΔw
p = λ × ||w'||_F                ▷ λ is small like 0.05
if ||w' − w_0|| > p then
    w' = w_0 + (w' − w_0)/||w' − w_0|| · p
end if
φ_difference = L(w') − L(w_0)
```

## 4 Experiments

For comparison, we implement each Sharpness-based optimization as a fine-tuning objective on the multilingual mBERT base variant (`bert-base-multilingual-cased` from huggingface) (Devlin et al., 2019) in addition to mT5 model (`google/mt5-small`) (Xue et al., 2021). We use a linear classification layer of size 768x3 where the output dimension is equal to the number of labels. We adopt a two-step training approach in our experiments. First, we fine-tune the model on the English language part of the XNLI dataset to optimize the model to learn the task specifically in English. Subsequently, we perform a zero-shot transfer of the fine-tuned model on the rest of the 14 languages to facilitate an evaluation of the generalization of models.

### 4.1 Data, Model details, and Settings

For this work, we used the XNLI dataset (Conneau et al., 2018) that includes data samples from the MultiNLI dataset (Williams et al., 2018) and their translated versions in 14 different languages (Arabic "ar", Bulgarian "bg", German "de", Greek "el", Spanish "es", French "fr", Hindi "hi", Russian "ru", Swahili "sw", Thai "th", Turkish "tr", Urdu "ur", Vietnamese "vi", Chinese "zh"). We only train the models on the English ("en") subset of the dataset. We use the data of these 14 languages only for inference and evaluation of the models.

We fine-tune pretrained mBERT models for 15 epochs each with a batch size of 32, with a learning rate of $2 \times 10^{-5}$, and select best checkpoint on validation. The objective function we use for the baseline model with the classification layer is the AdamW optimizer (Loshchilov and Hutter, 2019) with cross-entropy loss, the mBERT+FIM model has an additional loss as Fisher Penalty, the mBERT+SAM model uses the SAM optimizer and mBERT+MVR uses the MVR algorithm for fine-tuning. We use the hyperparameters and code presented in XTREME[2] and MVR codebase[3]. We run the models with 8 random seeds and present the average performance of these models (Figure 6). In Algorithm 1, the amount of Gaussian noise we add to model weights during calculating sharpness is controlled using a scale that we empirically find (among [0.001, 0.005, 0.01, 0.02]) for each model, with $n$ equal to 0.05.

We fine-tuned the MT5 model (`google/mt5-small` using Huggingface's library over 15 epochs. The XNLI dataset was

[2]https://github.com/google-research/xtreme

[3]https://github.com/cindyxinyiwang/multiview-subword-regularization

processed using a function to tokenize inputs, and the optimizer utilized was Adafactor with a learning rate scheduler. Adafactor optimizer's ability to adapt learning rates is helpful with larger models like T5 in multi-lingual settings. We trained the model with a batch size of 8, accumulating gradients over 4 steps.

Additional experiments were run on PAWS-X dataset (Yang et al., 2019) which has 7 languages: German "de", English "en", Spanish "es", French "fr", Japanese "ja", Korean "ko", Chinese "zh". We use similar experimentation of fine-tuning on english and doing a zero-shot transfer on 6 other languages as defined above for this dataset. We used Huggingface's models: mBERT (`bert-base-multilingual-cased`), RoBERTa (`roberta-base`), and XLM (`xlm-mlm-en-2048`) using Adam optimizers.

**Results**

To evaluate how each of the selected measures correlates with cross-lingual generalization, we first compare these measures with held-out test accuracy. In Table 1, we present the correlation coefficients (using `numpy.corrcoef`) of margin vs. accuracy and sharpness vs. accuracy. We notice that having a higher margin is exceptionally correlated to achieving great performance on unseen language data. Hence, we assume the margin to indicate the generalization performance of a given model. Similarly, sharpness captures a noteworthy negative correlation with test performance.

| Model | Correlation with Accuracy | |
|---|---|---|
| | Margin | Sharpness |
| Baseline | 0.801 | -0.845 |
| mBERT+MVR | 0.818 | -0.793 |
| mBERT+SAM | 0.874 | -0.584 |
| mBERT+FIM | 0.954 | -0.671 |
| mT5 + Adafactor | 0.912 | -0.410 |

Table 1: Correlation coefficients between Margin & Test Accuracy, and Sharpness & Test Accuracy on the XNLI dataset.

We notice similar results by extending our similar experimentation to Paraphrase Identification, PAWS-X dataset (Yang et al., 2019) with 3 different models: mBERT (`bert-base-multilingual-cased`), RoBERTa (`roberta-base`) (Liu et al., 2019), and XLM (`xlm-mlm-en-2048`) (CONNEAU and Lample, 2019) and analyze the validity of the flatness hypothesis, i.e. a flat optimum neighborhood would lead to a generalized model. In Figure 1, we confirm the strong relationship between Margin (indicating generalization) and Sharpness (indicating flatness) even when compared across all models and metrics, suggesting flat neighborhoods of model optimum can help in achieving higher margin values which correlate to better generalization. More findings about visualizations are in Appendix A.1.

| Model | Correlation with Accuracy | |
|---|---|---|
| | Margin | Sharpness |
| mBERT | 0.998 | -0.289 |
| RoBERTa | 0.997 | -0.708 |
| XLM-R | 0.995 | -0.622 |

Table 2: Correlation coefficients between Margin and Sharpness with Test Accuracy on the PAWS-X dataset.

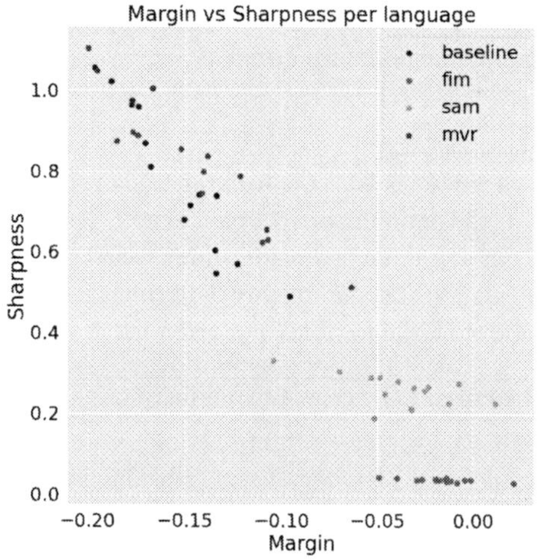


Figure 1: Scatter plot of Margin values and Sharpness ($\phi_{\text{difference}}$) values for each mBERT model (on XNLI dataset) with different objectives language-wise to show the relationship between sharpness and generalization.

We can interpret sharpness as the inverse of flatness, providing us the verdict that flatness of the minimum in which the fine-tuned model is, would help the model perform better on unseen language data. When we evaluate similar models trained with different objectives across languages, we ob-

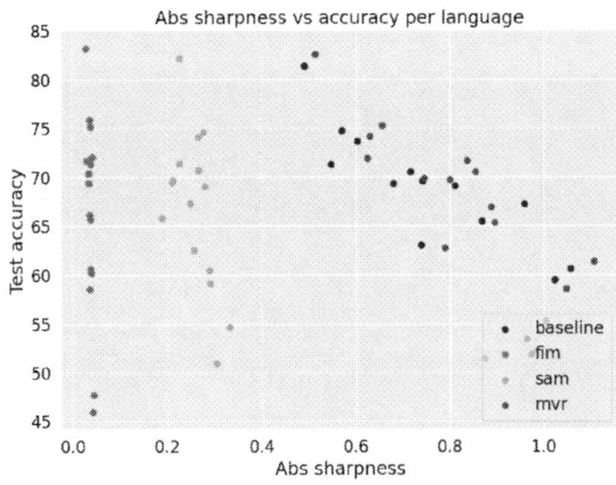


Figure 2: Scatter plot of difference-based sharpness measure with test performance for all models combined.

serve that the relationships between measures are likely dependent on the optimization objective functions used during fine-tuning. In coherence with both Figure 1 and 2, overall, we see that min-max based optimization methods including FIM and SAM, have the lowest sharpness values, compared to the baseline and the regularization method MVR.

In Figure 3, we create scatter plots for mBERT models where in each scatter plot, we plot the model's margin based on the validation set for each language, and we plot the accuracy of that model on the test set on the XNLI dataset. We observe that the margin measure exhibits a consistent correlation with test performance across all the models analyzed.

As can be seen in the scatter plots for sharpness (proposed difference-based sharpness) and accuracy in Figure 4, findings further indicate a negative correlation between sharpness and test performance, suggesting that lower sharpness values are associated with better generalization, represented as model performance on unseen data.

## 5 Conclusion

Enabling cross-lingual knowledge transfer is an important step towards extending the applicability of NLP models to more languages. Despite recent efforts to develop better optimization methods for improving the generalization of language models in new languages or domains; these techniques try different types of methods to achieve higher performance such as sharpness-based minimizations, reducing gradient of loss functions, or consistency regularization. Evaluating these techniques thoroughly without a standardized methodology remains a difficult task. This work aims to uncover insights into how to measure cross-lingual generalization by exploring suitable measures that work well under different settings. Our experiments studying model loss landscape and parameter properties find strong relationships between the margin, sharpness in the loss minima neighborhood, and zero-shot cross-lingual downstream task performance, both on validation and test sets, supporting strong applicability to evaluate models before deploying them in new languages.

## Limitations

The algorithm presented in our paper, the difference-based sharpness measure, is a great novelty for more robust sharpness computation, however, we would like to acknowledge that a few variables in the algorithm still require tuning heuristically, including the noise scale and the multiplication coefficient required to compute the projected radius. Secondly, the mean-based margin distance is only applicable to classification tasks. Due to the limited scope of this project, we leave the development of generalization measures more suitable for generative tasks to future work.

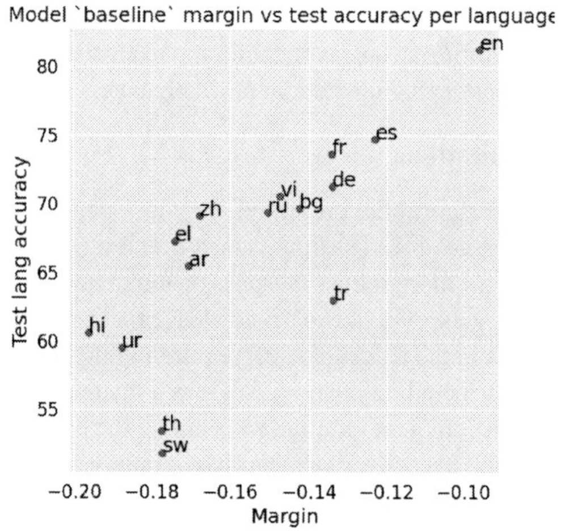


(a) Correlation visualization for Baseline(mBERT + AdamW)

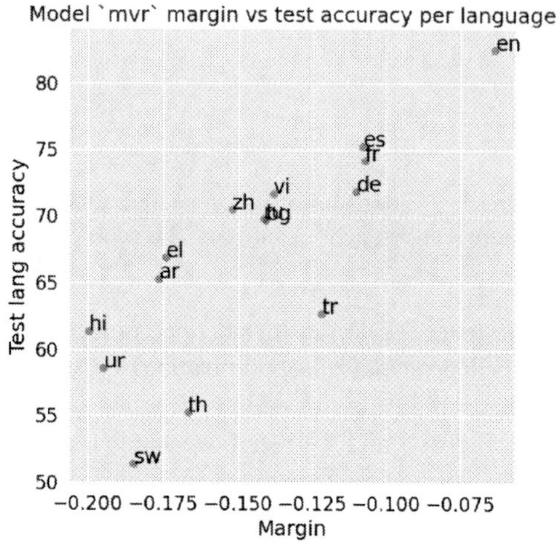


(b) Correlation visualization for mBERT + MVR model

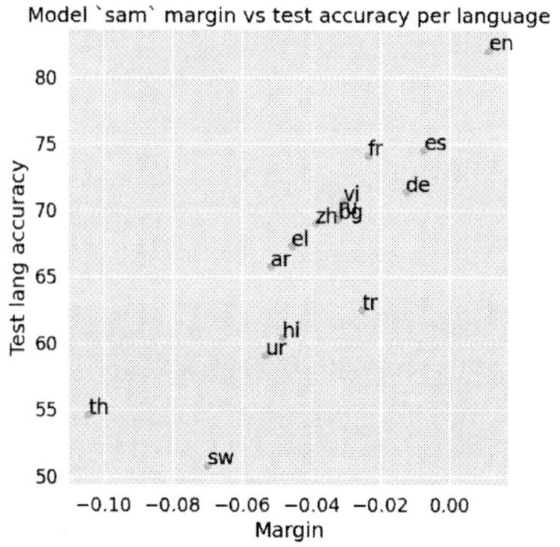


(c) Correlation visualization for mBERT + SAM model

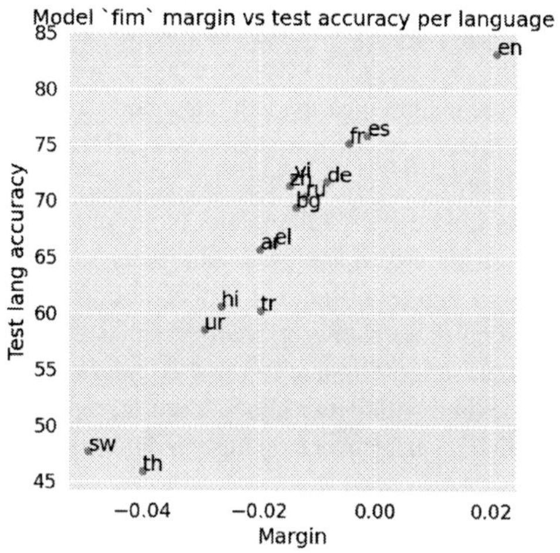


(d) Correlation visualization for mBERT + FIM model

Figure 3: Scatter plots of margin of individual models and their corresponding performance on test set language-wise on XNLI dataset.

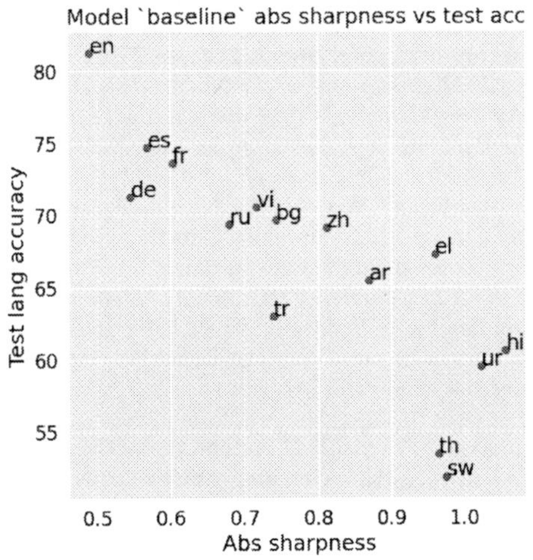


(a) Correlation visualization for Baseline (mBERT + AdamW)

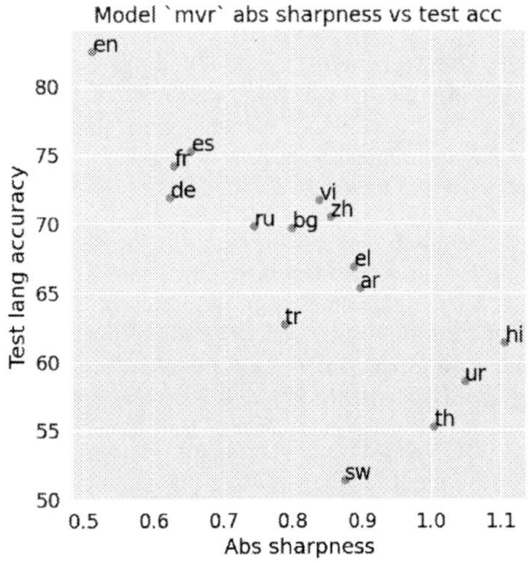


(b) Correlation visualization for mBERT + MVR model

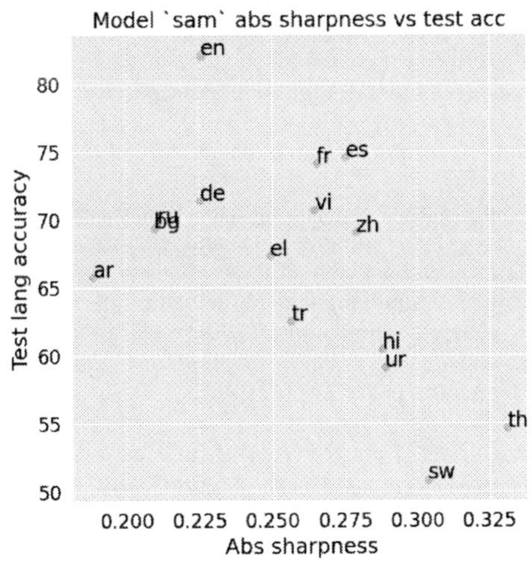


(c) Correlation visualization for mBERT + SAM model

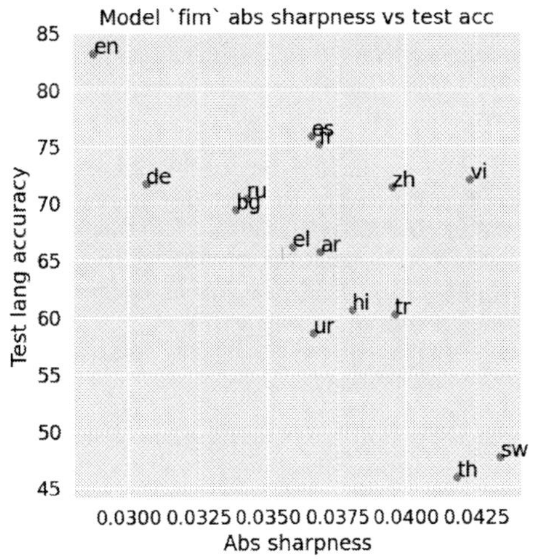


(d) Correlation visualization for mBERT + FIM model

Figure 4: Scatter plots of the proposed difference-based sharpness ($\phi_{\text{difference}}$) of individual models and their corresponding performance on test set language-wise on XNLI Dataset.

## References


Armen Aghajanyan, Akshat Shrivastava, Anchit Gupta, Naman Goyal, Luke Zettlemoyer, and Sonal Gupta. 2021. Better fine-tuning by reducing representational collapse. In *International Conference on Learning Representations*.

Léon Bottou. 2012. Stochastic gradient descent tricks. *Neural Networks: Tricks of the Trade: Second Edition*, pages 421–436.

Junbum Cha, Sanghyuk Chun, Kyungjae Lee, Han-Cheol Cho, Seunghyun Park, Yunsung Lee, and Sungrae Park. 2021. Swad: Domain generalization by seeking flat minima. *Advances in Neural Information Processing Systems*, 34:22405–22418.

Pratik Chaudhari, Anna Choromanska, Stefano Soatto, Yann LeCun, Carlo Baldassi, Christian Borgs, Jennifer Chayes, Levent Sagun, and Riccardo Zecchina. 2019. Entropy-sgd: Biasing gradient descent into wide valleys. *Journal of Statistical Mechanics: Theory and Experiment*, (12):124018.

Alexis CONNEAU and Guillaume Lample. 2019. Cross-lingual language model pretraining. In *Advances in Neural Information Processing Systems*, volume 32. Curran Associates, Inc.

Alexis Conneau, Ruty Rinott, Guillaume Lample, Adina Williams, Samuel R. Bowman, Holger Schwenk, and Veselin Stoyanov. 2018. Xnli: Evaluating cross-lingual sentence representations. In *Proceedings of the 2018 Conference on Empirical Methods in Natural Language Processing*. Association for Computational Linguistics.

Jacob Devlin, Ming-Wei Chang, Kenton Lee, and Kristina Toutanova. 2019. BERT: Pre-training of deep bidirectional transformers for language understanding. In *Proceedings of the 2019 Conference of the North American Chapter of the Association for Computational Linguistics: Human Language Technologies, Volume 1 (Long and Short Papers)*, pages 4171–4186, Minneapolis, Minnesota. Association for Computational Linguistics.

Laurent Dinh, Razvan Pascanu, Samy Bengio, and Yoshua Bengio. 2017. Sharp minima can generalize for deep nets. In *International Conference on Machine Learning*, pages 1019–1028. PMLR.

Erik Englesson and Hossein Azizpour. 2021. Generalized jensen-shannon divergence loss for learning with noisy labels. *Advances in Neural Information Processing Systems*, 34:30284–30297.

Ronald Aylmer Fisher. 1925. Theory of statistical estimation. In *Mathematical proceedings of the Cambridge philosophical society*, volume 22, pages 700–725. Cambridge University Press.

Pierre Foret, Ariel Kleiner, Hossein Mobahi, and Behnam Neyshabur. 2021. Sharpness-aware minimization for efficiently improving generalization. In *International Conference on Learning Representations*.

Edward J Hu, Phillip Wallis, Zeyuan Allen-Zhu, Yuanzhi Li, Shean Wang, Lu Wang, Weizhu Chen, et al. 2022. Lora: Low-rank adaptation of large language models. In *International Conference on Learning Representations*.

Hang Hua, Xingjian Li, Dejing Dou, Chengzhong Xu, and Jiebo Luo. 2021. Noise stability regularization for improving bert fine-tuning. In *Proceedings of the 2021 Conference of the North American Chapter of the Association for Computational Linguistics: Human Language Technologies*, pages 3229–3241.

Kuan-Hao Huang, Wasi Ahmad, Nanyun Peng, and Kai-Wei Chang. 2021. Improving zero-shot cross-lingual transfer learning via robust training. In *Proceedings of the 2021 Conference on Empirical Methods in Natural Language Processing*, pages 1684–1697, Online and Punta Cana, Dominican Republic. Association for Computational Linguistics.

P Izmailov, AG Wilson, D Podoprikhin, D Vetrov, and T Garipov. 2018. Averaging weights leads to wider optima and better generalization. In *34th Conference on Uncertainty in Artificial Intelligence 2018, UAI 2018*, pages 876–885.

Stanislaw Jastrzebski, Devansh Arpit, Oliver Astrand, Giancarlo B Kerg, Huan Wang, Caiming Xiong, Richard Socher, Kyunghyun Cho, and Krzysztof J Geras. 2021. Catastrophic fisher explosion: Early phase fisher matrix impacts generalization. In *Proceedings of the 38th International Conference on Machine Learning*, volume 139 of *Proceedings of Machine Learning Research*, pages 4772–4784. PMLR.

Haoming Jiang, Pengcheng He, Weizhu Chen, Xiaodong Liu, Jianfeng Gao, and Tuo Zhao. 2020a. Smart: Robust and efficient fine-tuning for pre-trained natural language models through principled regularized optimization. In *Proceedings of the 58th Annual Meeting of the Association for Computational Linguistics*, pages 2177–2190.

Yiding Jiang, Behnam Neyshabur, Hossein Mobahi, Dilip Krishnan, and Samy Bengio. 2020b. Fantastic generalization measures and where to find them. In *International Conference on Learning Representations*.

Jean Kaddour, Linqing Liu, Ricardo Silva, and Matt J Kusner. 2022. When do flat minima optimizers work? *Advances in Neural Information Processing Systems*, 35:16577–16595.

Nitish Shirish Keskar, Jorge Nocedal, Ping Tak Peter Tang, Dheevatsa Mudigere, and Mikhail Smelyanskiy. 2017. On large-batch training for deep learning: Generalization gap and sharp minima. In *5th International Conference on Learning Representations, ICLR 2017*.

Hao Li, Zheng Xu, Gavin Taylor, Christoph Studer, and Tom Goldstein. 2018. Visualizing the loss landscape of neural nets. *Advances in neural information processing systems*, 31.

Lijun Liang, Juntao Li, Yue Wang, Qi Meng, Tao Qin, Wei Chen, Min Zhang, Tie-Yan Liu, et al. 2021. R-drop: Regularized dropout for neural networks. *Advances in Neural Information Processing Systems*, 34:10890–10905.

Yinhan Liu, Myle Ott, Naman Goyal, Jingfei Du, Mandar Joshi, Danqi Chen, Omer Levy, Mike Lewis, Luke Zettlemoyer, and Veselin Stoyanov. 2019. Roberta: A robustly optimized BERT pretraining approach. *CoRR*, abs/1907.11692.

Ilya Loshchilov and Frank Hutter. 2019. Decoupled weight decay regularization. In *International Conference on Learning Representations*.

Mehryar Mohri, Afshin Rostamizadeh, and Ameet Talwalkar. 2012. *Foundations of Machine Learning*. The MIT Press.

Ido Nachum, Jonathan Shafer, Thomas Weinberger, and Michael Gastpar. 2024. Fantastic generalization measures are nowhere to be found. In *The Twelfth International Conference on Learning Representations*.

Vaishnavh Nagarajan and J. Zico Kolter. 2019. Generalization in deep networks: The role of distance from initialization. *arXiv:1901.01672 [cs.LG]*.

Jungsoo Park, Gyuwan Kim, and Jaewoo Kang. 2022. Consistency training with virtual adversarial discrete perturbation. In *Proceedings of the 2022 Conference of the North American Chapter of the Association for Computational Linguistics: Human Language Technologies*, pages 5646–5656.

Henning Petzka, Michael Kamp, Linara Adilova, Cristian Sminchisescu, and Mario Boley. 2021. Relative flatness and generalization. *Advances in neural information processing systems*, 34:18420–18432.

Boris T Polyak and Anatoli B Juditsky. 1992. Acceleration of stochastic approximation by averaging. *SIAM journal on control and optimization*, 30(4):838–855.

Claude E Shannon. 1948. A mathematical theory of communication. *The Bell system technical journal*, 27(3):379–423.

Asa Cooper Stickland and Iain Murray. 2021. Regularising fisher information improves cross-lingual generalisation. In *Proceedings of the 1st Workshop on Multilingual Representation Learning*, pages 238–241.

V. N. Vapnik and A. Ya. Chervonenkis. 1971. On the uniform convergence of relative frequencies of events to their probabilities. *Theory of Probability & Its Applications*, 16(2):264–280.

Xinyi Wang, Sebastian Ruder, and Graham Neubig. 2021. Multi-view subword regularization. In *Proceedings of the 2021 Conference of the North American Chapter of the Association for Computational Linguistics: Human Language Technologies*, pages 473–482.

Colin Wei, Jason D. Lee, Qiang Liu, and Tengyu Ma. 2018. On the margin theory of feedforward neural networks. *arXiv:1810.05369 [stat.ML]*.

Adina Williams, Nikita Nangia, and Samuel Bowman. 2018. A broad-coverage challenge corpus for sentence understanding through inference. In *Proceedings of the 2018 Conference of the North American Chapter of the Association for Computational Linguistics: Human Language Technologies, Volume 1 (Long Papers)*, pages 1112–1122. Association for Computational Linguistics.

Linting Xue, Noah Constant, Adam Roberts, Mihir Kale, Rami Al-Rfou, Aditya Siddhant, Aditya Barua, and Colin Raffel. 2021. mT5: A massively multilingual pre-trained text-to-text transformer. In *Proceedings of the 2021 Conference of the North American Chapter of the Association for Computational Linguistics: Human Language Technologies*, pages 483–498, Online. Association for Computational Linguistics.

Yinfei Yang, Yuan Zhang, Chris Tar, and Jason Baldridge. 2019. PAWS-X: A cross-lingual adversarial dataset for paraphrase identification. In *Proceedings of the 2019 Conference on Empirical Methods in Natural Language Processing and the 9th International Joint Conference on Natural Language Processing (EMNLP-IJCNLP)*, pages 3687–3692, Hong Kong, China. Association for Computational Linguistics.

Elad Ben Zaken, Yoav Goldberg, and Shauli Ravfogel. 2022. Bitfit: Simple parameter-efficient fine-tuning for transformer-based masked language-models. In *Proceedings of the 60th Annual Meeting of the Association for Computational Linguistics (Volume 2: Short Papers)*, pages 1–9.

Bo Zheng, Li Dong, Shaohan Huang, Wenhui Wang, Zewen Chi, Saksham Singhal, Wanxiang Che, Ting Liu, Xia Song, and Furu Wei. 2021. Consistency regularization for cross-lingual fine-tuning. In *Proceedings of the 59th Annual Meeting of the Association for Computational Linguistics and the 11th International Joint Conference on Natural Language Processing (Volume 1: Long Papers)*, pages 3403–3417.

# A Appendix

## A.1 Visualization results

Previous work (Nagarajan and Kolter, 2019; Jiang et al., 2020b) suggests that a lower Frobenius distance from initialization would lead to better generalization. As Figure 5 shows, we fail to observe a strong direct relationship between generalization and Frobenius distance from initialization. However, the model trained with Fisher Penalty as an additional objective function that has a high distance from initialization overall performed poorly than others. We also see that models trained with Fisher Penalty, SAM, and MVR optimizers tend to be more stable than the baseline model, with Fisher Penalty resulting in the most stable model when trained multiple times (with different seeds, see Figure 6), and SAM achieving generally the best average zero-shot task accuracy.

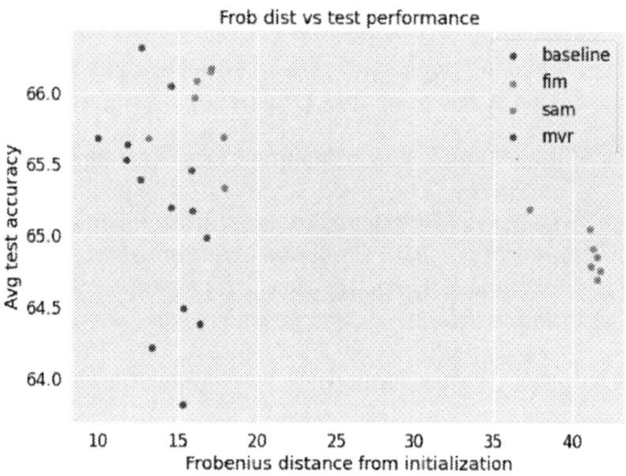


Figure 5: Scatter plot of Frobenius distance from initialization and Test accuracy for each model type (trained multiple times independenty).

## A.2 Additional experiments

To compare all models together, using the difference-based sharpness measure, on language-wise performance, we observe it is dependent on the learning algorithms used during training in Figure 2.

We used the Jiang et al.'s $\alpha$-based sharpness algorithm for the experiment and optimized the threshold loss values for our experimental setting. The results of the correlation coefficient (using `numpy.corrcoef`) for $\alpha$-based sharpness and test accuracy are shown in Table 3 and Figure 7. We notice that $\alpha$-based sharpness values occur at extreme points (for example, for mBERT+FIM model, sharpness values are low whereas for the

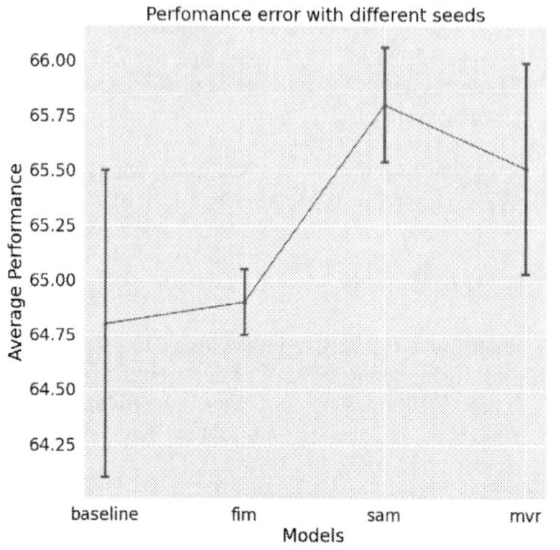


Figure 6: Average test performance (and deviations) of models when trained multiple times with different seeds.

| Model | Correlation coefficient of $\alpha$-sharpness with accuracy |
|---|---|
| Baseline | 0.249 |
| mBERT+MVR | -0.471 |
| mBERT+SAM | -0.166 |
| mBERT+FIM | -0.440 |

Table 3: Correlation coefficients between $\alpha$-sharpness (Jiang et al., 2020b) & Test Accuracy on the XNLI dataset.

Baseline or mBERT+MVR model, sharpness values are much larger). Apart from being a computationally expensive algorithm, we failed to see a strong relationship of $\alpha$-based sharpness with performance in Baseline and mBERT+SAM models.

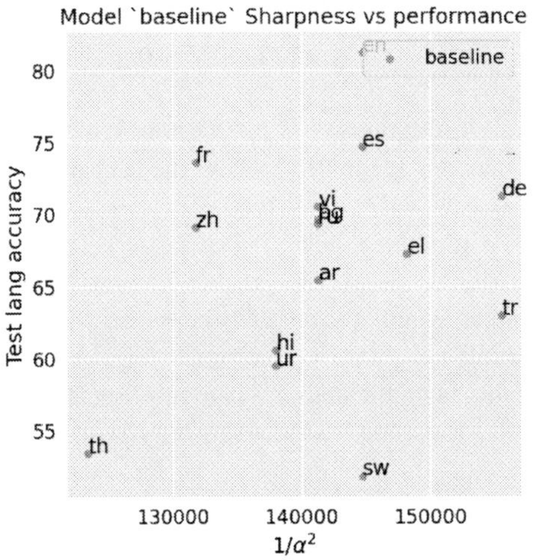


(a) Correlation visualization for Baseline (mBERT + AdamW)

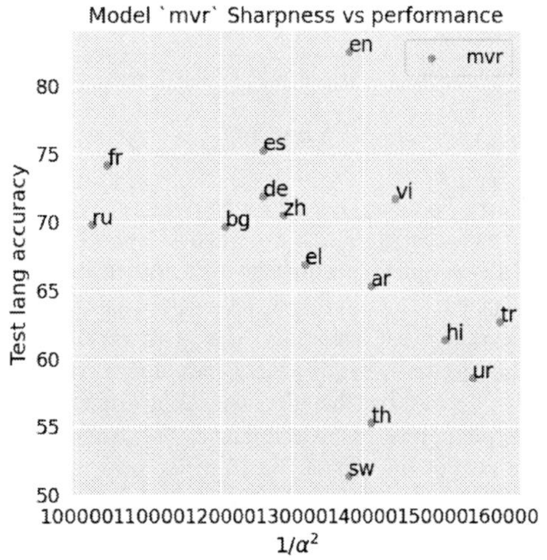


(b) Correlation visualization for mBERT + MVR model

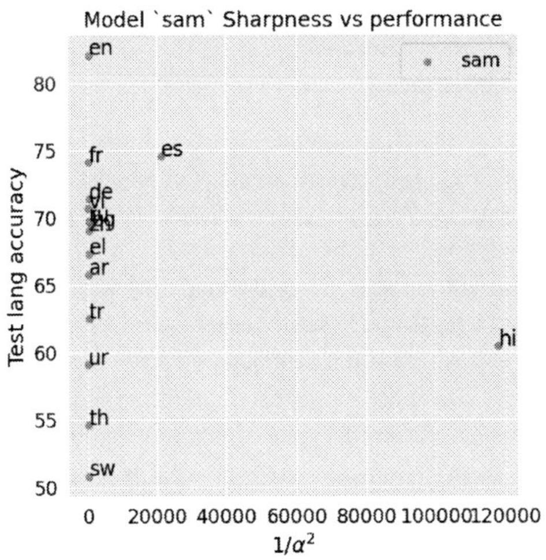


(c) Correlation visualization for mBERT + SAM model

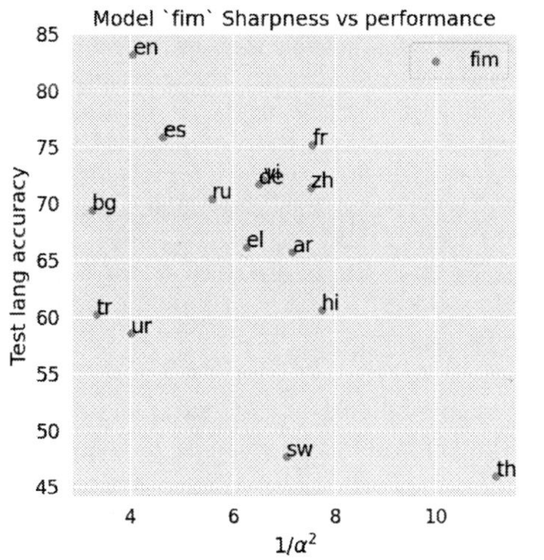


(d) Correlation visualization for mBERT + FIM model

Figure 7: Scatter plots of Jiang et al. (2020b) based $\alpha$-sharpness measure (we are only considering $\frac{1}{\alpha^2}$ here) of individual models and their corresponding performance on test set language-wise.

# Detecting and Translating Language Ambiguity with Multilingual LLMs

**Behrang Mehrparvar**
University of Amsterdam
behrang.mehrparvar@student.uva.nl

**Sandro Pezzelle**
ILLC
University of Amsterdam
s.pezzelle@uva.nl

## Abstract

Most languages could be ambiguous, which means the same conveyed text or speech, results in different actions by different readers or listeners. In this project, we propose a method to detect the ambiguity of a sentence using translation by multilingual LLMs. In particular, we hypothesize that a good machine translator should preserve the ambiguity of sentences in all target languages. Therefore, we investigate whether ambiguity is encoded in the hidden representation of a translation model or, instead, if only a single meaning is encoded. In our experiments, we have been able to predict the ambiguity of sentences with high accuracy using machine translation without direct use of semantics and only based on the reconstruction error of a function that maps the forward and backward translation hidden representations to each other. The potential applications of the proposed approach span i) detecting ambiguous sentences, ii) fine-tuning existing multilingual LLMs to preserve ambiguous information, and iii) developing AI systems that can generate ambiguity-free languages when needed.

## 1 Introduction

Language ambiguity is defined as the potential of different actions as a response to a single text by different people, based on their interpretations (Ceccato et al., 2004). This definition aligns with the semantic, syntactic, pragmatic tests along with identity tests defined in (Zwicky and Sadock, 1975) to identify ambiguous sentences.

Several research studies have been focusing on the ambiguity of language. For a comprehensive review on resolving ambiguities in NLP, refer to (Yadav et al., 2021). (Wang, 2011) have studied lexical and syntactic ambiguity in the Korean language. They proposed adding new words as a solution for lexical and syntactic ambiguities. (Ceccato et al., 2004) proposed a prototype for an ambiguity identification tool. They defined sentence ambiguity of a sentence, as a function of number of senses of each word in that sentence. Furthermore, Yadav et al. (2021) have proposed a comprehensive taxonomy of different types of language ambiguities.

| Ambiguous | Disambiguation |
|---|---|
| "Give me the bat!" (Lexical) | "Give me the baton!" |
| "The professor said on Monday he would give an exam" (Syntactic) | "The professor said that on coming Monday he would give an exam" |
| "Jane saw the man with a telescope" (Semantic) | "Jane saw the man by using a telescope" |
| "I like you too!" (Pragmatic) | "I like you too like others do!" |
| "The prof said she would give us all A's." (Vagueness) | "The prof said the TA would give us all A's." |
| "Proposal" to "voorstel" and "aanzoek" (Translational) | "Research proposal" |

Table 1: Various types of language ambiguity (Yadav et al., 2021) and their disambiguated versions.

In many languages including English, sentences do not always correspond to a unique set of possible behaviors and actions by different readers/listeners, which as we define, leads to language ambiguity. Table 1 lists different types of language ambiguities based on (Yadav et al., 2021), including examples and their disambiguated versions.

Language ambiguity brings up misunderstandings and conflicts in real-world interactions such as political, commercial, and cultural interactions (Bowe et al. (2014), Bachmann-Medick (1996)). This misunderstanding can lead to either wasting of huge amount of time in negotiation between the



*Proceedings of the Fourth Workshop on Multilingual Representation Learning (MRL 2024)*, pages 310–323
November 16, 2024 ©2024 Association for Computational Linguistics

parties for conflict resolution or even in the worst case results in conflicting actions (Kimmel (2006)). By using the powerful tools in NLU and NLP using language models, it could be possible to solve these issues.

The main research questions being investigated in this project are:

**Question 1:** *Do state-of-the-art Transformer-based MT models properly encode whether a sentence in the source language is (non-) ambiguous?*

**Question 2:** *Are both semantic validity and ambiguity preserved by the translation of these models, when the sentence is translated into a target language, and then translated back?*

**Question 3:** *Can we predict the ambiguity of a sentence by translating it into another language looking at the learned hidden representations?*

The main contribution of this work is proposing a solution that detects ambiguous sentences in different typos, without direct use of semantics. Furthermore, through our experiments, we conclude that ambiguity of the sentences are preserved in the hidden representation of the multilingual LLM translation model.

## 2 Related work

Before explaining the proposed approach, we review the related literature, consisting of ambiguity in NLP, ambiguity in machine translation, and an overview of multilingual LLMs.

### 2.1 Ambiguity in machine translation

Language ambiguity is a key aspect explored in machine translation (Baker et al. (1994), Jaspaert (1984)).

With the goal of disambiguation in translation, in Baker et al. (1994), the authors propose a source language analyzer component in their machine translation system that incorporates a controlled lexicon, a controlled grammar, and a semantic domain model.

One of the key points in dealing with ambiguity in translation is choosing the representation of the ambiguous sentence. The way we represent the sentence, directly influences the method we propose to detect ambiguity and/or disambiguate the sentence. Emele and Dorna (1998) suggest using a form of hierarchical recursive representation similar to a syntactic tree, to preserve the ambiguities between source and target language. In cases where the target language cannot preserve the ambiguity, the authors propose local disambiguation by asking the human user to specify the correct intention of the source sentence. In Boguslavsky et al. (2005), the authors propose a rule-based machine translation system that use a morphological structure and dependency tree structure to interactively disambiguate sentences.

Apart from syntactic structures, lexical representation of sentences is also crucial in disambiguation. In Sammer et al. (2006), the authors propose using human assistance in lexical ambiguity resolution in machine translation. They develop a system composed of a controlled language lexicon composed of words, word senses, their translations, and a short, intuitive gloss or set of clue words to help the user select the correct word sense during interaction with the machine translation system. Měchura (2022) investigates gender, number, and formality ambiguities in translation. In these cases, according to the paper, the machine translator either decided on a random or statistically biased translation which requires to ask the human the right questions to disambiguate the text manually.

Unlike Baker et al. (1994), our method is not rule-based and hard-coded which results in a more flexible ambiguity detection method. Also, contrary to Sammer et al. (2006), we do not require a predefined lexicon for detecting ambiguous words. Unlike Emele and Dorna (1998) and Boguslavsky et al. (2005),our approach however represents the sentences in forms of vector representations in the LLM but still do not directly rely on these representations in detecting ambiguity.

In this project, we do not provide direct solutions for disambiguation. As of future work, similar to Měchura (2022), our method can be considered as a human-assisted machine translation (HAMT) solution defined in Alzeebaree (2020) which the user is asked to disambiguate detected ambiguous sentences in the input text. Also, the machine translation model we use is trained based on the interlingua approach.

### 2.2 Ambiguity in the Era of LLMs

Language ambiguity, as a subset of semantic underspecification (Egg, 2010) which is introduced as the possibility for a linguistic signal to convey only part of the information needed for communication to succeed ((Hada et al., 2023)).

Liu et al. (2023) have proposed a benchmark for evaluating pre-trained language models to recognize ambiguity and disentangle possible meanings. They capture the ambiguity of the sentences through their entailment relations with other sentences. They have covered different ambiguity types including pragmatic, lexical, syntactic, scopal, coreference, figurative, and other ambiguities. Based on their benchmark, they realized that disambiguation of sentences using state-of-the-art LLMs is still very challenging.

More recently, in Wildenburg et al. (2024), the authors use perplexity measures to identify underspecified sentences from the pairs in their proposed DUST dataset. Based on Egg (2010), they define four types of underspecified sentences.

In (Pezzelle, 2023) the author has investigated how multi-modal models deal with semantic underspecification and how communicative approaches would provide solutions to this type of task. In Hutchinson et al. (2022), the authors also investigated semantic underspecification in text used to generate images. They studied a taxonomy of the family of multi-modal tasks and provided a list of risks and concerns regarding ambiguity in multimodal text and image tasks.

Our work builds on this previous research investigating how LLMs deal with ambiguity. However, we make a step further, and consider how ambiguity is represented by current models across various languages. To the best of our knowledge, ours is the first work studying ambiguity in multilingual LLMs.

### 2.3 Multilingual Large Language Models

With the advent of Transformer-based language models, multilingual models have been proposed. These models are trained with data from many languages and can perform machine translation among many other NLP tasks with higher performance, compared to traditional approaches (Liu et al. (2024), Liao et al. (2024)).

As multilingual LLMs are trained on data from multiple languages, the mechanism of how these models perform certain tasks has been recently studied. Knowing the internal mechanism could provide us insight into the ambiguity encoded in the representation of the hidden layers of the LLM.

Choenni et al. (2023) have studied how individual languages in multilingual LLMs benefit from each other as in cross-lingual sharing at the data level. They found that multilingual LLMs rely on data from multiple languages during fine-tuning which can be useful in real-world translation models. Furthermore, in Zhang et al. (2023), the authors studied how knowledge transfer happens in multilingual LLMs during translation while limited multilingual training data leads to advanced multilingual capabilities. According to their finding, LLMs struggle to provide accurate results in translation-variant tasks. Liu et al. (2024) have studied the connections of multilingual activation patterns in LLMs at the level of language families. Similar to Tang et al. (2024), they have discovered (non-)language-specific neurons in the LLMs which capture meanings, regardless of specific target language.

Finally, Zhao et al. (2024) have studied the representation of multilingual LLMs across the layers of the model and realized that the first layers understand the questions by converting the multilingual input to English, the intermediate layers perform problem-solving, mainly in English, and in the last layers, the models generate the response according to the original language. Knowing the outcome of their results in finding the responsibility of different layers of multilingual LLMs could help us choose the representation of the right layer for our experiments.

In Qi et al. (2023), the authors study the cross-lingual consistency of factual knowledge and propose a metric to evaluate knowledge consistency across languages independently from accuracy. Tanwar et al. (2023) study cross-lingual in-context learning.

Finally, Zhu et al. (2023), (Zhu et al., 2024) and Gao et al. (2024) have studied multilingual machine translation in LLMs. Through their approach, they where able to improve zero-shot translation performance by learning language-agnostic representations in the multilingual LLMs.

## 3 Proposed method

In this project, we aim at testing how language ambiguity is represented in multilingual LLMs. We propose language translation as an action performed by LLM agents. Accordingly, we propose a four-step approach in detecting language ambiguity, as illustrated in figure 1:

1. **Translation**: Translate the input text from the source language into the target languages using a multilingual LLM. Then extract the hidden representation from the LLM.

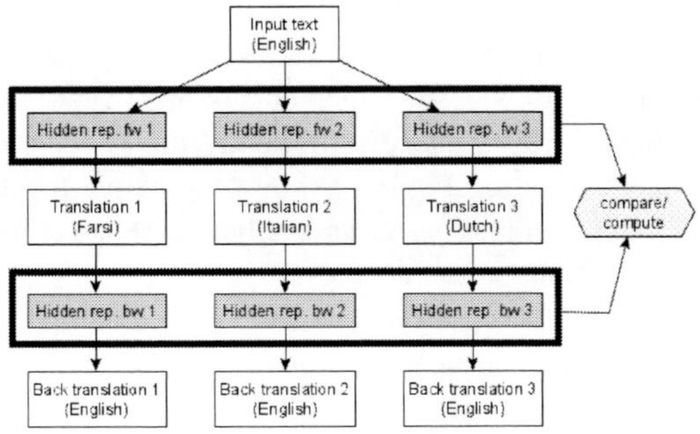


Figure 1: Proposed approach in language ambiguity detection using LLM translation consisting of four steps: 1) translating the text into the target languages, 2) translating back the new texts into the source language, 3) comparing the pairwise representations, 4) computing the overall measure of ambiguity.

2. **Back-translation**: Translate back the output texts of the first step from the target language into the source language using the same LLM. Then extract the hidden representation of the state of the LLM as a vector.

3. **Mapping function**: Compute a function that maps the two representations above. Note that due to the both complexity of the LLM and also various types of information stored in the representations such as semantics, syntax, language information, etc., we do not expect an identity function to be able to map the representations, even in case of unambiguous sentences.

4. **Ambiguity evaluation**: Compute an overall measure of ambiguity based on the properties of the mapping function. We hypothesize that the mapping function learns high-level feature encoding how ambiguous a sentence is, independently of its meaning. Therefore, we can use features of this mapping function to quantify how much ambiguity was preserved in the translation and back-translation.

Considering $n$ different meanings for input text $t_A$ and $m$ different interpretations of the output text $t_B$, in the worst case we would have $n \times m$ different translation meaning pairs, which complicates the problem of ambiguity in translation. As it has been noted in section 4.3, the translation process by itself can be a source of ambiguity.

The LLM works as a function $f(.)$ defined in equation (1):

$$r \mapsto f(t, l_s, l_t) \quad (1)$$

where $t$ is the input text, $l_s$ is the source language, $l_t$ is the target language, and $r$ is the vector representation of the hidden state of the LLM. By applying the translation function $f(.)$ in steps 1 and 2 listed above, the representation vectors can be found as in equation (2):

$$\begin{aligned} r_A &= f(t_A, l_1, l_2) \\ r_B &= f(t_B, l_2, l_1) \end{aligned} \quad (2)$$

where $t_A$ is the input text and $t_B$ is the generated output text from the translation using the LLM in step 1.

The hidden representation $r$ consists of a distributed representation of multiple factors, not only including the semantics (Bau (2022), Zhang (2024)) and it is not easy to simply disentangle these factors and manually extract the representation of the input text $t$ from the representation $r$. Also as the representation $r$ contains factors such as the information about the source and target language, the translation task, etc., we can not directly compare the two representations $r_A$ and $r_B$ to detect ambiguity in the text. Therefore we propose a different approach in detecting ambiguity.

In the first step, we define a function $g(.)$ that maps the two representations to each other as illustrated in equation (3):

$$r_B = g(r_A) \quad (3)$$

where $r_A$ and $r_B$ are the representations found from equation (2) and $g(.)$ is the mapping function.

To find the function $g(.)$, we learn a simple auto-encoder with a single hidden layer of size $s_H$, input size of $s_A$ and output size of $s_B$. Note that as the translation in steps 1 and 2 are both performed using the same LLM, we have $s_A = s_B$.

The auto-encoder maps the input translation representation $r_A$ to the output translation representation $r_B$. The error of the network implementing $g(.)$ is defined as the normalized mean squared error (NMSE) of the elements of the two representations $r_A$ and $r_B$ (the actual equations can be found in the Appendix A).

We define the function $c(.)$ as complexity of the function $g(.)$ as follows:

$$c(g) = s_H / s_A \quad (4)$$

where $s_H$ and $s_A$ are the sizes (number of neurons) in the hidden layer $H$ and input $r_A$ of the neural network implementing the $g(.)$ function.

By learning function $g(.)$, for each text $t_A$ in the input dataset, we can evaluate the translation error $e(.)$ for each setting of the network complexity $c(.)$ with different hidden layer sizes. Figure 2 reports the error of the function against its complexity.

The main idea for using an auto-encoder is based on the assumption that: (1) We expect the auto-encoder will behave differently for ambiguous vs unambiguous sentences; (2) in particular, we conjecture that model size and the target language will affect differently the model when dealing with ambiguous vs unambiguous sentences.

We propose using a simple neural network model to predict ambiguity using the data points in the elbow chart in figure 2 as input in a supervised manner.

### 3.1 Experiments

The Dataset of semantically Underspecified Sentences by Type (DUST)[1] contains a balanced number of ambiguous and unambiguous English sentences. We use a multi-language translation model such as Facebook M2M100[2] (Fan et al., 2020) to translate each sentence from English to other possible languages and translate them back to English. The model is trained on any pairs of 100 languages in a supervised manner with 15.4B parameters has resulted a high performance compared to English-Centric approaches. The pairs of sentences are selected from different sources mentioned in (Fan et al., 2020). The scope of the paper is to study ambiguity detection in LLM translation for the first time, therefore we chose one model not necessarily the state-of-the-art. Therefore, future work should indeed compare various models. We consider German, Greek, Persian, Spanish, French, Hindi, Italian, Korean, Dutch, Russian, Turkish, Croatian, Romanian and Chinese as our target languages. After translation, we extract the hidden states of the LLM for the two translation steps as defined in equation (5):

$$T_A = \{t_A^j\}, R_A = \{r_A^j\}, R_B = \{r_B^j\} \quad (5)$$

[1] https://github.com/frank-wildenburg/DUST

[2] https://huggingface.co/facebook/m2m100_418M

After learning the network for the function $g(.)$, we feed all the $r_A$'s to the network and capture the outputs $r'_B$'s. Using equations (4) and (6), we find the complexity and error for each sample and each network size. Figure 2 shows the elbow for the mapping functions of an ambiguous sentence and its unambiguous version.

For classification, we used either a neural network or a logistic regression model. Further details about the classification experiments are explained in section 4.2.

#### 3.1.1 Qualitative Analysis

As an analysis of the experiment before, for the misclassified samples, the two authors of the paper, who are proficient in two languages (Farsi and Italian) out of the set reported above, verified if the corresponding sentence in the target language is (A) semantically valid and (B) (non-)ambiguous. Semantic validity is verified by asking the human user whether the sentence is correctly translated, and ambiguity is verified by asking whether the translated sentence is (still) ambiguous or not.

### 3.2 Evaluation

We translate ambiguous and unambiguous English sentences to the languages listed above and investigate whether the meaning has changed through analysis of the hidden states of the multilingual LLMs.

Based on our evaluation protocol, if we obtain high accuracy in predicting the ambiguity of ambiguous sentences, we can conclude that the model is able to properly encode ambiguity in its hidden representations (research question 1). Furthermore, the high accuracy shows that predicting ambiguity using multilingual LLM translation models is possible (research question 3).

Human error analysis will help us shed light on the research question 2.

## 4 Results

In this section, we provide the results of our experiments.

### 4.1 Discriminability

In the first step of our analysis, we examined the discriminability of reconstruction error of the best auto-encoder per each language in predicting ambiguity of the sentences. Figure 5 illustrates the distribution of reconstruction error along languages for

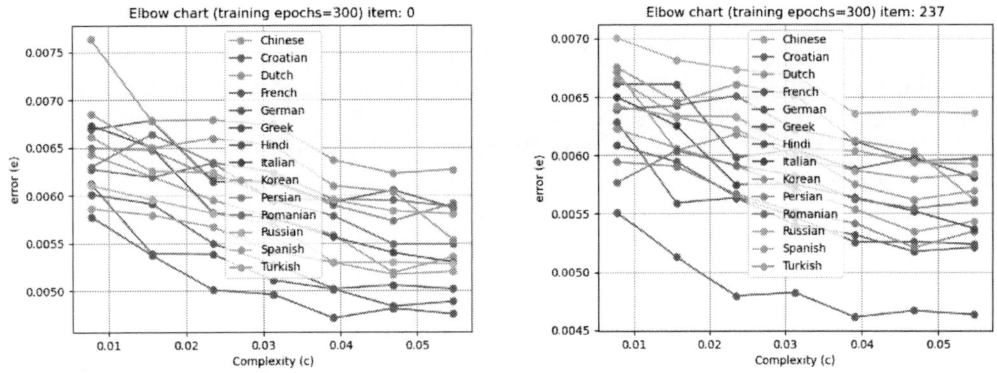


(a) "Andrei picked up the chair or the bag and the telescope" (ambiguous)

(b) "Andrei picked up the chair, or both the bag and the telescope" (unambiguous)

Figure 2: Illustration of the mapping function for an ambiguous sentence and its unambiguous version.

| Language | t-test | p-value |
|---|---|---|
| German | -0.341 | 0.33 |
| Greek | 0.510 | 0.610 |
| Persian | -1.95 | 0.051 |
| Spanish | -0.087 | 0.931 |
| French | -1.072 | 0.285 |
| Hindi | 1.828 | 0.069 |
| Italian | -0.821 | 0.413 |
| Korean | 1.864 | 0.063 |
| **Dutch** | -2.253 | **0.025** |
| Russian | -0.905 | 0.366 |
| Turkish | -1.557 | 0.121 |
| Croatian | -1.034 | 0.452 |
| Romanian | -1.594 | 0.112 |
| **Chinese** | -3.307 | **0.001** |

Table 2: T-test statistics indicating discriminability of reconstruction error of best auto-encoder for ambiguity. We test significance at $pvalue < 0.05$.

each class. To evaluate the discriminability, we performed t-test statistics by verifying pseudo-normal distribution of data. The detailed results are listed in table 2.

Based on the t-test results, we can conclude that mean reconstruction errors for separate target languages are not informative enough to discriminate ambiguous and unambiguous sentences, except for a limited number of languages.

### 4.2 Classification

To determine the most informative variables for classification, we performed several experiments, each including a different setting composed of the options listed in Appendix B.

Table 3 shows the results of classification in all experiment settings. The detailed analysis of the findings for these experiments is provided in section 5.

### 4.3 Source of Ambiguity

After classifying the data, we investigated the source of misclassification using annotation for the Italian and Persian languages. Accordingly, we found both machine translation and also the incapability of the target language itself in preserving the ambiguity, as the sources of misclassification. We only performed a preliminary and arguably limited annotation, but in future work we chould recruit many more participants and conduct a much larger-scale human analysis. Figure 3 illustrates these results.

From the misclassified sentences (examples shown in table 6), considering two target languages (Italian and Persian) we found the following outcomes:

- Ambiguity was lost in 44.68% of the Italian and 51.02% of the Persian target sentences (out of misclassified ambiguous sentences).

- From the misclassified sentences that the ambiguity was lost, in the Italian target language, 85.71% of the loss was because of the translation model and the sentence could be written in an ambiguous sense by a native human. However, none of the loss of ambiguity was because of the translation in the Persian target language and the native Persian human was

| Input | Input variable | Output | Model | Accuracy | F-Measure |
|---|---|---|---|---|---|
| Persian | Differences | Amb. Vs unamb. | LR | 57.81% | 0.578 |
| Best AE | Values | Amb. Vs unamb. | LR | 66.67% | 0.667 |
| Along languages | Differences | Amb. Vs unamb. | LR | 85.87% | 0.859 |
| Whole | Differences | Amb. Type | LR | 92.83% | 0.928 |
| Whole | Differences | Amb. Vs unamb. | LR | 88.19% | 0.882 |
| Best AE | Values | Amb. Vs unamb. | NN | 73.21% | 0.732 |
| Whole | Values | Amb. Vs unamb. | NN | 81.99% | 0.820 |
| Whole | Values | Amb. Type | NN | 78.26% | - |
| Whole | Differences | Amb. Type | NN | 93.04% | 0.925 |
| Whole | Differences | Amb. Vs unamb. | NN | 94.94% | 0.949 |

Table 3: Classification results for different settings. For classifying ambiguous vs unambiguous sentences the chance level accuracy is 50.0% and for ambiguity type it is 36.58%

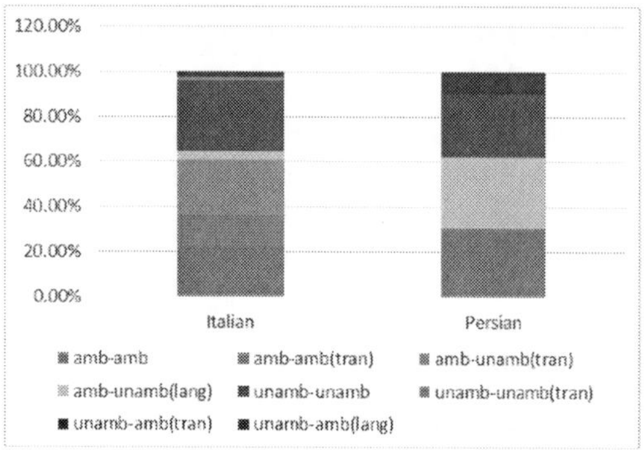


Figure 3: Misclassified samples distribution - format: source-target(problem): *amb*: ambiguous, *unamb*: unambiguous, *tran*: source of misclassification is wrong machine translation, *lang*: source of misclassification is target language incapability in transferring ambiguity.

also unable to translate the ambiguity into the target language due to the innate difference between English and Persian languages.

- From the unambiguous misclassified sentences, in 7.69% of the cases, ambiguity was introduced in Italian translation, none of which was because of wrong translation by the machine, but because of the innate difference between the target language and English. This percentage increases in Persian to 26.67% of the unambiguous misclassified sentences which was similarly due to the innate difference in languages and not because of machine translation.

- We can conclude that 68.49% of the misclassified sentences in total were correctly translated in terms of ambiguity in Italian while 58.23% in Persian, from which 78.26% (for Italian) and 0.0% (for Persian) was because of a machine translation problem.

## 5 Discussion

Based on the results of our classification experiments shown in table 3, we achieved the following findings:

1. Single language translation is not informative enough in predicting ambiguity. By moving from one language (Persian) to all languages, we achieved 85.87% accuracy (from 57.81%). This could be due to the effect of adding more informative input features (information about other language translations) to the classification algorithm.

2. Single best auto-encoder is not informative enough in predicting ambiguity. The accuracy has changed from 66.67% to 88.19% by introducing more auto-encoder models even with lower complexities. Adding more features about the gradual change over the complexity of the auto-encoder model could explain this phenomenon.

3. Adding reconstruction error differences between languages improves accuracy. By adding this information we achieved 88.19% accuracy compared to 85.87%. Accordingly, adding more features about the properties of the mapping function mesh improved the accuracy.

4. Reconstruction error differences is more informative than their values. These phenomena can be observed from the results by improving from 81.99% to 94.94% accuracy. We

can conclude that the shape of the mapping function is informative not the position of it. However, we would expect that a nonlinear complex classifier would also be able to pick this feature.

5. A simple linear model can perform relatively close to a complex neural network model. The accuracy of the complex model was 94.94% compared to 88.19% for the linear model. Learning more complex and nonlinear features actually helped the classification.

6. Predicting more detailed classes improves the accuracy in linear models. For the linear model, the accuracy have changed from 88.19% (F-measure 0.820) to 92.83% (F-measure 0.928) by changing to multi-class classification. It can be explained by classifying more detailed regions in the misclassified regions. For more details on the distribution of the classes along the main two principle components, refer to figure 6. For the neural network however, the classification result decreased from 94.94% to 93.04% by moving to multi-class classification. Compared to the increase of accuracy in the linear model, we can explain that the neural networks have been already able to learn the nonlinear boundaries in the input space and already got a high accuracy in two-class classification.

Moving back to our initial research questions, based on the results in table 3, we can claim that it is possible to predict sentence ambiguity using machine translation. However, we can not claim that the semantic validity and ambiguity is preserved by translation for all target languages and it highly depends on the language. Finally, we conclude that the ambiguity of the sentence is actually encoded in the hidden representation of the LLMs, as the ambiguity is predictable from these representations.

The main contribution of the project is predicting ambiguity of the sentences, without direct use of semantics. As explained in section 3 this feature is achieved by classifying the ambiguity based on the shape of the mapping function. As a consequence, the algorithm does not require extensive training data to cover the whole semantic. Furthermore, the approach is potentially much more generalizable to unseen sentences with unseen semantics. Also, the model would be robust to changes to the input distribution as it is independent of the semantics.

## 6 Future work

One future direction method is to investigate in more details the source of misclassification for all fourteen target languages other than Italian and Persian. Other than that, detecting the source of ambiguity in sentences in terms of words could be an interesting direction. Furthermore, extending the method to different source languages other than English could also be considered as future work.

One of the potential applications of an ambiguity detection method could be in automatic translation of critical documents e.g. legal, political, commercial, where the user is asked to clarify the ambiguity of the source language manually, to prevent misunderstanding and potential conflicts.

Fine-tuning existing multilingual large language models to preserve ambiguity in sentences could be another potential application of the proposed method.

Finally, the trained classifier model can potentially be used as a partial loss function for designing and optimizing ambiguity-free AI-generated human languages investigated at Synaptosearch[3]. In order to do so, for each input sentence generated by the AI, the ambiguity is measured using the model and the gradient with respect to the input is calculated and used to optimize the loss function term related to ambiguity.

Ambiguity can be considered of a strength of the language in cases such as providing efficient means of communication or when it is used as amphibology in literature. However, in critical political, commercial and cultural cases and social media, unintended ambiguity results in misunderstandings and conflicts. The outcome of the misunderstanding could lead to spending a lot of time in negotiation to elaborate the meaning, or in worse case conflicting actions.

One major organization that can benefit from the proposed research is the United Nations (UN) where different countries with different languages interact with each other. Considering automatic translation in such organizations where a speech/text is translated into many languages, detecting and informing the potential ambiguities to both the speaker/writer and the listener/reader, would prevent potential misunderstandings, tedious negotiations, and conflicting actions between the nations and parties in the long term (Bowe et al. (2014), Kimmel (2006)).

[3]https://synaptosearch.com/

## References


Yaseen Alzeebaree. 2020. Lexical and Structural Ambiguity in Machine Translation: An Analytical Study. *Eastern Journal of Languages, Linguistics and Literatures*, 1(1).

Doris Bachmann-Medick. 1996. Cultural misunderstanding in translation: Multicultural coexistence and multicultural conceptions of world literature. *Erfurt Electronic Studies in English*, 7(1996):1–15.

Kathryn Baker, Alexander Franz, Pamela Jordan, Teruko Mitamura, and Eric Nyberg. 1994. Coping with ambiguity in a large-scale machine translation system. In *COLING 1994 Volume 1: The 15th International Conference on Computational Linguistics*.

Anthony Bau. 2022. *Interactions Between Syntax and Semantics in Language Models*. Ph.D. thesis, Massachusetts Institute of Technology.

Igor M Boguslavsky, Leonid L Iomdin, Alexander V Lazursky, Leonid G Mityushin, Victor G Sizov, Leonid G Kreydlin, and Alexander S Berdichevsky. 2005. Interactive resolution of intrinsic and translational ambiguity in a machine translation system. In *International Conference on Intelligent Text Processing and Computational Linguistics*, pages 388–399. Springer.

Heather Bowe, Kylie Martin, and Howard Manns. 2014. *Communication across cultures: Mutual understanding in a global world*. Cambridge University Press.

Mariano Ceccato, Nadzeya Kiyavitskaya, Nicola Zeni, Luisa Mich, and Daniel M Berry. 2004. Ambiguity identification and measurement in natural language texts. Publisher: University of Trento.

Rochelle Choenni, Dan Garrette, and Ekaterina Shutova. 2023. How do languages influence each other? Studying cross-lingual data sharing during LLM fine-tuning. *arXiv preprint arXiv:2305.13286*.

Markus Egg. 2010. Semantic underspecification. *Language and Linguistics Compass*, 4(3):166–181. Publisher: Wiley Online Library.

Martin C Emele and Michael Dorna. 1998. Ambiguity preserving machine translation using packed representations. In *36th Annual Meeting of the Association for Computational Linguistics and 17th International Conference on Computational Linguistics, Volume 1*, pages 365–371.

Angela Fan, Shruti Bhosale, Holger Schwenk, Zhiyi Ma, Ahmed El-Kishky, Siddharth Goyal, Mandeep Baines, Onur Celebi, Guillaume Wenzek, Vishrav Chaudhary, Naman Goyal, Tom Birch, Vitaliy Liptchinsky, Sergey Edunov, Edouard Grave, Michael Auli, and Armand Joulin. 2020. Beyond english-centric multilingual machine translation. *Preprint*, arXiv:2010.11125.

Pengzhi Gao, Zhongjun He, Hua Wu, and Haifeng Wang. 2024. Towards boosting many-to-many multilingual machine translation with large language models. *arXiv preprint arXiv:2401.05861*.

Rishav Hada, Varun Gumma, Adrian de Wynter, Harshita Diddee, Mohamed Ahmed, Monojit Choudhury, Kalika Bali, and Sunayana Sitaram. 2023. Are large language model-based evaluators the solution to scaling up multilingual evaluation? *arXiv preprint arXiv:2309.07462*.

Ben Hutchinson, Jason Baldridge, and Vinodkumar Prabhakaran. 2022. Underspecification in scene description-to-depiction tasks. *arXiv preprint arXiv:2210.05815*.

Lieven Jaspaert. 1984. About the treatment of ambiguity in machine translation. *ITL-International Journal of Applied Linguistics*, 64(1):1–21.

Paul R Kimmel. 2006. Culture and conflict. *The handbook of conflict resolution: Theory and practice*, pages 625–648.

Baohao Liao, Christian Herold, Shahram Khadivi, and Christof Monz. 2024. Ikun for wmt24 general mt task: Llms are here for multilingual machine translation. *arXiv preprint arXiv:2408.11512*.

Alisa Liu, Zhaofeng Wu, Julian Michael, Alane Suhr, Peter West, Alexander Koller, Swabha Swayamdipta, Noah A Smith, and Yejin Choi. 2023. We're afraid language models aren't modeling ambiguity. *arXiv preprint arXiv:2304.14399*.

Weize Liu, Yinlong Xu, Hongxia Xu, Jintai Chen, Xuming Hu, and Jian Wu. 2024. Unraveling Babel: Exploring Multilingual Activation Patterns within Large Language Models. *arXiv preprint arXiv:2402.16367*.

Michal Měchura. 2022. A taxonomy of bias-causing ambiguities in machine translation. In *Proceedings of the 4th Workshop on Gender Bias in Natural Language Processing (GeBNLP)*, pages 168–173.

Sandro Pezzelle. 2023. Dealing with semantic underspecification in multimodal NLP. *arXiv preprint arXiv:2306.05240*.

Jirui Qi, Raquel Fernández, and Arianna Bisazza. 2023. Cross-Lingual Consistency of Factual Knowledge in Multilingual Language Models. *arXiv preprint arXiv:2310.10378*.

Marcus Sammer, Kobi Reiter, Stephen Soderland, Katrin Kirchhoff, and Oren Etzioni. 2006. Ambiguity reduction for machine translation: Human-computer collaboration. In *Proceedings of the 7th Conference of the Association for Machine Translation in the Americas: Technical Papers*, pages 193–202.

Tianyi Tang, Wenyang Luo, Haoyang Huang, Dongdong Zhang, Xiaolei Wang, Xin Zhao, Furu Wei, and Ji-Rong Wen. 2024. Language-Specific Neurons: The Key to Multilingual Capabilities in Large Language Models. *arXiv preprint arXiv:2402.16438*.

Eshaan Tanwar, Manish Borthakur, Subhabrata Dutta, and Tanmoy Chakraborty. 2023. Multilingual llms are better cross-lingual in-context learners with alignment. *arXiv preprint arXiv:2305.05940*.

William Shi-Yuan Wang. 2011. Ambiguity in language. *Korea Journal of Chinese Language and Literature*, 1:3–20.

Frank Wildenburg, Michael Hanna, and Sandro Pezzelle. 2024. Do Pre-Trained Language Models Detect and Understand Semantic Underspecification? Ask the DUST! *arXiv preprint arXiv:2402.12486*.

Apurwa Yadav, Aarshil Patel, and Manan Shah. 2021. A comprehensive review on resolving ambiguities in natural language processing. *AI Open*, 2:85–92. Publisher: Elsevier.

Xiang Zhang, Senyu Li, Bradley Hauer, Ning Shi, and Grzegorz Kondrak. 2023. Don't trust ChatGPT when your question is not in English: A study of multilingual abilities and types of LLMs. In *Proceedings of the 2023 Conference on Empirical Methods in Natural Language Processing*, pages 7915–7927.

Xulang Zhang. 2024. Disentangling syntactics, semantics, and pragmatics in natural language processing.

Yiran Zhao, Wenxuan Zhang, Guizhen Chen, Kenji Kawaguchi, and Lidong Bing. 2024. How do Large Language Models Handle Multilingualism? *arXiv preprint arXiv:2402.18815*.

Wenhao Zhu, Shujian Huang, Fei Yuan, Shuaijie She, Jiajun Chen, and Alexandra Birch. 2024. Question Translation Training for Better Multilingual Reasoning. *arXiv preprint arXiv:2401.07817*.

Wenhao Zhu, Hongyi Liu, Qingxiu Dong, Jingjing Xu, Lingpeng Kong, Jiajun Chen, Lei Li, and Shujian Huang. 2023. Multilingual machine translation with large language models: Empirical results and analysis. *arXiv preprint arXiv:2304.04675*.

Arnold M Zwicky and Jerrold M Sadock. 1975. Ambiguity tests and how to fail them. In *Syntax and Semantics volume 4*, pages 1–36. Brill.

## A Normalized mean squared error

The network error is computed using Normalized mean squared error defined in equation (6):

$$e(r_A, r_B) = \frac{1}{s_A} \sum_{i=0}^{s_A} \frac{(r_A^i - r_B^i)^2}{\overline{r_A}\,\overline{r_B}}$$
$$\overline{r_A} = \frac{1}{s_A} \sum_{i=0}^{s_A} r_A^i \qquad (6)$$
$$\overline{r_B} = \frac{1}{s_B} \sum_{i=0}^{s_B} r_B^i$$

where $r_X^i$ is the $i$'th element of representation $r_X$ and $s_X$ is the size (number of neurons) of $r_X$.

## B Experiment settings

The experiment settings consisted of several options defined in table 4.

| Setting | Options |
|---|---|
| Input type | - Single language across all auto-encoder models<br>- All languages only for the best auto-encoder<br>- Only relations across languages<br>- Whole mapping functions |
| Input variable | - Reconstruction error<br>- Reconstruction error difference |
| Output | - Ambiguous vs Unambiguous<br>- Ambiguity type |
| Model | - Logistic regression<br>- Neural network |
| Cross-validation | - 10-fold |

Table 4: Experiment settings for ambiguity classification

## C Additional figures

Considering several possibilities of translating (un)ambiguous sentences, we summarize 6 states that can be found in table 5 and figure 4.

According to figure 4, for unambiguous sentences, state $sU0$ is desirable and for ambiguous source sentences, for all target languages, either of the states $sA0$ or $sA2$ is desirable. In other words, if a sentence is ambiguous, it should be either ambiguous in all target languages, or none of them.

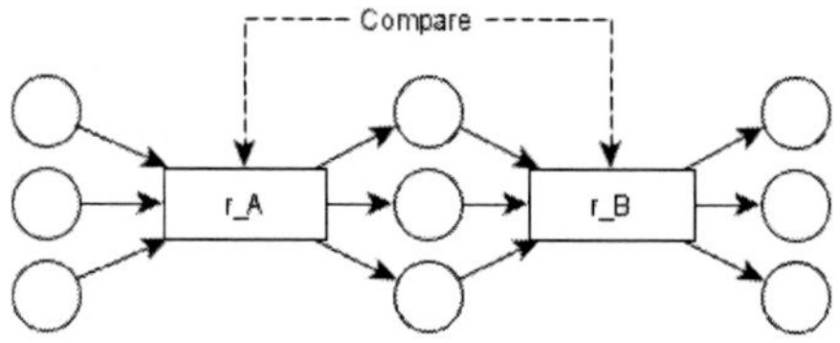


(a) State sA0

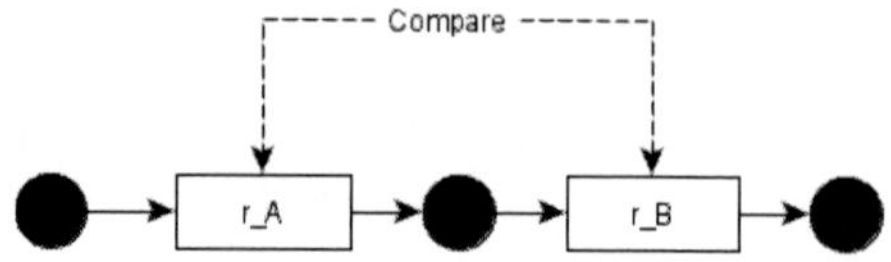


(b) State sU0

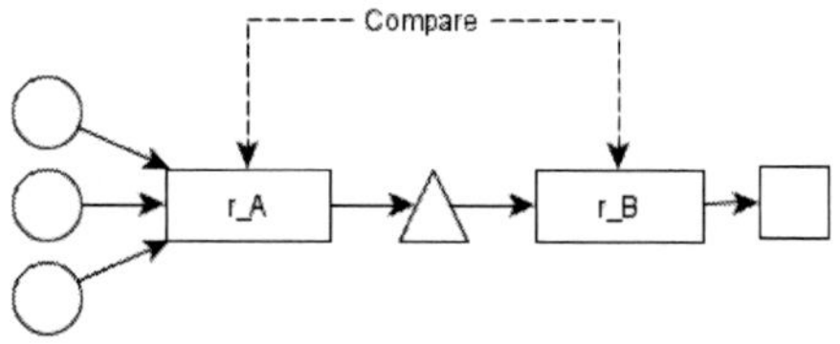


(c) State sA1

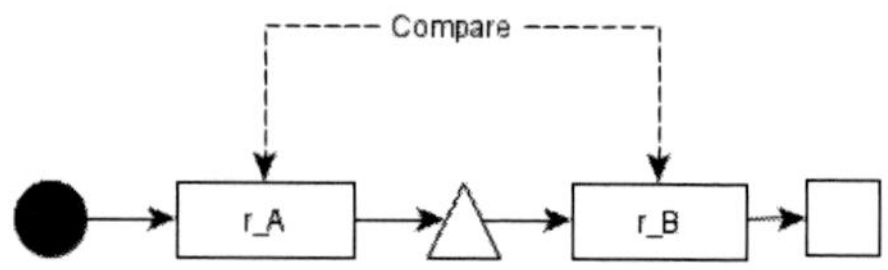


(d) State sU1

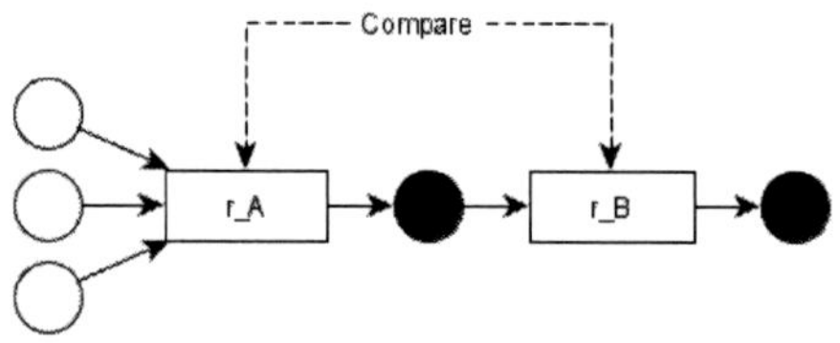


(e) State sA2

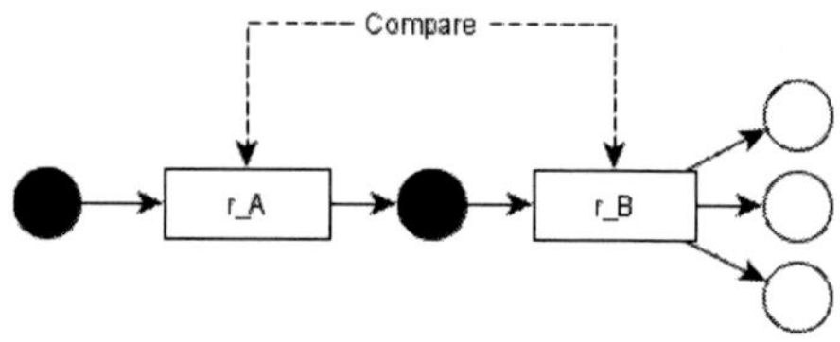


(f) State sU2

Figure 4: Possible states of the 2-step translation approach proposed in the project. White circles indicate certain meanings associated to an ambiguous sentence. Black circles indicate a biased meaning from possible meanings of an ambiguous sentence. Rectangles indicate the internal hidden states of a translation step. Triangles and squares indicate incorrect translations. For detailed description about the possible states refer to table 5.

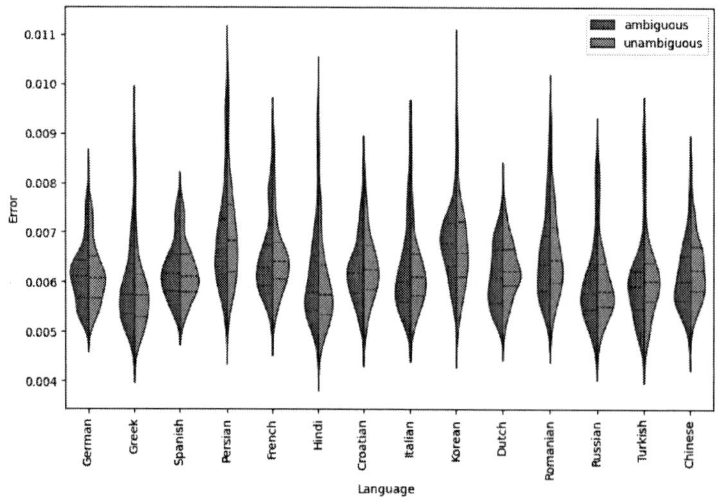


Figure 5: Discriminability of reconstruction error along language for the best auto-encoder. Languages other than Dutch and Chinese are not significantly separable according to the p-value in table 2.

Table 5: Possible states of the 2-step translation approach proposed in the project.

| Tag | Source | Target | Case study | Hyp. Score | Notes |
|---|---|---|---|---|---|
| **sA0** | Ambiguous | Ambiguous | 26% | 0 | Perfect hypothetical translation and rich target language. But score doesn't detect ambiguity. |
| **sA1** | Ambiguous | Incorrect | 38% | 1 | Incorrect translation in step 1. |
| **sA2** | Ambiguous | Unambiguous | 36% | ? | If the score is 1, then we could conclude that ambiguity is encoded in the representation and the representation is not biased towards certain meanings. Also reaching this state might be because of the unambiguity in the target language by itself. |
| **sU0** | Unambiguous | Unambiguous | 30% | 0 | |
| **sU1** | Unambiguous | Incorrect | 70% | 1 | Only one sentence in case study; not reliable statistically. |
| **sU2** | Unambiguous | Ambiguous | 0% | 1 | Very rare, but possible. |

| Input Text | Input ambiguity | Target language | Back translation | Back-translation ambiguity | Error state |
|---|---|---|---|---|---|
| Andrei and Danny moved the yellow bag and chair | Amb. | Persian | Andrew and Danny transferred the yellow bag and the chair. | Unamb. | sA2 |
| Andrei and Danny held the green chair and bag | Amb. | Italian | Andrei and Danny have the green chair and the bag. | Unamb. | sA2 |
| Andrei looked at Danny moving a yellow bag | Amb. | Persian | Andrew looked at Danny that the yellow bag was rolling around. | Wrong | sA1 |
| Andrei held the bag, and either the telescope or the chair | Unamb. | Persian | Andrei kept the bag, or a telescope or a chair. | Wrong | sU1 |
| Andrei picked up the chair, or both the bag and the telescope | Unamb. | Italian | Andrei took the chair, either the bag or the telescope. | Wrong | sU1 |
| Danny moved the telescope that was on the bag | Unamb. | Persian | He moved the telescope on the bag. | Amb. | sU2 |
| Danny left the chair while holding a green bag | Unamb. | Italian | Danny left the chair holding a green bag | Amb. | sU2 |

Table 6: Example of possible error states in translation and back translation.

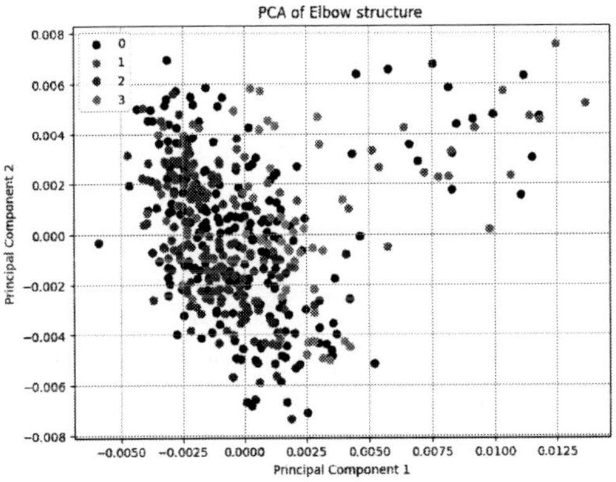


Figure 6: Data distribution over two main principle components

# MLT-DR: Multi-Lingual/Task Demonstration Retrieval
# An Attempt towards Generalized Retriever for In-Context Learning

**Kazuma Hashimoto** **Arjun Reddy Akula** **Karthik Raman** **Michael Bendersky**
Google DeepMind, Mountain View
{kazumah,arjunakula,karthikraman,bemike}@google.com

**Abstract**

This paper presents Multi-Lingual/Task Demonstration Retrieval (MLT-DR) for in-context learning with Large Language Models (LLMs). Our goal is to investigate how dense demonstration retrieval models are generalized across languages and tasks. We first convert 81 tasks into a common format, covering various languages, task types, and domains. For 8 English-based tasks among them, we use machine translation to create synthetic multi/cross-lingual tasks, by translating the examples into non-English languages to explicitly cover more than 130 languages. We then use an instruction-tuned LLM to estimate utility of demonstrations for all the tasks to train the demonstration retrieval models. In our experiments, we show an interesting counterintuitive observation; to compute embeddings of demonstrations, using both the input and ground-truth output hurts the generalization ability of the retriever on unseen tasks whose output space is quite different from those in the seen task set. We also examine that our retriever robustly works even with LLMs that we did not touch during the development of the models.

## 1 Introduction

In-Context Learning (ICL) is an emergent strategy to make Large Language Models (LLMs) perform a task by showing its instruction and *demonstrations* (i.e., input-output pairs) without fine-tuning the LLMs (Brown et al., 2020; Zhao et al., 2021). A crucial research question in this line of work is how to select demonstrations for a new test input. A well-studied approach is to use a general or task-specific text encoder to retrieve demonstrations whose inputs are similar to the test input (Liu et al., 2022). Furthermore, such a text retriever can be effectively fine-tuned by estimating the utility of the demonstrations for a specific LLM (Rubin et al., 2022; Luo et al., 2023).

Li et al. (2023) and Wang et al. (2023) have made progress towards fine-tuning a single demonstration retriever for multiple tasks. They have even shown that the multi-task demonstration retrievers can be generalized on *unseen* datasets (that are *not* used in fine-tuning the retrievers). The key factor is that the unseen datasets share the output formats with those used in the fine-tuning.[1] What is the boundary of the generalization ability?

As an attempt to answer this question, we investigate capabilities of Multi-Lingual/Task Demonstration Retrieval (MLT-DR). We first collect 81 tasks from publicly available datasets,[2] covering diverse languages, task types, and domains. We apply a data augmentation technique to generate synthetic multi/cross-lingual tasks for 8 English-based tasks to improve the generalization ability on low-resource languages, by using machine translation for more than 130 languages. We then fine-tune a general multi-lingual text retriever with feedbacks from an LLM and evaluate fine-tuned models both on seen and unseen tasks.

The findings in our experiments are summarized as follows:

- A counterintuitive finding is that using both the input and ground-truth output to compute demonstration embeddings hurts the generalization ability on unseen tasks, especially when the output spaces are semantically non-trivial.

- The simple translation-based data augmentation helps preserve the generalization ability for low-resource languages (and cross-lingual ICL).

[1] Sentiment classification in a different domain, natural language inference in a different input style, code summarization for different programming languages, etc.

[2] We use the two terms, "tasks" and "datasets," interchangeably as in Wang et al. (2023).



*Proceedings of the Fourth Workshop on Multilingual Representation Learning (MRL 2024)*, pages 324–345
November 16, 2024 ©2024 Association for Computational Linguistics

- The fine-tuned retriever can be used for unseen LLMs, and thus we believe that our retriever will serve as a baseline, a building block to be combined with various techniques, starting points to try further fine-tuning, etc. for future research.

## 2 Multi-Task Demonstration Retrieval

A multi-task demonstration retriever $R$ is designed to estimates $s(d|x,t)$, a utility score of a demonstration $d$ given an input $x$ and its corresponding task $t$ (Li et al., 2023; Wang et al., 2023). It is a common practice to model this as a dense retrieval model (Karpukhin et al., 2020):

$$s(d|x,t) = E_q(x,t) \cdot E_c(d,t), \tag{1}$$

where $E_q$ is an encoder model for the query input, and $E_c$ for the demonstration candidate. We fine-tune a general dense retrieval model $R_0$; for our primary research question, we assume that $R_0$ can handle many languages and domains in diverse text formats (like mT5 (Xue et al., 2021)) and is trained by a general task-agnostic text retrieval objective (like Izacard et al. (2021)).

**Contrastive Learning** The dense retriever model is usually fine-tuned with contrastive learning (Karpukhin et al., 2020). The previous studies used various forms of contrastive learning; for example, Wang et al. (2023) used a combination of cross-attention and dense-retrieval models with a knowledge distillation technique. In this work, we follow a simple and well-established formulation in Yang et al. (2019). To do this, we construct a query set $\mathcal{Q}_t$ and a demonstration candidate set $\mathcal{C}_t$, by splitting the original training set of the task.

**Sampling candidates** We first sample demonstration candidates (from $\mathcal{C}_t$) for a query input $x \in \mathcal{Q}_t$, by combining two types:

- retrieval-based candidates and
- random candidates.

$\ell$ candidates are given by the baseline retriever $R_0$, and $m$ candidates by random sampling, resulting in $(\ell + m)|\mathcal{Q}_t|$ query-candidate pairs for the task $t$. $(\ell, m) = (10, 10)$ is the default setting, except that we use $(\ell, m) = (50, 50)$ for very small datasets.

**Scoring candidates** Next, we annotate the usefulness of a candidate $d$ to perform the task $t$ for $x$. The usefulness is scored by using an LLM:

$$u(d|x,y,t), \tag{2}$$

where $y$ is a gold output of $x$. We employ the incremental utility function in Hashimoto et al. (2024), where the scores are in the range of $[0.0, 1.0]$;

- $u(d|x,y,t) = 0.5$ means that $d$ does not affect the LLM's prediction,
- $u(d|x,y,t) > 0.5$ means a positive effect, and
- $u(d|x,y,t) < 0.5$ means a negative effect.

The utility scores are annotated in a task-specific fashion as described in Appendix A.1. We use the utility scores to select *positive* and *hard negative* candidates for the contrastive learning.

**Positive candidates** For $x$, a positive candidate $d_\mathrm{p}$ satisfies

$$u(d_\mathrm{p}|x,y,t) \geq 0.5 + \delta_1, \tag{3}$$

where $\delta_1 \in (0.0, 0.5]$ is a margin to ensure the quality of $d_\mathrm{p}$. The larger the margin value is, the more significant the contribution of $d_\mathrm{p}$ is. However, there is a trade-off; a large margin value reduces the number of the training examples we can use. We have tried different values in the development of our framework, and we empirically set $\delta_1 = 0.05$.

**Hard negative candidates** We pair $d_\mathrm{p}$ with a set of hard negative candidates $\{d_\mathrm{n}\}$, such that they satisfy

$$u(d_\mathrm{p}|x,y,t) - u(d_\mathrm{n}|x,y,t) \geq \delta_2, \tag{4}$$

where $\delta_2 \in [0.0, 1.0]$ is another margin to ensure the quality difference between the positive and hard negatives; we empirically set $\delta_2 = 0.1$.

**Multi-task fine-tuning** Consequently, we have a set of the tuples

$$(x, d_\mathrm{p}, \{d_\mathrm{n}\}) \tag{5}$$

for the task. Then the baseline retriever $R_0$ is fine-tuned to satisfy $s(d_\mathrm{p}|x,t) > s(d_\mathrm{n}|x,t)$ by the contrastive learning. The fine-tuning process is done by mixing the tuples from all the tasks we use for the retriever training.

## 3 The Role of Ground-Truth Outputs

There are two major dimensions in the design of the demonstration retriever in Section 2: what texts are fed into

1) the query encoder $E_q$ and

2) the candidate encoder $E_c$.

The former is relatively straightforward; we can concatenate a task instruction of $t$ and the query text: $[\text{Instruction}(t); x]$ as done in Li et al. (2023) and also in task-aware retrievers (Asai et al., 2023; Su et al., 2023).

For the candidate encoder, we find a standard practice in the previous studies (Rubin et al., 2022; Li et al., 2023; Luo et al., 2023; Wang et al., 2023); they concatenate the input and ground-truth output of the demonstration:

$$[\text{Instruction}(t); d_{\text{in}}; d_{\text{out}}],$$

where the instruction is used optionally for the multi-task learning cases. We may think that this is a natural and reasonable design; however, we cast doubt on this from a view point of the generalization ability on unseen tasks.

**Diversity in the output space** Let's think about tasks whose outputs are specifically designed for them. Classification is considered to be the most representative one. For some datasets, the output space is limited and not ambiguous:

- {"positive", "negative", "neutral"} in sentiment classification,
- {"entailment", "contradiction", "neutral"} in natural language inference, and
- {"sports", "music", ...} in topic classification.

For others, we see diverse, unlimited, and domain-specific labels: intent classification, relation classification, etc. It is often the case that such class labels are represented with simple words or short phrases, and they are not always comprehensive even for humans. Other example tasks are slot labeling and named entity recognition, where slot/entity labels can be arbitrary strings, and the output format can be designed in various ways (Raman et al., 2022). Is the candidate encoder robust in the diverse output space?

To answer this question, we compare the following three designs for the demonstration representations by the candidate encoder:

- STD: $[\text{Instruction}(t); d_{\text{in}}; d_{\text{out}}]$,

- DESC: $[\text{Instruction}(t); d_{\text{in}}; \text{Desc}(d_{\text{out}})]$,

- NO: $[\text{Instruction}(t); d_{\text{in}}]$.

**STD** is the standard approach in the previous work as mentioned above.

**DESC** is to replace $d_{\text{out}}$ with its description, $\text{Desc}(d_{\text{out}})$, to explain the meaning of the output (Rastogi et al., 2020; Gao et al., 2023b). We apply DESC to tasks with symbolic outputs (e.g., classification), and manually give a description for each output candidate. For example, in the DDI13 relation extraction task, we adapt the original definitions of the relation labels in the dataset paper (Herrero-Zazo et al., 2013); if we cannot find definitions even in the dataset papers, we refer to training examples to come up with the descriptions.

**NO** removes the use of $d_{\text{out}}$, which is *counterintuitive* against the common practice. During the development of DESC, we have observed that it is not trivial to provide comprehensive descriptions, and the actual examples themselves clearly tell us the meaning of the output space (Simard et al., 1992; Zhang et al., 2020). This motivates us to investigate NO solely based on the input representations.

## 4 Experimental Settings

### 4.1 LLM and Retriever

We use Flan-PaLM2 (S) (Google et al., 2023) as our main LLM, and follow the prompt design in Gao et al. (2023a). As the baseline (multi-lingual) retriever $R_0$, we use the t5x-retrieval code base (Ni et al., 2022) to fine-tune mT5 large (Xue et al., 2021) with a general text retrieval objective in Izacard et al. (2021) on the mC4 corpus (Xue et al., 2021). The retriever has 565M model parameters.

### 4.2 Tasks

**Seen tasks** To fine-tune our retrievers, we collect NLP tasks in diverse languages and domains from publicly available resources like Flan-v1 (Wei et al., 2021), MTEB (Muennighoff et al., 2023), those used in Li et al. (2023), and others, resulting in 81 tasks in total. The complete list of them is summarized in Table 1. For each task, we manually write a long task instruction to construct the prompt for the LLM, and a short task instruction (i.e., Instruction(t)) for the retriever.

| No. | Name | Type | Languages | Source | Scoring | $\lvert\mathcal{Q}_t\rvert$ | $\lvert\mathcal{C}_t\rvert$ |
|---|---|---|---|---|---|---|---|
| 01 | WMT14 en→fr (Bojar et al., 2014) | Machine translation | en, fr | Link | GLEU | 100,000 | 30,059,732 |
| 02 | WMT14 fr→en (Bojar et al., 2014) | Machine translation | en, fr | Link | GLEU | 100,000 | 30,059,732 |
| 03 | WMT16 en→de (Bojar et al., 2016) | Machine translation | de, en | Link | GLEU | 60,000 | 4,143,251 |
| 04 | WMT16 de→en (Bojar et al., 2016) | Machine translation | de, en | Link | GLEU | 60,000 | 4,143,251 |
| 05 | WMT16 en→ru (Bojar et al., 2016) | Machine translation | en, ru | Link | GLEU | 30,000 | 2,296,592 |
| 06 | WMT16 ru→en (Bojar et al., 2016) | Machine translation | en, ru | Link | GLEU | 30,000 | 2,296,592 |
| 07 | ANLI r1 (Nie et al., 2020) | Natural language inference | en [+MT] | Link | Probability | 8,473 | 8,473 |
| 08 | ANLI r2 (Nie et al., 2020) | Natural language inference | en | Link | Probability | 22,730 | 22,730 |
| 09 | ANLI r3 (Nie et al., 2020) | Natural language inference | en | Link | Probability | 30,000 | 70,459 |
| 10 | QNLI (Rajpurkar et al., 2018) | Natural language inference | en | Link | Probability | 30,000 | 74,543 |
| 11 | MNLI (Williams et al., 2018) | Natural language inference | en | Link | Probability | 30,000 | 100,000 |
| 12 | WNLI (Levesque et al., 2012a) | Natural language inference | en | Link | Probability | 317 | 318 |
| 13 | MRPC (Dolan and Brockett, 2005) | Paraphrase identification | en | Link | Probability | 200 | 3,268 |
| 14 | PAWS (Zhang et al., 2019) | Paraphrase identification | en | Link | Probability | 30,000 | 19,401 |
| 15 | Tatoeba (Artetxe and Schwenk, 2019) | Translation identification | sqi, fry, kur, tur, ... | Link | Probability | 30,000 | 177,554 |
| 16 | IMDB (Maas et al., 2011) | Sentiment classification | en | Link | Probability | 12,400 | 12,400 |
| 17 | SST2 (Socher et al., 2013) | Sentiment classification | en | Link | Probability | 30,000 | 37,149 |
| 18 | Yelp (Fast.AI) | Sentiment classification | en | Link | Probability | 30,000 | 100,000 |
| 19 | Tweet Sentiment Extraction (Kaggle) | Sentiment classification | en [+MT] | Link | Probability | 10,000 | 17,281 |
| 20 | AfriSenti (Muhammad et al., 2023a) | Sentiment classification | amh, hau, ibo, ... | Link | Probability | 30,000 | 33,685 |
| 21 | TweetEval-emoji (Barbieri et al., 2018) | Emoji classification | en | Link | Probability | 20,000 | 25,000 |
| 22 | TweetEval-emotion (Mohammad et al., 2018) | Emotion classification | en | Link | Probability | 1,600 | 1,657 |
| 23 | DialogEmotion (Kumar et al., 2024) | Multi-speaker emotion classification | en, hi | Link | F1 | 700 | 799 |
| 24 | Massive-intent (FitzGerald et al., 2022) | Dialog intent classification | af, am, ar, az, ... | Link | Probability | 30,000 | 100,000 |
| 25 | MTOP-domain (Li et al., 2021) | Dialog domain classification | de, en, es, fr, ... | Link | Probability | 30,000 | 43,928 |
| 26 | MTOP-intent (Li et al., 2021) | Dialog intent classification | de, en, es, fr, ... | Link | Probability | 30,000 | 43,928 |
| 27 | ATIS-intent (Price, 1990) | Multi-label dialog intent classification | en | Link | F1 | 2,000 | 2,189 |
| 28 | E2ENLG-reversed (Dušek et al., 2019) | Semantic parsing (text to dict) | en | Link | F1 | 16,662 | 16663 |
| 29 | WikiSQL (Zhong et al., 2017) | Semantic parsing (text/table to SQL) | en | Link | GLEU | 20,000 | 36,355 |
| 30 | BC5CDR (Li et al., 2016) | Named entity recognition (biomedical) | en | Link | F1 | 2,000 | 2,560 |
| 31 | BioNLP13PC (Ohta et al., 2013) | Named entity recognition (biomedical) | en | Link | F1 | 1,000 | 1,499 |
| 32 | JNLPBA (Huang et al., 2020) | Named entity recognition (biomedical) | en | Link | F1 | 9,000 | 9,346 |
| 33 | MultiCoNER2 (Fetahu et al., 2023) | Named entity recognition | de, fa, fr, ... | Link | F1 | 30,000 | 140,824 |
| 34 | CoNLL2003 (Tjong Kim Sang and De Meulder, 2003) | Named entity recognition | en | Link | F1 | 7,000 | 7,041 |
| 35 | MTOP-slot (Li et al., 2021) | Dialog slot labeling | en, fr, hi | Link | F1 | 19,000 | 19,811 |
| 36 | SNIPS-slot (Coucke et al., 2018) | Dialog slot labeling | en | Link | F1 | 6,000 | 7,084 |
| 37 | ATIS-slot (Price, 1990) | Dialog slot labeling | en | Link | F1 | 2,000 | 2,478 |
| 38 | SemRel (Hendrickx et al., 2010) | Relation classification (nominals) | en [+MT] | Link | Probability | 3,800 | 4,000 |
| 39 | DDI13 (Herrero-Zazo et al., 2013) | Relation classification (drugs) | en | Link | Probability | 8,000 | 10,779 |
| 40 | ChemProt (Islamaj Doğan et al., 2019) | Relation classification (chemical and protein) | en | Link | Probability | 9,000 | 10,460 |
| 41 | WordSeg (Bañón et al., 2020) | Word segmentation | en | Link | GLEU | 30,000 | 100,000 |
| 42 | FixPunct (Bañón et al., 2020) | Punctuation fix | en | Link | GLEU | 30,000 | 100,000 |
| 43 | CoLA (Warstadt et al., 2019) | Linguistic acceptability judgment | en | Link | Probability | 4,175 | 4,176 |
| 44 | CoNLL2000 (Tjong Kim Sang and Buchholz, 2000) | Syntactic phrase chunking | en | Link | F1 | 4,000 | 4,936 |
| 45 | Pronoun (Rahman and Ng, 2012) | Coreference resolution | en | Link | Probability | 561 | 561 |
| 46 | WSC (Levesque et al., 2012b) | Coreference resolution | en | Link | Probability | 252 | 252 |
| 47 | WinoGrande (Sakaguchi et al., 2019) | Sentence completion | en | Link | Probability | 20,099 | 20,099 |
| 48 | WiC (Pilehvar and Camacho-Collados, 2019) | Word sense disambiguation | en | Link | Probability | 2,614 | 2,614 |
| 49 | Python (Lu et al., 2021) | Code summarization | en | Link | GLEU | 30,000 | 100,000 |
| 50 | Java (Lu et al., 2021) | Code summarization | en | Link | GLEU | 30,000 | 100,000 |
| 51 | Go (Lu et al., 2021) | Code summarization | en | Link | GLEU | 30,000 | 100,000 |
| 52 | PHP (Lu et al., 2021) | Code summarization | en | Link | GLEU | 30,000 | 100,000 |
| 53 | Gigaword (Napoles et al., 2012) | Text summarization | en | Link | GLEU | 30,000 | 100,000 |
| 54 | SAMSum (Gliwa et al., 2019) | Dialog summarization | en | Link | GLEU | 7,366 | 7,366 |
| 55 | iDebate (Wang and Ling, 2016) | Debate summarization | en [+MT] | Link | GLEU | 859 | 800 |
| 56 | MultiHateCheck (Röttger et al., 2022) | Hate speech detection/classification | en, fr, hi, it, ... | Link | Probability | 20,055 | 20,055 |
| 57 | Toxic (Muennighoff et al., 2023) | Toxic text detection | en | Link | Probability | 24,900 | 24,900 |
| 58 | Countfact (O'Neill et al., 2021) | Counterfactual review detection | de, en, ja | Link | Probability | 7,500 | 7,718 |
| 59 | Irony (Van Hee et al., 2018) | Irony detection | en | Link | Probability | 1,400 | 1,462 |
| 60 | Offensive (Zampieri et al., 2019) | Offensive text detection | en | Link | Probability | 5,000 | 6,916 |
| 61 | Sarcasm (Abu Farha et al., 2022) | Sarcasm detection | ar, en | Link | Probability | 2,500 | 3,414 |
| 62 | SQuAD2 (Rajpurkar et al., 2018) | Reading comprehension | en | Link | GLEU | 30,000 | 100,119 |
| 63 | BoolQ (Clark et al., 2019) | Reading comprehension | en [+MT] | Link | Probability | 4,613 | 4,614 |
| 64 | DROP (Dua et al., 2019) | Reading comprehension (numerical) | en | Link | Probability | 29,635 | 46,621 |
| 65 | OpenbookQA (Mihaylov et al., 2018) | Reading comprehension | en | Link | Probability | 2,478 | 2,478 |
| 66 | Cosmos (Huang et al., 2019) | Reading comprehension (common sense) | en | Link | Probability | 12,531 | 12,531 |
| 67 | SciDocs (Cohan et al., 2020) | Relevance, re-ranking | en | Link | Probability | 30,000 | 99,159 |
| 68 | HotpotQA (Yang et al., 2018) | Relevance, re-ranking | en | Link | F1 | 30,000 | 60,447 |
| 69 | AI2 ARC-easy (Clark et al., 2018) | Closed-book question answering | en | Link | Probability | 1,025 | 1,026 |
| 70 | AI2 ARC-challenge (Clark et al., 2018) | Closed-book question answering | en | Link | Probability | 459 | 460 |
| 71 | TriviaQA (Joshi et al., 2017) | Closed-book question answering | en | Link | Probability | 30,000 | 108,184 |
| 72 | Math (Saxton et al., 2019) | Math question answering | en | Link | Probability | 30,000 | 100,000 |
| 73 | CommonGen (Lin et al., 2020) | Constrained text generation (common sense) | en | Link | GLEU | 30,000 | 37,189 |
| 74 | SNLI-en (Bowman et al., 2015) | Constrained text generation (entailment) | en | Link | GLEU | 10,112 | 33,106 |
| 75 | PIQA-qgen (Bisk et al., 2019) | Question/query generation | en [+MT] | Link | GLEU | 7,956 | 7,957 |
| 76 | arXiv (Muennighoff et al., 2023) | Multi-label topic/category classification | en | Link | F1 | 30,000 | 69,113 |
| 77 | medRxiv (Muennighoff et al., 2023) | Topic/category classification | en | Link | Probability | 5,000 | 16,229 |
| 78 | DBpedia (Lehmann et al., 2014) | Topic/category classification | en [+MT] | Link | Probability | 5,000 | 5,000 |
| 79 | Yahoo (Zhang et al., 2015) | Topic/category classification | en | Link | Probability | 14,575 | 14,575 |
| 80 | AG news (Zhang et al., 2015) | Topic/category classification | en | Link | Probability | 30,000 | 89,800 |
| 81 | TREC (Li and Roth, 2002) | Topic/category classification | en [+MT] | Link | Probability | 2,626 | 2,626 |

Table 1: The list of the 81 tasks used as *seen* tasks. "[+MT]" in the Languages column means that the dataset is used for the data augmentation described in Section 5.4.

| Name | Type | Notes |
|---|---|---|
| AfriSenti Zero (Muhammad et al., 2023b) | Sentiment classification (positive, negative, neutral) | Two **held-out African languages** are targeted, while 12 other African languages are used in a seen sentiment classification task (AfriSenti). |
| GoEmotions (Demszky et al., 2020) | Multi-label emotion classification (28 classes) | This is a **multi-label fine-grained** task, while a 4-way (single-class) classification task (TweetEval-emotion) is included in the seen tasks. |
| CLINC150 (Larson et al., 2019) | Dialog intent classification (150 classes) | Similar tasks (ATIS/MTOP/Massive-intent) are included in the seen tasks, and this is another task with multi-domain **fine-grained** classes. |
| Orcas-I (Alexander et al., 2022) | Search query intent classification (5 classes) | This is different from those in the seen tasks; the search queries are not always comprehensive and thus rely on **retrieval augmentation**. |
| MIT-R (Dataset link) | Dialog slot labeling (8 slot types) | Similar tasks (ATIS/MTOP/SNIPS-slot, E2ENLG-reversed) are used in the seen tasks, and this is expected to be the **easiest** unseen task. |
| SSENT (Barnes et al., 2022) | Polar expression extraction (positive, negative) | The task format is similar to that of MIT-R, but focuses on **polar (positive and negative) expressions** of hotel reviews in **Spanish**. |
| XML-MT (Hashimoto et al., 2019) | Machine translation (en→ja, en→fi) | Machine translation tasks (WMT14/16) are included in the seen tasks, but this focuses on **two other language pairs** and **XML-tagged texts**. |

Table 2: Tasks for the *unseen* task evaluation. "Notes" explain what aspects we focus on in the evaluation.

| | AfriSenti (46.30) | | | | DDI13 (18.18) | | | | ATIS-intent (35.49) | | | | MTOP-intent (48.46) | | | |
|---|---|---|---|---|---|---|---|---|---|---|---|---|---|---|---|---|
| $R_0$ | 49.24 | 51.39 | 52.78 | 54.98 | 19.92 | 23.59 | 25.52 | 28.8 | 70.31 | 87.16 | 91.74 | 95.48 | 84.22 | 88.55 | 90.55 | 92.55 |
| $R_{\mathrm{STD}}$ | +1.24 | +2.75 | +4.84 | +7.29 | +8.42 | +11.13 | +14.90 | +14.87 | +4.11 | +2.79 | +3.87 | +2.27 | +8.10 | +5.67 | +4.53 | +3.11 |
| $R_{\mathrm{DESC}}$ | +1.28 | +3.12 | +5.12 | +8.03 | +5.56 | +10.39 | +15.67 | +15.11 | +5.60 | +2.41 | +3.88 | +2.65 | +7.86 | +5.46 | +4.48 | +2.92 |
| $R_{\mathrm{NO}}$ | +1.43 | +3.07 | +4.97 | +7.74 | +7.46 | +11.06 | +12.89 | +16.14 | +6.61 | +3.24 | +3.87 | +2.87 | +8.32 | +6.07 | +4.97 | +3.50 |
| | Countfact (26.48) | | | | Offensive (53.44) | | | | BC5CDR (2.70) | | | | PHP (3.00) | | | |
| $R_0$ | 41.44 | 48.80 | 55.28 | 63.37 | 61.15 | 65.14 | 63.98 | 63.76 | 37.44 | 55.14 | 60.45 | 63.28 | 13.61 | 14.44 | 13.82 | 11.00 |
| $R_{\mathrm{STD}}$ | +5.34 | +9.47 | +9.79 | +6.90 | +1.26 | +2.21 | +3.46 | +1.99 | +7.87 | +4.21 | +1.49 | -1.08 | +1.68 | +1.39 | +1.54 | +0.55 |
| $R_{\mathrm{DESC}}$ | +4.92 | +9.48 | +9.81 | +4.79 | +0.72 | +1.80 | +4.00 | +1.32 | +7.76 | +4.01 | +2.01 | -0.83 | +1.75 | +1.54 | +1.51 | +1.38 |
| $R_{\mathrm{NO}}$ | +4.01 | +8.92 | +10.27 | +10.44 | +0.73 | +2.89 | +4.44 | +3.66 | +7.26 | +4.41 | +2.55 | +0.49 | +1.42 | +1.20 | +1.09 | +0.28 |

Table 3: Seen task results. The four numbers in the $R_0$ rows correspond to the scores by 1,3,5,10-shot ICL with the baseline retriever $R_0$. The rest of the rows show the absolute improvements by using the fine-tuned retrievers ($R_{\mathrm{STD}}$, $R_{\mathrm{DESC}}$, and $R_{\mathrm{NO}}$) based on the three types of the demonstration representations. The score next to the task name reports the LLM's zero-shot performance to know its knowledge about the task without any demonstrations.

**Unseen tasks** To evaluate the generalization ability of the demonstration retrievers from diverse angles, we use the tasks summarized in Table 2. The "Notes" in the table explain what kinds of unseen aspects we would like to test with the retrievers. For each task, we use the whole training set to construct the candidate set $C_t$; the AfriSenti Zero task does not have any training examples, and we use the AfriSenti task for the candidate set (i.e., a cross-lingual ICL setting). We describe more details in Appendix B.

## 5 Results

We evaluate the retrievers based on $k$-shot ICL with $k \in \{1, 3, 5, 10\}$. Unless otherwise stated, we simply use the top-$k$ retrieved demonstrations to construct the prompts for the LLM. All the evaluation scores are in the range of [0, 100], and Appendix C describes the metric for each task.

### 5.1 Evaluation on Seen Tasks

We first confirm the effectiveness of the fine-tuned retrievers on the seen tasks as in the previous studies (Li et al., 2023; Wang et al., 2023). We use a sentiment classification task in 12 African languages (AfriSenti), a relation extraction task in the biomedical domain (DDI13), two (single/multi-label) dialog intent classification tasks (ATIS/MTOP-intent), two binary (counterfactual/offensive) detection tasks (Countfact, Offensive), a named entity recognition task in the biomedical domain (BC5CDR), and a code summarization task (PHP).

Table 3 shows the results. It is consistent with the previous work that the fine-tuned retrievers perform significantly better than the baseline retriever. We hypothesized that the three types of the fine-tuned retrievers perform similarly on the seen tasks, and it is true in most of the cases. Overall, we did not observe the potential advantage of $R_{\mathrm{DESC}}$ in the results.

However, we sometimes see nontrivial gains by $R_{\mathrm{NO}}$, for example, in the COUNTFACT result. This is presumably because using the output labels is severely affected by overfitting. It is also interesting to see that $R_{\mathrm{NO}}$ works well even on tasks with more complex output space like BC5CDR.

| | AfriSenti Zero (39.43) | | | | GoEmotions (27.92) | | | | CLINC150 (70.58) | | | | Orcas-I (42.00) | | | |
|---|---|---|---|---|---|---|---|---|---|---|---|---|---|---|---|---|
| $R_0$ | 40.50 | 41.48 | 41.92 | 42.97 | 27.19 | 29.05 | 30.66 | 32.36 | 91.36 | 93.53 | 94.24 | 95.87 | 46.30 | 48.70 | 51.00 | 54.30 |
| $R_{\text{STD}}$ | -0.51 | -0.54 | -0.03 | -1.37 | +0.52 | +0.34 | -0.48 | -1.31 | -1.34 | -1.60 | -1.62 | -1.96 | -0.90 | -1.20 | -3.50 | -6.00 |
| $R_{\text{DESC}}$ | -1.00 | -0.27 | -0.32 | -1.81 | +0.53 | +0.53 | -0.04 | +0.74 | -0.69 | -1.31 | -1.08 | -2.11 | +1.40 | +0.90 | +0.50 | -0.30 |
| $R_{\text{NO}}$ | -0.41 | -1.32 | -1.25 | -0.44 | +0.34 | +0.61 | -0.05 | -0.09 | +2.35 | +2.14 | +1.78 | +0.40 | +0.70 | +0.50 | -1.00 | -0.80 |
| | MIT-R (1.09) | | | | SSENT (7.38) | | | | XML-MT enja (37.71) | | | | XML-MT enfi (23.56) | | | |
| $R_0$ | 40.14 | 49.34 | 54.54 | 60.46 | 24.66 | 27.52 | 30.33 | 27.32 | 52.10 | 55.54 | 56.19 | 56.08 | 36.43 | 39.00 | 39.86 | 40.00 |
| $R_{\text{STD}}$ | +6.44 | +6.10 | +4.68 | +1.83 | +3.21 | +3.02 | -0.21 | -2.10 | +0.36 | +0.93 | +0.31 | +0.55 | -0.23 | +0.26 | +0.08 | -0.43 |
| $R_{\text{DESC}}$ | +5.63 | +5.18 | +3.98 | +1.78 | +3.95 | +4.03 | +1.38 | +1.38 | +0.52 | +0.57 | +1.08 | +0.28 | -0.06 | -0.03 | +0.56 | -0.22 |
| $R_{\text{NO}}$ | +5.19 | +5.88 | +3.99 | +2.26 | +0.66 | +1.35 | -1.16 | +0.44 | +0.85 | +0.06 | +0.92 | +0.02 | +0.84 | +0.72 | +0.60 | -2.32 |

Table 4: Unseen task results with Flan-PaLM 2. The structure of this table is analogous to that of Table 3.

| | AfriSenti Zero (44.48) | | | | GoEmotions (28.26) | | | | CLINC150 (92.62) | | | | Orcas-I (49.10) | | | |
|---|---|---|---|---|---|---|---|---|---|---|---|---|---|---|---|---|
| $R_0$ | 55.83 | 55.81 | 54.42 | 54.03 | 31.61 | 33.50 | 35.57 | 37.97 | 96.22 | 97.22 | 97.51 | 97.73 | 59.00 | 60.90 | 61.90 | 65.4 |
| $R_{\text{NO}}$ | -0.75 | -2.61 | -3.00 | -3.37 | -0.33 | +0.34 | -0.12 | +0.10 | +0.54 | +0.85 | +0.56 | +0.56 | -0.90 | +0.50 | +0.80 | -0.30 |
| | MIT-R (8.60) | | | | SSENT (22.40) | | | | XML-MT enja (27.94) | | | | XML-MT enfi (24.16) | | | |
| $R_0$ | 64.93 | 68.45 | 72.85 | 75.25 | 44.96 | 50.34 | 52.22 | 53.91 | 58.45 | 62.51 | 63.10 | 63.94 | 42.90 | 45.47 | 45.90 | 47.34 |
| $R_{\text{NO}}$ | +3.48 | +2.98 | +2.23 | +1.65 | +0.93 | +1.49 | +1.05 | +3.68 | +1.37 | +0.58 | +1.01 | +0.97 | +0.57 | -0.07 | -0.40 | +0.23 |

Table 5: Unseen task results with Gemini 1.5 Pro. The structure of this table is analogous to that of Table 3.

### 5.2 Evaluation on Unseen Tasks

We then evaluate the retrievers on the unseen tasks. Table 4 shows the results, and below we summarize the key points.

- All the fine-tuned retrievers perform worse than $R_0$ on AfriSenti Zero. We hypothesize that "catastrophic forgetting" is caused by the fact that the two zero-shot languages (Oromo and Tigrinya) are never observed in the retriever fine-tuning process.

- It is surprising to see that $R_{\text{STD}}$ performs significantly worse than $R_0$ on fine-grained classification tasks whose labels are not easy to interpret. Especially, it fails on CLINC150, even when we have successful results on the intent classification tasks in Table 3. In contrast, $R_{\text{NO}}$ provides more robust results.

- It matches our expectation that all the fine-tuned retrievers perform well on MIT-R as explained in Table 2.

- Overall, the effects of using $R_{\text{DESC}}$ are not conclusive. We see the potential benefit on Orcas-I (whose label descriptions are helpful even for humans) and SSENT, while it does not help on CLINC150. It is possible that the provided label descriptions are not good enough, but this nontrivial process itself indicates that $R_{\text{DESC}}$ would not be the best way.

| | Natural Instructions (25.28) | | | |
|---|---|---|---|---|
| $R_0$ | 26.59 | 27.08 | 26.95 | 27.04 |
| $R_{\text{NO}}$ | +0.26 | +0.49 | +0.81 | +0.37 |

Table 6: Natural Instructions results.

- Based on the SSENT results, using the task output would be effective for some tasks. An interesting future work is to consider how to strike a balance between $R_{\text{STD}}$ and $R_{\text{NO}}$.

**More unseen tasks** We further perform evaluation on 20 unseen text generation tasks from Super Natural Instructions (Wang et al., 2022) to test the robustness of the demonstration retriever. The tasks include machine translation, text summarization, question answering, paraphrase generation, etc, and the datasets are *not* used in fine-tuning our retrievers. Table 6 shows the average scores across all the tasks, and we can see some gains by using $R_{\text{NO}}$. The size of the training set for a task is limited to around 6,000 examples in Super Natural Instructions, and thus this might not be the best setup for ICL; still, our retriever shows the robust results.

**Transfer ability** Following the previous work (Li et al., 2023; Wang et al., 2023), we test how $R_{\text{NO}}$ works with another LLM, Gemini 1.5 Pro (Reid et al., 2024). It should be noted that we have never touched the new LLM until we perform the final test evaluation. Table 5 shows the results, and we can see consistent trends. Gemini

| | ATIS-intent | | | COUNTFACT | | |
|---|---|---|---|---|---|---|
| $R_0$ | 87.16 | 91.74 | 95.48 | 48.80 | 55.28 | 63.37 |
| $R_{\text{NO}}$ | +3.24 | +3.87 | +2.87 | +8.92 | +10.27 | +10.44 |
| +cov. | +4.85 | +4.34 | +2.14 | +11.13 | +12.65 | +11.57 |
| | AfriSenti Zero | | | SSENT | | |
| $R_0$ | 41.48 | 41.92 | 42.97 | 27.52 | 30.33 | 27.32 |
| $R_{\text{NO}}$ | -1.32 | -1.25 | -0.44 | +1.35 | -1.16 | +0.44 |
| +cov. | -1.12 | -0.05 | -0.20 | +3.07 | +1.19 | +1.54 |

Table 7: Coverage-based selection results. $k = 1$ is not affected by this method, and we only show the scores with $k = 3, 5, 10$.

| | AfriSenti Zero (39.43) | | | |
|---|---|---|---|---|
| $R_0$ | 40.50 | 41.48 | 41.92 | 42.97 |
| $R_{\text{NO}}$ | -0.41 | -1.32 | -1.25 | -0.44 |
| $R_{\text{NO}}$+MT | +0.15 | +0.39 | +0.49 | +1.29 |
| | ATIS-intent hi,tr (29.67) | | | |
| $R_0$ | 62.18 | 79.09 | 84.39 | 89.26 |
| $R_{\text{NO}}$ | +3.11 | +2.44 | +2.57 | +1.27 |
| $R_{\text{NO}}$+MT | +5.72 | +3.82 | +3.02 | +2.47 |

Table 8: Cross-lingual ICL results with Flan-PaLM 2.

1.5 pro achieves much better baseline scores than those of Flan-PaLM 2 (S), but still $R_{\text{NO}}$ helps. It is encouraging that our fine-tuned retriever works well even for this much stronger LLM.

### 5.3 Compatibility with Existing Methods

We discuss the potential of using $R_{\text{NO}}$ as a basic building block in diverse scenarios for future work. In other words, we do not intend to claim that our retriever should be always used alone, and instead we believe that our retriever can be used along with existing methods.

For example, we consider the coverage-based demonstration selection method in Gupta et al. (2023), and we apply their "cosine" method to the top-retrieved candidates by $R_{\text{NO}}$. Table 7 shows the results, and the method works well with our retriever.

Other possible future directions are using our retriever for sequential selection models (Scarlatos and Lan, 2024; Liu et al., 2024), continual learning with more tasks and languages, and explicit adaptation to other LLMs.

### 5.4 Improved Language Coverage by Machine Translation

We have observed that the fine-tuning process degrades the generalization ability of the retriever on unseen languages. Our seen task set covers various languages as shown in Table 1, but still, English is dominant. How can we make our retriever more robust from this viewpoint? One solution is to add more and more tasks in many languages, but it is not a trivial effort.

To this end, we consider using machine translation for data augmentation as in the common practice (Balahur and Turchi, 2014; Lee et al., 2018). We describe our process below:

1. Select 8 tasks ($\sim$10% of the whole) from the seen task list in Table 1: ANLI r1, Tweet Sentiment Extraction, SemRel, iDebate, BoolQ, PIQA-qgen, DBpedia, and TREC; all the selected tasks are originally in English.

2. Use Google Translate[3] to translate the examples in the query set $\mathcal{Q}_t$ and the candidate set $\mathcal{C}_t$ for the selected task; for each example in $\mathcal{Q}_t$, we randomly sample $a$ target languages ($b$ ($> a$) for $\mathcal{C}_t$), and consequently we have multi-lingual query and candidate sets.[4]

3. Add the multilingual version of the 8 tasks to the seen task list; note that the new tasks are separated from the original English ones, and the utility estimation for the retriever fine-tuning is done solely within the synthetic data.

By this, the demonstration retriever is **exposed to more than 130 languages** during the fine-tuning.

We revisit the evaluation on AfriSenti Zero; this is considered to be a cross-lingual ICL evaluation, in that the languages in the query set and the candidate set are different. We add another cross-lingual ICL evaluation with the Hindi and Turkish variants of the ATIS-intent task, where we use the original English ATIS-intent for the candidate set.

Table 8 shows the results, and we can see that $R_{\text{NO}}$ with the data augmentation ($R_{\text{NO}}$+MT) performs the best. Hindi and Turkish are included in seen tasks (e.g., Massive-intent), but still the data augmentation helps. Note that using the synthetic data does not degrade the retriever's performance on other tasks.

In our checkpoint release, we will also provide a model that is based on even more languages for the data augmentation. The model covers more than 230 languages.[5]

[3]As of early June 2024, 132 non-English languages are supported at `https://cloud.google.com/translate/docs/languages`.

[4]In Appendix A.3, we describe details of this process

[5]`https://support.google.com/translate/answer/15139004`

## 6 Conclusion

We have presented our multi-lingual and multi-task demonstration retriever for in-context learning with LLMs. We showed the counterintuitive finding to improve the generalization ability of the demonstration representations, and improved multi/cross-lingual performance of the retriever by the translation-based data augmentation. We believe that our released models will be useful for future work.

## Limitations

**Task coverage** We did our best to collect as diverse tasks as possible. However, we would be able to find new tasks where our retriever does not work well. Our future effort will be to improve the task coverage or seek the use of instruction-tuned LLMs themselves (Gemini, GPT, Llama, etc.) as a retriever to leverage their generalization ability.

**Short task instruction** We assume the use of the short task instruction for our retriever. To handle new tasks that are quite different from those in our task set, we may need to come up with new short task instructions. In such a case, we suggest that the users refer to the complete list (in Appendix A.2) of all the instructions we used, to design the new instructions.

**Translation error in data augmentation** No machine translation systems (including Google Translate we used in our experiments) are perfect, and thus we expect that translation errors exist in our synthetic multi-lingual tasks. To avoid the potential negative effects by the translation errors, we did not use the synthetic data for validation and evaluation to test our retriever's quality.

## References


Ibrahim Abu Farha, Silviu Vlad Oprea, Steven Wilson, and Walid Magdy. 2022. SemEval-2022 Task 6: iSarcasmEval, Intended Sarcasm Detection in English and Arabic. In *Proceedings of the 16th International Workshop on Semantic Evaluation (SemEval-2022)*, pages 802–814.

Daria Alexander, Wojciech Kusa, and Arjen P. de Vries. 2022. ORCAS-I: Queries Annotated with Intent using Weak Supervision. In *Proceedings of the 45th International ACM SIGIR Conference on Research and Development in Information Retrieval*, SIGIR '22, page 3057–3066, New York, NY, USA. Association for Computing Machinery.

Mikel Artetxe and Holger Schwenk. 2019. Massively Multilingual Sentence Embeddings for Zero-Shot Cross-Lingual Transfer and Beyond. *Transactions of the Association for Computational Linguistics*, 7:597–610.

Akari Asai, Timo Schick, Patrick Lewis, Xilun Chen, Gautier Izacard, Sebastian Riedel, Hannaneh Hajishirzi, and Wen-tau Yih. 2023. Task-aware Retrieval with Instructions. In *Findings of the Association for Computational Linguistics: ACL 2023*, pages 3650–3675.

Alexandra Balahur and Marco Turchi. 2014. Comparative experiments using supervised learning and machine translation for multilingual sentiment analysis. *Computer Speech Language*, 28:56–75.

Marta Bañón, Pinzhen Chen, Barry Haddow, Kenneth Heafield, Hieu Hoang, Miquel Esplà-Gomis, Mikel L. Forcada, Amir Kamran, Faheem Kirefu, Philipp Koehn, Sergio Ortiz Rojas, Leopoldo Pla Sempere, Gema Ramírez-Sánchez, Elsa Sarrías, Marek Strelec, Brian Thompson, William Waites, Dion Wiggins, and Jaume Zaragoza. 2020. ParaCrawl: Web-Scale Acquisition of Parallel Corpora. In *Proceedings of the 58th Annual Meeting of the Association for Computational Linguistics*, pages 4555–4567, Online. Association for Computational Linguistics.

Francesco Barbieri, Jose Camacho-Collados, Francesco Ronzano, Luis Espinosa-Anke, Miguel Ballesteros, Valerio Basile, Viviana Patti, and Horacio Saggion. 2018. Semeval 2018 task 2: Multilingual emoji prediction. In *Proceedings of The 12th International Workshop on Semantic Evaluation*, pages 24–33.

Jeremy Barnes, Laura Ana Maria Oberländer, Enrica Troiano, Andrey Kutuzov, Jan Buchmann, Rodrigo Agerri, Lilja Øvrelid, and Erik Velldal. 2022. SemEval-2022 Task 10: Structured Sentiment Analysis. In *Proceedings of the 16th International Workshop on Semantic Evaluation (SemEval-2022)*.

Yonatan Bisk, Rowan Zellers, Ronan Le Bras, Jianfeng Gao, and Yejin Choi. 2019. PIQA: Reasoning about Physical Commonsense in Natural Language.

Ondřej Bojar, Christian Buck, Rajen Chatterjee, Christian Federmann, Liane Guillou, Barry Haddow, Matthias Huck, Antonio Jimeno Yepes, Aurélie Névéol, Mariana Neves, Pavel Pecina, Martin Popel, Philipp Koehn, Christof Monz, Matteo Negri, Matt Post, Lucia Specia, Karin Verspoor, Jörg Tiedemann, and Marco Turchi, editors. 2016. *Proceedings of the First Conference on Machine Translation: Volume 1, Research Papers*. Association for Computational Linguistics, Berlin, Germany.

Ondřej Bojar, Christian Buck, Christian Federmann, Barry Haddow, Philipp Koehn, Christof Monz, Matt Post, and Lucia Specia, editors. 2014. *Proceedings of the Ninth Workshop on Statistical Machine Translation*. Association for Computational Linguistics, Baltimore, Maryland, USA.

Samuel R. Bowman, Gabor Angeli, Christopher Potts, and Christopher D. Manning. 2015. A large annotated corpus for learning natural language inference. In *Proceedings of the 2015 Conference on Empirical Methods in Natural Language Processing*, pages 632–642, Lisbon, Portugal. Association for Computational Linguistics.

Tom B. Brown, Benjamin Mann, Nick Ryder, Melanie Subbiah, Jared Kaplan, Prafulla Dhariwal, Arvind Neelakantan, Pranav Shyam, Girish Sastry, Amanda Askell, Sandhini Agarwal, Ariel Herbert-Voss, Gretchen Krueger, Tom Henighan, Rewon Child, Aditya Ramesh, Daniel M. Ziegler, Jeffrey Wu, Clemens Winter, Christopher Hesse, Mark Chen, Eric Sigler, Mateusz Litwin, Scott Gray, Benjamin Chess, Jack Clark, Christopher Berner, Sam McCandlish, Alec Radford, Ilya Sutskever, and Dario Amodei. 2020. Language Models are Few-Shot Learners. In *Advances in Neural Information Processing Systems 33: Annual Conference on Neural Information Processing Systems 2020, NeurIPS 2020, December 6-12, 2020, virtual*.

Christopher Clark, Kenton Lee, Ming-Wei Chang, Tom Kwiatkowski, Michael Collins, and Kristina Toutanova. 2019. BoolQ: Exploring the Surprising Difficulty of Natural Yes/No Questions. In *Proceedings of the 2019 Conference of the North American Chapter of the Association for Computational Linguistics: Human Language Technologies, Volume 1 (Long and Short Papers)*, pages 2924–2936, Minneapolis, Minnesota. Association for Computational Linguistics.

Peter Clark, Isaac Cowhey, Oren Etzioni, Tushar Khot, Ashish Sabharwal, Carissa Schoenick, and Oyvind Tafjord. 2018. Think you have Solved Question Answering? Try ARC, the AI2 Reasoning Challenge.

Arman Cohan, Sergey Feldman, Iz Beltagy, Doug Downey, and Daniel S. Weld. 2020. SPECTER: Document-level Representation Learning using Citation-informed Transformers.

Alice Coucke, Alaa Saade, Adrien Ball, Théodore Bluche, Alexandre Caulier, David Leroy, Clément Doumouro, Thibault Gisselbrecht, Francesco Caltagirone, Thibaut Lavril, et al. 2018. Snips voice platform: an embedded spoken language understanding system for private-by-design voice interfaces. *arXiv preprint arXiv:1805.10190*.

Dorottya Demszky, Dana Movshovitz-Attias, Jeongwoo Ko, Alan Cowen, Gaurav Nemade, and Sujith Ravi. 2020. GoEmotions: A dataset of fine-grained emotions. In *Proceedings of the 58th Annual Meeting of the Association for Computational Linguistics*, pages 4040–4054, Online. Association for Computational Linguistics.

William B. Dolan and Chris Brockett. 2005. Automatically Constructing a Corpus of Sentential Paraphrases. In *Proceedings of the Third International Workshop on Paraphrasing (IWP2005)*.

Dheeru Dua, Yizhong Wang, Pradeep Dasigi, Gabriel Stanovsky, Sameer Singh, and Matt Gardner. 2019. DROP: A Reading Comprehension Benchmark Requiring Discrete Reasoning Over Paragraphs. In *Proceedings of the 2019 Conference of the North American Chapter of the Association for Computational Linguistics: Human Language Technologies, Volume 1 (Long and Short Papers)*, pages 2368–2378, Minneapolis, Minnesota. Association for Computational Linguistics.

Ondřej Dušek, David M. Howcroft, and Verena Rieser. 2019. Semantic Noise Matters for Neural Natural Language Generation. In *Proceedings of the 12th International Conference on Natural Language Generation*, pages 421–426, Tokyo, Japan. Association for Computational Linguistics.

Fast.AI. Yelp sentiment classification dataset.

Besnik Fetahu, Sudipta Kar, Zhiyu Chen, Oleg Rokhlenko, and Shervin Malmasi. 2023. SemEval-2023 Task 2: Fine-grained Multilingual Named Entity Recognition (MultiCoNER 2). In *Proceedings of the 17th International Workshop on Semantic Evaluation (SemEval-2023)*, pages 2247–2265, Toronto, Canada. Association for Computational Linguistics.

Jack FitzGerald, Christopher Hench, Charith Peris, Scott Mackie, Kay Rottmann, Ana Sanchez, Aaron Nash, Liam Urbach, Vishesh Kakarala, Richa Singh, Swetha Ranganath, Laurie Crist, Misha Britan, Wouter Leeuwis, Gokhan Tur, and Prem Natarajan. 2022. MASSIVE: A 1M-Example Multilingual Natural Language Understanding Dataset with 51 Typologically-Diverse Languages.

Lingyu Gao, Aditi Chaudhary, Krishna Srinivasan, Kazuma Hashimoto, Karthik Raman, and Michael Bendersky. 2023a. Ambiguity-Aware In-Context Learning with Large Language Models. *arXiv preprint cs.CL 2309.07900*.

Lingyu Gao, Debanjan Ghosh, and Kevin Gimpel. 2023b. The Benefits of Label-Description Training for Zero-Shot Text Classification. In *Proceedings of the 2023 Conference on Empirical Methods in Natural Language Processing*, pages 13823–13844, Singapore. Association for Computational Linguistics.

Bogdan Gliwa, Iwona Mochol, Maciej Biesek, and Aleksander Wawer. 2019. SAMSum Corpus: A Human-annotated Dialogue Dataset for Abstractive Summarization. In *Proceedings of the 2nd Workshop on New Frontiers in Summarization*, pages 70–79, Hong Kong, China. Association for Computational Linguistics.

Google, Rohan Anil, Andrew M. Dai, Orhan Firat, Melvin Johnson, Dmitry Lepikhin, Alexandre

Passos, Siamak Shakeri, Emanuel Taropa, Paige Bailey, Zhifeng Chen, Eric Chu, Jonathan H. Clark, Laurent El Shafey, Yanping Huang, Kathy Meier-Hellstern, Gaurav Mishra, Erica Moreira, Mark Omernick, Kevin Robinson, Sebastian Ruder, Yi Tay, Kefan Xiao, Yuanzhong Xu, Yujing Zhang, Gustavo Hernandez Abrego, Junwhan Ahn, Jacob Austin, Paul Barham, Jan Botha, James Bradbury, Siddhartha Brahma, Kevin Brooks, Michele Catasta, Yong Cheng, Colin Cherry, Christopher A. Choquette-Choo, Aakanksha Chowdhery, Clément Crepy, Shachi Dave, Mostafa Dehghani, Sunipa Dev, Jacob Devlin, Mark Díaz, Nan Du, Ethan Dyer, Vlad Feinberg, Fangxiaoyu Feng, Vlad Fienber, Markus Freitag, Xavier Garcia, Sebastian Gehrmann, Lucas Gonzalez, Guy Gur-Ari, Steven Hand, Hadi Hashemi, Le Hou, Joshua Howland, Andrea Hu, Jeffrey Hui, Jeremy Hurwitz, Michael Isard, Abe Ittycheriah, Matthew Jagielski, Wenhao Jia, Kathleen Kenealy, Maxim Krikun, Sneha Kudugunta, Chang Lan, Katherine Lee, Benjamin Lee, Eric Li, Music Li, Wei Li, YaGuang Li, Jian Li, Hyeontaek Lim, Hanzhao Lin, Zhongtao Liu, Frederick Liu, Marcello Maggioni, Aroma Mahendru, Joshua Maynez, Vedant Misra, Maysam Moussalem, Zachary Nado, John Nham, Eric Ni, Andrew Nystrom, Alicia Parrish, Marie Pellat, Martin Polacek, Alex Polozov, Reiner Pope, Siyuan Qiao, Emily Reif, Bryan Richter, Parker Riley, Alex Castro Ros, Aurko Roy, Brennan Saeta, Rajkumar Samuel, Renee Shelby, Ambrose Slone, Daniel Smilkov, David R. So, Daniel Sohn, Simon Tokumine, Dasha Valter, Vijay Vasudevan, Kiran Vodrahalli, Xuezhi Wang, Pidong Wang, Zirui Wang, Tao Wang, John Wieting, Yuhuai Wu, Kelvin Xu, Yunhan Xu, Linting Xue, Pengcheng Yin, Jiahui Yu, Qiao Zhang, Steven Zheng, Ce Zheng, Weikang Zhou, Denny Zhou, Slav Petrov, and Yonghui Wu. 2023. PaLM 2 Technical Report.

Shivanshu Gupta, Matt Gardner, and Sameer Singh. 2023. Coverage-based Example Selection for In-Context Learning. *arXiv preprint cs.CL 2305.14907*.

Kazuma Hashimoto, Raffaella Buschiazzo, James Bradbury, Teresa Marshall, Richard Socher, and Caiming Xiong. 2019. A High-Quality Multilingual Dataset for Structured Documentation Translation. In *Proceedings of the Fourth Conference on Machine Translation (Volume 1: Research Papers)*, pages 116–127.

Kazuma Hashimoto, Karthik Raman, and Michael Bendersky. 2024. Take One Step at a Time to Know Incremental Utility of Demonstration: An Analysis on Reranking for Few-Shot In-Context Learning. In *NAACL 2024*.

Iris Hendrickx, Su Nam Kim, Zornitsa Kozareva, Preslav Nakov, Diarmuid Ó Séaghdha, Sebastian Padó, Marco Pennacchiotti, Lorenza Romano, and Stan Szpakowicz. 2010. SemEval-2010 Task 8: Multi-Way Classification of Semantic Relations between Pairs of Nominals. In *Proceedings of the 5th International Workshop on Semantic Evaluation*, pages 33–38, Uppsala, Sweden. Association for Computational Linguistics.

María Herrero-Zazo, Isabel Segura-Bedmar, Paloma Martínez, and Thierry Declerck. 2013. The DDI corpus: An annotated corpus with pharmacological substances and drug–drug interactions. *Journal of Biomedical Informatics*, 46(5):914–920.

Lifu Huang, Ronan Le Bras, Chandra Bhagavatula, and Yejin Choi. 2019. Cosmos QA: Machine Reading Comprehension with Contextual Commonsense Reasoning. In *Proceedings of the 2019 Conference on Empirical Methods in Natural Language Processing and the 9th International Joint Conference on Natural Language Processing (EMNLP-IJCNLP)*, pages 2391–2401, Hong Kong, China. Association for Computational Linguistics.

Ming-Siang Huang, Po-Ting Lai, Pei-Yen Lin, Yu-Ting You, Richard Tzong-Han Tsai, and Wen-Lian Hsu. 2020. Biomedical named entity recognition and linking datasets: survey and our recent development. *Briefings in Bioinformatics*, 21(6):2219–2238.

Rezarta Islamaj Doğan, Sun Kim, Andrew Chatr-aryamontri, Chih-Hsuan Wei, Donald C Comeau, Rui Antunes, Sérgio Matos, Qingyu Chen, Aparna Elangovan, Nagesh C Panyam, Karin Verspoor, Hongfang Liu, Yanshan Wang, Zhuang Liu, Berna Altınel, Zehra Melce Hüsünbeyi, Arzucan Özgür, Aris Fergadis, Chen-Kai Wang, Hong-Jie Dai, Tung Tran, Ramakanth Kavuluru, Ling Luo, Albert Steppi, Jinfeng Zhang, Jinchan Qu, and Zhiyong Lu. 2019. Overview of the BioCreative VI Precision Medicine Track: mining protein interactions and mutations for precision medicine. *Database*, 2019:bay147.

Gautier Izacard, Mathilde Caron, Lucas Hosseini, Sebastian Riedel, Piotr Bojanowski, Armand Joulin, and Edouard Grave. 2021. Unsupervised dense information retrieval with contrastive learning. *arXiv preprint arXiv:2112.09118*.

Mandar Joshi, Eunsol Choi, Daniel Weld, and Luke Zettlemoyer. 2017. TriviaQA: A Large Scale Distantly Supervised Challenge Dataset for Reading Comprehension. In *Proceedings of the 55th Annual Meeting of the Association for Computational Linguistics (Volume 1: Long Papers)*, pages 1601–1611, Vancouver, Canada. Association for Computational Linguistics.

Kaggle. Tweet Sentiment Extraction.

Vladimir Karpukhin, Barlas Oguz, Sewon Min, Patrick Lewis, Ledell Wu, Sergey Edunov, Danqi Chen, and Wen-tau Yih. 2020. Dense Passage Retrieval for Open-Domain Question Answering. In *Proceedings of the 2020 Conference on Empirical Methods in Natural Language Processing (EMNLP)*, pages 6769–6781.

Shivani Kumar, Md Shad Akhtar, Erik Cambria, and Tanmoy Chakraborty. 2024. SemEval 2024 – Task

10: Emotion Discovery and Reasoning its Flip in Conversation (EDiReF).

Stefan Larson, Anish Mahendran, Joseph J. Peper, Christopher Clarke, Andrew Lee, Parker Hill, Jonathan K. Kummerfeld, Kevin Leach, Michael A. Laurenzano, Lingjia Tang, and Jason Mars. 2019. An Evaluation Dataset for Intent Classification and Out-of-Scope Prediction. In *Proceedings of the 2019 Conference on Empirical Methods in Natural Language Processing and the 9th International Joint Conference on Natural Language Processing (EMNLP-IJCNLP)*, pages 1311–1316.

Kyungjae Lee, Kyoungho Yoon, Sunghyun Park, and Seung-won Hwang. 2018. Semi-supervised Training Data Generation for Multilingual Question Answering. In *Proceedings of the Eleventh International Conference on Language Resources and Evaluation (LREC 2018)*, Miyazaki, Japan. European Language Resources Association (ELRA).

Jens Lehmann, Robert Isele, Max Jakob, Anja Jentzsch, Dimitris Kontokostas, Pablo Mendes, Sebastian Hellmann, Mohamed Morsey, Patrick Van Kleef, Sören Auer, and Christian Bizer. 2014. DBpedia - A Large-scale, Multilingual Knowledge Base Extracted from Wikipedia. *Semantic Web Journal*, 6.

Hector J. Levesque, Ernest Davis, and Leora Morgenstern. 2012a. The Winograd schema challenge. In *Proceedings of the Thirteenth International Conference on Principles of Knowledge Representation and Reasoning*, KR'12, page 552–561. AAAI Press.

Hector J. Levesque, Ernest Davis, and Leora Morgenstern. 2012b. The Winograd schema challenge. In *Proceedings of the Thirteenth International Conference on Principles of Knowledge Representation and Reasoning*, KR'12, page 552–561. AAAI Press.

Haoran Li, Abhinav Arora, Shuohui Chen, Anchit Gupta, Sonal Gupta, and Yashar Mehdad. 2021. MTOP: A Comprehensive Multilingual Task-Oriented Semantic Parsing Benchmark. In *Proceedings of the 16th Conference of the European Chapter of the Association for Computational Linguistics: Main Volume*, pages 2950–2962, Online. Association for Computational Linguistics.

Jiao Li, Yueping Sun, Robin J. Johnson, Daniela Sciaky, Chih-Hsuan Wei, Robert Leaman, Allan Peter Davis, Carolyn J. Mattingly, Thomas C. Wiegers, and Zhiyong Lu. 2016. BioCreative V CDR task corpus: a resource for chemical disease relation extraction. *Database: The Journal of Biological Databases and Curation*, 2016.

Xiaonan Li, Kai Lv, Hang Yan, Tianyang Lin, Wei Zhu, Yuan Ni, Guotong Xie, Xiaoling Wang, and Xipeng Qiu. 2023. Unified Demonstration Retriever for In-Context Learning. In *Proceedings of the 61st Annual Meeting of the Association for Computational Linguistics (Volume 1: Long Papers)*, pages 4644–4668.

Xin Li and Dan Roth. 2002. Learning Question Classifiers. In *COLING 2002: The 19th International Conference on Computational Linguistics*.

Bill Yuchen Lin, Wangchunshu Zhou, Ming Shen, Pei Zhou, Chandra Bhagavatula, Yejin Choi, and Xiang Ren. 2020. CommonGen: A Constrained Text Generation Challenge for Generative Commonsense Reasoning. In *Findings of the Association for Computational Linguistics: EMNLP 2020*, pages 1823–1840, Online. Association for Computational Linguistics.

Haoyu Liu, Jianfeng Liu, Shaohan Huang, Yuefeng Zhan, Hao Sun, Weiwei Deng, Furu Wei, and Qi Zhang. 2024. $Se^2$: Sequential Example Selection for In-Context Learning.

Jiachang Liu, Dinghan Shen, Yizhe Zhang, Bill Dolan, Lawrence Carin, and Weizhu Chen. 2022. What Makes Good In-Context Examples for GPT-3? In *Proceedings of Deep Learning Inside Out (DeeLIO 2022): The 3rd Workshop on Knowledge Extraction and Integration for Deep Learning Architectures*, pages 100–114.

Shuai Lu, Daya Guo, Shuo Ren, Junjie Huang, Alexey Svyatkovskiy, Ambrosio Blanco, Colin Clement, Dawn Drain, Daxin Jiang, Duyu Tang, Ge Li, Lidong Zhou, Linjun Shou, Long Zhou, Michele Tufano, MING GONG, Ming Zhou, Nan Duan, Neel Sundaresan, Shao Kun Deng, Shengyu Fu, and Shujie LIU. 2021. CodeXGLUE: A Machine Learning Benchmark Dataset for Code Understanding and Generation. In *Proceedings of the Neural Information Processing Systems Track on Datasets and Benchmarks*, volume 1.

Man Luo, Xin Xu, Zhuyun Dai, Panupong Pasupat, Mehran Kazemi, Chitta Baral, Vaiva Imbrasaite, and Vincent Y Zhao. 2023. Dr.ICL: Demonstration-Retrieved In-context Learning. *arXiv preprint cs.CL 2305.14128*.

Andrew L. Maas, Raymond E. Daly, Peter T. Pham, Dan Huang, Andrew Y. Ng, and Christopher Potts. 2011. Learning Word Vectors for Sentiment Analysis. In *Proceedings of the 49th Annual Meeting of the Association for Computational Linguistics: Human Language Technologies*, pages 142–150, Portland, Oregon, USA. Association for Computational Linguistics.

Todor Mihaylov, Peter Clark, Tushar Khot, and Ashish Sabharwal. 2018. Can a Suit of Armor Conduct Electricity? A New Dataset for Open Book Question Answering.

Saif Mohammad, Felipe Bravo-Marquez, Mohammad Salameh, and Svetlana Kiritchenko. 2018. Semeval-2018 task 1: Affect in tweets. In *Proceedings of the 12th international workshop on semantic evaluation*, pages 1–17.

Niklas Muennighoff, Nouamane Tazi, Loic Magne, and Nils Reimers. 2023. MTEB: Massive Text Embedding Benchmark. In *Proceedings of the 17th Conference of the European Chapter of the Association for Computational Linguistics*, pages 2014–2037, Dubrovnik, Croatia. Association for Computational Linguistics.

Shamsuddeen Muhammad, Idris Abdulmumin, Abinew Ayele, Nedjma Ousidhoum, David Adelani, Seid Yimam, Ibrahim Ahmad, Meriem Beloucif, Saif Mohammad, Sebastian Ruder, Oumaima Hourrane, Alipio Jorge, Pavel Brazdil, Felermino Ali, Davis David, Salomey Osei, Bello Shehu-Bello, Falalu Lawan, Tajuddeen Gwadabe, Samuel Rutunda, Tadesse Belay, Wendimu Messelle, Hailu Balcha, Sisay Chala, Hagos Gebremichael, Bernard Opoku, and Stephen Arthur. 2023a. AfriSenti: A Twitter Sentiment Analysis Benchmark for African Languages. In *Proceedings of the 2023 Conference on Empirical Methods in Natural Language Processing*, pages 13968–13981, Singapore. Association for Computational Linguistics.

Shamsuddeen Hassan Muhammad, Idris Abdulmumin, Seid Muhie Yimam, David Ifeoluwa Adelani, Ibrahim Said Ahmad, Nedjma Ousidhoum, Abinew Ali Ayele, Saif Mohammad, Meriem Beloucif, and Sebastian Ruder. 2023b. SemEval-2023 task 12: Sentiment analysis for African languages (AfriSenti-SemEval). In *Proceedings of the 17th International Workshop on Semantic Evaluation (SemEval-2023)*, pages 2319–2337, Toronto, Canada. Association for Computational Linguistics.

Courtney Napoles, Matthew Gormley, and Benjamin Van Durme. 2012. Annotated Gigaword. In *Proceedings of the Joint Workshop on Automatic Knowledge Base Construction and Web-scale Knowledge Extraction (AKBC-WEKEX)*, pages 95–100, Montréal, Canada. Association for Computational Linguistics.

Jianmo Ni, Gustavo Hernandez Abrego, Noah Constant, Ji Ma, Keith Hall, Daniel Cer, and Yinfei Yang. 2022. Sentence-T5: Scalable Sentence Encoders from Pre-trained Text-to-Text Models. In *Findings of the Association for Computational Linguistics: ACL 2022*, pages 1864–1874.

Yixin Nie, Adina Williams, Emily Dinan, Mohit Bansal, Jason Weston, and Douwe Kiela. 2020. Adversarial NLI: A New Benchmark for Natural Language Understanding. In *Proceedings of the 58th Annual Meeting of the Association for Computational Linguistics*, pages 4885–4901, Online. Association for Computational Linguistics.

Tomoko Ohta, Sampo Pyysalo, Rafal Rak, Andrew Rowley, Hong-Woo Chun, Sung-Jae Jung, Sung-Pil Choi, Sophia Ananiadou, and Jun'ichi Tsujii. 2013. Overview of the Pathway Curation (PC) task of BioNLP Shared Task 2013. In *Proceedings of the BioNLP Shared Task 2013 Workshop*, pages 67–75, Sofia, Bulgaria. Association for Computational Linguistics.

James O'Neill, Polina Rozenshtein, Ryuichi Kiryo, Motoko Kubota, and Danushka Bollegala. 2021. I Wish I Would Have Loved This One, But I Didn't – A Multilingual Dataset for Counterfactual Detection in Product Reviews.

Kishore Papineni, Salim Roukos, Todd Ward, and Wei-Jing Zhu. 2002. Bleu: a Method for Automatic Evaluation of Machine Translation. In *Proceedings of the 40th Annual Meeting of the Association for Computational Linguistics*, pages 311–318.

Mohammad Taher Pilehvar and Jose Camacho-Collados. 2019. WiC: the Word-in-Context Dataset for Evaluating Context-Sensitive Meaning Representations. In *Proceedings of the 2019 Conference of the North American Chapter of the Association for Computational Linguistics: Human Language Technologies, Volume 1 (Long and Short Papers)*, pages 1267–1273, Minneapolis, Minnesota. Association for Computational Linguistics.

Patti Price. 1990. Evaluation of spoken language systems: The ATIS domain. In *Speech and Natural Language: Proceedings of a Workshop Held at Hidden Valley, Pennsylvania, June 24-27, 1990*.

Altaf Rahman and Vincent Ng. 2012. Resolving Complex Cases of Definite Pronouns: The Winograd Schema Challenge. In *Proceedings of the 2012 Joint Conference on Empirical Methods in Natural Language Processing and Computational Natural Language Learning*, pages 777–789, Jeju Island, Korea. Association for Computational Linguistics.

Pranav Rajpurkar, Robin Jia, and Percy Liang. 2018. Know What You Don't Know: Unanswerable Questions for SQuAD. In *Proceedings of the 56th Annual Meeting of the Association for Computational Linguistics (Volume 2: Short Papers)*, pages 784–789, Melbourne, Australia. Association for Computational Linguistics.

Karthik Raman, Iftekhar Naim, Jiecao Chen, Kazuma Hashimoto, Kiran Yalasangi, and Krishna Srinivasan. 2022. Transforming Sequence Tagging Into A Seq2Seq Task. In *Proceedings of the 2022 Conference on Empirical Methods in Natural Language Processing*, pages 11856–11874.

Abhinav Rastogi, Xiaoxue Zang, Srinivas Sunkara, Raghav Gupta, and Pranav Khaitan. 2020. Towards scalable multi-domain conversational agents: The schema-guided dialogue dataset. In *Proceedings of the AAAI Conference on Artificial Intelligence*, volume 34, pages 8689–8696.

Machel Reid, Nikolay Savinov, Denis Teplyashin, Dmitry Lepikhin, Timothy Lillicrap, Jean-baptiste Alayrac, Radu Soricut, Angeliki Lazaridou, Orhan Firat, Julian Schrittwieser, et al. 2024. Gemini 1.5: Unlocking multimodal understanding across millions of tokens of context. *arXiv preprint arXiv:2403.05530*.

Paul Röttger, Haitham Seelawi, Debora Nozza, Zeerak Talat, and Bertie Vidgen. 2022. Multilingual HateCheck: Functional Tests for Multilingual Hate Speech Detection Models. In *Proceedings of the Sixth Workshop on Online Abuse and Harms (WOAH)*, pages 154–169, Seattle, Washington (Hybrid). Association for Computational Linguistics.

Ohad Rubin, Jonathan Herzig, and Jonathan Berant. 2022. Learning to retrieve prompts for in-context learning. In *Proceedings of the 2022 Conference of the North American Chapter of the Association for Computational Linguistics: Human Language Technologies*, pages 2655–2671.

Keisuke Sakaguchi, Ronan Le Bras, Chandra Bhagavatula, and Yejin Choi. 2019. WinoGrande: An Adversarial Winograd Schema Challenge at Scale.

David Saxton, Edward Grefenstette, Felix Hill, and Pushmeet Kohli. 2019. Analysing Mathematical Reasoning Abilities of Neural Models.

Alexander Scarlatos and Andrew Lan. 2024. RetICL: Sequential Retrieval of In-Context Examples with Reinforcement Learning.

Patrice Simard, Yann LeCun, and John Denker. 1992. Efficient Pattern Recognition Using a New Transformation Distance. In *Advances in Neural Information Processing Systems*, volume 5. Morgan-Kaufmann.

Richard Socher, Alex Perelygin, Jean Wu, Jason Chuang, Christopher D. Manning, Andrew Ng, and Christopher Potts. 2013. Recursive Deep Models for Semantic Compositionality Over a Sentiment Treebank. In *Proceedings of the 2013 Conference on Empirical Methods in Natural Language Processing*, pages 1631–1642, Seattle, Washington, USA. Association for Computational Linguistics.

Hongjin Su, Weijia Shi, Jungo Kasai, Yizhong Wang, Yushi Hu, Mari Ostendorf, Wen-tau Yih, Noah A. Smith, Luke Zettlemoyer, and Tao Yu. 2023. One Embedder, Any Task: Instruction-Finetuned Text Embeddings. In *Findings of the Association for Computational Linguistics: ACL 2023*, pages 1102–1121, Toronto, Canada. Association for Computational Linguistics.

Erik F. Tjong Kim Sang and Sabine Buchholz. 2000. Introduction to the CoNLL-2000 Shared Task Chunking. In *Fourth Conference on Computational Natural Language Learning and the Second Learning Language in Logic Workshop*.

Erik F. Tjong Kim Sang and Fien De Meulder. 2003. Introduction to the CoNLL-2003 Shared Task: Language-Independent Named Entity Recognition. In *Proceedings of the Seventh Conference on Natural Language Learning at HLT-NAACL 2003*, pages 142–147.

Cynthia Van Hee, Els Lefever, and Véronique Hoste. 2018. Semeval-2018 task 3: Irony detection in english tweets. In *Proceedings of The 12th International Workshop on Semantic Evaluation*, pages 39–50.

Liang Wang, Nan Yang, and Furu Wei. 2023. Learning to Retrieve In-Context Examples for Large Language Models. *arXiv preprint cs.CL 2307.07164*.

Lu Wang and Wang Ling. 2016. Neural Network-Based Abstract Generation for Opinions and Arguments. In *Proceedings of the 2016 Conference of the North American Chapter of the Association for Computational Linguistics: Human Language Technologies*, pages 47–57, San Diego, California. Association for Computational Linguistics.

Yizhong Wang, Swaroop Mishra, Pegah Alipoormolabashi, Yeganeh Kordi, Amirreza Mirzaei, Anjana Arunkumar, Arjun Ashok, Arut Selvan Dhanasekaran, Atharva Naik, David Stap, et al. 2022. Super-NaturalInstructions:Generalization via Declarative Instructions on 1600+ Tasks. In *EMNLP*.

Alex Warstadt, Amanpreet Singh, and Samuel R. Bowman. 2019. Neural Network Acceptability Judgments. *Transactions of the Association for Computational Linguistics*, 7:625–641.

Jason Wei, Maarten Bosma, Vincent Zhao, Kelvin Guu, Adams Wei Yu, Brian Lester, Nan Du, Andrew M Dai, and Quoc V Le. 2021. Finetuned Language Models are Zero-Shot Learners. In *International Conference on Learning Representations*.

Adina Williams, Nikita Nangia, and Samuel Bowman. 2018. A Broad-Coverage Challenge Corpus for Sentence Understanding through Inference. In *Proceedings of the 2018 Conference of the North American Chapter of the Association for Computational Linguistics: Human Language Technologies, Volume 1 (Long Papers)*, pages 1112–1122, New Orleans, Louisiana. Association for Computational Linguistics.

Yonghui Wu, Mike Schuster, Zhifeng Chen, Quoc V. Le, Mohammad Norouzi, Wolfgang Macherey, Maxim Krikun, Yuan Cao, Qin Gao, Klaus Macherey, Jeff Klingner, Apurva Shah, Melvin Johnson, Xiaobing Liu, Łukasz Kaiser, Stephan Gouws, Yoshikiyo Kato, Taku Kudo, Hideto Kazawa, Keith Stevens, George Kurian, Nishant Patil, Wei Wang, Cliff Young, Jason Smith, Jason Riesa, Alex Rudnick, Oriol Vinyals, Greg Corrado, Macduff Hughes, and Jeffrey Dean. 2016. Google's Neural Machine Translation System: Bridging the Gap between Human and Machine Translation. *arXiv preprint cs.CL 1609.08144*.

Linting Xue, Noah Constant, Adam Roberts, Mihir Kale, Rami Al-Rfou, Aditya Siddhant, Aditya Barua, and Colin Raffel. 2021. mT5: A Massively Multilingual Pre-trained Text-to-Text Transformer.

In *Proceedings of the 2021 Conference of the North American Chapter of the Association for Computational Linguistics: Human Language Technologies*, pages 483–498.

Yinfei Yang, Gustavo Hernandez Abrego, Steve Yuan, Mandy Guo, Qinlan Shen, Daniel Cer, Yun-hsuan Sung, Brian Strope, and Ray Kurzweil. 2019. Improving Multilingual Sentence Embedding using Bidirectional Dual Encoder with Additive Margin Softmax. In *Proceedings of the Twenty-Eighth International Joint Conference on Artificial Intelligence, IJCAI-19*, pages 5370–5378. International Joint Conferences on Artificial Intelligence Organization.

Zhilin Yang, Peng Qi, Saizheng Zhang, Yoshua Bengio, William Cohen, Ruslan Salakhutdinov, and Christopher D. Manning. 2018. HotpotQA: A Dataset for Diverse, Explainable Multi-hop Question Answering. In *Proceedings of the 2018 Conference on Empirical Methods in Natural Language Processing*, pages 2369–2380, Brussels, Belgium. Association for Computational Linguistics.

Marcos Zampieri, Shervin Malmasi, Preslav Nakov, Sara Rosenthal, Noura Farra, and Ritesh Kumar. 2019. SemEval-2019 Task 6: Identifying and Categorizing Offensive Language in Social Media (OffensEval). In *Proceedings of the 13th International Workshop on Semantic Evaluation*, pages 75–86.

Jianguo Zhang, Kazuma Hashimoto, Wenhao Liu, Chien-Sheng Wu, Yao Wan, Philip Yu, Richard Socher, and Caiming Xiong. 2020. Discriminative Nearest Neighbor Few-Shot Intent Detection by Transferring Natural Language Inference. In *Proceedings of the 2020 Conference on Empirical Methods in Natural Language Processing (EMNLP)*, pages 5064–5082.

Xiang Zhang, Junbo Zhao, and Yann LeCun. 2015. Character-level Convolutional Networks for Text Classification. In *Advances in Neural Information Processing Systems*, volume 28. Curran Associates, Inc.

Yuan Zhang, Jason Baldridge, and Luheng He. 2019. PAWS: Paraphrase Adversaries from Word Scrambling. In *Proceedings of the 2019 Conference of the North American Chapter of the Association for Computational Linguistics: Human Language Technologies, Volume 1 (Long and Short Papers)*, pages 1298–1308, Minneapolis, Minnesota. Association for Computational Linguistics.

Zihao Zhao, Eric Wallace, Shi Feng, Dan Klein, and Sameer Singh. 2021. Calibrate before use: Improving few-shot performance of language models. In *International Conference on Machine Learning*, pages 12697–12706.

Victor Zhong, Caiming Xiong, and Richard Socher. 2017. Seq2sql: Generating structured queries from natural language using reinforcement learning.

# Appendix

## A Seen Tasks

### A.1 Task List

Table 1 summarizes the 81 tasks we used to fine-tune the demonstration retriever. We started with datasets from Flan-v1 (Wei et al., 2021), MTEB (Muennighoff et al., 2023), and those in Li et al. (2023). We then further collected more datasets whose task formats are not well covered by our initial collection. In the following, we explain how to read the table.

**Name** We give a task name for each of them, while the names would not exactly match with those used in previous work.

**Type** We briefly describe the goal of every task by commonly-used terminologies.

**Languages** We collect datasets that use not only English, but also other languages to make our demonstration retriever work in as many languages as possible. Note that our retriever is based on mT5 (Xue et al., 2021) for the same purpose.

**Source** We provide the URL where we get the dataset for each task. The "Link" works only on PDF readers.

**Scoring** In the "Scoring candidates" paragraph in Section 2, we use the LLM to score a demonstration's usefulness for an input. We follow Hashimoto et al. (2024) to use different scoring functions, depending on the task types. We use the following three functions in this work:

- Probability– for tasks like single-class classification and multiple-choice selection, we use the probability value for generating the ground-truth output by the LLM: $p(y|x, t, d)$.
- F1– for tasks like text segmentation and multi-label classification, we use an F1 score by comparing the LLM's prediction (i.e., 1-shot prediction with $d$) against the ground-truth output, so that we can reward partially correct predictions.
- GLEU– for other text generation tasks, we use the GLEU score (Wu et al., 2016).

### A.2 Task Information

We briefly describe the information about each of the seen tasks, to mainly present our full (F) and short (S) task instructions used in our experiments. For all the data in any languages, we use the English-based instructions.

**No. 01–06** For the standard machine translation tasks, we use the following task instructions:

F: The goal of this task is to translate from [language 1] to [language 2].

S: Translation: [language 1] to [language 2].

**No. 07–09** For the ANLI tasks, we use the following task instructions:

F: The goal of this task is to judge if the hypothesis can be concluded, given the context. The output is "Yes", "No", or "It's impossible to say".

S: Natural language inference: context to hypothesis.

**No. 10** For the QNLI task, we use the following task instructions:

F: The goal of this task is to identify if the sentence correctly answers the question. The output is yes or no.

S: Natural language inference: sentence to question.

**No. 11** For the MNLI task, we use the following task instructions:

F: The goal of this task is to identify if the premise entails the hypothesis. The output is entailment, contradiction, or neutral.

S: Natural language inference: premise to hypothesis.

**No. 12** For the WNLI task, we use the following task instructions:

F: The goal of this task is to identify if text2 is true or false, given text1.

S: Natural language inference: text1 to text2.

**No. 13–14** For the paraphrase identification tasks, we use the following task instructions:

F: The goal of this task is to identify if sentence1 and sentence2 have the same meaning. The output is yes or no.

S: Paraphrase identification: sentence1 and sentence2.

**No. 15** For the Tatoeba task, we use the following task instructions:

F: The goal of this task is to identify if sentence1 is a translation of sentence2. The output is Yes or No.

S: Translation identification: sentence1 and sentence2.

We note that we used the test set of this task, and therefore our retrievers cannot be used for Tatoeba evaluation in any ways.

**No. 16–18** For the binary sentiment classification tasks, we use the following task instructions:

F: The goal of this task is to identify the sentiment given the text. The output is positive or negative.

S: Sentiment classification.

**No. 19–20** For the three-way sentiment classification tasks, we use the following task instructions:

F: The goal of this task is to identify the sentiment label of the tweet. The output is positive, negative, or neutral.

S: Sentiment classification.

**No. 21** For the TweetEval-emoji task, we use the following task instructions:

F: The goal of this task is to identify the emoji relevant to the tweet. The 20 possible emojis are ...

S: Emoji generation.

**No. 22** For the TweetEval-emotion task, we use the following task instructions:

F: The goal of this task is to identify the emotion of the tweet. The 4 possible emotions are anger, joy, optimism, or sadness.

S: Emotion classification.

**No. 23** For the DialogEmotion task, we use the following task instructions:

F: The goal of this task is to list all the speaker names who experience the specific emotion in the conversation. The output will be a #-separated list like "speaker_1#speaker_4#speaker_5".

S: Emotion detection: speakers.

**No. 24** For the Massive-intent task, we use the following task instructions:

F: The goal of this task is to identify the intent label of the user's input. The list of the 60 labels is: alarm_query, alarm_remove, alarm_set, audio_volume_down, audio_volume_mute, ...

S: User input intent classification.

**No. 25** For the MTOP-domain task, we use the following task instructions:

F: The goal of this task is to identify the domain of the user's input. There are 11 possible domains: alarm, calling, event, messaging, music, news, people, recipes, reminder, timer, weather.

S: User input domain classification.

**No. 26** For the MTOP-intent task, we use the following task instructions:

F: The goal of this task is to identify the intent of the user's input. There are 113 possible intents: ADD_TIME_TIMER, ADD_TO_PLAYLIST_MUSIC, ...

S: User input domain classification.

**No. 27** For the ATIS-intent task, we use the following task instructions:

F: The goal of this task is to identify user's intents from abbreviation, aircraft, airfare, ... If multiple intents are identified, the output will be a #-separated string: intent_1#intent_2#intent_3.

S: Multi-label intent classification.

**No. 28** For the E2ENLG-reversed task, we use the following task instructions:

F: The goal of this task is to extract attributes given a text about restaurant. The list of the 8 possible attributes are area, customerRating, eatType, familyFriendly, food, name, near, or priceRange. The output is a Python dictionary like {"attribute_1": "value_1", "attribute_2": "value_2", "attribute_3": "value_3"}

S: Attribute extraction.

**No. 29** For the WikiSQL task, we use the following task instructions:

F: The goal of this task is to convert the natural language question into an SQL query, based on the table.

S: Text/table to SQL generation.

**No. 30** For the BC5CDR task, we use the following task instructions:

F: The goal of this task is to copy the given text by tagging entities with XML tags. There are 2 entity types: Chemical, Disease. Then the output is like "word1 <Chemical>word2 word3</Chemical> word4 <Disease>word5</Disease>".

S: Named entity extraction: biomedical.

**No. 31** For the BioNLP13PC task, we use the following task instructions:

F: The goal of this task is to copy the given text by tagging entities with XML tags. There are 4 entity types: Cellular_component, Complex, Gene_or_gene_product, Simple_chemical. Then the output is like "word1 <Complex>word2 word3</Complex> word4 <Simple_chemical>word5</Simple_chemical>".

S: Named entity extraction: biomedical.

**No. 32** For the JNLPBA task, we use the following task instructions:

F: The goal of this task is to copy the given text by tagging entities with XML tags. There are 5 entity types: DNA, RNA, cell_line, cell_type, protein. Then the output is like "word1 <DNA>word2 word3</DNA> word4 <protein>word5</protein>".

S: Named entity extraction: biomedical.

**No. 33** For the MultiCoNER2 task, we use the following task instructions:

F: The goal of this task is to copy the given text by tagging entities with XML tags. There are 33 entity types: AerospaceManufacturer, AnatomicalStructure, ... Then the output is like "word1 <Artist>word2 word3</Artist> word4 <Drink>word5</Drink>".

S: Named entity extraction: Wikipedia.

**No. 34** For the CoNLL2003 task, we use the following task instructions:

F: The goal of this task is to copy the given text by tagging entities with XML tags. There are 4 entity types: Location, Miscellaneous, Organization, Person. Then the output is like "word1 <Location>word2 word3</Location> word4 <Person>word5</Person>".

S: Named entity extraction: news.

**No. 35** For the MTOP-slot task, we use the following task instructions:

F: The goal of this task is to copy the given text by tagging attributes with XML tags. There are 74 attribute types: AGE, ALARM_NAME, ... Then the output is like "word1 <AGE>word2 word3</AGE> word4 <CONTACT>word5</CONTACT>".

S: Attribute extraction.

**No. 36** For the SNIPS-slot task, we use the following task instructions:

F: The goal of this task is to copy the given text by tagging attributes with XML tags. There are 39 attribute types: album, artist, best_rating, ... Then the output is like "word1 <city>word2 word3</city> word4 <country>word5</country>".

S: Attribute extraction.

**No. 37** For the ATIS-slot task, we use the following task instructions:

F: The goal of this task is to copy the given text by tagging attributes with XML tags. There are 79 attribute types: aircraft_code, airline_code, ... Then the output is like "word1 <airport_code>word2 word3</airport_code> word4 word5".

S: Attribute extraction.

**No. 38** For the SemRel task, we use the following task instructions:

F: The goal of this task is to identify relation between the two entities marked by <e1></e1> and <e2></e2>. The possible relations are "e1:Cause e2:Effect", "e1:Effect e2:Cause", ... If the relation type is not one of the above, the output will be "Other".

S: Relation classification: e1 and e2.

**No. 39** For the DDI2013 task, we use the following task instructions:

F: The goal of this task is to identify the relation type of two drugs mentioned as @DRUG$ in the text. There are 4 relation types: advise, effect, int, mechanism. If there is no relation between the drugs, the answer is false.

S: Relation extraction: @DRUG$ and @DRUG$.

**No. 40** For the ChemProt task, we use the following task instructions:

F: The goal of this task is to identify the relation of @CHEMICAL$ and @GENE$ (or just @CHEM-GENE$) in the text. The answer is true or false.

S: Relation extraction: @CHEMICAL$ and @GENE$ (or @CHEM-GENE$).

**No. 41** For the WordSeg task, we use the following task instructions:

F: The goal of this task is to segment the words in the given characters. The output is like "word_1 word_2 word_3".

S: Word segmentation.

**No. 42** For the FixPunct task, we use the following task instructions:

F: The goal of this task is to generate the input text with punctuation.

S: Text punctuation.

**No. 43** For the CoLA task, we use the following task instructions:

F: The goal of this task is to identify if the input text is linguistically acceptable or not. The output is acceptable or unacceptable.

S: Linguistic acceptableness.

**No. 44** For the CoNLL2000 task, we use the following task instructions:

F: The goal of this task is to copy the given text by tagging syntactic phrases with XML tags. There are 11 phrase types: ADJP, ADVP, CONJP, INTJ, LST, NP, PP, PRT, SBAR, UCP, VP. Then the output is like "word1 <VP>word2 word3</VP> word4 <NP>word5</NP>".

S: Syntactic phrase chunking.

**No. 45** For the Pronoun task, we use the following task instructions:

F: The goal of this task is to identify what the pronoun corresponds to, given the sentence. The output is a phrase/entity in the sentence.

S: Coreference resolution: pronoun.

**No. 46** For the WSC task, we use the following task instructions:

F: The goal of this task is to identify if text1 and text2 are the same in the given context. The output is yes or no.

S: Text sense equivalence: text1 and text2 in context.

**No. 47** For the WinoGrande task, we use the following task instructions:

F: The goal of this task is to select one of the given options to complete the context.

S: Text completion.

**No. 48** For the WiC task, we use the following task instructions:

F: The goal of this task is to identify if the specified word has the same meaning in sentence1 and sentence2. The output is yes or no.

S: Word sense equivalence: word in sentence1 and sentence2.

**No. 49–52** For the code summarization tasks, we use the following task instructions:

F: The goal of this task is to write comment about the [language] code.

S: Code summarization: [language].

**No. 53** For the Gigaword task, we use the following task instructions:

F: The goal of this task is to extract a text segment that summarizes the input text.

S: Text summarization.

**No. 54** For the SAMSum task, we use the following task instructions:

F: The goal of this task is to summarize the dialogue.

S: Dialogue summarization.

**No. 55** For the iDebate task, we use the following task instructions:

F: The goal of this task is to generate a claim about the debate topic and the arguments.

S: Claim generation.

**No. 56** For the MultiHateCheck task, we use the following task instructions:

F: The goal of this task is to identify if the input text is hateful or non-hateful, and its activity type. The list of "hateful" types are derog_dehum, derog_impl, ... The list of "non-hateful" types are counter_quote, counter_ref, ... The output is "hateful:type" or "non-hateful:type".

S: Hate speech detection.

We note that we used the test set of this task, and therefore our retrievers cannot be used for MultiHateCheck evaluation in any ways.

**No. 57** For the Toxic task, we use the following task instructions:

F: The goal of this task is to identify if the input text is "toxic" or "not toxic".

S: Toxic conversation detection.

**No. 58** For the Countfact task, we use the following task instructions:

F: The goal of this task is to identify if the input text is counterfactual or not-counterfactual.

S: Counterfactual review detection.

**No. 59** For the Irony task, we use the following task instructions:

F: The goal of this task is to identify if the input tweet is irony or not. The output is Irony or Non-irony.

S: Irony tweet detection.

**No. 60** For the Offensive task, we use the following task instructions:

F: The goal of this task is to identify if the input tweet is offensive or not. The output is Offensive or Non-offensive.

S: Offensive tweet detection.

**No. 61** For the Sarcasm task, we use the following task instructions:

F: The goal of this task is to identify if an input text is sarcastic or non-sarcastic.

S: Sarcastic text detection.

**No. 62** For the SQuAD2 task, we use the following task instructions:

F: The goal of this task is to extract an answer phrase from the context to answer the question. If the question cannot be answered, then the output is "unanswerable".

S: Question answering.

**No. 63** For the BoolQ task, we use the following task instructions:

F: The goal of this task is to answer the question, given the title and text.

S: Question answering.

**No. 64** For the DROP task, we use the following task instructions:

F: The goal of this task is to answer the question, given the context.

S: Question answering.

**No. 65** For the OpenbookQA task, we use the following task instructions:

F: The goal of this task is to answer the question based on the fact. The output is one of the given options.

S: Multiple-choice question answering.

**No. 66** For the Cosmos task, we use the following task instructions:

F: The goal of this task is to answer the question, given the context. The output is one of the given options.

S: Multiple-choice question answering.

**No. 67** For the SciDocs task, we use the following task instructions:

F: The goal of this task is to identify if the candidate title is topically "Relevant" or "Not relevant" to the query title of a scientific document.

S: Relevance: candidate title to query title.

We note that we used the test set of this task, and therefore our retrievers cannot be used for SciDocs evaluation in any ways.

**No. 68** For the HotpotQA task, we use the following task instructions:

F: The goal of this task is to identify documents that are relevant to answering the question (QUESTION). The output is a #-separated list of the document IDs like "DOC_2#DOC_4".

S: Relevance: document IDs to question.

**No. 69–70** For the AI2 ARC tasks, we use the following task instructions:

F: The goal of this task is to answer the question. The output is one of the given options.

S: Multiple-choice question answering.

**No. 71** For the TriviaQA task, we use the following task instructions:

F: The goal of this task is to answer the question.

S: Question answering.

**No. 72** For the Math task, we use the following task instructions:

F: The goal of this task is to solve the math problem.

S: Math problem solution.

**No. 73** For the CommonGen task, we use the following task instructions:

F: The goal of this task is to generate a short text by using all the words in the input text.

S: Text generation: using all words.

**No. 74** For the SNLI-en task, we use the following task instructions:

F: The goal of this task is to generate a text that can be entailed by the input text.

S: Text generation: entailment.

**No. 75** For the PIQA-qgen task, we use the following task instructions:

F: The goal of this task is to generate a query that leads to the input text.

S: Query generation.

**No. 76** For the arXiv task, we use the following task instructions:

- F: The goal of this task is to identify all the categories about the arXiv article. There are 147 categories: astro-ph, astro-ph.CO, ... The output is a list of the categories separated by # like "category_1#category_2#category_3".
- S: Multi-label category classification.

This task is based on a very large dataset, and we used a part of it (`train_0.jsonl.gz`).

**No. 77** For the medRxiv task, we use the following task instructions:

- F: The goal of this task is to identify the category of the medRxiv article. There are 51 categories: addiction medicine, allergy and immunology, ...
- S: Category classification.

**No. 78** For the DBpedia task, we use the following task instructions:

- F: The goal of this task is to identify the topic of the input text. The output is one of the 14 topics: Company, Educational Institution, Artist, Athlete, ...
- S: Topic classification.

**No. 79** For the Yahoo task, we use the following task instructions:

- F: The goal of this task is to identify the topic about the community QA. The output is one of the 10 topics: Society & Culture, Science & Mathematics, Health, ...
- S: Topic classification.

**No. 80** For the AG news task, we use the following task instructions:

- F: The goal of this task is to identify the topic of the titled text. The output is one of the 4 topics: World, Sports, Business, Science/Tech.
- S: News topic classification.

**No. 81** For the TREC task, we use the following task instructions:

- F: The goal of this task is to identify what type of thing the question is asking about. The output is one of the 6 types: description, entity, abbreviation, human, numeric, location.
- S: Question topic classification.

### A.3 Multi-lingual Data Augmentation

We describe details about the data augmentation presented in Section 5.4.

**ANLI r1** The original input and output of this task are formatted as follows:

$x =$ context: "*context*" hypothesis: "*hypothesis*"

$y =$ Yes

We apply the translation to *context* and *hypothesis*, and keep the others in English. We set $(a, b) = (10, 20)$ for the target language sampling.

**Tweet Sentiment Extraction** The original input and output of this task are formatted as follows:

$x =$ *text*

$y =$ neutral

We apply the translation to *text*, and keep the others in English. We set $(a, b) = (4, 8)$ for the target language sampling.

**SemRel** The original input and output of this task are formatted as follows:

$x =$ ... *<e1>...</e1>* ... *<e2>...</e2>* ...

$y =$ e1:Effect e2:Cause

We apply the translation to ... *<e1>...</e1>* ... *<e2>...</e2>* ..., and keep the others in English. We filter out translated examples that result in not having the entity markers of e1 and e2. We set $(a, b) = (10, 20)$ for the target language sampling.

**iDebate** The original input and output of this task are formatted as follows:

$x =$ debate topic: "*debate topic*" arguments: "*arguments*"

$y =$ *claim*

We apply the translation to *debate topic*, *arguments*, and *claim*, and keep the others in English. We set $(a, b) = (20, 80)$ for the target language sampling.

**BoolQ** The original input and output of this task are formatted as follows:

$x =$ title: "*title*" text: "*text*" question: "*question*"

$y =$ *answer*

We apply the translation to *title*, *text*, *question*, and *answer*, and keep the others in English. We set $(a, b) = (10, 20)$ for the target language sampling.

**PIQA-qgen** The original input and output of this task are formatted as follows:

$x =$ *text*

$y =$ *query*

We apply the translation to *text* and *query*, and keep the others in English. We set $(a, b) = (10, 20)$ for the target language sampling.

**DBpedia** The original input and output of this task are formatted as follows:

$x =$ *text*

$y =$ Educational Institution

We apply the translation to *text*, and keep the others in English. We set $(a, b) = (10, 20)$ for the target language sampling.

**TREC** The original input and output of this task are formatted as follows:

$x =$ *text*

$y =$ human

We apply the translation to *text*, and keep the others in English. We set $(a, b) = (20, 40)$ for the target language sampling.

## B Unseen Tasks

Table 2 summarized the unseen tasks we used in our experiments, and in this section we provide further details of the tasks.

**AfriSenti Zero** For this task, we use the following task instructions:

F: The goal of this task is to identify the sentiment label of the tweet. The output is positive, negative, or neutral.

S: Sentiment classification.

These are identical to those of the AfriSenti task.

**GoEmotions** For this task, we use the following task instructions:

F: The goal of this task is to identify emotions in the text from admiration, amusement, anger, ... If multiple emotions are identified, the output will be a #-separated string: emotion_1#emotion_2#emotion_3.

S: Multi-label emotion classification.

**CLINC150** For this task, we use the following task instructions:

F: The goal of this task is to identify an intent given a user input. There are 150 intents: "current_location" "oil_change_when" "oil_change_how" ... Then the output is an intent label.

S: User input intent classification.

Unlike the previous work (Zhang et al., 2020; Hashimoto et al., 2024), we excluded all the out-of-scope examples from this task, and soley focus on the intent classification aspect.

**Orcas-I** For this task, we use the following task instructions:

F: The goal of this task is to identify the intent of the query with the search results (titles and URLs). The output is one of the 5 labels: Abstain, Factual, Transactional, Navigational, Instrumental.

S: Query intent classification.

**MIT-R** For this task, we use the following task instructions:

F: The goal of this task is to copy the given text by tagging attributes with XML tags. There are 8 attribute types: Amenity, Cuisine, Dish, Hours, Location, Price, Rating, Restaurant_Name. Then the output is like "word1 <Rating>word2 word3</Rating> word4 <Location>word5</Location>".

S: Attribute extraction.

**SSENT** For this task, we use the following task instructions:

F: The goal of this task is to copy the given text by tagging attributes with XML tags. There are 2 attribute types: Positive and Negative. Then the output is like "word1 <Negative>word2 word3</Negative> word4 <Positive>word5</Positive>".

S: Attribute extraction.

**XML-MT** For this task, we use the following task instructions:

F: The goal of this task is to translate an XML-tagged text from English to [target language] by preserving the XML structure. Both the input and output are like "word1 <tag-A>word2 word3</tag-A> word4 <tag-B>word5</tag-B>".

S: Translation: English to [target language].

## C Evaluation Metrics

This section describes the evaluation metric used for each task in our evaluation. All the scores are in the range of [0, 100].

### C.1 Seen Tasks

**AfriSenti** We use the label matching accuracy for this task.

**DDI13** We use an F1 score based on precision and recall of the non-false classes.

**ATIS-intent** We use a corpus-level F1 score for the multi-label classification task.

**MTOP-intent** We use the label matching accuracy for this task.

**Countfact** We use a corpus-level F1 score based on precision and recall of the “counterfactual” class.

**Offensive** We use a corpus-level F1 score based on precision and recall of the “Offensive” class.

**BC5CDR** We use a corpus-level F1 score based on precision and recall of the labeled entities.

**PHP** We use a corpus-level BLEU (Papineni et al., 2002) score for this text generation task.

### C.2 Unseen Tasks

**AfriSenti Zero** We use the label matching accuracy for this task.

**GoEmotions** We use a corpus-level F1 score for the multi-label classification task.

**CLINC150** We use the label matching accuracy for this task.

**Orcas-I** We use the label matching accuracy for this task.

**MIT-R** We use a corpus-level F1 score based on precision and recall of the labeled attributes.

**SSENT** We use a corpus-level F1 score based on precision and recall of the labeled attributes.

**XML-MT** We use the structured BLEU metric (Hashimoto et al., 2019).

# McGill NLP Group Submission to the MRL 2024 Shared Task: Ensembling Enhances Effectiveness of Multilingual Small LMs

**Senyu Li**[*1,2] **Hao Yu**[1,2] **Jessica Ojo**[1,2] **David Ifeoluwa Adelani**[1,2,3]
[1]Mila - Quebec AI Institute, [2]McGill University, [3]Canada CIFAR AI Chair
senyu.li@mail.mcgill.ca

## Abstract

We present our systems for the three tasks and five languages included in the MRL 2024 Shared Task on Multilingual Multi-task Information Retrieval: (1) Named Entity Recognition, (2) Free-form Question Answering, and (3) Multiple-choice Question Answering. For each task, we explored the impact of selecting different multilingual language models for fine-tuning across various target languages, and implemented an ensemble system that generates final outputs based on predictions from multiple fine-tuned models. All models are large language models fine-tuned on task-specific data. Our experimental results show that a more balanced dataset would yield better results. However, when training data for certain languages are scarce, fine-tuning on a large amount of English data supplemented by a small amount of "triggering data" in the target language can produce decent results.[1]

## 1 Introduction

In this paper, we present our submission for the MRL 2024 shared task[2]. The shared task includes the following three tasks: Named Entity Recognition (NER), Free-form Question Answering (FFQA), and Multiple-choice Question Answering (MCQA). Each task involves a final test set for five languages: Igbo, Swiss German, Turkish, Azerbaijani, and Yorùbá. Our systems are designed to support all of these languages simultaneously.

Our systems leveraged the remarkable success of transformer-based (Vaswani et al., 2017), pre-trained Language Models (LMs) such as BERT (Devlin et al., 2019) and T5 (Raffel et al., 2019), which have demonstrated outstanding performance in various Natural Language Processing (NLP) tasks in recent years. These models, with their large number of parameters and pre-training on vast datasets, have proven to be highly effective in extracting and representing information possessed by input sequences (Brown et al., 2020). Their strong generalization capabilities make them well-suited for fine-tuning on specific tasks, such as NER and translation. Multilingual pre-trained LLMs, like XLM-RoBERTa (Conneau et al., 2019), mT5 (Xue et al., 2021), and their variants, which were trained on extensive multilingual datasets, are particularly effective for multilingual tasks. These models capture semantic structures/knowledge shared across languages, enhancing their ability to transfer knowledge between languages. Fine-tuning these models for specific tasks allowed us to fully utilize their rich token-level and sentence-level semantic representations, which are essential for tasks requiring detailed language understanding. For instance, NER benefits from the token-level granularity learned during pretraining (Yan et al., 2019), while FFQA and MCQA require robust sentence-level comprehension, which these models provide (Robinson et al., 2023; Myrzakhan et al., 2024). The combination of pre-training on extensive multilingual corpora and task-specific fine-tuning enabled our system to achieve decent performance across all five target languages.

During the fine-tuning phase, in addition to hyper-parameter selection, our systems employed other strategies to promote a smoother and faster-converging learning process, such as using data from languages closely related to the target languages, applying curriculum learning (Bengio et al., 2009), and interleaving data from various languages to enhance model performance and smooth the learning process.

The experiment results show that different base models with a similar number of parameters exhibit varying advantages for different languages after fine-tuning. Ensembling the outputs from each model results in better and more robust overall performance. Additionally, given the limited availabil-

*Corresponding author

[1]Our codes will be made available at this link.

[2]The website of the shared task is available at this link.



*Proceedings of the Fourth Workshop on Multilingual Representation Learning (MRL 2024)*, pages 346–356
November 16, 2024 ©2024 Association for Computational Linguistics

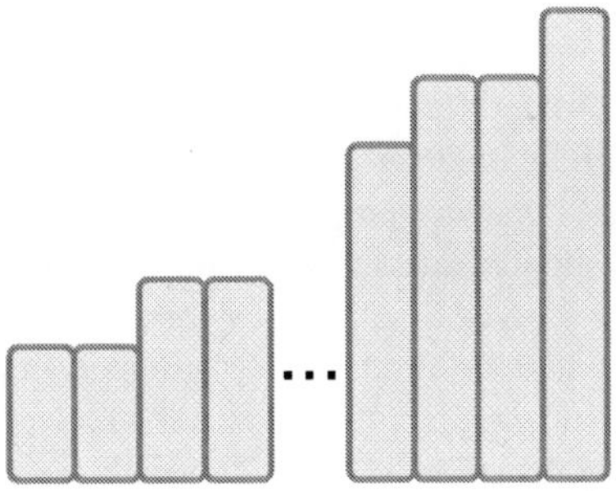

Figure 1: This figure illustrates the process of Curriculum Learning. Shorter data pieces appear earlier in the epoch, while longer data pieces are introduced later.

ity of data for certain languages, leveraging large amounts of task-specific data in English— which is the easiest to obtain— along with smaller amounts of data in the target language, allows knowledge transfer from English to the target language. This approach outperforms fine-tuning exclusively on the limited data available in the target language.

## 2 Background

In this section, we provide a brief overview of the background knowledge for the three tasks involved in the shared task, along with the three techniques we employed to facilitate the learning process.

**Named Entity Recognition** NER is an NLP task that focuses on identifying and categorizing specific tokens or phrases in a text as belonging to predefined entity types, such as persons (PER), organizations (ORG), locations (LOC), dates (DATE), and other relevant categories. A named entity refers to a real-world object or concept that can be recognized by its proper name within the text. For example, in the sentence "Barack Obama visited Paris in 2015," the named entities are "Barack Obama" (person), "Paris" (location), and "2015" (date). In this shared task, we only consider three entity tags: persons, organizations, and locations.

**Free-form Question Answering** FFQA involves providing answers to natural language questions based on the information given. This task assumes an information-seeking scenario, where users ask questions without knowing the answer in advance, and the system is responsible for finding a relevant answer based on information presented in the passage (if one exists). In this task, the system is given a question, a title, and a passage, and must either generate a text sequence for the correct answer or indicate that there is no answer for the question based on information available in the passage by generating the text sequence “no answer”. For example, consider the passage: "Tom went to the supermarket and bought two apples." If the question is "What did Tom buy in the supermarket?", the system should return the answer "Two apples." However, if the question is "Which supermarket did Tom visit?", the system should respond with "no answer," as the passage does not specify the name of the supermarket.

**Multiple-choice Question Answering** Similar to FFQA, MCQA assumes a scenario where users seek information by asking questions without knowing the answer and are given a question, title, and passage. However, unlike FFQA, the MCQA system is also provided with four potential options, and its task is to identify the correct one based on the information in the passage. For instance, consider the passage: "Tom went to the supermarket and bought two apples." If the question is "How many apples did Tom buy?" and the four options are "A. 1", "B. 2", "C. 3", and "D. 4", the system should return "B".

**Curriculum Learning** Curriculum learning (Bengio et al., 2009) is a machine learning strategy that gradually introduces a model to progressively more challenging data pieces over multiple training iterations. This method can often produce better results compared to using a randomly shuffled training set. This approach is effective in the sense that, the model begins by learning general concepts through simpler examples, and then incrementally incorporates more detailed and complex information as more difficult examples are introduced. For our systems, we define "difficulty" by the length of the input text, where longer text equates to greater complexity and comes later in the epoch, as shown in Figure 1. Since curriculum learning is a paradigm that focuses solely on the selection and ordering of training data, it can be integrated with various other machine learning techniques, like Interleaving Multilingual Data Pieces which we will introduce later in this section.

**Knowledge Transfer** Knowledge transfer in multilingual LLMs refers to the model's ability to leverage information, patterns, or representations learned in one language to enhance its performance or understanding in another. This happens because

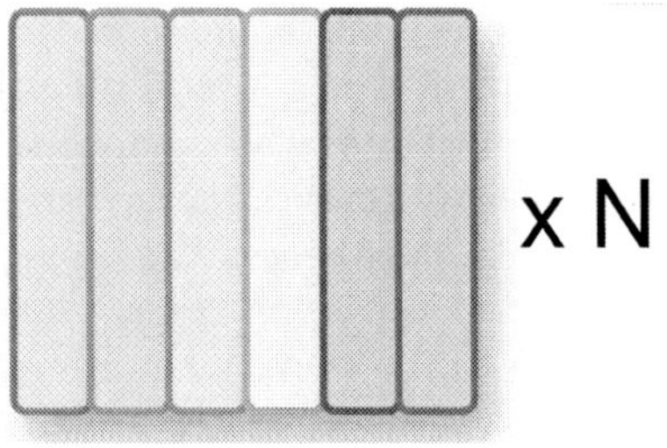


Figure 2: This figure illustrates the process of interleaving multilingual data. Each coloured tile represents a single data sample from a different language. This process is repeated for each data sample in every language, ensuring that each sample appears only once per epoch.

multilingual LLMs develop shared representations of concepts that can be applied across different languages. To facilitate the knowledge transfer for our base models, we fine-tuned the base models on diverse multilingual data. This includes a relatively small amount of data for the target languages, additional data for languages closely related to the target languages, and a large amount of data from high-resource languages like English.

**Interleaving Multilingual Data Pieces** Interleaving Multilingual Data Pieces is a machine learning technique used to train multilingual models by interleaving data from various languages during training. This approach promotes cross-lingual knowledge transfer by encouraging the model to develop shared linguistic representations and structures, which improves its ability to generalize across languages. It is especially effective in cross-lingual information retrieval scenarios, allowing the model to utilize common features across languages and enhance performance in low-resource language settings. An illustration of this approach can be found in Figure 2

## 3 Methods

In this section, we provide a detailed illustration of each system we implemented for the three tasks involved in MRL 2024.

### 3.1 Models Included

**XLM-RoBERTa** XLM-RoBERTa (Conneau et al., 2019) is a transformer-based masked language model, which is a multilingual version of the RoBERTa model, designed to handle text in multiple languages by extending the BERT architecture.

**Afro-XLMR** AfroXLMR (Alabi et al., 2022) is a variant of the XLM-RoBERTa model specifically tailored for African languages. While XLM-RoBERTa is designed to work across 100 languages, it may underperform for African languages due to limited data in these languages during training. AfroXLMR addresses this by focusing on improving the model's performance in African linguistic contexts, by using MLM adaptation of XLM-R-large model on 17 African languages, covering the major African language families and three high-resource languages. Previous work(Adelani et al., 2022) has empirically demonstrated that this model performs strongly in NER for African languages.

**mT5** The mT5 (Multilingual Text-to-Text Transfer Transformer) (Xue et al., 2021) is a variant of the T5 (Text-to-Text Transfer Transformer) architecture. mT5 is pre-trained on a massive multilingual dataset covering 101 languages from the Common Crawl corpus, which enables it to perform a wide range of natural language processing tasks. It operates using a text-to-text framework, where all tasks are framed as feeding text inputs and generating text outputs.

**mT0** The mT0 (Multilingual T0) (Muennighoff et al., 2023) is a variant of the T0 model, designed to extend its zero-shot and few-shot learning capabilities to a multilingual context. It is based on the T5 architecture but trained to follow natural language instructions using multilingual data, allowing it to generalize across a wide range of languages and tasks without requiring task-specific training.

**AfriTeVa V2** AfriTeVa V2 (Oladipo et al., 2023) is a multilingual sequence-to-sequence model derived from the T5 architecture, designed to support African languages. AfriTeVa V2 was pretrained on Wura which contains 20 languages, including 16 African languages, including Yorùbá and Igbo, alongside globally spoken languages like English and French.

### 3.2 Named Entity Recognition

We fine-tuned three models for the NER task: `xlm-roberta-large`, `afro-xlmr-large`, and `afro-xlmr-large-76L`. A linear layer was added to the final hidden states of the Transformer encoder for each model, followed by a softmax activation to predict the probability distribution for each token.

During training, each input sequence was first tokenized, meaning that each token was either tokenized as a whole or split into multiple tokens. For tokens that form parts of a word, only the first token is used for prediction. For example, if the word "eating" is tokenized into "eat" and "ing," only the prediction for "eat" will be considered as the final prediction for the word "eating" and the loss will be calculated only for the token "eat"

For the tokens in the test set, we gathered predictions from each model and applied majority voting. The prediction that occurred most frequently was selected as the final output for that token. In the case of a tie, where all three models produced different predictions, we chose the prediction from `afro-xlmr-large`, which is the best-performing model in the development phase.

### 3.3 Free-form Question Answering

We fine-tuned two models for the Free-form Question Answering task: mT5 Large and AfriTeVa V2 Large. The models were trained using a sequence-to-sequence (seq2seq) text generation approach. During training, the model was optimized to minimize the cross-entropy loss between the predicted tokens and the actual target tokens. The input data formatting template is shown in Table 1.

For the final submission, we chose to use the fine-tuned AfriTeVa V2 Large for the two African languages and mT5 Large for the other three non-African languages. This decision was based on the fact that AfriTeVa V2 Large is specifically adapted for African languages, while mT5, being designed for more general language tasks, performs better with non-African languages.

### 3.4 Multiple-choice Question Answering

We finetuned 3 models for the Multiple-choice Question Answering task: mT5 Large, mT0 Large and AfriTeVa V2 Large. The models were trained using the seq2seq text generation approach. Similar to the finetuning for FFQA, The input data formatting template is shown in Table 1

During the fine-tuning phase, we modified the target output that the model was optimized to predict. Instead of solely predicting the letter corresponding to the correct choice, we adjusted the model to predict both the letter and the text associated with the choice. For example, given the passage: "Tom went to the supermarket and bought two apples." and the question: "How many apples did Tom buy?" with the four options: "A. 1", "B. 2", "C. 3", and "D. 4", rather than training the model to predict only the letter "B," we trained it to predict "B. 2". During inference, we extracted the first token generated (the letter) as the final prediction. This adjustment led to improved performance and faster convergence during the development phase compared to using the original target text.

| FFQA |
|---|
| Task: free-form QA<br>Context: [Passage]<br>Question: [Question] |
| **MCQA** |
| Context: [Passage]<br>Question: [Question]<br>A. [Text of choice A]<br>B. [Text of choice B]<br>C. [Text of choice C]<br>D. [Text of choice D] |

Table 1: Input templates for MCQA and MMQA.

For each question in the test set, we collected predictions from each model and applied majority voting. The prediction that occurred most frequently was selected as the final answer for that question. In case of a tie, where all three models produced different predictions, we chose the prediction from mT5 Large, as it was the best-performing model during the development phase.

## 4 Experiment

In this section, we provide detailed information about our implementation, including the computational resources used to run the experiments, the specifics of the training process, and the datasets used to train the models for each of the three tasks. Additionally, we will present the results on the test set provided by the organizers of this shared task, along with an analysis of the experimental results.

### 4.1 Setup

We used one Nvidia A100 80G GPU for all experiments. We used the Trainer of huggingface transformers to fine-tune all the models.

### 4.2 Datasets

This section lists all the datasets used to train models for each of the three tasks. All datasets are publicly available. For datasets that were not associated with any papers, we listed them in the Ap-

| Models | AZ | YO | TR | IG | ALS | Avg | Mdn |
|---|---|---|---|---|---|---|---|
| **Named Entity Recognition** | | | | | | | |
| Ours | **0.821** | **0.857** | **0.826** | 0.093 | **0.789** | 0.677 | **0.821** |
| CUNI | 0.573 | 0.805 | 0.778 | **0.740** | 0.704 | **0.720** | 0.740 |
| **Free Form Question Answering** | | | | | | | |
| Ours | 0.421 | 0.361 | 0.399 | 0.331 | 0.421 | 0.377 | 0.399 |
| 0-shot Llama-3.1-instruct 7B | 0.536 | 0.468 | 0.472 | 0.536 | 0.425 | 0.485 | 0.472 |
| 4-shot Llama-3.1-instruct 7B | 0.501 | 0.373 | 0.451 | 0.520 | 0.435 | 0.452 | 0.451 |
| 0-shot Llama-3.1-instruct 70B | **0.540** | 0.508 | 0.491 | 0.491 | 0.478 | 0.498 | 0.491 |
| 4-shot Llama-3.1-instruct 70B | 0.506 | 0.436 | 0.460 | **0.616** | **0.488** | **0.513** | 0.488 |
| 0-shot gemma-2 27b | 0.448 | 0.490 | 0.423 | 0.347 | 0.474 | 0.434 | 0.448 |
| 4-shot gemma-2 27b | 0.453 | 0.458 | 0.425 | 0.449 | 0.478 | 0.458 | 0.453 |
| 0-shot aya-101 13B | 0.398 | 0.444 | 0.370 | 0.318 | 0.419 | 0.390 | 0.398 |
| 4-shot aya-101 13B | 0.404 | 0.451 | 0.364 | 0.453 | 0.422 | 0.434 | 0.422 |
| 0-shot o1-preview | 0.535 | **0.525** | **0.520** | 0.428 | 0.458 | 0.480 | **0.520** |
| **Multiple Choice Question Answering** | | | | | | | |
| Ours | 0.969 | 0.853 | 0.816 | **0.969** | 0.777 | 0.879 | 0.853 |
| FT mT5 large | 0.966 | 0.848 | 0.810 | 0.965 | 0.778 | 0.876 | 0.848 |
| FT mT0 large | 0.966 | 0.824 | 0.830 | 0.965 | 0.769 | 0.869 | 0.830 |
| FT AfriTeVa V2 large | 0.807 | 0.784 | 0.592 | 0.949 | 0.580 | 0.772 | 0.784 |
| 0-shot Llama-3.1-instruct 7B | 0.969 | 0.731 | 0.884 | 0.954 | 0.788 | 0.849 | 0.884 |
| 4-shot Llama-3.1-instruct 7B | 0.931 | 0.737 | 0.701 | 0.933 | 0.782 | 0.827 | 0.782 |
| 0-shot Llama-3.1-instruct 70B | 0.979 | 0.896 | 0.939 | 0.959 | 0.917 | 0.932 | 0.939 |
| 4-shot Llama-3.1-instruct 70B | 0.976 | 0.881 | 0.966 | 0.963 | **0.923** | 0.932 | 0.963 |
| 0-shot gemma-2 27b | 0.979 | 0.891 | 0.946 | 0.963 | 0.886 | 0.925 | 0.946 |
| 4-shot gemma-2 27b | **0.983** | 0.905 | 0.932 | 0.967 | 0.898 | 0.932 | 0.932 |
| 0-shot aya-101 13B | 0.969 | 0.881 | 0.905 | 0.967 | 0.834 | 0.906 | 0.905 |
| 4-shot aya-101 13B | 0.969 | 0.860 | 0.871 | 0.967 | 0.834 | 0.898 | 0.871 |
| 0-shot o1-preview | 0.976 | **0.911** | **0.973** | 0.967 | 0.922 | **0.941** | **0.967** |

Table 2: The final results of each model on the test set for each task.

pendix B. For the final submission, we integrated the validation set provided by the organizers into our training set to reduce the gap between the training set and the test set.

#### 4.2.1 Named Entity Recognition

We used data of 10 languages from 5 datasets to fine-tune models for the NER task. For each dataset, we masked out NER tags that were not included in this shared task.

**MasakhaNER 2.0** MasakhaNER 2.0 (Adelani et al., 2022) is a human-annotated NER dataset for 20 African languages. For our study, we utilized the Yorùbá and Igbo data in this dataset. Additionally, we included data in Naija, Hausa, and chiShona to facilitate knowledge transfer.

We chose to include Naija, Hausa, and chiShona in our training data because Hausa and Naija are the top two transfer languages for Yorùbá, while chiShona is the best transfer language for Igbo (with Yorùbá as the second-best), as shown in the study by Adelani et al..

**CoNLL03** CoNLL03 (Tjong Kim Sang and De Meulder, 2003) consists of annotations of NER tags across English and German languages. In our experiments, we used the data from both languages.

**Turkish Wiki NER Dataset** Turkish Wiki NER dataset (Altinok, 2023) is an NER dataset which contains 20,000 manually annotated sentences selected from TWNERTC dataset (Sahin et al., 2017).

**UZNER** UZNER(Yusufu et al., 2023) is a benchmark manually dataset specifically designed for NER tasks in the Uzbek language.

#### 4.2.2 Free-form Question Answering

**XTREME-UP** XTREME-UP (Ruder et al., 2023) is a benchmark focus on the scarce data across 88 languages and 9 tasks. We used the Indonesian and English data of the "qa in lang" task in this dataset.

**MLQA** MLQA (Lewis et al., 2019) is an extractive QA evaluation benchmark contain across 7 languages. We used German data of this dataset.

**XQuAD** XQuaAD (Artetxe et al., 2019) is a cross-lingual question answering dataset composed of paragraphs and question-answer pairs selected from SQuAD v1.1 (Rajpurkar et al., 2016) translated into ten languages. We used German and Turkish data of this dataset.

**NaijaRC** NaijaRC (Aremu et al., 2024) is a multiple-choice reading comprehension dataset consisting of questions from high school reading comprehension exams in three native Nigerian languages. We used the Igbo, Yorùbá, and Hausa data from this dataset.

**Belebele** Belebele (Bandarkar et al., 2024) is a multilingual multiple-choice machine reading comprehension dataset. We transformed it into an FFQA dataset by removing the multiple-choice options and setting the text associated with the correct option as the target answer. We used the Azerbaijan, Igbo, Indonesian, English, German, Turkish, Uzbek, Yorùbá, and Hausa data from this dataset. We filtered out some questions if the question is not a closed question.

#### 4.2.3 Multiple-choice Question Answering

**Belebele** For MCQA, we used the data from the same set of languages as for the FFQA dataset.

**Cosmos QA** Cosmos QA (Huang et al., 2019) is a commonsense-based reading comprehension dataset in English, formulated as multiple-choice questions.

**RACE** RACE (Lai et al., 2017) is a large-scale reading comprehension dataset in English

### 4.3 Results

The Table 2 demonstrates the final results of our model and other LLMs applied to these tasks. Currently, there is a lack of final results from the official leaderboard. We will only include the FFQA and MCQA results.

#### 4.3.1 Free-form Question Answering

Our model achieved an average F1 score of 0.377 across all five languages. The performance varied across languages, with the highest scores observed for Azerbaijani and Swiss German (both 0.421), followed by Turkish (0.399), Yorùbá (0.361), and Igbo (0.331).

Compared to the baseline models, our system's performance was generally lower. The best-performing baseline was the 4-shot Llama-3.1-instruct 70B model, with an average F1 score of 0.513. The 0-shot o1-preview model also performed well, achieving the highest score for Azerbaijani (0.535) and competitive scores for other languages.

#### 4.3.2 Multiple-choice Question Answering

Our MCQA system demonstrated strong performance, achieving an average accuracy of 0.879 across all languages. The system performed exceptionally well on Azerbaijani (0.969) and Igbo (0.969), followed by Yorùbá (0.853), Turkish (0.816), and Swiss German (0.777).

Among the individual models we fine-tuned, mT5 large performed the best with an average accuracy of 0.876, closely followed by mT0 large at 0.869. The AfriTeVa V2 large model, despite being specifically adapted for African languages, showed lower overall performance (0.772) but performed well on Igbo (0.949).

Our ensemble system outperformed all of our individual fine-tuned models, demonstrating the effectiveness of the ensemble approach. However, some of the larger baseline models, particularly the 0-shot o1-preview and the 4-shot versions of Llama-3.1-instruct 70B and gemma-2 27b, achieved higher average accuracies (0.941, 0.932, and 0.932 respectively).

#### 4.3.3 Named Entity Recognition

Our NER system demonstrated strong performance across most languages in the shared task and achieved the highest F1 scores for four out of the five languages (Azerbaijani, Yorùbá, Turkish, and Swiss German) among all participant teams.

### 4.4 Analysis

#### 4.4.1 Named Entity Recognition

**Investigate Igbo Anomaly** A detailed analysis of our model's behaviour on Igbo data is crucial. This could include examining the training data and the model predictions.

**Ensemble Method Refinement** Given the strong performance of our system in most languages, further refinement of our base methods could potentially improve the final results, especially if we can address the models' performance issue on Igbo. Incorporating elements from our system and CUNI's system might result in a more robust and universally effective NER model for diverse languages.

#### 4.4.2 Free-form Question Answering

**Language-specific performance** Our system's performance varied across languages, with better results for Azerbaijani and Swiss German compared to African languages like Yorùbá and Igbo. This disparity might be due to differences in the quality or quantity of training data available for each language.

**Gap with larger models** The significant performance gap between our system and larger models like Llama-3.1-instruct 70B highlights the advantage of massive pre-training and model size in tackling complex FFQA tasks.

**Zero-shot vs. few-shot** Interestingly, for some baseline models (e.g., Llama-3.1-instruct 7B), the zero-shot performance was better than the few-shot performance. This suggests that for some languages, providing examples might not always lead to improved performance and could potentially introduce biases.

#### 4.4.3 Multiple-choice Question Answering

**Strong overall performance** Our MCQA system demonstrated robust performance across all languages, with particularly high accuracies for Azerbaijani and Igbo. This suggests that our approach of fine-tuning multilingual models and using ensemble methods is effective for MCQA tasks.

**Ensemble effectiveness** The superior performance of our ensemble system compared to individual fine-tuned models validates our approach of combining predictions from multiple models to improve overall accuracy.

**Language-specific variations** The performance variations across languages (e.g., lower accuracy for Swiss German) indicate that language-specific challenges persist even in MCQA tasks. This could be due to factors such as linguistic complexity, dataset quality, or the model's pre-training data distribution.

**Competitiveness with larger models** While some larger baseline models outperformed our system, the performance gap is smaller compared to the FFQA task. This suggests that our approach is particularly effective for MCQA, where the task structure might allow for better utilization of fine-tuning on limited data.

**AfriTeVa V2 performance** The specialized AfriTeVa V2 model showed strong performance on Igbo but underperformed on non-African languages. This highlights the trade-off between language-specific models and more general multilingual models.

## 5 Conclusion

Our study on multilingual multi-task information retrieval revealed key insights across NER, FFQA, and MCQA tasks. In the MCQA task, our ensemble models demonstrated particular strength, outperforming individual fine-tuned models. This underscores the benefits of combining predictions from multiple models to boost accuracy and robustness. For NER, our system showed strong performance across most languages, achieving the highest F1 scores in four out of five languages compared to the other participating systems. However, we observed a significant performance drop for Igbo, highlighting the challenges of consistent performance across diverse languages. We observed variable performance across tasks, with challenges particularly evident in FFQA and significant differences across languages, especially in low-resource settings. This variability was also present in NER, where our model's performance on Igbo lagged significantly behind other languages.

Looking forward, our findings suggest several promising areas for improvement. Enhancing FFQA performance through better fine-tuning strategies and exploring cross-lingual transfer methods is crucial. Developing task-specific model architectures that can better capture the nuances of each task while maintaining multilingual capabilities could lead to significant advances. Improving data augmentation and efficient fine-tuning approaches, especially for low-resource languages, remains a key challenge. Increasing model interpretability will be vital to better understand and address performance discrepancies across languages and tasks. For NER, investigating the causes of the performance anomaly in Igbo and refining our ensemble method could create a more universally effective model across diverse languages. While our approach shows promise, particularly for MCQA and most languages in NER, there is substantial room for further research. The goal remains to develop robust, multilingual, multi-task information retrieval systems that can overcome language barriers, address performance inconsistencies, and improve access to global information across a wide range of languages and task types.

## Acknowledgements

This research was supported by MILA compute. David Adelani is supported by the Canada CIFAR AI Chair program. We are grateful to OpenAI for providing API credits through their Researcher Access API programme to Masakhane for the evaluation of GPT LLMs.

## References

David Adelani, Graham Neubig, Sebastian Ruder, Shruti Rijhwani, Michael Beukman, Chester Palen-Michel, Constantine Lignos, Jesujoba Alabi, Shamsuddeen Muhammad, Peter Nabende, Cheikh M. Bamba Dione, Andiswa Bukula, Rooweither Mabuya, Bonaventure F. P. Dossou, Blessing Sibanda, Happy Buzaaba, Jonathan Mukiibi, Godson Kalipe, Derguene Mbaye, Amelia Taylor, Fatoumata Kabore, Chris Chinenye Emezue, Anuoluwapo Aremu, Perez Ogayo, Catherine Gitau, Edwin Munkoh-Buabeng, Victoire Memdjokam Koagne, Allahsera Auguste Tapo, Tebogo Macucwa, Vukosi Marivate, Mboning Tchiaze Elvis, Tajuddeen Gwadabe, Tosin Adewumi, Orevaoghene Ahia, and Joyce Nakatumba-Nabende. 2022. MasakhaNER 2.0: Africa-centric transfer learning for named entity recognition. In *Proceedings of the 2022 Conference on Empirical Methods in Natural Language Processing*, pages 4488–4508, Abu Dhabi, United Arab Emirates. Association for Computational Linguistics.

Jesujoba O. Alabi, David Ifeoluwa Adelani, Marius Mosbach, and Dietrich Klakow. 2022. Adapting pre-trained language models to African languages via multilingual adaptive fine-tuning. In *Proceedings of the 29th International Conference on Computational Linguistics*, pages 4336–4349, Gyeongju, Republic of Korea. International Committee on Computational Linguistics.

Duygu Altinok. 2023. A diverse set of freely available linguistic resources for Turkish. In *Proceedings of the 61st Annual Meeting of the Association for Computational Linguistics (Volume 1: Long Papers)*, pages 13739–13750, Toronto, Canada. Association for Computational Linguistics.

Anuoluwapo Aremu, Jesujoba O. Alabi, Daud Abolade, Nkechinyere F. Aguobi, Shamsuddeen Hassan Muhammad, and David Ifeoluwa Adelani. 2024. Naijarc: A multi-choice reading comprehension dataset for nigerian languages.

Mikel Artetxe, Sebastian Ruder, and Dani Yogatama. 2019. On the cross-lingual transferability of monolingual representations. *CoRR*, abs/1910.11856.

Lucas Bandarkar, Davis Liang, Benjamin Muller, Mikel Artetxe, Satya Narayan Shukla, Donald Husa, Naman Goyal, Abhinandan Krishnan, Luke Zettlemoyer, and Madian Khabsa. 2024. The belebele benchmark: a parallel reading comprehension dataset in 122 language variants.

Yoshua Bengio, Jerome Louradour, Ronan Collobert, and Jason Weston. 2009. Curriculum learning. In *Proceedings of the 26th Annual International Conference on Machine Learning (ICML)*, pages 41–48. ACM.

Tom B. Brown, Benjamin Mann, Nick Ryder, Melanie Subbiah, Jared Kaplan, Prafulla Dhariwal, Arvind Neelakantan, Pranav Shyam, Girish Sastry, Amanda Askell, Sandhini Agarwal, Ariel Herbert-Voss, Gretchen Krueger, Tom Henighan, Rewon Child, Aditya Ramesh, Daniel M. Ziegler, Jeffrey Wu, Clemens Winter, Christopher Hesse, Mark Chen, Eric Sigler, Mateusz Litwin, Scott Gray, Benjamin Chess, Jack Clark, Christopher Berner, Sam McCandlish, Alec Radford, Ilya Sutskever, and Dario Amodei. 2020. Language models are few-shot learners. *CoRR*, abs/2005.14165.

Alexis Conneau, Kartikay Khandelwal, Naman Goyal, Vishrav Chaudhary, Guillaume Wenzek, Francisco Guzmán, Edouard Grave, Myle Ott, Luke Zettlemoyer, and Veselin Stoyanov. 2019. Unsupervised cross-lingual representation learning at scale. *CoRR*, abs/1911.02116.

Jacob Devlin, Ming-Wei Chang, Kenton Lee, and Kristina Toutanova. 2019. BERT: Pre-training of deep bidirectional transformers for language understanding. In *Proceedings of the 2019 Conference of the North American Chapter of the Association for Computational Linguistics: Human Language Technologies, Volume 1 (Long and Short Papers)*, pages 4171–4186, Minneapolis, Minnesota. Association for Computational Linguistics.

Lifu Huang, Ronan Le Bras, Chandra Bhagavatula, and Yejin Choi. 2019. Cosmos qa: Machine reading comprehension with contextual commonsense reasoning.

Guokun Lai, Qizhe Xie, Hanxiao Liu, Yiming Yang, and Eduard Hovy. 2017. RACE: Large-scale ReAding comprehension dataset from examinations. In *Proceedings of the 2017 Conference on Empirical Methods in Natural Language Processing*, pages 785–794, Copenhagen, Denmark. Association for Computational Linguistics.

Patrick Lewis, Barlas Oguz, Ruty Rinott, Sebastian Riedel, and Holger Schwenk. 2019. Mlqa: Evaluating cross-lingual extractive question answering. *arXiv preprint arXiv:1910.07475*.

Niklas Muennighoff, Thomas Wang, Lintang Sutawika, Adam Roberts, Stella Biderman, Teven Le Scao, M Saiful Bari, Sheng Shen, Zheng Xin Yong, Hailey Schoelkopf, Xiangru Tang, Dragomir Radev, Alham Fikri Aji, Khalid Almubarak, Samuel Albanie, Zaid Alyafeai, Albert Webson, Edward Raff, and Colin Raffel. 2023. Crosslingual generalization through multitask finetuning. In *Proceedings of the 61st Annual Meeting of the Association for Computational Linguistics (Volume 1: Long Papers)*, pages 15991–16111, Toronto, Canada. Association for Computational Linguistics.

Aidar Myrzakhan, Sondos Mahmoud Bsharat, and Zhiqiang Shen. 2024. Open-llm-leaderboard: From multi-choice to open-style questions for llms evaluation, benchmark, and arena.

Akintunde Oladipo, Mofetoluwa Adeyemi, Orevaoghene Ahia, Abraham Owodunni, Odunayo Ogundepo, David Adelani, and Jimmy Lin. 2023. Better quality pre-training data and t5 models for African languages. In *Proceedings of the 2023 Conference on Empirical Methods in Natural Language Processing*, pages 158–168, Singapore. Association for Computational Linguistics.

Colin Raffel, Noam Shazeer, Adam Roberts, Katherine Lee, Sharan Narang, Michael Matena, Yanqi Zhou, Wei Li, and Peter J. Liu. 2019. Exploring the limits of transfer learning with a unified text-to-text transformer. *CoRR*, abs/1910.10683.

Pranav Rajpurkar, Jian Zhang, Konstantin Lopyrev, and Percy Liang. 2016. Squad: 100,000+ questions for machine comprehension of text.

Joshua Robinson, Christopher Michael Rytting, and David Wingate. 2023. Leveraging large language models for multiple choice question answering.

Sebastian Ruder, Jonathan Clark, Alexander Gutkin, Mihir Kale, Min Ma, Massimo Nicosia, Shruti Rijhwani, Parker Riley, Jean-Michel Sarr, Xinyi Wang, John Wieting, Nitish Gupta, Anna Katanova, Christo Kirov, Dana Dickinson, Brian Roark, Bidisha Samanta, Connie Tao, David Adelani, Vera Axelrod, Isaac Caswell, Colin Cherry, Dan Garrette, Reeve Ingle, Melvin Johnson, Dmitry Panteleev, and Partha Talukdar. 2023. Xtreme-up: A user-centric scarce-data benchmark for under-represented languages. In *Findings of the Association for Computational Linguistics: EMNLP 2023*, page 1856–1884. Association for Computational Linguistics.

H. Bahadir Sahin, Caglar Tirkaz, Eray Yildiz, Mustafa Tolga Eren, and Ozan Sonmez. 2017. Automatically annotated turkish corpus for named entity recognition and text categorization using large-scale gazetteers.

Erik F. Tjong Kim Sang and Fien De Meulder. 2003. Introduction to the CoNLL-2003 shared task: Language-independent named entity recognition. In *Proceedings of the Seventh Conference on Natural Language Learning at HLT-NAACL 2003*, pages 142–147.

Ashish Vaswani, Noam Shazeer, Niki Parmar, Jakob Uszkoreit, Llion Jones, Aidan N Gomez, Łukasz Kaiser, and Illia Polosukhin. 2017. Attention is all you need. In *Advances in neural information processing systems*, volume 30, pages 5998–6008.

Linting Xue, Noah Constant, Adam Roberts, Mihir Kale, Rami Al-Rfou, Aditya Siddhant, Aditya Barua, and Colin Raffel. 2021. mT5: A massively multilingual pre-trained text-to-text transformer. In *Proceedings of the 2021 Conference of the North American Chapter of the Association for Computational Linguistics: Human Language Technologies*, pages 483–498, Online. Association for Computational Linguistics.

Hang Yan, Bocao Deng, Xiaonan Li, and Xipeng Qiu. 2019. TENER: adapting transformer encoder for named entity recognition. *CoRR*, abs/1911.04474.

Aizihaierjiang Yusufu, Liu Jiang, Abidan Ainiwaer, Chong Teng, Aizierguli Yusufu, Fei Li, and Donghong Ji. 2023. Uzner: A benchmark for named entity recognition in uzbek. In *Natural Language Processing and Chinese Computing*, pages 171–183, Cham. Springer Nature Switzerland.

# A Prompt

## A.1 Zero-Shot Prompt

### A.1.1 FFQA Prompt

```
You are an AI assistant designed
   to answer questions based on
   given passages.
Your task is to provide accurate
   and concise answers to
   questions using only the
   information provided in the
   passage.
If the passage doesn't contain
   enough information to answer
   the question, respond with '
   The passage does not provide
   sufficient information to
   answer this question.'
```

```
Do not use any external knowledge
    or make assumptions beyond
   what is explicitly stated in
   the passage. Response should
   be in one line without any
   additional information and
   response in source language.

Passage: {Passage}

Question: {Question}

Your answer:
```

#### A.1.2 MCQA Prompt

```
You are an AI assistant designed
   to answer multiple-choice
   questions.
Your task is to select the most
   appropriate answer from the
   given options (A, B, C, D)
   based on the question provided
   .
Analyze the question and options
   carefully before making your
   selection.
Your response should only contain
    the letter of the correct
   option (A, B, C, or D).
If none of the options seem
   correct or if there isn't
   enough information to make a
   selection, respond with '
   Unable to determine the
   correct answer based on the
   given options.'

Passage: {Passage}
Question: {Question}
Options:
A) {OptionA}
B) {OptionB}
C) {OptionC}
D) {OptionD}
Answer:
```

### A.2 Few-Shot Prompt

#### A.2.1 FFQA Prompt

```
You are an AI assistant designed
   to answer questions based on
   given passages.
Your task is to provide accurate
   and concise answers to
   questions using only the
   information provided in the
   passage.
If the passage doesn't contain
   enough information to answer
   the question, respond with '
   The passage does not provide
   sufficient information to
   answer this question.'
Do not use any external knowledge
    or make assumptions beyond
   what is explicitly stated in
   the passage. Response should
   be in one line without any
   additional information and
   response in source language.

Passage: {Passage1}
Question: {Question1}
Answer: {Answer1}

Passage: {Passage2}
Question: {Question2}
Answer: {Answer2}

Passage: {Passage3}
Question: {Question3}
Answer: {Answer3}

Passage: {Passage4}
Question: {Question4}
Answer: {Answer4}

Passage: {Passage}
Question: {Question}
Answer: "
```

#### A.2.2 MCQA Prompt

```
You are an AI assistant designed
   to answer multiple-choice
   questions.
Your task is to select the most
   appropriate answer from the
   given options (A, B, C, D)
   based on the question provided
   .
Analyze the question and options
   carefully before making your
```

```
    selection.
Your response should only contain
    the letter of the correct
    option (A, B, C, or D).
If none of the options seem
    correct or if there isn't
    enough information to make a
    selection, respond with '
    Unable to determine the
    correct answer based on the
    given options.'

Passage: {Passage1}
Question: {Question2}
Options:
A) {OptionA1}
B) {OptionB1}
C) {OptionC1}
D) {OptionD1}
Answer: A)

Passage: {Passage2}
Question: {Question2}
Options:
A) {OptionB2}
B) {OptionA2}
C) {OptionC2}
D) {OptionD2}
Answer: B)

Passage: {Passage3}
Question: {Question3}
Options:
A) {OptionC3}
B) {OptionB3}
C) {OptionA3}
D) {OptionD3}
Answer: C)

Passage: {Passage4}
Question: {Question4}
Options:
A) {OptionD4}
B) {OptionB4}
C) {OptionC4}
D) {OptionA4}
Answer: D)

Passage: {Passage}
Question: {Question}
Options:
A) {OptionA}
B) {OptionB}
C) {OptionC}
D) {OptionD}
Answer:
```

## B Additional Datasets

### B.1 NER

LocalDoc/azerbaijani-ner-dataset[3]

### B.2 FFQA

LocalDoc/databricks-dolly-azerbaijan (closed qa)[4]

[3]https://huggingface.co/datasets/LocalDoc/azerbaijani-ner-dataset

[4]https://huggingface.co/datasets/LocalDoc/databricks-dolly-azerbaijan

# CUNI and LMU Submission to the MRL 2024 Shared Task on Multi-lingual Multi-task Information Retrieval

**Katharina Hämmerl**[λ,μ,*] **Andrei Manea**[κ] **Gianluca Vico**[κ]
**Jindřich Helcl**[κ] **Jindřich Libovický**[κ]

[κ]Faculty of Mathematics and Physics, Charles University, Czech Republic
[λ]Center for Information and Language Processing, LMU Munich Germany
[μ]Munich Center for Machine Learning (MCML), Germany
haemmerl@cis.lmu.de {manea,vico,helcl,libovicky}@ufal.mff.cuni.cz

## Abstract

We present the joint CUNI and LMU submission to the MRL 2024 Shared Task on Multi-lingual Multi-task Information Retrieval. The shared task objective was to explore how we can deploy modern methods in NLP in multi-lingual low-resource settings, tested on two sub-tasks: Named-entity recognition and question answering. Our solutions to the subtasks are based on data acquisition and model adaptation. We compare the performance of our submitted systems with the translate-test approach which proved to be the most useful in the previous edition of the shared task. Our results show that using more data as well as fine-tuning recent multilingual pre-trained models leads to considerable improvements over the translate-test baseline. Our code is available at `https://github.com/ufal/mrl2024-multilingual-ir-shared-task`.

## 1 Introduction

Over the past few years, large language models (LLMs) have attracted a fair share of attention from the research community. This is mainly caused by the remarkable in-context learning properties these models exhibit, especially in languages where there is plenty of data available (Wei et al., 2022).

Very recently, research advances have shown promising results in low-resource language processing by leveraging LLMs trained primarily on English data (Cahyawijaya et al., 2024; Nguyen et al., 2024, inter alia). Meanwhile, massively multilingual approaches also started to deliver good results (Zaratiana et al., 2024; Üstün et al., 2024). The MRL 2024 Shared Task on Multi-lingual Multi-task Information Retrieval aims to build upon this trend in tasks of named-entity recognition (NER; § 2) and question answering (QA; § 3) for Alsatian, Azerbaijani, Igbo, Indonesian, Turkish, Uzbek, and Yoruba.

In both subtasks, our submissions include fine-tuned mulitlingual models, compared to a translate-test baseline (Helcl and Libovický, 2023).

## 2 Named Entity Recognition

The goal of the NER subtask was to detect and classify words and phrases into one of three categories: person (PER), organization (ORG), and location (LOC). Unlike the previous year's edition, date and time entities were omitted from the task.

For development, the organizers released validation data in Alsatian, Azerbaijani, Turkish, and Yoruba, each of around 120 sentences.

We experiment with the translate-test approach and compare it with the most recent massively multilingual models (§ 2.1). We collect additional training data for the shared languages (§ 2.2) and fine-tune the best-scoring multilingual model (§ 2.3).

### 2.1 Baseline Models

**Translate-test.** Using the label-projection method from Helcl and Libovický (2023), we translate the validation data to English, then test two pre-trained models on them: An English SpaCy pipeline[1] and (English-only) GliNER[2] (Zaratiana et al., 2024). See Table 1, "Translate + Spacy" and "Translate + GliNER" for the respective validation set results.

**Multilingual Models.** We further test a multilingual baseline model from the UniversalNER project (Mayhew et al., 2024), as well as multilingual GliNER[3] (Zaratiana et al., 2024) on the original validation data. The model from UniversalNER is a version of XLM-R$_{large}$, fine-tuned on all of the project's annotated training data. Multilingual GliNER is an open-type NER model intitialised from mDeBERTa-v3$_{base}$ (He et al., 2023)

* Part of KH's work on this paper was done during a research visit to CUNI.

[1] `en_core_web_lg`

[2] `urchade/gliner_large-v2.1`; 459M parameters

[3] `urchade/gliner_multi-v2.1`; 209M parameters



*Proceedings of the Fourth Workshop on Multilingual Representation Learning (MRL 2024)*, pages 357–364
November 16, 2024 ©2024 Association for Computational Linguistics

| Method | als | aze | tur | yor | Avg. |
|---|---|---|---|---|---|
| Translate + Spacy | 43.7 | 51.7 | 42.6 | 52.0 | 47.5 |
| Translate + GliNER | 30.7 | 48.2 | 46.9 | 44.1 | 42.5 |
| Universal NER | 56.9 | 67.8 | 62.9 | 55.0 | 62.5 |
| Multiling. GliNER | 61.5 | 67.8 | 63.5 | 63.0 | 64.3 |
| ↳ + tuning | 71.5 | 69.2 | 74.2 | 74.0 | 72.2 |

Table 1: Results of the explored methods on the shared task validation data.

| Parameter | Value |
|---|---|
| Learning rate | $5 \times 10^{-6}$ |
| Weight decay | 0.01 |
| Epochs | 5 |
| Batch size | 16 |
| Warmup ratio | 0.1 |

Table 2: Hyperparameters used for the final tuned GliNER model.

and fine-tuned on Pile-NER (Zhou et al., 2024). The validation set results from these models are also listed in Table 1. Based on these initial results, we select Multilingual GliNER for further tuning.

### 2.2 Datasets

For fine-tuning Multilingual GliNER, we use a selection of NER datasets in different languages. We found relevant data for all target languages except Alsatian and decided to use Standard German data instead.

**MasakhaNER2.** Adelani et al. (2022) provide a high-quality NER dataset for 20 African languages. The data includes labels for *person*, *organisation*, *location* and *date* in the BIO format. Since the shared task does not include date labels, we discard those from the data before feeding it to our model. We use the Yoruba (6.8k) and Igbo (7.6k) training splits for the final tuned model. The validation splits (around 1k each) are also used for evaluation during model fine-tuning.

**PolyglotNER.** PolyglotNER (Al-Rfou et al., 2015) is a large, automatically created NER dataset for 40 languages. It includes labels for *person*, *organisation*, and *location*. We convert the labels to the BIO format before training. We use parts of the Turkish and German subsets in the final tuned model. In order to keep the training data to a similar size as Yoruba and Igbo, we only take around 10k examples for the training itself, and around 1k examples for validation during model fine-tuning.

**LocalDoc NER.** LocalDoc NER (LocalDoc, 2024) is an extensive collection of Azerbaijani NER data with 24 entity types. Since the shared task data includes only the target entities *person*, *organisation*, and *location*, we discard all other entity types, and transform the data to the BIO format, before feeding the data to our model. Since this leaves us with a somewhat large proportion of "empty" examples (with no labels other than "O"), we then discard such examples with a 50-50 chance. The original dataset includes almost 100k examples, but we only use around 10k examples for training in order to keep a similar proportion of training data as the other languages. We use an additional 1k examples for validation during model fine-tuning.

**Additional Datasets.** We further experimented with UZNER (Yusufu et al., 2023) and SwissNER (Vamvas et al., 2023) data for Uzbek and Swiss German, respectively, but found that including this data did not noticeably improve performance on the validation languages, so the final tuned model does not include them.

### 2.3 Model Tuning

We attempt tuning with different combinations of data, different learning rates, weight decay, and number of epochs. Table 2 shows the hyperparameters used in the selected model. Due to the comparatively small size of the base model (209M parameters), and limited training data especially for the smallest sets used, each training run is quite fast: Between one and two hours depending on epochs and data mix, on a single GPU.

### 2.4 Results

The validation results are presented in Table 1. The fine-tuned GliNER scores the best on all languages in the validation set, on average 8 $F_1$ points better than the pre-trained version. Multilingual models, even without fine-tuning, significantly outperformed translate-test baselines.

Based on these results, we submitted outputs of the fine-tuned GliNER to the shared task.

Table 3 shows test set results released by the organisers. Although our model is actually outpaced on most of the test languages by the system from McGill, we win on consistency, for an average performance lead of 4.2 $F_1$ points. Our result on Azerbaijani falls furthest behind, which may indicate that the distribution of the LocalDoc dataset

| Team | als | az | ig | tr | yo | Avg. |
|---|---|---|---|---|---|---|
| CUNI | 70.4 | 57.3 | **73.9** | 77.8 | 80.5 | **71.9** |
| McGill | **78.9** | **82.1** | 9.3 | **82.6** | **85.7** | 67.7 |
| Ifeoma | 0.8 | 2.0 | 2.0 | 4.0 | 0.8 | 1.9 |

Table 3: Results on the NER test set. The value for each language is the F1 metric.

was too different from the shared task set.

## 3 Question Answering

The goal of this task is to answer questions within a given context in two scenarios: First, select the correct answer from a set of four choices (multiple-choice questions). Second, generate a free-form answer in natural language (open questions).

The organizers provided 200 multiple-choice questions for all languages except Uzbek. All correct options in the development data were labeled as "A". To balance the dataset, we shuffle the ordering of the options in the data and report the performance on this shuffled dataset. Additionally, around 100 single-reference open questions for all languages were provided.

We experiment with LLMs in the zero-shot setup both in the task languages and when translating the test into English (§ 3.1). Then, we collect QA datasets that are available for the task languages (§ 3.2). We use the data to fine-tune the models (§ 3.3). Finally, we experiment with ensembling of the models outputs in the zero-shot setup (§ 3.4).

### 3.1 Zero-shot LLMs

We select a few multilingual LLMs tested on both the original and translated validation sets: Aya-101 (Üstün et al., 2024) and 4 versions of the LLaMA model (Touvron et al., 2023). Aya-101 is an encoder-decoder model trained in multiple tasks and 101 languages, while LLaMA is a causal language model.

**Multiple Choice Questions.** For this task, we extract the probability score for each option: "A)," "B)," "C)," or "D)." To do so, we use a prompt consisting of the context, the question, and the answer options. This is followed by "The correct answer is:". This way, we increase the chance that the next generated token is one of the answer letters. We translate this prompt into each task language so that the prompt and the question are in the same language.

We know the next token might not necessarily be in our range, as Wang et al. (2024) state. To overcome this, we use the system prompt: "You are an assistant trained to read the following context and answer the question with one of the options A), B), C) or D).". Upon inspection of the generated text, we found a minimal number of cases (1-2) where the generated answer starts with a different token.

We extract the probabilities of the four tokens corresponding to the options, and re-normalize them with softmax. Then, we choose the option with the maximum score. Another strategy is to generate text using nucleus sampling and extract the first label. This results in slightly lower accuracy for all languages; therefore, we use the probability scores.

**Open Questions.** For the open-question scenario, we use a different system prompt: "You are an assistant trained to read the following context and provide a succinct, accurate, and clear response in the same language." The user prompt consists only of the context and the question.

We use temperature 0.6, nucleus sampling with top $p$ of 0.9, and maximum new tokens 80.

**Translate test.** We translate the multiple choice validation set into English using NLLB-200-3.3B (Team et al., 2022) and then use the same mentioned models as a baseline. Long samples are split into sentences with an English SpaCy pipeline[4] to fit the NLLB context size. The translations are then appropriately concatenated to have the context and the questions together. The prompt is in English, while in the multilingual case, it is translated into each input language.

### 3.2 Datasets

We use additional datasets for multiple-choice questions to fine-tune the LLaMA models and Aya-101. Similarly to the NER task, we use Standard German data instead of Alsatian, but we do not have Azerbaijani data. We also use additional English data. The domain of some datasets is broader than that of this shared task because these datasets can test for knowledge or include multiple-choice sentence completion. We standardize the format of all the datasets, including this shared task dataset: we combine the short text with the question and add

[4] en_core_web_sm

the prefixes "A)," "B)," "C)," and "D)" to the four possible answers.

**MMLU.** MMLU (Hendrycks et al., 2021b) (Hendrycks et al., 2021a) contains English multiple-choice questions testing various branches of knowledge. In contrast to this shared task, it does not contain a separate text with the information to answer the question. Moreover, some samples are about sentence completion, or the context is not always sufficient to answer the question. This set contains 115700 English samples.

**AFRIMMLU.** AFRIMMLU (Adelani et al., 2024) is a translation of MMLU in several African languages. We use the Igbo and Yoruba splits, which contain 608 examples.

**M_MMLU.** M_MMLU (Dac Lai et al., 2023) is a machine-translated version of MMLU. We use the Indonesian portion, which contains 14798 samples.

**MMLU_TR.** M_MMLU (Alhajar, 2024) is a Turkish machine-translated version of MMLU which contains 15263 samples.

**Belebele.** Belebele (Bandarkar et al., 2024) is a multiple-choice question dataset about reading comprehension. Each sample contains a short text, a question, and four possible answers (from 1 to 4, converted to A, B, C, and D). We use 900 samples for the following languages: Tosk Albanian (language code ALS), German, English, Igbo, Indonesian, Turkish, Uzbek, and Yoruba.

**EXAMS.** EXAMS (Hardalov et al., 2020) is a dataset that contains high school-level multiple-choice questions. Each sample has a short test, a question, and four possible answers. However, the short text does not answer the question, as the dataset aims to test knowledge. We use 1964 Turkish samples.

**QASC.** QASC (Khot et al., 2020) is a multiple-choice question dataset about grade school science questions. We use 9060 unique English samples with a short fact, a question, and eight possible answers. To adapt it for this task, we randomly discard four wrong answers from each sample and relabel the remaining ones.

**NaijaRC.** NaijaRC (Aremu et al., 2024) is a multiple-choice question dataset about reading comprehension. As the dataset for this shared task, NaijaRC contains a short text, a question, and four possible answers. We used 89 Igbo samples and 191 Yoruba samples.

| Model | Method | als | aze | ibo | tur | yor | Avg. |
|---|---|---|---|---|---|---|---|
| LLaMA | score | **83.0** | **83.5** | **88.0** | 88.2 | **87.5** | **86.0** |
| | gen. | 80.5 | 81.0 | 86.5 | **89.2** | **87.5** | 83.7 |
| Aya 101 | score | 85.5 | **96.0** | **95.0** | 88.2 | **90.5** | **91.0** |
| | gen. | **88.0** | 95.0 | 92.5 | **89.2** | 87.5 | 90.5 |

Table 4: Comparison of the *score* versus *generate* (gen.) method in the zero-shot multilingual inference. LLaMA model refers to 3.1 8B version.

### 3.3 Model Tuning

In the multiple-choice task scenario, we fine-tune the models using Low-Rank Adaptation (LoRA; Hu et al., 2021). We format the data in the same way as in the zero-shot experiments. After the context, questions, and multiple choices, we repeat the correct answer with "The right answer is X):" prepended.

For training the model using LoRA, we set rank $r$ to 64, scaling factor $\alpha$ to 16. We use a dropout of 0.1, with no bias, and we only adapt the attention layers. We tested the fine-tuned models on the open task with the prompt mentioned in Section 3.1.

Table 7 and 8 contains the preliminary results of the test set. These were the only submissions that were publicly listed on Codabench.

**Multilingual Fine-tuning.** We compile the training dataset from all datasets listed in the previous section, except for EXAMS, which we omit so Turkish is not overrepresented.

**Monolingual Fine-tuning.** We fine-tune the multilingual models with monolingual data to make a comparison. We train each model for 8 epochs with a learning rate of $2 \cdot 10^{-4}$ and tested on the same language. Since we do not have Azerbaijani data, this language is not included. For Alsatian, we use Standard German and Tosk Albanian (ALS), which was included by accident because of the same unofficial abbreviation as the ISO code for Alsatian.

### 3.4 Ensembling

For the multiple-choice scenario, we experiment with model ensembling to increase robustness.

**Three Models.** We combine the scores of our best models: LLaMA 3.0 70B, LLaMA 3.1 70B, and Aya 101. Each model outputs scores for each answer choice. We merge the scores with either

| | Model | als | aze | ibo | tur | yor | Avg. |
|---|---|---|---|---|---|---|---|
| Translate-test | LLaMA 3.0 8B | 55.0 | 80.0 | 86.0 | 87.7 | 74.0 | 76.5 |
| | LLaMA 3.1 8B | 52.0 | 81.5 | 87.5 | 85.1 | 75.5 | 76.3 |
| | Aya 101 | 49.0 | 79.0 | 85.0 | 81.0 | 73.5 | 73.5 |
| Multilingual Zero-Shot | LLaMA 3.0 8B | 84.5 | 88.0 | 91.5 | 90.8 | 80.5 | 87.3 |
| | LLaMA 3.0 70B | 92.5 | 96.5 | 93.0 | 95.4 | 83.5 | 92.2 |
| | LLaMA 3.1 8B | 83.0 | 83.5 | 88.0 | 88.2 | 87.5 | 86.0 |
| | LLaMA 3.1 70B | 92.5 | 96.5 | 93.0 | 95.4 | 83.5 | 92.2 |
| | Aya 101 | 85.5 | 96.0 | 95.0 | 88.2 | 90.5 | 91.0 |
| Multilingual Tuned | LLaMA 3.1 8B | 78.0 | 94.5 | 89.5 | 85.6 | 79.0 | 85.3 |
| Monolingual Tuned | LLaMA 3.1 8B | 85.0 | — | 95.0 | 80.5 | 82.5 | — |
| | Aya 101 | 85.5 | — | 91.0 | 73.8 | 85.0 | — |
| Three Models | hard | 92.0 | **99.5** | 94.5 | **96.4** | 92.0 | 94.9 |
| | soft | **93.0** | **99.5** | **95.5** | **96.4** | **92.5** | **95.4** |
| Three Prompts | Aya 101 | 86.5 | 97.0 | 94.5 | 89.7 | 90.5 | 91.7 |
| | LLaMA 3.1 70B | 92.5 | 97.5 | 91.5 | **96.4** | 89.5 | 93.5 |

Table 5: Results for the multiple choice model on the validation set, using the *score* method

| | Model | Metric | als | aze | ibo | tur | yor | ind | uzb | Avg. |
|---|---|---|---|---|---|---|---|---|---|---|
| Multilingual Zero-Shot | LLaMA 3.1 8B | ChrF | 27.7 | 61.7 | 37.7 | 52.3 | 25.3 | 42.2 | 49.6 | 42.3 |
| | | RougeL | 9.1 | 55.3 | 28.7 | 35.9 | 15.9 | 35.5 | 38.8 | 31.3 |
| | | BERTscore | 64.5 | 83.6 | 70.3 | 67.0 | 66.2 | 69.7 | 72.4 | 70.5 |
| | LLaMA 3.1 70B | ChrF | **32.1** | **69.5** | **57.0** | **53.4** | 33.2 | 41.7 | 56.9 | **49.1** |
| | | RougeL | **22.5** | **70.7** | **43.2** | **46.3** | 23.4 | 36.4 | 46.4 | **41.3** |
| | | BERTscore | **85.0** | **96.1** | **86.5** | **91.1** | 82.8 | 83.5 | 87.1 | **87.5** |
| | Aya 101 | ChrF | 22.4 | 53.2 | 24.5 | 42.0 | **34.8** | **44.1** | **60.2** | 40.2 |
| | | RougeL | 16.7 | 52.4 | 25.0 | 39.2 | **29.1** | **43.6** | **48.1** | 36.3 |
| | | BERTscore | 82.5 | 91.6 | 83.5 | 89.1 | **84.8** | **86.5** | **87.8** | 86.5 |
| Multilingual Tuned | LLaMA 3.1 8B | ChrF | 24.6 | 34.0 | 22.0 | 22.8 | 17.9 | 39.8 | 31.1 | 27.5 |
| | | RougeL | 15.2 | 31.2 | 15.5 | 19.3 | 13.1 | 33.0 | 19.2 | 20.9 |
| | | BERTscore | 67.9 | 72.1 | 65.1 | 50.3 | 63.9 | 72.5 | 64.7 | 65.22 |

Table 6: Results for the open question models on the validation set.

| Team | als | az | ig | tr | yo | Avg. |
|---|---|---|---|---|---|---|
| isidoratourni | **0.92** | **0.98** | **0.98** | **0.97** | **0.92** | **0.95** |
| CUNI | **0.92** | **0.98** | **0.98** | 0.96 | 0.86 | 0.93 |
| McGill NLP Group | 0.78 | 0.97 | 0.97 | 0.82 | 0.85 | 0.88 |

Table 7: Preliminary results of multiple-choice questions leaderboard, extracted from Codabench. The final column is the weighted accuracy.

| Team | als | az | ig | tr | yo | Avg. |
|---|---|---|---|---|---|---|
| CUNI | **0.43** | **0.61** | **0.68** | **0.55** | **0.47** | **0.54** |
| McGill NLP Group | 0.42 | 0.42 | 0.33 | 0.4 | 0.36 | 0.38 |

Table 8: Preliminary results of open questions leaderboard, extracted from Codabench. The final column is the weighted average of all the metrics.

*hard* or *soft* voting. In *hard* voting, we select the choice with the highest score for each model and then choose the final answer with a majority vote. In *soft* voting, we average the scores for each choice and then select the one with the maximum score.

**Three Prompts.** Since the models produce answers in different formats, we use two additional prompts. In addition to the original, "The correct answer is: ", we add "It is: " and the empty prompt. We translate the prompts into the shared task languages and use them with the model. We average the probabilities for the respective prompts and return the option with the maximum score.

### 3.5 Results

Table 4 shows the difference between the scoring method and the generated for the multiple-choice tasks. The results were much better with scoring, allowing us more flexibility, such as using *soft* voting in ensembling models.

After tuning the models, we observe a performance drop in every language. We believe this is due to a domain mismatch between the training and shared task test data. Therefore, we decided to proceed with the zero-shot setup. Table 5 shows the performance on the validation set in the multiple-choice task. For the submission, three models *soft* voting was selected as the best submission.

Table 6 contains the result from the open task, with the best submission being LLaMA 3.1 70B (zero-shot).

## 4 Conclusions

We presented our submissions to the MRL Shared Task on Multi-lingual Multi-task Information Retrieval. Our methods based on data acquisition and fine-tuning of multilingual pre-trained models achieve good results compared to the translate-test approach, which was the key idea of the winning system from 2023 (Helcl and Libovický, 2023). For NER, we achieved our best results by finetuning state-of-the-art models specifically for the shared task languages and entities. In the QA subtask, we achieved our best results using the LLMs in the zero-shot setup.

## Acknowledgments

This work was supported by the Charles University project PRIMUS/23/SCI/023 and SVV project number 260 698.

## References

David Adelani, Graham Neubig, Sebastian Ruder, Shruti Rijhwani, Michael Beukman, Chester Palen-Michel, Constantine Lignos, Jesujoba Alabi, Shamsuddeen Muhammad, Peter Nabende, Cheikh M. Bamba Dione, Andiswa Bukula, Rooweither Mabuya, Bonaventure F. P. Dossou, Blessing Sibanda, Happy Buzaaba, Jonathan Mukiibi, Godson Kalipe, Derguene Mbaye, Amelia Taylor, Fatoumata Kabore, Chris Chinenye Emezue, Anuoluwapo Aremu, Perez Ogayo, Catherine Gitau, Edwin Munkoh-Buabeng, Victoire Memdjokam Koagne, Allahsera Auguste Tapo, Tebogo Macucwa, Vukosi Marivate, Mboning Tchiaze Elvis, Tajuddeen Gwadabe, Tosin Adewumi, Orevaoghene Ahia, and Joyce Nakatumba-Nabende. 2022. MasakhaNER 2.0: Africa-centric transfer learning for named entity recognition. In *Proceedings of the 2022 Conference on Empirical Methods in Natural Language Processing*, pages 4488–4508, Abu Dhabi, United Arab Emirates. Association for Computational Linguistics.

David Ifeoluwa Adelani, Jessica Ojo, Israel Abebe Azime, Jian Yun Zhuang, Jesujoba O. Alabi, Xuanli He, Millicent Ochieng, Sara Hooker, Andiswa Bukula, En-Shiun Annie Lee, Chiamaka Chukwuneke, Happy Buzaaba, Blessing Sibanda, Godson Kalipe, Jonathan Mukiibi, Salomon Kabongo, Foutse Yuehgoh, Mmasibidi Setaka, Lolwethu Ndolela, Nkiruka Odu, Rooweither Mabuya, Shamsuddeen Hassan Muhammad, Salomey Osei, Sokhar Samb, Tadesse Kebede Guge, and Pontus Stenetorp. 2024. Irokobench: A new benchmark for african languages in the age of large language models. *Preprint*, arXiv:2406.03368.

Rami Al-Rfou, Vivek Kulkarni, Bryan Perozzi, and Steven Skiena. 2015. Polyglot-NER: Massive multilingual named entity recognition. *Proceedings of the 2015 SIAM International Conference on Data Mining, Vancouver, British Columbia, Canada, April 30- May 2, 2015.*

Mohamad Alhajar. 2024. mmlu_tr-v0.2. https://huggingface.co/datasets/malhajar/mmlu_tr-v0.2.

Anuoluwapo Aremu, Jesujoba O. Alabi, Daud Abolade, Nkechinyere F. Aguobi, Shamsuddeen Hassan Muhammad, and David Ifeoluwa Adelani. 2024. Naijarc: A multi-choice reading comprehension dataset for nigerian languages. *Preprint*, arXiv:2308.09768.

Lucas Bandarkar, Davis Liang, Benjamin Muller, Mikel Artetxe, Satya Narayan Shukla, Donald Husa, Naman Goyal, Abhinandan Krishnan, Luke Zettlemoyer, and Madian Khabsa. 2024. The belebele benchmark: a parallel reading comprehension dataset in 122 language variants. In *Proceedings of the 62nd Annual Meeting of the Association for Computational Linguistics (Volume 1: Long Papers)*, pages 749–775, Bangkok, Thailand. Association for Computational Linguistics.

Samuel Cahyawijaya, Holy Lovenia, and Pascale Fung. 2024. LLMs are few-shot in-context low-resource language learners. In *Proceedings of the 2024 Conference of the North American Chapter of the Association for Computational Linguistics: Human Language Technologies (Volume 1: Long Papers)*, pages 405–433, Mexico City, Mexico. Association for Computational Linguistics.

Viet Dac Lai, Chien Van Nguyen, Nghia Trung Ngo, Thuat Nguyen, Franck Dernoncourt, Ryan A Rossi, and Thien Huu Nguyen. 2023. Okapi: Instruction-tuned large language models in multiple languages with reinforcement learning from human feedback. *arXiv e-prints*, pages arXiv–2307.

Momchil Hardalov, Todor Mihaylov, Dimitrina Zlatkova, Yoan Dinkov, Ivan Koychev, and Preslav Nakov. 2020. EXAMS: A multi-subject high school examinations dataset for cross-lingual and multilingual question answering. In *Proceedings of the 2020 Conference on Empirical Methods in Natural Language Processing (EMNLP)*, pages 5427–5444, Online. Association for Computational Linguistics.

Pengcheng He, Jianfeng Gao, and Weizhu Chen. 2023. DeBERTav3: Improving DeBERTa using ELECTRA-style pre-training with gradient-disentangled embedding sharing. In *The Eleventh International Conference on Learning Representations*.

Jindřich Helcl and Jindřich Libovický. 2023. CUNI submission to MRL 2023 shared task on multi-lingual multi-task information retrieval. In *Proceedings of the 3rd Workshop on Multi-lingual Representation Learning (MRL)*, pages 302–309, Singapore. Association for Computational Linguistics.

Dan Hendrycks, Collin Burns, Steven Basart, Andrew Critch, Jerry Li, Dawn Song, and Jacob Steinhardt. 2021a. Aligning ai with shared human values. *Proceedings of the International Conference on Learning Representations (ICLR)*.

Dan Hendrycks, Collin Burns, Steven Basart, Andy Zou, Mantas Mazeika, Dawn Song, and Jacob Steinhardt. 2021b. Measuring massive multitask language understanding. *Proceedings of the International Conference on Learning Representations (ICLR)*.

Edward J. Hu, Yelong Shen, Phillip Wallis, Zeyuan Allen-Zhu, Yuanzhi Li, Shean Wang, Lu Wang, and Weizhu Chen. 2021. Lora: Low-rank adaptation of large language models. *Preprint*, arXiv:2106.09685.

Tushar Khot, Peter Clark, Michal Guerquin, Peter Jansen, and Ashish Sabharwal. 2020. Qasc: A dataset for question answering via sentence composition. *arXiv:1910.11473v2*.

LocalDoc. 2024. Azerbaijani NER dataset (Revision 7bf7e0a).

Stephen Mayhew, Terra Blevins, Shuheng Liu, Marek Suppa, Hila Gonen, Joseph Marvin Imperial, Börje Karlsson, Peiqin Lin, Nikola Ljubešić, Lester James Miranda, Barbara Plank, Arij Riabi, and Yuval Pinter. 2024. Universal NER: A gold-standard multilingual named entity recognition benchmark. In *Proceedings of the 2024 Conference of the North American Chapter of the Association for Computational Linguistics: Human Language Technologies (Volume 1: Long Papers)*, pages 4322–4337, Mexico City, Mexico. Association for Computational Linguistics.

Xuan-Phi Nguyen, Mahani Aljunied, Shafiq Joty, and Lidong Bing. 2024. Democratizing LLMs for low-resource languages by leveraging their English dominant abilities with linguistically-diverse prompts. In *Proceedings of the 62nd Annual Meeting of the Association for Computational Linguistics (Volume 1: Long Papers)*, pages 3501–3516, Bangkok, Thailand. Association for Computational Linguistics.

NLLB Team, Marta R. Costa-jussà, James Cross, Onur Çelebi, Maha Elbayad, Kenneth Heafield, Kevin Heffernan, Elahe Kalbassi, Janice Lam, Daniel Licht, Jean Maillard, Anna Sun, Skyler Wang, Guillaume Wenzek, Al Youngblood, Bapi Akula, Loic Barrault, Gabriel Mejia Gonzalez, Prangthip Hansanti, John Hoffman, Semarley Jarrett, Kaushik Ram Sadagopan, Dirk Rowe, Shannon Spruit, Chau Tran, Pierre Andrews, Necip Fazil Ayan, Shruti Bhosale, Sergey Edunov, Angela Fan, Cynthia Gao, Vedanuj Goswami, Francisco Guzmán, Philipp Koehn, Alexandre Mourachko, Christophe Ropers, Safiyyah Saleem, Holger Schwenk, and Jeff Wang. 2022. No language left behind: Scaling human-centered machine translation. *Preprint*, arXiv:2207.04672.

Hugo Touvron, Thibaut Lavril, Gautier Izacard, Xavier Martinet, Marie-Anne Lachaux, Timothée Lacroix, Baptiste Rozière, Naman Goyal, Eric Hambro, Faisal Azhar, Aurelien Rodriguez, Armand Joulin, Edouard Grave, and Guillaume Lample. 2023. Llama: Open and efficient foundation language models. *Preprint*, arXiv:2302.13971.

Ahmet Üstün, Viraat Aryabumi, Zheng Yong, Wei-Yin Ko, Daniel D'souza, Gbemileke Onilude, Neel Bhandari, Shivalika Singh, Hui-Lee Ooi, Amr Kayid, Freddie Vargus, Phil Blunsom, Shayne Longpre, Niklas Muennighoff, Marzieh Fadaee, Julia Kreutzer, and Sara Hooker. 2024. Aya model: An instruction fine-tuned open-access multilingual language model. In *Proceedings of the 62nd Annual Meeting of the Association for Computational Linguistics (Volume 1: Long Papers)*, pages 15894–15939, Bangkok, Thailand. Association for Computational Linguistics.

Jannis Vamvas, Johannes Graën, and Rico Sennrich. 2023. SwissBERT: The multilingual language model for Switzerland. In *Proceedings of the 8th edition of the Swiss Text Analytics Conference*, pages 54–69, Neuchatel, Switzerland. Association for Computational Linguistics.

Xinpeng Wang, Bolei Ma, Chengzhi Hu, Leon Weber-Genzel, Paul Röttger, Frauke Kreuter, Dirk Hovy, and Barbara Plank. 2024. "my answer is C": First-token probabilities do not match text answers in instruction-tuned language models. In *Findings of the Association for Computational Linguistics ACL 2024*, pages 7407–7416, Bangkok, Thailand and virtual meeting. Association for Computational Linguistics.

Jason Wei, Yi Tay, Rishi Bommasani, Colin Raffel, Barret Zoph, Sebastian Borgeaud, Dani Yogatama, Maarten Bosma, Denny Zhou, Donald Metzler, Ed H. Chi, Tatsunori Hashimoto, Oriol Vinyals, Percy Liang, Jeff Dean, and William Fedus. 2022. Emergent abilities of large language models. *Transactions on Machine Learning Research*. Survey Certification.

Aizihaierjiang Yusufu, Jiang Liu, Abidan Ainiwaer, Chong Teng, Aizierguli Yusufu, Fei Li, and Donghong Ji. 2023. UZNER: A benchmark for named entity recognition in Uzbek. In *Natural Language Processing and Chinese Computing*.

Urchade Zaratiana, Nadi Tomeh, Pierre Holat, and Thierry Charnois. 2024. GLiNER: Generalist model for named entity recognition using bidirectional transformer. In *Proceedings of the 2024 Conference of the North American Chapter of the Association for Computational Linguistics: Human Language Technologies (Volume 1: Long Papers)*, pages 5364–5376, Mexico City, Mexico. Association for Computational Linguistics.

Wenxuan Zhou, Sheng Zhang, Yu Gu, Muhao Chen, and Hoifung Poon. 2024. UniversalNER: Targeted distillation from large language models for open named entity recognition. In *The Twelfth International Conference on Learning Representations*.

Ahmet Üstün, Viraat Aryabumi, Zheng-Xin Yong, Wei-Yin Ko, Daniel D'souza, Gbemileke Onilude, Neel Bhandari, Shivalika Singh, Hui-Lee Ooi, Amr Kayid, Freddie Vargus, Phil Blunsom, Shayne Longpre, Niklas Muennighoff, Marzieh Fadaee, Julia Kreutzer, and Sara Hooker. 2024. Aya model: An instruction finetuned open-access multilingual language model. *Preprint*, arXiv:2402.07827.

# Findings of the 2nd Shared Task on Multi-lingual Multi-task Information Retrieval at MRL 2024


**Francesco Tinner**
University of Amsterdam
14497425@uva.nl

**Raghav Mantri**
New York University
raghav.mantri@nyu.edu

**Mammad Hajili**
Microsoft
mammadhajili@microsoft.com

**Chiamaka Chukwuneke**
Lancaster University, UK

**Dylan Massey**
University of Zurich
dylan.massey@uzh.ch

**Benjamin A. Ajibade**
University of Alabama
baajibade@crimson.ua.edu

**Bilge Deniz Kocak**
Villanova University
bkocak1@villanova.edu

**Abolade Dawud**
Masakhane
aboladedawud@gmail.com

**Jonathan Atala**
Anglia Ruskin University
Olaatala7@gmail.com

**Hale Sirin**
Johns Hopkins University
hsirin1@jhu.edu

**Kayode Olaleye**
University of Pretoria
kayode.olaleye@up.ac.za

**Anar Rzayev**
KAIST
rzayev.anar1@kaist.ac.kr

**David Adelani**
McGill University
david.adelani@mcgill.ca

**Duygu Ataman**
New York University
ataman@nyu.edu



## Abstract

Large language models (LLMs) demonstrate exceptional proficiency in both the comprehension and generation of textual data, particularly in English, a language for which extensive public benchmarks have been established across a wide range of natural language processing (NLP) tasks. Nonetheless, their performance in multilingual contexts and specialized domains remains less rigorously validated, raising questions about their reliability and generalizability across linguistically diverse and domain-specific settings. The second edition of the Shared Task on Multilingual Multitask Information Retrieval aims to provide a comprehensive and inclusive multilingual evaluation benchmark which aids assessing the ability of multilingual LLMs to capture logical, factual, or causal relationships within lengthy text contexts and generate language under sparse settings, particularly in scenarios with under-resourced languages. The shared task consists of two subtasks crucial to information retrieval: Named entity recognition (NER) and reading comprehension (RC), in 7 data-scarce languages: Azerbaijani, Swiss German, Turkish and Yorùbá, which previously lacked annotated resources in information retrieval tasks. This year specifally focus on the multiple-choice question answering evaluation setting which provides a more objective setting for comparing different methods across languages.


## 1 Introduction

Recent advancements in organizing online knowledge facilitated by Large Language Models (LLMs) have fundamentally reshaped the way we approach information retrieval. This functionality creates exciting potential for new applications for education and media supporting seamless access to information on diverse subjects. However, this functionality is largely to limited in high-resourced languages, preventing equal access to potential applications in



*Proceedings of the Fourth Workshop on Multilingual Representation Learning (MRL 2024)*, pages 365–376
November 16, 2024 ©2024 Association for Computational Linguistics

many under-resourced or studied languages across the world (Yong et al., 2023). Recently, initiatives for creating standardized benchmarks for evaluating natural language processing (NLP) systems in a more linguistically inclusive setting had been proposed by corpora like XTREME (Hu et al., 2020) and XTREME-UP (Ruder et al., 2023). Although these data sets bring together large multilingual corpora they lack in generative human prepared data related to information access.

The 2nd Shared Task on Multi-lingual Multi-task Information Retrieval (MMIR), provides a benchmark for evaluating multi-lingual large language models (LLMs) in terms of their applicability for information retrieval in various under-resourced and typologically diverse languages. Purely constructed using human annotated data consisting of examples of reading comprehension questions and named entity recognition in various context and languages, MMIR benchmark presents a challenging new task for testing and improving LLMs. As evaluation resource we use Wikipedia which we find representative of the inclusion of languages online. We pick five languages with varying degrees of resources and linguistic typology from three different language families: Azerbaijani and Turkish (Turkic), Igbo and Yoruba, (Niger-Congo) and Swiss German (Germanic), and produce annotations in two tasks crucial for IR: named entity recognition (NER) and reading comprehension (RC). We present our data curation and annotation process as well as the findings of the evaluation in the resulting benchmark including prominent LLMs trained on multi-lingual multi-task settings: LLAMA (Dubey et al., 2024), Aya (Üstün et al., 2024) and Gemini (Reid et al., 2024). Extending the data sets and competition from 2023, this year's edition allowed submissions both in open-ended and multiple-choice question answering to allow a more fine-grained and objective analysis. we received 3 submissions in the multiple-choice and 2 submissions in the open-ended RC tasks. The NER task also received 2 submissions. We provide more details on the data sets and a comparison of competing systems.

## 2 Tasks

MMIR shared task provides a multi-task evaluation format to assess information retrieval capabilities of LLMs in terms of two tasks: named entity recognition (NER) and reading comprehension (RC).

| Narendrabhai Damodardas Modi ni Mínśítà àgbà India kẹrìnlá àti mínísítà àgbà tí India lọ́wọ́ lọ́wọ́ lati ọdun 2014. O jẹ oloselu kan lati Bharatiya Janata Party , agbari-iṣẹ oluyọọda ara ilu Hindu kan. Oun ni Prime Minister akọkọ ni ita ti Ile-igbimọjọ ti Orilẹ-ede India lati ṣẹgun awọn ofin itẹlera meji pẹlu opoju to kun ati ekeji lati pari diẹ sii ju ọdun marun ni ọfiisi lẹhin Atal Bihari Vajpayee . |
|---|

Table 1: Example of named entities in Yorùbá language. PER , LOC , and ORG are in colours red, green, and blue respectively. We make use of Label Studio for annotation (Tkachenko et al., 2020-2022).

### 2.1 Named Entity Recognition (NER)

Named Entity Recognition (NER) is a classification task that identifies text phrases referring to specific entities or categories (e.g., dates, names of people, organizations, or locations). This is essential for systems handling entity look-ups for tasks like knowledge verification, spell-checking, or localization. Our training data in the shared task relies on the XTREME-UP dataset (Ruder et al., 2023) which is the most comprehensive data set that combines annotated data from MasakhaNER (Adelani et al., 2021b) and MasakhaNER 2.0 (Adelani et al., 2022) in a wide range of under-resourced languages including: Amharic, Ghomálá, Bambara, Ewe, Hausa, Igbo, (Lu)Ganda, (Dho)Luo, Mossi (Mooré), Nyanja (Chichewa), Nigerian Pidgin, Kinyarwanda, Shona, Swahili, Tswana (Setswana), Twi, Wolof, Xhosa, Yorùbá and Zulu.

The objective of the system is to tag the named entities in a given text, either as a person (PER), organization (ORG), or location (LOC). The NER data this year remains as same with 2023.

### 2.2 Reading Comprehension (RC)

RC is a challenging task often requiring different levels of natural language comprehension and reasoning for answering a given question based on a span of information distributed across a given context. Here we focus on the information-seeking scenario where questions can be asked without knowing the answer. It is the system's task to locate a suitable answer passage (if any). We provide 4 options for each question, where the systems are asked to pick one of the 4 answers as the correct one. Examples can be found in Table 2.

Information-seeking question-answer pairs typically display limited lexical and morphosyntactic overlap between the question and answer, as they

| Context | Question | Options |
|---|---|---|
| Zaqatala" qəzeti redaksiyası 1923-cü ilin mart ayından fəaliyyətə başlamışdır. İlk əvvəllər "Zaqatala kəndlisi" adlanan qəzet sonralar "Kolxozun səsi", "Bolşevik kolxozu uğrunda", "Qırmızı bayraq" və s. başlıqlarla fəaliyyət göstərmişdir. 1991-ci ilin oktyabr ayından isə "Zaqatala" adı ilə fəaliyyətini davam etdirir. Hal-hazırda "Zaqatala" qəzeti redaksiyasında 5 nəfər çalışır. | İndi qəzetdə neçə nəfər çalışır? | **(1) İndi "Zaqatala" qəzetində 5 nəfər işləyir.** (2) "Zaqatala" qəzetinin hal-hazırki işçi sayı 7-dir. (3) İndi "Zaqatala" qəzetində 20 nəfər işləyir. (4) "Zaqatala" qəzetinin işçilərinin sayı bilinmir. |
| Noch de jüngere Version isch de Eurytos vom Herakles töödt woore. Us Raach nämmli, well de em sini Töchter Iole nöd hett wöle gee, hett er d Stadt Oichalia eroberet, de Eurytos und all sini Söö töödt und d Iole graubt. | Was isch de Grund gsi für di tötig vom Eurytos? | (1) Will de Eurytos de Herakles ermordet het. (2) Will das eh jüngeri Version vo de Gschicht isch gsi. **(3) Will de Eurytos am Herakles nöd sis Töchterli - d Iole - het welle geh.** (4) Will de Eurytos vom Herakles töödt woore isch. |
| A bi Aisha Adamu Augie ni Zaria, Ipinle Kaduna, Nigeria, Augie-Kuta jẹ ọmọbinrin oloogbe Senator Adamu Baba Augie (oloselu / olugbohunsafefe), ati Onidajọ Amina Augie (JSC). Augie-Kuta bere si ni nifẹ si fọtoyiya nigbati baba rẹ fun u ni kamẹra ni ọdọ. | Ki ni ibaṣepọ to wa laarin Aisha Adamu Augie ati Senator Adamu Baba Augie? | (1) Aisha Adamu j ìyàwó Senator Adamu Baba Augie **(2) Aisha Adamu jẹ ọmọ fun Senator Adamu Baba Augie** (3) Aisha Adamu jẹ àbúrò Senator Adamu Baba Augie (4) Aisha Adamu j ọbàkan Senator Adamu Baba Augie |

Table 2: Examples from the RC validation data in different languages. Correct answers indicated in **bold.**

| Language | Family |
|---|---|
| Azerbaijani | Turkic |
| Igbo | Niger-Congo |
| Swiss German | Indo-European |
| Turkish | Turkic |
| Yorùbá | Niger-Congo |

Table 3: List of languages and language families.

are composed independently. This makes them ideal for evaluating languages with diverse typological features. In this task, the system receives a question, title, and passage, and must either provide the correct answer or indicate that no answer is present in the passage. Currently, the XTREME-UP benchmark includes data in Indonesian, Bengali, Swahili, and Telugu (Ruder et al., 2023), requiring competing systems to infer information from different language annotations. Our benchmark also contains correct text answers from 2023 edition (Tinner et al., 2023) for open-ended RC evaluation. This year we extend the benchmark in four languages with multiple-choice RC annotations. We allow both types of output for submission to the shared task.

## 3 Languages

Table 3 provides an overview of the variety in our data set in terms of language families.

### 3.1 Azerbaijani (AZ)

Azerbaijani, part of the Turkic language family, is mainly spoken in Azerbaijan and Iran. It shares many linguistic traits with other Turkic languages, particularly those in the Western Oghuz group like Turkish, Gagauz, and Turkmen. Azerbaijani features agglutinative morphology, uses a Subject-Object-Verb (SOV) word order, and lacks gender in its grammar. In Azerbaijan, the Latin script has been used since 1991, while Iranian Azerbaijanis use the Arabic script. This study's data preparation focuses on texts in the Latin script.

### 3.2 Igbo (IG)

Igbo, part of the Benue-Congo group within the Niger-Congo language family, is spoken by over 27 million people, primarily in southeastern Nigeria, as well as parts of Equatorial Guinea and Cameroon. While there are several dialects, Central Igbo, standardized in 1962, is the most widely used. Standard Igbo includes 28 consonants and 8 vowels, with two tones: high (marked by an acute accent) and low (marked by a grave accent), though these tones are usually not represented in writing. Igbo has been featured in various language benchmarks, such as MasakhaNER (Adelani et al., 2021b, 2022), AfriQA (Ogundepo et al., 2023), MasakhaPOS (Dione et al., 2023), AfriSenti (Muhammad et al., 2023).

### 3.3 Swiss German (ALS)

Swiss German, part of the Alemannic dialects within the Germanic language family, poses a significant challenge for multilingual NLP due to its non-standardized nature. It varies greatly in lexicon, phonetics, morphology, and syntax, with no official orthography. Individuals often write words based on their interpretation of phonetics, resulting in inconsistent spellings. Unlike Standard German, Swiss German is not an official language of Switzerland and is primarily used in spoken or informal contexts, with formal writing done in Standard German. Due to this, textual resources are scarce. A notable exception is a text corpus for PoS tagging, compiled from sources like Alemannic Wikipedia, novels, reports, and articles (Hollenstein and Aepli, 2014). Further resources are only available in spoken format, including the SDS-200 corpus (Plüss et al., 2022), Swiss Parliaments Corpus (Plüss et al., 2020), SwissDial corpus (Dogan-Schönberger et al., 2021), Radio Rottu Oberwallis corpus (Garner et al., 2014), ArchiMob corpus (Samardžić et al., 2016), SST4SG-350 (Plüss et al., 2023).

### 3.4 Turkish (TR)

Turkish, the most widely-resourced language in the Turkic family, is known for its agglutinative morphology and Subject-Object-Verb (SOV) word order. It has no grammatical gender but includes a complex case system. Verbs are inflected to show tense, mood, and person, while personal pronouns are used for person reference. Key linguistic features include vowel harmony, palatalized consonants, and phonemic vowel length, which influences word meaning. Turkish lacks definite or indefinite articles, relying on context for clarity. Despite its uniqueness compared to Indo-European languages, its use of the Latin script allows for easier comparisons. Corpus studies in Turkish include plenty monolingual (Aksan et al., 2012) and parallel resources (Tyers and Alperen, 2010; Cettolo et al., 2012; Ataman, 2018). Turkish NLP resources include many inclusive tree banks, such as for Universal Dependencies (Sulubacak et al., 2016; Sulubacak and Eryiğit, 2018), semantic parsing (Şahin and Adalı, 2018) and a WordNET (Ehsani et al., 2018). It is also included in prominently used public multilingual benchmarks including the mc4 corpus (Raffel et al., 2019), and it is recognized in benchmarks, such as for machine translation (Cettolo et al., 2013; Bojar et al., 2017) and morphological analysis (Pimentel et al., 2021). There are also annotated resources for Turkish which were created through automatic annotation using label transfer from other languages or translating existing resources, in tasks including natural language inference (Conneau et al., 2018), NER (Sahin et al., 2017), and summarization (Scialom et al., 2020).

| | | # Sentences/ # Passages | | # Tokens | |
|---|---|---|---|---|---|
| **Lang** | **Task** | Val | Test | Val | Test |
| AZ | NER | 126 | 124 | 7,774 | 8,200 |
| | RC-OE | 202 | 291 | 13,268 | 25,487 |
| | RC-MC | 202 | 291 | 16,147 | 31,447 |
| IG | NER | 711 | 143 | 54,526 | 11,668 |
| | RC-OE | 202 | 748 | 15,620 | 58,963 |
| | RC-MC | 202 | 748 | 21,987 | 79,761 |
| ALS | NER | 130 | 166 | 8,761 | 11,610 |
| | RC-OE | 202 | 651 | 16,949 | 50,045 |
| | RC-MC | 202 | 651 | 21,113 | 58,182 |
| TR | NER | 113 | 151 | 7,375 | 11,736 |
| | RC-OE | 197 | 148 | 16,336 | 12,384 |
| | RC-MC | 197 | 148 | 22,059 | 16,169 |
| YO | NER | 100 | 303 | 4,166 | 11,490 |
| | RC-OE | 202 | 673 | 20,497 | 67,816 |
| | RC-MC | 202 | 673 | 22,891 | 79,529 |

Table 4: Dataset statistics for the validation and test splits. NER annotations are at the sentence level while RC questions include passages and questions related to the passage. RC-MC denote the multiple-choice setting where the question is accompanied with 4 potential answers for systems to pick the correct answer.

### 3.5 Yorùbá (YO)

Yorùbá part of the Volta-Niger subgroup of the Niger-Congo language family, is spoken by over 45 million people, primarily in southwestern Nigeria, as well as in Benin and Togo. It ranks among the top five most spoken African languages, after Nigerian Pidgin, Swahili, Hausa, and Amharic (Eberhard et al., 2021). Yorùbá makes use of the Latin script with modified alphabet: it omits the letters "c,q,v,x,z" and adds "ẹ, gb, ọ, ṣ". The language is tonal, the tones includes high, low, and neutral. The high (as in à) and low (as in á) tones are indicated when writing texts in the language. The tones are important for the correct understanding and pronunciation of the words in Yorùbá. Despite the importance of the tones, many texts written online do not support the writing of the tonal marks, and this may pose a challenge on some downstream NLP applications e.g. machine translation (Adelani et al., 2021a) and text-to-speech (Ogunremi et al., 2023).

## 4 Data Preparation

The textual data for the generative task are based on Wikimedia downloads[1]. RC annotations are prepared by sampling articles, splitting into paragraph-wise for question and answer annotations. In the extension of the benchmark this year, we annotate additional questions and wrong answer options for creating the multiple-choice QA setting (Tinner et al., 2023). For the NE annotation, we ensure we sample only biographical articles and also only include articles available in all six languages.

We use Label Studio for RC and NER annotation (Tkachenko et al., 2020-2022) with the tag set (Person (PER), Organization (ORG), Location (LOC)) and ensure an annotation overlap of 2% for NER. The question-answer pairs were always produced from two separate annotators. We recruited two annotators per language, for IG and TR respectively four annotators contributed, and five persons annotated YO. The resulting data statistics for the validation and test splits can be found in Table 4. The scripts used to obtain the data, as well as pre- and post-processing methods required to create and export Label Studio annotation projects is included in this GitHub repository [2].

## 5 Experimental Methodology

### 5.1 Baseline Systems

**GPT-4** OpenAI (2023) is a large-scale, multimodal AI model capable of processing both text and image inputs to generate text outputs. GPT-4 achieves human-like performance on various professional and academic benchmarks. It is a

[1] https://dumps.wikimedia.org/

[2] https://github.com/Fenerator/wikiDataProcessingForQAandNER

Transformer-based model, pre-trained to predict the next word in a sequence. A post-training alignment phase enhances its factual accuracy and ensures it behaves according to specific guidelines. Key to its development was creating infrastructure and optimization methods that scale reliably. The instruction training is based on Reinforcement Learning from Human Feedback (RLHF), similar to InstructGPT (Ouyang et al., 2022).

**Gemini-1.5 Pro** (Reid et al., 2024) is a mid-size multimodal model optimized for scalability across various tasks, performing on par with the 1.0 Ultra, the largest model to date. It introduces a breakthrough feature in long-context understanding, with a standard 128,000 token context window. Built on cutting-edge research in Transformer and Mixture of Experts (MoE) architecture, Gemini 1.5 uses multiple smaller "expert" neural networks instead of a single large one, enhancing efficiency and performance.

**LLAMA-3.2** (Touvron et al., 2023) is a set of large language models (LLMs) that have been pre-trained and fine-tuned, with 1B and 3B models handling multilingual text only, while the 11B and 90B models accept both text and image inputs and produce text outputs.

**Claude 3.5 SonnetV2** is an AI language model developed by Anthropic, designed to handle complex tasks and conversations while prioritizing user safety and ethical AI use. It is named after Claude Shannon, a pioneer in information theory. The model is built with a focus on creating helpful, honest, and harmless interactions, with an emphasis on reducing biased or harmful outputs. Its architecture supports advanced reasoning, summarization, and in-depth conversations, making it ideal for a wide range of applications.

| | **Prompt Template** |
|---|---|
| mT0 | `<CONTEXT> <QUESTION>` |
| GPT-4 | I will provide you with a passage and a question, please provide a precise answer<br>Passage: <CONTEXT><br>Question: <QUESTION> |

Table 5: Zero-shot prompt template used to obtain open-ended answers from the systems.

| | **Prompt Template** |
|---|---|
| mT0 | <CONTEXT> <QUESTION> |
| GPT-4 | I will provide you with a passage and a question, please provide a precise answer<br>Passage: <CONTEXT><br>Question: <QUESTION><br>Answers:<br><A> ...<br><B> ...<br><C> ...<br><D> ... |

Table 6: Zero-shot prompt template used to obtain answers in the multiple-choice setting.

### 5.2 Evaluation

We evaluate and report results in the generative task using ROGUE-L (Lin and Hovy, 2003), chrF (Popović, 2015), chrF+, chrF++ (Popović, 2017), and BERTScore (Zhang et al., 2019) F1 computed with RoBERTaBase (Liu et al., 2019) [3] embeddings. Implementation is based on HuggingFace's evaluate library[4]. Overall performance in the NER task is computed in terms of precision, recall and F-1 scores using the CoNLL Evaluation Scripts[5], implemented in accordance with (Tjong Kim Sang and Buchholz, 2000). We obtain a final score per task and system by weighting the performance per language inversely by the total number of tokens in the test sets per language.

### 5.3 Submissions

The shared task received five submissions in the NER task, including CUNI-LMU (Charles University and LMU Munich) and McGill (McGill University) with system descriptions, and three submissions without descriptions, labeled as (Ifeoma, Omkar, SandboxAQ. RC task received three submissions in the multiple-choice QA subtask (RC-MC), from McGill, SandboxAQ and CUNI, and two submissions in the open-ended RC task by CUNI and McGill (RC-OE).

## 6 Results

We evaluate the overall system performance on the generative task using automatic metrics weighted by the number of articles in the test set containing individual context used for answering the RC questions Table 7 and Table 9. Detailed results per

[3] https://huggingface.co/roberta-base

[4] https://github.com/huggingface/evaluate

[5] https://github.com/sighsmile/conlleval

| System | ChrF | ChrF+ | ChrF++ | RougeL | BERT F1 |
|---|---|---|---|---|---|
| Claude 3.5 SonnetV2 | 0.51 | 0.50 | 0.47 | 0.42 | 0.89 |
| GPT-4 | 0.45 | 0.44 | 0.42 | 0.36 | 0.87 |
| Gemini 1.5 Pro | 0.42 | 0.41 | 0.38 | 0.40 | 0.86 |
| Llama 3.2 90B | 0.45 | 0.43 | 0.41 | 0.41 | 0.87 |
| CUNI | **0.48** | **0.46** | **0.45** | **0.42** | **0.88** |
| McGill | 0.33 | 0.32 | 0.31 | 0.36 | 0.84 |

Table 7: RC-OE system evaluation. Results indicate weighted average of the metrics over 6 languages. Results are weighted by the number of paragraphs in the testset.

system and language for the open-ended RC task are presented in Table 8. We also present NER results for the system submission in Table 10.

**NER** The winning system in the NER task is **McGill University** system which deploys an ensemble of XLM-R-Large (Conneau et al., 2020), AfroXLMR (Alabi et al., 2022), and AfroXLMR-76L (Adelani et al., 2024) models fine-tuned on the collection of NER data sets, if we consider the median performance, winning 4 (out of the 5 languages).

**RC-OE** The RC-OE task is a competitive challenge and both McGill and CUNI, although CUNI has a slightly better performance. In this case, McGill system is comprised of fine-tuned mt5-large (Xue et al., 2021) and AfriTeVA V2 large (Oladipo et al., 2023) models, fine-tuned as ensemble on the publicly available multilingual QA data sets. CUNI system , on the other hand, uses an ensemble of LLAMA models and Aya-101 (Üstün et al., 2024). In the overall evaluation, we find **CUNI** system performs best across languages.

**RC-MC** The winning team for the multi-choice QA is **SandboxAQ** achieving an average performance of 95% accuracy score. The performance of the CUNI team is competive with only $-2.0$ point less than that of the winner. On the otherhand, McGill team came third with worse overall result especially for ALS.

## 7 Conclusion and Future Work

We presented a new multi-lingual multi-task benchmark on information retrieval from Wikipedia in five languages from typologically-diverse and low-resourced language families in the open-ended or multiple-choice QA and NER tasks. We organized a shared task to call for system development on this challenging benchmark where we conducted a detailed analysis on how state-of-the-art LLMs perform in language understanding and generation under low-resourced settings. In addition to finding strong evidence on fall backs in both understanding and generation capabilities of LLMs in low-resourced languages, we also find it crucial to invest in better automatic evaluation metrics for generation in different languages. While we do not find this task to be solved, we plan to keep the competition open and promote more investment into the progress of information retrieval for languages with non-prominent and low-resourced characteristics.

## Limitations

We have presented a multilingual evaluation benchmark for information retrieval which was created relying on Wikipedia articles in different languages. Using Wikipedia has inherent limitations such as limitations in variety of content and styles across languages making it challenging to ensure a uniform difficulty level for comprehension questions. Additionally, relying solely on Wikipedia may introduce biases, as certain languages might have more comprehensive or detailed articles than others. Moreover, evaluating language models on Wikipedia-centric benchmarks may not fully reflect their generalization abilities, as the models might excel at leveraging the more structured and well-formulated information found on Wikipedia but may struggle more with more diverse and unstructured text from other sources. These limitations underscore the need for diverse and contextually rich benchmarks to provide a comprehensive assessment of LLMs across multiple languages.

## Ethics Statement

All annotators were provided with clear instructions and guidelines to ensure the responsible and unbiased annotation of the data. We ensured eth-

| System | Language | ChrF | ChrF+ | ChrF++ | RougeL | BERT F1 |
|---|---|---|---|---|---|---|
| CUNI | ALS | 0.37 | 0.37 | 0.34 | 0.24 | 0.85 |
| CUNI | AZ | 0.55 | 0.55 | 0.52 | 0.51 | 0.92 |
| CUNI | IG | 0.63 | 0.63 | 0.61 | 0.62 | 0.91 |
| CUNI | TR | 0.48 | 0.48 | 0.45 | 0.43 | 0.90 |
| CUNI | YO | 0.38 | 0.38 | 0.36 | 0.35 | 0.86 |
| McGill | ALS | 0.32 | 0.31 | 0.30 | 0.32 | 0.84 |
| McGill | AZ | 0.29 | 0.27 | 0.26 | 0.33 | 0.85 |
| McGill | IG | 0.35 | 0.35 | 0.34 | 0.39 | 0.83 |
| McGill | TR | 0.24 | 0.24 | 0.23 | 0.26 | 0.83 |
| McGill | YO | 0.34 | 0.34 | 0.33 | 0.39 | 0.84 |
| Claude 3.5 SonnetV2 | ALS | 0.33 | 0.34 | 0.31 | 0.20 | 0.84 |
| Claude 3.5 SonnetV2 | AZ | 0.59 | 0.58 | 0.55 | 0.50 | 0.91 |
| Claude 3.5 SonnetV2 | IG | 0.68 | 0.68 | 0.66 | 0.65 | 0.92 |
| Claude 3.5 SonnetV2 | TR | 0.51 | 0.51 | 0.47 | 0.41 | 0.89 |
| Claude 3.5 SonnetV2 | YO | 0.42 | 0.41 | 0.39 | 0.36 | 0.86 |
| Gemini 1.5 Pro | ALS | 0.36 | 0.35 | 0.32 | 0.29 | 0.84 |
| Gemini 1.5 Pro | AZ | 0.51 | 0.50 | 0.47 | 0.48 | 0.90 |
| Gemini 1.5 Pro | IG | 0.45 | 0.44 | 0.42 | 0.48 | 0.87 |
| Gemini 1.5 Pro | TR | 0.42 | 0.41 | 0.37 | 0.35 | 0.87 |
| Gemini 1.5 Pro | YO | 0.38 | 0.37 | 0.35 | 0.36 | 0.86 |
| Llama 3.2 90B | ALS | 0.41 | 0.40 | 0.37 | 0.32 | 0.86 |
| Llama 3.2 90B | AZ | 0.52 | 0.51 | 0.48 | 0.49 | 0.91 |
| Llama 3.2 90B | IG | 0.45 | 0.45 | 0.44 | 0.48 | 0.86 |
| Llama 3.2 90B | TR | 0.47 | 0.46 | 0.43 | 0.42 | 0.90 |
| Llama 3.2 90B | YO | 0.44 | 0.43 | 0.41 | 0.43 | 0.87 |

Table 8: RC-OE system evaluations for all languages.

ical practices by providing clear guidelines and obtaining informed consent. We appreciate their contributions, and ethical treatment remains a key focus in our research.

## Acknowledgements

We thank Google Deepmind Gemini Academic Program for the compute provided for conducting our analysis. We also thank HumanSignal for providing us access to Label Studio's Enterprise version which allowed us execute the large-scale collaboration to perform human annotations in multiple tasks. Lastly, we thank Damilola Oluwaseun Oloyede, Nagihan Lule, Ece Yurtseven, Mehmet Can Dadan, and Saliha Muradoglu for their contributions to the dataset creation.

## References

David Adelani, Hannah Liu, Xiaoyu Shen, Nikita Vassilyev, Jesujoba Alabi, Yanke Mao, Haonan Gao, and En-Shiun Lee. 2024. SIB-200: A simple, inclusive, and big evaluation dataset for topic classification in 200+ languages and dialects. In *Proceedings of the 18th Conference of the European Chapter of the Association for Computational Linguistics (Volume 1: Long Papers)*, pages 226–245, St. Julian's, Malta. Association for Computational Linguistics.

David Adelani, Graham Neubig, Sebastian Ruder, Shruti Rijhwani, Michael Beukman, Chester Palen-Michel, Constantine Lignos, Jesujoba Alabi, Shamsuddeen Muhammad, Peter Nabende, et al. 2022. Masakhaner 2.0: Africa-centric transfer learning for named entity recognition. In *Proceedings of the 2022 Conference on Empirical Methods in Natural Language Processing*, pages 4488–4508.

David Adelani, Dana Ruiter, Jesujoba Alabi, Damilola Adebonojo, Adesina Ayeni, Mofe Adeyemi, Ayodele Esther Awokoya, and Cristina España-Bonet. 2021a. The effect of domain and diacritics in Yoruba–

| System | ALS | AZ | IG | TR | YO | Avg. |
|---|---|---|---|---|---|---|
| SandboxAQ | 92.0 | 98.0 | 98.0 | 97.0 | 92.0 | **95.0** |
| CUNI | 92.0 | 98.0 | 98.0 | 96.0 | 86.0 | 93.0 |
| McGill | 78.0 | 97.0 | 82.0 | 97.0 | 85.0 | 88.0 |
| Claude 3.5 SonnetV2 | 91.0 | 98.0 | 95.0 | 95.0 | 92.0 | 94.0 |
| Gemini 1.5 Pro | 91.0 | 96.0 | 96.0 | 96.0 | 90.0 | 93.0 |
| Llama 3.2 90B | 91.0 | 97.0 | 96.0 | 95.0 | 89.0 | 93.0 |

Table 9: RC-MC system evaluation. Results indicate weighted average of the metrics over 5 languages. Results are weighted by the number of paragraphs in the test set.

| System | ALS | | | AZ | | | IG | | |
|---|---|---|---|---|---|---|---|---|---|
| | pre | rec | F1 | pre | rec | F1 | pre | rec | F1 |
| CUNI | 77.07 | 64.74 | 70.37 | 69.88 | 49.49 | 57.31 | 69.88 | **79.86** | **73.97** |
| Ifeoma | 65 | 1.18 | 0.84 | 1.6 | 2.75 | 2.02 | 1.74 | 2.44 | 2.03 |
| McGill | **81.83** | **76.15** | **78.89** | **78.93** | **85.43** | **82.05** | **97.3** | 4.86 | 9.27 |
| SandboxAQ | 65.8 | 48.6 | 55.9 | 63.7 | 42.6 | 51 | 51.3 | 39.7 | 44.8 |
| Omkar | 1 | 1.3 | 1.1 | 2.1 | 3.03 | 2.48 | - | - | - |

| System | TR | | | YO | | | | |
|---|---|---|---|---|---|---|---|---|
| | pre | rec | F1 | pre | rec | F1 | Avg | Med |
| CUNI | **85.38** | 71.46 | 77.8 | 78.61 | 82.55 | 80.53 | **71.996** | 73.97 |
| Ifeoma | 3.04 | 5.91 | 4.02 | 0.69 | 1 | 0.82 | 1.946 | 2.02 |
| McGill | 84.19 | **81.12** | **82.62** | **85.81** | **85.56** | **85.69** | 67.704 | **82.05** |
| SandboxAQ | 62.1 | 44.7 | 52.0 | - | - | - | 50.925 | 51.5 |
| Omkar | 3.8 | 5.5 | 4.5 | 1.7 | 1.7 | 1.7 | 2.445 | 2.09 |

Table 10: Test results for NER. Averages are weighted by number of tokens per language. Best results are in bold. *Avg: Average. Med: Median.*


English neural machine translation. In *Proceedings of Machine Translation Summit XVIII: Research Track*, pages 61–75, Virtual. Association for Machine Translation in the Americas.

David Ifeoluwa Adelani, Jade Abbott, Graham Neubig, Daniel D'souza, Julia Kreutzer, Constantine Lignos, Chester Palen-Michel, Happy Buzaaba, Shruti Rijhwani, Sebastian Ruder, et al. 2021b. Masakhaner: Named entity recognition for african languages. *Transactions of the Association for Computational Linguistics*, 9:1116–1131.

Yesim Aksan, Mustafa Aksan, Ahmet Koltuksuz, Taner Sezer, Ümit Mersinli, Umut Ufuk Demirhan, Hakan Yilmazer, Gülsüm Atasoy, Seda Öz, Ipek Yildiz, et al. 2012. Construction of the turkish national corpus (tnc). In *LREC*, pages 3223–3227.

Jesujoba O. Alabi, David Ifeoluwa Adelani, Marius Mosbach, and Dietrich Klakow. 2022. Adapting pre-trained language models to African languages via multilingual adaptive fine-tuning. In *Proceedings of the 29th International Conference on Computational Linguistics*, pages 4336–4349, Gyeongju, Republic of Korea. International Committee on Computational Linguistics.

Duygu Ataman. 2018. Bianet: A parallel news corpus in turkish, kurdish and english. In *LREC 2018 Workshop*, page 14.

Ondřej Bojar, Rajen Chatterjee, Christian Federmann, Yvette Graham, Barry Haddow, Shujian Huang, Matthias Huck, Philipp Koehn, Qun Liu, Varvara Logacheva, Christof Monz, Matteo Negri, Matt Post, Raphael Rubino, Lucia Specia, and Marco Turchi. 2017. Findings of the 2017 conference on machine translation (WMT17). In *Proceedings of the Second Conference on Machine Translation*, pages 169–214.

Mauro Cettolo, Christian Girardi, and Marcello Federico. 2012. Wit3: Web inventory of transcribed and translated talks. In *Proceedings of the Conference of European Association for Machine Translation (EAMT)*, pages 261–268.

Mauro Cettolo, Jan Niehues, Sebastian Stüker, Luisa

Bentivogli, and Marcello Federico. 2013. Report on the 10th iwslt evaluation campaign. In *Proceedings of the 10th International Workshop on Spoken Language Translation: Evaluation Campaign*.

Alexis Conneau, Kartikay Khandelwal, Naman Goyal, Vishrav Chaudhary, Guillaume Wenzek, Francisco Guzmán, Édouard Grave, Myle Ott, Luke Zettlemoyer, and Veselin Stoyanov. 2020. Unsupervised cross-lingual representation learning at scale. In *Proceedings of the 58th Annual Meeting of the Association for Computational Linguistics*, pages 8440–8451.

Alexis Conneau, Ruty Rinott, Guillaume Lample, Adina Williams, Samuel Bowman, Holger Schwenk, and Veselin Stoyanov. 2018. Xnli: Evaluating cross-lingual sentence representations. In *Proceedings of the 2018 Conference on Empirical Methods in Natural Language Processing*, pages 2475–2485.

Cheikh M. Bamba Dione, David Ifeoluwa Adelani, Peter Nabende, Jesujoba Alabi, Thapelo Sindane, Happy Buzaaba, Shamsuddeen Hassan Muhammad, Chris Chinenye Emezue, Perez Ogayo, Anuoluwapo Aremu, Catherine Gitau, Derguene Mbaye, Jonathan Mukiibi, Blessing Sibanda, Bonaventure F. P. Dossou, Andiswa Bukula, Rooweither Mabuya, Allahsera Auguste Tapo, Edwin Munkoh-Buabeng, Victoire Memdjokam Koagne, Fatoumata Ouoba Kabore, Amelia Taylor, Godson Kalipe, Tebogo Macucwa, Vukosi Marivate, Tajuddeen Gwadabe, Mboning Tchiaze Elvis, Ikechukwu Onyenwe, Gratien Atindogbe, Tolulope Adelani, Idris Akinade, Olanrewaju Samuel, Marien Nahimana, Théogène Musabeyezu, Emile Niyomutabazi, Ester Chimhenga, Kudzai Gotosa, Patrick Mizha, Apelete Agbolo, Seydou Traore, Chinedu Uchechukwu, Aliyu Yusuf, Muhammad Abdullahi, and Dietrich Klakow. 2023. MasakhaPOS: Part-of-speech tagging for typologically diverse African languages. In *Proceedings of the 61st Annual Meeting of the Association for Computational Linguistics (Volume 1: Long Papers)*, pages 10883–10900, Toronto, Canada. Association for Computational Linguistics.

Pelin Dogan-Schönberger, Julian Mäder, and Thomas Hofmann. 2021. Swissdial: Parallel multidialectal corpus of spoken swiss german.

Abhimanyu Dubey, Abhinav Jauhri, Abhinav Pandey, Abhishek Kadian, Ahmad Al-Dahle, Aiesha Letman, Akhil Mathur, Alan Schelten, Amy Yang, Angela Fan, et al. 2024. The llama 3 herd of models. *arXiv preprint arXiv:2407.21783*.

David M. Eberhard, Gary F. Simons, and Charles D. Fennig. 2021. Ethnologue: Languages of the world. twenty-third edition.

Razieh Ehsani, Ercan Solak, and Olcay Taner Yildiz. 2018. Constructing a wordnet for turkish using manual and automatic annotation. *ACM Transactions on Asian and Low-Resource Language Information Processing (TALLIP)*, 17(3):1–15.

Philip N. Garner, David Imseng, and Thomas Meyer. 2014. Automatic speech recognition and translation of a swiss german dialect: Walliserdeutsch. In *Interspeech*.

Nora Hollenstein and Noëmi Aepli. 2014. Compilation of a Swiss German dialect corpus and its application to PoS tagging. In *Proceedings of the First Workshop on Applying NLP Tools to Similar Languages, Varieties and Dialects*, pages 85–94, Dublin, Ireland. Association for Computational Linguistics and Dublin City University.

Junjie Hu, Sebastian Ruder, Aditya Siddhant, Graham Neubig, Orhan Firat, and Melvin Johnson. 2020. Xtreme: A massively multilingual multi-task benchmark for evaluating cross-lingual generalisation. In *International Conference on Machine Learning*, pages 4411–4421. PMLR.

Chin-Yew Lin and Eduard Hovy. 2003. Automatic evaluation of summaries using n-gram co-occurrence statistics. In *Proceedings of the 2003 human language technology conference of the North American chapter of the association for computational linguistics*, pages 150–157.

Yinhan Liu, Myle Ott, Naman Goyal, Jingfei Du, Mandar Joshi, Danqi Chen, Omer Levy, Mike Lewis, Luke Zettlemoyer, and Veselin Stoyanov. 2019. Roberta: A robustly optimized BERT pretraining approach. *CoRR*, abs/1907.11692.

Shamsuddeen Hassan Muhammad, Idris Abdulmumin, Abinew Ali Ayele, Nedjma Djouhra Ousidhoum, David Ifeoluwa Adelani, Seid Muhie Yimam, Ibrahim Said Ahmad, Meriem Beloucif, Saif M. Mohammad, Sebastian Ruder, Oumaima Hourrane, Pavel Brazdil, Felermino D'ario M'ario Ant'onio Ali, Davis C. Davis, Salomey Osei, Bello Shehu Bello, Falalu Ibrahim, Tajuddeen Rabiu Gwadabe, Samuel Rutunda, Tadesse Destaw Belay, Wendimu Baye Messelle, Hailu Beshada Balcha, Sisay Adugna Chala, Hagos Tesfahun Gebremichael, Bernard Opoku, and Steven Arthur. 2023. Afrisenti: A twitter sentiment analysis benchmark for african languages. *ArXiv*, abs/2302.08956.

Odunayo Ogundepo, Tajuddeen R. Gwadabe, Clara E. Rivera, Jonathan H. Clark, Sebastian Ruder, David Ifeoluwa Adelani, Bonaventure F. P. Dossou, Abdou Aziz DIOP, Claytone Sikasote, Gilles Hacheme, Happy Buzaaba, Ignatius Ezeani, Rooweither Mabuya, Salomey Osei, Chris Emezue, Albert Njoroge Kahira, Shamsuddeen H. Muhammad, Akintunde Oladipo, Abraham Toluwase Owodunni, Atnafu Lambebo Tonja, Iyanuoluwa Shode, Akari Asai, Tunde Oluwaseyi Ajayi, Clemencia Siro, Steven Arthur, Mofetoluwa Adeyemi, Orevaoghene Ahia, Aremu Anuoluwapo, Oyinkansola Awosan, Chiamaka Chukwuneke, Bernard Opoku, Awokoya Ayodele, Verrah Otiende, Christine Mwase, Boyd Sinkala, Andre Niyongabo Rubungo, Daniel A. Ajisafe, Emeka Felix Onwuegbuzia, Habib Mbow, Emile Niyomutabazi, Eunice

Mukonde, Falalu Ibrahim Lawan, Ibrahim Said Ahmad, Jesujoba O. Alabi, Martin Namukombo, Mbonu Chinedu, Mofya Phiri, Neo Putini, Ndumiso Mngoma, Priscilla A. Amuok, Ruqayya Nasir Iro, and Sonia Adhiambo. 2023. Afriqa: Cross-lingual open-retrieval question answering for african languages.

Tolulope Ogunremi, Kola Tubosun, Anuoluwapo Aremu, Iroro Orife, and David Ifeoluwa Adelani. 2023. Ìròyìnspeech: A multi-purpose yorùbá speech corpus.

Akintunde Oladipo, Mofetoluwa Adeyemi, Orevaoghene Ahia, Abraham Owodunni, Odunayo Ogundepo, David Adelani, and Jimmy Lin. 2023. Better quality pre-training data and t5 models for African languages. In *Proceedings of the 2023 Conference on Empirical Methods in Natural Language Processing*, pages 158–168, Singapore. Association for Computational Linguistics.

OpenAI. 2023. Gpt-4 technical report. *ArXiv*, abs/2303.08774.

Long Ouyang, Jeff Wu, Xu Jiang, Diogo Almeida, Carroll L. Wainwright, Pamela Mishkin, Chong Zhang, Sandhini Agarwal, Katarina Slama, Alex Ray, John Schulman, Jacob Hilton, Fraser Kelton, Luke E. Miller, Maddie Simens, Amanda Askell, Peter Welinder, Paul Francis Christiano, Jan Leike, and Ryan J. Lowe. 2022. Training language models to follow instructions with human feedback. *ArXiv*, abs/2203.02155.

Tiago Pimentel, Maria Ryskina, Sabrina J Mielke, Shijie Wu, Eleanor Chodroff, Brian Leonard, Garrett Nicolai, Yustinus Ghanggo Ate, Salam Khalifa, Nizar Habash, et al. 2021. Sigmorphon 2021 shared task on morphological reinflection: Generalization across languages. In *Proceedings of the 18th SIGMORPHON Workshop on Computational Research in Phonetics, Phonology, and Morphology*, pages 229–259.

Michel Plüss, Jan Deriu, Yanick Schraner, Claudio Paonessa, Julia Hartmann, Larissa Schmidt, Christian Scheller, Manuela Hürlimann, Tanja Samardžić, Manfred Vogel, and Mark Cieliebak. 2023. STT4SG-350: A speech corpus for all Swiss German dialect regions. In *Proceedings of the 61st Annual Meeting of the Association for Computational Linguistics (Volume 2: Short Papers)*, pages 1763–1772, Toronto, Canada. Association for Computational Linguistics.

Michel Plüss, Manuela Hürlimann, Marc Cuny, Alla Stöckli, Nikolaos Kapotis, Julia Hartmann, Malgorzata Anna Ulasik, Christian Scheller, Yanick Schraner, Amit Jain, Jan Deriu, Mark Cieliebak, and Manfred Vogel. 2022. SDS-200: A Swiss German speech to Standard German text corpus. In *Proceedings of the Thirteenth Language Resources and Evaluation Conference*, pages 3250–3256, Marseille, France. European Language Resources Association.

Michel Plüss, Lukas Neukom, and Manfred Vogel. 2020. Swiss parliaments corpus, an automatically aligned swiss german speech to standard german text corpus. *ArXiv*, abs/2010.02810.

Maja Popović. 2015. chrf: character n-gram f-score for automatic mt evaluation. In *Proceedings of the tenth workshop on statistical machine translation*, pages 392–395.

Maja Popović. 2017. chrf++: words helping character n-grams. In *Proceedings of the second conference on machine translation*, pages 612–618.

Colin Raffel, Noam Shazeer, Adam Roberts, Katherine Lee, Sharan Narang, Michael Matena, Yanqi Zhou, Wei Li, and Peter J. Liu. 2019. Exploring the limits of transfer learning with a unified text-to-text transformer. *arXiv e-prints*.

Machel Reid, Nikolay Savinov, Denis Teplyashin, Dmitry Lepikhin, Timothy Lillicrap, Jean-baptiste Alayrac, Radu Soricut, Angeliki Lazaridou, Orhan Firat, Julian Schrittwieser, et al. 2024. Gemini 1.5: Unlocking multimodal understanding across millions of tokens of context. *arXiv preprint arXiv:2403.05530*.

Sebastian Ruder, Jonathan H Clark, Alexander Gutkin, Mihir Kale, Min Ma, Massimo Nicosia, Shruti Rijhwani, Parker Riley, Jean-Michel A Sarr, Xinyi Wang, et al. 2023. Xtreme-up: A user-centric scarce-data benchmark for under-represented languages. *arXiv preprint arXiv:2305.11938*.

Bahadir Sahin, Mustafa Tolga Eren, Caglar Tirkaz, Ozan Sonmez, and Eray Yildiz. 2017. English/turkish wikipedia named-entity recognition and text categorization dataset. *Mendeley Data, V1*.

Gözde Gül Şahin and Eşref Adalı. 2018. Annotation of semantic roles for the turkish proposition bank. *Language Resources and Evaluation*, 52:673–706.

Tanja Samardžić, Yves Scherrer, and Elvira Glaser. 2016. ArchiMob - a corpus of spoken Swiss German. In *Proceedings of the Tenth International Conference on Language Resources and Evaluation (LREC'16)*, pages 4061–4066, Portorož, Slovenia. European Language Resources Association (ELRA).

Thomas Scialom, Paul-Alexis Dray, Sylvain Lamprier, Benjamin Piwowarski, and Jacopo Staiano. 2020. Mlsum: The multilingual summarization corpus. In *2020 Conference on Empirical Methods in Natural Language Processing (EMNLP)*, pages 8051–8067. Association for Computational Linguistics.

Umut Sulubacak and Gülşen Eryiğit. 2018. Implementing universal dependency, morphology, and multiword expression annotation standards for turkish language processing. *Turkish Journal of Electrical Engineering and Computer Sciences*, 26(3):1662–1672.

Umut Sulubacak, Memduh Gökırmak, Francis Tyers, Çağrı Çöltekin, Joakim Nivre, and Gülşen Eryiğit. 2016. Universal dependencies for turkish. In *Proceedings of COLING 2016, the 26th international conference on computational linguistics: Technical papers*, pages 3444–3454.

Francesco Tinner, David Ifeoluwa Adelani, Chris Emezue, Mammad Hajili, Omer Goldman, Muhammad Farid Adilazuarda, Muhammad Dehan Al Kautsar, Aziza Mirsaidova, Müge Kural, Dylan Massey, et al. 2023. Findings of the 1st shared task on multilingual multi-task information retrieval at mrl 2023. In *Proceedings of the 3rd Workshop on Multi-lingual Representation Learning (MRL)*, pages 310–323.

Erik F. Tjong Kim Sang and Sabine Buchholz. 2000. Introduction to the CoNLL-2000 shared task chunking. In *Fourth Conference on Computational Natural Language Learning and the Second Learning Language in Logic Workshop*.

Maxim Tkachenko, Mikhail Malyuk, Andrey Holmanyuk, and Nikolai Liubimov. 2020-2022. Label Studio: Data labeling software. Open source software available from https://github.com/heartexlabs/label-studio.

Hugo Touvron, Thibaut Lavril, Gautier Izacard, Xavier Martinet, Marie-Anne Lachaux, Timothée Lacroix, Baptiste Rozière, Naman Goyal, Eric Hambro, Faisal Azhar, et al. 2023. Llama: Open and efficient foundation language models. *arXiv preprint arXiv:2302.13971*.

Francis M Tyers and Murat Serdar Alperen. 2010. South-east european times: A parallel corpus of balkan languages. In *Proceedings of the LREC workshop on exploitation of multilingual resources and tools for Central and (South-) Eastern European Languages*, pages 49–53.

Ahmet Üstün, Viraat Aryabumi, Zheng-Xin Yong, Wei-Yin Ko, Daniel D'souza, Gbemileke Onilude, Neel Bhandari, Shivalika Singh, Hui-Lee Ooi, Amr Kayid, et al. 2024. Aya model: An instruction finetuned open-access multilingual language model. *arXiv preprint arXiv:2402.07827*.

Linting Xue, Noah Constant, Adam Roberts, Mihir Kale, Rami Al-Rfou, Aditya Siddhant, Aditya Barua, and Colin Raffel. 2021. mT5: A massively multilingual pre-trained text-to-text transformer. In *Proceedings of the 2021 Conference of the North American Chapter of the Association for Computational Linguistics: Human Language Technologies*, pages 483–498, Online. Association for Computational Linguistics.

Zheng-Xin Yong, Cristina Menghini, and Stephen H Bach. 2023. Low-resource languages jailbreak gpt-4. *arXiv preprint arXiv:2310.02446*.

Tianyi Zhang, Varsha Kishore, Felix Wu, Kilian Q Weinberger, and Yoav Artzi. 2019. Bertscore: Evaluating text generation with bert. *arXiv preprint arXiv:1904.09675*.

# Author Index

**Association for Computational Linguistics**
209 N. Eighth Street
Stroudsburg, Pennsylvania 18360

ISBN 979-8-3313-0848-3

9 798331 308483

CURRAN ASSOCIATES INC.
proceedings.com